New Approaches to Teaching Italian Language and Culture

New Approaches to Teaching Italian Language and Culture: Case Studies from an International Perspective

Edited by

Emanuele Occhipinti

Cambridge Scholars Publishing

New Approaches to Teaching Italian Language and Culture: Case Studies from an International Perspective, Edited by Emanuele Occhipinti

This book first published 2008 by

Cambridge Scholars Publishing

12 Back Chapman Street, Newcastle upon Tyne, NE6 2XX, UK

British Library Cataloguing in Publication Data
A catalogue record for this book is available from the British Library

ISBN (10): 1-84718-638-6, ISBN (13): 9781847186386

In loving memory of my mother Lina and my brother Massimo.

TABLE OF CONTENTS

Part II: Teaching Italian with Technology

Part III: Teaching Italian Translation

Part V: Teaching Italian Culture Through Film

Part VI: Teaching Italian Culture Through Songs

LIST OF TABLES AND FIGURES

INTRODUCTION

EMANUELE OCCHIPINTI

The aim of this collection of essays is to fill a major gap in existing scholarship and textbooks devoted to the teaching of Italian language and culture. Although in the past there have been monographic issues of journals like *Italica*[1] devoted to some aspects of Italian pedagogy,[2] there has never been a systematic collection of essays on this topic with such a variety of contributions in a single volume.

In today's world the need to incorporate a rigorous study of foreign languages is more and more strongly felt: in schools and universities across the world it is standard for students to be expected to be proficient in at least one foreign language and also, often, to attend courses on aspects of culture and diversity. Additionally, in recent years, more and more scholars have become interested in effective language teaching methodology, and many universities are starting to hire people with specialized degrees in language pedagogy and Second Language Acquisition rather than PhDs in literature. This calls for specialized texts that can provide studies and examples of effective pedagogy of language teaching and testing that instructors and teacher trainers from different academic backgrounds can use in their classes.

In the past decade, the study of Italian has grown everywhere in the world,[3] especially in the U.S., with a 22.6% increase since 2002, and the number of students reaching 78,368 in 2006[4] (rising from 11,000 in the

---

[1] *Italica* is an American journal, published four times a year with articles on Italian language, literature and linguistics.

[2] See, for example, *Italica* 77, no. 4 (2000), 78, no. 4 (2001) on some aspects of Italian pedagogy, and 83, no, 1 (2006) on teaching film and culture.

[3] For a thorough analysis of teaching methods of Italian in the world see Paolo E. Balboni and Matteo Santipolo eds., *L'italiano nel mondo. Mete e metodi dell'insegnamento dell'italiano nel mondo. Un'indagine qualitativa* (Roma: Bonacci editore, 2003).

[4] See the MLA report at http://www.mla.org/pdf/release11207_ma_feb_update.pdf See also Nelly Furman, David Goldberg, and Natalia Lusin, "Enrollments in

'60s), placing Italian as the fourth most studied foreign language after Spanish, French and German.[5]

This volume offers case studies that present a coherent and organized overview of contemporary Italian pedagogy, integrating the expertise of scholars in the fields of language methodology and language acquisition from Italy and four major countries where the study of Italian has a long tradition: Australia, Canada, Great Britain and U.S. The twenty-four essays, divided into six main parts, offer tremendous variety, and an up-to-date approach to the teaching of Italian as a foreign language or L2[6] incorporating both theoretical aspects of pedagogy and practical ones, including examples of specific syllabi.

Part I ("Curricular Innovations") explores new teaching approaches in the Italian curriculum. The five essays in this section answer the need to update curricula with innovative and stimulating activities that take into consideration the latest studies in language learning. The first chapter examines the principles of CBI (Content-based Instruction), from the history of its development, dating back to 1965 in French programs in Canada, to its use today. The chapter focuses on its implementation at The Ohio State University in order to eliminate the division between elementary courses devoted solely to the teaching of language, and more advanced ones devoted to the teaching of literature. This method allows students to progress with their natural language learning of the four skills while integrating authentic materials in all courses levels. The old and new curricula are compared and discussed with reasons for the change. In the appendix, a syllabus and a grid for oral and written assessment are provided.

The second chapter presents data from research on task-based instruction of intermediate Italian. The study follows a three-phase task: a pre-task activity in which the tasks are explained and students are exposed to authentic oral material; a during-task activity in which students actually

---

Languages Other Than English in United States Institutions of Higher Education, Fall 2006," http://www.mla.org/pdf/06enrollmentsurvey_final.pdf

[5] See Mario Calabresi, "USA, la rivincita dell'italiano: è boom di corsi all'università," *La repubblica*, April 23, 2007.

[6] The term "Foreign Language" refers to the teaching of a foreign language in schools in a foreign environment (for example Italian taught in the U.S., Great Britain, Australia, etc.). "L2" refers to the teaching of a language spoken in the context where foreign speakers live (for example Italian taught in Italy, Canton Ticino in Switzerland and areas of Istria). See Paolo E. Balboni, *Didattica dell'italiano a stranieri* (Roma: Bonacci and Università per stranieri di Siena, 1994), 13-4.

perform the task that is recorded on video or audio; and a post-task activity in which students work on the transcripts of their activities and on grammar points introduced by the instructor. Thus, the structured input and output of the TBI model creates the basis for a more natural way to acquire fluency and improve accuracy.

The third chapter expands on the notion that the best way to learn a foreign language is to put students in contact with real-life situations. The chapter deals with an innovative and flexible approach called "Project Work" that aims at integrating the theory of the language with its practical use in every day life. The didactic methodology of Project Work was applied to a class of Erasmus[7] students of Italian L2 in an Italian University. The chapter presents data obtained from the implementation of Project Work in which students were asked to assist in organizing a conference on second language acquisition with a series of related tasks including creating and distributing brochures and planning a cultural itinerary. The advantages of such a method are manifold, since students must incorporate their linguistic knowledge with a systematic use of different grammatical structures in a cooperative way, in which they not only need to interact with each other, but also with the world outside the classroom. Role-play became an essential part of this method because this helped the learner to act in a real situation (for example, students had to make phone calls in order to ask for estimates).

Chapter Four explores the effectiveness and challenges of the "Conversation Hour Program" at The College of New Jersey in the U.S. The Conversation Hour builds on studies that show that shorter and more frequent contact with the foreign language is crucial to master what has been learned. Even though the author had to face some bureaucratic and organizational issues including, among other things, the preparation and supervision of the coordinators, in the end the experiment became a permanent reality expanding to all foreign languages taught at the College. The teaching approach was aimed to foster the five Cs (Communication, Cultures, Connections, Comparisons and Communities) recommended by ACTFL (American Council on the Teaching of Foreign Languages) with activities ranging from vocabulary building to short dialogues and role-plays.

---

[7] The Erasmus project was created in 1987 and is named after the famous scholar Erasmus of Rotterdam who lived and studied in many parts of Europe for the purpose of expanding his experience and knowledge. The program offers generous grants and allows students to study for a semester or an academic year in a European University, other than his/her own, and have the credits earned recognized in the home institution.

The fifth and last chapter of the first section explores linguistic structures and their relationship to L2 development. The essay discusses what stages should be followed so that grammatical structures can be acquired at the appropriate level, without teaching structures that are too advanced, in order to speed the learning process. The progression is successfully achieved with Processability Theory that allows the instructor to teach structures at the right level according to a hierarchal sequence: lemma access, category, phrasal and sentence procedures. The experiment was carried out in a primary school in Sydney, Australia, in two Italian courses for 12 weeks. At the end of the experiment, children had learned in three months what they had not learned during a previous three-year period.

Part II ("Teaching Italian with Technology") deals with the fundamental tool of technology, integrated in nearly every curriculum thanks to the availability of computers and internet connections in tech-enhanced classrooms. The chapters in this section introduce some innovative projects, through the discussion of outcomes and goals. The first chapter explores the potential of WebCT a web-based tool with hyperlinks, images and colors, with the purpose of stimulating interest and improve effective learning of Italian at the University of Birmingham, UK. The experiment proved successful by boosting students' confidence and interest thanks to a vast array of activities including discussion boards and online exercises with electronic feedback.

The second chapter discusses the development of "Azione!," a web-based program of Italian film and television segments used in the elementary and intermediate Italian language courses at Yale University. The program was designed to allow students going abroad to be more comfortable in real-life situations and teach them to "listen selectively" and "listen for specific content." The topics of the segments range from health, environment and technology, travel, and politics to growing up and the family, and the flexibility of the program facilitates its integration with any textbook. Students have the ability to expand and reinforce their knowledge with activities of increasing difficulty. Furthermore, the unabridged clips help them to become accustomed to the normal speed of the language, with exposure to various accents and regional differences.

"Confronti" is the name of an innovative project, and topic of the third chapter of this section, developed cooperatively among the University of Padova, the University of Pennsylvania and Middlebury College in the U.S., and based on the *Cultura* French Project created at MIT in Cambridge, Massachusetts. The goal of integrating culture into the curriculum is achieved through a common website and communication tools like Skype and webcams. Using these tools, students across the ocean can take advantage of their particular expertise to discuss topics such as stereotypes, family, school, private and public spaces, regionalism, immigration and emigration. In this context, students are responsible for discovering differences and similarities while the instructor takes the role of facilitator. The advantages are many: enthusiastic involvement, the opportunity to understand a different culture while reflecting on one's own, and closer connections with students from a different country.

The last chapter on technology is devoted to research at the University of Montréal in Canada on the use of iPods and podcasting to learn Italian. Like with every technological tool, some challenges are present, but there are numerous advantages to using a tool that the majority of young people own: thanks to its small size and large memory, the iPod can be used to store hours of audio and video materials that accommodate many learning styles. Students can listen not only to songs, but also to recorded lessons and authentic language material, allowing them to learn in a quiet environment. Instructors can offer more content to advanced and motivated students and students with learning disabilities.

The four chapters of **Part III ("Teaching Italian Translation")** explore the challenges of teaching translation courses. Translation has gone through various phases: from being appreciated to being regarded as an old fashioned and ineffective method for language teaching. Today, many language experts consider the exercise of translation not only useful but also fundamental for improving students' reading and writing skills as well as their cross-cultural awareness, and some argue that it can be considered a "fifth linguistic ability." Chapter Ten describes the challenges surrounding a collaborative online learning course at the University of Strathclyde in Scotland, where students were faced with changes in the course structure over a period of three years, and analyzes the outcomes and drawbacks.

Chapter Eleven focuses on how translation can benefit the learning of Italian and how translation techniques can in fact help learners to achieve a high level of expertise, contributing to "metalinguistic reflection," broadening vocabulary and helping students to analyze cultural differences, develop "textual competence" and master more sophisticated stages of the learning process.

Chapter Twelve expands on the benefits of translation, presenting a case study of teaching methodology used in seminars for undergraduates to hone their translation skills in their final year of a three-year degree course in "Civiltà e Lingue Straniere Moderne" at the University of Parma. The seminars are geared towards students who translate from Italian into

English, and train students through readings of an array of texts from literary to technical, scientific, political, and legal. Chapter Thirteen is a "hands on" example of how to help students analyze specialized language, in this case legal and journalistic, with its unique use of technical, lexical and morphosyntactic terms. This, of course, bears some problems since English is not the students' native language, and the risk of misinterpretations or poor translation is very high. The methodology proposed helps students in the process of decoding and encoding thanks to some techniques that are analyzed in detail, such as "cloze method" to strengthen grammatical structures; "multiple choice" and "error correction" exercises to facilitate students' critical thinking; and "back translation" to help students notice discrepancies.

Part IV ("Teaching Italian Culture") is devoted to examples on how to effectively teach Italian culture in every foreign language curriculum. As Swiderski points out,

> Whatever presence culture may have in the language classroom, those who enter the classroom expect culture. They have explicit expectations, expressed perhaps as a wish to learn about the ways and lives of the people who speak the language to be learned, or as a need to know how to behave and how not to behave while among these people. Students expect to receive this information, and teachers expect to teach it. This is the outright cultural act of language teaching/learning set within the cultural environment of the classroom.[8]

The five essays consider how Italian culture is taught in the States, and provide some useful examples on how to improve its effectiveness. "Visual literacy" (introduced in chapter fourteen) is a skill to develop in order to decode images. The same skill can be applied to film—a medium that employs visual and cultural messages—and chapter twenty-one introduces "visual thinking," or the ability to facilitate the analysis and description of a film before its interpretation, as an important skill in the teaching of film. Students must therefore be encouraged to think critically, and should be able to "read" an image through a series of exercises, which the author describes in detail. Students should then be able to make hypotheses and recognize similarities and differences between the two cultures. In the end, students may, for example, come to the conclusion that when the same object is used at different times in different cultures, it

---

[8] Richard M. Swiderski, *Teaching Language, Learning Culture* (Westport, CT: Bergin & Garvey, 1993), 19.

may become two completely different objects, even if these objects have the same semantic definition.

Chapters Fifteen and Nineteen discuss two cultural courses developed and taught in two different American universities. Chapter Fifteen analyzes a fifth-semester culture course ("Women in Italy 1930s-2000s: history, sociology, law, anthropology, cinema, dance and songs") taught at Wellesley College. The interdisciplinary nature of the course makes it a model for cultural courses that incorporate a variety of visual media such as films, documentaries, dance shows, interviews, political posters, militant slogans and murals, etc. Through guided discussions and oral presentations that include visual tools, students are engaged in thinking critically and "visually." The same concepts are applied in the cultural course examined in chapter nineteen, taught at the University of Washington: an interdisciplinary survey of Italian culture from the pre-Roman era to the contemporary time. The purpose of this course is to develop a cultural awareness focusing on historical, political and religious facts and their enormous impact on the artistic and literary world.

"Intercultural competence" (chapter sixteen) is another fundamental skill that students should develop in order to experience a reality different from their own when they travel abroad. When abroad, students experience a dynamic process including three different steps: stress, adaptation and growth. The case study presents some tools that instructors can use to prepare students for the new experience, with the support of data from a two-month summer program of Columbia University students who visited Venice. A website was created in order to provide useful information about the host country and Ca'Foscari University. Also, pre-departure meetings tested students' attitudes and expectations. In Venice, students were matched with "cultural partners" for support and exchange of experiences. Through a series of "social communication" activities students were able to discuss with their teachers and cultural partners their expectations, fears and surprises. Keeping a journal in which they registered their perspectives while experiencing this different reality further enabled students to confront their fears and develop an intercultural awareness.

As we have seen, integrating culture into the curriculum is not as easy as it can initially seem, especially when instructors need to assess students' cultural competence. In chapter seventeen, a third-year Italian culture course is analyzed, and assessment suggestions are offered employing a combination of formats to ensure that students' grasp of the materials covered in class is assimilated.

The "IVC, Chiavi di lettura" project (chapter eighteen), developed at Emory University in the U.S., takes a step forward in implementing the Modern Languages Association suggestion to integrate culture with the teaching of language and literature. Culture is presented in order to learn the language, and students are asked to make comparisons and connections through art, politics, religion and theater, among other disciplines. Indeed, this authentic and interdisciplinary cultural material provides the context in which grammatical rules are embedded and acquired in an intuitive manner. In this way, the process of grammatical teaching occurs in a passive mode and students can think about formal rules in a later phase. The advantage of this method is that the learner's process mimics first language acquisition in a dynamic and natural way.

Part V ("Teaching Italian Culture Through Film") and **Part VI ("Teaching Italian Culture Through Songs")** are concerned with how to successfully integrate culture with two of the most effective media: films and songs, and how these media can be used to teach cultural competency. Chapter Twenty is a case study of a curriculum change at Macquarie University in Sydney, which integrated films into all levels of Italian courses. The essay explores some of the most up-to-date and frequently used film manuals, and it analyzes the effectiveness of some activities and assessments of proficiency, such as plot summaries, film reviews, short answer quizzes, letters, research projects and oral presentations. The aim of the study is to see how students responded to this curriculum change, and to support the integration of movies into language teaching. The author ultimately makes the case that love stories, quests, coming of age films, and films where the main characters are children, teenagers or young adults were most effective.

Chapter Twenty-two is a detailed analysis of two movies, *La finestra di fronte* (*Facing Windows*) and *Una giornata particolare* (*A Special Day*) that, because of their thematic similarities and depictions of particular moments in Italian history (Fascism and the Holocaust) can be used to explain the historical background of certain events and how these events shaped Italian political developments. Films in this case help students to contextualize what they learn and images help them to better remember historical facts.

The last two chapters take into consideration how songs can be used both to integrate culture and grammar into the curriculum (while trying to overcome the existing dichotomy between "big C" culture thought of as Art, Literature and Opera and "small c" culture seen in the popular culture that is an integral part of students' lives) and to strengthen students' listening and comprehension abilities.

Chapter Twenty-three demonstrates how music can be beneficial to language learners because it stimulates parts of the brain conducive to learning a foreign language. Its utility is based on the assumption (studies by Alfred Tomatis are mentioned) that every language has a different frequency and that the contact with frequencies other than the ones of our own language can lead to better production of different sounds. The course illustrated in this chapter, taught in Italy to Erasmus students, was centered on main topics, with songs used as an introduction to different cultural realities. The preview and follow-up activities—key-word listening, dictations, use of rhymes and phonetic symbols, rewriting texts and role-playing to cite just a few—proved very useful for a general understanding of Italian culture and the reinforcement of grammatical rules, increasing students' attention and performance.

Finally, the last chapter shows how songs can form the basis of an entire course on language and culture. The purpose of the course ("Italian Freaks and Punks: History of Italian Culture and Civilization from 1950s to 2005 retold by Protest Songs") is twofold: using "protest songs" is useful for familiarizing students with some possibly unknown yet critical moments in Italian history of the last fifty years, such as differences between dialect and standard language, economic and cultural development, students and workers protesting for better living conditions, and feminism. The songs are also used for reviewing difficult grammatical rules pertaining to the subjunctive, conditional, imperative with pronouns, passato prossimo/imperfect.

The chapters of this book, despite their differences, share the enduring theme that the teaching of language and culture should be a natural process, with a holistic exchange between teachers and students. To quote Stephen D. Krashen, "We teach language best when we use it for what it was designed for: communication."[9] After much progress and many changes in the theory of language teaching in past few decades, Krashen's words from 1981 still represent a valid assumption that illustrates one, if not the main, goal of this collection.

DREW UNIVERSITY, USA

---

[9] Stephen D. Krashen, *Second Language Acquisition and Second language Learning* (http://www.sdkrashen.com/SL_Acquisition_and_Learning/index.html), 11.

PART I:

CURRICULAR INNOVATIONS

CHAPTER ONE

ELIMINATING THE "GAP" THROUGH CURRICULAR INNOVATION

JANICE M. ASKI AND HEATHER WEBB

Introduction

The dilemma that has plagued Italian programs and has been discussed repeatedly at roundtable discussions at national conferences is how to bridge the 'gap' between elementary language courses and intermediate/advanced content (usually literature) courses. The key to the solution must be related to two erroneous assumptions that curricula with this gap make about L2 acquisition: 1) an L2 can be acquired after one or two years of classroom language study and 2) students cannot take content courses until they have mastered the language. In this traditional curriculum most learners are unlikely to succeed, since, as SLA research has demonstrated, a foreign language cannot usually be mastered after such a brief period of classroom study. Moreover, since language courses typically employ a communicative approach and therefore focus on interpersonal communication, students are ill-prepared for the discourse of academic content courses.[1] The ensuing frustration has been identified as a major source of attrition between the lower-level language courses that satisfy the language requirement and enrollments in the major.[2]

---

[1] James Cummins, *Bilingualism and Special Education: Issues in Assessment and Pedagogy* (Clevedon, England: Multilingual Matters, 1984). James Cummins, "Language Proficiency, Bilingualism, and Academic Achievement," in *The Multicultural Classroom: Readings for Content-Area Teachers*, ed. P. Richard-Amato & M. A. Snow (New York: Longman, 1992), 16-26.

[2] Beatrice C. Dupuy, "Content-Based Instruction: Can it Help Ease the Transition from Beginning to Advanced Foreign Language Classes?" *Foreign Language Annals* 33, no. 2 (2000): 205-23. Diane Musumeci, "Language and Linguistics in the Italian Curriculum," *Italica* 73, no. 4 (1996): 493-507.

In the Italian program at The Ohio State University (OSU) this artificial division between language and content instruction has been eliminated by adopting Content-Based Instruction (CBI), in which the study of language is integrated into courses that focus on content, such as history, film, and literature. While CBI can be adopted in a variety of ways and degrees, at OSU we have adapted all post-elementary courses to the CBI model, and courses that focus exclusively on language, such as "Grammar and Conversation" and "Grammar and Composition," no longer exist. By the same token, there are no courses that focus exclusively on content; faculty teach content while attending to students' developing language skills in every course. In this way, the study of language continues uninterrupted throughout the undergraduate program.

This essay begins with a brief introduction to CBI. First, the history of the development of this model and its current manifestations in the United States are outlined, then the principles of CBI and the research supporting its effectiveness in foreign language education are examined. This is followed by a case study of the changes implemented in the Italian program at OSU. A comparison of the old, traditional curriculum and the new CBI curriculum is accompanied by a discussion of the reasons for the change and the organization of the program. After describing the program that is in place, this essay concludes by exploring the challenges of curricular revision from a traditional language program to CBI, and describing how the faculty at OSU collectively confronted and are overcoming these challenges.

A brief introduction to Content Based Instruction

Dueñas[3] states that integrating language and content is not a novel pedagogical approach in the field of general education, but it is a relative newcomer to second/foreign language teaching. Using content to learn both language and subject matter originated in Canada circa 1965 in immersion programs that were developed for English speakers learning French, Canada's other official language. CBI appeared on the language teaching scene in the late 1980s and gained popularity in the 1990s.[4] For

---

[3] Maria Dueñas, "The Whats, Whys, Hows and Whos of Content-Based Instruction in Second/Foreign Language Education," *International Journal of English Studies* 4, no. 1 (2004): 73-96.

[4] For the distant origins of CBI, see Diane Musumeci, *Breaking Tradition: An Exploration of the Historical Relationship between Theory and Practice in Second Language Teaching* (San Francisco: McGraw Hill, 1997). She traces the principles that characterize CBI to three educators of the 15th-17th centuries who were

many years integrating language and content remained primarily an ESL and K-12 endeavor,[5] but it is becoming increasingly popular in secondary schools and has seen explosive growth in post-secondary institutions.

Met, Brinton and Holten, and Dueñas[6] point out that the term "content-based instruction" is commonly used to describe approaches that integrate language and content instruction, but that this term is not always used consistently. As examples, Met[7] notes that for Crandall and Tucker CBI is an approach that integrates the presentation of subject matter topics or tasks within the context of second/foreign language teaching while Curtain and Pesola limit use of the term to curriculum concepts being taught in the foreign language.[8] Moreover, the definitions of content also vary in that for some it must be academic subject matter while for others it needs to be material that is cognitively engaging but not necessarily academic.[9]

The differences among the various manifestations of CBI demonstrate the flexibility of the framework. Met[10] conceives of this flexibility in terms of a continuum of the relative role of content and language. At one extreme are total immersion programs that are primarily content driven, and at the other are language courses that frequently use content for language practice and are therefore language driven. She finds that sheltered courses, the adjunct model, and theme-based courses fall

---

proponents of pedagogical reform: Guarino Guarini (1374-1460), Ignatius of Loyola (1491-1556), and Johannes Amos Comenius (1592-1670). She suggests that their innovations were ultimately ignored as the "other" pedagogical practice of teaching Latin through memorization of grammar rules and vocabulary and translation came to be understood as the traditional approach to language teaching.

[5] Maiheng Shen Dietrich, "Integrating Content into the Language Classroom" in *Content, Tasks and Projects in the Language Classroom*, eds. R. Jourdenais and S. Springer (Monerey, CA: Monerey Institute of International Studies, 2005), 47-60.

[6] Myriam Met, "Content-Based Instruction: Defining Terms, Making Decisions" NFLC Reports. http://www.nflc.org (accessed 1/4/07). Donna Brinton and Christine Holten, "Into, Through and Beyond: A Framework to Develop Content-Based Material," *English Teaching Forum* 35 (1997): 10-25. Dueñas, "The Whats, Whys, Hows and Whos."

[7] Met, "Content-Based Instruction."

[8] Jodi Crandall and G. Richard Tucker, "Content-Based Instruction in Second and Foreign Languages" in *Foreign Language Education: Issues and Strategies*, eds. Amado Padilla, Hatford H. Fairchild and Concepcion Valadez (Newbury Park, CA: Sage, 1990), 35-54. Curtain, H. A. and Carol Ann Pesola. *Languages and Children: Making the Match* (New York: Longman, 1994).

[9] See the University of Minnesota's website on CBI (http://www.carla.umn.edu/cobaltt/cbi.html) for various definitions of what qualifies as content in CBI.

[10] Met, "Content-Based Instruction."

between the two extremes in different degrees. In sheltered courses, which fall to the right of immersion and partial immersion programs, students are taught content using linguistically sensitive teaching strategies, so the priority is mastery of the content but language learning is also attended to. The adjunct model of language/content integration falls in the middle of the continuum, since students are expected to learn content while developing language proficiency. They are taught and tested on subject matter by a content instructor and taught and tested on language by a language instructor. Theme-based courses are closest to the language-driven extreme, since these courses are organized around themes that are selected to contribute to language growth. These courses are taught by language teachers and learning of the content is incidental.

Despite the different approaches to CBI, Jourdenais and Shaw[11] provide a list of the defining characteristics of CBI that are shared by its various manifestations:

- learners are exposed to language while learning about other content areas
- content areas are relevant to learners' academic and/or professional needs
- language is contextualized through these relevant content areas, and thus is also relevant to learner needs
- support is provided for learners' linguistic development
- a focus is placed on developing academic and/or professional language proficiency
- authentic materials are used to present content matter (the use of authentic materials lends itself to the integration of skills, to increased motivation, and to increased cognitive and linguistic complexity).

These features of CBI offer the ideal conditions for learning a second language (as long as they are carried out appropriately). Grabe and Stoller[12] highlight seven strong rationales for using CBI that follow from

---

[11] R. Jourdenais and P. Shaw, "Dimensions of Content-Based Instruction in Second Language Education" in *Content, Tasks and Projects in the Language Classroom*, eds. R. Jourdenais and S. Springer (Monterey, CA: Monterey Institute of International Studies, 2005), 2.

[12] William Grabe and Fedricka L. Stoller, "Content-Based Instruction: Research Foundations, 1-15" CoBaLTT Modules: Principles—Reading: Grage & Stoller 1997. http://carla.acad.umn.edu/cobaltt/modules/index.html?principles/main.html (accessed 2/3/07).

these characteristics. They note that 1) CBI provides a setting in which students are exposed to a considerable amount of comprehensible input while learning content, which makes second language learning consistent with most other academic learning contexts. 2) CBI allows for explicit language instruction that is integrated with content instruction in a relevant, purposeful context. 3) Learners call on their own prior knowledge to learn additional language and subject matter. 4) Students are motivated to learn when confronted with complex and interesting information and demanding activities. 5) CBI supports a variety of learning approaches, such as cooperative learning, experiential learning, and project-based learning. 6) CBI is a flexible and adaptable approach that gives instructors the opportunity to meet the interests and needs of the instructor and the students. 7) CBI lends itself to student-centered activities, which increase student involvement.

These strong rationales predict the success of CBI, which is borne out by research. Grabe and Stoller[13] and the University of Minnesota's website on CBI[14] summarize the research from a variety of related disciplines that support the CBI approach. A major source of support for CBI comes from second language acquisition research, such as Krashen's comprehensible input hypothesis, Swain's output hypothesis that resulted from her work on French immersion programs in Canada, and Cummins' notion of Cognitive Academic Language Proficiency.[15] Research on the instructional strategies employed in CBI, such as cooperative learning, extensive reading, and the incorporation of a variety of thinking skills and learning strategies, have been shown to have a positive influence on second language development. Support for CBI also comes from educational and cognitive psychology. Grabe and Stoller (12-13) highlight five research areas (cognitive learning theory, depth-of-processing research, discourse comprehension processing research, motivation, attribution and interest research, and expertise research) that each provide support for CBI. The overwhelmingly positive evidence in favor of the CBI model of instruction is responsible for its explosive growth and for the decision to use CBI in the Italian undergraduate curriculum at OSU. In the next section, we will describe how we adapted CBI to meet our faculty and students' needs.

---

[13] Ibid.

[14] See note 9 above.

[15] Grabe and Stoller, "Content-Based Instruction," 2-3.

A case study: the Italian program at the Ohio State University

The desire for a change in the intermediate and advanced Italian curriculum at OSU has been building over several years. Like programs across the country, we have seen steady increases in Italian enrollments. Since 1995, enrollments at the intermediate level have increased by about 10-20 students per year, but from 2004/2005 to 2005/2006, there was a much larger increase: from 121 students to 164 students (43 students). Our courses in English have gone from enrolling 50 students in 2004/2005 to enrolling 311 in 2005/2006.

Another aspect that has contributed to the need for change at the intermediate level of OSU Italian is the thriving, growing study abroad program. Many of our minors and majors choose to go abroad and come back in search of new challenges from the Italian department on campus. Roughly 50 students[16] participate in our study abroad program in Lecce each summer, and we have recently begun to send students to programs that accommodate students who wish to study abroad during the academic year. As more and more students benefit from the study abroad experience, we find ourselves with more sophisticated students in the classroom.

Our goal in Italian at OSU is to offer stimulating courses that attract undergraduates and fulfill their expectations to acquire Italian and learn about Italian culture, society, history, literature, film, etc. However, we found that our previous courses and requirements fell short of serving the needs of our growing population of linguistically sophisticated learners, and that an expanded and diversified program at the intermediate and advanced levels was necessary in order to maintain the interest of our new student demographic.

We aimed for a new program that would continue to build proficiency while also providing a solid background in Italian studies. By doing this, we hoped that even more students would consider minoring or majoring in Italian and that, by diversifying our offerings, we would make it easier for students to see how a degree in Italian fits into their overall program of study. Table 1-1 shows the most relevant changes to our program, side-by-side with the previous offerings.

---

[16] Not all participants are majors or minors, but a large percentage of students in the Italian program study abroad before graduating.

Previous Undergraduate Curriculum	CBI Undergraduate Curriculum
202: Italian conversation and composition	Italian 202: Contemporary Italian society
206: Business Italian	
401: Review grammar and composition	Italian 401: Modern Italian media (repeatable to 10 credits)
402: Intermediate Italian conversation and composition	Italian 402: The sounds of Italian
420: Thematic approaches to modern Italian literature and culture (repeatable to 15 cr.)	Italian 420: Italian culture through the ages
	Italian 421: Reading Italy: Italian literature and culture (repeatable to 10 cr.)
	Italian 423: The Italian language yesterday and today
	Italian 425: The regions of Italy
	Italian 450: Italian theater workshop
601: Modern Italian syntax	Italian 601: Structures of the Italian language
602: Italian translating	
603: Advanced Italian conversation and composition	
604: Italian phonology	
	Italian 613: Italian cinema
	Italian 614: Survey of Italian literature
	Italian 615: Italian identities

Table 1-1. Side by side comparison of the old and new curriculum at OSU.

As the comparison shows, the new curriculum includes significant innovation. At the 400-level "Review grammar and composition" has been replaced with "Modern Italian media" and "Intermediate Italian conversation and composition" has been replaced with "The sounds of Italian," a linguistics course that focuses on phonetics and phonology with the goal of improving pronunciation. The course "Thematic approaches to modern Italian literature and culture" has been replaced with four new courses. Similar changes have been made at the 600-level so that, in accordance with the CBI model, all courses are organized around academic subject matter and the study of grammar and the development of the four language skills are incorporated into each course.

Our 200-level course, "Contemporary Italian society," which all students are required to take before moving into the 400-level, appears to serve as the traditional "bridge" course in our new curriculum. The term, "bridge," however, suggests that there is a stark contrast between our 100-level elementary courses and the intermediate-level courses, which is not the case at OSU. Before revamping our intermediate courses, our first-year courses were modified so that the exclusive use of Italian by our instructors and graduate teaching assistants was facilitated, learners spend more time doing meaningful, communicative activities, learners are exposed to extensive comprehensible input by following interactive presentations on culture, which in turn also improve students' cultural competence, and time is spent in class working on reading and writing skills. In order to successfully develop cultural competence and the four skills in this way, the grammar scope for the first year had to be reduced.[17] However, this change is concordant with research in SLA, which has shown that grammatical competence develops over time, not after one or even two exposures to grammar points. By reducing the amount of grammar in the first year, we created more time in the curriculum to develop the four language skills. Moreover, by adopting the CBI model for our intermediate and advanced students, we now have time to review structures and present more cognitively complex constructions when students are more likely to be ready to process them. That is, the more challenging grammar points that are not covered in the first year will be covered in future courses, and the grammar that is covered in the first year will be recycled during the rest of the sequence. Thus, the 200-level course continues what has begun in the first year: the development of the four skills and language study and serves as a transition to the intermediate level by developing content topics and emphasizing the refinement of reading skills and of writing and editing skills.

Since we eliminated all courses that focus exclusively on grammar,[18] the challenge was how to incorporate the continued study of grammar throughout the curriculum. Having identified the sorts of cultural awareness that we want our students to have, we determined the ways in which grammar could be incorporated into the study of this desired

---

[17] For a detailed rationale for the reduction of the grammar scope of the elementary-level Italian courses, see Janice M. Aski and Alessia Colarossi, "Doing it All in the First Year: Curricular Decisions for Italian Elementary Language Instruction" *Italica* 84, no. 1(2007): 22-41.

[18] The course, "Structures of Italian," is a linguistics course that focuses on the syntax of simple sentences and of complex constructions, such as indirect discourse, hypothetical constructions, and *fare/lasciare* + infinitive.

content. That is, we identified which grammatical structures would most likely appear in readings or emerge from discussions on each course topic. Research shows that formal features of the language are more likely to be learned and acquired if they are presented and practiced in the meaningful context in which they are encountered.[19] That is, exposing students to decontextualized language instruction that is separate from the meaningful language use provided by the content has minimal cffcct. For this reason, for example, the *passato remoto* and the passive were assigned to the course on the history of the language, since these structures are encountered often in these texts, *piacere, dovere/potere/volere,* and imperatives were assigned to the media course, since they are heard in dialogues in movies and television programs, and ordinal numbers and comparatives are presented in the culture course that provides an overview of the major historical periods (Medieval, Baroque, etc.). Thus, we aim to allow for natural patterns of repetition and the introduction of new structures through the coordination of all our courses. The distribution of grammar points throughout the curriculum is shown in Table 1-2.[20]

202	present perfect (and the remote past) ***da/per*+time** imperfect vs. present perfect **past perfect** indefinite **adjectives** and pronouns
401	*dovere/potere/volere* (present perfect and **other tenses, correct usage**) *piacere* and **verbs similar to *piacere*** object pronouns/double object pronouns formal/informal imperative (**with object pronouns**)

19 Patsy Lightbown, "The Importance of Timing in Focus on Form," in *Focus on Form in Classroom Second Language Acquisition*, eds. C. Doughty and J. Williams (Cambridge: Cambridge University Press, 1998), 177-196. Roy Lyster, *Learning and Teaching Languages Through Content: A Counterbalanced Approach* (Amsterdam, John Benjamins, 2007). Daryl M. Rodgers, "Developing Content and Form: Encouraging Evidence from Italian Content-Based Instruction," *The Modern Language Journal* 90 (2006): 373-386.

20 Once the distribution of grammatical structures was established, the faculty chose a grammar text that would be assigned for all courses beyond the elementary level so that students would not have to buy a different grammar text for each course. This text is used primarily as a grammar resource. Since in CBI grammar practice activities are embedded in the context of the content being studied (see below), these activities will be provided by the instructors.

420	comparatives of inequality with *di* and ***che*** **comparatives of equality** prepositions ordinal numbers relative pronouns (*che* and ***cui***)
421	subjunctive (all tenses)—**they have not had the *trapassato del congiuntivo*** ***la concordanza dei tempi*** **conjunctions followed by the subjunctive** **subjunctive vs. infinitive**
423	remote past **passive** and impersonal *si* future e **future of probability** **future anterior** (recognition only)
601	***fare/lasciare*+infinitive** conditional: present and **past** *periodo ipotetico* (**hypotheticals of impossibility**) **direct and indirect discourse (past conditional as "future in the past")**
613	subjunctive (all tenses) ***la concordanza dei tempi*** **conjunctions followed by the subjunctive** **subjunctive vs. infinitive**
614	**direct and indirect discourse (past conditional as "future in the past")** **the infinitive, the gerund and the past participle**
615	*periodo ipotetico* (**hypotheticals of impossibility**) ***fare/lasciare*+infinitive**

Table 1-2. Distribution of grammar points throughout the curriculum (*Items in bold are new material; they were not taught in the first year).

The complexity of the grammatical structures presented increases as learners move up the curriculum[21] with the expectation that as learners' proficiency improves they will have more attentional resources to devote

[21] Determining the complexity of particular structures is a sticky issue. See Janice M. Aski, "Alternatives to Mechanical Drills for the Early Stages of Language Practice in Foreign Language Textbooks," *Foreign Language Annals* 38, no.3 (2005): 333-43 for discussion of this topic. The progression in our curriculum reflects the order of grammatical structures, which in terms of complexity is primarily intuitive, that is found in most textbooks.

to processing more complex constructions. In addition, although it is expected that structures that cause difficulty will be reviewed as they emerge in all courses, in some cases review is overtly incorporated into the curriculum. That is, most of grammar covered in the 600-level is review of the constructions that are traditionally difficult for North American learners of Italian.

With these changes in the curriculum came changes in the major and minor requirements. Above all, we wanted to ensure that students did not take courses in a random order. In the old curriculum, students could take courses in essentially any order, so they could leave the elementary level and bypass the 200-level. Increased enrollments in Italian have allowed us to require students to go through each level of the curriculum, building the necessary language skills for different kinds of content as they go.[22] Moreover, previously students were not required to take a particular number of courses at any level. Now all majors must take two courses on the 600-level on our campus, which will ensure that by the time of degree they will have acquired the skills necessary to speak, read, write and understand Italian and be well-versed in varied aspects of Italian culture.

By coordinating our courses and degree requirements, we are convinced that our majors and minors will leave our program with a structured background in a variety of aspects of Italian studies. However, arriving at this newly structured curriculum with a new pedagogical approach did not happen over night. The faculty at OSU worked together for approximately three years to develop this program. The next section explains the developmental process.

Making curricular change happen

At OSU, revamping the entire post-elementary curriculum using the CBI model was a long process that required the participation and cooperation of the entire faculty. Many of the challenges we faced are outlined by Stoller[23] who describes case studies of a variety of CBI models and lists the following challenges that were common to all:

---

[22] At the moment, the prerequisite for most of the 600-level courses is 420, 421 or 423 because our population of students is not large enough to only allow students at the end of their course of study into the 600-level. However, 600-level courses will be offered less frequently, and students will be advised strongly to take all their 400-level courses before moving into the 600-level.

[23] Federicka L Stoller, "Content-Based Instruction: Perspectives on Curriculum Planning," *Annual Review of Applied Linguistics* 24 (2004): 261-83.

- The identification and development of appropriate content
- The selection and sequencing of language items dictated by content sources rather than a predetermined language syllabus
- The alignment of content with structures and functions that emerge from the subject matter (Short, 1999)[24]
- The choice of appropriate materials and the decision to use (or not to use) textbooks
- Faculty development that assists language instructors in handling unfamiliar subject matter and content-area instructors in handling language issues
- Language- and content-faculty collaboration
- The institutionalization of CBI in light of available resources and the needs of faculty and students
- Systematic assessment to demonstrate (1) students' language and content learning and (2) program effectiveness

The process of selecting the content to be covered in our undergraduate curriculum began by researching Italian programs throughout the country for innovative ideas. In addition, we identified what we believed our undergraduate majors should know about Italy, Italian, and Italian studies while keeping in mind the areas of interest/expertise of the faculty. After establishing the content topics, grammatical structures were assigned to each course as described above.

Once these features, which constituted the foundation of the program, were in place, we sought student input. We elicited feedback primarily on the choice of content topics and the new method of presenting grammar. This is a crucial step in program development since, as Babbit and Williams Mlynarczyk[25] point out, successful program design assesses (and meets) student needs. We held two more focus groups with undergraduate students of Italian during the three-year process, and each time modifications were made in accordance with their ideas and concerns. In addition, at the end of the process we asked an expert on CBI from another university to review our proposal. The external reviewer provided invaluable suggestions that improved our proposal significantly.

---

[24] Deborah Short, *New Ways in Teaching English at the Secondary Level* (Alexandria, Va.: Teachers of English to Speakers of Other Languages, 1999).
[25] Marcia Babbit and Rebecca Williams Mlynarczyk. "Keys to Successful Content-Based Programs," in *Content-Based College ESL Instruction*, ed. Loretta F. Kasper (Mahwaw, New Jersey: Lawrence Erlbaum, 2000), 55-72.

After having incorporated student feedback into the general plan, each faculty member began creating a sample syllabus for the courses in her/his area of expertise. This allowed us to identify the most suitable authentic Italian texts and sources for each course and unify assessment procedures so that grammar and content were both tested and attention was paid to the development of each of the fours skills. In addition, we developed an introduction to CBI and the philosophy of our approach that would appear on each syllabus, because we feel that it is important for students to understand the methodology by which they will learn language and content. (A sample course description from the syllabus for "Italian 420: Italian Culture through the Ages" is provided in Appendix A. The rubrics that follow the syllabus were developed in the Department of French and Italian at OSU). The syllabi that we developed serve as models for future iterations of the courses. Faculty members are asked to follow the spirit of the models, but are free to develop the courses as they wish. That is, everyone is asked to incorporate the designated grammar points, test grammar as well as content, and focus on and evaluate the four language skills, but they are free to develop the content as they feel appropriate.

In order to assess the overall effectiveness of our program over time, we implemented a program-wide assessment plan that requires each Italian major to create a web-based portfolio into which s/he will deposit a predetermined number of essays from each level of instruction (200, 400, and 600). Faculty will have access to the portfolios, and when students graduate, their essays will be examined by a committee. This tool together with the department-wide summative assessment procedures, such as exit surveys and oral exams, will allow us to assess whether the program goals for student achievement are being met.

At this point it is clear that this type of curricular development requires collaboration among the faculty.[26] All instructors must be willing to abandon the traditional division between lower-level language and upper-level content courses[27] and be willing to adopt CBI principles for teaching content as well as language. Dupuy points out that "... instructors must ...

[26] See Yuko Goto Butler, "Content-Based Instruction in EFL Contexts: Considerations for Effective Implementation," *JALT Journal* 27, no. 2 (2005): 227-45. Sagliano, Michael, Stewart Timothy and Julie Sagliano. "Professional Training to Develop Content-Based Instruction in Higher Education," *TESL Canada Journal* 16, no. 1 (1998): 36-53.

[27] Byrnes, Heidi. "Meaning and Form in Classroom-Based SLA Research: Reflections from a College Foreign Language Perspective," in *Form and Meaning: Multiple Perspectives*, eds. James Lee and Albert Valdman (Boston: Heinle & Heinle, 2000), 125-79.

have a strong understanding of and dedication to CBI principles. They must be willing to shelter content, [and] provide students with a variety of activities in which they can purposefully make use of the target language..." Wilcox Peterson also describes what content instructors ideally need to know to successfully implement CBI, including how to activate background knowledge, the importance of comprehensible input, and approaches to integrating content and language.[28] There is a general consensus in the literature that providing input is not enough; learners also need to attend to how meaning is formed in order for language development in the CBI model to be effective.[29] In particular, instructors need to understand and develop effective means for focusing on form while working with the content material, which, as noted above, research studies have identified as a necessary factor for second language development. Moreover, as Swain's[30] output hypothesis suggests, learner output is also essential for restructuring interlanguage, which means that instructors also need to focus on developing and expanding pushed output in the classroom. However, the biggest challenge for instructors will be to avoid drifting to the extremes of teaching language or content exclusively and succumbing to the temptation to rely on materials and lesson plans that have been developed over the years that may not be appropriate for CBI.[31]

In order to equip instructors with the instructional methodology that research has shown to be successful and to unify instruction across the

---

[28] Dupuy, "Content-Based Instruction," 219. Wilcox Peterson, Pat. "Knowledge, Skills and Attitudes in Teacher Preparation for Content-Based Instruction," in *The Content-Based Classroom: Perspectives on Integrating Language and Content* (New York: Longman 1997), 173.

[29] Brinton and Holten, "Into, Through and Beyond." Goto Butler, "Content-Based Instruction." Lesser, Michael J. "Learner Proficiency and Focus on Form during Collaborative Dialogue," *Language Teaching Research* 8, no. 1 (2004): 55-81. Master, Peter. "Grammar in Content-Based Instruction," in *Content-Based College ESL Instruction*, ed. Loretta F. Kasper (Mahwaw, New Jersey: Lawrence Erlbaum, 2000), 93-106. Pica, Teresa. "Subject-Matter Content: How Does it Assist the Interactional and Linguistic Needs of Classroom Language Learners?" *The Modern Language Journal* 86, no. 1 (2002): 1-19.

[30] Meryl Swain. "The Output Hypothesis: Just Speaking and Writing Aren't Enough," *The Canadian Modern Language Review* 50 (1993): 68-83.

[31] These challenges are discussed by Dupuy, "Content-Based Instruction," Kasper, *Content-Based College ESL Instruction*, Master, "Grammar in Content-Based Instruction," and Brinton, Donna M., Marguerite Ann Snow and Majorie Bingham Wesche, *Content-Based Second Language Instruction* (New York: Newbury House, 1989).

curriculum, all faculty and instructors of Italian at OSU that teach at the intermediate and advanced levels will participate in a training meeting led by the director of the Italian language program. The faculty will then convene once per quarter to discuss problems that arise and share materials and instructional approaches.[32]

Concluding remarks

It is up to the faculty in every program to assess their program's effectiveness and decide whether a change is necessary. At OSU we felt that our curriculum had fallen behind the times and needed to be updated to come into line with current research in foreign language pedagogy and second language acquisition. Although there are still many unresolved issues in these research areas, they have given us many insights into how languages are learned and how they can be taught more effectively.

We decided to adopt the CBI model of instruction because it is highly recommended by research in terms of its effectiveness, and it is a flexible model that could be adapted (relatively easily) to our needs. Leaver and

---

[32] The packet that accompanies the training meeting will include the following readings: Dueñas, "The Whats, Whys, Hows and Whos," Brinton and Holten, "Into, Through and Beyond." Fredricka Stoller, "Content-Based Instruction: A Shell for Language Teaching or a Framework for Strategic Language and Content Learning? CoBaLTT Modules: Principles–Reading: Stoller 2002. http://www.carla.umn.edu/cobaltt/modules/strategies/Stoller2002/READING1/stoller2002.htm (accessed 2/3/07). Diane Musumeci, "Second Language Reading and Content Area Instruction: The Role of Second Language Reading in the Development of Communicative and Subject Matter Competence," in *Language and Content Discipline—and Content-Based Approaches to Language Study*, eds. Merle Krueger and Ryan Frank (Washington: D.C. Heath and Company, 1993), 169-180. Lyster, *Learning and Teaching Languages through Content: A Counterbalanced Approach*, Chapters 2-4. For additional information and examples of how to integrate focus on form and content, see, among others, Lyster, Ibid., Pica, "Subject Matter Content," and Mary Schleppegrell and Mariana Achugar. "Learning Language and Learning History: A Functional Linguistic Approach," *TESOL Journal* 12, no. 2 (2003): 21-7. For activities, examples of successful reading strategies and suggestions for how to access content, see Brinton and Holten, "Into, Through and Beyond," Jiaying Howard "Developing Reading Activities: Making Content Reading Accessible to Language Learners," in *Content, Tasks and Projects in the Language Classroom: 2004 Conference Proceedings*, eds. R. Jourdenais and S. Springer (Monerey, California: Monterey Institute of International Studies, 2005), 35-45. Musumeci, "Second Language Reading," and Schleppegrell and Achugar, "Learning Language."

Stryker[33] point out that "CBI may be implemented effectively in many different ways, depending on the setting, the resources available, the language proficiency of the students, and its appropriateness in achieving the overall objectives of a program of study." There is an increasing number of programs that are adopting the CBI platform in different degrees. For example, the German Department at Georgetown University has taken CBI a step beyond the OSU program. They revamped their entire curriculum and developed a content-oriented curriculum that spans the entire four-year language sequence, including the elementary level.[34] Although renovating an entire curriculum may not be plausible for all programs, steps can be taken to incorporate CBI into a curriculum that is already in place, such as creating CBI transitional courses.[35] For example, Musumeci[36] describes a second-year, two-course CBI sequence in the Italian program at the University of Illinois at Champaign-Urbana that serves as a bridge between the elementary language courses and intermediate/advanced (primarily) literature courses that focus on content. Bueno recounts her experiences in the Spanish Department of a Midwestern state university transforming a third-year composition and conversation course into a CBI course.[37]

---

[33] Betty Lou Leaver and Stephen Stryker. "Content_Based Instruction for Foreign Language Classrooms," *Foreign Language Annals* 22 (1989): 271.

[34] See their website, http://www3.georgetown.edu/departments/german/programs/curriculum/index.htm l, for a detailed description of the transition, which took place from 1997-2000, and of the characteristics of the CBI program that they implemented.

[35] Gisela Hoelchel-Alden, "Turning Professional: Content-Based Communication and the Evolution of a Cross-Cultural Language Curriculum," *Foreign Language Annals* 33 (2000): 614-21.

[36] Musumeci, "Content Language Learning," and Musumeci, "Language and Linguistics." See Rodgers, "Developing Content and Form" for a recent (positive) assessment of the program outcomes at the University of Illinois at Champaign-Urbana.

[37] Kathleen A. Bueno, "Creating Community and Making Connections in the Third-Year Spanish Course: A Content-Based Approach," *Foreign Language Annals* 35, no. 3 (2002): 333-42. For citations or reports of other experiences instituting CBI at post-secondary institutions, see Dueñas, "The Whats, Whys, Hows and Whos," Grabe and Stoller, "Content-Based Instruction," Met, "Content-Based Instruction," Stoller, "Content-Based Instruction," and Stephen B. Stryker and Betty Lou Leaver "Introduction," in *Content-Based Instruction in Foreign Language Education: Models and Methods*, eds. Stephen B. Stryker and Betty Lou Leaver (Georgetown: Georgetown University Press, 1997), 2-28.

The type of transition that takes place is particular to each program and crucially depends on the motivation and dedication of most (preferably all) the faculty members who will teach in the new curriculum or the course(s) that has/have been crafted to fit the CBI model. As awareness of second language issues grows and faculty learn the value of comprehensible input and realize that students cannot learn all the grammar of the Italian language in one year or in a few grammar-focused intermediate/advanced courses, attention will increasingly turn to a model in which language and content instruction go hand in hand.

THE OHIO STATE UNIVERSITY, USA

APPENDIX A

Syllabus

This syllabus demonstrates how the four language skills are developed in a content course. The grammar topics are strategically placed in the course to coincide with their appearance in the course materials.

Italian 420: Italian Culture through the Ages
5 Credit Hours

Professor:
French and Italian
Hagerty Hall
E-mail:
Office hours:
Date/time final exam:

Course Description:
Welcome to Italian 420! The instructional approach taken in this course and in all of the intermediate and advanced Italian courses is *Content-Based Instruction*, which is a holistic approach to foreign language education; that is, you will develop your language skills while learning about a particular topic. This course provides an overview of the major historical periods (Medieval, Baroque, etc.) through readings and discussions of significant events in each period. Students will learn about a variety of historical figures and their contribution to Italian culture. Oral skills are refined through class discussion and oral presentations. Students will develop writing skills by writing several essays throughout the course and particular attention will be given to the continued development of effective reading skills. New vocabulary will be derived from the texts and topics that you will discuss. Grammar will be reviewed as necessary, but a certain number of structures will be targeted for focused review or presentation. The *Targeted Structures* for this course are: comparatives of inequality with *che*, comparatives of equality, ordinal numbers, and relative pronouns.

Goals:
The goals of this course are to improve reading, speaking, listening, and writing skills through the analysis of issues in Italian culture and history as revealed in the material studied.

Language:
This coursc will bc conducted entirely in Italian.

Texts:
Easy Italian Reader: A Three-Part Text for Beginning Students, Riccarda Saggese, New York, 2006.
L'Italia dal Fascismo ad Oggi, Daniela Bartalesi-Graf, Perugia, 2005.

Internet sources: numerous websites will be used—see schedule for details

Grammar text: Marchegiani Jones, Irene and Francesca Italiano. 2007. *Crescendo*. 2nd ed. Boston: Thomson Heinle. (Also on reserve in the Main Library.)

Students may wish to purchase an Italian dictionary if they do not already have one.

Note: Do not resell *Crescendo* if you are continuing in Italian. This text will be assigned in all intermediate-level courses and will be a useful text to consult in the advanced courses.

Methods of Evaluation:

Quality of class participation, including oral presentations:	15%
Quizzes:	20%
Compositions:	20%
Midterm:	20%
Final:	25%

Grading scale:

A 93-100	B+ 88-89	B- 80-82	C 73-77	D+ 68-69	E 64-0
A- 90-92	B 83-87	C+ 78-79	C- 70-72	D 65-67	

Participation (attendance, quality of classroom interaction): Regular attendance and participation in class are essential for learning a foreign language. Therefore, students should prepare carefully for class by completing all assignments in advance and being ready to participate actively and thoughtfully in class.

Homework: Homework will be assigned each class period to be discussed and/or submitted during the following class period (unless otherwise instructed). Late homework will not be accepted. If you miss class, you must contact a classmate to find out the material covered and assigned and come to the next class meeting with the work completed.

Oral presentations: Each student will prepare an oral presentation on a topic selected from a list prepared by the instructor (topics will include the authors, cities, composers, and the literary works studied, etc.) The presentation must include visuals and/or realia (Power Point preferred) and last approximately 10 minutes. Presentations will be graded using the attached rubric.

Quizzes: Regular quizzes will test content, grammar and vocabulary.

Compositions: There will be four compositions, which will be graded using the rubric attached to this syllabus. Before turning in each composition, there may be an in-class writing workshop in which students will edit and discuss each other's papers and during which time the instructor will provide feed-back to each student. Students who are Italian majors may submit the last composition to their on-line assessment portfolio.

Exams: There will be a midterm and a final exam, both of which will test the course content as well as the grammar and vocabulary discussed. Students should note the date and time of the final exam. The date and time of the final exam are determined by the university and cannot be changed. There should be no conflicts with exams in other courses.

Academic Misconduct:
It is the responsibility of the Committee on Academic Misconduct to investigate or establish procedures for the investigation of all reported cases of student academic misconduct. The term "academic misconduct" includes all forms of student academic misconduct wherever committed; illustrated by, but not limited to, cases of plagiarism and dishonest

practices in connection with examinations. Instructors shall report all instances of alleged academic misconduct to the committee (Faculty Rule 3335-5-487). For additional information, see the Code of Student Conduct (http://studentaffairs.osu.edu/info_for_students/csc.asp).

Disability Services:
Students with disabilities that have been certified by the Office for Disability Services will be appropriately accommodated, and should inform the instructor as soon as possible of their needs. The Office for Disability Services is located in 150 Pomerene Hall, 1760 Neil Avenue; telephone 292-3307, TDD 292-0901; http://www.ods.ohio-state.edu/.

Schedule (pages numbers correspond to *Saggese*, unless otherwise noted):

WEEK ONE:
Introduction

Rome
Grammar: ordinal numbers
Homework 1: Saggese, pp. 61-62. Answer questions on p. 63. Do grammar exercises.

Rome
Grammar: comparatives of equality
Homework 2: Grammar exercises, Saggese, pp. 64-65. Answer questions on p. 65, Do grammar exercises.

WEEK TWO:
Julius Caesar
Homework 1: Saggese, pp. 66-67. Answer questions on p. 68. Read Ripasso, p. 68 and answer questions on p. 69. Do Cruciverba, p. 70.

Pax romana
First quiz: vocabulary and grammar points from the readings that were discussed in class
Homework 2: Saggese, pp. 71-73. Answer questions on p. 74.
First essay: Do some research on the Internet and write a description of some currently visible medieval aspects of an Italian city (e.g. a cathedral, a piazza, a baptistery, a palazzo). Print a picture as well. 250 words.

The medieval city
In class: share essays and images in the form of oral presentations.
Homework 1: Read Saggese, pp. 75-76. Respond to questions on p. 77, Read Saggese, pp. 78-79. Respond to questions on p. 80.

WEEK THREE:
Medieval culture and religiosity, Saint Francis of Assisi
In class: watch some of Zeffirelli's film about St. Francis
Grammar: comparatives of inequality with *che*
Revision of first essay due.
Homework 2: Read Francis' "Cantico delle creature" on LiberLiber
http://www.liberliber.it/biblioteca/f/francesco_d_assisi/il_cantico_di_frate_sole/html/cantico.htm
Saggese, pp. 81-83, answer questions on pp. 83-84. Do grammar exercises.

Marco Polo and Venice
Homework 1: Read Ripasso 2 pp. 84-85 and answer questions pp. 85-86. Do cruciverba, p. 87. Read Day One, Introduction, Decameron, paragraphs 8-12 in Decameron Web.

The Black Death
Essay #2, draft 1 due.
Quiz #2 on vocabulary, grammar and reading comprehension
Homework 2: Read pp. 88-90 and answer questions on p. 90.
http://www.arte.go.it/mostre/botticelli/index.htm : this reading will be divided up amongst the class

WEEK FOUR:
Botticelli and Lorenzo il Magnifico
Homework 1: pp. 91-93, answer questions on pp. 93-94. Do Cruciverba, p. 94

Cristoforo Colombo
Revision of Essay #2 due.
Homework 2: Study for midterm.

Midterm
Homework 1: read biographies of Leonardo and Michelangelo in LiberLiber. Look at their art in **www.wga.hu**

WEEK FIVE:

Leonardo and Michelangelo

In class: oral presentations of individual art works by students
Grammar: relative pronouns (*che*)
Homework 2: pp. 95-97. Answer questions on p. 98. Do grammar exercises.

Galileo

First draft of Essay #3 due.
Grammar: relative pronouns (*cui*)
Homework 1: Read pp. 99-101. Answer p. 101, Do grammar exercises.

Masaniello

Quiz #3
Homework 2: Read pp. 102-104. Answer p. 104. Read 105-106. Answer pp. 106-107. Do cruciverba, p. 108.

WEEK SIX:

Carlo III di Borbone

Revision of Essay #3 due.
Homework 1: 109-112. Questions, p. 113.
Watch "Le cinque giornate di Milano," first episode, on Raiclick: http://www.raiclicktv.it/raiclickpc/secure/folder.srv?id=1716

L'unità d'Italia

Homework 2: 114-116, questions, p. 116.
Watch "Napoli e la sua provincia" on Raiclick:
http://www.raiclicktv.it/raiclickpc/secure/folder.srv?id=251

Different realities, North and South

Relative pronouns (*il quale*)
First draft of Essay #4 due.
Homework: pp. 117-119, questions, p. 119. Ripasso, p. 119-120, questions p. 120. Cruciverba, p. 121, grammar exercises.

WEEK SEVEN:

Modernization and Emigration

Quiz #4
Homework: Bartalesi-Graf, pp. 17- 26, questions, p.28.
Watch "Il giovane Mussolini" on Raiclick:
http://www.raiclicktv.it/raiclickpc/secure/folder.srv?id=1721

Fascism
Revision of Essay #4 due.
Grammar: ordinal numbers
Homework: Bartalesi-Graf pp. 29-37. Do grammar exercises.

Le donne e la guerra
Homework: Bartalesi-Graf pp. 66-78 and all questions.

WEEK EIGHT:
"Boom economico"
Homework: Bartalesi-Graf pp. 83-88 and all questions and exercises.

After the war—first-hand descriptions
Homework: Bartalesi-Graf pp. 111- 122 and all questions

From 1960-1980
Homework: Bartalesi-Graf pp. 126-133 and all questions and exercises.

WEEK NINE:
1968—in their own words
Homework: Bartalesi-Graf pp. 164-177 and all questions

The last 25 years
Homework: Bartalesi-Graf pp. 178-188 and all questions

Tangentopoli
Homework: Bartalesi-Graf pp. 233-240 and all questions

WEEK TEN:
Immigration in the last 25 years
Homework: Bartalesi-Graf pp. 263-273 and all questions

The mafia
Homework: prepare an oral presentation on one of the main themes covered in this class.

Conclusions
Homework: study for the final!

FINAL EXAM

French/Italian Evaluation of oral work

Name:____________Grade:______

Categorical Rubric

Amount of language used

A Student communicates significantly more than required to fulfill the task.

B Student communicates more than required to fulfill the task.

C Student communicates an adequate amount to fulfill the task.

D Student communicates, but amount is less than adequate.

F There is not enough speech to evaluate.

Fluency/Fluidity

A Speech is smooth and flowing. No hesitation or rephrasing.

B Speech is smooth for the most part. Occasional hesitancy. Some rephrasing.

C Speech is generally hesitant and often choppy.

D Speech is extremely hesitant and choppy. Frequent pauses and/or unfinished phrases.

F Speech is limited to isolated words or short phrases. No fluidity whatsoever.

Pronunciation

A No or very little mispronunciation that interferes with comprehension.

B Mispronunciation rarely results in misunderstanding.

C Several mispronunciations resulting in some confusion and misunderstanding.

D Frequent mispronunciation resulting in consistent confusion and misunderstanding.

F Mispronunciation makes comprehension impossible.

Vocabulary

A Student uses a wide range of vocabulary appropriately.

B Student uses a fairly wide range of vocabulary, most of which is used appropriately.

C Student uses an adequate range of vocabulary, but sometimes inappropriately.

D Student uses a very limited range of vocabulary and often inappropriately.

F Student shows no command of vocabulary.

Grammar

A No or few grammatical errors.
B Some grammatical errors that do not result in misunderstanding.
C Several grammatical errors resulting in occasional misunderstanding.
D Many grammatical errors resulting in frequent confusion and misunderstanding.
F Grammatical errors so frequent that communication is totally impeded.

Prepared role play/skits

A Exchange is very well connected and clear with no hesitations.
B Exchange is well connected with very few hesitations.
C Exchange is somewhat choppy due to misunderstandings between participants.
D Exchange is unconnected and extremely choppy due to misunderstandings between participants.
F Student is unable to maintain her/his end of dialogue. Totally unconnected.

Prepared Presentation

A Presentation is well organized and content is covered in depth with elaboration and detail.
B Presentation is fairly well organized and content is covered in sufficient depth.
C Presentation is somewhat organized and content is mostly covered adequately.
D Presentation lacks organization and does not cover many significant aspects of the topic.
F Presentation is disorganized and misses most significant aspects of the topic.

French/Italian Evaluation of written work
Name:_______________Grade:______
Categorical Rubric

Content

A	Significant, interesting, well conceived, appropriate to assignments, stays on task. Rich in specific details and examples.
B	Generally good work, but some facts or arguments may be unsupported, or some repetitions or clichés may be apparent.
C	Only adequate development of content and arguments, shows occasional carelessness.
D	Inadequately or insufficiently developed. No effort to make content significant to the topic at hand. Reader may be unsure of writer's message.
E	Wildly inappropriate or incoherent content.

Grammar

A	Good use of grammar, successful effort to use new forms and structures.
B	Effort to use new forms, occasional errors do not impede comprehension.
C	Grammar communicates adequately, but limited in range; frequent errors.
D	Meaning often confused; errors very frequent and significant; needs major work.
E	Unintelligible.

Vocabulary

A	Good use of vocabulary, successful effort to use new forms and idioms.
B	Effort to use new forms, occasional errors do not impede comprehension, but at times poorly calqued from English.
C	Limited range of vocabulary, frequent errors and calques from English, or poor dictionary work.
D	Very limited vocabulary, meaning often confused; errors very frequent, needs major work.
E	Unintelligible.

Style and Organization

A	Well-organized paragraphs and use of topic and summary sentences, convincing, easy to follow, highly readable.
B	Good evidence of structuring of paragraphs, with some unwieldy patterns.

C	Some attempts at organization, but few topic, development, or summary sequences. Difficult to read.
D	Style is awkward, lack of organization undermines intelligibility, hard to follow.
E	No evidence of planning in paragraph or sentence structure.

Typographic Accuracy

A	Good attention to details
B	Spelling, punctuation errors do not impede comprehension
C	Frequent errors in spelling and/or punctuation errors: use Spellcheck!
D	Unacceptably sloppy; accents not typed; use Spellcheck!
E	Not intelligible.

Suggestions for next time:

CHAPTER TWO

TASK-BASED INSTRUCTION OF INTERMEDIATE ITALIAN: A RESEARCH-SUPPORTED MODEL

TOM MEANS

Introduction

This article addresses the need to better define what we mean by task-based instruction (TBI) of Italian. Accordingly it presents a well-defined, research-supported model of TBI of intermediate Italian. This model has the working title of "Input-heavy TBI."

TBI of Italian at present is a very generalized pedagogical notion: many instructors of Italian consider 'task-based' work to entail the occasional use of tasks in place of exercises as a means of practice in a grammar-based syllabus. The pedagogical plan presented here will share an alternative that is truly task-based: students learn by doing. This TBI model is based on a three-phase task cycle of *pre-task, during-task, and post-task.* The TBI model of intermediate Italian presented here is based on empirical studies demonstrating the beneficial effects of its various components. Second Language Acquisition (SLA) research generally concurs that classroom instruction should emulate authentic language use, language that is dynamic and constantly changing. TBI sets the stage for the acquisition of such dynamism by forcing students to transact tasks in realistic ways, in real time. The model's balance of structured input (important for developing interpretation skills) with structured output (important for developing production skills) appears to show a way forward for our attempts to catalyze our students' potential for achieving accuracy and fluency.

Each phase of the TBI model will be presented briefly below. This section will be followed by a brief overview of Traditional Instruction (TI). Next, the theoretical and empirical foundations of each phase of the TBI model will be presented with some concrete examples. The final section in this chapter will be a summary of the original research that supports this model.

A definition

An essential definition of TBI can be reached by looking at a TBI syllabus: The object and focus of a TBI syllabus is the performance of concrete tasks. Compare this to TI, where the object and focus of the syllabus is the textbook's chapters and the grammatical points therein. Another common definition of TBI is that it is a system of instruction in which students act primarily as language *users*; compare this to TI, where students act primarily as language *learners*.[1]

The model of TBI presented in this chapter has the working title of Input-heavy TBI, because beyond the above-stated focus of performing concrete tasks, there is also a focus on copious input in all media: aural, textual, visual, web-based. The present model and the original research that informs it[2] provide some proof that "Classrooms can become places where learners talk about real things and learn about each other [in the target language] ... moving away from teacher-fronted to teacher-assisted interactions"[3]

Three-phase cycle of TBI

This TBI model is based on a three-phase task cycle of *pre-task, during-task, and post-task*. This is an adaptation of J. Willis'[4] three phases of pre-task, task cycle, and language focus. Each phase will be presented briefly below, and then treated in depth in the following section.

A pre-task phase:

- tasks are explained in both English and Italian;
- the lexical and grammatical tools to accomplish this task are provided;

---

[1] Kris Van den Branden, *Task-based Language Education: From Theory to Practice* (Cambridge: Cambridge University Press, 2006).
[2] Tom Means, "A comparative study on the effectiveness of task-based and traditional instruction of Italian: Findings on accuracy and fluency" Unpublished PhD dissertation (Rutgers University, New Jersey, 2006).
[3] James Lee and Bill VanPatten, *Making Communicative Language Teaching Happen* (New York: McGraw Hill, 2004), 72.
[4] Jane Willis, *A Framework for Task-Based Learning.* (Harlow: Longman, 1996).

- lengthy exposure to authentic oral speech and/or text is given in a relevant context;
- task-relevant activities are performed;
- successful demonstration of task is provided to learners;
- pre-task planning is performed individually and/or in pairs.

A during-task phase:

- learners, on their own, perform the task;
- performance is recorded on video and/or audio;
- task is accomplished.

A post-task phase:

- learners prepare transcripts of their own performance;
- learners give self-report and/or self-assessment;
- teacher presents relevant grammar points;
- learners work on relevant focus-on-form exercises;
- learners revise their self-transcriptions and hand in final "paper" for the task cycle;
- learners also hand in the recorded task performance.

Across the three phases, conditions are created for natural learning to occur: there is authentic exposure to extended input, opportunities for spontaneous output, and there is a focus on more formal, planned language.[5] In order to ground this cycle in the reader's mind, I will now share an example of a task that has been used in normal foreign-language classroom settings, and under rigorous research conditions: "Present how your partner celebrated his/her last 3 birthdays, in a one-to-two minute oral presentation, without notes."

This task has been operationalized as a 4-class lesson plan that lasts for approximately 6 contact hours. Following is the complete outline of a task cycle of Input-heavy TBI:

---

[5] Ibid.

Input-heavy TBI, Three Phase Task Cycle

I. Pre-task
   a. Introduce lesson-final task
   b. Watch/read pertinent target language material (Structured Input)
   c. Input A ; Activity A
   d. Teacher-led brainstorm
   e. Input B; Activity B
   f. Input C; Activity C
   g. Input D; Activity D
   h. (Watch successful demonstration of task [on video])
   i. Pre-task planning (individual and/or pairs)

II. During-task
   a. Do task (with time pressure; if task is oral, do not read notes)
   b. Record performance on audio/video

III. Post-task
   a. Prepare self-transcript, Version A (in pairs); Start self-correction (if written)
   b. (Watch task demonstration again; read native transcript)
   c. Group report/assessment
   d. Teach relevant grammar points; do relevant grammar exercises
   e. Revise self-transcription, Version B

Table 2-1. Input-heavy TBI.

Differences between TBI and Traditional Instruction (TI)

TBI has evolved from Communicative Language Teaching (CLT) which has been the dominant general approach to language teaching in the United States since the 1970's. CLT evolved from the post-ALM (Audio Lingual Method) notion that language learning occurs from meaning negotiation, and that the best way to harness this in language classrooms is through putatively natural communication, where students are simply exposed to natural samples of the target language. CLT is also the mother approach of TI, which is how Italian is currently taught in most university settings in the United States[6]. As CLT evolved throughout the 1980's and 1990's a strong version (resembling TBI) appeared alongside a weak version (resembling TI). The architecture of TBI is considered a strong version of CLT because it maintains a priority on meaning. The

[6] Means.

architecture of TI is considered a weak version of CLT because it has replaced the original priority on meaning with a priority on form. TI is also commonly cited as Presentation, Practice, Production (PPP) and is generally presented as a three-part cycle in the literature[7].

TI: Three-part cycle

The basic order of TI (also referred to as PPP) is to:

- present a discrete grammatical item;
- practice that discrete point;
- produce that language in a relatively 'free' context, with learners interacting in pairs or groups, often to complete a written exercise and/or an oral communication task.

D. Willis[8] describes how the TI (PPP) methodology appears to allow for three important elements contributing to language learning:

1. it allows for a precise focus on specific target forms of the language;
2. it encourages students to speak with some attention to form;
3. it provides opportunities for language use in a communicative context.

As stated above, the architecture of TBI is considered a strong version of CLT because it maintains a priority on meaning. I will later refer to this priority as one in which fluency development comes before accuracy development. The architecture of TI/PPP is considered a weak version of CLT because it prioritizes grammatical form over meaning, thus it prioritizes accuracy development over fluency development.[9] The TBI presented in this chapter falls under the label Focus on Form instruction,[10]

---

[7] Jane Willis and Dave Willis, eds. *Challenge and Change in Language Teaching* (Oxford: Heinemann Macmillan, 1996); Ron Sheen, "Focus on form—a myth in the making," *ELT Journal* 57 (2003): 225-33; Ron Sheen, "Focus on formS as a means of improving accurate oral production," in A. Housen and M. Pierrard, eds., *Investigations in Instructed Second Language Acquisition* (New York: Mouton de Gruyter, 2005); Michael Swan, "Legislation by Hypothesis: The case of task-based instruction" *Applied Linguistics* 26, no. 3 (2006): 376-401.

[8] Willis and Willis.

[9] In SLA research, a general definition of *fluency* is "the capacity to communicate in real time," likewise a general definition of *accuracy* is "the ability to formulate the target language according to native speaker norms."

[10] Michael Long and Peter Robinson, "Focus on form: Theory, research, and practice," In Catherine Doughty and Jessica Williams, eds. *Focus on Form in Classroom Second Language Acquisition* (Cambridge: Cambridge University Press, 1998).

where the goal of the language lesson is meaning, but some attention is given to form.

One of the principles of TBI is that it is a form of instruction in which meaning is primary and form is secondary. Contrarily in TI, the reverse is true: form is primary and meaning is secondary. This follows another key principle of TBI: that students' accuracy development should *follow* their fluency development. This would be instead of the opposite approach implicit in TI, that fluency development will follow accuracy development.

In TBI, all learners are aware of the fact that their units of analysis[11] are the tasks to be performed, recorded and transcribed; thus their focus is primarily on creating meaning and fluency. In TI, all learners are aware of the fact that their units of analysis are the chapters and grammatical topics to be covered in the textbook; thus their focus is primarily on the forms and accuracy therein. The following table, Table 2-2, aims to clarify and expand upon the foci of these types of instruction:

	Task-based Instruction (TBI)	**Traditional Instruction (TI)**
Also referred to as:	Focus on Form	Focus on Forms; PPP
Directionality:	Meaning >Form; Fluency > Accuracy	Form > Meaning; Accuracy > Form
Type of syllabus:	Analytic	Synthetic
Unit of analysis:	Task Performance	Textbook chapter, Grammar Point
Order of events:	Do, then analyze	Analyze, then do

Table 2-2. Types of instruction presented in this chapter.

The following table, Table 2-3, adapted from Ellis,[12] illustrates general descriptions of how TBI and TI programs traditionally view their respective units of analysis, tasks and textbook chapters.

[11] Michael Long and Graham Crookes, "Three approaches to task-based syllabus design," *TESOL Quarterly,* 26 (1991): 27-55.

[12] Rod Ellis, "Task-based research and language pedagogy," *Language Teaching Research* 4, no. 3 (2000): 197.

	Tasks (TBI)	Textbook Chapters (TI)
Orientation	Linguistic skills are developed through engaging in communicative activity	Linguistic skills viewed as a prerequisite for learning communicative abilities
Focus	Propositional content and pragmatic communicative meaning	Linguistic form and semantic meaning
Center	Meaning-centered and student-centered.	Form-centered and teacher-centered
Goal	Achievement of a communicative goal	Manifestation of code knowledge
Outcome-evaluation	Performance evaluated in terms of whether the communicative goal has been achieved	Performance evaluated in terms of conformity to the code
Real-world relationship	Direct and obvious relationship between the activity that arises from the task and natural communicative activity	Internalization of linguistic skills serves as an investment for future use

Table 2-3. Units of analysis presented in this chapter.

The Role of Input and Output in TBI

Before moving on to a concrete example of how a task cycle is implemented, I would like to note the crucial role of input in this model of TBI: it is predominantly input-based—learners spend approximately two thirds of their time comprehending, elaborating and negotiating audio, video and written input. This is important to note because it could seem somewhat paradoxical that a "production-based" methodology like TBI has such an emphasis on comprehension.

This model of TBI contains a focus on copious input *and* meaningful output because current research[13] suggests that an effective balance of structured input and structured output will better lead to acquisition than the traditional focus on production. This model of TBI, "Input-heavy TBI" is an attempt to strike this balance. Research has shown the superior learning effects on foreign language learners who receive copious amounts of relevant target-language input. Such input is believed to promote the growth of grammatical competence[14].

The model's three crucial stages are presented in some detail in the following section, where each sub-phase is couched in the concrete example of the "birthday" task. The theory and research behind each sub-phase is also presented when relevant. At this point, the reader will get the most use of the following examples by first glancing at the TBI outline provided above, Table 2-1.

Pre-task Phase: Introduce lesson-final task

As the cycle commences, students are reminded that this cycle will last approximately 6 classroom hours in its entirety. The pre-task phase is initiated by presenting the lesson-final task to the students. In a foreign-language setting, the teacher would present the task to the students in both

---

[13] Bill VanPatten, *From Input to Output: A teacher's guide to SLA* (New York: McGraw Hill, 2003); Merrill Swain, "The output hypothesis and beyond: Mediating acquisition through collaborative dialogue," In James Lantolf, ed. *Sociocultural Theory and Second Language Learning* (Oxford: Oxford University Press, 2000): 97-114; Kara Morgan-Short and Harriet Wood Bowden, "Processing instruction and meaningful output-based instruction," *Studies in Second Language Acquisition*, 28, (2006): 31-65.

[14] Bill VanPatten, and Terry Cadierno, "Explicit instruction and input processing," *Studies in Second Language Acquisition*, 15, (2003): 225-43; Terry Cadierno, "Formal instruction from a processing perspective: An investigation into the Spanish past tense," *Modern Language Journal*, 19 (1995):179-93; Alessandro Benati, "A comparative study of the effects of processing instruction and output-based instruction on the acquisition of the Italian future tense," *Language Teaching Research*, 5, (2001): 95-127; Alessandro Benati, "The effects of processing instruction and its components on the acquisition of gender agreement in Italian," *Language Awareness*, 13, no. 2 (2004);Alessandro Benati, "The effects of processing instruction, traditional instruction, and meaningful-based output instruction on the acquisition of English past simple tense," *Language Teaching Research*, 9 (2005): 67-93.

English and Italian, "Present how your partner celebrated his/her last 3 birthdays, in a one-to-two minute oral presentation, without reading your notes."

The provision of the lesson-final task at the start of the task cycle brings out the benefits of what Lee and VanPatten[15] refer to as the "gazebo effect:" Students are made aware that the purpose of the following activities is to build something (compared to the construction of a gazebo), and the rest of the activities in the pre-task phase are equivalent to the hammer and nails that would be required to build the gazebo. Lee and VanPatten[16] believe that such concretization of the purpose of instructional activities will lead to greater attention and noticing[17] in the pre-task phase.

This follows the motivational basis[18] behind using tasks as the unit of analysis in a syllabus: "... instructors and learners can point to it and say, 'When we can do this task, we have reached the goal for this lesson.'"[19]

Watch/read pertinent target language material (Structured Input)

As soon as students understand the focus of the task cycle, and accordingly begin to think of the relevant vocabulary and structures they will need to perform the task, the instructor has achieved the establishment of a framework that will allow him/her to present the input-heavy phase of the cycle. The structured input adopted in this model does not strictly adhere to the same definition provided by VanPatten[20], but instead aims to provide general exposure of the theme to the learners in the form of lengthy, authentic input.

The pre-task phase is the stage that is most marked by the abundant and rich input that SLA research has shown to be effective for interlanguage growth[21]. Accordingly, it is the lengthiest of the three stages; as each task cycle lasts approximately four 90-minute lessons, or 6 contact

---

[15] Lee and VanPatten.

[16] Ibid.

[17] Richard Schmidt, "Attention," in Peter Robinson, ed. *Cognition and Second Language Instruction.* (Cambridge: Cambridge University Press, 2001).

[18] Zoltan Dornyei, "The motivational basis of language learning tasks," in Peter Robinson, ed. *Individual Differences and Instructed Language Learning* (Amsterdam: John Benjamins, 2002).

[19] Lee and VanPatten, 77.

[20] Bill VanPatten, *Input Processing and Grammar Instruction.* (New York: Ablex: 1996).

[21] See note 14 above.

hours, the pre-task stage occupies approximately the first 3.5 hours of this time. Its aim is essentially to take learners through input and activities that incrementally build the necessary skills and language required to complete the lesson-final task.

As evident on the TBI outline above, the pre-task phase consists of 4-6 subtasks. These subgoals take the learners through the types of exposure, interaction and activities they will need to know in order to successfully perform the lesson-final task at the end of the pre-task phase. In planning the subtasks for each task cycle, one should always heed Lee and VanPatten's suggestion to "remember that language acquisition always begins with input. Regardless of whether vocabulary, grammar, or some other aspect of language is the focus, we will want to start with input."[22]

This follows the larger cognitive scheme of building up the learners' interlanguage system through the 'raw material' of input, and then providing the learners with opportunities to access that system, in an increasingly fluent and accurate way, through output channels.[23] Accordingly, each subtask provides abundant input, opportunity for negotiation via collaborative dialogue,[24] and some sort of focus-on-form through a relevant activity.

In adherence to the principle of providing rich input, the types of language used in the pre-task phase are of several stamps, e.g., extended (recorded) dialogues of Italians engaged in informal chats, as well as more formal monologues (on audio or video), and a range of different kinds of related writing samples, e.g., postcards, emails, notes, short stories. This speaks to the importance of rich input:

> As beginners progress, they need access to more and more complex input, so that the internal processes can continue to map new forms and structures onto meaning.[25]

Students are constantly reminded that it is not important for them to understand everything; in fact, it is precisely in this type of cognitive "stretching" to comprehend that learning is most likely to take place (the zone that Krashen refers to as $i + 1$).[26]

---

[22] Lee and VanPatten, 85.
[23] Ibid.
[24] Swain 2000.
[25] VanPatten, 2003: 94.
[26] Stephen Krashen, *Principles and practice in second language acquisition.* (New York: Pergammon, 1982).

Each instructor of Italian will bring different resources to the pre-task phase; one excellent resource is the lengthy dialogues in *Linea diretta.*[27]. The average length of these listening activities is two-to-three minutes. In these dialogues one hears Italians speaking at a natural pace, with natural dialogue characteristics: interruptions, hesitations, repetitions, background noise, etc. Students should be forewarned that they will not understand everything, and that they are not supposed to: They are being trained to listen for informational purposes, to get information and then *do* something with that information. In the subsequent activities they will be asked to identify, confirm, and transform information obtained through the listening activities. Students should also be informed that the teacher will replay the dialogue several times.

Input A; Activity A

Continuing with the "birthday" task example, at this point the instructor would carefully select an extended dialogue that mentions parties, events, social gatherings, etc. If at all possible, one would select a dialogue or a film clip that focuses explicitly on someone's birthday party. This (video) clip or recorded dialogue should be played for the students several times, with a task-relevant activity implemented in between each listening.

Following are some suggestions on how to utilize such a challenging clip: in the first listening, students are challenged to comprehend the basic points of the dialogue; after the first listening the teacher is asked to comment on only the naturalness of the dialogue, before passing quickly to the second listening. After the second listening, the teacher asks everyone to pair up with one other student seated to his/her side. The instructor informs the students that they will have 2 minutes to discuss what they understood, what doubts they have, what they could/could not follow, etc. The instructor encourages the pairs to communicate in the target language. Following Swain[28] such orchestration leads to the emergence of collaborative dialogue. This pattern is repeated after the third listening also, with a new conversation partner. Following the outline, these activities constitute "Activity A."

---

[27] Corrado Conforti and Linda Cusimano, *Linea Diretta.* (Perugia, Italy: Edizioni Guerra, 2005).

[28] Swain 2000; Swain, "The Output Hypothesis: Theory and Research," in Eli Hinkel, ed. *Handbook of Research in Second Language Teaching and Learning.* (Mahway, New Jersey: Lawrence Erlbaum, 2005).

This type of pair-activity, "You will have 2 minutes to discuss, with your task partner, the dialogue you just heard," is a key feature in this model's pre-task phase and is typically implemented several times for *each* task. It is the creation of a context that aims to develop the learners' 'zone of proximal development,' defined by Lantolf as:

> The difference between what a person can achieve when acting alone and what the same person can accomplish when acting with support from someone else.[29]

This metaphor, originally proposed by Vygotsky,[30] addresses one of the key ingredients in language learning-mediation: people working together (peers in this case) to co-construct contexts and meanings that they would not arrive at alone. This zone is frequently referred to as 'collaborative dialogue' and is defined by Swain as:

> It is knowledge-building dialogue ... dialogue that constructs linguistic knowledge. It is what allows performance to outstrip competence. It is where language use and language learning can co-occur. It is language use mediating language learning. It is cognitive activity and it is social activity.[31]

Teacher-led brainstorm

As evidenced on the outline of the task cycle, this 'set' of extended listening activities constitutes Input/Activity A of the pre-task phase. The instructor then leads a vocabulary brainstorming activity on relevant vocabulary that will be useful for the task performance. This follows Newton's recommendations[32] for developing vocabulary in a TBI approach. The provision of pre-task, teacher-led brainstorming is another key aspect of this model. Omaggio-Hadley[33] suggests that providing students with opportunities for brainstorming activities will help students develop greater "fluency of ideas." Such a condition is proposed to alter the learners' production strategies.

---

[29] Lantolf, 17.
[30] L.S. Vygotsky, *Mind in Society*. (Cambridge, MA: Harvard University Press, 1978).
[31] Swain 2000: 97.
[32] Jonathan Newton, "Options for vocabulary learning through communication tasks," *ELT Journal* 55 (2001): 30-7.
[33] Alice Omaggio Hadley, *Teaching Language in Context* (New York, Heinle & Heinle, 2001).

This activity also allows for the introduction of relevant lexical chunks and linking words, suggested by Peter Skehan[34] to be one of the main features of the mind's exemplar-based mode (the other mode, in his proposed Cognitive Theory, is the mind's rule-based mode). The instruction of lexical chunks allows for the immediate application of useful and practical language such as "all of a sudden," "after that," and "to finish the night."

Baigent[35] describes a study in which she investigated her learners' use of multi-word chunks in four tasks, and the effect of different task types on the chunks produced. Results support the hypothesis that the use of multi-word chunks helped fluency.

These chunks are also referred to as *contextually coded exemplars*, *lexical phrases*, *collocations*, and *polywords*.[36] As mentioned above in relation to Skehan's Cognitive Theory, the theoretical framework for this model of TBI, chunks such as these are assumed to be stored as one unit in the memory-based mode, and therefore require very little processing space. This ties back to the Skehanian theory in which TBI is framed in the present model: If learners can exploit the large memory capabilities of their lexical/memory cognitive mode, their fluency should notably increase. This may be a simple question of repetition: Skehan has argued that much of human language is repetitive, and this recycled language comes at a lower processing expense:

> Much of language production is based on *a redundantly organized memory system*, and that speakers frequently avoid having to engage in clause-internal processing (demanding as this is), through the use of memorized chunks of language.[37]

Time Pressure

One key aspect of the pre-task phase that is not apparent on the outline above is its time-pressure component. Each activity is given a precise time limit, e.g., "You will have two minutes to discuss, with your task partner,

---

[34] Peter Skehan, *A Cognitive Approach to Language Learning* (Oxford: Oxford University Press, 1998).

[35] Maggie Baigent, "Multi-word Chunks in Oral Tasks," in Corony Edwards and Jane Willis, eds. *Teachers Exploring Tasks in English Language Teaching* (Basingstoke, Palgrave Macmillan, 2005).

[36] Dave Willis, *Rules, Patterns and Words* (Cambridge: Cambridge University Press, 2003).

[37] Skehan, 35.

the dialogue you just heard. Try to clear up any confusion and use this time to summarize what you think you heard." The teacher should time each activity with a stopwatch. Essentially the inclusion of a time-pressure component to this model's activities and tasks speaks to TBI's stated goal of achieving a high degree of representativeness. In the real world, operating on real time—online, so to speak—there is almost always a degree of pressure to create fluent speech without undue hesitation. This methodological variable should contribute to the TBI learners' increased ability to produce spontaneous language, one of the overarching goals of TBI.

Input/Activity B, C, D

Input/Activity B, C and D vary according to the type of skills necessary for the upcoming task performance. At all points of the pre-task phase, the teacher's priorities in choosing the activities center around the students' development of task-relevant vocabulary and structures. As justified above in terms of the larger cognitive scheme, all of these activities contain some sort of focus on output, oral or written, *after* some sort of input flood.

Following is a simple principle for what type of output these activities should generate: Learners must produce language that communicates something real (has meaning) to someone else. Lee and VanPatten refer to this as:

> output created by the learner [that is] purposeful: Because it contains a message, someone in some way must respond to the content of the message. [38]

The authors go on to suggest activities that will create such authentic message exchanges: filling out a grid or chart based on what was said; indicating agreement or disagreement; determining the truth of a statement, etc.

Overall, the focus of the pre-task activities (Activities A-D) is to engage the learners in manipulating copious information on the task topic, and to introduce and reactivate relevant vocabulary. Again, in each of these activities the learners first receive some sort of extended input and are then asked to create some sort of output.

---

[38] Lee and VanPatten, 175.

Watch successful demonstration of task [on video]

In this sub-phase, a successful task demonstration is provided by the teacher, or a prerecorded version of the task is played in which native speakers perform the task. The demonstration is integral to the TBI model because of its provision of target-language behavior. The demonstrator uses language and communication strategies in a natural way, and students are comforted by an example of what they are supposed to do.

Students essentially watch the demonstrator successfully perform the task. For the "birthday" task presented in this chapter, the teacher would record himself while speaking spontaneously for 90 seconds in front of the class about his friend's last three birthdays. The language demonstrated is colloquial, rife with fillers and linkers, clear, and most importantly, successful. This demonstration is assumed to ease the cognitive processing load during the task to come[39] and should increase fluency and accuracy.

Similar to the facilitative role of lexical chunks mentioned above, such a task demonstration promises to liberate more cognitive resources for other aspects of the learners' performance. It is hoped that through such demonstrations, students will 'learn' to do what native speakers do; imperative not only for motivational reasons,[40] but also to give students some experience with samples of spontaneous speech.

After the task demonstration, the teacher asks students to comment on it. In this process, learners often question the many filler words employed by the native speakers in the task demonstrations. Such devices in Italian are the filler and linker words like *allora* (so, therefore), *comunque* (anyway, so), *ecco* (here we are, okay) and *dunque* (so, well then). These words are used continuously by native speakers in authentic discourse. The learners' noticing of them, and the class's subsequent metalinguistic discussion of them, lead to their employment of some of them in the learners' task performances.

Pre-task planning (individual and/or pairs)

Providing learners with a planning period immediately before their task performance grants them a moment to marshal all of their resources and think seriously about their upcoming assignment. The planning subphase fills a psychological role, giving learners a moment to relax in

---

[39] Rod Ellis, *Task-Based Language Learning and Teaching* (Oxford: Oxford University Press, 2003).

[40] Dornyei.

silence and plan what they want to do and say; it also fills a lexical role, giving students some tranquil moments to mobilize all of the relevant vocabulary to be employed in the task. According to the research summarized by Ellis,[41] the provision of unguided planning seems to be the most advantageous; students in this model of TBI are thus provided with one-to-two minutes of silent, unguided planning before beginning the task performances, i.e., the teacher does not guide the students on what they should think about or how they should plan their performance.

During-task Phase: Record performance on audio/video

All students must perform the task without explicitly reading notes while their performance is recorded on audio and/or video. They are asked to present for a minimum of one minute and a maximum of two minutes. Time is controlled by the teacher's use of a stopwatch. Continuing with the "birthday" task as an example, each student has to present how his/her partner celebrated the last three birthdays, without explicitly reading notes.

One notes that this phase is the slimmest of the three stages; it is also the richest. This phase gives space for the potential of TBI to be a learner-centered pedagogy that fosters individuals' ability to speak spontaneously. Spontaneous oral speech is generally accepted as the most accurate picture of a learner's internal grammar:

> Mainstream SLA has viewed spontaneous oral language use as the best source of data for investigating interlanguage development. It is one thing to demonstrate ... controlled-production and entirely another to demonstrate ... spontaneous-production.[42]

A prerequisite for allowing this important language to emerge is the decentralization of the teacher that is a cornerstone of TBI. At this pivotal during-task phase, the teacher must withdraw and allow natural, spontaneous language to emerge. In fact, a significant amount of TBI literature is dedicated to the discussion of the teacher's decentralized role[43]. The role of a TBI teacher is that of architect and resource person. If

---

[41] Rod Ellis, ed. *Planning and Task Performance in a Second Language* (Philadelphia: John Benjamins, 2005).

[42] Rod Ellis, *Instructed Second Language Acquisition: Learning in the Classroom* (Malden, MA: Blackwell, 2001): 34.

[43] Virginia Samuda, "Guiding relationships between form and meaning during task performance: The role of the teacher," in Martin Bygate, Peter Skehan, and Merrill

the challenging but all-important goal of foreign language instruction is to foster an ability in our students to create *spontaneous oral speech*, it logically follows that this crucial part of the instruction cycle should leave the learner to his/her own devices.

Post-task: Prepare self-transcript, Version A (in pairs); Start self-correction (if written)

The post-task phase is initiated with the students' transcription of their performance. This aspect of the post-task phase ensures attention to form as proposed by Lynch.[44] Students listen to their respective performance, recorded on digital voice recorders distributed to each pair before the performance, and are asked to transcribe everything they said in their one-to-two minute performance.

The purpose of the post-task phase in this TBI cycle is to allow for a focus on form which should result in more accurate language. The placement of grammar analysis at the end of the cycle speaks to the central belief of TBI—that form should follow meaning. D. Willis[45] refers to this meaning-to-form directionality as a natural progression from the holistic to the specific.

At this point the students are focused on form; they have already successfully performed their task with a focus on meaning. The assumption is that now there should be a greater occurrence of noticing of detail. These activities are assumed to help change the way in which learners direct their attention—reminding them that fluency is not the only goal during task completion, and that accuracy has importance too[46].

As a form of modified output,[47] these transcriptions focus learners' attention on forms of the language which they have already processed for meaning. Instead of a teacher "presenting" language to learners as "new," a language analysis activity like transcribing encourages learners to reflect on the language they have already experienced.[48] In this model, as the learners work on their transcripts with their task partners and/or teacher, a

---

Swain, eds. *Researching Pedagogic Tasks, Second Language Learning, Teaching and Testing* (Harlow: Longman, 2001).

[44] Tony Lynch, "Seeing what they meant: Transcribing as a route to noticing," *ELT Journal* 55, (2002).

[45] Willis and Willis.

[46] Lynch 2002; Lynch, "Learning from the transcripts of an oral communication task," *ELT Journal* 61, no. 4 (2007).

[47] Swain 2000.

[48] Lynch 2002; Lynch 2007.

less inhibiting natural form of feedback arises: conversation with their task partner or teacher about what they said and/or the changes they are considering.

The transcription's inherent recycling of output (the first modality is oral speech, recorded; the second modality is written speech, transcribed), allows us to say with greater certainty that the merits of Swain's Output Hypothesis[49] are being realized. Swain posits such merits of output as essentially pushing learners to process language on a deeper level, with more mental effort, than processing input would do alone. Her claim essentially is that learners' own output can serve as "an attention-getting device which brings to their awareness something that they need to know"[50]

Watch task demonstration again; read native transcript

More target-like exposure is provided through a subsequent viewing of the task demonstration (performed by the teacher in person, or by native speakers on video) and a transcript of the fluent speaker's task demonstration is available for inspection. Students are asked to compare the language documented in their transcript with the target-like language documented in the native speakers' performance and transcript.

By analyzing transcripts of fluent speakers carrying out tasks, learners are able to identify typical features of spontaneous spoken language. Such exposure also, crucially, demonstrates to learners that no one—not even native Italians—speaks in perfect, measured sentences. When the learners see, in black and white, through videos and video transcripts, that even native speakers talking in real time back-track, hesitate, and compose in short chunks, making use of common lexical phrases, students should acquire the 'license' to speak in a similar, imperfect fashion.

At this point in the post-task phase, students have listened to the recording of their performance and transcribed it. They are then given further exposure to the native speaker's task demonstration (in person or on video, and print) and they are encouraged to learn from the cognitive conflict[51] that this juxtaposition presents. At this point a direct comparison of transcripts is performed (students' transcripts with natives'), and

---

[49] Swain 2005.

[50] Catherine Doughty, "Cognitive underpinnings of focus on form," in Robinson 2001.

[51] Agustina Tocalli-Beller and Merrill Swain, "Reformulation: the cognitive conflict and L2 learning it generates," *International Journal of Applied Linguistics*, 15, no. 1 (2005).

students can use this model to revise their original transcript and 'write in' what they could have, or should have, said.

Group report/assessment

At this point in the cycle, teacher and students openly and explicitly discuss grammatical form for the first time. The timing is appropriate because students have been forced to document what their performance sounded like and looked like, and consequently they have a greater awareness for and appreciation of the grammatical forms that could have facilitated their task performance. After some sort of language report or assessment (while the students are transcribing, the teacher should circulate around to each student and underline mistakes and awkward phrasings), relevant grammar points are presented and learners work on relevant grammar exercises.

Teach relevant grammar points; do relevant grammar exercises

Immediately following the group report/assessment, these activities are the most traditional and grammar-point explicit ones of the cycle. Attention to form is ensured by the naturally-occurring need for form that all students feel after their (imperfect) performance and transcription of their task. The teacher will have selected appropriate exercises for the students to do individually and in pairs, e.g., fill-in-the-blank, create complete sentences, etc.

Revise self-transcription, Version B

This revision of the transcript (Version B) is the equivalent of the final paper for the task cycle. Students are asked to rewrite their first transcript. They are essentially cleaning it up—grammatically, lexically, mechanically—and they are invited to include words and forms they did not use in the actual performance, but now with a better understanding of the relevant grammar and vocabulary, realize they should have. This speaks to the value of task recycling which has been proven to improve accuracy and fluency.[52] This is their opportunity to refine their accuracy

[52] Tony Lynch and Joan Maclean, "A case of exercising: Effects of immediate task repetition on learners' performance," in Bygate and others, eds. 2001.

and hand in a polished, written version of their task transcript as the 'final paper' for the task cycle.

For teachers interested in how a TBI course could be graded, let us assume that you could complete 10 task cycles in one semester (each task cycle should last about 6 hours): at the end of the semester, each student will have 10 oral reports and 10 written reports on which to be graded. A scoring rubric could easily be devised isolating points for fluency and points for accuracy. Students will know how they will be scored and will be motivated to perform in a fluent and accurate way. This concludes the task cycle developed for TBI.

Research summary

This section will briefly summarize the original research[53] conducted to test the efficacy of this TBI model. A longitudinal, method-comparison experimental research study was conducted with two groups: a control group learned intermediate Italian with a TI/PPP methodology, and an experimental group learned intermediate Italian with a TBI methodology. Both groups met for 9 weeks under rigorous research conditions.

It was predicted that both types of instruction would have beneficial effects on learner performance, but that the task-based group would display an overall superior performance after treatment. The research design was a true experimental design and, as such, did not utilize existing Italian classes for its treatment groups. The decision to pursue a true experimental design (rather than a quasi-experimental design utilizing existing Italian classes) is justified by the research team's desire to create a highly representative treatment. In order to achieve this high degree of representativeness, while also answering the call for more longitudinal research in instructed SLA, it was deemed necessary to treat the subjects for an extended period, i.e., nine weeks. Such an extended treatment would not have been possible with the 'borrowed' subjects found in a quasi-experimental design.

The independent variable of this study was type of instruction, and it had two forms: TBI and TI. The same instructor taught both treatment groups. There were two dependent variables: a) learners scores on grammatical gender agreement accuracy and b) oral and written fluency counts, with all scores collected across three times: pretest, posttest, and delayed posttest. One student level was included, intermediate Italian as a foreign language.

---

[53] Means.

Subjects were recruited to apply for participation in the study through email messages, flyers, and several announcements published in an Italian-American weekly newspaper circulated in New Jersey and New York. The announcements were worded in such a way as to encourage only qualified people, i.e., intermediate-level students of Italian, to contact the research team. All interested parties were required to fill out a bio-questionnaire to ensure that all eventual research subjects met the following inclusion criteria:

- raised in an English-speaking only home;
- past experience with the Italian language consisted of only 2-3 years of high school Italian, or 2-3 semesters of college Italian, or an equivalent self-study experience;
- age of first (consistent) contact with Italian was post-pubescent;
- subjects would be available for the 9-week study, and would not have any contact with the Italian language, outside of the treatment, for the 9-week period;
- past experience with the Italian language consisted of mostly classroom contact.

The participants (n = 22) were aged between 19 and 72 (mean = 40) and the bios were matched across treatment groups. The TI treatment (n = 10) began with 13 students but three of the students dropped out due to personal/professional conflicts; the TBI treatment (n = 12) began with 15 students but three of the students did not attend the final data collection session, rendering their data invalid.

Both groups met for a total of 13.5 hours of treatment and 4.5 hours of testing. To measure results, a battery of language tests was created (it included two controlled-production measures, and two spontaneous-production measures) and used in a pre-, post-, and delayed posttest design (testing for both immediate and sustained effect). The results showed that, for accuracy, on all four tests, results were nearly equal across both treatment groups, with a marginal advantage displayed by the TBI group. For fluency (measured as syllables per minute for the two oral fluency measures, and words per minute for the one written fluency measure), on the three tests that were amenable to such a measure, the TBI group demonstrated significantly greater gains. The findings from this small-scale study confirm that TBI better promotes the acquisition of fluency than TI in intermediate Italian as a foreign language.

The data collected clearly illustrate the different fluency-building effects the respective treatments had: *TBI better prepares students for the challenge of producing spontaneous oral speech.*

Conclusions

This chapter has described and explained a new approach to TBI, with concrete examples and theoretical and empirical justifications. It is hoped that this model has provided the reader with sufficient information on Input-heavy TBI so that he/she can experiment with it in the appropriate context.

As documented in the final section, this new approach has been tested under rigorous research conditions in a fine-grained, longitudinal method comparison research study. The findings of that study bear out the claims of TBI: it better promotes fluency than TI. However, this initial study was only one small-scale study, and the usual problems of generalizability across structures and learners apply.[54]

If we are to better understand how different teaching approaches result in different types of knowledge, we must meet the challenge of fine-grained method comparison research studies that last for entire 15-week semesters, and entire sequences of 2, 3, and 4 semesters. This need simultaneously speaks to the requirement that future studies strike a keen balance between internal and external validity.

For Italian-language pedagogy, the present model of TBI and the research findings that inform it are important because of their provision of a comprehensive model of TBI that is research-based. The descriptive and replicable model of intermediate-level TBI that this case presents is a first attempt toward a standardizing of what, exactly, is meant by TBI of Italian, and how such a line of research might best proceed.

MARLBORO COLLEGE, VERMONT, USA

---

[54] Robert DeKeyser, ed. *Practice in a Second Language: Perspectives from Applied Linguistics and Cognitive Psychology* (Cambridge: Cambridge University Press, 2007).

CHAPTER THREE

WHAT CAN BE OBTAINED FROM PROJECT WORK? A CASE STUDY

ASSUNTA GIUSEPPINA ZEDDA

Introduction

Project work[1] is a very flexible didactic approach which can be used alongside the main language teaching methods without substituting them. When applied to the linguistic field, the study of a second language is aimed at carrying out a project making it becomes an authentic means of information to be used in achieving aims. Project work makes the most of communicative activities which are the means for developing linguistic abilities "used interdependently and cumulatively not necessarily in any prescribed order"[2] and at the same time to recycle previous skills and

---

[1] Diana L. Fried-Booth, *Project Work* (New York: Oxford University Press, 1986, 2nd ed., 2002); Simon Haines, *Project for the EFL Classroom: Resource Material for Teachers* (Walton-on-Thames - UK: Nelson, 1989); Jane Henry, *Teaching Through Project* (London: Kogan Page, 1994); May M. T. Lee, Benjamin K. W. Li, and Icy K. B. Lee, *Project Work: Pratical Guidelines* (Hong Kong: The Hong Kong Institute of Education, 1999); Michael Legutke, "Szenarien für Einen Handlungsorientierten Fremdsprachen-unterricht," in *Englischunterricht*, ed. Gerhard Bach and Johannes-Peter Timm (Tübingen/Basel: Francke, 1989), 103-28; N. S. Prabhu, *Second Language Pedagogy* (Oxford: Oxford University Press, 1987); Franca Quartapelle, "Definire il Progetto," in *Didattica per Progetti*, ed. Franca Quartapelle (Milano: Franco Angeli, 1999), 65-87; Fredricka Stoller, "Project Work: A Means to Promote Language Content," *English Teaching Forum* 35, no. 4 (1997): 2-9; Fredricka Stoller, "Establishing a Theoretical Foundation for Project-Based Learning in Second and Foreign Language Contexts," in *Project-Based Second and Foreign Language Education: Past, Present and Future*, ed. Gulbahar H. Beckett and Paul Chamness Miller (Greenwich - CT: Information Age Publishing, 2006), 19-40.

[2] Fried-Booth 2002, 25.

knowledge to be used in natural contexts[3]. Projects involve pre-communicative, communicative and instrumental/managerial linguistic tasks[4] and are an ideal way of promoting students' learning autonomy and consenting differences in style and preferences in form.[5]

Project work (PW) means learning a foreign language through interaction, with the teacher, with the class, with the real world and its main aim is to overcome the existing gap between the language taught in class (study) and that used outside (use). It pushes out the boundaries by bringing students into direct contact with authentic language and experiences not usually available within the four walls of a classroom using textbooks.[6] As it is focused on the learner, the teacher takes on a different role, becoming more of a facilitator and advisor than a pedagogue and expert.[7] Projects can be proposed to students of all ages at all levels of linguistic knowledge in a variety of instructional settings including general, academic, specific and occupational, vocational, professional purposes, in addition to pre-service and in-service teacher training.[8] Duration is very varied, from one day to a whole year and, depending on the amount of teacher input, we can have a structured project where the teacher chooses the topic and plans the phases; semi-structured, where the students have a certain number of responsibilities although the topic and methodology have been given to them; and unstructured, where the learners "design, conduct, analyse and present their findings on a topic of their own choosing using information they have located themselves."[9] Projects in L2 (second language) which have the advantage of exploiting the mother tongue community are distinct from projects in FL (foreign language) which need a great deal of planning due to the lack of native speakers or because the students all share the same L1.[10] Each PW ends up with a final product (e.g. a video, website, class newspaper, radio programme, written report, oral presentation, audio guide, wall display) to

---

[3] Haines 1989, 1.

[4] Legutke 1989, 104.

[5] Peter Skehan, "Differenze Individuali e Autonomia di Apprendimento," in *L'Autonomia nell'Apprendimento Linguistico*, ed. Luciano Mariani (Firenze: La Nuova Italia, 1994), 19-38: 33.

[6] Fried-Booth 2002, 6.

[7] Henry 1994, 12.

[8] Stoller 1997, 4

[9] Henry 1994, 14-5.

[10] Gabriele Ridarelli, "Project work," in *C'era una volta il Metodo: Tendenze Attuali nella Didattica delle Lingue Straniere*, ed. Carlo Serra Borneto (Roma: Carocci, 1998), 173-87: 177.

be presented either to an authentic external audience or within the learning context.

Project work is not only interesting but also intellectually challenging, engaging students in a number of cognitive and meta-cognitive skills such as conceptualizing, inquiring, problem solving, planning, reading, observing, judging, enquiring, collaborating, thinking and so on[11].

According to Stoller, "project work" is one of the many labels given to classroom approaches that incorporate projects and together with experiential and negotiated language learning, investigative research, problem-solving learning, project approach or project-based approach reveals many of the features commonly attributed by literature to project-based learning (PBL):

> It has been equated, by some, with in-class group work, out-of-class activities, cooperative learning, task-based instruction, a vehicle for fully integrated language and content learning, and a mechanism for cross-curricular work. For some, project work involves fairly non-elaborated tasks; for others project work entails elaborate sets of sequenced tasks during which students are actively engaged in information gathering, processing, and reporting, with the ultimate goal of increased content knowledge and language mastery[12].

Sometimes PW is not properly appreciated:[13] for some teachers, it means plenty of preparation which may not be worth the effort,[14] while for some students it suggests toil and boredom with minimal benefit. However, experience shows that PW can be as meaningful and manageable as it is interesting and challenging, once teachers know the tricks of the trade and once students have been on the receiving end of them[15].

---

[11] Lee, Li and Lee 1999, 8-11.

[12] Stoller 2006, 21.

[13] Icy K. B. Lee, "Project Work in Second/Foreign Language Classrooms," *Canadian Modern Language Review* 59, no. 2 (2002): 282-290, 282.

[14] Janet Louise Eyring, "Is Project Work Worth It?," *ERIC* EDRS ED no. 407-838 (1997): 1-55, 10. In fact, some results from Eyring show a greater waste of time on the different activities in a project carried out in an academic setting e.g. "Presentation of the syllabus": PW 10.47 hours vs. ESL-Regular 0.35 minutes. However, the project work students felt greater satisfaction with this approach than the comparison group students, but the goals they accomplished were mostly non-academic goals such as having more time for sightseeing or having a lighter work load.

[15] Lee, Li, and Lee 1999, 7.

Studies on positive outcomes of PBL

Project based learning is spreading to all levels of teaching in Italy. As a general approach to the different disciplines, it is being introduced gradually in schools as a possible form of Dewey's *didattica attiva*[16] and as a continuation of the *laboratory.*[17] However, the journey towards establishing projects negotiated with students has been long and has swung for years between the wish to renew the school environment and the difficulty in integrating project policy in individual schools.[18] As an approach to foreign languages, there are various exchange projects between European schools and universities (e.g. *Comenius*, *Socrates*, *Erasmus*) and the number of projects in content and language integrated learning (*CLIL*) is ever increasing, even in schools which are not specifically linguistically orientated.[19] At university, the development of PW is particularly evident in post-graduate studies, in particular in Masters and post-graduate education courses. On the other hand, similar experiences in undergraduate courses are quite occasional and left up to the teacher's individual initiative, and are rarely concerned with the field of second language study.

If, on one hand there is a certain impetus to use projects in the linguistic field, on the other hand, there are few studies which document such a use.[20] Very few of these contain empirical data on the benefits of

---

[16] Leo van Lier, "Foreward," in *Project-Based Second and Foreign Language Education: Past, Present and Future*, ed. Gulbahar H. Beckett and Paul Chamness Miller (Greenwich-CT: Information Age Publishing, 2006), xi-xvi: xi. The action-based and experiential learning initiated by Dewey, Kilpatrick and others at the beginning of the 1900s in the USA, did not differ greatly from models elaborated in Europe in the preceding centuries or at the same time as great educators such as Comenius, Pestalozzi, Montessori, Piaget and Vygotsky.

[17] Daniela Bertocchi, "Progettare per Apprendere," in *Didattica per Progetti*, ed. Franca Quartapelle (Milano: Franco Angeli, 1999), 39-63: 54.

[18] Franca Quartapelle, "Il Cammino verso la Progettualità," in *Didattica per Progetti*, ed. Franca Quartapelle (Milano: Franco Angeli, 1999), 13-37: 23.

[19] Carmel M. Coonan, *La Lingua Straniera Veicolare* (Torino: UTET, 2002); Daniela Cornaviera, Claudio Marangon, and Gianna Miola, *Apprendo in Lingua 2. Educazione Bilingue: L'Uso Veicolare della Lingua Straniera. La Formazione. Quaderno 1* (Castagnole di Paese-TV: Tipolitografiche N.T.L., 2004); Graziano Serragiotto, *C.L.I.L. Apprendere Insieme una Lingua e Contenuti non Linguistici* (Perugia: Guerra Edizioni, 2003).

[20] Francesca Brotta, "L2 Project Work in L1 Context," *Problems and Experiences in the Teaching English* 2, no.2 (1985); Caterina Cangià, *L'Altra Glottodidattica: Bambini e Lingua Straniera fra Teatro e Computer* (Firenze: Giunti, 1998); Gisella

project work. Nevertheless, we can extract some statements from the available studies which support the quality of the approach and its positive results: interdisciplinary involvement, job satisfaction, enthusiasm, enjoyment, responsible action, motivation linked to interest, problem solving skills, professionalising experiences, a combination of the experiential dimension and deeper examination of content, plurality of concrete opportunities for interaction, the learning of Italian as an educational experience, a form of inclusion and integration for non Italian speaking students, development of interaction, socialisation and autonomy, harmonic and creative collaboration mediated by new technology, dynamism of relationships inside and outside the classroom, active participation and cooperation. These benefits can accompany and sometimes overlap those listed by Stoller[21] who, analysing 16 studies, finds eight advantages which can be commonly attributed to PBL by teachers (Tab. 3-1).

Although it is not always easy to say in advance what students will learn during a project, the majority of benefits which emerge from studies correspond with the goals that the teachers expect to achieve when they propose PW.[22]

The aim of this study is to present some positive results obtained through the use of project work.

Langé and Francesca Costa, *CLIL Scienze: Science in English for Upper Secondary Schools* (Milano: Ghisetti & Corvi Editori, 2007); Annalisa Latela, "CLIL e Insegnamento dell'Italiano come Seconda Lingua nella Scuola Elementare," *ITALS* 2, no. 6 (2004): 33-50; Marina Medi, "Sperimentare il Microcredito nell'Area di Progetto", *Strumenti Cres* 35, no. suppl. *Mani Tese* (2003), under "results," Home > Attività > Educazione allo sviluppo > Cres > Strumenti > Archivio (accessed September 17, 2007); Paola Polselli, "Cronaca di un Diario Collettivo," *ITALS* 3, no. 9 (2005): 67-87; Fiorenza Quercioli, "Italianizzazione e Content and Language Integrated Learning: Un Nuovo Orientamento Glottodidattico per i Programmi Americani in Italia," *ITALS* 2, no. 6 (2004): 63-84; Assunta G. Zedda, "Le Nuove Tecnologie e l'Ecologia dell'Apprendimento Linguistico: Uno Studio con Project Work," *RILA* 2-3 (2006): 301-321; Assunta G. Zedda, "Il Project Work: Una Metodologia di Insegnamento Linguistico," *ITALS* 3, no. 9 (2005.): 89-114.

21 Stoller 2006, 24-7.

22 For a review, see Gulbahar H. Beckett, "Beyond Second Language Acquisition: Secondary School ESL Teacher Goals and Actions for Project-Based Instruction," in *Project-Based Second and Foreign Language Education: Past, Present and Future*, ed. Gulbahar H. Beckett and Paul Chamness Miller (Greenwich - CT: Information Age Publishing, 2006), 55-70: 56-8.

Advantages commonly attributed to PBL	
1.	Authenticity of experience and language.
2.	Intensity of motivation, involvement, engagement, participation, enjoyment, creativity.
3.	Enhanced language skills; repeated opportunities for output, modified input, and negotiated meaning; purposeful opportunities for an integrated focus on form and other aspects of language.
4.	Improved abilities to function in a group, including social, cooperative and collaborative skills.
5.	Increased content knowledge.
6.	Improved confidence, sense of self, self-esteem, attitude toward learning, comfort using language, satisfaction with achievement.
7.	Increased autonomy, independence, self-initiation, and willingness to take responsibility for own learning.
8.	Improved abilities to make decision, be analytical, think critically, solve problems.

Table 3-1. Outcomes of PBL.

Methodology

a. Participants and setting

The project was carried out in an Italian university, in an intermediate level L2 Italian class. The learners involved (10), aged between 20 and 24 and 3 males to 7 females, were nearly all "*Erasmus*" students from Europe (French, German, English and Spanish speakers). They had a medium to high cultural level, came from different study areas (art, languages, literature, history, pedagogy, agriculture) and language skills were mixed. The PW took place in the 2nd semester during a semi-intensive course (6 weeks) which would allow them to follow courses more easily in the various faculties they attended. L2 Italian courses do not have a final exam, so the PW had 0 credits.

The students had computers with software and other technology such as a digital recorder to record some utterances, internet access to find texts and images, a video-camera to film some role-plays, a telephone and a printer with a scanner. Their IT laboratory was adapted as much as possible to the project's needs by introducing what technology was missing. Nevertheless, nothing could be done about the Internet line, telephone and rigidity of the computer station, except to move to appropriate places when necessary.

b. The project

The *encounter project*,[23] by linking the class with the outside world through real and concrete interactions, respects the principle that language learning is basically a social and communicative activity.[24] Ours was to solve some logistical problems related to the organisation of an international scientific conference on SLA (Second Language Acquisition), in the creation and successful distribution of posters and brochures, collection of tourist information for conference folders and the creation of a pamphlet about the cultural itinerary for the conference trip (final products). The students were introduced to the methods and were told that a certain amount of responsibility and involvement was expected. They discussed and defined products, aims and work strategies based on knowledge, possibility and time. They made decisions, carried out tasks and visits (to printers, public offices, schools, bookshops) becoming more collaborative and independent and specialising in small groups towards a particular final product. In turn they made notes on group discussions in their own register, also useful for updating absentees, and they supervised and corrected each other's performance. Except for the teacher's assessment of the final products, during the PW there was self-evaluation of *in progress* results aimed at correcting set up, changing decisions and redefining plans. Among other things, the learners also organised the end of course trip.

The very nature of the PW led to the adoption of a procedural syllabus,[25] i.e. a syllabus based on students carrying out tasks with their available linguistic means in that particular moment. In this way, the gradual evolution of their interlanguage (IL) will be determined by the continuous effort to use it[26] and the natural evolutive sequences of the interlanguage[27] will be respected as much as the learner's "*inner syllabus*."[28] The choice of a procedural syllabus did not mean complete

---

[23] Michael Legutke and Howard Thomas, *Process and Experience in the Language Classroom* (London: Pergamon Press, 1991).
[24] Gabriele Pallotti, "La Classe dans une Perspective Écologique de l'Acquisition," *Acquisition et Interaction en Langue Étrangerè* 16 (2002): 165-197, 171.
[25] Prabu (quot.) 1987, 87-95; Jack C. Richards and Richard Schmidt, *Dictionary of Language Teaching & Applied Linguistics* (London: Longman, 2002), 421.
[26] Gabriele Pallotti, *La Seconda Lingua* (Milano: Bompiani, 1998), 296.
[27] Stephen D Krashen, *The Input Hypothesis: Issues and Implications* (London: Longman, 1985).
[28] S. Pit Corder, *Error analysis and interlanguage* (Oxford: Oxford University Press, 1981), 11.

abandonment of structures which, although not planned beforehand, were dealt with before each different stage of the project. We can say that linguistic needs emerged naturally (role-play scripts, letters of request, drafts, Italian software etc.). Structures, functions and specific vocabulary were focused on at opportune moments. Analysis of interlanguage ("errors") was carried out together on transcripts of recorded texts.

c. Data collection

Data was collected to document the PW experiment in an "*Erasmus*" type class with students on brief migratory projects, relationship dynamics were based above all on their common L1 and limited socialization with the target community. The recording of results was considered useful for future projects.

Data came from the teacher's diary notes and from audio-video recordings of the students in action (organisation, preparation for external visits, computer work, telephone calls, collection of materials etc.). All students agreed to be recorded although with different degrees of participation: Nina-**DE**, Pierre-**BE**, Maria-**ES**, Melanie-**AT**, Alex-**UK**, Karin-**AT**, Miguel-**ES**, Dan-**IE**, Bea-**ES** and Eli-**IE** (pseudonyms).

In a video-taped role-play, Nina and Melanie prepare to request estimates through telephone calls or visits to a printer's. Nina makes a phone call to collect this information. Other partial results are presented later. For full data refer to those already published in other studies.[29]

d. Data analysis

Analysis was carried out especially on samples of interlanguage which were chosen because they highlighted a particular result. Nevertheless, as we will see, the project's benefits are presented in groups as they are not singular or independent from others.

The audio-video recorded dialogues were transcribed using the simplified Jeffersonian system.[30] Some transcripts were revised and commented on by the students to have a better idea of the context and the

[29] Zedda 2005, 99-112; 2006, 301-21.

[30] George Psathas and Tim Anderson, "The 'Practices' of Transcription in Conversation Analysis," *Semiotica* 78 (1990): 75-99; "[ ]" out of dialogue comments in italics; ":" lengthening of a sound or syllable; "-" word-ending missing; "#" short pause (#: 1 second; ##: 2 seconds; etc.); "( )" word not heard clearly or incomprehensible: (x) one word; (xx) two words; (xxx) three or more words; "..." cuts.

physical actions that accompanied them, especially in the dialogues recorded outside the classroom. Analysis of the role-play was carried out with the aid of a table (Tab. 3-2) in three columns: "functions" (personal, interpersonal, etc.), "acts" (greetings, thanking, giving information, etc.) and "expressions" (good morning, thank-you very much, we would like to have a poster printed, etc.)

FUNCTIONS	ACTS	EXPRESSIONS

Table 3-2. Functional analysis.

Findings

It is not easy to record the effects of PW and it is even more difficult to understand the effects that new technology (NT) has on SLA due to the complexity of the variables involved (e.g. early obsolescence). It is impossible to measure the benefits using traditional methods, whereas we can evaluate them through careful ethnographic documentation. This must come from contextualised research which is compatible with an ecological approach to SLA and focuses more on relationships and processes than on products and results.[31] This ecological view tries to capture the links between psychological, social and environmental processes, concentrating on socio-cognitive, socio-cultural and symbolic- ritualistic aspects of SLA. This means that, concerning NT, no effort to develop hardware and software is needed, nor is it necessary to increase the *quantity* of PCs in the classrooms (in accordance with commercial, political and institutional logic).[32] Instead, it is necessary to pay attention to the *quality* of the environment in which NT is not considered as an alternative or substitute for the teacher, but an instrument that aids and simplifies the teaching/ learning process with stimuli not found elsewhere.[33]

For example, concerning *quantity*, 10 students were put into 3 groups at 3 of the 12 available PC stations. Also, when the groups were formed, (based on IT competence and different L1) disparity in PC access emerged

[31] Leo van Lier, "A tale of Two Computer Classrooms: The Ecology of Project-Based Language Learning," in *Ecology of Language Acquisition*, ed. Jonathan H. Leather and Jet van Dam (Amsterdam: Kluwer, 2002), 49-63: 51-2.

[32] Many experts think that information technology is often "oversold and underused", e.g. Larry Cuban, *Oversold and Underused: Computers in the Classroom* (Cambridge - MA: Harvard University Press, 2001).

[33] Van Lier 2002, 49-50; Paolo E. Balboni, *Didattica dell'Italiano a Stranieri* (Roma: Bonacci, 1994), 106-15.

between students of different genders: 2 out of 3 males declared themselves competent vs. 1 female out of 7.[34] This is a problem affecting heuristic abilities[35] which should be considered before an exclusively numerical one if equal opportunities are to be guaranteed. As far as *quality* is concerned, the classroom used was a common space full of individual spaces with computers arranged in rows (4) like the old language laboratories of the 1970s: large monitors hid the students' faces and backs, limiting their chance to interact in front or behind them. In this way the bases for correct relations between human beings and social situations which must be characterised by interaction, reciprocal adaptation and exchange were compromised. In fact, SLA is a process of re-socialisation, which, through interaction, signs and meanings of the new social group, provides the learner with the semiotic instruments and interpretative mechanism in order to re-signify and re-produce meanings in relation to that group's norms.[36] How is it possible to engage in this process without interacting and without looking each other in the eye? To overcome this problem, chairs were placed in the large access aisle to computers in order to hold face to face discussions.

a. Some results

Interaction is therefore very important and is also the greatest contribution that PW and NT can make together with the development of collaboration, cooperation, socialisation, independence and diversity of actions. In fact, using a computer, a tape recorder or the internet also means carrying out actions which are not customary in a language class.

The scenes annotated below portray the students involved in different research activities or their preparation.

- Maria, with little experience, sits at the computer and takes orders from Pierre using the imperative, Nina supervises and corrects them.[37] The interaction is managed independently without the teacher and controlled

---

[34] Zedda 2006, 310.

[35] Council of Europe, *Common European Framework of Reference for Languages: Learning, Teaching, Assessment* (Cambridge: Cambridge University Press, 2001), 132.

[36] Wan Shun Eva Lam and Claire Kramsch, "The Ecology of an SLA Community in a Computer-Mediated Environment," in *Ecology of Language Acquisition*, ed. Jonathan H. Leather and Jet van Dam (Amsterdam: Kluwer, 2002), 141-58: 146-47.

[37] Zedda 2006, 310-12.

by the group: peer correction is decidedly less risky than teacher correction (*sì? no- professora? Ohohoh [ride] ### ho ditto mille volte la professora*) and is used both on how to carry out the task (*ohoh no- devi dito ## xxxx ha detto [viene interrotta]*) and on structure (*si dice professoressa::: Pierre*). Verbal actions are enriched by physical and visual actions (computer operations) but, unlike the *total physical response,* they have a direct, practical and authentic meaning (*vai qui ## [indica con il dito un punto sul monitor]*). On analysis, a process of socialisation towards the internal culture of the class is noted,[38] i.e. towards those norms or behaviour models appropriate to the class as a "social group" (*me spiace; oh scusi, scusi*) and as "a learning community": the cooperative behaviour in finishing a task together and the collaborative behaviour (*no- preoccupare; tu empari ### no- è problema correccione*) aimed at the support of the weakest group member (*huff iò no- esso niente*).

- With Nina, Karin and Pierre on the internet searching for texts and images for the cultural pamphlet for the conference trip,[39] we can see interaction and cooperation aimed at expressing their own opinion (*questo me pare molto interessante*), making choices and proposals (*va bene prendiamo?*), making decisions (*sì dopo decisiamo do-*). There is harmony in relations, initiative (*possiamo modificare forse*) and independent action which shows confidence and competence within the class community. In fact, in this case, the use of language creates Nina's symbolic identity when she expresses specific knowledge of her study area (*cupola anche # tholos; no, no- cupula cu # po # la*). Language and identity have become a symbolic *ensemble* in the process of self identification and education in the class[40], attributing her with the role of expert that the peer group is able to recognise even jokingly (*tu fai accademìa no?* [*battuta di spirito*]).

- Pierre makes a phone call to ask for an estimate for the educational trip. He interacts with a native, familiarising himself with the norms of the external community.[41] Interaction with the extra-scholastic world is aimed at making requests (*volemo sapere quanto costa (e)n otobus per un*

[38] Anna Ciliberti, "Incontro di Culture e Processi di Socializzazione nella Classe Multilingue," in *Le Lingue in Classe: Discorso, Apprendimento e Socializzazione*, ed. Anna Ciliberti, Rosa Pugliese, and Laurie Anderson (Roma: Carocci, 2003), 57-73: 65-6.
[39] Zedda 2006, 317-18.
[40] Lam and Kramsch 2002, 153.
[41] Zedda 2005, 108-9.

giorno?#; ma è otobus piccolo?), obtaining information (*bene vi costa # 360 euro*; *sì, sì quello grande è da 55 posti e vi verrebbe a costare 420 euro*) and replying successfully to the interlocutor's requests (*el 27 de marzo*; *itinerario per visitare xxxx e xxxx*). Pierre also gets a discount on the original price through two indirect requests (*ma eh:: poca differenzia*; *è un po' caro eh::*) and correctly interprets the interlocutor's move when he puts him on hold to talk to the owner. In fact he communicates to his colleagues: "*Forse meno il prezzio.*" In this exchange, Pierre has learnt that in Italy it is possible to propose a native cultural model, storing information for future use (it would have been the same if he had discovered that Italians don't ask for discounts). In fact, when a learner studies the spoken language also from the target community he has to establish relationships with it that allow him to interpret it[42] and in that way, interaction with natives represents the privileged means by which the cultural norms of a certain social environment can be internalized.[43]

- Maria has been absent and works with Pierre to update a file. Pierre is already an expert and has been asked to show her the task and its simplicity, mediated at first by the teacher.[44] As well as interaction, cooperation and collaboration, responsibilisation is also observed (## *per favore Pierre puoi spiegare come abbiamo fatto*) which means more involvement and promotion of learner independence. In fact, the teacher has transmitted the positive idea that the task is easy (*sì, l'abbiamo un po' cambiato ma non è difficile; è molto semplice*), the students proceed without external help, finish the task successfully and reinforce confidence in their abilities (Pierre: "*è faccile?*" Maria: "*sì*"). In the future, a sense of self- effectiveness and expectation of success should allow students (especially Maria) to make other positive evaluations of the work to be done, leading then towards learner independence (*learning to learn*) seen not just as a linguistic skill but one that is present in all disciplines.[45]

- Nina, Maria and Alex prepare for a visit to a tourist information board with a role-play; they had received some information from the teacher and had previously prepared a list of requests.[46] We can observe

---

[42] Ciliberti 2003, 65.
[43] Pallotti 2002, 171-72.
[44] Zedda 2006, 312-13.
[45] Luciano Mariani and Graziella Pozzo, *Stili, Strategie e Strumenti nell' Apprendimento Linguistico: Imparare a Imparare e Insegnare a Imparare* (Firenze: La Nuova Italia, 2002), 59.
[46] Zedda 2005, 110-12.

interaction, cooperation in the task and independence. In the organisational phase (*ok prima doviamo decidere ruoli*) they divide the work by preference (*io fa studente*) or mood (*uhm va bene sì # si no è problema vado a scrivìre # controllo uhm: sono po' stanco scussa*). In the acting phase, Nina is more alert, she has accepted the remaining role (*ok, ok Maria [ride] io sono l'altro*) and she overlaps Maria in the controlling role intervening in Alex's work (*ma cosa serve il materiale # devi dire cosa serve # tu non hai detto per congresso*). This comment has a meta-communicative nature and highlights the double role of the student in simulated discussions: learner and character at the same time.[47] The comment also has a meta-cognitive nature and shows that the process of independence is in progress. The ability to *learn to learn* therefore emerges, which means the acquisition and use of learning strategies which can be used in all contexts and for all our lives.[48] Among these there are meta-cognitive strategies, those operations which allow the student to plan, evaluate and control the product and its learning process.[49] Even Alex's implicit request for feedback using facial expression (*uhm bello # eh quando possiamo prendere? [guarda Maria]*) and Maria's response (*buene [a voce bassa]*) can be considered under the heading of learner independence, or more specifically socio-affective strategies used both towards oneself (control of reaction, self-monitoring, rewards etc.) and towards others when we resort to interlocutors for explanations, confirmation, help, etc.[50]

- Miguel, Alex and Dan have to collect informative material from an association which has been warned of their arrival.[51] Here the interaction requires *negotiation of meaning*, a conversational activity used when there are comprehension difficulties which are expressed through "requests for

---

[47] Rosa Pugliese, Anna Ciliberti, and Laurie Anderson, "Le Attività Riflessive nelle Classi di Lingua," in *Le Lingue in Classe: Discorso, Apprendimento, Socializzazione*, ed. Anna Ciliberti, Rosa Pugliese and Laurie Anderson (Roma: Carocci, 2003), 93-108: 104-5.

[48] Luciano Mariani and Paola Tomai, *Il Portfolio delle Lingue: Metodologie, Proposte, Esperienze* (Roma: Carocci Faber, 2004), 37-39; Luciano Mariani, "I Fili di un Discorso sull'Autonomia," in *L'Autonomia nell'Apprendimento Linguistico*, ed. Luciano Mariani (Firenze: La Nuova Italia,1994), 1-18: 6-8.

[49] J. Michael O'Malley and Anna Uhl Chamot, *Learning Strategy in Second Language Acquisition* (Cambridge: Cambridge University Press, 1990), 118-21; 144-45.

[50] Mariani and Pozzo 2002, 75-8.

[51] Zedda 2005, 101-2.

clarification" or "confirmation of understanding."[52] During the presentation, Miguel is observed speaking quickly to introduce the group (*siamo studenti Erasmus siamo faziendo un progieto alla...*) and the usher has difficulty and asks for clarification (*chi siete:::?*): the Spanish interference and the word "*Erasmus*" are not common to him. Alex intervenes by repeating more slowly and substituting the word "*Erasmus*" with "foreigners" (*siamo studenti stranieri # nostra professoressa ha detto ## prendere il materiale culturale* [...]). The first difficulty is overcome but the usher asks for confirmation of understanding repeating "*materiale culturale?*" Later the usher *pour parler* asks Dan a double question (*e siete stranieri così avete detto?* [*tutto d'un fiato*]) preceded by "*mi sennò qua vi perdete ##*". Dan, probably cognitively overloaded, shows some doubt (*uhm? sì # cosa:*). But after the usher's simplification strategy (*siete studenti stranieri?*), he understands easily and even adds some additional information: *sì, sì io da Irlanda*. A similar event occurs immediately afterwards. A clerk asks the students: "*e buste ne avete portato?*" using a difficult syntactic structure due to its remarkable order: *dislocazione a sinistra*. In fact the object complement (*buste*) is moved forwards in place of the subject and with the pronoun (*ne*) used to repeat and emphasise it. Miguel asks for clarification (*eh non è capito, scussa #*), the clerk repeats and adds synonyms (*buste # buste?*"; "*...una borsa dove mettere*") and finally simplifies (*avete portato le buste? [ride]*) favouring Miguel's ability to analyse (*no portato buste [ride]*).

b. A telephone call and a role-play

A telephone call is compared to a role-play (carried out previously) to show how this technique effectively prepared the learner to face a real life situation. Normally a role-play (RP) is a "pedagogical" type of task which only indirectly refers to the learner's external needs. However, in this case, it is directly connected to the students' needs outside the classroom as it actually becomes a reality task "about the objective" or "as a trial."[53] It can be categorised as a *spontaneous role-play* as the learners keep their own identity. It is also of the "open" variety because it specifies the situation, the purpose and the roles but not the direction or result of the interaction, and also because the comunicative acts evolve over multiple turns and their sequential organization is contingent on the interlocutor's uptake involving both interactive functions and interpersonal functions. It is not

[52] Pallotti 1998, 132-33.
[53] Council of Europe 2001, 192.

by chance that the potential of RP is greatly exploited in L2 developmental pragmatics research on communicative acts.[54]

After taking part in the preparatory RP, Nina crossed the classroom boundaries with a telephone call (Tab. 3-3) to a printer's to request an estimate for producing a conference poster.[55] During the telephone call, she had to take notes on the incoming information. Other students had carried out the same research by visiting the printers in person. To prepare for this, everyone had compiled scripts containing the things they had to ask, how to introduce themselves, how to ask for and give information, etc. Afterwards, they practised in some role-plays, one of which was filmed and transcribed: the teacher played the printer, Nina was the customer and Melanie supervised the exercise by suggesting and adding things.

Telephone call "*Printer's*" (duration 3,5 minutes)	
Nina:	pronto sono Nina Weber # una studentessa Erasmus # freq- [*interrotto*]
Tel1:	le passo l'interno
Nina:	[*attesa*]
Tel2:	pronto
Nina:	ok pronto sono una studentessa Erasmus # frequento il corso di italiano per stranieri dell'Università di xxxxx # facciamo un **progetto vorremo** realizzare **un una locandina** vo- [*interrotto*]
Tel2:	le passo l'addetto
Nina:	sì, grazie:: [*commenta nell'attesa*] anche questo numero sbagliato [*ride*]
Tel3:	sì dica
Nina:	sono Nina Weber:: una studentessa Erasmus frequento il corso di italiano per stranieri dell'Università di xxxxx # facciamo un progetto **vorremmo** realizzare una locandina eh:: **vorrei** sapere **i prezzi** per minimo **50 pezzi** del- della locandina con **carta colorata** e con un'**imaccine** e col questa immacine è anche colorata # vorremo usare **un colore** # eh:: il **formato** è **A3** # ehm:: *quanto costano questi locandi(ni)*?
Tel3:	50 pezzi ha detto?
Nina:	Sì
Tel3:	50 euro con stampa a colore
Nina:	[*scrive*] 50 euro:: # stampata a colori
Tel3:	poi dipende ##
Nina:	ok ## e *quando noi prendiamo 100*?
Tel3:	allora sarebbero 80 euro #

[54] Gabriele Kasper and Kenneth R. Rose, "Pragmatics Development in a Second Language," *Language Learning. A journal of research in language studies* 52, no. suppl. 1 (2002): 1-341, 86-7.

[55] Zedda 2006, 313-15.

Nina:	ehm ## [*scrive*] 80 euro ok # ehm *che tipo di stampa è*?
Tel3:	possiamo fare **offset** o **quadricromia** dipende dalla carta [*esegue la sua produzione velocemente*]
Nina:	[*lo interrompe*] mo- momento devo scrivere [*si agita*] ehm [*scrive*] quatro- quatrocromia con questa carta # ehm ***gramatura di carta***?
Tel3:	150 grammi
Nina:	150 grami ok::: [*rallenta la voce*] ahm *quanto tempo occorre per stampare*?
Tel3:	non più di mezza giornata
Nina:	mezza cionnata? [*tono stupito*]
Tel3:	beh noi abbiamo # i nostri tempi sono molto veloci
Nina:	[*lo interrompe*] sì, sì:: [*ride*] sembra po- uhm troppo poco # ok
Tel3:	[*ride*] l'impianto è grande
Nina:	[*scrive*] ok # cio-
Tel3:	come avete preparato il **file**?
Nina:	abbiamo preparato il Word
Tel3:	[*rumori*] (xxx) ('na) bozza subito
Nina:	uhm # ok:: e con **la bozza** ok::
Tel3:	poi vediamo eventualmente facciamo noi le modifiche e non ti preoccupare per la velocità [*ride*]
Nina:	[*ride*] ok penso questo era tutto
Tel3:	bene siamo qui
Nina:	grazie, grazie ## arrivederci

Table 3-3. Transcript of the telephone call "Printer's."

As we can see, the telephone call is quite long and well sustained given that making phone calls is one of the most *challenging* types of communication for a language learner (no visual contact, exclusively verbal communication, line interference). But Nina is not uncomfortable, on the contrary she is confident in her management of the interaction, even when she gets agitated and asks the interlocutor to slow down his flow of information ([*lo interrompe*] *mo- momento devo scrivere*). In terms of effectiveness, it is a positive result that Nina always replies appropriately and that there is only one, even banale, *breakdown* in communication (*50 pezzi ha detto?*) when faced with the speech of a stranger at a distance who uses technical terminology. Moreover, it should be noticed that her utterances are also understood by Tel3 who replies equally appropriately. Involvement can be seen in the precise and prompt questions and answers, whereas the relaxed, cordial atmosphere can be detected in some humorous comments made by Nina (*anche questo numero sbagliato [ride]*; *mezza cionnata?*; *sì, sì:: [ride] sembra po- uhm troppo poco*) which the interlocutor replies to wittily and changing to the informal register ([*ride*] *l'impianto è grande*; ...*non ti preoccupare per la velocità* [*ride*]). Nina demonstrates her ability to establish relationships with the target community and this allows her to know how to interpret it correctly, to interact with it effectively and finally to participate in its life.[56]

But how did this learner manage to carry out such a difficult exchange with so much success? The "*Printer's*" role-play shows how the preparatory activity supplied her with the tools for a successful communicative interaction in real life. To demonstrate this, a functional analysis has been made in terms of "macro-purposes" or "macro-functions", which are categories used to define the functional use of dialogues formed by sequences of phrases, even long ones.[57] Within the role-play the "communicative acts"[58] and the relative linguistic expressions have been identified with the key words necessary for the activity highlighted in bold. The results of the analysis are shown in the following table 4 which contains a synthesis of the relevant communicative acts in the order that they appear in the role-play (**N**: Nina; **M**: Melanie; **I**: teacher).

This is certainly a dynamic and loquacious role-play (1906 words) in which all the key words produced in the telephone call can be found. In particular the presence of some technical words in the RP can explain why, although Nina does not use them in her phone call, she is able to understand them when produced by the worker: the preparatory work serves this purpose too. This leads to the evaluation of the results of the project work not only in terms of productive competence but also in terms of receptive skills.

Almost all the structures in the telephone call were previously produced in the role-play. In the phone call, they are more accurate: for example, *vorrem(m)o* vs. *vogliamo*; *un colore* vs. *una colore* (f. Ger. *Farbe*); *una locandina* vs. *il locandino/un locandina* (n. Ger. *Plakat*); *carta colorata* vs. *carta leggero* (n. Ger.); *la bozza* vs. *il bozo* (m. Ger. *Entwurf*); *i prezzi* vs. *le prezzi* (Ger. m.); 50 *pezzi* vs. *le pezzi* (Ger. n.); *quanto tempo occorre* vs. *quanto tempo occorro*. We can see that some wrong structures present in the role-play alternate with their correct forms, which is what happens when the structures have not yet been learnt properly or automated by the learner. Some of these errors can be explained by the interference of gender in the use of the article before

[56] Ciliberti 2003, 64-6.
[57] Council of Europe 2001, 155.
[58] Paolo E. Balboni, *Le Sfide di Babele: Insegnare le Lingue nelle Società Complesse* (Torino: UTET Libreria, 2002), 75.

nouns which have a different gender from Italian in Nina's L1,[59] with a tendency to liken the "neuter" gender of German to the "male" one in Italian (e.g. *dare un* ***offerto***, Ger. n., *Angebot*). Nina's increased accuracy in the phone call can be explained by the fact that learners usually have better results on repetition of the same task,[60] but also by the *focus on form* activity carried out in class on the role-play transcript. The substantial use of the doubtful "forse (maybe)" in the RP leads back to the moment during the PW when there were still many things to decide and few certainties, but also to the increased difficulty experienced in the first performance of such a complex interactive task.

Role-play "*Printer's*" (duration 18 minutes)		
FUNCTIONS	**ACTS**	**EXPRESSIONS**
Personal function	Introducing oneself	**N:** - siamo studenti di Erasmus frequentiamo un corso per italiano per stranieri;
Interpersonal function	Greetings and leave-taking.	**N e M:** - buongiorno; **N:** - abbiamo finito, non mi ricordo altre cose; **I:** - allora forse ci sentiamo per telefono la prossima volta; - **N:** ok, arrivederci; **I:** - arrivederci
	Thanking	**N:** - grazie; - grazie mille; - grazie; **M:** molto gentile.
	Accepting proposals	**N:** - ah va bene;
	Maintaining contact	**N:** - ho capito; **I:** - ho capito; **N:** - sì, ok, ho capito, adesso; - ah, va bene, ok, ho capito; - sì, certamente; - *forse* [*ridono e guardano la scaletta*] un momento per favore.
	Apologising	**N:** - scusi [*ride*];
Regulatory-instrumental function	Expressing intentions, wishes	**N:** - **vogliamo** realizzare **un # una locandina** e un depliant; - **vogliamo** realizzare # abbiamo domande per questo **progetto**; - **vogliamo** fare *forse* **una colore**.

[59] Marina Chini and Stefania Ferraris, "La Morfologia del Nome," in *Verso l'Italiano: Percorsi e Strategie di Acquisizione*, ed. Anna Giacalone Ramat (Roma: Carocci, 2003), 37-69: 56.
[60] Martin Bygate, "Effects of Task Repetition on the Structure and Control of Oral Language," in *Researching Pedagogic Tasks*, ed. Martin Bygate, Peter Skehan and Merrill Swain (Harlow: Pearson Education, 2001), 23-49.

Referential function	Asking for information	**N:** - *forse* loro fanno? - **per favore potrebbe** dirci **i prezzi** per un **depliant** senza e con **immacine** e senza e con colore; - *forse* lei **potrebbe** farci vedere **un:: locandina** cià realizzato; - *forse* lei **potrebbe dare un offerto** eh; **I:** - che **formato** la locandina?; **N:** - ma ci sono altri **formati**?; - anche con un'immacine *forse* lei **potrebbe** dire **le prezzi** anche senza immacine; - **i prezzi** si cambia **quando** noi stampiamo o vogliamo di più depliant?; **I:** - vi piace la **carta lucida** o la **carta opaca**?; **M:** - è possibile ehm fare l'**ordinazione per telefono?**; **N:** - quando dobbiamo dare il **file** con **il bozo**?; - quanto costa questo lavoro **di composi- # composito**?; - per un'ora per lavoro**?**; - e questo (ref. *file*) è a posto?; **M:** - quando il **lavoro è** fini- **fini::to**?; **N:** - quanto tempo **occorro**?; - **I:** vi serve **una bozza**? la volete?; - avete finito? avete altre cose?; **N:** - no, no, ah, mi ricordo dobbiamo dare un **acconto**?
	Giving information	**N:** - facciamo un progetto; - ok, abbiamo fatto **un bozza**…noi non sappiamo come dobbiamo fare il **file**; - ma non sappiamo **le pezzi**; - (dobbiamo) fare questo con **una carta leggero**, penso è meglio e **questa locandina** facciamo 'na carta pesante perché *forse* **anche fuori**; **I: bicolore…**fare una **stampa plotter... costi tipografici**; **N:** - ma *forse* **vogliamo** prendere solo **un colore** e stampare, non fare **un plotter**; - abbiamo pensato prendiamo *forse* 50 **dei locandine** e *forse* 150 **delle depliant**; - per il depliant penso un po' # # **leggero** va bene, ma per **il locandino** *forse* **c'è fuori** eh un po' pesante; - abbiamo pensato **formato** A3; **N:** - **vorrei** informarla che non abbiamo molti soldi per disposizione; - *forse* noi prendiamo 200 o 250; **I:** - farvi uno **sconticino**, ma se voi prendete 200 oppure 300 pezzi posso fare uno **sconto**; **N:** - noi **vogliamo** provare fare una telefonata, esercitazione con nostra professoressa, ma dopo sicuramente **andiamo a** fare l'**ordinazione**; **I:** - le 4 pagine possono essere anche una separata dall'altra, poi noi facciamo un **lavoro di composizione**; **N:** - ah, **l'**abbiamo fatto in **word**.

	Asking for explanations	**I:** locandine **quante aveva detto**? (*comprehension check*); **N:** - ok, facciamo **i paghine** sempre uno per uno e non insieme?; - **I:** ah, **i tempi di consegna**? (*comprehension check*).
	Giving explanations	**N:** - non molto **leggera**, **leggero** (ref. *carta*) **così, così**; - 50 (*clearing up*); **I:** - se non siete in grado di farle da sole, le lasciate separate; **M:** sì (*clearing up*);
	Asking for reassurance	**N:** - **c'è nienti problemi** perché **vorre-vorremmo** questo lavoro **alle** 20 **del** marzo # **non ci sono problemi** perché è dopo pasqua::?; - siete quasi pronti?; - ma quando noi portiamo qua il file, siete puntuali? [*ride*].
	Giving reassurance	**I:** - no, no, diciamo che va bene; - se voi riuscite a darmi in anticipo il file… dunque, meglio 10 giorni prima anziché una settimana; - [ride] sì, sì, sapendo qual è il periodo di consegna meglio 10 giorni che una settimana.
Meta-linguistic functions	Reflections about communication	**M:** [*voce bassa*] **per un congresso**; - **N:** ah, **per un congresso** # hai racione; - aspetta, aspetta [*a voce bassa mentre il "tipografo" fa i conti*]; **M:** - (**acconto**) [*voce bassa*].

Table 3-4. Analysis of functions, acts and expressions with key words.

Concerning functions, the phone call contains nearly all those present in the role-play with a smaller number of communicative acts which basically depends on the content of the phone call: for example, the replies given did not bring about the necessity to ask for/give reassurance about delivery times or ask for/give explanations about the preparation of files or the thickness of the paper. The phone call does not have a meta-linguistic function, contrary to the role-play, in which it shows the double role of the students (actors and learners) and in which the interaction has a more didactic nature. It surely cannot be sustained that the role-play was the only source for learning all these functions, many of which could already have been known by Nina. However, we can see how these functions appear with more precision and confidence in the real phone call, following their *rehearsal* in the RP. Many functions that were tried out in the role play are then effectively used in the phone call, which means that preparatory RPs really are useful in preparing for real life: in this way, role play ceases to be a purely formal didactic activity, and becomes an integral part of project work with its practical and contextualised communicative aims.

Conclusion

The final outcome of this PW appears positive. Significant results have been found in different areas: development of productive and receptive skills (*meaningful input and output*), learner independence (*learning to learn*), ability to work in groups (cooperation and collaboration) and socialisation. Although not specifically analysed, contributions in terms of the integration of basic skills, involvement, development of new relationships outside the L1 group, ability to take on a role, the closer relationship between guided learning and the spontaneous acquisition of L2 (adoption of a procedural syllabus) can all be observed.

Project work has significantly contributed to the creation of chances for interaction, which, although carried out with limited means (those available to the students), proves to be very beneficial. In fact, participating in conversational exchanges eases comprehension and favours the learning process and the development of interlanguage.[61]

Interaction has also allowed a symbolic use of L2 as an instrument which offers students the chance to emerge and establish themselves in the classroom system and other related systems, instigating a process of re-socialisation as a response to social norms and conventions of the host cultures in an ecological context which meant to integrate physical, social and cultural spaces.

LANGUAGE CENTRE (CLA)
UNIVERSITY OF SASSARI, ITALY

Other References

Amati, Anna "La Didattica per Progetti: Una Strategia di Rinnovamento." *Strumenti Cres* (suppl. *Mani Tese*) no. May (1998): 3-9.

De Bartolomeis, Francesco *Lavorare per Progetti.* Firenze: La Nuova Italia, 1989.

---

[61] Susan M. Gass, "Input and Interaction," in *Handbook of Second Language Acquisition*, ed. Catherine J. Doughty and Michael H. Long (Malden: Blackwell, 2003), 224-55.

Merli, Monica "La Didattica per Progetti come Sostegno alla Motivazione dei Discenti in College e Programmi Americani in Italia," *ITALS* 2, no. 5 (2004): 63-82

Quercioli, Fiorenza "La Didattica per Progetti nella Gestione della Classe Plurilingue," *Didattica & Classe Plurilingue* 3, Aug-Oct (2002), under "results," http://associazioni.comune.firenze.it/ilsa/dcp_agott02/art_quer.htm (accessed September 18, 2007).

CHAPTER FOUR

THE CONVERSATION HOUR: THE MAKING OF AN EXPERIMENT

SIMONA WRIGHT

Introduction

The Conversation Hour program was developed at our institution, a small liberal arts college in the Northeast, out of the necessity to increase student exposure to foreign languages, in this specific case, to Italian. As it is generally the case in American undergraduate education, our college has a language requirement.[1] Within this requirement, courses formerly carried a load of three credits, meeting for 80 minutes twice a week. Although this structure had been in place since the introduction of foreign language instruction, it was becoming more and more apparent that it was insufficient to produce in the students a satisfactory level of language proficiency. Numerous studies published in the 1990s confirmed the faculty's empirical observations and demonstrated how better results in language learning were produced with shorter but more frequent exposure to the target language.

My realization of the shortcomings of our college's academic structure for effective language learning and my exposure to innovative foreign language teaching methodologies motivated me to carry out a personal experiment by introducing an additional contact hour into the Italian curriculum. This hour was constructed as an "out-of-class" conversational experience whose goal was to provide students with much needed language practice outside of the traditional academic constraints. Advanced students were to lead this conversation period, students whose

[1] Language requirements vary by school and department. At our institution, the School of Culture and Society leads the effort to internationalize the campus and the curriculum with a three-semester language requirement.

skills were situated between the intermediate high and advanced mid level of the ACTFL scale.[2]

Several challenges, both organizational and pedagogical, emerged in this developing stage of the Conversation Hour. In this chapter, I will discuss those challenges and explore the way in which they were met. As will become clear in the course of this study, the success of the program hinged on the symmetrical functioning of both administrative and academic dimensions, and needed the support of both faculty and college administrators.

The Administrative Component

The structural organization of the Conversation Hour constituted the first area of consideration, as it involved scheduling, hiring, payroll, curricular and professional development. From the academic side, the CH component was to become an integral part of the course, and as such had to appear in the syllabus as an, albeit mildly, assessed element.

Initially only a relatively small group of students, those studying Italian, was impacted by the additional hour of instruction. The lack of symmetry between the requirements in Italian and those in the other languages was, for some students, difficult to accept, while the vast majority seemed to recognize the validity of adding an hour of stress-free conversation to their linguistic experience.

The concerns of the minority were mainly scheduling ones, as some of the students were unable to fit the CH into their already busy schedules. If the CH was to continue, it had to become recognized as a regular hour of instruction and as such needed to appear on the students' schedule when registering for classes.

In a semester of 14 weeks, ten[3] weekly meetings (10) were scheduled in the evenings. Small groups with a maximum of ten students would meet under the supervision of Conversation Hour Leaders who had been previously selected and interviewed by a faculty member and subsequently hired by the Director of the Tutoring Center.[4] The support of the Director

---

[2] See American Council on the Teaching of Foreign Languages (ACTFL), *Program Standards for the Preparation of Foreign Language Teachers*, 2002, 129-33.

[3] Conversation Hour meetings begin in the third week of the semester and end the week prior to the semester end. This delayed start allows the Conversation Hour Coordinators to staff new sections, to train the Payroll Coordinator, and to attend to unexpected emergencies prior to the beginning of the program.

[4] The Center provides free academic tutoring to students.

of the Tutoring Center was essential in the successful organization and implementation of the initial stages of the Conversation Hour. The Center provided the space where the meetings were to take place, hired the Conversation Hour Leaders, provided administrative and support services, coordinated the schedule and the payroll, and finally funded the entire project.

With the passing of time the Conversation Hour gained popularity and was adopted by other language programs, a fact that resulted in an exponential growth in the number of sections, CH Leaders, and administrative services. The rapid changes made the re-organization and restructuring of the program absolutely necessary. It became apparent that the Tutoring Center could not support such growth. At the same time, the expansion of the program to other languages made closer supervision of the academic side necessary.

Conversations involving the Dean of the School of Culture and Society, the Director of the Tutoring Center, and the Chair of the Modern Languages Department resulted in the decision to move the entire program, including its budget, to Modern Languages, thus giving our department complete administrative and academic control. This move transformed the Conversation Hour program in a positive way by placing complete control over the scheduling and hiring of CH Leaders, direct involvement into the pedagogical dimension of the CH, including curricular development, training and professional enhancement, and control over the budget into the hands of the Modern Languages Department.[5]

In a propitious sequence of events, simultaneous to the implementation of the Conversation Hour in Italian the college administration spearheaded a comprehensive curricular transformation, which involved a radical re-thinking of the academic requirements and an intensification of the curriculum. All academic courses were redesigned following a 4-credit unit model, which called for an additional "contact" hour.

The Modern Languages Department participated in the curricular transformation with the reassessment of, among other things, the basic language sequence, where the Conversation Hour was formally introduced.[6] Thus, the addition of required conversation hours to our elementary and intermediate language courses responded both to the

---

[5] Among the possible disadvantages to the move is an expansion of the responsibilities of the Modern Language Department Chair.

[6] Some programs required that the Conversation Hour be offered also at the intermediate level, a decision that produced the need for more proficient instructors and the hiring of adjunct faculty on a need base.

College's mandate for curricular strengthening and restructuring and to our Department's desire to remedy what was felt as the main limitation of our language program: insufficient student exposure to the target language.

After the Modern Languages Department approved the implementation of the CH in the basic sequence for all languages, it presented the administration with an implementation plan that confirmed the move of all administrative and academic responsibilities under its supervision, and requested permission to hire two CH Coordinators,[7] and a student who would work as CH Payroll Coordinator.

The CH Coordinators' responsibilities are to supervise the hiring of all Conversation Hour Leaders, to coordinate the schedule of all CHs, to organize and offer workshops on second language acquisition, to monitor the academic quality of the leaders' performance by conducting regular CH observations, to provide instructional material appropriate to every level and language, to develop evaluative tools, to collect relevant data, and to give regular reports on the status and progress of the CH to the Chair of the Modern Languages Department, the ML Department, and the Dean of Culture and Society (see Appendix 2). In turn, the student Payroll Coordinator is responsible for the collection and monitoring of all the CH leaders' timesheets and their timely transmission to the Office of Payroll.

The CH Payroll Coordinator is hired from a reliable and capable pool of Business students. The CH Coordinators are experienced instructors conversant with the current methodologies of Second Language Acquisition and with the national standards of foreign language teaching (ACTFL). Beside their administrative duties, in fact, their contract includes a teaching load of three courses per year and the responsibility of continuing their professional development by becoming and retaining their status as ACTFL certified OPI interviewers.

Immediately after the hiring of the CH Coordinators, the CH schedule was uploaded in the system that students access to register for their courses. On the students' screen, the CH would appear as a co-curricular activity that is clearly linked to the hour of foreign language instruction. Every CH has an enrollment capacity of ten students and all CHs in that particular level are open to students, independently of the lecture/discussion section in which they enroll, to allow for maximum scheduling flexibility.

To sum up, the issues related to the organizational and administrative side of the Conversation Hour were defined by the formalization of this

---

[7] The two Conversation Hour Coordinators are responsible respectively for Spanish, which has a major, and for all remaining languages (French, Italian, German, Arabic, Japanese, Chinese, and Russian).

additional time period into the students' schedule, a move for which the Department of Modern Languages sought the support, both conceptual and financial, of the college administration. It is important to reiterate here that the collaboration of the administration, which came in the form of personnel hiring (CH Leaders, CH Coordinators, CH Payroll Coordinator), additional funds for the Modern Languages Department's budget, and total freedom in the supervision of all aspects of the process (staffing, hiring, payroll, program assessment, staff supervision and development), was instrumental in the successful implementation and functioning of the "fourth" contact hour of conversation.

Academics

A number of academic and instructional questions had to be confronted before offering the Conversation Hour: they can be separated in two main categories relating respectively to the students who would attend the activities and those who would lead them. In the first category the main issue was the development of a methodological approach, which would have, on one hand, determined both the content and the structure of the experience and on the other, redefined the role of the students in it.

It must be said at this point that the transformation of the curriculum in the Modern Languages Department went hand in hand with a shift in the methodological approach in foreign language teaching. For several years some faculty members had been utilizing the Communicative Approach in their classes and had championed it as the most effective teaching methodology in foreign language acquisition. Curricular transformation promoted a departmental review of the methodology and a commitment to professional development that included participation at several workshops on foreign language teaching methodology, on ACTFL standards, and on NCATE requirements for the preparation of language teachers. A formal departmental endorsement of the Communicative Approach, with a consequent realignment of the curriculum, was the result of this thorough process.

In symmetry with recent trends in pedagogy and teaching methodology,[8] the Communicative Approach challenges the traditional

---

[8] See M. Canale & Swain, "Theoretical Bases of Communicative Approaches to Second Language Teaching and Testing," *Applied Linguistics 1*: 1-47; M. Krashen, S. *Principles and Practice of Second Language Acquisition* (Oxford: Pergamon Press, 1982); K. E. Johnson, *Understanding Communication in Second Language Classrooms* (New York: Cambridge University Press, 1995); J. C. Richard & T.

methods of foreign language instruction in American education[9] and seeks to re-conceptualize the learner's role by calling for a learning experience that is student-centered and student-focused (see Appendix 1). Complementing this approach was the introduction of the five language goals, better known as the 5 Cs (Communication, Cultures, Connections, Comparisons, and Communities), endorsed by the American Council on the Teaching of Foreign Languages.[10]

The Conversation Hour was to become an extension of the communicative classroom and provide a learning environment that was both collaborative and dynamic, but most importantly centered on activities focused on the three communicative modes outlined in the first goal, Communication, of the ACTFL standards.[11]

Before and After

When the development of the Conversation Hour was in its initial stages, i.e. it was offered only by the Italian program, a rather small section if compared with Spanish, I had interviewed a number of very competent and enthusiastic students who were to become CH Leaders. They were all talented, mature, hardworking individuals, and had demonstrated, in class and outside, an uncommon commitment to the language. After being hired by the Director of the Tutoring Program, they

---

Rodgers, *Approaches and Methods in Language Teaching* (New York: Cambridge University Press, 2000).

[9] See A. Coleman, *The Teaching of Modern Foreign Languages in the United States* (New York: Macmillan, 1929).

[10] See the *Standards for Foreign Language Learning in the 21st Century*, 1999. These standards were developed as a collaborative effort by nine foreign language associations representing around 40,000 members. See also the *Program Standards for the Preparation of Foreign Language Teachers*, published by the American Council on the Teaching of Foreign Languages (ACTFL), 2001, 2-4.

[11] Ibid., 3. The first goal of the ACTFL standards is centered on Communication and describes what students should know and be able to do through the class activities. As the standards clearly indicate, foreign language learning shifts with these goals from a "focus on language and culture to one of communication and culture." The first of the five goals, Communication, is further subdivided in three communicative modes: "The *interpersonal* mode is characterized by two-way communication and active negotiation of meaning among individuals in written and spoken form. The *interpretive* mode focuses on the understanding and interpretation of oral and printed texts, in which no active negotiation of meaning is possible. The *presentational* mode refers to the oral and written presentation of information, concepts, and ideas to an audience of listeners and readers."

were to meet weekly in my office to discuss how to structure the hour and how to develop activities that would be student-centered and student-focused, eliciting the highest amount of participation and language practice. Since the CH was created to support the regular foreign language classes, no new material was introduced in the conversation hours but rather, previously presented material was reviewed in oral, aural, and TPR activities.

A considerable amount of time was dedicated to the selection and development of communicative activities that were aimed at providing the needed student output in the target language. With this in mind, the Conversation Hour was segmented in three parts, the first dedicated to short readings, the second centered on vocabulary building activities through language trees, fill-ins, questions and answers, brief exchanges and descriptions, the third and final one centered on the student production and performance of descriptions, short skits, and presentations.

When the Conversation Hour received the endorsement of the administration and became a formalized element of the curriculum, the Department of Modern Languages requested that two Conversation Hour Coordinators and a Payroll Coordinator be hired to assume the academic and administrative management of the program.

Upon their hiring, the Conversation Hour Coordinators took over the coordinating role I had carried out and continued to meet weekly with the CH leaders to discuss activities, strategies, and second language acquisition techniques. These meetings were recognized as units of professional development, with attached credit hours, and officially integrated in the CH Leaders' schedule.

Conversation Hour Leaders' Training

The support for the Conversation Hour by the Modern Languages Department was constant throughout the formalization process and led to the organization of several methodology workshops presided by the faculty. The objective of the workshops, which are offered twice per semester, is to continue to train CH Leaders in Second Language Acquisition theory and to provide a forum where experiences, questions, and concerns can be shared. The workshops, which are highly interactive, have proven instrumental to allow CH leaders to acquaint themselves with the principles of the Communicative Approach and the ACTFL standards for foreign language teaching.

As the Modern Language Department views the CH as a great opportunity for student professional development, it was decided to include the requirement of leading a CH in MDL 390 (Foreign Language Acquisition and Related Methodologies), a course required for students majoring in Spanish Teaching. The practicum component of the CH complements well the theoretical structure of the course and was positively received by the majors. In addition, some seniors have, over the years, completed an Independent Study that involved leading a section of Conversation Hour, developing a complete portfolio of communicative activities (covering the entire semester), and writing a self-reflective essay based on SLA theory, empirical experience, and an evaluation of the methodology used.

As complete standardization was never an objective in the establishment of the Conversation Hour, the development of activities based on the same fundamental principles for each language program was, however, left to the individual Language Program Directors, who works in concert with his/her respective CH Coordinators.

Data Collection, Evaluation, and Assessment

While it was paramount to continue to develop the expertise of CH Leaders and to support them with student-centered activities aligned with the ACTFL goals, it became also essential to assess both the students' participation in and the effectiveness of the Conversation Hour. Class attendance is taken by CH Leaders who are not responsible for grading students but for providing a record of the students' presence. Student participation is thus assessed in a quantitative rather than qualitative manner. CH Leaders are given four different symbols (V-; V; V+; and 0), which correspond respectively to 1) present at low level of participation, 2) present at average level of participation, and 3) present at high level of participation, and 4) absent.

Faculty members can monitor the students' attendance and participation throughout the semester thanks to the college's instructional network (SOCS), which includes a virtual board where assignments, activities, and messages can be posted by CH Coordinators and faculty, and be viewed by CH Leaders and students. Successful participation in all CH meetings is recognized as 10% of the students' final grade.

From the very beginning, it was understood and agreed upon among the faculty that the CH should not become reason for additional testing. As it was not considered a separate component of the learning experience but rather an expansion of the class time, the CH's effectiveness was to be observed exclusively in the students' successful language production in class and evaluated by the individual professor, at the level of his or her lecture/discussion section, through general class activities and oral proficiency interviews.

However, assessment of the CH's success and reception among the students was however important. For this reason, the CH Coordinators and the Modern Languages Department collaborated in the development of a questionnaire that is handed out with the college and department evaluation forms at the end of every semester. The questionnaire's main objectives are to measure the effectiveness of the teaching strategies, to collect evidence of students' successful input, and to assemble data for further analysis andimprovement of the CH (see Appendix 3).

To date, the general view among Modern Languages faculty and students is that the implementation of the CH has significantly improved the amount of students' language output by providing needed time for practice in the target language. By adding a fourth hour of exclusive language production to their traditional class meetings, students have the opportunity not only to improve their practical understanding of the material presented in class but can also, thanks to a stress-free and relaxed environment, start to overcome the fears associated with speaking in a foreign language.

As the success of the CH became evident, all language programs, except Spanish, decided to add this co-curricular activity to their intermediate and advanced courses. The challenge in this respect was to find CH leaders that were linguistically as well as methodologically competent. A solution was tailored for each individual language, as needs and competencies differ greatly from program to program. In German, a skilled group of exchange students was hired, while in French adjunct faculty accepted the additional activity as overload. For Italian, Arabic, Chinese, and Japanese, the respective program coordinators selected a cohort of competent bilingual students.

Student Professional Development

The success of the CH program has had positive and somewhat unexpected effects on the Leaders, as the professional experience gathered during the CH has encouraged some of them to pursue a minor or major in the target language, a teaching career or graduate studies in the target language after graduation. On the one hand, many students become interested in the CH leadership as they complete the elementary sequence and are encouraged to apply for the position once the necessary proficiency level is reached. On the other, the understanding that CH Leaders need to continue their language studies has increased the interest for intermediate and advanced classes and this resulted in the development of new intermediate and advanced courses and the establishment of new minors.

Another important position available to students since the implementation of the program is that of the CH Payroll Coordinator, who is responsible for the management of the CH Leaders' payroll records. The student hired in this position is generally a Business major in his/her sophomore year that will work in the MLD offices until graduation. The hiring process for this position is accompanied by a semester internship to be completed in the department prior to the actual hiring.

This is a management experience of primary significance for a student planning to work in the business world, as the responsibilities of the position include the upkeep of critical college records, the oversight of the CH payroll office, and the development of good organizational and interpersonal skills involved in managing a payroll of over 60 workers. Students graduating from the college with this experience in their background were offered excellent career opportunities.

Conclusions

The development and implementation of the Conversation Hour have presented the department of Modern Languages with both challenges and opportunities. From the pedagogical point of view, the addition of such a program has greatly improved the students' chances for success in learning a foreign language while from the professional perspective the experience of leading a CH has produced increased interest in the pursuit of language studies. The additional administrative load in the department, scheduling, hiring, payroll, oversight of academic quality, was divided between the chair (program oversight), and the newly hired personnel. The Conversation Hour proved to be a testing ground for the relations between administration and faculty, which developed into a productive collaboration that proved instrumental to the initiative's success. The faculty involvement in the academic side of the Conversation Hour guarantees a program that matches the academic needs of the students with the objectives of each language curriculum. Methodologically, the alignment of the Conversation Hour with the methodological approach endorsed by the department ensures that the national standards for the teaching of foreign languages are met at all levels of the academic experience.

Finally, the addition of the Conversation Hour serves the overarching objectives of the college, as outlined in its mission: the development of citizens with a global understanding of the multilingual and multicultural realities of our world.

THE COLLEGE OF NEW JERSEY, USA

APPENDIX

1. Conversation Hour Activities (Samples)
CHs are generally held in smart classrooms to allow for the use of internet and to facilitate access to computer based activities

Italian 101

Goal: Through vocabulary building activities (brainstorming, word associations, etc.), guided input, Q/A, short dialogues, have students describe their hometowns and an Italian town in a short narrative.

CH Leader models target behavior by describing his/her home town.

Patterns needed:
La mia città è piccola/grande/bella/moderna.
Nella mia città c'è/ci sono // non c'è/non ci sono ....
La mia città ha/non ha un/uno/una/un'....

Students play word games to review the vocabulary of town and country:
Word associations:
Intorno alla piazza
In un piccolo paese
Students compile lists of nouns for these semantic areas.

Question-answer activity
CHLeader asks students questions such as:
Cosa c'è nella tua città?
Che cosa non c'è nella tua città?

CH Leader pairs students for a short exchange. Students will ask each other five questions about each other's hometown and write a brief report. The report will subsequently be presented to the larger group.

Every 4 reports the CH Leader will ask the class to give information on the students' town: questions can range from: Che cosa c'è (non c'è) nella città di Martha? Dov'è.....? Com'è la città? Etc.

CH Leader calls for each student to describe his or her hometown. CH Leader invites students to ask at least 5 questions after each presentation.

Then CH Leader shows students a picture (video) of Rome and asks students to describe it, creating a 5-8 sentence narrative to present in class.

Italian 102

Goal: Through vocabulary building activities (brainstorming, word associations, etc.), guided input, Q/A, short dialogues, have students describe their food habits, compare them with those of Italians, and perform a skit in an Italian restaurant.

Students brainstorm a series of words, verbs, and idiomatic expressions related to food and food habits. CH Leaders writes them on the board.

With pictures taken at an Italian market or with a PowerPoint presentation, CH Leader asks questions related to food in the United States and in Italy (market versus supermarket, freshness of products, times and content of meals).

CH Leader asks students to form pairs and ask each other' s food preferences. Students will report their findings to the class, which will take note and report in turn (after 4 students have reported on their workmates)

CH Leader distributes a menu from an Italian restaurant (found on the web). In group of three (two customers and a waiter), students create a skit considering 1) the different customer's preferences (vegetarian—on a diet—food allergies—and so on) and perform it in groups (at least three times).

CH Leader selects 3 groups to act out the skit.

Italian 103

Goal: Through vocabulary building activities (brainstorming, word associations, etc.), guided input, Q/A, short dialogues, have students talk about their travels and describe the services offered by an "agriturismo."

CH Leader writes and circles three words on the board (aeroporto-passaporto-hotel-valigia-visto etc) and invites students to brainstorm on related words and idiomatic expressions.

CH Leader introduces a photo from the activity material (All'aeroporto di Roma) and asks students to create a story about the arrival of the people in the photo (they lost their luggage—their friends did not meet them as planned—need to find taxi, bank, maps, etc.)

CH Leader asks students to create a guided dialogue containing questions about their travels—where they went over the summer, what they did, how they traveled, how they made reservations, where they will travel next year.

Students perform the dialogue going around the class and finding at least three different partners (after the skit is performed once the guided dialogue is erased from the board)

CH Leader shows the brochure of a hotel or a the website of an "agriturismo": students will find information pertaining to the location, prices, services, offered by the "agriturismo"/hotel and describe them to the class in a Q/A session led by the CH Leader.

2. CH Report

The Role of Conversation Hours in the MLD and at ____________
Submitted by __________ and ___________
with the assistance of ____________

1. Role in the Modern Language program

The Conversation Hour is the response of the Modern Languages Department to the College's call for academic transformation. The department recognized the college's plan for curricular enhancement as an opportunity to provide students with an additional contact hour. The Conversation Hour represents the fourth credit for our 100 and, in some languages, 200 and 300 level language courses.

The department stands behind the commitment to the Conversation Hour and recognizes the curricular addition to be in compliance with the mandate for transformation. In some languages, Web pages were developed for each level to serve both the faculty members and the CH Leaders. In the less commonly taught languages, instructors work closely with CH Leaders to provide activities that support the goals of the course. The CH Coordinators organize regular orientations and workshops held by faculty members.

Conversation Hours in the MLD are therefore an essential part of our academic requirement for which students pay tuition. Material covered in the CHs is based on the material presented in the corresponding courses. By improving student proficiency in foreign languages, the CH program supports the College's stated mission to prepare students for leadership in a multicultural, global world characterized by genuine cross-cultural interaction, a laudable goal which requires the ability to communicate in other languages.

2. Role of the Conversation Hour Program in the education of students

During the current semester, 827 students, approximately 15% of the student body, are enrolled in conversation hours in Arabic, Chinese, French, German, Italian, Japanese, and Spanish. This figure is usually slightly higher in the fall semester. The enrollment in conversation hours in the spring of 2006 is illustrated in the following graph.

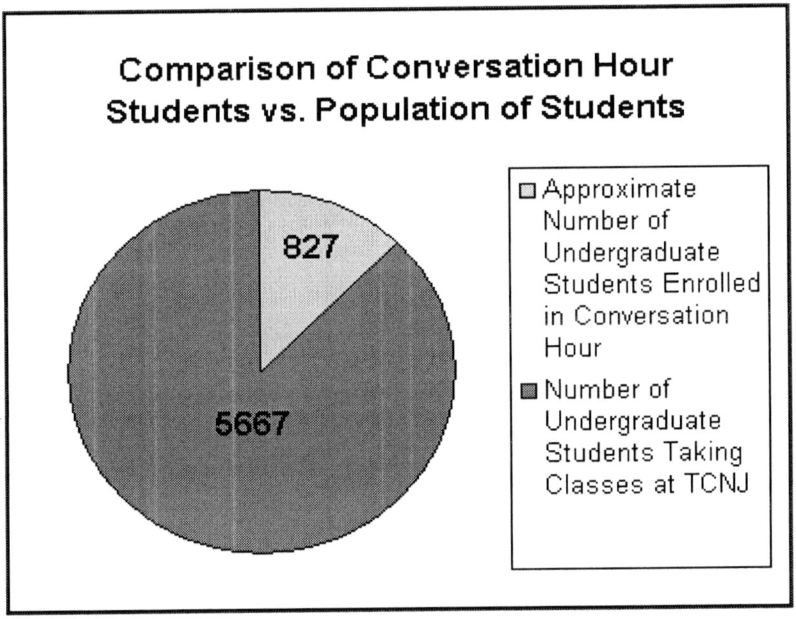

Table 4-1. Students vs. Population of Students.

3. Scope of the Conversation Hour Program

The CH program involves approximately 1400 student work hours per semester including the time used by the Conversation Hour Payroll Coordinator. This number is increasing as more courses are adding the CH component.

The Conversation Hour program is fully integrated into the academic mission of the Department. In Spanish, students enrolled in Methodology (Spanish 390) and Advanced Oral Proficiency (Spanish 302), are required to lead a CH as part of their course work. In Spanish and Italian, leading of CHs now forms an essential part of an independent study in language pedagogy.

Occasionally it is necessary to hire an adjunct, either because of a scheduling emergency or because the level of language proficiency required for a 300 level CH is beyond the abilities of our CH Leaders. However, the courses taught as part of our students' coursework usually balance expenses incurred by hiring adjuncts.

4. Administration

The CH program is run by two Coordinators (one for Spanish, one for the other languages) whose time is split between teaching and coordinating and by a Payroll Coordinator who works 15 hours a week and whose duties are detailed in Supplement A of this document.

5. Educational value of the Conversation Hour Program for students enrolled in ML

Conversation hours have had a very positive effect on our language program by giving our students an extra contact hour a week. The informal atmosphere of the peer-led CH encourages students to take more risks in speaking. Faculty members have noticed an increased willingness on the part of students to participate orally in class. (See Supplement B of this document)

CHs are scheduled, as far as possible, on days when the regular class does not meet, thus insuring that students have contact with the foreign language three times a week.

CH hours are carefully monitored and supervised to ensure that they are fulfilling the goals that the course coordinators have set for them. One of the projects for next year is to examine the possibility of including the material of the Conversation Hours on course examinations.

6. Educational value of the Conversation Hour Program for CH Leaders

The experience of leading a CH has benefited our advanced students both professionally and personally. Leading a CH has given them the opportunity to put their knowledge of the foreign language to use in a challenging class situation.

Especially for those students interested in languages other than Spanish, whose schedules may not allow them to take electives, the opportunity to lead a CH helps them maintain and improve their language skills.

CH Leaders report that leading a CH affords them the opportunity for personal and professional growth and regard it as a valuable experience for their career after graduation. It is clear from their commentsthat the opportunity to lead a CH has substantially and substantively enriched their educational experience at the college.

Supplement A
Responsibilities of the Payroll Coordinatorof the Conversation Hour Program

a) Create and maintaining a file system for timesheets, attendance and record-keeping regarding program and leaders
Administering payroll for students
Coordinate budget with office of Budget and Finance
b) Coordinate hiring process and paperwork related to hiring process with Career Services
c) Coordinate payroll process with Payroll
d) Make sure students receive timesheets every week
e) Ensure students turn in timesheets every week
f) Keep track of CH leader attendance and payment
g) Make sure students receive paychecks each pay period
h) Resolve conflicts and answering questions for students regarding their pay
i) Communicating with leaders regarding CH Leader/student
j) Manage attendance and the payroll process
k) Resolve issues or finding answers to questions students have with career services regarding their employment as CH Leaders
l) Communicate with students every day via email and telephone answering questions/reminding CH Leaders about timesheets, paychecks, and attendance
m) Answer questions concerning CH program policies
n) Communicate with other offices when necessary regarding students concerns
o) Make copies of CH materials for leaders
p) Maintain mailboxes for the CH materials as needed
q) Present at CH Leader meetings throughout the year to explain CH Attendance and Payroll Process
r) Hold office hours for students to contact with questions, for the payroll process to occur and to allow leaders to log in their attendance for the students

s) Create materials to explain the payroll/attendance process and to answer any possible questions the CH Leaders may have
t) Assist ________and ________ with the creation of budget reports and the analysis of financial information regarding CH program
u) Research information for professors via correspondence with Records& Registration and Student Accounts
v) Use databases and Payroll statistics to obtain necessary information for budget report
w) Attend meetings at the CH and MLD levels about the performance and operation of the program

Supplement B
Student Evaluations

Conversation Hour Survey—Italian
Frequency Table

1) I am taking this Modern Language Course as:

		Frequency	Percent	Valid Percent	Cumulative Percent
Valid	General Education	15	40.5	40.5	40.5
	Undergraduate Elective	3	8.1	8.1	48.6
	Requirement in UG Major/Minor	16	43.2	43.2	91.9
	Option in UG Major/Minor	2	5.4	5.4	97.3
	Elective in Graduate	1	2.7	2.7	100.0
	Total	37	100.0	100.0	

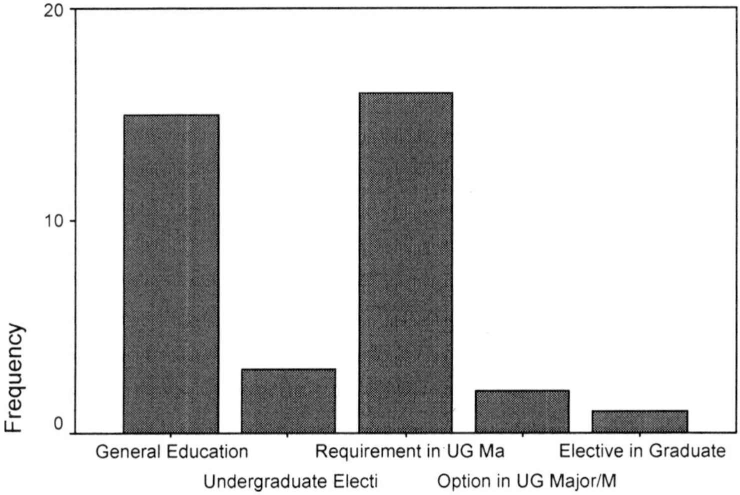

2) The CH Leader had a variety of activities available for each class meeting:

		Frequency	Percent	Valid Percent	Cumulative Percent
Valid	Strongly Disagree	1	2.7	2.7	2.7
	Disagree	4	10.8	10.8	13.5
	Undecided	3	8.1	8.1	21.6
	Agree	17	45.9	45.9	67.6
	Strongly Agree	12	32.4	32.4	100.0
	Total	37	100.0	100.0	

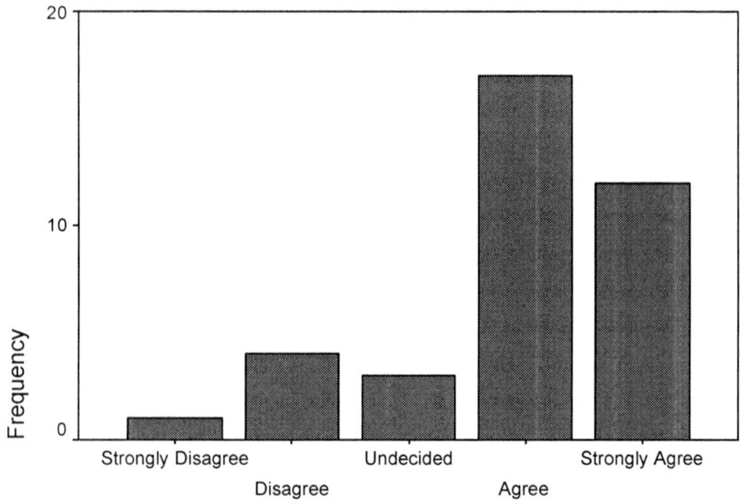

3) The CH Leader moved from activity to activity without wasting time:

		Frequency	Percent	Valid Percent	Cumulative Percent
Valid	Disagree	3	8.1	8.1	8.1
	Undecided	6	16.2	16.2	24.3
	Agree	16	43.2	43.2	67.6
	Strongly Agree	12	32.4	32.4	100.0
	Total	37	100.0	100.0	

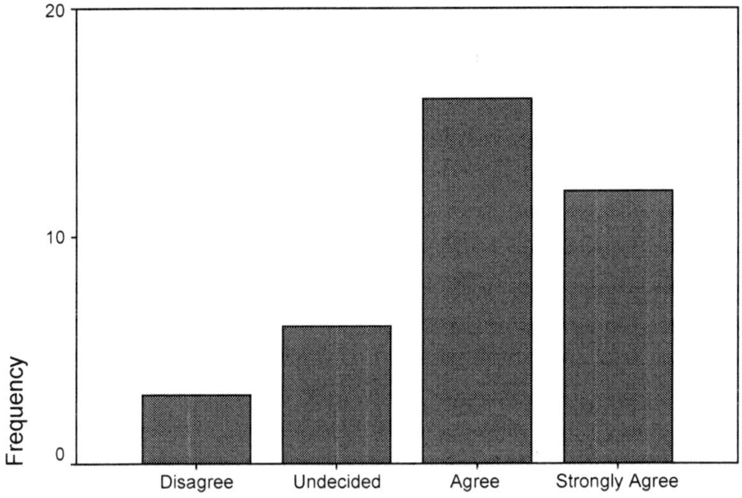

4) The CH Leader met each of his or her classes on time:

		Frequency	Percent	Valid Percent	Cumulative Percent
Valid	Undecided	5	13.5	13.5	13.5
	Agree	10	27.0	27.0	40.5
	Strongly Agree	22	59.5	59.5	100.0
	Total	37	100.0	100.0	

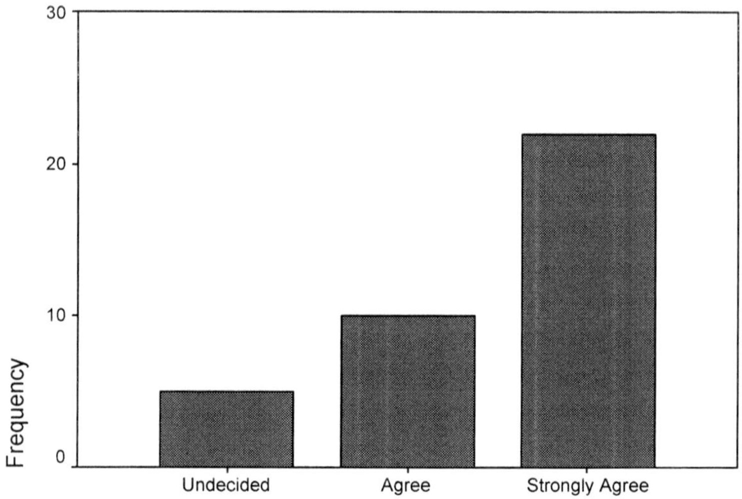

5) The CH Leader always used the full 50 minutes allotted:

		Frequency	Percent	Valid Percent	Cumulative Percent
Valid	Strongly Disagree	2	5.4	5.4	5.4
	Disagree	3	8.1	8.1	13.5
	Undecided	3	8.1	8.1	21.6
	Agree	14	37.8	37.8	59.5
	Strongly Agree	15	40.5	40.5	100.0
	Total	37	100.0	100.0	

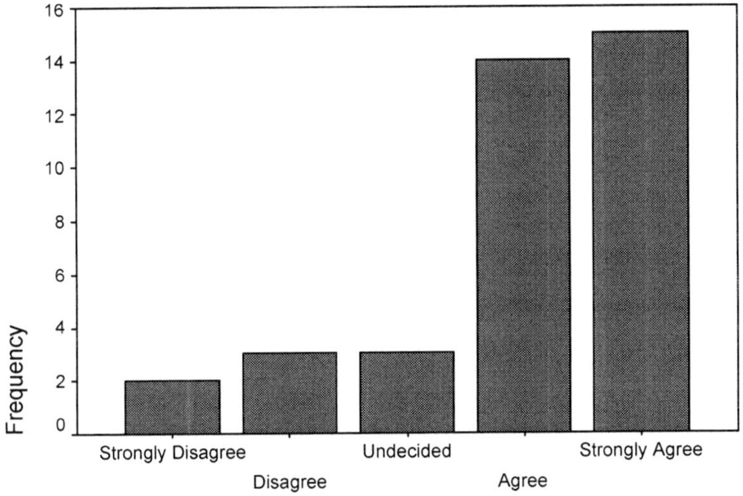

6) The CH Leader shows enthusiasm for the language taught:

		Frequency	Percent	Valid Percent	Cumulative Percent
Valid	Strongly Disagree	2	5.4	5.4	5.4
	Undecided	5	13.5	13.5	18.9
	Agree	7	18.9	18.9	37.8
	Strongly Agree	23	62.2	62.2	100.0
	Total	37	100.0	100.0	

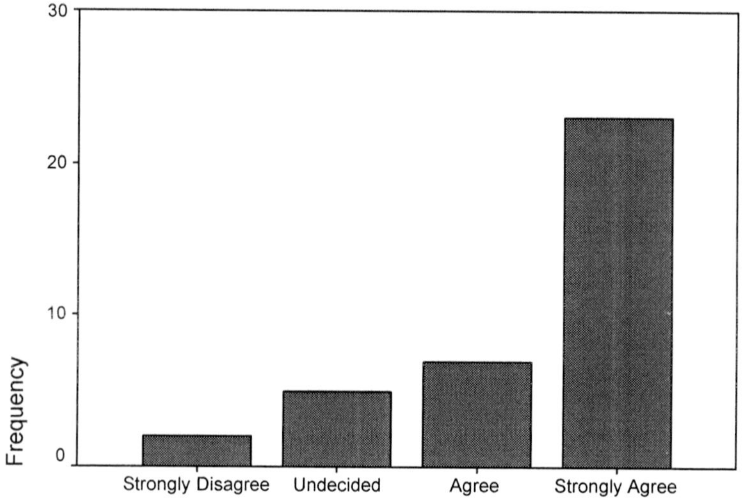

7) The CH Leader used the foreign language almost all of the time:

		Frequency	Percent	Valid Percent	Cumulative Percent
Valid	Strongly Disagree	1	2.7	2.7	2.7
	Undecided	8	21.6	21.6	24.3
	Agree	18	48.6	48.6	73.0
	Strongly Agree	10	27.0	27.0	100.0
	Total	37	100.0	100.0	

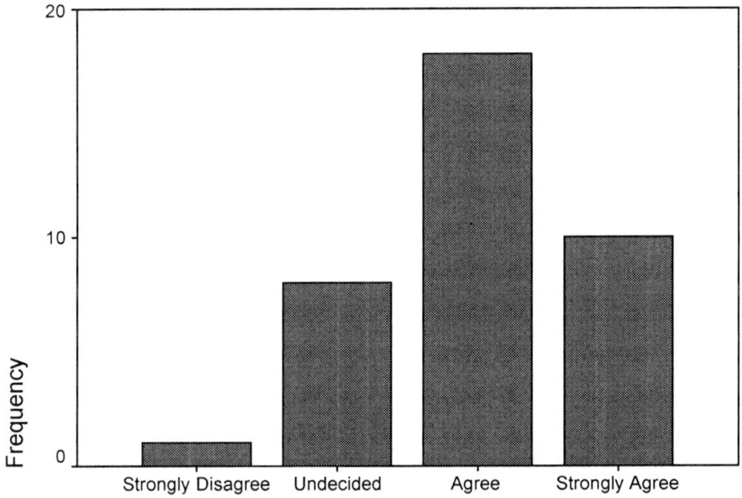

8) The CH Leader encouraged me to use the foreign language almost all of the time:

		Frequency	Percent	Valid Percent	Cumulative Percent
Valid	Strongly Disagree	1	2.7	2.8	2.8
	Disagree	1	2.7	2.8	5.6
	Undecided	6	16.2	16.7	22.2
	Agree	16	43.2	44.4	66.7
	Strongly Agree	12	32.4	33.3	100.0
	Total	36	97.3	100.0	
Missing	System	1	2.7		
Total		37	100.0		

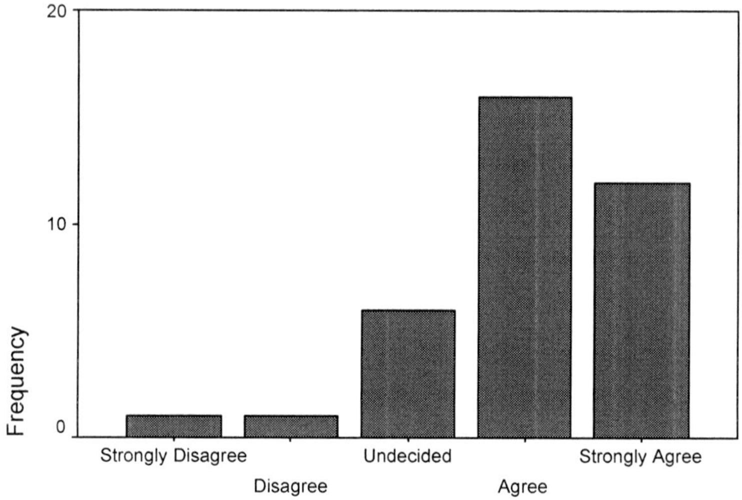

9) The CH Leader encouraged me to use the foreign language almost all of the time:

		Frequency	Percent	Valid Percent	Cumulative Percent
Valid	Strongly Disagree	1	2.7	2.7	2.7
	Disagree	5	13.5	13.5	16.2
	Undecided	6	16.2	16.2	32.4
	Agree	8	21.6	21.6	54.1
	Strongly Agree	17	45.9	45.9	100.0
	Total	37	100.0	100.0	

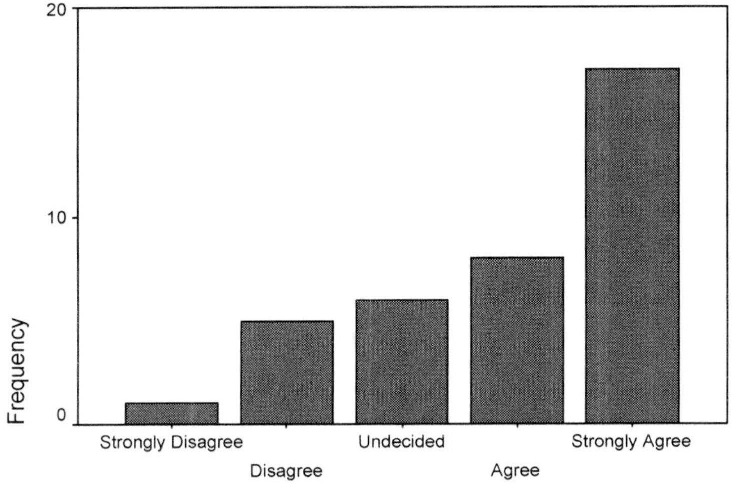

10) I believe that the CH meetings have helped me develop my speaking ability in the language I am studying:

		Frequency	Percent	Valid Percent	Cumulative Percent
Valid	Strongly Disagree	5	13.5	13.9	13.9
	Disagree	2	5.4	5.6	19.4
	Undecided	8	21.6	22.2	41.7
	Agree	13	35.1	36.1	77.8
	Strongly Agree	8	21.6	22.2	100.0
	Total	36	97.3	100.0	
Missing	System	1	2.7		
Total		37	100.0		

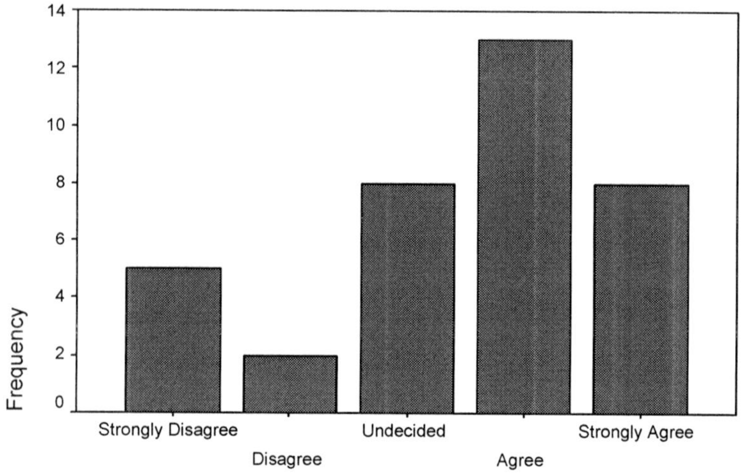

11) I believe that the activities in the CH helped me understand the language better:

		Frequency	Percent	Valid Percent	Cumulative Percent
Valid	Strongly Disagree	5	13.5	13.5	13.5
	Undecided	6	16.2	16.2	29.7
	Agree	15	40.5	40.5	70.3
	Strongly Agree	11	29.7	29.7	100.0
	Total	37	100.0	100.0	

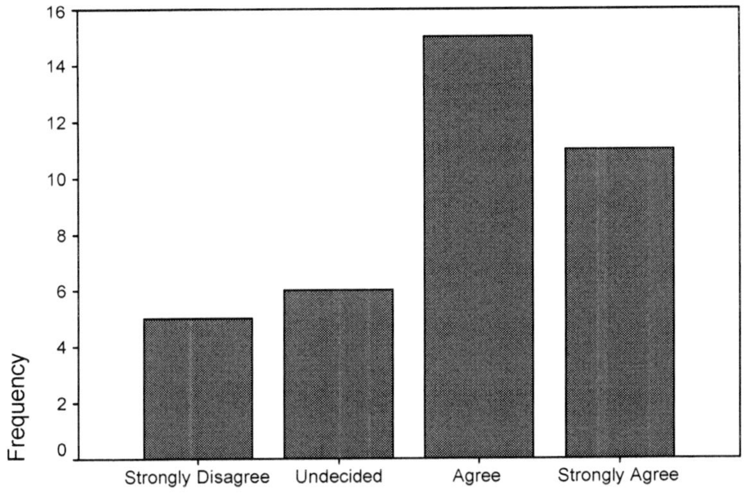

12) I was treated fairly, impartially, and with respect by the CH Leader:

		Frequency	Percent	Valid Percent	Cumulative Percent
Valid	Disagree	1	2.7	2.7	2.7
	Undecided	5	13.5	13.5	16.2
	Agree	9	24.3	24.3	40.5
	Strongly Agree	22	59.5	59.5	100.0
	Total	37	100.0	100.0	

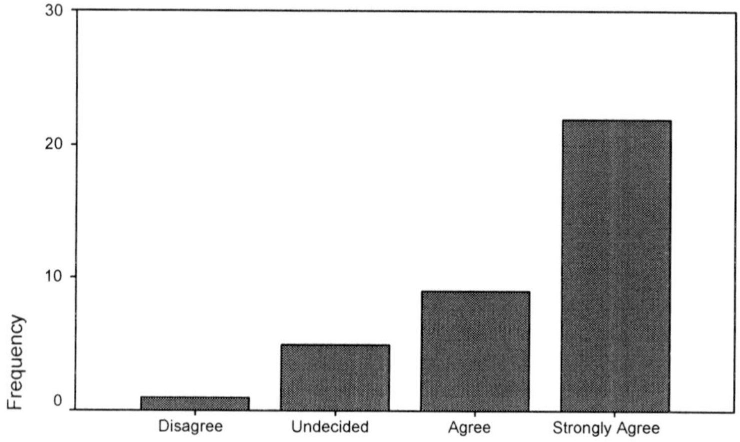

13) I feel more confident in speaking the language because of my work in the CH:

		Frequency	Percent	Valid Percent	Cumulative Percent
Valid	Strongly Disagree	2	5.4	5.4	5.4
	Disagree	5	13.5	13.5	18.9
	Undecided	8	21.6	21.6	40.5
	Agree	14	37.8	37.8	78.4
	Strongly Agree	8	21.6	21.6	100.0
	Total	37	100.0	100.0	

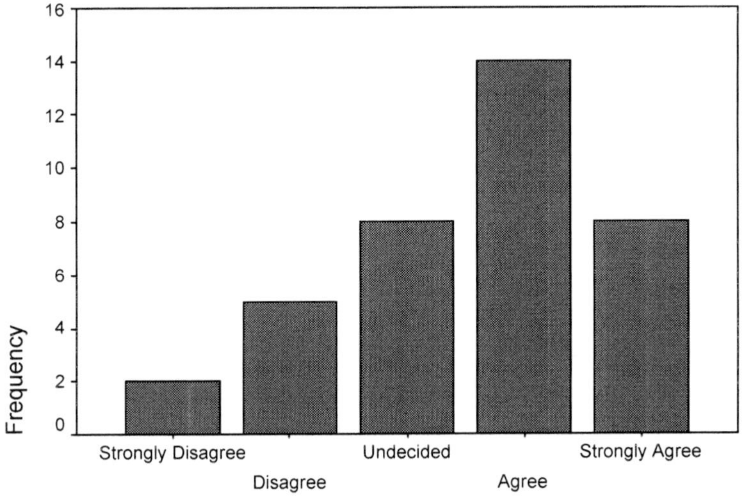

14) I believe that my work in the CH has had a positive influence on my participation in the recitation sections of my language course:

		Frequency	Percent	Valid Percent	Cumulative Percent
Valid	Strongly Disagree	3	8.1	8.1	8.1
	Disagree	4	10.8	10.8	18.9
	Undecided	9	24.3	24.3	43.2
	Agree	14	37.8	37.8	81.1
	Strongly Agree	7	18.9	18.9	100.0
	Total	37	100.0	100.0	

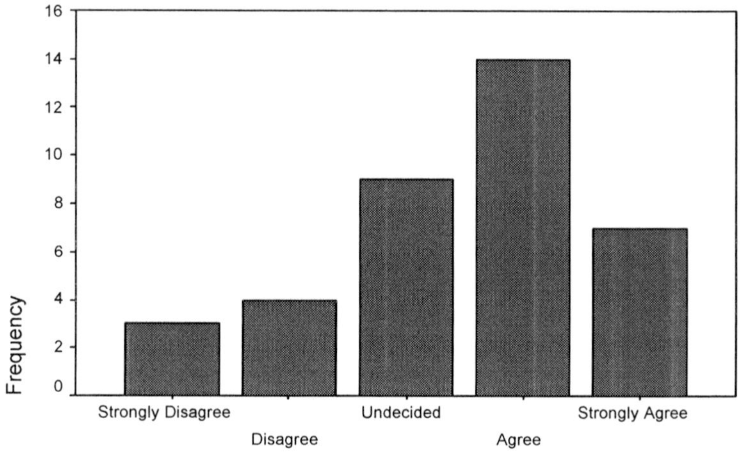

15) I believe that the CH meetings helped me get a higher grade in my language course:

		Frequency	Percent	Valid Percent	Cumulative Percent
Valid	Strongly Disagree	4	10.8	10.8	10.8
	Disagree	6	16.2	16.2	27.0
	Undecided	10	27.0	27.0	54.1
	Agree	10	27.0	27.0	81.1
	Strongly Agree	7	18.9	18.9	100.0
	Total	37	100.0	100.0	

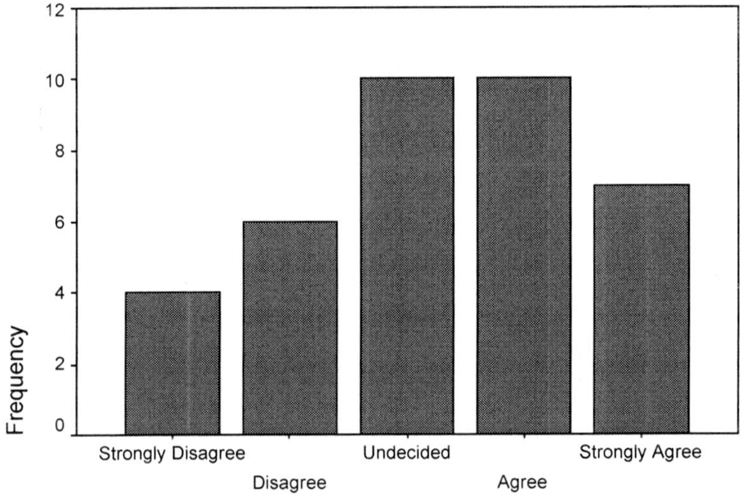

16) The work of the CH was usually related to the work of the recitation session:

		Frequency	Percent	Valid Percent	Cumulative Percent
Valid	Strongly Disagree	2	5.4	5.4	5.4
	Disagree	2	5.4	5.4	10.8
	Undecided	8	21.6	21.6	32.4
	Agree	15	40.5	40.5	73.0
	Strongly Agree	10	27.0	27.0	100.0
	Total	37	100.0	100.0	

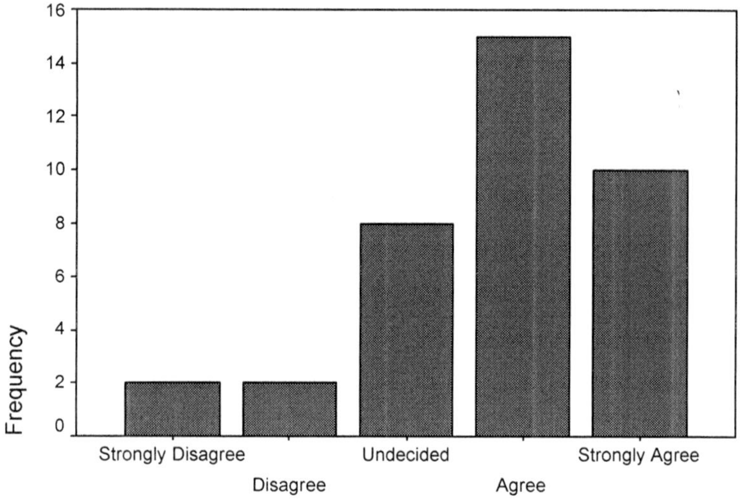

CHAPTER FIVE

TEACHING LEARNABLE GRAMMAR

CAMILLA BETTONI AND BRUNO DI BIASE

Introduction

Language teachers know only too well that learners do not always learn what they are taught, nor do they learn as fast as they might. In their attempt to cope with this problem, busy with heavy classroom and preparation work, teachers tend to rely ever more closely on official programmes and methodologies. Yet these are often organised according to established tradition rather than fresh scientific evidence. Failure among L2 learners is quite common, and can of course be due to many different factors, both linguistic and extra-linguistic. In this chapter, we wish to contribute to the rapidly growing body of language teaching research, which aims at identifying constraints on learning. In particular, we will discuss two factors which we believe crucially affect the learning of grammar:

- which linguistic structures should be targeted for instruction?
- how should they be treated in class?

To answer the first question, we refer to Manfred Pienemann's Teachability Hypothesis[1] subsumed under his Processability Theory.[2] This wider theory (PT from now on) claims that, because structures are hierarchically arranged in speech production, they are acquired only when learners are developmentally ready to process them. On the other hand, the Teachability Hypothesis (TH from now on) shows that teaching failure can

[1] Manfred Pienemann, "Psychological Constraints on the Teachability of Languages," *Studies in Second Language Acquisition* 6 (1984): 186-214.
[2] Manfred Pienemann, *Language Processing and Second Language Development: Processability Theory* (Amsterdam: John Benjamins, 1998).

be prevented, and learning success can be promoted if the syllabus respects universal sequences of development, and instruction focuses on learnable features. We will therefore start by showing how PT determines which structures can be learned at which stage of development, and by specifying an Italian L2 schedule regarding nominal morphology. Having shown how—despite varying characteristics of the learners and types of intervention—universally determined developmental considerations need to inform the morphosyntactic component of the syllabus, we will then answer the second question. This brings into the fore the one dimension that can vary: the speed of learning, and we will discuss the advantages of moderating developmentally not only the syllabus but also the feedback to learners. On the basis of our empirical data, we claim that more efficient, faster learning can be promoted if a targeted learnable structure is not only repeatedly comprehended and produced in context, but also accompanied by corrective feedback in communicative contexts.

The Theory

Processability Theory offers a principled and parsimonious account of morphosyntactic developmental sequences in interlanguage. As such, it is one of the nine theories of Second Language Acquisition (SLA from now on) selected for discussion by VanPatten and Williams in the most recent introduction to this field.[3] Originally accounting for German L2 and English L2, it is now tested typologically on different languages such as Swedish,[4] Arabic,[5] Chinese,[6] and Japanese.[7] Recently, developmental sequences have been worked out also for Italian.[8]

[3] Bill VanPatten and Jessica Williams, "The Nature of Theories," in *Theories of Second Language Acquisition*, eds. Bill VanPatten and Jessica Williams (Mahwah, NJ: Lawrence Erlbaum, 2007), 1-16.
[4] Cf., among others, Gisela Håkansson, "Modern Times in L2 Swedish. On the Acquisition of Swedish Morphology and Syntax in Formal and Informal Settings," in *Eurosla 7 Proceedings: Views on the Acquisition and Use of a Second Language*, eds. Lourdes Diaz and Carmen Pérez (Barcelona: Universitat Pompeu Fabra, 1997), 39-50.
[5] Cf., among others, Feti Mansouri, "Agreement Morphology in Arabic as a Second Language: Typological Features and their Processing Implications,", in *Cross-Linguistic Aspects of Processability Theory*, ed. Manfred Pienemann (Amsterdam: John Benjamins, 2005), 117-54.
[6] Cf., among others, Yanyin Zhang, "Processing Constraints, Categorical Analysis, and Second Language Acquisition of the Chinese Adjective Suffix *de* (ADJ)," *Language Learning* 54 (2004): 437-68.

According to PT, the production of L2 structures requires a set of cognitive (hence universal, non-language specific) processing procedures which learners develop in an implicational order—that is, each lower-level procedure is a pre-requisite for the next higher level one, and stages cannot be skipped. This L2 processability hierarchy is based on the general architecture of the human language processor. As such, it is parallel to a universal hierarchy of key grammatical encoding procedures which are implicationally arranged in language generation.[9] These procedures are activated in the following sequence:

1) lemma access,
2) category procedure,
3) phrasal procedure,

---

[7] Cf., among others, Satomi Kawaguchi, "Argument Structure and Syntactic Development in Japanese as a Second Language," in *Cross-linguistic Aspects of Processability Theory*, ed. Manfred Pienemann (Amsterdam: John Benjamins, 2005), 253-99.

[8] Cf., among others, Bruno Di Biase, "Focusing Strategies in Second Language Development: A classroom-based Study of Italian L2 in Primary School," in *Developing a Second Language: Acquisition, Processing and Pedagogy of Arabic, Chinese, English, Italian, Japanese, Swedish*, ed. Bruno Di Biase (Melbourne: Language Australia, 2002), 95-120; Bruno Di Biase and Satomi Kawaguchi, "Exloring the Typological Plausibility of Processability Theory: Language Development in Italian Second Language and Japanese Second Language," *Second Language Research* 18, 3 (2002): 272-300; Camilla Bettoni and Bruno Di Biase, "Sviluppo Obbligato e Progresso Morfosintattico: Un Caso di Processabilità in Italiano L2," *ITALS. Didattica e Linguistica dell'Italiano come Lingua Straniera* III, 7 (2005): 27-48; Camilla Bettoni and Bruno Di Biase, "Lessico Verbale e Questioni di Processabilità in Italiano L2," in *Lessico e Apprendimenti. Il ruolo del lessico nella linguistica educativa*, eds. Monica Barni, Donatella Troncarelli and Carla Bagni (Milano: Franco Angeli, 2008), 260-67; Camilla Bettoni, Bruno Di Biase and Stefania Ferraris, "Sviluppo Sintattico e Sviluppo Morfologico: Ipotesi di Corrispondenze nella Processabilità dell'Italiano L2," in *Competenze Lessicali e Discorsive nell'Acquisizione di Lingue Seconde*, ed. Giuliano Bernini, Lorenzo Spreafico and Ada Valentini (Perugia: Guerra Editore, in press); Bruno Di Biase, "Developmentally Moderated Focus-on-Form," paper presented at the *5th Pacific Second Language Forum*, University of Queensland, Brisbane, Australia, July 4-6, 2006; Bruno Di Biase and Camilla Bettoni, "Funzioni Discorsive e Processabilità in italiano," in *Imparare una Lingua. Recenti Sviluppi Teorici e Proposte Applicative*, eds. Marina Chini, Anna De Meo, Paola Desideri and Gabriele Pallotti (Perugia: Guerra Editore, 2006), 209-33.

[9] Cf. Willem Levelt, *Speaking: From Intention to Articulation.* (Cambridge, MA: MIT Press), 1989.

4) sentence procedure.

This means that a word needs to be added to the L2 lexicon before its grammatical category can be assigned—plainly, before the learner recognises it as a noun, verb, adjective, etc. The grammatical category of a lemma and its main feature(s) are needed before a phrasal procedure can be activated—that is, before the learner recognises that certain words are grouped together into phrases. Only when a phrasal procedure is in place, can the learner assign the function of the phrase within the sentence[10]—that is, mark a phrase as subject, object, etc.

While native speakers do all this effortlessly, learners must construct and automatise each of these procedures in their target language. They cannot rely on their L1 for this, because, while the procedures are universal, they are deployed in language-specific ways. For instance Italian nouns mark the gender of the referent grammatically, while English or Chinese do not. For reasons of space we will not go further into the theory, which now includes also interfaces between syntax and discourse-pragmatics elaborated by Manfred Pienemann, Bruno Di Biase and Satomi Kawaguchi.[11] Suffice it to say here that the L2 grammatical structures that depend on these procedures will be acquired in the order just outlined. For example, when the category procedure is in place, very likely the plural marking on nouns (*bambino* vs *bambini*) and the past marking on verbs (*mangia* vs *mangiato*) will emerge at about the same time. Also for reasons of space, we will not show all the structures that depend on these procedures, but will concentrate on the acquisition of plural marking on Italian nominal structures, such as nouns and adjectives, as shown in Table 5-1.

---

[10] Pienemann 1998, 80.

[11] Manfred Pienemann, Bruno Di Biase and Satomi Kawaguchi, "Extending Processability Theory," in Pienemann ed. 2005, 199-252.

Stage		t_1	t_2	t_3	t_4
4	Sentence procedure	–	–	–	information exchange across phrases
3	Phrasal procedure	–	–	information exchange within phrase	information exchange within phrase
2	Category procedure	–	category + affix	category + affix	category + affix
1	Word / lemma	lemma access	lemma access	lemma access	lemma access

Table 5-1. Developmental stages according to Processability Theory.

For the development of Italian L2 nominal morphology, PT predicts the following sequence. To begin with, at Stage 1, learners produce either unanalysed formulaic chunks, such as "*mi chiamo Tom,*" or separate words that may be juxtaposed without grammatical encoding, as in (1). In communicative settings, young learners especially will embed them in L1 structures, as in (2).[12]

(1) R le stelle sono? ... arrabbiate proviamo il triangolo com'è il triangolo
A una triangolo è arrabbiate
R è arrabbiato. e i triangoli come sono?
A due tringolo arrabbiate

(2) does your animali hop? is your animali a mammal?

At Stage 2, learners assign a category to their lemmas, and notice that, in their morphologically rich target Italian, word endings often vary. So they start annotating some alternation. To begin with, of course, they are unable to capture all the features of a lemma, and will deal only with the more conceptually transparent ones. That is, on nouns, they will mark the number first rather than the gender, which in Italian is often arbitrary and

[12] Examples of learners' production are from Bruno Di Biase, "Il Lessico nello Sviluppo dell'Italiano L2," *Italiano e Scuola–Italian at School: Bulletin for Teachers of Italian* 2, 1 (1997): 15-23; and Di Biase 2002.

conceptually opaque (e.g., the grammatical gender of *sole* <the sun> is masculine in Italian but feminine in German). Nor will learners be able to mark soon all values for each feature. That is, it is highly unlikely that the plural will be marked on all classes of nouns.[13] Most likely, they will start from the default values in a one-to-one correspondence between form and function. So they will assign the plural value using the *-i* ending on all nouns. Nevertheless, it is clear that grammar is thus emerging, albeit only within the word itself, since every lexical item is still treated separately, as the elements of an utterance are not yet grouped into sentence constituents. So learners may now mark the plural, as in (3),[14] thus alternating *orso* with *orsi*:

(3) il tre orsi come back

They may even alternate *bianco* with *bianchi*; yet they will be unable to string *orsi bianchi*.

At Stage 3, with the activation of the phrasal procedure, constituents start appearing, learners recognise the categorical head of a phrase, and are thus able to annotate grammatically the values of its internal elements. In the Italian nominal system, this annotation needs to be marked over the phrase, since most elements that modify or specify the head noun (articles, quantifiers, adjectives, etc.) must unify their information about number and gender with the noun itself. For example, in (4), the learner (L) appears to do this productively, as he marks the plural value in the single lexical item (4c), with a juxtaposed numeral (4a), over the phrase in more than one occasion (4g, k), and contrastively (4g vs 4e):

(4) a. L tre triangoli
b. R di che colore?
c. L rossi
d. R bravissima *(shows card with green triangle)*

---

[13] Examples of classes in Italian are nouns with endings in *-o/-i* (*bambino/bambini*), *-a/-e* (*casa/case*), *-e/-i* (*elefante/elefanti*), *-a/-i* (*problema/problemi*), and other classes as small as the latter.

[14] The Italian article system is formally so complex that it is best not to consider it as indexical of category procedure. As a matter of fact, it is also the last one to be acquired by children learning Italian L1; cf. Elena Pizzuto and Maria Cristina Caselli, "The Acquisition of Italian Morphology: Implications for Models of Language Development," *Journal of Child Language* 19 (1992): 491-557; and Maria Cristina Caselli, Laurence B. Leonard, Virginia Volterra and Maria Grazia Compagnoli, "Towards Mastery of Italian Morphology: A Cross-sectional Study," *Journal of Child Language* 20 (1993): 337-93.

e. L un triangolo verde
f. R sì *(shows green squares)*
g. L due quadrati verdi
h. R bravissima *(shows yellow triangle)*
i. L un triangolo giallo
j. R brava *(shows red crosses)*
k. L tre croci *rossi

By the way, this last turn (4k) shows that the gender and class features of nouns (in this case, *croce/croci* 'cross/crosses' <gender=feminine>) are not yet annotated by this learner. Hence, until these lexical annotations are in place, the default plural *-i* will continue to be generalized on the adjective.[15]

Continuing now our main description, at Stage 4, the exchange of information takes place between different kinds of constituents. This is clearly seen where a full referential Subject agrees with the predicate adjective (*i triangoli sono verdi* 'the triangles<pl;f> are green<pl;f>') or with the past participle of an intransitive verb (*i bambini sono partiti* 'the children AUXbe left<pl;m>'). These structural outcomes, however, are difficult for learners, and are only mentioned here to complete the developmental schedule, but will receive no further comment in this paper.

One crucial point that needs to be understood clearly about these stages is the criterion used by PT for determining the emergence of a particular stage.[16] According to PT, a learner is deemed to have reached a stage when s/he uses a structure belonging to that stage in a productive (that is, non formulaic) manner. This is substantially different from saying that a learner has full mastery of that stage, which would mean that s/he is able not only to use productively all the structures belonging to that stage, but also to mark accurately all their features and values. Thus, for our nominal plural considered here, emergence means that learners use one ending (usually the default one) in a generalized way across the board (cf. examples and discussion in (4) above). On the other hand, mastery means that all relevant, non-default endings are also correctly used, which of course is achieved very late. As a matter of fact, most learners will progress to the following stage well before they master all the form-function mapping for the stage they are on. Just as some specific lexical

---

[15] For an informative discussion on the complexities of the notion of inflectional classes in Italian, cf. Paolo D'Achille and Anna Maria Thornton, "La Flessione del Nome dall'Italiano Antico all'Italiano Contemporaneo," in *Italia Linguistica Anno Mille, Italia Linguistica Anno Duemila*, eds. Nicoletta Maraschio and Teresa Poggi-Salani (Roma: Bulzoni, 2003), 211-30.
[16] Pienemann 1998, 138ff.

features may not be acquired even by advanced learners, who will continue to say, for example, **la problema* ('the<sing;f> problem<sing;m>') thus contradictorily attributing feminine gender to a grammatically masculine noun on the basis of perceived prosodic association of the *-a* ending of the noun *problema* with feminine gender. Taken in isolation, this would show that the advanced learner failed a Stage 3 phrasal unification, but this view would soon be corrected on the basis of a fuller performance analysis.

Having thus established the developmental sequences, the TH maintains that classroom teaching can promote successful learning in two ways:

a) it can push the range of form-function mappings beyond the default structures that belong to the current stage of development—that is, annotate further feature and value pairs in the lexicon, such as gender, class—and thus increase accuracy;
b) it can accelerate the progression from the current stage to the next one.

How can the teacher help learners do this most efficiently?

The teacher's intervention

Few researchers today would agree with Stephen Krashen[17] that an exclusively communicative approach would produce best results in language learning, or, against him, support the worst case scenario of the traditional grammar-translation method that he so successfully disparaged. Yet between these two extremes, in the context of a widely accepted meaning-based or communicative setting, the current literature reports a lively debate on the precise role that teacher's intervention can play for best results with some form focused instruction.

One of the best known and influential proposals is Michael Long's,[18] who claims that the most effective approach for language learning is a Focus on Form (FonF) which "overtly draws attention to the linguistic elements as they arise incidentally in lessons whose overriding focus is on

[17] Stephen D. Krashen, *Principles and Practice in Second Language Acquisition*. Oxford: Pergamon, 1982.

[18] Michael Long, "Focus on Form: A Design Feature in Language Teaching Methodology," in *Foreign Language Research in Crosscultural Perspective*, eds. Kees de Bot, Claire Kramsh and Ralph B. Ginsberg (Amsterdam: John Benjamins, 1991), 33-52.

meaning or communication"—where the *incidental* drawing of attention to a feature of the linguistic code, by the teacher or by one or more students, is "triggered by perceived problems with comprehension or production."[19] Thus Long's FonF is different from Focus on Forms (FonFs), where the forms themselves, rather than the meaning, are the focus of instruction, and are first presented in an ordered syllabus and then subjected to corrective feedback. On the contrary, since FonF arises from communication breakdowns, it does not relate to a particular instructional programme or syllabus per se (as many practitioners may have thought when it was first formulated), but deals with grammatical features according to more or less unpredictable needs, and could in principle deal with any aspect of linguistic form: pronunciation, stress, syllabification, lexical choice, or any of the possible ways in which the form of the required word fails to communicate. As such, FonF is then essentially limited to offering *feedback*. Other researchers, such as Doughty and Williams,[20] interpret FonF in a broader sense which refers not only to a feedback technique but also to an ordering principle for broader based intervention, such as the construction of a syllabus. Thus they maintain that FonF and FonFs are not mutually exclusive approaches but rather polar end points of a continuum, where the first entails a focus on formal elements of language, and the second is limited to such focus.

In this debate, our proposal is threefold. First, the universal developmental path identified by PT should inform a key (morphosyntactic) component of an L2 programme which clearly targets a structure at a time. Secondly, this component should be embedded in a task-based communicative approach. And, thirdly, incidental corrective feedback should not take place randomly on any structure but be limited to the structure currently targeted by the programme.[21] Our hypothesis is then that not just Long's FonF technique can make a difference to the learning progress, but also its grammatical 'content'. In other words, faster learning

---

[19] Michael Long and Peter Robinson, "Focus on Form: Theory, Research and Practice," in *Focus on Form in Second Language Acquisition*, eds. Catherine Doughty and Jessica Williams (Cambridge: Cambridge University Press, 1998), 15-41.

[20] Catherine Doughty and Jessica Williams, "Issue and Terminology," in Doughty and Williams eds. 1998, 1-11.

[21] Here we are referring to feedback on morphosyntax. Of course, if there is a genuine communication problem caused by a lexical gap or by mispronunciation, the teacher should help.

can be promoted when repeated comprehension and production[22] of a particular *learnable structure*, in context, is accompanied also by *targeted feedback* concentrating primarily on that structure.

The experiment

To test our hypothesis, we report on a longitudinal quasi-experimental project attempting to couple developmental readiness for a specific grammatical feature with form-focusing on that very feature. In this study, conducted in a primary school in Sydney, Australia, Italian L2 lessons in grade 3 are video-taped for 12 weeks in two classes, one experimental, and the other for control. Both classes are held by the same teacher, and are generally very similar in terms of socio-economic and ethnic background of the pupils.[23] There are altogether 18 pupils participating in the project, 9 in each class, all tested both before and four-to-six weeks after the differential intervention of the observation period.

Before the intervention, at Time 1, all children had received instruction in Italian L2 for about three years, which typically consisted of two sessions of about 40-50 minutes per week. Computing this into hours, and allowing for normal attrition (assemblies, pupil-free days, sports carnivals, presentations, etc.) the total is about 230 hours per class—which is no little time. The L2 content of this programme is usually organised around some themes within the wider school programme, from the 'human society and its environment' key learning area (e.g., seasons and the weather, with clothes used in different weather conditions, etc.). Teaching approaches include 'communicative' and occasionally mild 'grammatical' approaches in a rather eclectic mix, as described by Di Biase and de Rachewiltz.[24] Yet, despite this long period of tuition, thoughtful programme and varied methodology, at Time 1, only few children are actually beginning to vary the form of nouns or adjectives. Having found that the word/lemma and formulaic Stage 1 was stable across the board, and that the children knew a range of basic vocabulary and expressions (e.g., greetings), they were

[22] Cf. Michel Paradis, *A Neurolinguistic Theory of Bilingualism* (Amsterdam: John Benjamins, 2004), 34-61. According to him, providing contexts for repeated production-comprehension of a specific structure or construction may help establish a neural path for it, which may be the reason why focusing on form seems to work.

[23] No pupils of Italian background happened to be included in the project.

[24] Bruno Di Biase and Claudia de Rachewiltz, "Italian at School: A Survey of NSW Co.As.It. Teachers," *Italiano e Scuola—Italian at School: Bulletin for Teachers of Italian* 1, no. 3 (1998): 12-3.

deemed 'developmentally ready' to learn the clearer features and default values identified as pertaining to PT Stage 2, and then to procede to Stage 3.

Among nominal features, number was chosen for the purpose of developmental measurement, because it is conceptually transparent and its *-i* ending has a clearer form/function correspondence than other endings. By contrast a feature such as gender is conceptually opaque more often than not.[25] Then only the major classes of nouns and adjectives[26] were targeted for instruction, as summarised in Table 5-2.

Singular	Plural	Gender	Example
Nouns			
-o *-a* *-e*	*-i* *-e* *-i*	masculine feminine masc / fem	*libro* *casa* *pane*, *neve*
Adjectives			
-o *-a* *-e*	*-i* *-e* *-i*	masculine feminine masc / fem	*rosso* *rossa* *verde*

Table 5-2. Italian Noun and Adjective forms (major classes only).

As for the behaviour by the teacher, the two classes are similar in all but one respect, i.e. feedback interventions. Instructions for general procedural intervention in both classes included the following:

- use Italian as the medium of instruction. You need to speak consistently in Italian for pupils to receive the necessary input, and hence the chance to learn the language. Learners will only *notice* the focused structures if previously they had the chance to *hear* them;
- after hearing, the learner needs to actually *produce*.[27] Learner's production is crucial for memorisation, over and above

[25] Of course, noun gender could not be totally ignored, as it is inherently marked.

[26] Nigel Vincent, "Italian," in *The Major Languages of Eastern Europe*, ed. Bernard Comrie (London: Routledge, 1990), 269-92.

[27] Cf. Merrill Swain, "Communicative Competence: Some Roles of Comprehensible Input and Comprehensible Output in its Development," in *Input in Second Language Acquisition*, eds. Susan M. Gass and C.G. Madden (Rowley, MA: Newbury House, 1985), 235-252; and Merrill Swain, "The Output Hypothesis and

understanding what the teacher says. Encourage pupils to communicate verbally in Italian, hence to listen and speak, before reading and writing;

- so, a *communicative* approach is essential for the project to succeed;
- *repeated* production is crucial for automatising the retrieval of lexical items from memory, as well as for rule formation and any other *procedural* component of learning. Repeated production is the only way learners can build their procedural resources (automatic skills) in the L2;
- you need to devote regularly about 10 minutes at the start of each lesson to FonF grammar teaching. Always include revision of structures previously focused on. However, this is the time for introducing the new FonF structure for the week, and maximizing *learner speaking*, rather than teacher speaking;
- during this 10 minute FonF phase, it is important that the tasks be stimulating and fast-paced. That is, rather than requiring all pupils to have a turn, it may be necessary to separate them into groups, so as to give them all a chance to participate and produce;
- application of FonF should include 'input enhancement', intonational or visual highlighting, but always respect the priority 'aural' (listening/speaking) *before* 'visual' (reading/ writing);
- the syllabus for both classes is identical. The schedules supplied for the research project constitute a graded list of FonF grammar structures only, that is *what* morphosyntactic structure to focus on and *when*, but they do not represent your programme as a whole.

An excerpt of the schedule suggested for use in both classes is shown in Table 5-3.

Beyond: Mediating Acquisition Through Collaborative Dialogue," in *Sociocultural Theory and Second Language Learning*, ed. James P. Lantolf (Oxford: Oxford University Press, 2000), 97-114.

Term 1	Consolidate	FonF structure	Ex.	Notes and tasks
13 March Lexical level (single word)	Lexicon Use lexical items already known	Sing and Plur of Masc Nouns *-o* Noun *-o* > Noun *-i*	*libro-libri*	Get learner to use numbers rather than articles. If pupil says 'due libro', emphasize 'due libri'. Use picture/word matching and memory games.
20 March Lexical level (single word)	Lexicon Use lexical items already known	Sing and Plur of Masc Adjectives *-o* Adj *-o* > Adj *-i*	*nero-neri*	Show two black cats, and asks for cats' colour. If pupil says '*nero*' or '*due gatto nero*', emphasise '*neri*'.
27 March Phrasal level: singular	Lexicon Use lexical items already known	Agreem of Singular Noun *-o* and Adjective *-o* Sing Masc Nouns *-o* + Sing Masc Adj *-o*	*libro nuovo*	Point out final vowel in any Noun+Adj pair ending in *-o*. In recast ignore plurals and ignore articles.
3 April Phrasal level: plural	Lexicon Use lexical items already known	Agreem of Plural Noun *-i* and Adjective *-i* Plur Masc Nouns *-i* + Plur Masc Adj *-i*	*libro nuovo* > *libri nuovi*	Create a microsystem which is regular: i.e., no feedback on feminine cases and other irregular endings even if they come up: if learner says *pizza buono*, ignore it; in *due pizza buoni*, give no feedback on *pizza* sing.[28]; ignore *matiti*

Table 5-3. Excerpt of form focused instruction schedule.

[28] When introducing the plural, textbooks usually present both genders together. We are proposing here that the plural be presented first in default form only. Once this is learned, the feminine plural can be introduced. In this example, although phrasal agreement is targeted, the feminine singular *pizza* should not be given feed back; that is, since the learner's form cannot be corrected into *pizzi* (which is the targeted ending), it is best ignored.

The only difference in teacher's intervention between the two classes is that in the experimental class FonF feedback is directed exclusively to the targeted structures, while the control group receives the usual corrective feedback on any error or communication problem the teacher feels spontaneously moved to correct. More specifically, instructions to the teacher include the following:

Experimental Group

- first, during the 10 minute FonF period, feedback should apply *only* to structures specified in the programme, both the newly introduced ones and the revised ones. Reward correct answers;
- other structures may be recast *without emphasis*;
- then, throughout the communicative lesson, FonF feedback should continue on the *same* structures only but *incidentally*. That is, as you continue with the usual programme, you need to keep your ear open on the chance occurrence of the specific FonF structure you are targeting, and pick up (for learners to notice) on such occurrences especially when a problem in communication, comprehension or production arises;
- other than the targeted structures you may also recast lexical gaps or pronunciation causing misunderstanding, but—of course—only incidentally, implicitly and without emphasis.

Control Group

- first, during the 10 minute FonF period, recast may be used *on any structure* without emphasis. Reward correct answers;
- then, recasts may be used also throughout the lesson, but with no input enhancement of FonF structures at any time.

In order to ascertain that there are actual differences in FonF teacher intervention with the two groups, detailed observations were scored on the basis of ten recorded videotapes. A trained research assistant counted instances of verbal behaviour according to a prepared schedule using the following categories:

- teacher does not intervene;
- questions;
- supplies positive feedback (with form);
- requests repetition;

- provides cue;
- provides form;
- recasts with emphasis;
- repeats wrong form with emphasis;
- requests clarification (*what?*);
- requests explanation (*why?*);
- corrects explicitly (*NOT this but THAT*).

Here are a couple of examples of teacher FonF feedback that we deem effective: in (5) the teacher first gives a verbal clue in the form of a question; secondly, she repeats the wrong form with question intonation, and gives again a verbal clue; then, thirdly and fourthly, the correction becomes explicit, followed by a verbal clue; and finally, positive feedback is given with the repetition of the correct forms. In (6), she first repeats the wrong form and gives a verbal clue, then supplies positive feedback and the correct form.

(5) T questa è una gonna .. e queste?
[this is a skirt. And these <pl,f>?]
Adr due gonni
[two skirts<pl,m>]
T due gonni? .. una gonna . due ...?
[two skirts<pl,m>? one skirt<sing,f>, two...?]
Adr gonna
[skirt<sing,f.>]
T no .. è come una zebra . due zebre .. una gonna …?
[no, it's like one zebra<sing,f>, two zebra<pl,f>, one skirt<sing,f> ...?]
Adr due gonni
[two skirts<pl,m>]
T no.. due…? chi lo sa?
[no. Two..? Who knows it?]
Lau due gonne?
[two skirts<pl,f>]
T sì . due gonne .. una gonna . due gonne
[yes. Two skirts<pl,f>, one skirt<sing,f>, two skirts<pl,f>]

(6) Mat i pantaloni grigio
[the grey pants]
T grigio?
[grey<singular>?]
Mat grigi
[grey<plural>]
T bravo .. i pataloni grigi

[good, grey<plural>]

Testing—both at pre-intervention Time 1, and delayed post-intervention Time 2—occurred outside of class, where one child at a time talked to the researcher. Data were collected using a variety of communicative tasks, such as story telling, guessing and describing animals.

The results

Pre-intervention, Time 1 test results are shown in Table 5-4. The low numbers of plural morphological markers confirm what we have already mentioned above. That is, previous L2 instruction, received over a two-to-three year period, provides a broad lexical basis but no grammatical development that can be measured in overt language production. In Processability terms, learners in both groups are at Stage 1, that is, they can comprehend and produce invariant words (overwhelmingly nouns, some adjectives, some greeting expressions, and practically no verbs), but not yet form variation. That is, they cannot produce plural forms, nor—naturally enough—the agreement of these forms, as required by the L2.

	Nouns		Adjectives	
Informants	*-i*	*-e*	*-i*	*-e*
Control group				
Amy	0	3	0	1(?)
Car	1	0	0	0
Chr	0	1	1	0
Coum	0	0	0	0
Jor	1	0	0	0
Jos	0	0	0	1?
Kie	0	1(?)	0	0
Nik	1	2	0	1
Olg	0	0	0	0
Experimental group				
Adr	0	3	0	0
Ale	0	0	0	0
Alli	0	0	0	0
Chrs	0	0	0	0
Katv	0	0	0	0
Lau	0	0	0	0
Matw	0	0	1?	0
Sar	0	1	0	1
Sop	0	1	0	0

Table 5-4. Time 1: Production of plural forms (out of about 20 chances).

Post-intervention, Time 2 (delayed posttest) results are shown in Table 5-5. Even though at Time 1 both groups are almost perfectly matched in terms of developmental readiness, by Time 2 the experimental group has made more consistent progress to the next developmental stages. All informants in the experimental group reach Category Procedure Stage 2, and are thus able to mark plurals in both nouns and adjectives. On the other hand, not all the children in the control group have reached this stage, although in all fairness many do have. This result, by the way, means that even FonF general intervention during a ten minute grammar period at the beginning of each lesson can work, and achieve better results in three months than without it in the previous three years.

	Nouns		Adjectives	
Informants	*-i*	*-e*	*-i*	*-e*
Control group				
Amy	7	2(?)	5	0
Car	2	0	5	0
Chr	0	0	0	0
Coum	0	0	0	0
Jor	7	1	11	1
Jos	15	0	15	0
Kie	7	1(?)	12	0
Nik	5	3	8	0
Olg	0	2	0	0
Experimental group				
Adr	6	1	6	2
Ale	2	2	2	0
Alli	3	4	7	5
Chrs	17	0	7	1(?)
Katv	3	3	4	6
Lau	5	2	3	1
Matw	4	2	3	2(?)
Sar	3	1	2	3
Sop	5	2	2	0

Table 5-5. Time 2: Production of plural forms (out of about 20 chances).

Furthermore, Table 5-6 shows that there is overall progress also to Stage 3, which is characterised by agreement within the Noun Phrase between the noun and the adjective.[29] However, as in table 5, here too progress is stronger in the experimental group than in the control one. After 3 months of instruction (altogether no more than 36 hours), all learners in the experimental group (9 out of 9) have successfully reached Stage 3, while in the control group two thirds (6 out of 9) have done so. Notice also that the experimental group is more advanced in another way:

[29] In the table, the simple fraction in the 'Noun + Adjective' column represents the successful production of the default *-i* plural agreement; the figure preceded by '+' means that a successful (non-default) *-e* agreement was produced; and the total number of contexts for agreement is given after the slash. Let us take the learner Jor, for example: he produces a total of 11 plural agreement contexts, of which 9 are successfully marked, 8 with the default *-i* ending, plus one case with the non-default *-e* ending.

while in the control group most plural markers are represented by the default *-i/-i* agreement, in the experimental group learners are more adventurous, and try out more often also the *-e/-e* agreement, which applies to a subgroup of feminine gender nouns matching a subgroup of adjectives. This increases accuracy.

Control group		Experimental group	
Informants	Noun + Adjective	Informants	Noun + Adjective
Amy	4/11	Adr	4+1/12
Car	3/12	Ale	2+1/9
Chr	0/10	Alli	3+1/9
Coum	0/11	Chrs	10/14
Jor	8+1/11	Katv	4+2/11
Jos	14/16	Lau	4+1/9
Kie	9+1/15	Matw	3+2/9
Nik	5/8	Sar	3/7
Olg	0/13	Sop	3/8

Table 5-6. Time 2: Production of phrasal plural agreement.

Finally, looking at tables 5 and 6 together, we can see that, among the three learners in the control group who at T2 have not made it to Stage 3, Olg is the only one who, having produced two plurals with different nouns, has just made it to Stage 2; while Chr and Coum do not show any progress away from Stage 1. This is an important point, as it shows—once again—that PT implicational stages are fully respected: while progress to Stage 2 does not imply achievement of Stage 3, all learners at Stage 3 have reached Stage 2.

Conclusion

Our experiment shows that pursuing consistenly in the right way the learning of a single appropriate feature can speed up grammatical learning significantly: children in our primary school classes have learned in three months grammatical features they had not learned in three years. With the 10 minute FonF intervention—systematically targeting only the developmentally appropriate plural feature within a communicative classroom context—all but two of the children in the control group progress from Stage 1 to Stage 2 on the default targeted feature *-i.*[30] With the addition of developmentally moderated feedback in the experimental group, further progress is also measured in so far as, at Time 2, all the learners in the experimental group are able to handle also non default *-e* endings on either or both nouns and adjectives. By contrast, in the control group, only five learners can handle it on the noun, and one of thesealso on the adjective. The same applies to the development from Stage 2 to Stage 3: the extra negative feedback offered to the experimental group results in more learners progressing to the higher stage with the default value, and in better accuracy on the non-default ones.

Having seen what happens in the earlier stages, we can suggest how the teacher can help learners to progress further. She can choose to proceed in two different ways: working to take her learners from Stage 3 to Stage 4 by targeting inter-phrasal agreement on default one-to-one form-function mapping, or improve on the accuracy of Stages 2 and 3 features where non-default form-function mapping applies. The progress shown from Stage 2 to Stage 3 among the experimental group suggests that there is certainly no need to wait for full accuracy on one stage before proceeding to the next. On the other hand, some gradual consolidation of non-default values, as well as some expansion of vocabulary items, would seem preferable to a fast jump forward.

In short, we believe that a combination of two elements in L2 instruction is critical for more efficient L2 learning: the use of a principled, psycholinguistically plausible developmental schedule for the L2, which is then used systematically to moderate form-focused feedback. In other words, let us refrain from teaching structures that are too far ahead of the learners' current level, and let us concentrate instead on teaching, within a communicative context, structures that are either just at the learner's stage or at the stage immediately above.

UNIVERSITY OF VERONA, ITALY
UNIVERSITY OF WESTERN SYDNEY, AUSTRALIA

---

[30] Olg, from the control group, is again the exception: she uses the *-e* ending as her default.

PART II:

TEACHING ITALIAN WITH TECHNOLOGY

CHAPTER SIX

ENHANCING THE STUDENT EXPERIENCE THROUGH TECHNOLOGY: MAKING LANGUAGE LEARNING MORE MEANINGFUL THROUGH A DEPARTMENTAL VLE

CLELIA BOSCOLO, ALISON DAVIES, KELLY SMITH

Introduction

Students require contextualized interactive and reflective activities that satisfy a variety of learning styles to develop and utilize newly acquired language skills.[1] It is becoming increasingly evident that computer-based learning has the potential to enhance foreign language (FL) and second language (L2) learning by providing a diverse range of tools to support different tasks and activities, increasing motivation for learning, and by enabling different levels of social interaction.[2] However, as Kern (2006)

---

[1] A.L. Wenden, "Metacognitive Knowledge and Language Learning," *Applied Linguistics* 19, no. 4 (1998): 515-37

[2] R. Kern, "Perspectives on Technology in Learning and Teaching Languages," *TESOL Quarterly* 41, no. 1 (2006): 183-210. See also: C. Richards, "The Design of Effective ICT-Supported Learning Activities: Exemplary Models, Changing Requirements, and New Possibilities," *Language Learning & Technology* 9, no. 1 (2005): 60-79; H. Shang, "Email Dialogue Journaling: Attitudes and Impact on L2 Reading Performance," *Educational Studies* 31, no.2 (2005): 197-212; B. Skinner and R. Austin, "Computer Conferencing—Does it Motivate EFL Students?" *ELT Journal* 53, no.4 (1999): 270-78; and M. Warschauer, "Computer-Mediated Collaborative Learning: Theory and Practice," *The Modern Language Journal* 81, no. 4 (1997): 470-81

argues, "it is not the technology per se that is effective or ineffective but the particular ways in which the technology is used."[3]

This chapter will describe a Virtual Learning Environment (VLE) section (course) within WebCT, developed by one of the authors, Clelia Boscolo, in the Department of Italian Studies, Centre for European Languages and Cultures, University of Birmingham. The section was designed to facilitate Italian language learning by providing students with additional resources that enhanced their existing and more traditional face-to-face classroom activities. The online facilities aimed to accommodate all learning styles by providing a variety of visual, auditory, and logical language tasks and provided students with comprehensive online feedback and notice boards for course information.

As the educator responsible for the WebCT section, Clelia Boscolo will present her perspectives on how these online facilities enabled students to develop and improve their language skills more effectively than by traditional teaching methods alone. The commentary will include the rationale behind the design and pedagogy choices of activities within three categories: a) grammar and vocabulary exercises, b) writing exercises, and c) listening and reading exercises. The lessons learnt from the development and implementation of each type of activity will be discussed. Student experiences of the section will also be presented to provide important insights into the impact of using computer-based materials upon their self-confidence and independence in language learning.

Overview

Computer-based learning can take a variety of forms including email, the use of Virtual Learning Environments (VLEs), and emerging "Web 2.0" technologies supporting activities such as pod-casting or social networking. Yu and Yu[4] found that students who received documents and course information through email did not remain as passive recipients of information but started to become actively engaged with reflection and discussion through the electronic medium. Yu and Yu suggested that email, as a form of asynchronous communication, provided time for

---

[3] Ibid., 189; see also: Richards, op. cit.; and U. Felix, "Teaching Languages Online: Deconstructing the Myths," *Australian Journal of Educational Technology* 19, no. 1 (2003): 118-38.

[4] F. Yu and H. Yu, "Incorporating E-mail into the Learning Process: its Impact on Student Academic Achievement and Attitudes," *Computers & Education* 38 (2002): 117-26.

reflection, and facilitated organization and re-organization of thought. In addition, Yu and Yu argued that the anonymity provided by computer mediated learning through tools such as email is particularly useful for shy students who may be less forthcoming in face-to-face settings.[5] Yu and Yu's participants were not language students, but others, such as Warschauer[6] and Shang,[7] have made similar conclusions for L2 learners. For example, Warschauer writes that computer mediated communication (CMC) merges the interactional and reflective aspects of language within a single medium, overcoming the historical divide between speech and writing. He explains that with CMC, "human interaction now takes place in a text-based form,"[8] which is easily re-moulded and re-evaluated by its participants as they engage in the language learning process.

Shang investigated L2 learning using email dialogue journaling to enhance reading performance. Here, English language students in Taiwan enrolled on a reading course were required to read an article, summarize it, and discuss their summaries via email with a self-selected peer. 44% of students reported that they enjoyed the email task, and 56% considered that the email dialogue had improved their reading. A path analysis suggested that positive attitudes towards using email for learning increased motivation and confidence to acquire knowledge. Furthermore, student survey responses suggested that students' understanding of text improves through discussion and sharing of ideas. Similar results were found by Skinner and Austin,[9] who suggested that involvement with computer conferencing (CC; here through a dedicated software system called "First Class"), can improve three aspects of motivation: communication and community, personal confidence, and overcoming writing apprehension.

Shang, however, cautions against the conclusion that all students should be required to use email as a learning tool because of the anxiety that some students experience using computers. Part of this anxiety can be caused by viruses or hardware problems, lack of access, or lack of computer knowledge. This suggestion may be tempered by the findings of Skinner and Austin which showed that once they were used to CC, students felt less stressed and more confident than in other learning situations.

Although a large group of Shang's students reported that they enjoyed the email dialogue journal task, 49% of respondents reported that they

---

[5] Yu and Yu, op. cit.
[6] Warschauer, op. cit.
[7] Shang, op. cit.
[8] Warschauer, op. cit., 472.
[9] Skinner and Austin, op. cit.

disliked it. The reasons given for this dislike included the time required to undertake the task, and the fact that some students did not consider their peer partner to be qualified enough to provide competent feedback. This latter result led Shang to suggest that language corrections be made by teachers, rather than students themselves.

Student Evaluation Feedback

Student views and experiences of developing their language skills through the use of the WebCT section were gathered by questionnaire. The questionnaire was delivered to a total of 50 undergraduate students in the Department of Italian Studies; responses were received from 36 students.

The questionnaire was divided into two sections. The first section contained a combination of closed and open-ended questions about the usability of online resources both on and off campus. Students were asked, for example, about ease of access, what they liked most and least about the online resources, and if the resources could be improved in any way for future cohorts.

The second section presented students with more specific questions, again open-ended, about the different exercises that were available online to help students develop their language skills. These questions were organised into three types or categories: Grammar and Vocabulary Exercises; Writing Exercises; and Listening and Reading Exercises. Students were asked to comment in their own words on how these different exercises had helped and/or hindered their language learning.

The feedback from students was collected in March 2007, at the end of Semester 2 and when students were coming to the end of their academic year of study. The responses were collected and have been used below to illustrate if and how the student experience matched the educator's aspirations and expectations.

Overview of the Use of Technology for Italian Language Learning and Teaching

VLEs such as WebCT provide a suite of tools and features that can support a variety of learning activities. These include asynchronous and synchronous discussion tools, self-assessment quiz tools for multiple choice and other simple question types, and more formal assessment tools for students to submit essays and presentation work.[10]

The learning activities supported by the WebCT section that are described in this chapter have been guided by the underlying mission to provide greater opportunities for students to develop their language skills that traditional contexts and methods do not allow as easily. Furthermore, building on the notion that the effectiveness of technology is determined by how it is used, particular consideration was given to the ways in which the design of a WebCT section would impact on student language learning. For example, consideration was given to the overall structure of the section. Here, rather than provide a separate section for different years of study, levels of learning, or for different modules of study, all Italian language students were given access to the same section. The overarching section was sub-divided using folders and appropriate icons by year, then by module, by level if necessary, and then by type of activity. Careful thought went into each of the activities that were chosen to populate each part of the WebCT section as described in the Educator's Commentary below.

Educator's Comments:

> The modules for which I was responsible were of two types: the straightforward language courses, where the aim was to learn Italian as quickly and accurately as possible; and two written language options, which were both 'text based' and involved translation from Italian into English, summarizing from English into Italian, and essay writing in Italian. For the first type of modules, I divided the activities according to skills: grammar, listening, reading, writing, vocabulary and oral work, and kept the same divisions at all levels (First, Second, Final year/Beginners, Intermediate and Advanced), so that students could practice the skill they felt or were told they needed to improve. I really wanted all the exercises that I designed to be 'learning opportunities' rather than just 'testing opportunities,' so I made the lexis I used relevant (similar to that used in students' course books), interesting, and meaningful. For example, I designed tasks that required students to ask for a single train ticket, rather than to say 'stroke the cat'. For the second type of modules, I realized that WebCT offered a perfect opportunity to do something that is virtually impossible in a conventional teaching setting. Once summaries, translations, essays or any other creative piece of work in the target

---

[10] G. Salmon, *E-tivities: the Key to Active Online Learning* (London: Kogan Page Limited, 2002).

language had been handed in, marked and discussed in class, I asked students to enter electronically the corrections that I had made in pen (most work is word-processed) and then send the new corrected pieces back to me. This in itself was a pedagogically useful exercise in that physically correcting their own mistakes reinforces the learning of the correct form and finally gets students to move away from 'the mark' towards concentrating on 'the piece.' I then collected all these pieces in a file and posted them on WebCT. This had two positive outcomes. First, it instilled a sense of pride and 'authorship' in the students (all pieces were credited with the author's name). Second, and more importantly, it allowed students to see how their peers had dealt with the various difficulties in the summaries/translations/compositions in question, and to benefit from this by maximizing their exposure to multiple examples of correct target language prose. As writing and translation competence is notoriously harder to learn and, in particular, to improve upon, I felt that this was an excellent advantage offered by WebCT. In the modules where I used this approach, the students' work was of an extremely high standard and greatly praised by the external examiner, who was surprised to learn that some of the work had been produced by students who had started Italian as absolute beginners only the year before. For the materials in each module, I decided to exploit the Assessment Tool and to create many individual exercises for students to either test their learning (Grammar and Vocabulary), or gain extra practice (Listening and Reading). In the first year, all material was used for practice and was not formally assessed, but by using the assessment tool, students were provided with useful and immediate feedback on their work. Once students become familiar with this type of activity, it is hoped that the assessment tool can be used for formal assessment, thereby reducing marking time for staff. The multiple module structural design of the section was chosen to give students an overall view of their degree course at any time and to convey the point that each course or module is part of a whole and cannot be taken separately. Being able to access the entire section allows students to 'have a look' at activities in subsequent years or to try more difficult (or easier) exercises if they want to. Although some activities were required components for certain levels and modules, all students of Italian could choose to engage if they decided it was useful to their learning. For example, a 'grammar queries' theme was included in a asynchronous discussion board. The theme was open and accessible to all students to post their queries, or to offer answers, suggestions, and explanations in response to other students' queries. This opportunity for students to explain something to their peers became a powerful way of testing their own understanding, further helping their learning, and improving their memory skills. Pedagogically, this approach to section design reinforces the principle that learning should not be a compartmentalized or a self-centred, isolated exercise and encourages students to consider themselves independent learners with the potential to take charge of and be responsible for their own learning. In addition, by designing the section in this way, it was hoped that the sense of community which already exists within the small Department of Italian Studies would be maintained and further developed into a learning context where everyone strives towards the common goal that learning is for life, not just for a degree. In addition to the pedagogical benefits that computer-based language learning has created for students and staff, students have also benefited from the administrative function of the WebCT section. Students could find all paper-based information online at any time and staff could ensure that all programme and module information was up to date. The section therefore provided an integrated central location for all information pertaining both to language learning and to the logistics of study. For the modules that I was not responsible for, I simply uploaded material sent to me by colleagues following a standardized format. Several colleagues quickly came to realize the advantages of a medium like WebCT and began to exploit it in more productive ways than just as a notice board. For example, the use of a single WebCT section provided a useful forum to view and share practice, as it allowed staff to view real and active examples of innovative use of the tools that WebCT supports. Some staff have actively engaged with WebCT as a consequence of viewing the work included in the section and are exploring how they can use it themselves to promote active learning; other staff have not yet engaged but it is hoped that they may do so in the future. I hope that in future years, when computer-based learning becomes better established, these colleagues will also succumb to 'peer and student pressure' (another advantage, perhaps, of having a single section!), and begin to use WebCT more actively and imaginatively.

Exploiting the WebCT Tools

a) Grammar and Vocabulary Exercises

It is imperative that the choice of tool is driven by the pedagogic needs of students. As a web-based resource, WebCT can be used to exploit some of the more basic but powerful features of the Internet (including the use of hyperlinks, images and colour) to enhance the learning experience. The use of colour and imagery was particularly important to the educator and was used in the Grammar and Vocabulary Exercises both to set the scene for learning, and to provide important cues to feedback. The Educator's Commentary below describes the thought processes behind the look and feel of these exercises, and begins to explore how the different tools and features were chosen.

Educator's Comments:

In preparation for all the exercises in the section (Grammar and Vocabulary, Writing, Listening and Reading), it was important to consider how the resources could be made as appealing and as colourful as possible to encourage a relaxed and positive approach from students. For the Grammar and Vocabulary Exercises in particular, the use of colour and images helped 'liven up' the presentation and aid student learning. I also varied the types of questions as much as possible, even in the same assessment (multiple choice, short answer etc). As mentioned above, I chose to use the exercises to reiterate and reinforce the points made in lessons and based the vocabulary exercises on the vocabulary from students' course books so that the materials would be immediately useful and relevant. To make these exercises more interesting and challenging, I arranged the questions into 'sets', so that every time the students attempted a vocabulary exercise, they would be asked to produce 20 words chosen at random from a set of around 100. This made repeating the exercise as many times as they wanted meaningful and challenging, as the actual exercise would be different each time. However, the small chance that, after several attempts, they would be asked the same question again, meant that further learning and reinforcement were taking place. Students and instructors could also check on progressive improvements in the score, which acted as a confidence boost. I also entered comprehensive feedback on wrong answers, to reinforce students' language learning.

Student views:

Students were very positive about the online Grammar and Vocabulary Exercises, suggesting that their language learning improved due to the immediate feedback they received on their submitted work, which showed them where they were going wrong. As one student noted, "I could complete exercises at home and get a mark immediately which was useful." This feedback encouraged students to "evaluate the results" whenever they submitted completed exercises, which in turn, helped them to engage in a reflective process that encouraged deeper learning than previously. Students also felt that the web-based exercises helped them to "consolidate what [they] had learnt in class" by enabling them to apply theoretical work in practical ways. Furthermore, students liked the presentation and layout of the exercises, describing them as "very clear and enjoyable." Students found the colourful and bold presentation of resources "made it fun", which again, encouraged them to engage in the learning process more thoroughly. This presentation, combined with clear and easy-to-navigate materials ultimately meant that students could use

WebCT with ease, thus avoiding the problem of technology itself, rather than the learning process, becoming the focus.

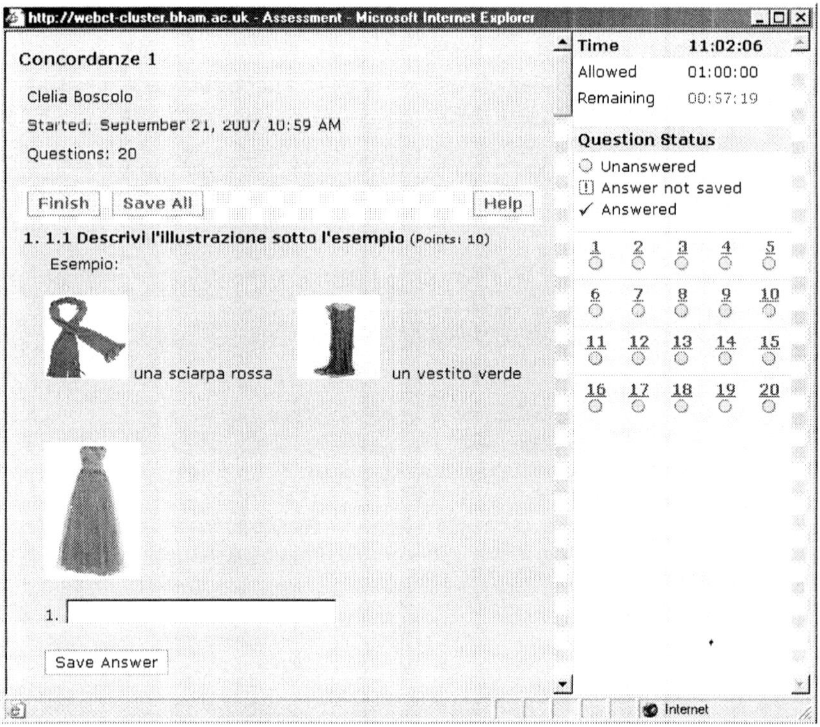

Figure 6-1. An example of an early stage short-answer question presented through WebCT showing the use of colourful images to illustrate grammatical concepts.

The flexibility that computer based learning offers learners is well documented.[11] Unsurprisingly, therefore, students found that working online gave them the flexibility of completing the exercises in their own time and space, commenting that "you could go back and do them as many

[11] G. Salmon, *E-Moderating: The Key to Teaching and Learning Online* (London: Kogan Page Limited, 2000). See also: A. Davies and K. J. Smith, "Drivers and Barriers to the Uptake of Learning Technologies: Staff Experiences in a Research-Led University," O'Donoghue, J. (ed) *Technology Supported Learning & Teaching: A Staff Perspective*. (USA: Idea Group Inc, 2005).

times as you wanted/needed to." This facility to go back to the exercises made the online resources a useful revision tool and means of learning from their mistakes. In addition to this, the online facility enabled students to gain confidence by repeating the exercises in their own private space away from their peers; a confidence that in turn, fed into their interactions with peers in the "public space" of the classroom.

b. Writing Exercises

A VLE provides a number of tools that can be used to support writing exercises. One example is provided below where a journal discussion was set up within WebCT for students to post diary entries. Students posted a diary entry (Figure 2a), which was commented on by their teacher (Figure 2b) using different colours to provide different levels and types of feedback. Note that this task differs from some forms of dialogue journal in that the feedback is provided by the teacher, rather than by student peers. This form of feedback is recommended by Shang[12] (see introduction above).

An additional benefit of using the journal discussion tool within WebCT was that students were able to collect their entries and their teacher's comments in a single, private space. Within this space, students were able to think about contributions before submitting them, could hide and reveal feedback comments, reflect on their learning, and ask for further clarifications from the teacher as required and at their own pace. This further demonstrates Warschauer's[13] assertion that online communications can help bring reflection and interaction together in a way that is difficult to support through non-electronic means.

Educator's Comments:

> Writing is a notoriously difficult skill to encourage and to make meaningful and perhaps the one that yields the poorest results. Writing has to be accurate, well-structured, and coherent and is a distillation and concentration of all things learnt. Students are reluctant to produce much and find it hard, yet they have to do it from early on in their learning. In order to encourage a greater, more meaningful and relaxed production, I exploited the opportunities offered by the 'journal' type discussion board. In this feature, each student could have a virtual page that only s/he and the tutor have access to. I called the discussion board "Caro Diario..." and

---

[12] Shang, op. cit.

[13] Warschauer, op. cit.

asked students to write diary entries at least once a week. To try and home in on the topics we were covering in the language classes, I asked the entries to be specific. For example, I would ask students to talk about a person or place that they knew (nouns, adjectives, physical description, present tense), how they spent today/yesterday/last weekend (past tense, sequence of events), describe a party that went wrong (imperfect, perfect), and what they would do the following weekend (future). Each entry was cut and pasted into a comment, where it was corrected and commented on using different colours and then sent back to the student. Several students chose, unprompted, to print these pages out and keep them in a sort of portfolio. It is difficult to understate the impact and usefulness of this exercise: students absolutely loved it, made it their own, started writing extensive pieces (some over 1500 words!), and even varied the type of writing by including dialogues and poems. For me, it was truly rewarding to see how much they had improved over the year and how relaxed and natural their writing was.

> Questo giovedì è il ventesimo compleanno del mio ragazzo e ho organizzato una cena di sorpresa per lui, con tutti gli amici dal hockey su ghiaccio, dal suo appartamento e la casa mia ed alcuni vecchi amici. È all'oscuro e so che sarà una sorpresa meravigliosa! Dopo la cena, andremo nella città per alcune bevande ma devo essere a letto prima perché ho un esame venerdi - che scherzo! Venerdì sera, andiamo a un concerto in Manchester (conosci Snow Patrol?) quindi dopo il mio esame, devo correre alla stazione ferroviaria per essere in Manchester alle 7. Dopo il concerto andiamo nella città con un'amica che vive lí e poi, dopo un po'di spese per natale, voliamo a Francia il 18 dicembre. Che settimana occupata! In mezzo a tutto il questo, devo trovare il tempo per rivedere! Buona Fortuna, Eli!

Figure 6-2a. An early, original diary entry (two months into the course) entered into WebCT by a student.

A second type of open discussion board was used within the WebCT course for students to manage and set up their own discussion topics and threads. Use of a discussion tool in this way can help students' writing skills, help students form communities of practice with the potential to bring about positive social relations,[14] provide a 'real' or authentic experience derived from the personal interests of participants,[15] and can encourage anxious or shy learners to participate.[16]

---

[14] See Skinner and Austin, op. cit.; Warschauer, op. cit.

[15] Skinner and Austin, op. cit.

[16] Yu and Yu, op. cit.; Salmon, op. cit., 2002; Gonzalez-Bueno, M. "The Effects of Electronic Mail on Spanish L2 Discourse," *Language Learning & Technology* 1, no. 2 (1998): 55-70; and Warschauer, op. cit.

Questo giovedì è il ventesimo compleanno del mio ragazzo e ho organizzato una cena a sorpresa per lui, con tutti gli amici della squadra di hockey su ghiaccio, del suo appartamento e di casa mia ed alcuni vecchi amici. È all'oscuro e so che sarà una sorpresa meravigliosa! Dopo cena, andremo in centro a bere qualcosa ma devo andare a letto presto perché ho un esame venerdì - che scherzo! Venerdì sera, andiamo a un concerto a Manchester (conosci Snow Patrol?) quindi dopo il mio esame, devo correre alla stazione ferroviaria per essere a Manchester alle 7. Dopo il concerto andiamo in centro con un'amica che vive lí e poi, dopo un po'di spese per natale, prendiamo l'aereo per la Francia il 18 dicembre. Che settimana intensa! In mezzo a tutto questo, devo trovare il tempo per ripassare! Buona Fortuna, Eli!

Sì, buona fortuna, Eli!

Careful not to repeat errors that I have already corrected before: I have marked them in green. Ma anche questo è un bel testo, brava!

Figure 6-2b. The same diary entry corrected and commented on by the educator. Note the use of colour to highlight different types of error. Here green was used to highlight errors that had been made and corrected in a previous entry; red was used to highlight new types of correction. The original and corrected entries are displayed next to each other in WebCT, which facilitates comparison. All previous entries and comments are kept in chronological sequence and are always immediately available to both the student-author and the instructor: the former can easily look back at his/her earlier production or check earlier corrections, the latter can easily track the individual student's progress and check whether previous errors are being repeated.

There are, however, some potential pitfalls with use of open discussion boards. For example, negative messages or "flames" can set back learning and social cohesion, and students may be put off by "information overload" where too many messages are posted which can hinder organisation and reflection.[17] For most commentators, however, the positive aspects of providing opportunities for many-to-many communication outweigh the negative.

The two examples of writing exercises above used the asynchronous journal discussion tool to support and facilitate learning. The final example in this section exploits the web-based nature of WebCT and uses simple HTML formatting and hyperlinks to provide higher-level cues and

[17] Warschauer, op. cit.

information beyond simple text. In the activity reported here, students were required to produce summaries in Italian of news articles and similar types of materials written in English. Texts were shown as HTML web pages and colour was used to mark items deemed important and necessary to the final summary, and to highlight interesting aspects of each language as shown in Figure 3 below. Hyperlinks were also used (dark blue underlined letter codes) to enable students to view and interact with additional information and glossary notes without detracting from the flow of the original text.

Police recover frescoes stolen from Pompeii

By Bruce Johnston in Rome

Italian police yesterday recovered two ancient Roman frescoes - already packed for export - days after thieves had torn them from the walls[U1] of an important villa in Pompeii.
The frescoes, stolen from a villa known as the House of the Chaste Lovers, were found at a building site half a mile from the ruins of the ancient city[U2].
Among the clues said to have led police to the frescoes was a half-eaten[CB3] takeaway pizza that the thieves left behind[CB4] in the ancient villa. Police are believed to have made inquiries with the pizzeria.
Experts were busy assessing the damage yesterday and determining whether[U5] the frescoes could be fixed back[CB6] to the walls.
The House of the Chaste Lovers, whose main fresco features two clothed lovers, has been under excavation since 1987 but has never been open to the public.
The theft, described as the worst in Pompeii in years, caused severe damage to the villa. Besides tearing two central scenes from the walls the intruders badly damaged several other frescoes.
They broke in at night at the weekend. The next day, administrators said, the floors of the villa were found littered with bits of broken fresco[CB7], leading them to think that vandals[CB8] had struck.
But two frescoes, finely painted between AD 45 and 79 in Pompeii's "third" and "fourth" styles, had been brutally hacked away[CB9].
Antonio D'Ambrosio, head of excavations, said the thieves, while removing a central scene of a cockerel pecking at a pomegranate from the south wall of one room, badly damaged the rest of the wall. A marine scene in the same room was also damaged.

(The Telegraph, 9th April, 2003)

Figure 6-3a. Example of an English text to be summarised in Italian, presented and marked up via WebCT. The most important parts of the text that should be carried into the summary are highlighted in blue. Green is used to highlight points of complex lexis, often with links to further information and suggestions given in square brackets after the highlighted text.

Text 2

Si trovavano in un cantiere edile vicino agli Scavi, già imballati e pronti per essere trasferiti all'estero

Pompei. recuperati gli affreschi rubati

I due reperti sono stati danneggiati dai ladri

NAPOLI - Sono stati recuperati i due reperti archeologici rubati venerdì notte negli Scavi di Pompei. I carabinieri li hanno trovati in un cantiere edile vicino agli Scavi, già imballati e pronti per essere trasferiti all'estero. Dopo un primo esame della Soprintendenza archeologica di Pompei, è risultato subito evidente che i due affreschi sono stati danneggiati dai ladri durante il trasporto. "Non sappiamo ancora se si potrà ricomporre in maniera completa il quadro pittorico" ha esordito il soprintendente Piero Giovanni Guzzo. Saranno i tecnici del laboratorio di restauro a verificare le possibilità di reinserimento nelle pareti che li ospitavano.

"I due pannelli" spiega Guzzo "sono ambedue danneggiati come già si immaginava dopo i primi sopralluoghi. Ora bisognerà controllare i frammenti ritrovati dove sono stati asportati con le lacune che si osservano sui pannelli ritrovati oggi, in maniera da vedere se si fosse perduto qualche particolare e se tra i frammenti ritrovati e i pannelli il quadro pittorico sia completo. Al momento" aggiunge "non si sa ancora se si potrà ricomporre in maniera completa. Inizieremo immediatamente le verifiche".

Secondo il soprintendente è comunque "molto importante che, in poche ore dalla notizia del furto, grazie ai carabinieri, sia stato possibile il ritrovamento". Sul furto, Guzzo avanza qualche dubbio. "L'ultimo furto negli Scavi" sottolinea, "era stato compiuto cinque anni fa. Come allora anche adesso si stava pensando a una riorganizzazione dei servizi di vigilanza e del lavoro

Figure 6-3b. An extract of an Italian text on the same subject as that shown in Figure 3a. Important items of lexis and structures are again highlighted in blue. Students can compare the two texts and use the highlighted words and phrases to help them summarise the story presented in Figure 3a into Italian.

Summaries 2006-2007
Week 8–News Events–Group B

Text 1

I carabinieri hanno ritrovato gli affreschi rubati da Pompei.
Ieri la polizia italiana ha recuperato i due affreschi antichi che alcuni ladri avevano rubato alcuni giorni prima.
Gli affreschi, rubati dalla 'Casa dei Casti Amanti,' sono stati trovati in un cantiere edile vicino a Pompei.
Un indizio che ha aiutato la polizia a trovarli è stata una pizza mangiucchiata che i ladri avevano abbandonato.
Gli esperti hanno valutato ieri il danno per decidere se gli affreschi potranno essere ricomposti.
La 'Casa dei Casti Amanti,' una villa che non è mai stata aperta al pubblico, è stata molto danneggiata. I ladri hanno rovinato anche altri affreschi.
Hanno fatto irruzione di notte durante il fine settimana. I custodi pensavano che fossero stati dei vandali perché il pavimento era coperto di affreschi rotti.
Ma due pannelli, che risalgono agli anni il 45 e il 79 dC, erano stati asportati dai muri.
Il direttore degli scavi ha detto che i ladri hanno danneggiato gravemente il muro mentre toglievano un affresco che rappresenta un gallo. Anche una scena marina nella stessa camera è stata rovinata.

Figure 6-3c. Example of a student's summary in response to the activity described in Figures 3a and 3b.

Student Views:

For students who used the writing exercises, the diary feature captivated their interest and was considered to be the most useful of all the resources. Students considered writing a diary entry as "more interesting than handing in a piece of written work" and described the diary feature as "useful practice" in helping them to develop their writing skills. As with the Grammar and Vocabulary Exercises, students found that the diary feature was "easy to use" due to the clear and colourful presentation. One student commented that "it's clearer seeing online corrections and all diary entries are stored neatly and clearly on WebCT," which in turn, helped them to "write more accurately and faster." In addition to improving their writing skills, students commented that the diary facility helped them to expand their informal vocabulary.

Students were also positive about the discussion boards, suggesting that they were useful for their year abroad and gave them the opportunity to confer with other year groups about the course. Some students, however, felt that more encouragement and information about how to use the resources were needed so that more students would use the discussion boards more frequently.

Listening and Reading Exercises

Educator's Comments:

The listening and reading exercises were designed to give additional listening and reading practice which would be convenient for the students to do in their own time. Listening and reading are both quite time-consuming activities and can only be done sparingly in the context of the language class. It is important that students listen to longer chunks of spoken language than the one to two minute pieces that can usually be managed in class. It is also important that they are allowed to manage their listening if we want their skill to develop. For this reason, I embedded an audio or video file into the body of the assessment, so that students could control it themselves—stop, go back, listen again—in order to answer the questions. The fact that they could do these exercises on their own made them more relaxed and consequently, more receptive. The reading exercises were straight text-based comprehension exercises, mainly designed to offer students easily accessible texts on topics they had covered during the course and at levels suitable for them. Educators always insist that in order to improve, students should "read" a lot, but when the students ask for clarification on 'what' they should read, they are often told 'anything, it's all useful.' This is clearly untrue, as it is unrealistic to expect a first-year student to read a newspaper or a novel, and it is frustrating and demoralizing for the student, who feels unable to read what is erroneously deemed a 'simple' text. Reading, like all skills, needs to be developed gradually, using texts which are challenging but within the student's actual possibilities. The reading exercises were then prepared bearing these principles in mind and using a format similar to the one students would encounter in their examinations. In this way, they were able to practise and develop their reading skills in their own time and without requiring additional marking time on the instructor's part. As a result, students read a lot more than they would have done otherwise.

Student Views:

Students suggested that the listening and reading exercises were helpful in three key ways. First, like the Grammar and Vocabulary exercises, the Listening and Reading exercises provided useful practice for their exams. Students commented that the exercises provided another important dimension to their language learning by enabling them to "gain experience in hearing speech" and thus prepare them for the aural examinations. Second, the exercises enabled students to access and complete them on or off campus in their own time. As one student noted, "you could access the exercises anywhere and re-do them at your leisure." This opportunity of completing the exercises at students' own leisure was an important factor in contributing to the more relaxed and receptive atmosphere found by the educator above. Third, students commented that the exercises allowed them to read as well as listen to dialogue at the same time, which aided them in the language learning process by tapping into different types of learning at the same time.

Students therefore found the listening and reading exercises very useful, although some suggestions were made on how they could be improved upon. Some students suggested, for example, that the listening exercises could be shorter in length, and that exercises with different levels of difficulty would be useful to help them see improvements in their language acquisition.

Conclusions and Future Developments

> It was a very interesting course, which helped me not only to increase my knowledge of Italian, but it was also great practice… I haven't got any suggestions to change it—I am very content with it (Student).

The comment above encapsulates the views of most students who were introduced to the online resources during their Italian studies. Students commented that they found the course "extremely helpful in achieving better language acquisition" and "the most interesting out of all [their] modules." Integrating online resources into the Department of Italian Studies has therefore proved to be a positive experience for students and staff. At the heart of this success has been the drive to encourage independent learning that accommodates a variety of different learning styles through contextual, interactive and flexible resources.

The use of computer based resources has enabled students to develop self-confidence in their language learning through a greater sense of community with their peers and with staff. This sense of 'community' amongst students has been made possible through the creation of a single section for all students to see and through discussion boards that encourage students to post their comments and queries to their peers and to staff. Student self-confidence has been further enhanced by the flexibility of the resources, which have given students the opportunity to work at their own pace and in their own time, and by providing opportunities to practise their language skills through an abundance of additional material. Finally, by opening up new and exciting possibilities for students in the Department of Italian (and not forgetting immense amounts of staff enthusiasm), they have engaged more fully in an active learning process that has, in turn, brought their understanding and learning experience alive.

In terms of future developments, it is anticipated that the most successful exercises (diary, sample work) will be extended to other groups in the Department of Italian in the near future. It is hoped that the possibilities for oral practice will be expanded by introducing the voice tool Wimba, and by creating free-standing exercises that are associated with the diary discussion board, which will encourage students to participate in a mixture of spoken and written entries.

Acknowledgements

First and foremost, thanks are due to Bob Hunter and the Learning Development Unit at the University of Birmingham, who made this project possible by supporting it financially. Without their research grant, we would not have been able to devote time to its design. In the early stages, Marc Griffith was a patient and inspiring WebCT tutor. Dealing with someone who was not only a competent technician but above all a teacher, made it all less frightening. Nowadays, William Miller is an equally patient and resourceful "wizard", when it comes to solving technical problems. Clelia's son Edwin was brilliant and very patient, too, at helping her design some of the pictures and icons just as she wanted them. The biggest thanks, though, go to her hard-working, funny, enthusiastic, challenging students, who tried it all, used it all, put up with it all and came out smiling at the end of it!

University of Birmingham, UK

CHAPTER SEVEN

AZIONE! TEACHING LISTENING SKILLS THROUGH VIDEO: A WEB-BASED PROGRAM OF FILM AND TELEVISION SEGMENTS DESIGNED FOR ITALIAN LANGUAGE COURSES AT YALE UNIVERSITY

AMELIA MOSER

The following article discusses the genesis, development, and implementation of *Azione!*, a web-based program of Italian film and television clips currently used in the elementary and intermediate Italian language curricula at Yale University. *Azione!* is designed to improve students' listening comprehension skills and to stimulate discussion using vocabulary from the standard first-year textbook.[1]

Azione! was created thanks to an Instructional Innovation Grant from the Center for Language Study at Yale University awarded to Rachele Pierro and the author.[2] The program can be seen on-line at the following site: www.cls.yale.edu/azione.

---

[1] Graziana Lazzarino, Maria Cristina Peccianti, Janice M. Aski, and Andrea Dini, *Prego! An Invitation to Italian.* 6th ed. (Boston and New York: McGraw Hill, 2004).

[2] I would like to thank the Center for Language Study staff for their assistance in helping us realize this program. Above all, I am grateful to Vincent Cangiano, Language Study Specialist, and Chris Meyer, Programmer/Analyst, for their instruction on digitizing and uploading video to the website; Bradley Gano, Associate Director, for his aid in the organizational aspects of the program; and Steven Melillo, Sr. Multimedia Technician, for his technical support. I would also like to thank the Yale Italian Department for their support, especially Professors Giuseppe Mazzotta and Risa Sodi.

Focusing on Needs

Language instructors in the Yale Italian Program expressed the need for listening comprehension materials that would bolster students' skills in their aural comprehension of natural, native speech—an ability which instructors sensed was not addressed successfully in textbooks. Many students intend to spend time in Italy for a summer, semester, or year, and faculty members believed it was essential to offer them more in and out-of-class opportunities to hear normal rate-speed native speech early in their studies so that the transition during their stay in Italy would proceed as smoothly as possible. Instructors, in fact, observed that a frequent complaint of students returning from study abroad (and also a common concern expressed by those about to depart for a stay in Italy) was that—while they were confident in their grammar, reading, and writing abilities—they believed that during their pre-departure course of study they had not acquired adequate skills to understand native speakers. We also discovered that students often felt overwhelmed when confronted with native speech because they had not been trained to listen selectively for the most important information. *Azione!* was designed to teach students how to listen selectively by providing them with brief "full-immersion" experiences.

It is an inevitable (and yet necessary) reality of any early-level language class that most of the speech students hear in the classroom and at home while listening to course videos is artificial in speed, vocabulary, setting, and diction. While teachers work diligently to build students' grammar, lexical knowledge, writing abilities, and conversational skills, they often find that there is not enough time in class sessions to address listening strategies on a consistent basis. Several instructors in the program noted that, while desiring to integrate such activities into classroom studies, they were faced with three obstacles:

- After addressing the necessary grammar and conversation activities required by the syllabus, only a limited amount of time, usually no more than 15 minutes, remained in any given lesson for listening activities.
- Readily available materials for listening comprehension required much more time to adapt into classroom activities than instructors considered feasible. Because of these time-constraints, instructors felt obliged to limit authentic listening activities to occasional events scheduled on the days following an exam, when at least thirty to forty minutes could

be devoted to a full listening experience which would include a pre-activity, viewing of a video more than once, and a post-activity.
- Students tended to be able to follow native speech only for limited amounts of time, whereas the majority of material at the instructors' disposal exceeded this restricted listener threshold. Viewings of longer videos, therefore, were often assigned at home for lab-work. But instructors also expressed the need to be able to follow-up with students in class by watching at least sections of the video together, having noted that this is the most effective way to teach listening strategies.

When designing *Azione!*, we took these concerns regarding time constraints into consideration and created a program which offers the following:

- Brief video clips that would not exceed students' threshold for listening time. (Most clips do not exceed three minutes)
- Clips that present the general context reflected in the lexical material already covered in the textbook. This characteristic allowed teachers to review vocabulary already covered as opposed to introducing completely new lexical material in the pre-activity phase. Also, because success in listening comprehension is heavily based on students' prior knowledge of terms and expressions, the authors felt the lexical correlation between text and *Azione!* would be key.
- A program aimed at emphasizing content and not grammar, since the latter is sufficiently addressed in the textbook.

Teaching Listening

Listening is a complex activity requiring learners to decode and process oral messages while also accessing previous knowledge. It is known that there are several different styles of listening and that people tend to listen differently. To construct activities that promote student listening, it is first important to understand what is meant by "good listening skills." Studies show that interpretation of aural input occurs at three levels: a lexical level (where the listener attempts to infer meaning by recognizing known vocabulary), a base or schematic level (where a listener acquires conceptual understanding by linking utterances), and an interpersonal level (where a listener infers possible motivations or intentions of the speaker).[3] As mentioned above, language learners are exposed to different types of listening activities depending on whether the activities are conducted in the classroom (tending to be constructed and artificial) or in a native-speaker setting (prone to be faster-paced and not student-focused). If an instructor's goal is to incorporate authentic listening activities into the language curriculum, he or she might do well to make note of Penny Ur's recommendations regarding real-life listening. Ur indicates that real-life listening is defined by the following: first, students must be afforded ample environmental cues, second, listening segments must be presented in brief parts, and third, students must respond in some way to what they are listening.[4] While every instructor may dream of the day when it will possible to pair each student with a native speaker discussion partner even in the early stages of learning, this, as we know well, is rarely feasible at the present time. The next best thing, of course, is the use of video clips, given that they expose students to environmental clues and can also be shown in short segments:

> Video clips can serve various purposes; they can help students infer main ideas of communicative events, figure out the meaning of unknown words, organize information extracted from linguistic input, and build schemata for the situational context.[5]

***

Listening in the classroom has been shown to be the most frequently used language skill[6] and the one that, more than reading ability and overall

---

[3] Michael Rost, *Listening in Language Learning* (London/NY: Longman, 1990), 83-4.

[4] Penny Ur, *Teaching Listening Comprehension* (Cambridge: Cambridge University Press, 1984), 2-10.

[5] Michelle Kitajima Johnston and Mary Ann Lyman-Hager, "Theory-Driven Use of Digital Video in Foreign Language Instruction," *CALICO Journal* 16, no.1 (1998): 40. See also Alice Omaggio Hadley, *Teaching Language in Context* (Boston, MA: Heinle & Heinle Publishers, 1993), 82, 380-2. One point, however, at which the video listening activity falls short when compared to a conversation with a native speaker is that, when watching a video, the student is not a direct participant in the conversation he is witnessing. Given this limitation, the instructor must provide ways of evoking reciprocity in the student in any video-watching activity.

[6] See Sanford E. Taylor, *Listening: What Research Says to the Teacher* (Washington, DC: National Education Association, 1964).

academic achievement, determines student success.[7] And yet because listening in the L1 is more a habit than a conscious choice,[8] L2 students may not be able to easily transfer their L1 listening technique(s) into the foreign language classroom. Strategies, such as inferring from context or intonation, predicting from visual cues, and listening for only pre-selected information, are certainly key in helping students acquire the ability to decipher aural input in L2[9], but studies have proven that lexical background is the most important factor in determining whether a student can **successfully** listen to L2 speech.[10] With this in mind, teachers—especially those at the elementary levels—should first focus on helping students build their vocabulary knowledge since, as Bonk concluded in an article on this topic, it is highly unlikely that a learner with low percentage of lexis familiarity "would be able to get the gist after one listening, whether or not that person was an effective user of listening strategies."[11] Instructors might then decide that if students find it too difficult to understand native speech, it would be more helpful to review general vocabulary rather than focusing solely on finding new listening strategies.

With this in mind, we wanted users of *Azione!* to expect **not** to understand every spoken word, but rather to listen for specific content. To this purpose, when the video clips are shown at the elementary level, students are instructed to read the comprehension questions before viewing the clips in order to train themselves to listen selectively. Because the comprehension questions address only the essential points of the scenes, such exercises are aimed at helping learners understand only

---

[7] See Martha Smith Conaway, "Listening: Learning Too and Retention Agent," in *Improving Reading and Study Skills*, ed. Ann S. Algier and Keith W. Algier (San Francisco: Jossey-Bass, 1982).

[8] Ellen J. Langer, "Rethinking the role of thought in social interaction," in vol. 2 of *New Directions in Attribution Research*, ed. by John H. Harvey, William John Ickes, and Robert F. Kidd (Hillsdale, NY: Erlbaum, 1980), 35-58. In discussion of the role of conscious thinking and awareness in social interactions, Langer avers that much of human interactive behavior (including listening) occurs automatically, without the participant being aware of the skills he is actively using. See also Richard M. Shiffrin and Walter Schneider, "Controlled and automatic human information processing, II: Perceptual learning, automatic attending, and a general theory," *Psychological Review* 84 (1977): 127-90.

[9] Ernesto Macaro, "Research on Listening," Chap. 7 in *Teaching and Learning a Second Language. A Review of Recent Research* (London/NY: Continuum, 2003), 160-71.

[10] William J. Bonk, "Second Language Lexical Knowledge and Listening Comprehension," *International Journal of Listening* 14 (2000): 16.

[11] Ibid., 18.

central messages. Following the goal of teaching selective listening, we intentionally avoided exhaustive vocabulary lists, preferring to furnish students with only those words essential for achieving general comprehension. In this way, listeners would have to rely on their previous long-term lexical knowledge and not short-term recall from the vocabulary list on the *Azione!* web page. The only words included on the provided vocabulary lists were those not presented in the textbook, but yet which were crucial to the students' understanding of the general meaning of the video. *Azione!*'s main goal, thus, is to help train learners to listen for what they know, while discouraging them from feeling overwhelmed by what they do not know. In such a way, students discover that it is possible to comprehend general meaning even if one is not able to understand each individual word pronounced.

As indicated in previous research, selective listening activities function best when the follow-up exercise is very focused on clear choices.[12] Questions are, for obvious reasons, powerful tools in order to guide learners in selective listening, especially when they are presented before the listening activity commences.[13] Strategies used in listening at the L2 level not only give learners the opportunity to understand more fully, they also reinforce motivation and self-confidence and increase a student's sense of autonomy and agency within the learning process.[14]

Unique Characteristics of Azione!

In their early studies of the Italian language, students are accustomed to hearing standardized speech and thus have difficulty when traveling in Italy where they are confronted with regional accents they have never before encountered. *Azione!* was also designed to offer students the opportunity to become familiar with several regional differences.

Before creating our program, we were aware of many similar video-based programs available for classroom use which address serious and sensitive cultural issues and thus rightfully require substantial time to integrate into a lesson plan. These materials most certainly have their place in the curriculum, but we desired to create a program that could easily be introduced as a short segment of any given lesson without requiring

---

[12] Michael Rost, *Listening in Language Learning* (London/NY: Longman, 1990), 232.

[13] Ibid., 166.

[14] Christine Goh, "Second Language Listening Expertise," in *Expertise in Second Language Learning and Teaching*, ed. Keith Johnson (Hampshire/NY: Palgrave Macmillan: 2005), 160.

teachers to plan extensive pre and post-activities. Therefore, in order to make *Azione!* easily adaptable, most of the video clips are humorous and compatible with a lively, up-beat classroom setting. In fact, segments were chosen not only for their pedagogical value and their relevance to the themes addressed in the textbook, but also for their entertainment value. Serious issues are touched on at times, but only when they represent a part of Italian society that the authors felt would interest Yale students and would relate to their everyday life.

Summary of Program Contents:

Unit 1 Health
Unit 2 The Home
Unit 3 The Environment and Technology
Unit 4 Comedy: Benigni
Unit 5 Art and Archeology
Unit 6 Travel Humor
Unit 7 Love and Humor
Unit 8 Politics and Government
Unit 9 The Italian School System
Unit 10 Growing Up
Unit 11 The Family

In summation, the general goals and objectives of *Azione!* are:

- To help students learn and practice listening comprehension strategies by teaching them skills in selective listening.
- To offer elementary learners the opportunity to become familiar with the speech of many regions in Italy.
- To offer an alternative lab exercise made specifically for Yale students which integrates well with the grammar textbook.
- To introduce students to Italian film.
- To create a program that can be used for both at-home work and in-class activities.

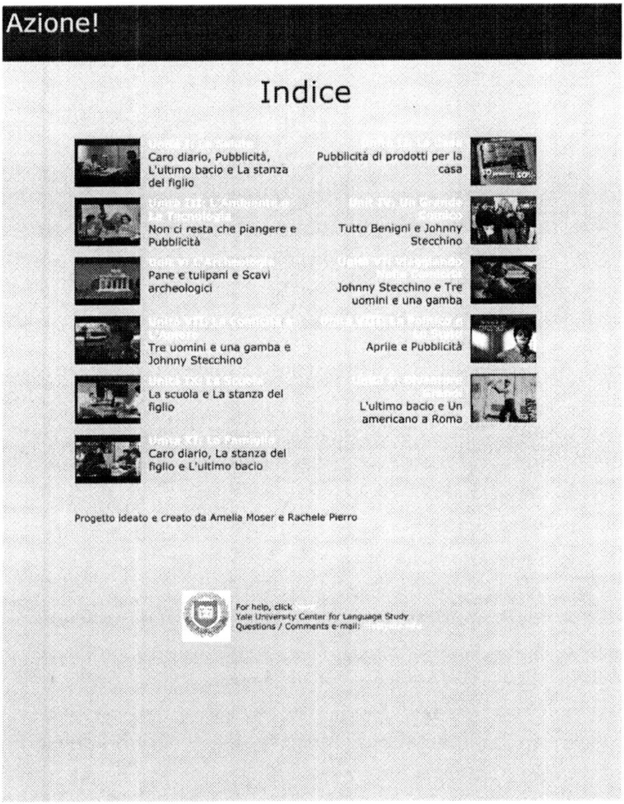

Figure 7-1. The *Azione!* webpage.

Design and Integration of the Program

We originally calculated that one semester and a summer would be necessary to develop and complete all stages of the project, but found that the project was much more labor-intensive and actually required an entire year. This was partly due to the large amount of material selected and also to difficulties faced in gathering such materials. Before making final video selections, topics were chosen based on the issues addressed in the textbook, *Prego*, yet the authors tried to follow *Prego* only loosely so that, if at any time the textbook were to change, the program could be adapted to another language textbook.[15] The selection and viewing of films which addressed these topics became the most time-consuming aspect of the project. In fact, an appropriate two-minute clip was often only identifiable after analyzing several hours of video. We also taped and viewed many hours of TV shows and commercials from various channels of Italian television. After selecting all material, we then wrote the activities and vocabulary lists, and finally uploaded all work onto a web-based template called VISION, recently designed by the Yale Center for Language Study. VISION (Video Software for Instruction Online) is multimedia courseware that aims to improve and test aural comprehension of authentic materials by presenting selected video clips. The template allows for each clip to be accompanied by a previewing section (with an introduction and new vocabulary guide), and a post-viewing section (with a cultural and grammatical commentary, general comprehension questions, and true/false and multiple choice questions sets).

Implementation of the Program

Originally intended to be used during the second semester of first-year Italian, *Azione!* has now been expanded to both the first and second years of instruction. The decision to extend its use was mainly due to the wide range of materials presented and to their varying difficulty. While using the program, instructors have noted that (depending on the class level and make-up) certain students have initially felt overwhelmed and anxious about engaging in real-life listening activities for fear of not understanding as well as their classmates and, as a result, of feeling diminished in front of their peers. Since listening anxiety has been shown to be a determining factor in students' difficulty with successful listening,[16] it is recommended that teachers address this issue by implementing pre-listening activities. Most importantly instructors are trained to inform students that the goal of the program is to teach the strategy of selective listening and that learners are not expected to understand every word in the clip, but that the challenge they are given is only to identify cues (lexical, physical, and cultural) already reviewed and learned in the course of their previous study. In-class pre-activities, which can be initiated and concluded in three to five minutes, include a discussion of the title of the video clip and the

[15] In fact, because *Azione!* is a webpage and not printed material, it can easily be updated or tailored to fit new pedagogical needs.

[16] Goh, "Second Language Listening Expertise," 74; Anita Jones Vogely, "Listening Comprehension Anxiety: Students' Reported Sources and Solutions," in *Foreign Language Annals* 31, no.1 (1998): 67-80.

context of the scene, after which students are encouraged to think of words and situational dynamics that may appear. Instructors can reiterate key vocabulary words by writing them on the board so that students have a visual prompt in their mind before listening. During the listening exercise, however, it is recommended that all pre-activity vocabulary be erased from the board so that students will experience a more 'real-life listening' experience. Instructors should also direct students to the brief vocabulary list provided to the left of each video. In the early stages of video watching it may be useful to have students simply watch the video without the audio with the intent of verifying the amount of information they can determine from cultural behaviors and situations. With the audio turned off, instructors can also ask students to engage in video narration, problem solving, or decision making activities to help them become more aware of how to build these communicative strategies.[17] An exercise which might be implemented for advanced learners is dictation (both opened or closed) which is associated with better comprehension.[18]

As the semester proceeds and students become more accustomed to viewing the program, instructors can experiment with just how much pre-activity work they need to do, perhaps opting to limit such tasks in order to assess students' abilities under different circumstances. In general, twice a month, students watch selected clips at home, answer questions about the clips, and email their responses to the instructor who then corrects their work. The clips are discussed briefly the following day in class, and any problems with comprehension are addressed at that time. In addition, instructors often view the program in class and have students work in small groups in order to decipher the meaning of these new clips. The video clips, thus, serve not only as the subject of individual lab work, but also as the inspiration for group activities, vocabulary games, and grammar review.

Composition of the Program

The Program is comprised of 11 thematically divided units, each divided into a varying number of lessons, for a total of 40 lessons. The levels of the lessons are mixed within the units for more flexible use at

---

[17] See Kitajima and Lyman-Hager, "Theory-Driven Use of Digital Video in Foreign Language Instruction," 41.

[18] Bonk, "Second Language Lexical Knowledge and Listening Comprehension," 23.

both the elementary and intermediate levels. Most students are able to answer all questions correctly after viewing the clip 2 or 3 times.

1. **Description of Clips:** Each lesson contains a 30 second to around 3 minute video clip from film or television media (commercials and a travel show).
2. **Ancillary Activities Accompanying the Clips:** Each lesson contains pre-viewing activities (including vocabulary lists) and 7-10 post-viewing activities (including general comprehension questions, true/false and/or multiple choice questions).

The titles of each Unit and lesson are as follows:

I. *La salute* [Health] (Chapter. 9, *Prego*)
   1. Scena 1: Medicina→*Caro diario* I [A phone call to the specialist/In the doctor's office]
   2. Scena 2: Medicina→ *Caro diario* II [Health tips]
   3. Scena 3: L'igiene→ Pubblicità "Day Gum" [TV ad for anti-cavity gum]
   4. Scena 4: La bellezza→ *L'ultimo bacio* I [The aesthetics of piercing]
   5. Scena 5: La psicologia→ *La stanza del figlio* [Interpretation of dreams]

II. *La casa* [The Home] (Chapter 12, *Prego*)
   1. Scena 2: Pubblicità "Finish" [TV ad for dishwasher soap]
   2. Scena 3: Pubblicità "Vanish" [TV ad for house cleaner]
   3. Scena 4: Pubblicità "Rex" [TV ad for household appliances]
   4. Scena 5: Pubblicità "Emmelunga" [TV ad for furniture store]

III. *L'ambiente e la tecnologia* [The Environment and Technology] (Chapter 13, *Prego*)
   1. Scena 1: *Non ci resta che piangere* I [Meeting Leonardo da Vinci]
   2. Scena 2: *Non ci resta che piangere* II [Helping Leonardo invent the train]
   3. Scena 3: *Non ci resta che piangere* III [Teaching Leonardo about the thermometer]

4. Scena 4: Pubblicità Telefonino [TV ad for cellphones]
5. Scena 5: Pubblicità Incendio [TV ad for prevention of forest fires]

IV. *Un grande comico* [A Great Comic] (Chapter 14, *Prego*)
1. Scena 1: "Sereno variabile I" [about Benigni, Part One]
2. Scena 2: "Sereno variabile II" [about Benigni, Part Two]
3. Scena 3: *Johnny Stecchino* I [Insurance Fraud]
4. Scena 4: *Johnny Stecchino* II [Getting caught]

V. *L'archeologia* [Archeology] (Chapter 15, *Prego*)
1. Scena 1: *Pane e tulipani* [A visit to the temple at Paestum]
2. Scena 2: *Ercolano* [The Roman Baths]
3. Scena 3: *Pompei* [A Roman Taverna or Diner]

VI. *Viaggiando nella Comicità* [Travel Humor] (Chapter 15, *Prego*)
1. Scena 1: *Johnny Stecchino* [Pit stop]
2. Scena 2: *Tre uomini e una gamba* I [Getting ready to leave for the car trip]
3. Scena 3: *Tre uomini e una gamba* II [Seat belt discussion]
4. Scena 4: *Tre uomini e una gamba* III [Car accident]

VII. *La comicità e l'amore* [Breaking up and falling in love]
1. Scena 1: *Tre uomini e una gamba* [At lunch]
2. Scena 2: *Johnny Stecchino* [Maria visits Dante's place]

VIII. *La politica e lo stato* [Politics and Government] (Chapter 16, *Prego*)
1. Scena 1: *Aprile* I [Berlusconi's political speech]
2. Scena 2: *Aprile* II [Activist speech at Hyde Park, London]
3. Scena 3: Pubblicità Europa [TV ad for the EU]

IX. *La scuola* [The School System] (Chapter 3, *Prego*)
1. Scena 1: *La scuola* I [End-of-the-year examination]
2. Scena 2: *La scuola* II [Last day of school]
3. Scena 3: *La stanza del figlio* [Getting a call from the principal]

X. *Diventare grandi* [Growing Up] (Chapter 17, *Prego*)
   1. Scena 1: *L'ultimo bacio* I [Imagining the future]
   2. Scena 2: *Un americano in Italia* [The "kid" who won't grow up]
   3. Scena 3: *L'ultimo bacio* II [Wedding speech]

XI. *La famiglia* [The Family] (Chapter 3 and Chapter 18, *Prego*)
   1. Scena 1: *Caro diario* I [Toddlers in control of their parents]
   2. Scena 2: *La stanza del figlio* [Pressures on young adults to be competitive]
   3. Scena 3: *La stanza del figlio* [Breakfast at the table]
   4. Scena 4: *L'ultimo bacio* [Dinner with the whole family]

Examples of Clips and Ancillary Activities

Unit 11/Lesson 1 *Caro diario*: Toddlers in control of their parents/ Children on the Phone

- Intended for second semester elementary level
- Can be used with the grammar point "Passato remoto"
- Possible follow-up activities: Students create fairy tales using the 'passato remoto' and animal characters. Students practice leaving messages on answering machines.
- A follow-up video that could be shown in class: Scene from *Johnny Stecchino* in which the mobsters make the same animal sounds as the adults in Moretti's film.

Unit 11/Lesson 2 *La stanza del figlio*: Pressures on young adults to be competitive / A Tennis Match

- Intended for second semester elementary level or first semester intermediate level.
- Possible follow-up activity: A class debate on competition: Is competition good or bad? Are students too competitive? What kinds of pressure do students have to deal with (from family, friends, classmates, professors, and/or society-at-large)?
- A follow-up reading on the theme of competition: Alberto Moravia's short story "La concorrenza" (appropriate for intermediate level)

Unit 3/Lesson 2 *Non ci resta che piangere*: Leonardo Da Vinci and the Train

- Intended for the intermediate level

- Allows students to hear different accents: Benigni-Tuscan; Troisi-Neapolitan.
- Possible follow-up activity: Students organize a weekend trip to Tuscany on different budget levels; Students discuss time travel; Encourage students to work with original texts by presenting them with Neapolitan songs and/or proverbs in dialects.

Unit 5/ Lesson 3 Pompeii: A Typical Roman Taverna or Diner

- Intended for the intermediate level
- Follow-up activity: Web site: www.pompeisepolta.com; Review the recipe for *garum*, a typical Roman fish sauce described in the video clip; Students discuss strange eating habits or invent unusual recipes; Students invent a conversation between two Romans in Pompeii in one of the settings described in the video (bath, forum, private house, gym, or street).

Building Learner Confidence

The benefits of real-life listening activities are many, yet one advantage may not at first seem evident: to build listener confidence. Indeed, because through these exercises students become gradually and comfortably aware of the difference between classroom speech and 'real-life' speech, they are then able to appreciate their own improvement in understanding un-modified native speaker speech and, as a result, begin to attain advanced listening skills. While it is true that students, at times, will request the teacher to modify speech heard in the videos (either by rephrasing in more comprehensible language or by slow repetition verbatim), studies have shown that in a real-life situation a learner may interpret such modifications on the part of a native speaker as a gesture of condescension or of social distancing.[19] Instructors would do well to remind themselves of this complex dynamic when deciding whether or not to modify any native speech heard on the video. Although control of the rate of speed of the audio could be a possible addition to future programs like *Azione!* (a recent study showed that this option may be beneficial for elementary listeners[20]), we specifically did not include it because doing so

---

[19] See Wolfgang Klein, *Second Language Acquisition* (Cambridge: Cambridge University Press, 1987) and Anne Anderson and Tony Lynch, *Listening* (Oxford: Oxford University Press, 1988).

[20] Yong Zhao, "The Effects of Listeners' Control of Speech Rate on Second Language Comprehension," in *Research in Technology and Second Language*

would encourage the word-for-word listening strategy which was not the aim of our program.

COLUMBIA UNIVERSITY, USA

Other References

Anderson, Anne and Tony Lynch. *Listening*. Oxford: Oxford University Press, 1988.

Kirtley Johnston, Michelle, James B. Weaver, III, Kittie W. Watson, and Larry B. Barker. "Listening Styles: Biological or Psychological Differences?" *International Journal of Listening* 14 (2000): 32-46.

McDonough, Steven. "Training Language Learning Expertise." In *Expertise in Second Language Learning and Teaching*. Edited by Keith Johnson, 150-63. Hampshire & N.Y., Palgrave Macmillan: 2005.

Rivers, Wilga M. *Teaching Foreign Language Skills*. Chicago/London: University of Chicago Press, 1968.

Thompson, Irene, and Joan Rubin. "Can Strategy Instruction Improve Listening Comprehension?" *Foreign Language Annals* 29.3 (1996): 331-42.

Education, ed. Yong Zhao (Greenwich, CT: Information Age Publishing, 2005), 178.

CHAPTER EIGHT

*CONFRONTI*NG NEW TECHNOLOGIES: A CROSS-CULTURAL TELECOLLABORATIVE PROJECT ACROSS THE OCEAN

SILVIA CARLOROSI, FRANCESCA HELM, NICOLETTA MARINI-MAIO AND KATHRYN K MCMAHON

Introduction

Confronti, an intermediate Italian curriculum, was first developed at the University of Pennsylvania in 2000 under the direction of Kathryn McMahon and Nicoletta Marini-Maio. For the prior two decades, instruction in basic language courses at Penn had been organized around the proficiency principle as articulated in the ACTFL Proficiency Guidelines. The primary objectives focused on developing students' functional communicative competence, and work concentrated on preparing students to attain a specified level on the ACTFL scale in each of the four skills.[1] As the new century came, a need was felt to move the curriculum "beyond proficiency." Within the pedagogical landscape in the US many figures called for an increased focus on content, and stressed the need to engage students intellectually in their language learning, whether it be through culture and context,[2] the importance of literacy,[3] or the

[1] Interestingly enough, the ACTFL Provisional Guidelines included a "fifth" skill, Culture. In the final version, however, it disappeared as it was deemed too difficult to determine a hierarchy of assessable performances for culture learning.
[2] Claire Kramsch, *Context and Culture in Language Teaching* (Oxford: Oxford University Press, 1993).
[3] Richard Kern, *Literacy and Language Teaching* (Oxford: Oxford University Press, 2000).

development of "multiple literacies."[4] Before designing the new curriculum at Penn, the authors administered several questionnaires to students in order to gauge their motivations for learning Italian; a desire to learn more about Italian history and culture ranked very high. The goal for the new curriculum became, then, to place culture learning at the center, rather than at the periphery, to challenge the students with engaging materials, and to integrate the language learning activities around the culture core.

Certainly most language professionals espouse the importance of teaching and learning culture, and many affirm that language and culture are indeed inseparable. In recent years, there has been renewed interest in bringing culture learning to the fore. In the United States, the *National Standards for Foreign Language Education*, first published in 1996 is now in its third edition entitled *Standards for Foreign Language Learning in the 21st century*[5]. Originally intended as a document to guide curriculum design at the K-12 level, it has extended its range to K-16 and is increasingly used for the elaboration of college and university curricula. Developed under the sponsorship of ACTFL, it represents a remarkable consensus among virtually all professional language-teaching organizations for both commonly and less-commonly taught languages in the US. It moves beyond the earlier Proficiency Guidelines to delineate five content areas, the Five Cs (one of which is Culture), to be included in foreign language curricula, thus opening up language study to areas of intellectual inquiry well beyond a narrowly-defined skills approach. (See below "The American Side") The document makes a strong appeal for the place of culture in the curriculum: "The United States must educate students who are linguistically and culturally equipped to communicate successfully in a pluralistic American society and abroad."[6]

In May of 2007, the Modern Language Association released a report entitled "Foreign Languages and Higher Education: New Structures for a Changed World" examining the state of language teaching in the US in a

---

[4] Heidi Byrnes, "Constructing Curricula in Collegiate Foreign Language Departments", in H. Byrnes, ed., *Learning Foreign and Second Languages: Perspectives in Research and Scholarship* (New York: The Modern Language Association of America, 1998).

[5] *Standards for Foreign Language Learning in the 21st Century: Including Arabic, Chinese, Classical Languages, French, German, Italian, Japanese, Portuguese, Russian, and Spanish.* 3rd ed., rev. (Yonkers, NY: National Standards in Foreign Language Education Project, 2006).

[6] National Standards, Executive summary:
http://www.actfl.org/i4a/pages/index.cfm?pageid=3324

post 9/11 era, and giving strong support to "*a broad, intellectually driven approach to teaching language and culture.*"[7] (Italics added.) It continues:

> Not surprisingly, "the need to understand other cultures and languages" was identified by Daniel Yankelovich as one of five imperative needs to which higher education must respond in the next ten years if it is to remain relevant. "Our whole culture," Yankelovich says, "must become less ethnocentric, less patronizing, less ignorant of others, less Manichaean in judging other cultures, and more at home with the rest of the world. Higher education can do a lot to meet that important challenge." In May 2005 Senator Daniel Akaka made a similar point: "Americans need to be open to the world; we need to be able to see the world through the eyes of others if we are going to understand how to resolve the complex problems we face." In the current geopolitical moment, these statements are no longer clichés. The MLA is prepared to lead the way in the reorganization of language and cultural education around these objectives.[8]

The report goes on to recommend that the Foreign Language curriculum should produce "educated speakers who have deep translingual and transcultural competence," and the authors envision a future which "will situate language study in cultural, historical, geographic, and cross-cultural frames within the context of humanistic learning," and consider that more students will be motivated to continue their study of the language "if courses incorporate cultural inquiry at all levels."[9]

Until recently there has been a lack of a principled pedagogy for teaching culture. Language teachers are all too familiar with the challenges of teaching and assessing culture, with the many different definitions and approaches advocated. [See both Kramsch[10] and Risager[11] for useful overviews of the question.] In many instances, culture teaching has been unsystematic and haphazard. Vicki Galloway once described the menu of approaches as a choice from:

> **The Frankenstein Approach** : A taco from here, a flamenco dancer from there, a gaucho from here, a bullfight from there.

---

[7] MLA Ad Hoc Committee on Foreign Languages. "Foreign Languages and Higher Education: New Structures for a Changed World." http://www.mla.org/flreport p. 1

[8] Ibid., 1-2.

[9] Ibid., 3-4.

[10] Claire Kramsch, "Culture in Language Teaching", in K. Brown, K., ed., *Encyclopedia of Language and Linguistics* (Oxford: Elsevier Ltd, 2006), 322-29.

[11] Karen Risager, *Language and Culture Pedagogy: From a National to a Transnational Paradigm* (Clevedon: Multilingual Matters Ltd, 2007).

The 4-F Approach: Folk dances, festivals, fairs and food.
The Tour Guide Approach: The identification of monuments, rivers, and cities.
The "By-the-Way" Approach: Sporadic lectures or bits of behavior selected indiscriminately to emphasize sharp differences. [12]

Even though more recent materials have introduced an awareness of sociolinguistic appropriateness, in most curricula the treatment of culture does not lead students to a deep knowledge and understanding of the target culture, or perhaps more important, of how culture works.

The *Standards* proposes a systematic approach to the teaching of culture.[13] Simply learning about "practices" (socially appropriate patterns of interaction and behavior) or "products" ("the tangible or intangible creations of a particular culture") is insufficient. It is important that students understand how "practices" and "products" are rooted in the underlying values, attitudes, conceptions, and beliefs of a particular culture, referred to as "perspectives", and that these three are all interrelated and intertwined. The goal for the students, thus, is to be able to view aspects of the target culture through the eyes of the members of that culture.

This approach harkens back to a metaphor of culture used in the past in intercultural training, that of the iceberg model of the nature of culture.[14] In this model, the tip of the iceberg that is above the waterline is that which is primarily in awareness, i.e., the practices and products. The remaining part of the iceberg (or nine-tenths of it) is out of sight below the water line. This submerged structure is analogous to that part of culture that is out of conscious awareness, often referred to as deep culture and corresponding to the perspectives referred to above. It is precisely the part of culture which is unconscious and taken for granted, that can often lead to cultural misunderstandings. Galloway signals the complex nature of culture:

> Cultures are powerful human creations, affording their members a shared identity, a cohesive framework for selecting, constructing, and interpreting perceptions, and for assigning value and meaning in consistent fashion. The complex systems of thought and behavior that people create and

---

[12] Vicki B. Galloway, as quoted in Alice Omaggio Hadley, *Teaching Language in Context,* 3rd ed. (Boston: Heinle & Heinle/Thomson Learning, 2001), 348-49

[13] *Standards,* 50.

[14] Indrei Fatiu and Irene Rodgers, "A workshop on Cultural Differences", in *AFS Orientation Handbook* Vol. 4 (New York : AFS Intercultural Programs Inc., 1984), 14.

> perpetuate in and for association are subtle and profound, so elementally forged as to be endowed by their bearers with the attributes of universal truth: Things that fit into this cultural framework are given the labels "human nature," "instinct," "common sense," "logic". Things that don't fit are different, and therefore either illogical, immoral, nonsensical, or the result of a naïve and inferior state of development of "human nature."[15]

It is such "things that don't fit" that students abroad frequently react to with expressions such as "that doesn't make any sense!", "that's stupid!", failing to grasp the logic of the other culture, and the underlying cultural framework of values and beliefs.

If by definition the "deep culture" is out of awareness, how can we help our students access it? In the illustration of the iceberg model of culture, a fish is seen swimming next to the iceberg (and a diving bird is flying above). The fish is there to remind the intercultural trainer to remark to the audience, "If you want to know what water is, don't ask a fish, for all it knows is water;" of course the bird knows both air and water, and this leads to a discussion of the value of experiencing another culture in order to truly fathom one's own. It is through the ability to compare our own culture with others, that we can begin to hypothesize about the differences in an effort to understand them. As Mikhail Bakhtin has written:

> In the realm of culture, outsidedness is a most powerful factor in understanding. It is only in the eyes of another culture that a foreign culture reveals itself fully and profoundly. A meaning only reveals its depths once it has encountered and come into contact with another foreign meaning. They engage in a kind of dialogue which surmounts the closedness and one-sidedness of these particular meanings, these cultures. [16]

This principle is embodied in the National Standards as well, where the fourth C stands for "Comparisons," both in the realm of language and of culture; in the case of the latter, the goal is that students "recognize that cultures use different patterns of interaction and can apply this knowledge to their own culture."

---

[15] Vicki B. Galloway, "Toward a Cultural Reading of Authentic Texts" in H. Byrnes, ed., *Languages for a Multicultural World in Transition.* Reports of the Northeast Conference on the Teaching of Foreign Languages (Lincolnwood, IL: National Texbook Company, 1992), 88.

[16] Bakhtin as quoted in Bauer, and Lynne deBenedette, Gilberte Furstenberg, Sabine Levet, Shoggy Waryn, "The *Cultura* Project" in. Julie A. Belz and Steven L. Thorne eds. *Internet-mediated Intercultural Foreign Language Education* (Boston, MA: Thomson Heinle, 2006), 34.

In the past, experiential learning of another culture was in large part reserved for students studying abroad, and the development of intercultural awareness still remains one of the primary reasons for students to study in the target culture. With the advent of new technologies such as Internet, email, chats, videoconferencing, Skype, however, it is now possible to create that direct contact between members of different cultures through virtual means. We are now in the second decade of internet-mediated learning and it is not surprising that a plethora of projects have developed to bridge the geographical distances, allowing learners from different backgrounds to learn from each other. Many of these projects have involved tandem exchanges with students matched one-on-one for written interaction with the goal of linguistic improvement.

However, the emphasis on intercultural learning in these exchanges has grown to the extent that J. Belz and S. Thorne have developed a new acronym, ICFLE (Intercultural Foreign Language Education) to designate cases where "interaction with members of the studied culture forms the leading classroom activity."[17]

The most elaborated model for internet-mediated intercultural learning, and certainly the most venerable one, having begun in 1997, is the *Cultura* Project in French which was developed at MIT.[18] It was the direct inspiration for the *Confronti*[19] curriculum in addition to having spawned versions in Spanish and Russian. Here the exchange is class-to-class. A distinct advantage of the forum-based model is that it provides access to a greater variety of viewpoints, and breaks down the notion of the target culture being a homogeneous bloc. Students on either side can express disagreement among themselves, and it becomes evident to those on the other side that any "national" culture is composed of many sub-cultures.[20]

---

[17] Julie A. Belz, and Steven L. Thorne, eds. 2006, *Internet-mediated Intercultural Foreign Language Education* (Boston, MA: Thomson Heinle 2006), ix-x.

[18] Gilberte Furstenberg, Sabine Levet, Kathryn English, and Katherine Maillet, "Giving a virtual voice to the silent language of culture: The Culture Project," *Language Learning & Technology* 5 no.1 (2001): 55-102. See also the Cultura site at http://web.mit.edu/french/culturaNEH/

[19] Fans of Beppe Severgnini's journalistic intercultural explorations in the *Corriere della sera* will recognize in our project name the title of one of his many books, *Confronti* (1996). We would like to thank him wholeheartedly for allowing us to use this title for our project.

[20] Beth Bauer, Lynne deBenedette, Gilberte Furstenberg, and Sabine Levet, Shoggy Waryn, "The Cultura Project," in *Internet-mediated Intercultural Foreign Language Education*, eds. Julie A. Belz and Steven L. Thorne (Boston, MA: Thomson Heinle, 2006), 34.

The *Cultura* model consciously follows a constructivist approach[21] in which the teacher is no longer a font of knowledge; instead, students are encouraged to go through a process of cultural exploration and discovery.

The *Confronti* project

The *Confronti* project is based on the *Cultura* model, it offers web-enhanced intercultural exchanges, carried out through a website, specifically created by the University of Pennsylvania (See Figure 8-1 http://ccat.sas.upenn.edu/italian/index.html). Students of English from Italian high schools and universities, and American students of Italian access the *Confronti* project online and collaboratively construct their knowledge.

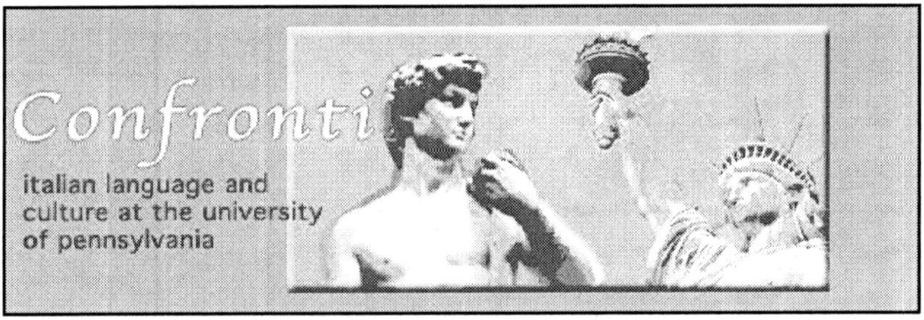

Figure 8-1. The *Confronti* webpage.

The *Confronti* website consists of three sections, which allow students to respond to questionnaires, compare their answers, and engage in forum discussions. After groups of Italian and American students have been paired up, they fill out the questionnaires provided in the website: Stereotypes Italy, Stereotypes USA, Word Associations, Sentence Completion, and Situation Reactions. Figure 8-2 shows excerpts from a questionnaire sample page:

[21] Dorit Kaufman, "Constructivist Issues in Language Learning and Teaching," *Annual Review of Applied Linguistics* 24 (2004): 303–19.

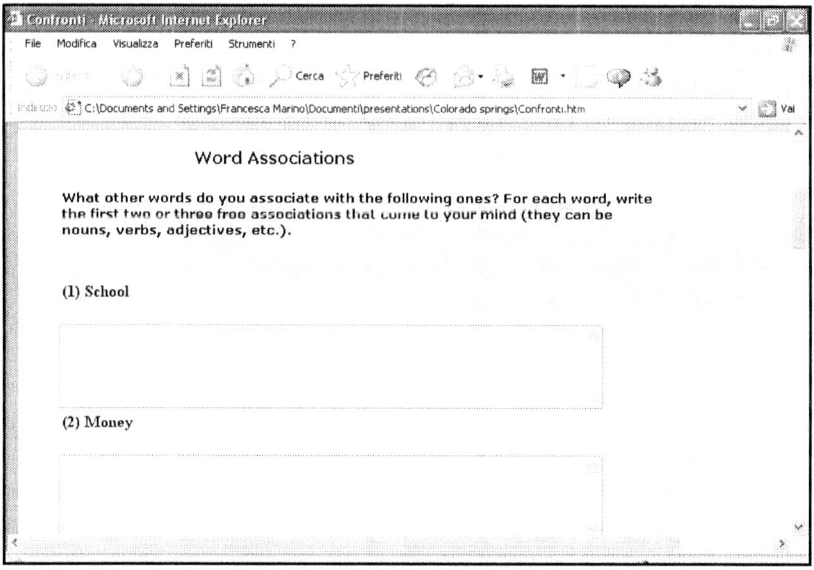

Figure 8-2. The Word Association Questionnaire.

The questionnaires are designed to provide comparative data for the students to analyze and interpret. The data generated from the questionnaires can be viewed on a single web page for each questionnaire, in a side-by side format. The View and Compare pages provide data for class discussions in which students use the answers as linguistic materials, inputs for the analysis of specific cultural topics, pre-reading activities, raw data for the building of charts and other meaningful activities (see Figures 8-3 and 8-4).

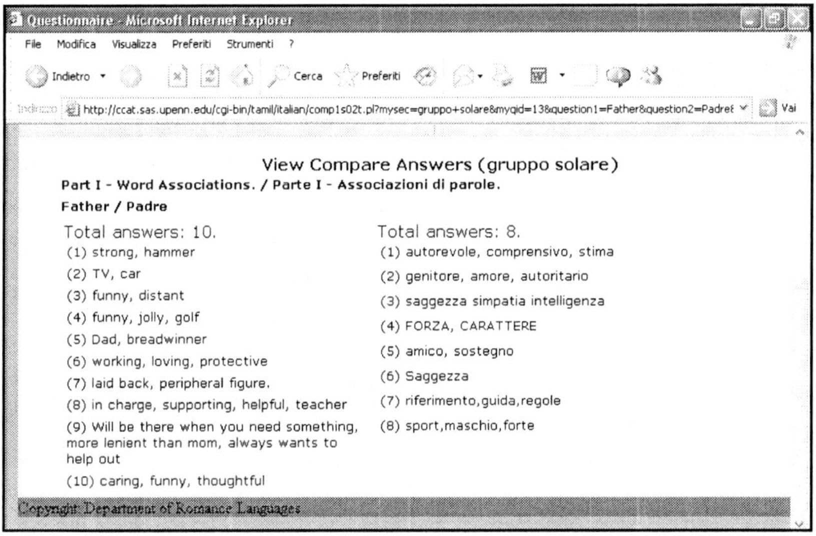

Figure 8-3. Word Association answers on Father/Padre in the View and Compare pages.

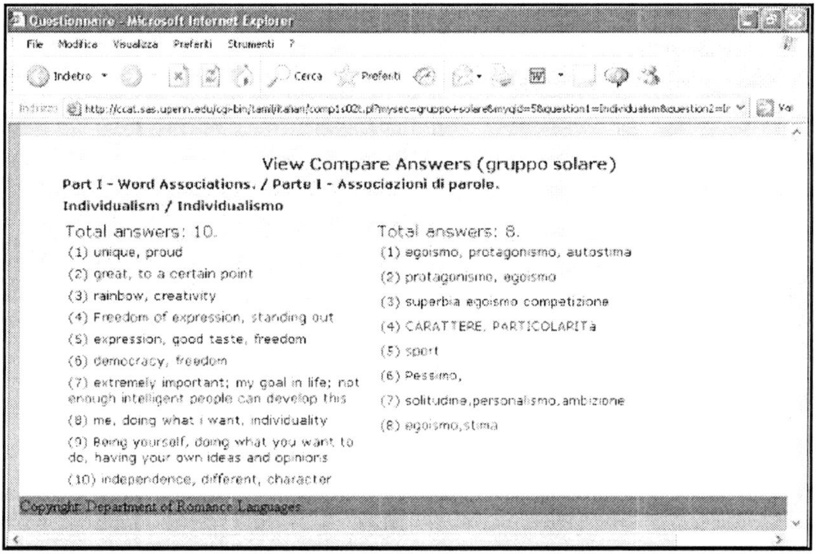

Figure 8-4. Word Association answers on Individualism/Individualismo in the View and Compare pages.

In the last section of the *Confronti* website, students engage in asynchronous forum exchanges with their international counterparts about issues which emerge from discussion of the *Confronti* data or of other materials that they have read, listened to, seen, or analyzed in conjunction with the information elicited in the View and Compare pages. In this project, the students on one side are supposed to turn to those on the other side for help in understanding or clarifying questions about intercultural similarities and differences. Ideally the forum functions as a place where students are able to express their interest, their puzzlement, their curiosity, their hypotheses about the other culture and where through an exchange of views the students on both sides arrive at a better understanding of not only the other culture, but also their own (see Table 8-1).

Forum: Part I - Association of words / Parte I - Associazioni di parole
Subject: Individualism/Individualismo
5 responses (gruppo solare)

(1) Hi,
While reading your responses to the word association for individualism, we wondered how the political climate in Padova compares to the rest of Italy. We feel that Middlebury is more liberal than the rest of America. This would mean that our answers may not be representative of all Americans' opinions. Therefore we wanted to know if there is a similar situation between Padova and Italy. Do you think your answers are representative of all of Italy?
Your friends,
XXXXXXXXXXXXXX
(Email:XXXXX@middlebury.edu, Nationality:USA)

(2) Hi all,
Noah and I were wondering about your responses to the word individualism. We found that you had negative associations with the word, that you often often gave it a connotation of ego. We thought this was interesting because it has a very different connotation for us. We feel that for Americans individualism is viewed as a positive thing because of a common history that has placed an emphasis on the necessity for individual initiative. We were wondering how your culture/history has influenced your views of individualism. Thanks
-XXXXXXXX
(Email:XXXXXX@middlebury.edu, Nationality:USA)

3) Ciao amici,
credo che Padova sia rappresentativa della situazione italiana in generale. Infatti, dal punto di vista degli studenti universitari,si notano differenti orientamenti politici anche a seconda della facoltà a cui appartengono. Analizzando invece la

cittadinanza di Padova notiamo la prevalenza dell'orientamento conservatore. Sabato scorso Padova è stata, come esempio attuale, la sede di 4 diverse manifestazioni. I neofascisti, il corteo del collettivo antifascista degli studenti di scienze politiche, i disobbedienti e anarchici dei centri sociali occupati.
Nelle altre città italiane si presentano situazioni simili, soprattutto le città nelle quali ci sono le università. Per esempio, a differenza di Padova, Bologna è una città storicamente di sinistra sia da parte della cittadinanza che dal popolo studentesco.
Di conseguenza potete capire che viviamo in un contesto nel quale c'è la prevalenza di un solo orientamento, cosa che favorisce il pluralismo. Questo può anche spiegare il grande numero di partiti esistenti in Italia, a differenza di altri paesi europei.
Esistono diversi orientamenti politici anche nelle vostre università? è grande la percentuale di studenti che s'interessa attivamente alla formazione politica (per esempio partecipando a corsi o gruppi politici)?
Grazie e a presto!
XXXXXXXX
(Email:XXXXXX@gmail.com, Nationality: ITALY)

Table 8-1. Forum discussion of Word Association answers on Individualism/Individualismo.

The language used in the three sections of the *Confronti* website is the native language of the students (or to be more specific, the language spoken in the country where students live). This prevents unavoidable linguistic discrepancies in the target language from becoming too obvious and creates necessary parity between the users. The language used outside the *Confronti* website (namely during class-time, for homework, papers, etc.) has always been the target language.

When students have questions on the View and Compare data, rather than responding with his or her own hypothesis about the answer, the *Confronti* instructor encourages the students to speculate, asks them to work collaboratively to explore why they may have found a certain answer strange or bizarre, and then directs them to the forum to engage in a direct dialogue. This project, thus, calls for a somewhat different pedagogical role for the instructor than many of us are used to. Instead of being the immediate authority and conveyor of knowledge, we are rather in the role of advisor and guide, helping our students through a process of exploration and discovery where the process of inquiry is as important—and perhaps even more important—than the actual outcome or answer.

Confronti hinges upon the underlying principle of intercultural communication and the activities carried out online are at the core of the curriculum; however, *Confronti* is not simply a web project, and the learning process does not happen on the web alone. A great deal of the work is done in the classroom. *Confronti* is in fact a multifold curriculum that reflects several approaches and methods. It provides students with an ample selection of materials, spanning from Italian literature to statistics. These materials and the related activities are associated to a meaningful context.[22] *Confronti* is content—and context-based for its emphasis on cultural topics, and includes the "focus on form" method for language accuracy.[23] Furthermore, the work carried out in *Confronti* requires a great deal of collaboration among students, whose learning process is boosted by a series of concrete tasks performed inside or outside the class.[24]

Although the core curriculum remains the same for its focus on intercultural matters, *Confronti* does not require the two partners involved to share the same content and program, therefore the American and Italian partners developed their own syllabi in order to respond to the universities' specific needs and demands. However they have often shared readings, video clips, and other materials, in Italian or in English, that students then discussed in the forum boards.

For five years from 2000 up to 2004, *Confronti* established cross-cultural exchanges through asynchronous forums and videoconferences between the University of Pennsylvania and various Italian institutions, among which the most active were the University of Padova and the Bocconi University of Milan. In 2006, then, Middlebury College and Padova University adopted the project and developed it further using up-to-date technology, which allowed synchronous conversations through Skype. In accordance with the original spirit of *Confronti*, this article describes both the case studies of the University of Pennsylvania and Middlebury College vis-à-vis the Italian experience of the University of Padova (see Table 8-2).

---

[22] For the importance of context and culture in language teaching and learning, see Claire Kramsch, *Context and Culture in Language Teaching* (Oxford: Oxford University Press, 1993) and "Language and Culture: A Social Semiotic Perspective." *ADFL Bulletin* 33, no.2 (2002): 8-15.

[23] Catherine Doughty, "Acquiring Competence in a Second Language: Form and Function." in *Learning Foreign and Second Languages,* ed. Heidi Byrnes, (New York: Modern Language Association of America, 1998), 128-56.

[24] With regard the role of task in Foreign Language Teaching see Heidi Byrnes, "The Role of Task and Task-based Assessment in a Content-oriented Collegiate Foreign Language Curriculum." *Language Testing* 19, no.4 (2002): 419-37.

University of Pennsylvania 2000-2004	University of Padova, Italy 2002-2004	Middlebury College Fall 2006	University of Padova, Italy Fall 2006
Intermediate: third and forth semester of Italian at Upenn (103 and 104)	2nd year English for students majoring in Modern Languages.	Intermediate: third semester of Italian at Middlebury College (250)	1st year English Language for students at Faculty of Political Science.
Research institution. Language requirement enforced, students need to take 4 semesters of (or have equivalent competence in) a foreign language.	Students have to take English exams for all 3 years of degree course.	Liberal Arts College. Emphasis in foreign languages at the College level. No language requirement. Most students major in foreign languages.	English is a course requirement for degree courses in Political Science.
Course objectives: Develop intercultural awareness. Focus on communicative skills in the modal framework of the National Standards (interpersonal, interpretative, and presentational).	Course objectives: to reach level B2 (Common European Framework of Reference CEFR) in reading, writing, listening, spoken production and interaction, also to develop intercultural awareness.	Course objectives: Develop intercultural awareness. Focus on communicative skills in the modal framework of the National Standards (interpersonal, interpretative, and presentational).	Course objectives: to reach level B1 of Common European Framework for reading skills only.
4/6 classes for each semester, from 2000 to 2004. No. of students enrolled in each class: 10 to18. Compulsory attendance.	No. of students enrolled in course: c.100, divided into 4 classes of 25..	3 classes of 9 to15 students each in fall 2006. Compulsory attendance.	No. of students enrolled in courses: 200. About 40 regularly attending students.

The course is mandatory either to complete the language requirement or to proceed to the upper division courses (third and fourth year)	Exams are mandatory, attendance is not compulsory.	The course is mandatory to proceed to the upper division courses (third and fourth year)	Exams are mandatory, attendance is not compulsory.
Frequent quizzes (weekly or biweekly) and term texts at the end of each Module. No final exam. Final project.	Continuous assessment in place of part of exam to encourage attendance. To be eligible students must complete all tasks set. Students also have to take part of final exam.	Frequent quizzes (weekly). No final exam. Final project.	Presentation about an issue related to *Confronti* instead of 10-minute oral exam based on course reader. Students were required to commit to *Confronti* project for whole duration.
Number of contact hours per week: 3, in a smart classroom.	No. of contact hours per week: 5. 2 of these hours in multimedia laboratory for *Confronti* project.	Number of contact hours per week: 3, in a smart classroom.	No. of contact hours per week: 5. 2 of these hours in multimedia laboratory for *Confronti* project.
Instructors: courses held by lecturers, and graduate students. The instructors met weekly to discuss teaching strategies, set short terms goal, design tests and quizzes, and plan tasks and the final project	Same instructor for all groups.	Instructors: course held by lecturers, and professors. They met weekly to discuss teaching strategy, select texts, set short term goals, and identify specific language points for practice	Same instructor for all groups.

Table 8-2. *Confronti* partnerships described in this paper.

The American Side

The American *Confronti* curriculum is organized into six modules: I Stereotypes, II Family, III School, IV Private and Public Spaces, V Regionalism, VI Immigration and Emigration. These modules are identified to be carried out in the time frame of two semesters, and are aimed to guide students to investigate the target culture through various media and materials (articles, literature excerpts, video and audio clips,) while making a comparison with their own culture. Grammar accuracy is deductively built up through exercises based on various readings and on the authentic language used by the Italian partners in their questionnaire answers and in the forums. In addition, students practice specific grammar topics based on their performance, communicative needs, and errors ("focus on form" approach). As mentioned above, the *Confronti* curriculum has been designed within the framework of the Five Cs of the National Standards: Communication, Cultures, Connections, Comparisons and Communities. In particular, it emphasizes the following areas of the content standards, objectives included in levels 1 and 3: "Present information, concepts, and ideas to an audience of listeners or readers on a variety of topics" (Communication, Standard 1.3); "Demonstrate an understanding of the relationship between the products and the perspectives of the culture studied" (Cultures, Standard 2.2); "Acquire information and recognize the distinctive viewpoints that are only available through the foreign language" (Connections, Standard 3.2); "Demonstrate understanding of the concept of culture through comparisons of the culture studied and their own" (Comparisons, Standard 4.2); and use "the language both within and beyond the school setting" (Communities, Standard 5.1).[25]

With these goals in mind, both at the University of Pennsylvania and at Middlebury College *Confronti* was adopted in the intermediate Italian courses (see Table 8-2 for details). Although they were quite similar in their agenda, the experiences at the University of Pennsylvania and Middlebury College differed to some extent and reached different results in meeting the standards, especially considering their diverse contexts and the unequal focus on the foreign language within the academic community (see Table 8-2).

At the University of Pennsylvania, in the years 2000-2004, most of the intermediate sections and instructors were involved in experimenting the new *Confronti* curriculum. The Italian partners involved in the early phase

---

[25] *Standards*, 4.

were different for each class, consisting mainly of universities and high schools in northern and central Italy (Padova, Perugia). Other Italian individuals not affiliated to any school or university discovered the *Confronti* questionnaires and forums online and asked to join the project. The additional category of Italian "participants at large" was created to include this group. Despite these dissimilarities class activities would typically follow the same six-module sequence, all classes were conducted entirely in Italian, and learners were required to use only the target language, except in their initial questionnaires and forum contributions.

At the beginning of the semester both Italian and American students responded to the *Confronti* questionnaires on cultural issues, which remained on-line as reference material throughout the semester. Instructors then presented students with a text to analyze, that could be a piece of literature, a visual or audio text, or even data from major research agencies' reports (such as ISTAT). A meaningful example from the first module (Stereotypes) is the unit on "Women and Men," where the American and Italian students compared their views on masculine and feminine images, roles, and perceptions. The variety of the material allowed students to meet with different textual genres, used as starting points for building and exercising grammar accuracy (form), while at the same time posing questions on a specific cultural issue in line with the Module investigated (content). Subsequently learners were asked to view and compare the *Confronti* data on the same issue. At that point, the instructors, coherently with their role of cultural mediators rather than of experts who offered answers, used class time for discussions with students who were then guided to pose their queries or points of view on the online forums, opening the dialogue to their Italian partners.

During Module II (Family) for example, learners were presented with the challenge of comparing how the media portray women and men. To this aim students analyzed various advertisements from Italian magazines through guided questions, that made them consider the target public, the product advertised, and the object of the advertisement. Figure 8-5 shows a sample of the ads used with the guided questions provided in Table 8-3:

Figure 8-5. Sample of ads.

Lavoro sul testo
Qual è il prodotto di questa pubblicità? Quali immagini vedi in questa pubblicità? Come sono disposte queste immagini? Che cosa suggeriscono la posizione e la grandezza delle immagini? Che relazione c'è tra prodotto e destinatario? A chi si rivolge la pubblicità, secondo te? Confronta questa pubblicità con le altre mostrate in classe: si rivolgono tutte allo stesso destinatario? Qual è il messaggio trasmesso dalla pubblicità? Es. : "Se compri questo prodotto...." (continua tu!)
Progetti
1. Crea una pubblicità usando ingredienti simili. Dovrai spiegare alla classe la logica usata. 2. Trova delle pubblicità americane di prodotti simili e analizza le differenze e le analogie fra le pubblicità italiane e quelle americane.

Table 8-3. Guided Questions.

The instructor's main goal was to guide the students to develop their own points of view, without supporting any previously formed opinions. Class activities then expanded the analysis to American advertisements of men which students brought to class and students' first hand experiences. This prepared learners to further investigate the *Confronti* data on the same subject, "American Men and Italian Men," through questions which asked them to identify differences and similarities in the answers, looking for similar words or adjectives thus expanding their vocabulary ("Leggi bene le risposte italiane, e cerca le parole che non conosci sul dizionario. Poi cerca tra le risposte in inglese i sinonimi degli aggettivi usati dagli italiani: c'è qualche cosa che non compare? Quali aggettivi compaiono più frequentemente nella parte in italiano e quali nella parte in inglese? C'è qualcosa che non capisci? C'è qualcosa che ti incuriosisce e che vorresti chiedere agli italiani?").

After this analysis, students would be then ready to engage first in small group discussions, and then larger class discussions. These have always proved to be the most interesting and stimulating for students, who by that time have the grammar, vocabulary and cultural proficiency to fully support their points of view. By this point it was the students themselves who wanted to post their reflections and ask Italians for explanations on puzzling points through the "*Confronti*" forum. The forums in this section were particularly meaningful and showed a high level of sophistication. Table 8-4 reports an example from the forum section, where students discuss the role of the father in Italian and American societies, emphasizing the different contexts and perceptions:

Forum: Part I - Association of words / Parte I - Associazioni di parole **Subject: Father/Padre** **4 responses** (gruppo solare)
(1) We noticed a difference in the responses in the word associations about fathers. The American idea of a father seems to be more funny, jolly, laid-back, and thoughtful, while the Italian ideas associated with fathers seems more authoritative, strong, more associated with rules and leadership. Does this seem like a fair assessment? Is an Italian father thought of more as the leader, the foundation for the father, the one who makes the rules? There also seem to be some similar ideas of the father between the two sets of responses - in both cases there seems to be some feeling of fathers as the "breadwinner" of the family. (Email:XXXXXXX@middlebury.edu, Nationality: USA on: 24-OCT-06) (2) Anche secondo il mio punto di vista in Italia la figura del genitore (padre) è quella di un uomo autoritario, anche se per certi aspetti questa descrizione non corrisponde più ai genitori dei tempi "moderni". Nel passato (mi riferisco ai miei nonni) ho intuito una certa forma di rispetto assoluto nei confronti del padre, questo rispetto veniva accentuato in molti casi dal "lei" che si dava al padre quando ci si rivolgeva a lui. In molti casi le madri che godevano di poca emancipazione nella società assumevano una (sic) posizione pesantemente subordinata a quella del marito. Tutto ciò contribuisce a formare la figura del padre autoritario che lavorando in molti casi fuori casa contribuiva a guadagnare i soldi per il pane quotidiano (sic). Nella società attuale la situazione è mutata, la figura della donna oggi assume posizioni decisamente più elevate ed è meno legata alla figura del marito. Il matrimonio è ormai un rituale che diminuisce con il passare degli anni, quindi è anche inappropriato parlare di marito e moglie. Il trend della nostra società è quello di una convivenza in cui i conviventi sono sullo stesso piano lavorativo, votati entrambi alla carriera nel mondo dell'occupazione a discapito di uan diversità che permetta la crescita dei figli, cosa che avviene in età sempre più avanzata rispetto a qualche decennio fa. (Email:XXXXXXXX@gmail.com, Nationality: ITALY on: 03-NOV-06) (3) Ciao!Riguardo le associazioni di parole, esse ci hanno dato la possibilità di far emergere quali sono gli stereotopi che abbiamo rispetto alla figura del padre. Analizzando le risposte sembra evidente che americani e italiani vedono per lo più diversamente la figura paterna. Questo a mio avviso è dovuto alla storia, al cinema, alla letteratura, all'arte che ci hanno offerto per molto tempo l'immagine di una famiglia patriarcale. Ora, nonostante i rapporti siano cambiati e siano in continua evoluzione grazie all'emancipazione della donna, al progresso e ad altri fattori permane l'idea del padre autoritario e forte. Sono anche dell'idea però, che la diversa concezione del padre sia data anche dal diverso rapporto che ognuno di noi instaura con lui. Concludo dicendo che se noi attribuiamo degli aggettivi a padre pensando alla nostra relazione con lui e non all'idea generale che se ne ha nel

proprio paese, possano emergere delle opinioni più veritiere e non stereotipate che metterebbero italiani e americani d'accordo.
(Email:XXXXXXXX@yahoo.it, Nationality: ITALY on: 03-NOV-06)

Table 8-4. Forum.

Confronti revealed itself to be a success amongst students, boosted their interest in the language and culture, enriched their social perspective of Italy. Their enthusiasm for Italian culture and their newly found understanding of it, explicitly come to light in their class evaluations. As one student says:

> "I enjoyed the readings in class, especially the discussions that follow because they help in my understanding of the material. It is also nice to connect the stories to our own experiences of Italian culture."

Another underlines: "Approaching material in various ways (discussion, *Confronti*, readings etc.) gives me a more complete understanding of Italian culture."[26]

The ultimate success of the curriculum was reflected in the high student participation in the various activities proposed outside the classroom. At the end of every semester, despite some technical difficulties, it was in fact possible to hold videoconferences with the Italian partners, where numerous students engaged in face to face dialogue with their friends overseas. Furthermore, the University of Pennsylvania, in collaboration with the Center for Italian Studies and the Italian Consulate, organized two conferences, in January 2001 and April 2003, with the journalist Beppe Severgnini, author of several texts on Italian vis-a-vis American culture that were used as class material for analysis and discussion. Students' participation in these activities was remarkably active: the author heightened their enthusiasm in the language and culture, while addressing and discussing with them the same issues they had focused on in class. At that point students were not only prepared to discuss them, but also eager to debate using their own knowledge.

These conferences proved to be the perfect place for assessing the students' achievements in the Standard 5.1, Communities. On these occasions learners successfully "used the language both within and beyond

[26] Students' comments from Midterm class evaluations for Ital 130 F 2002 (Instructor Silvia Carlorosi).

the school settings."[27] The same result was achieved also thanks to a final project, which required them to connect with the community of Italians recently moved to the States, and Italian-Americans in Philadelphia. Students were asked to look for immigrants, analyze their original geographical location, interview them, draw their personal story, comment on it and interact with them. Everyone tackled the assignment enthusiastically and with dedication, since at that point of the year they were intellectually ready to encounter and communicate with a representative of their target culture who had also personally confronted the same cultural and social issues analyzed in class. Furthermore, the multicultural environment of the students' identities, their personal views of and experiences with immigration made the topic especially attractive to them. Their final projects proved not only original in form (many shot videos, included images, authentic documents etc.), rich in information, but also touched abstract problems that interested students personally. Most of them were interested in knowing the reaction of the community to their expectations and problems adapting to the American culture, as they asked questions in the line of: "Hai avuto dei problemi ad integrarti nella cultura americana?" "Quali erano le tue aspettative e si sono avverate?"

All the students' final projects have been presented to the school community as well as to the Italian-American community of Philadelphia, which includes some of the people they had actually interviewed. Learners introduced clearly their projects in public, explaining their abstract and sometimes complex ideas on cultural integration, and successfully communicated with a heterogeneous audience, which included their student peers, teachers, Italians abroad, and Italian-Americans, thus demonstrating the ability to "present information, concepts, and ideas in Italian to an audience of listeners or readers on a variety of topics" as Standard 1.3, Communication states.[28] By the same token, during the entire academic year, learners showed evidence of being able to "understand and interpret written and spoken language on a variety of topics" (Communication, Standard 1.2) as they have been exposed to a variety of texts, literary, analytical, and visual, whose comprehension was assessed through questionnaires, quizzes, and tests.[29] During class discussions and in the assigned compositions of various typologies (narrative, creative, and argumentative writing) they could reassess their understanding of the topics examined and express informed opinions.

---

[27] *Standards*, 4.
[28] Ibid.
[29] Ibid.

Various class activities during the year also helped to assess the achievements of the goals set in Cultures and Connections's Standards. Students demonstrated evidence of understanding "the relationship between the products and perspectives of the culture studied" (Culture, Standard 2.2) specifically in forums and class discussions.[30] For instance, after analyzing the on-line answers of Italian students on "what symbolizes Italy," American students noted that none of their Italian partners had mentioned the Italian flag. On the contrary the "stars and stripes" flag was the most frequently cited symbol in the American students' answers to "what symbolizes America." This striking discrepancy urged the Americans to open a forum on how Italians perceived their nationality, which revealed to be one of the richest in social, cultural, and historical information exchanged by both parts. At their partners' requests, Italian students explained in detail how for them the flag is still a symbol loaded with political significance that dates back to the Fascist era (see Table 8-5).

Forum: Part 1 - Impressions-USA / Impressioni-USA Subject (6) Is/are there any thing(s) which symbolize Italy for you? / Qual è l'oggetto che secondo te rappresenta l'America di oggi? 3 responses (gruppo solare)
(1) Perché pochi di voi hanno indicato la Statua della Libertà come oggetto che rappresenta l'America? Non è per voi rappresentativa come lo sembra a noi? XXXXXXXX, XXXXXXXX (2) That is a good question that I do not think I will have a good enough answer to, but I am going to respond anyway. The Statue of Liberty was of much importance during the immigration period in which mostly everyone from Europe came through New York, which is where the statue is located. So, basically, we have moved on. I think the object that most people usually think of when they think "America" is the flag. It is the one thing of America that remains constant in our ever evolving society. (Email:XXXXXX@upenn.edu, Nationality: USA) (3) Per noi Italiani la bandiera italiana non è molto significativa come per voi,f orse perchè essa viene associata a Mussolini e al Fascismo e soprattutto al

[30] Ibid.

Nazismo che rappresenta un'epoca in cui vennero uccise molte persone ingiustamente.L'Italia dal nostro punto di vista viene meglio rappresentata dal Colosseo, Roma e altri luoghi e monumenti famosi. XXXXXXXX & XXXXXXXX

Table 8-5. Forum.

Forums, questionnaires, and class discussions, also proved to be the best place to assess learners' achievement on Connections, (Standard 3.2). Through the various materials presented in class or available on line on the *Confronti* website, students were able to "acquire information" and during their analyses and class discussions to "recognize the distinctive viewpoints that are only available through the foreign language and its cultures."[31] However, a distinctive place where students could prove their achievement was during the video conferences with their Italian friends. This was the best place for them to ask specific practical questions on their institutions and routines, but also engage in more abstract inquiries on their school systems, educational habits and activities. As mentioned before, video conferences proved to be an ideal tool to boost students' enthusiasm, allowing them to visually meet their friends, thus creating a closer connection with them.

Similar class and out-of-class activities were used to train students to be able to "understand the concept of culture through comparisons of the culture studied and their own" (Comparisons, Standards 4.2).[32] Learners compared and contrasted political, social and educational issues in Italy and in their own country, through the analyses and comparisons of various literary, audio and visual texts. A specific activity on immigration and emigration proved to be particularly valuable for this scope. In order to show the students the different attitudes towards immigration that Italians have, namely the striking separation between who is in favor and who is against it, students confronted with various materials, and specifically read an article that emphasized the paradox that Italy is living these days: Italians seem to be strongly against illegal immigration, but on the other hand, they do not know how to welcome legal immigrants, because the political, social, and physical structures are not adequately equipped to

[31] Ibid.

[32] Ibid.

face this new phenomenon.[33] After pre-readings and at home activities aimed to activate students' schemata on the "immigration" topic and familiarize them with the vocabulary, they were ready to discuss the topic in class. This discussion, first in small groups, then as a class, was probably one that the students enjoyed most, and led to a more complex activity: a debate on immigration, with students formally taking positions for or against. In this context they were able to give their opinions, bring personal experiences in the discussion, while finding themselves actively involved in a debate without an official right answer, but which allowed them to argue according to their own personal positions. At the end of such a complex and structured lesson unit, students could give their informed opinions based not only on their personal experience, but also on previous readings. What made this class unit especially successful and formally productive was also their personal involvement and relation with the subject, thanks once more to the multicultural environment that exists in the community of the University of Pennsylvania, and to the fact many of the students are related to immigrants in the States.

In conclusion, we could assess that the level of students' achievement also depended on their own involvement, as well as the teachers on both ends, and the final results obtained by the different American classes involved in the project were somewhat uneven. The major cause for this was the lack of a unifying textbook that would serve as a structured guide for those instructors that depended more on such a teaching tool. Communication with other schools and universities, also, has not always been easy, and students and instructors on both sides experienced occasional difficulties interacting, not only because of the sometime uneven language level, but also because of the different communicative styles: on some occasions, the tone or the gist of their counterparts' comments in the forum discussions raised questions about "appropriateness" and "political correctness" among students and instructors. Such discussions, nevertheless, once more demonstrated the need to break cultural barriers at every level, and were used as learning opportunities for students, who could immediately comment and react in order to avoid misunderstandings. Furthermore, these exchanges were effectively used as first hand evidence of the need to avoid misunderstanding when training new instructors.

When moved to Middlebury College in the Fall of 2006, the *Confronti* curriculum was equally successful. Students achieved not only all the

---

[33] Piero Ostellino, "Immigrazione: Rigore nella civiltà: Clandestini No accoglienza sì" in *Corriere della sera*, March 20th 2000.

Standards set at the beginning, but even higher outcomes, particularly with regard to Standard 5.2, Communities, showing evidence of "becoming life-long learners by using the language for personal enjoyment and enrichment."[34] We argue that the different context, structure of the language program, and students' interests and profiles may have been the causes of this divergence in the attained goals. The University of Pennsylvania and Middlebury College are two different types of academic institutions. While the University of Pennsylvania is a top research institution, whose urban campus is set in the city of Philadelphia, Middlebury College is a prestigious liberal arts college that owes much of its worldwide recognition to its teaching of foreign languages with up-to-date pedagogic approaches and technology, and whose community of students and professors stands out for being an intimate, self sustaining one. Students who are admitted to the College community are usually interested in becoming proficient in more than just one foreign language. There is not a language requirement, but students enrolled in language courses do so for their own academic interest. They thus focus on language proficiency from day one and the whole College revolves around the importance of giving students opportunities to practice and be immersed in the foreign cultures and languages studied, with language houses, tables, events, films, conferences, and many other communal activities that bring students together, and make them feel part of a small community of their own, in close contact with their target language.

The classroom environment itself invites interactive learning, with computers and internet available for each student, in such a way that students can feel virtually part of the target culture community. Such a learning environment was ideal to develop *Confronti* and bring it to elevated levels, and building a real virtual community. Although the web site template (with the on line questions, view and compare and forums), the division in modules, and the typical lesson structure remained unchanged, students could take advantage of using new technologies that were intended to facilitate exchanges with Italy. Namely, Skype was introduced to make getting in touch with Italian partners easier and faster. Learners were given specific tasks, such as gathering data or information on students' living habits, and personal first hand opinions, while dealing with the Family Module, to then report to the class. Although the instructors could not exploit all the potential of this new form of synchronous communication, mainly since the Italian partners did not have the same facilitated internet access, introducing students to such a

[34] *Standards*. 4.

synchronous means for conversation led them to engage in spontaneous, meaningful conversations with their Italian partners. With or without a specific task to fulfill, some of the students had long and prolific conversations or chats, where they felt free to talk about anything, switching codes and even engaging in necessary practice of scaffolding to make the conversation flow and be comprehensible. The transcript from the Skype conversation shown in Table 8-6 is a clear example of such a spontaneous conversation:

[12/6/2006 5:57:35 PM] X says: hai viaggiato agli Stati Uniti?
[12/6/2006 5:57:50 PM] Z says: no mai purtroppo
[12/6/2006 5:58:02 PM] Z says: ma spero un giorno
[12/6/2006 5:58:03 PM] X says: ahh si
[12/6/2006 5:58:16 PM] Z says: com'è li la vita?
[12/6/2006 5:58:19 PM] X says: si, e un bel paese
[12/6/2006 5:58:32 PM] Z says: i ragazzi
[12/6/2006 5:58:36 PM] Z says: ?
[12/6/2006 5:58:39 PM] X says: la vita e' molto occupata per tutti, ogni giorno
[12/6/2006 5:59:01 PM] Z says: anche qui
[12/6/2006 5:59:05 PM] X says: i ragazzi sono diverenti e intelligenti e carini, in generale
[12/6/2006 5:59:11 PM] X says: ma non molto romantici
[12/6/2006 5:59:23 PM] Z says: abbiamo il primato
[12/6/2006 5:59:29 PM] X says: gli uomini italiani piacciono le donne americane?
[12/6/2006 5:59:53 PM] Z says: non ho capito
[12/6/2006 6:00:44 PM] X says: hmmm, gli uomini italiani vogliono incontrare o avere una relazione con le donne americane?
[12/6/2006 6:01:01 PM] Z says: tu mi chiedi se agli uomini it. piacciono le donne americ.?
[12/6/2006 6:01:07 PM] X says: si... agli
[12/6/2006 6:01:08 PM] Z says: si
[12/6/2006 6:01:28 PM] X says: scusi
[12/6/2006 6:01:38 PM] Z says: perdonata
[12/6/2006 6:01:43 PM] X says: si, ho detto che il mio italiano non e' perfetto!

Table 8-6. Transcript from the Skype conversation.

Conversations like this demonstrated that the college community was genuinely interested in making connections with Italians, using Italian for their own personal fulfillment and enjoyment, thus aspiring to become a real virtual community across the ocean.

Furthermore, prolific class discussions and forums carried out through the semester, mirrored students' excellent results in both form and content: their outcomes increased as they reached the proposed standards enthusiastically. As their class evaluations testify, every single student underlined how, at the end of the class, they felt more confident in every aspect of language and culture "My Italian grammar improved greatly" a student writes, "as well as my understanding of Italian culture. I can definitely communicate much better."[35] The great majority of these students continued to study Italian culture and literature, many planned a semester or a year abroad, while their awareness of being a community grew stronger, and all of them considered crucial their involvement with the *Confronti* curriculum.

The Italian side

Padova University has been involved in the *Confronti* exchange since 2002, with 8 classes of undergraduate students majoring in Modern Languages communicating with students at Penn, and more recently (2006-2007) students from the Faculty of Political Science communicating with students at Middlebury.

The reference point for language curricula in most schools and universities in Italy is the Common European Framework of Reference for Languages: Learning, teaching, assessment (CEFR).[36] The impact of the CEFR in Europe has been enormous, particularly as regards language curricula and assessment, but unfortunately intercultural competence (IC) is given little prominence in this important document, as Guilherme [37] writes:

> it is implied in this document that the cultural component and the development of intercultural competence are part of 'general competences,' a background knowledge that the language user/learner is expected to possess/acquire but that may not be materialised in the foreign language classroom. As far as the critical dimension of foreign culture education is concerned, it is neither explicitly nor implicitly included in the document, not is it hindered or valorised.

---

[35] Final evaluations for Ital 250 sec. C (instructor Silvia Carlorosi).

[36] Council of Europe, *Common European Framework of Reference for Languages: Learning,Tteaching, Assessment* (Cambridge: Cambridge University Press, 2001).

[37] Manuela Guilherme, *Critical Citizens for an Intercultual World* (Clevedon: Multilingual Matters, 2002), 149.

A result of this is that IC has been omitted from many school and university language curricula. However the situation is beginning to change and with the increasingly important notion of democratic citizenship in Europe being promoted in recent years by the Council of Europe, the issue of IC in the CEFR is being raised once again.[38]

The model of intercultural communicative (ICC) competence which is most commonly found in European foreign language teaching contexts is Byram's model[39], also due to Byram's work with the Council of Europe. This model of ICC has five main components, or "savoirs" as Byram describes them and can be summarized as follows:

· Intercultural attitudes (savoir être)—curiosity and openness, readiness to suspend disbelief about other cultures and belief about one's own intercultural attitudes;
· Knowledge (savoirs)—of social groups and their products and practices in one's own and interlocutor's country;
· Skills of interpreting and relating (savoir comprendre): ability to interpret a document or event from another culture, to explain it and relate it to documents or events from one's own;
· Skills of discovery and interaction (savoir apprendre/faire): ability to acquire new knowledge of a culture and to operate this knowledge in real-time communication;
· Critical cultural awareness (savoir s'engager): an ability to evaluate, critically and on the basis of explicit criteria, perspectives, practices and products in one's own and other cultures and countries.

One of the main reasons for introducing the *Confronti* project to English language classes was the belief in the importance of developing learners' ICC both for their personal and also academic and professional development. The comparative approach offered by the *Confronti* project and the opportunities for direct interaction were seen to offer opportunities to develop all of Byram's savoirs.

Although the Italian students involved in *Confronti* were majoring in foreign languages, few had traveled abroad, and though they have the opportunity to spend a year abroad as part of the Erasmus program,[40] only a minority choose to do so as residence abroad is not a course requirement.

---

[38] Michael Byram, ed., *Intercultural Competence* (Strasbourg: Council of Europe, 2003).
[39] Michael Byram, *Teaching and Assessing Intercultural Communicative Competence* (Clevedon : Multilingual Matters, 1997).
[40] http://ec.europa.eu/education/programmes/llp/erasmus/erasmus_en.html

The *Confronti* exchange was therefore seen as an important opportunity for these students to have an intercultural exchange. But it would be mistaken to assume that an online intercultural exchange such as *Confronti* is merely a substitute for an experience abroad. On the contrary, it is an authentic intercultural experience of the kind our learners will increasingly experience in the internet-connected world they live and work in, hence the importance of acquiring skills for communicating in this fast-changing intercultural environment. Online communication comes in many forms and each form has its own culture of use. *Confronti* also offered the Italian learners, many of whom were much less technologically 'connected' than their American partners, the opportunity to learn to communicate through new media.

The Italian university context is very different from the American one, and language classes are no exception. *Confronti* was first introduced to second-year students enrolled in the three-year degree course *Lingue e Culture Moderne*. There were over 100 students in the second year of the course, but they were sub-divided into smaller groups, of about 25 students, for language classes. Attendance was not obligatory (as for most Italian university students), but students were offered 5 contact hours a week over two 10-week semesters. To encourage students to attend lessons regularly continuous assessment was introduced, whereby students who attended at least 80% of lessons could be assessed on work carried out during the semester instead of doing part of the second-year exam. The approach was "blended" with students having to do online work as well as attend lessons. Contact hours were divided between traditional classroom lessons and lessons using the multi-media language laboratories of the university language centre where students are introduced to, and work with the computer conferencing software which is used in language courses. At the end of second-year English students are expected to have reached level B2 (as defined in the CEFR) for the skills of reading, writing, speaking and listening, though this is often not the case.

Although the *Confronti* project does not require students to share the same curriculum, it is difficult for telecollaboration projects to work unless they are an integral part of the curriculum so it was decided to build part of the second year English syllabus around the *Confronti* project and the topics that were raised in discussions. Due to different semester dates the Italian students had little lead up time for the *Confronti* project so preparation of individual and group profiles was the first activity students were required to do, followed by completion of the Questionnaires. The data was then discussed in class, and learners were also given specific tasks to work on in groups related to the data and also on some of the materials the American students also used, as well as readings related to intercultural communication and the development of intercultural competence. While almost all of the students' written production on the *Confronti* site was in their own language, the oral and written production in class and in the lab was in English.

Learners were required to keep learning diaries throughout the semester. The reason for this was a belief in the importance of reflection for the development of intercultural competence and awareness, it is not sufficient for learners to simply interact, they also need the opportunity to reflect, as Little writes "the components of intercultural competence may well be opaque in the absence of reflected intercultural experience."[41]

Each week students in Padova had to send their reflections on the exchange and their learning to a conference in *FirstClass* (the conferencing software used). At times students were given specific prompts to help focus their reflections, some of these were taken from the European Language Portfolio,[42] for instance reflecting on previous intercultural experiences, or on the relationship between language and culture, but they were free at all times to also write about anything else they wanted. The diaries were not assessed for content, but at the end of the semester students were required to hand in either a summary of their diaries, or all of their weekly diaries. The diaries also provided valuable feedback for the instructor on how the exchange was progressing in the students' eyes, and allowed any necessary adjustments to be made.

The learners took great care over their diaries, both the appearance and the content, with learners writing an average of 1,000 words. Looking back over their diaries before handing them in for assessment made learners aware of the progress they had made and the changes in attitude they experienced. Several students reported increased intercultural awareness and a desire to continue this type of experience, as these quotes from students illustrate:

> The *Confronti* Project has been very interesting and useful. I have learned a lot from this experience : to be careful when we deal with something we don't know , because we can create wrong opinions and most of all we can wrongly trust on stereotypes and cliches!!

---

[41] David Little and Barbara Simpson. *European Language Portfolio, The intercultural component and Learning how to learn* (Strasbourg: Council of Europe Language Policy Division, 2003).

[42] Council of Europe, Language Policy Division. European Language Portfolio. http://www.coe.int/t/dg4/portfolio/Default.asp?L=E&M=/main_pages/welcome.html

> Concluding, I really feel it is a pity we probably won't have the chance to experience such a thing again, but I hope we will keep in contact with the American students on the forums and let this exchange continue somehow.

They appreciated the fact that they were not only learning a language with which to communicate but also a new medium which they saw as opening up new horizons and opportunities for them. As one student reported in her diary:

> This form of socialization helped me in the practice of computer....Perhaps it can be a stupid remark, but when you want to communicate something you should be able to use this interactive channel of communication... it was terrible!! But now I know how to send a message or to reply and open a link.

The *Confronti* exchange provided a great deal of authentic language for the students to process, and from the beginning of the project students began noting new vocabulary in their diaries, as this student's diary entry illustrates:

> I have learnt also some new words: "outgoing" that means friendly and sociable, "cunning" that means astuteness, shrewdness and other expressions like "laid-back people" and "encased in a protective bubble".

The diaries have also proved a valuable source of evidence of the development of aspects of intercultural competence, particularly the 'less visible' components such as attitude and critical cultural awareness.[43]

The Padova students also had to write an intercultural report, which counted towards their final assessment. In this report they were required to research in more detail an issue from an intercultural viewpoint, comparing Italian and American perspectives on this issue. They were to use data from the *Confronti* forums and also the video conferences that were held, but they also had to look at other resources such as ISTAT or Eurostat, which provided a broader perspective than just that of their partner groups. Report titles created by the students included: Attitudes to cheating; Underage drinking; Italian and American Lifestyles; Living at home; Immigration.

The video conferences proved to be perhaps the most motivating part of the exchange for many of the learners in Padova. Being able to see their

---

[43] Francesca Helm, "Language and culture in an online context: What can learner diaries tell us about intercultural competence?" in *Language and Intercultural Communication.* (forthcoming).

American peers (see Fig. 6) and talk to them, exchange opinions and even share jokes with them was a valuable experience as this learner reported "This week has begun amazingly! We've speaken to Penn Students and for the first time I've seen their faces and listened to their voices."

Figure 8-6. An American student waves at Italian students during a video conference.

The experience in 2006-7 with students of English in the Faculty of Political Science was quite a different experience from that with students graduating in *Lingue e Culture Moderne*. First of all there was the issue of number of students—there were nearly 200 students enrolled for the course and it was not until lessons actually started that it was actually clear how many students were going to attend the course. *Confronti* was an optional component of the course, which students could choose to become involved in and gain credits for. Those who wanted to become involved had to commit themselves to attend the 2-hour weekly lessons which were dedicated to the project for the whole semester and had to prepare a presentation for their end of course evaluation.

About 40 students decided to become involved and these were split into three groups and had exchanges with three different classes at Middlebury. The students at Padova were very different from the Middlebury students: many of them were mature, working students; their level was English was from beginner to pre-intermediate and few of them felt comfortable with technology. Despite these differences the exchanges were fairly successful, with some interaction in the forums, though perhaps not as much as the students would have liked, some students engaging in chat sessions outside lesson times and a group video-conference in Skype.

Nuts and bolts

The *Confronti* project and the opportunities for communication offered by new technologies led to many successful outcomes on both sides of the Ocean. These outcomes included enhanced student motivation, perceived success in language learning, increased intercultural awareness, interest in other cultures, and, particularly for many students in Padova, a greater degree of computer literacy.[44] Yet it would be dishonest to say that the project did not also have problems. Several issues emerged which we feel need to be taken into consideration when embarking on such projects if they are to be successful, otherwise there is the risk of losing students' interest and motivation and even reinforcing negative attitudes and stereotypes.[45]

On the Italian side, computer literacy is still an issue for some students, though these are increasingly a small minority, and special training should be provided for these students before the course starts. Access to Internet however is an issue for many students. Padova University does not have sufficient facilities to provide easy Internet access to all students, nor do student residences. Many students who were living at home had Internet access though in many cases this was not a high-speed connection; those who lived in student accommodation often did not have access. While we are writing, moreover, the Italian government is designing a new law which will require that all blogs be legally registered and will actually end up limiting the use of some telecollaborative tools. As a consequence of these legal matters, for instance, the University of Padova may remove Skype from the language laboratory computers.

Despite these difficulties however, in some partnerships the Italian students were more active in the exchanges than their American peers. This could have been due to the fact that the Italian students were given time during class to contribute to the forum while for the American students it was a homework activity. Another reason could be that the novelty of computer-mediated-communication was a motivating factor for

---

[44] Francesca Helm, "The integration of videoconferencing and online tools in a journey of cross-cultural understanding" in C. Taylor, C. Taylor Torsello, M. Gotti (eds) *I Centri Linguistici: approcci, progetti e strumenti per l'apprendimento e la valutazione* (Trieste, Academic Press, 2005), 515.

[45] Robert O'Dowd, "Understanding 'the other side': Intercultural learning in a Spanish-English e-mail exchange" *Language Learning and Technology* 7, no.2 (2003): 118-44.

many Italian students, while for the majority of American students it was not a novelty.

Another issue was that of literacies. Though some of the Italian students had experience of using e-mail, none of them had experience of discussion lists or forums and for some groups it was not easy to get the discussion going. Students needed guidance on how to take part effectively in e-mail exchanges and keeping discussion going, and once this was provided there seemed to be more interaction in the forums. Telecollaboration researchers, such as O'Dowd[46] have commented on the need for the teacher to take a more active role than that of 'guide on the side', for instance in the provision of guidelines for interpreting email messages from another culture as well as for writing effective messages. The *Confronti* developers, in fact, provide teachers with suggestions and advice to give students when participating in the forums. These, together with examples of effective and not so effective messages were found to be very helpful by the students and led to more fruitful discussions.

The fact that the academic calendars of American and Italian universities are quite different means that there is little time for exchanges and that they start the project at different stages of their courses. The Italian students jumped straight into the project and completed the questionnaires in the first lessons of the semester and had to explore topics as they arose while the American students had explored some of the topics before the exchange began and thus had a broader knowledge of certain issues than the Italian students. On the other hand, the Italian students had more time at the end of the project to focus on selected issues which had emerged during the project and thus could dedicate more time to research and writing their intercultural reports. It would have been interesting for the students on both sides to prepare their reports for each other, even to work collaboratively in the production of these reports, but the limited time available made this impossible.

The time difference between America and Italy made synchronous communication difficult to organize. Video conferences and Skype sessions had to be scheduled outside regular class hours which meant that they occurred less frequently than instructors would have liked and that attendance was not 100%, but nonetheless many students did experience synchronous communication and particularly appreciated the experience.

Another issue is that different teachers' approach the *Confronti* project in different ways, some giving more importance to participation in the exchange than others. This can lead to imbalanced exchanges with

---

[46] Ibid.

frustration and a loss of interest for those students who are involved in an exchange where there is little interaction. While not sharing a curriculum gives teachers the freedom to organize the *Confronti* project around their institutional requirements, a shared curriculum and assessment of work done on the *Confronti* project would assure more active participation. A unifying textbook could serve as a structured guide for those instructors that depend more on such a teaching tool.

An important issue is that of language. While the use of the L1 for the exchange is a fundamental characteristic of the *Cultura* approach, some students on both sides, in particular those with higher proficiency, found it quite frustrating not being able to try out their L2 communication skills with their peers. The only opportunity they had was on the student pages of the *Confronti* site, and during some of the video conferences when it was decided that 50% of the conference would be in English and 50% in Italian. However, given that the Italian groups contained students of mixed abilities, and all of them had studied English for much longer than the American students had been studying Italian, the L1-L1 formula generally worked well. Nearly all the students in both the groups were happy with *Confronti*, they all managed to participate in the exchange and everyone gained something from it. Opportunities to use the target language were not lacking for class discussions, and the language provided in the questionnaires and forums constituted an idiomatic, vibrant, and unquestionably authentic source both for language learning and sociocultural reflection. Finally, on the Italian side learning diaries and final reports were all in English and on the American side the essays and the final projects were all in Italian.

Not all the students in the Italian groups were actually Italian. There were some students from Croatia, Serbia, Albania and Romania, some of whom initially participated very little in the exchanges. Discussion with these students revealed that some felt that they had little to contribute to the questionnaires and forums as they were not Italian and hence they felt their contributions would not be of interest to the Penn students (see Helm 2005). On the contrary, the international students and the recent immigrants in the American groups participated with enthusiasm in the exchanges and their diversity contributed greatly to the success of the exchanges. This discrepancy may be due to several factors. For historical and sociocultural reasons, Americans see immigration as an added value to their culture, while Italians, who are currently facing a huge immigration rate, are still struggling with the notion of diversity. In the Italian context, it is reasonable to assume that the non-Italian citizens did not feel a sense of belonging to the group nor did they want to expose themselves as culturally diverse individuals, fearing to arise hostility or be stigmatized for their diversity. Furthermore, American students' communicative style on several occasions was less direct than that of their Italian peers, particularly in discussions involving sociocultural taboos like ethnic diversity.[47] The lack of directness may have encouraged the non-American or immigrant students to express themselves freely. Overall, although they are not easy to handle, such issues of sociocultural nature find in *Confronti* a natural platform of intercultural investigation, which may foster the understanding not only of the foreign culture, but also of one's own.

Conclusion and future of *Confronti*

This paper illustrated the *Confronti* telecollaborative project developed at the University of Pennyslvania according to the basic principles of *Cultura* and recently adopted at Middlebury College. The description of how this project was carried out both on the American side and on the Italian side at the University of Padova shows that telecollaboration is conducive to reciprocal cultural understanding as well as language learning. Despite the difficulties deriving from students' unequal access to and familiarity with the Internet, uneven teachers' motivation, asymmetrical semesters, time difference, and partial use of the L1 in the exchanges, *Confronti* has in fact proved to be a flexible tool, which can be adapted to the American and Italian pedagogical contexts, namely the *Standards* and the Common European Framework.

The articulation of *Confronti* in a one-year six-module program at the intermediate level—a year traditionally considered problematic within the Italian curriculum in the US—is an important feature of this project.[48] In the American *Confronti* telecollaboration and its related activities merge with the analysis and interpretation of a full array of texts—from literature to statistics—in the class environment. Both for the telecollaborative

---

[47] The issue of directness and indirectness in intercultural communication has been emphasized by H. Byrnes, (1986). "Interactional style in German and American conversations," *Text*, 2 (1), 189-206.

[48] Belz emphasizes the lack of studies on the curricular articulation of telecollaborative courses and Schulz points out that the alternation of computer-mediated and face-to-face instruction have important effects on the learning environment when intercultural matters and language are involved. See J. Belz, "Telecollaborative Language Study: A Personal Overview of Praxis and Research," *Selected Papers from the 2004 NFLRC Symposium*. INTERNET <http://www.nflrc.hawaii.edu/networks/nw44/belz.htm>; 12/09/2006. Schulz is quoted in Belz.

exchanges and the variety of the proposed materials *Confronti* was for some students a valuable opportunity to develop a non superficial understanding of Italian culture before fulfilling the language requirement and quit the study of the foreign language. For other students, on the other hand, *Confronti* was the first approach to sophisticate sociocultural, literary, and historical concepts before accessing the upper division courses. Sharing some of this material with the Italian partners was particularly meaningful for the forums and the consequent class discussions and written essays.

One last word about the synchronous computer mediated activities introduced in the project via teleconferencing and Skype. Holding synchronous chats goes against the guidelines outlined in the *Cultura* model, which state that the forums must be necessarily asynchronous in order for the students to have the time to think and elaborate on their thoughts before posting their reactions to the forums. However, despite the technical difficulties, we hope to maintain Skype (or instant messaging) and videoconferencing as essential tools of the project. While forums remain a crucial component of *Confronti*, the telecollaborative practice of the project has in fact shown that synchronous computer mediated activities are effective in many ways: they make students familiarize and develop the sense of belonging to a community, promote processes of scaffolding (corrections of inaccuracies, questions, and suggestions), overcome the barriers of written communication, and contribute to pull down stereotypical assumptions.[49]

Finally, the history of the project at the University of Pennsylvania, Middlebury College, and University of Padova shows that the future of *Confronti* lies in its developers,' instructors, and partners' ability to adjust to new contexts, technical tools, and emerging circumstances. As O'Dowd argues, "very often it will be this flexibility and willingness to react to problems that will mean the difference between success and failure in online collaboration."[50] We could not agree more.

University of Maryland, USA
University of Padova, Italy
Dickinson College, USA
University of Pennsylvania, USA

[49] With this regard, see also O'Dowd, "Negotiating Sociocultural and Institutional Contexts: The Case of Spanish-American Telecollaboration," *Language and Intercultural Communication*, 5, no. 1 (2005): 49-50.
[50] Ibid., 54.

CHAPTER NINE

PODCASTING AND IPOD IN TEACHING AND LEARNING ITALIAN LANGUAGE, CULTURE AND LITERATURE: A RESEARCH STUDY AT UNIVERSITÉ DE MONTRÉAL, CANADA

JACQUELINE SAMPERI MANGAN

Figure 9-1. Photo by J. Samperi Mangan, ©2007.

Since the birth of iPod in 2001, the growth in the use of this little marvel has been phenomenal. The iPod impact has been worldwide and across many fields. Millions of people own an iPod and listen to their own choice of music. The iPod has challenged the traditional music industry and its economy, and has changed the way people listen to music. With an iPod, people do not need to rely on radio stations or home entertainment systems to surround themselves with the music they like. They have it all on their personalized iPod collection.

The use of iPod is spreading to surprising areas of interest. Today there are companies that put together a music selection on iPod for sale to babys' nurseries, to upscale shops, hair salons and hotels, and even special selections of music to accompany surgery. As Activair[1] co-founder Lara Wiesenthal explains:

> We're creating playlists to accompany surgery. The iPod is truly the key element in this project. Each surgery is unique, and the iPod's playlist feature allows us to style music for the various aspects of surgery.[2]

The iPod is taking hold in the car industry as well, as manifacturers offer iPod compatibility in most of their new vehicles.

The use of the iPod has also influenced and already evolved in the field of education. It isn't affecting only how people listen, but it is starting to impact on how people learn. This is where the iPod "consumption" becomes interesting for educators and institutions. Does the iPod and podcasting offer some possible teaching devices? Would podcasting be useful to students and their teachers? Aside from music, could a student learn a subject or even a language from listening to his or her iPod? These are all questions that many professionals and educators try to answer by exploring possibilities that the iPod could offer.

Some universities started to look at this seriously when, in 2004, Duke University in Durham, N.C. made worldwide headlines by offering iPods to all incoming freshmen.[3] Duke University was soon followed by Georgia College & State University and by Drexel University in Philadelphia. Today iPods are given or rented to students in several colleges and universities around the world. The use of iPods in the learning comunities is controlled in systems ranging from loose to highly structured. In most

---

[1] Based in New York, Wiesenthal calls Activaire a "music stylist." The service provides music to a half-dozen boutiques and jewelers in New York, Paris and California. From her library of nearly 100 GB of songs, Wiesenthal can tailor about 30 hours of music for each client. She often creates special playlists for different moods—upbeat or mellow—or different times of the day.
http://www.activaire.com/ (accessed September 9, 2007).

[2] Leander Kahney, "The Cult of iPod" in Playlist, November 2nd, 2005.
http://playlistmag.com/features/2005/11/02/cult/index.php (accessed September 9, 2007).

[3] "Duke Digital Initiative: iPods at Duke"
http://www.duke.edu/ddi/projects/ipod.html (accessed September 5, 2007).

cases students are encouraged to download audio files, class schedules and assignments, as well as readings and even podcasts of recordings of professors and fellow students.[4] The universities are adapting to a "shrinking world" by using e-Learning to reach off campus by using learning platforms to enhance traditional teaching on campus. The iPod is one of the new technologies that serve to enhance and supplement teaching in higher education.[5]

Figure 9-2. Photo by J. Samperi Mangan, ©2007.

As much as university professors have discovered the possibilities of the iPod in enhancing and supplementing their teaching, educators of younger students have discovered some unpleasant "side-effects." The use

---

[4] Pierre-André Normandin, "L'université dans la main," in *Le Soleil*: Québec, mardi 06 mars 2007.
http://www.cyberpresse.ca/article/20070306/CPSOLEIL/70306248&SearchID=73274421881724 (9 September 2007).

[5] Aixa M. Pascual, "Universities tap into Pods' potential as learning tool," in *The Atlanta Journal-Constitution*, February 11, 2007.
http://ipod.gcsu.edu/zzzzMedia/Press_Articles/AJC.pdf (accessed September 10, 2007).

of iPods in primary and secondary schools has, in fact, been generally discouraged mainly for fear of social isolation and because teenagers especially tend to tune into themselves instead of focusing on the teacher in class.[6] One other obvious "side-effect" of iPods in school is the cheating problem. Sneaking peeks and other traditional methods give way to recordings.

> Devices including iPods and Zunes can be hidden under clothing, with just an earbud and a wire snaking behind an ear and into a shirt collar to give them away, according to school officials.[7]

At the Univerité de Montréal in Canada, the largest French university outside France, with over 55,000 students, interest in new technologies such as the use of iPod and iTunes U is emerging. In the year 2007, two research projects on iPod and podcasting were conducted and one research project on iTunes U is in process.

As an Italian literature, language and culture professor, I have been working on the two distinct but parallel projects on the use of iPod in teaching and learning at the Université de Montréal.[8]

The first research, with the *Interdisciplinary Research Center on Emerging Technologies* (CITÉ)[9] in partnership with the *Centre d'études et de formation en enseignement supérieur* (CEFES)[10] of the Université de Montréal, explored the uses of podcasting in university teaching, and

---

[6] Linda Doherty and Jordan Baker, "No more songs in their pockets: school bans iPods" in *The Sydney Morning Herald*, March 22, 2005. http://www.smh.com.au/articles/2005/03/21/1111253959952.html (accessed September 9, 2007).

[7] "Schools ban iPods to stop cheaters" Associate Press Friday, April 27, 2007 http://www.cbc.ca/news/story/2007/04/27/tech-schools.html (accessed September 10, 2007).

[8] Interdisciplinary Research Center on Emerging Technologies, "Étude de la baladodiffusion dans l'éducation: usages et pratiques des étudiants universitaires," Université de Montréal, 2007. http://www.cite.umontreal.ca/main.html (accessed August 30, 2007).

[9] The *Interdisciplinary Research Center on Emerging Technologies* (CITÉ) at the University of Montréal is a new center at the Faculty of Arts and Science that is breaking fresh ground by bringing together, from different disciplinary horizons, leading researchers in emerging technologies and multimedia. http://www.cite.umontreal.ca/ (accessed October 10, 2007).

[10] The *Centre d'études et de formation en enseignement supérieur* (CEFES) at the University of Montréal is a research center dedicated to the study of learning and performance. It forms, assists, councel and develops teaching for faculty members. http://www.cefes.umontreal.ca/ (accessed October 9, 2007).

especially the uses of the iPod by students. The project looked at the relation youth have with information technologies and the way they integrate them into their studies. The teachers' perspective towards new technologies was also examined.[11]

The results of the research help to understand the notions of mobility and freedom that are associated with mobile digital multimedia devices, and the practices and interactions that they encourage in students' daily lives. As is the case with other universities that try to develop the pedagogical aspect of the new technologies, services have been put up to help with the tools of the new technologies. The *Centre d'études et de formation en enseignement supérieur* (CEFES) is responsible for this support, as is the *Educational Technology Service* at University of California at Berkley or *Duke Digital Initiative* of Duke University. This project was been made possible with the financial support of the *Canadian Foundation for Innovation.*[12]

Five classes participated in this research. The Italian language class, an English language class, a pharmacology, communication, and an industrial design class, were part of this study.[13] Later this article will focus on the impact of this technology as experienced in the Italian language class.

The second research done at the *Université de Montréal* on the use of iPod was carried forward with the *Comité local d'intégration pédagogique* (CLIP)[14] and consisted in an exploration project on podcasting as a teaching support in foreign languages. The project committee exmined the use of podcasting as support for the teaching of German, Spanish, Italian and Portuguese at the *Direction de l'enseignement des langues et de*

---

[11] M. Broad, M. Matthews and McDonald, A. "Accounting education through an online-supported virtual learning environment," *Active learning in higher education,* 5 (2), London: SAGE Publications, 2004.

[12] Canada Foundation for Innovation Official Web Site. http://www.innovation.ca/index.cfm (accessed October 9, 2007).

[13] André H. Caron, "I'm using my iPod for studying—.really!" André Caron launches a podcasting project, Université de Montréal, mars 2007. http://www.umontreal.ca/english/news_digest/2006-2007/20070212/podcasting.html (accessed September 8, 2007).

[14] The *Comité local d'intégration pédagogique* (CLIP) at Université de Montréal is a program open for researches on the integration, bettering and valorizing of the teaching of professors on contract. http://www.ebsi.umontreal.ca/clip/index.html (accessed September 10, 2007).

cultures étrangères (DELCE)[15] at the Université de Montréal. But of course, the applications are transferable to any spoken language.

Since the University of Montréal is focusing aggressively on the internationalisation of its studies and supports and encourages a great number of its students to spend a semester in a foreign university,[16] the studies about podcasting and iPod are on the crest of the interest. Podcasting, in fact, offers the foreign language students much authentic content from various cultures and countries, and increases the material and time of the lessons, thus offering a perfect language base for students heading for a semester in a foreign university.

Research methodology

The research methodology sought to combine comments from the students' perspective with the findings of the teacher's perspective in the use of iPod and podcasting. The objectives of the combined researches were:

- to understand the student's perception of this media;
- to verify to which measure the iPod is integrated into the language course;
- to identify the uses that the students would make of the iPod, and their information and communicative practices when using this particular technology;
- to identify the benefits that students can derive from such a learning tool;
- to identify the benefits that language teachers can derive from such a teaching tool;
- to verify the contribution that such a media can bring to the teaching of languages in general;
- to determine what pedagogical adjustments a language teacher has to plan and work with when integrating iPod and podcasting into his or her classroom.

---

[15] Direction de l'ensegnement des langues et de cultures étrangères, Official Web Site, Université de Montréal. http://www.delce.umontreal.ca/ (accessed October 10, 2007).

[16] Vice-rectorat de l'Université de Montréal, "Stratégie d'internationalisation de 2e generation," pdf document. November 2006. http://www.intl.umontreal.ca/StrategieInternUdeMnov2006.pdf (accessed October 9, 2007).

The questions of the combined researches were:

- What are the communication and information practices of the students?
- What are the perceptions of the students towards the new technology in class?
- What use will the students make of the podcasting and the iPod, will they have a conventional use or will they adopt new uses?
- What are the advantages and disadvantages of this new technology from the students' point of view?
- What are the advantages and disadvantages of this new technology from the teacher's point of view?

Collection and analysis of data

The students of the Italian language course were given three questionnaires to complete:

- the first was a preliminary questionnaire collecting demographic data, assessing the student's technological knowledge and his/her mobility;
- the second questionnaire, at half session, consisted in maintaining a day-to-day statistical journal of the iPod use for a week;
- and the third questionnaire was given to the students at the end of the course to assess the results of the use of such technology in class.

After the course was finished, students were asked to participate in small focus groups to share information and experience, and to answer a few more questions. From a group of 28 students, 26 answered the first questionnaire, 20 students answered the second and 17 students answered the third. For the focus groups, the Italian students shared with the students from the English, pharmacology, communication, and industrial design courses, who had also participated individually in the CITÉ-CEFES research. The qualitative analysis of the data collected is partially complete, while the quantitative analysis is complete and shows the statistics of the pool of research.

iPod and Zen Vision M

All sudents in the research of CITÉ-CEFES were lent an iPod or a Zen for four months, the length of the course. The models of iPod from Apple and Zen Vision M from Creative had been chosen by CITÉ-CEFES after a study done on podcasting in the fall 2006 by the same Center. Students who had access to Mac products received iPods, others received Zen. For the purpose of this article, the term iPod includes the Zen apparatus and service.

Server

A central server of the university was used to upload all materials from teachers and students which in turn was then ready to be downloaded separately by iPod users and by Zen users. Technicians were available for questions and technical help.

Techniques and materials

Every participating professor had the freedom to choose the appropriate techniques and contents of the course and adapt them to the pedagogy for that particular course. This was positive in two respects: the research analysis would presumably gather different results from different approaches, thus greater variety; and it gave the professors the opportunity to search for original materials and pedagogical methods for his/her particular class. A relatively small language class has a very different dynamic than an auditorium filled pharmacology pre-med class. Adding to the variety, Professor Philippe Lemay from Industrial Design was away from Montreal in Nova Scotia the entire semester and decided to create a podcast for every lesson that the students would download onto their video iPods to watch and listen to. Professor Lemay thus taught the entire course at a considerable distance from his students in Montreal. Professor Daniel Thirion from the Faculty of Pharmacy opted instead for the production of short capsules of information and directed his students to them to reinforce the contents of his lectures. Professor Sorel Friedman decided to introduce short video-clips of English programs to her students. For the Italian language class, Professor Jacqueline Samperi offered a variety of different materials to download:

- all exercices and readings in audio form from the assigned textbook;

- a love story on audio: *Storia d'Amore;*[17]
- a thriller story on audio: *Delitto in Piazza del Campo;*[18]
- pop and opera songs from personal CD's and from YouTube;
- video clips purchased from Dall'Italia Rai International;
- the oral presentations of some students.

The students of Italian were motivated by bonus points if they would use the podcasting, rather than being penalized for not using it. All course material, information and FAQ's had been added to a class blog which the students could access from the internet.

The primary objective was to discover which kind of podcasting the students would prefer and how they would use the extra material on their iPod to help themselves learn Italian.[19] At the end of the course the students could put their oral presentation on podcasting with audio and video.

Another objective was to present authentic material to students and add to the cultural aspect of learning a language by showing video clips of Italy and the regions. And finally, it was hoped that with their iPod the students would listen to readings and stories over and over, as well as practice their understanding and reading skills.[20] Repetition is crucial to the learning of a new language, but it is even truer when the student has a hearing impairment or a mental handicap. Such was the case for one student in the Italian class who has a learning disability and found it particularly beneficial to hear the lesson several times.

Learning took place both in and out of the classroom. Language learning is a process. It takes time to acquire language skills. The iPod combined with class time helped students become more adept more quickly.

---

[17] Cinzia Medaglia and Achim Seiffarth, *Storia D'Amore* (Genova: Cideb Editrice, 1998).

[18] Maria Luisa Banfi and Simona Gavelli, *Delitto in Piazza del Campo* (Genova: Cideb Editrice, 2000).

[19] Charles Coté, "As-tu baladodiffusé ton devoir?" in Nouvelle Tendance de *La Presse*: Montréal, dimanche 11 février 2007. http://www.cyberpresse.ca/article/20070211/CPACTUALITES/702110564&SearchID=73272342706337 (accessed September 9, 2007).

[20] Anne Drolet, "Étudier avec son baladeur numérique," in *Le Soleil*: Québec, vendredi 09 février 2007. http://www.cyberpresse.ca/article/20070209/CPSOLEIL/70209271&SearchID=73273540325196 (accessed September 9, 2007).

At the end of the course a questionnaire was given to students to fill out with questions on the iPod and Podcasting. Some questions were:

- What do you think about the iPod and Podcasting as a tool of learning?
- Have the new strategies of learning using podcasting helped you in your acquiring the language?
- What have you appreciated most among the strategies of learning with the iPod and podcasting?
- What did you appreciate least among the strategies of learning with the iPod and podcasting?
- Would you have added material to the podcasting? What would you have added?
- For what did you use your iPod most?

Results

Results from the Italian class were markedly positive. All the material proposed had been consulted and explored by enthusiastic students. The most creative element of the research, where the students had to produce oral and visual materials on the iPod by themselves, was the favorite among the students. Two students created a short video spoof along an "American Idol" theme with a love story twist. In this case the students taped themselves acting out the story in Italian dialogue, and they put some background music they composed themselves. It was surely a lot of work, but the results were amazing and very rewarding. Another student prepared and uploaded a virtual tour of the Vatican museums. Since she is a full-time student of Art History at the Université de Montréal, this was a natural choice combining her passion for art with the Italian course. Her creation included an audio and video presentation. The student created her video section by putting an exhibit of pictures of Rome and the Vatican and its treasures, and her Italian description of the art was especially enhanced by soft Vivaldi music in the background. Students were provided evaluation sheets to grade their peers on pronunciation, grammar, vocabulary as well as originality and creativity. Thus the creative aspect of the program attracted more attention than the materials already prepared for them.

The promotional videos from *Dall'Italia Rai International* elicited the least interest because the subjects were not directly related to course activities, but rather were seen as extra material with cultural purposes.

Contrary to the promotional videos, the two stories, *Storia D'Amore*[21] and *Delitto in Piazza del Campo*,[22] had a great success in class as well as outside the class. One chapter per week was "dripped" to the students so that they would concentrate on the material and not rush ahead. No reading was available, and the students had to discuss the stories in groups in class. Before the final chapters of the two stories, the students were asked to choose one story and to write an ending to it, presenting the ending in class. This particular activity had high quality results with students in class, and the several endings that they wrote were as realistic and interesting, if not more so, than the actual final chapters.

As expected, the Italian pop songs attracted a great deal of student interest. The songs were accompanied by the lyrics on the class blog and the students did some exercises in filling in missing words to the songs, while listening to the songs over and over on the iPod. The benefits of using the iPod in an academic context could be summarized as follows:

- the mobility factor of the iPod is the most critical feature of this media;
- extra authentic material can be added to language courses;
- repetition of language drills and phonemes is possible;
- self-paced learning is facilitated;
- students with reading and/or other disabilities are assisted;
- a richer learning environment is offered;
- professors are able to offer extra content to advanced and highly motivated learners;
- guest speakers can present a lecture, even lectures from other countries;
- exposure to the foreign language is increased;
- occasionally absent students are able to keep abreast of the class work;
- thousand of minutes of recorded foreign language contents can be heard anytime by students;
- photos, giving a visual reference, aid the study of location, and culture, climate and more;
- the iPod and the Zen can be used as a hard drive to transport data;
- live recordings of interviews, lessons, etc. can be downloaded on the home computer;

[21] Cinzia Medaglia and Achim Seiffarth, 1998.
[22] Maria Luisa Banfi and Simona Gavelli, 2000.

- students can record lessons instead of writing class notes;
- the combination of text, audio and video formats supports a wide range of learning styles;
- recorded video (such as demonstrations and visual aids) can be placed on iPod;
- and the small size, large memory capacity, as well as the mobility of the iPod allows much more efficient and easy access to all lessons recorded during class time, which then can be viewed or listened to at a later time to aid study.

The challenges of using the iPod in an academic context could be summarized as follows:

- much material is limited by copyrights;
- if any information is lost or changed on the computer, the iPod will mimic the computer it is assigned to;
- if the student has a question or a concern about the material/lesson viewed or listened to on the iPod, he/she is incapable of easily contacting the professor;
- the battery life wears out and if the student forgets to charge the iPod, there is nothing he/she can do but go home and recharge it;
- occasionally the time the iPod takes to upload information is quite long and if the student has a busy schedule this is inconvinient;
- the students found that uploading self-produced material can be cumbersome;
- recordings in class were not of high quality;
- writings downloaded onto the iPod are not readable because the characters are too small on the screen;
- videos are not ideal to watch on an iPod while walking or crossing a street, it requires concentration which distracts the student and could be hazardous;
- minus the mobility factor of the iPod, the material would be available on the computer at home or in the language lab;
- it is impossible for the professor to directly monitor the use of the iPod by students;
- technical training was required for students and professor;
- this technology is new for support and technical staff as well and glitches on their side are likely;

- large institutions like Universities often have different technology services, infrastructures, and politics across faculties.

Considerations

The following are some considerations that arose from the research pertaining to the use of iPod in the Italian language and culture class:

- The use of iPod and podcasting to learn a language is very useful in giving the students extra authentic materials which they can use outside the classroom, and as a complement to the formal teaching.
- Personal creativity and particular interests can be incorporated into the course by the students themselves, thus providing greater involvement in the often tedious discipline of language acquisition.
- The mobility factor of the iPod is the most interesting feature of this media, because it can be used anywere at anytime, even in an environment without electricity.
- The use of iPod and podacsting is extremely beneficial, particularly for drills of repetition for both regular and slower students.
- The students of the Italian class have all concurred that the use of the iPod cannot and should not substitute the professor in the language class, though this may not apply to other classes and faculties.
- Students found that the technical aspect is crucial to a smooth functioning of the use of iPod and the podcasting and if the technical support is not solid, frustrations may lead them to not try and they might even abandon the use of their iPod for the purpose of learning.
- Watching a lengthly video such as a movie is not advised on iPod, unless the student is on a long trip where they are a passanger.
- From the professor's point of view, the iPod is a great tool that helps to complement the formal instruction in class.
- The use of the iPod in class and outside would be more efficient if supported by other media, such as a class blog and/or WebCT and iTunesU.

- The time when all these media will converge is not far distant, but it takes time for universities to organize the proper infrastructure and technical support to launch this kind of elaborate academic learning environment.
- One thing coming out of this research is clear : language courses are the ones that might benefit most from the use of iPod by bringing the student experience closer to a language immersion.

Conclusion

Most students found the use of the iPod for the Italian course to be very useful but would not appreciate having the entire course on podcasting, but only as providing extra material to assist them learn the language. Most students found that the technical aspect of this research was difficult and frustrating at the beginning. For example, students did not know how to download from the server, or they had technical problems. Most of the class had not had an iPod before and were probably not ready to use one in class. They seemed confused and frustrated very easily. The difficulties arise not only because the students do not know how to use an iPod, but the University technical support and particularly the web platform has to be improved and updated. As Leicester University Online's director, Professor Gilly Salmon says: "As you begin to scale up, you are having to develop the technology to pull it all together."[23]

At the end of the course though, some students were able to put their own oral presentation on podcasting and this means that they were able to produce by themselves a podcast for the class to see on their iPods. This particular experience led to an idea for use in a subsequent course. The Italian Intermediate course scheduled for fall 2007 is proposing to create a virtual tour of "Little Italy" in Montreal to be integrated into the iTunes U project of the Université de Montréal.[24] This virtual tour on iTunes U will be created by the students themselves and will be part of a larger class project which will include interviews with students from Italy visiting at the Université de Montréal. Some questions on the interviews could ask visiting students their first impression of Canada, their likes and dislikes of

---

[23] "Universities adapt to a shrinking world," *The Guardian*, Tuesday March 7, 2006.http://education.guardian.co.uk/elearning/story/0,,1724616,00.html (accessed October 8, 2007).

[24] Projet Pilote du Centre d'études et de formation en enseignement supérieur CEFES, Université de Montréal, Automne 2007.
http://www.cefes.umontreal.ca/tic_enseignement/ItunesU_accueil.htm (accessed October 10, 2007).

the new culture, their difficulties with living in this city and what impact the experience has on them. This could lead further to acquiring the same information from Canadian students in Italy and become a resource for students looking to study abroad and ties in nicely with the internationalization policy of the Université de Montréal.[25]

Highly appreciated were the different materials put on the iPod by the students themselves. These materials include photos, stories, videos, phonetic excercises, music, songs, lectures, and selfproduced podcasting. This was very thrilling for the students. They felt that they were constructing part of the curriculum, and indeed they were.

UNIVERSITY OF MONTRÉAL, CANADA

[25] Vice-rectorat de l'Université de Montréal, "Stratégie d'internationalisation de 2e generation," pdf document. November 2006. http://www.intl.umontreal.ca/StrategieInternUdeMnov2006.pdf (accessed October 9, 2007).

PART III:

TEACHING ITALIAN TRANSLATION

CHAPTER TEN

TEACHING ITALIAN TRANSLATION: A CHALLENGE

LUCIANA D'ARCANGELI

Introduction

The "Thinking Italian Translation" course,[1] focus of this paper, was first approved in 2002 and taught by a colleague.[2] Being a relatively new course, it has, over the years, benefited the most from the continuing professional development courses I have attended for both the Certificate and Diploma in Advanced Academic Studies. First, it was enriched with a student website in 2002; this was designed and created for the tutor, implemented successfully, and is still running.[3]

The following year the course was divided into two parallel classes taught by myself and a colleague, and its duration was extended from 10 weeks to 20 weeks. The website was modified to allow for the set-up of on-line exercises thus extending previous use made of the web-site as on-line discussion, communication and help site where translation problems could be "aired." Given the different level of commitment to the use of technology between existing tutors the support given to new initiatives was "uneven" between the two groups.

In 2004 the course and end-of-year examination was further modified to allow for more non-literary content and the class was brought from 20 to 40 hours in order to allow for peer discussion (vicarious learning) of set work. This worked very well, with many of the students acquiring real

---

[1] Based on the book by the same name by S. Hervey, I. Higgins, S. Cragie, P. Gambarotta, *Thinking Italian Translation. A Course in Translation Method: Italian to English* (London: Routledge, 2000).

[2] See Appendix A for syllabus.

[3] See http://groups.msn.com/ThinkingItalianTranslation

translation skills that would allow them to work in the sector. The ongoing changes, the website and the effort put into this course has been much appreciated by the students who have repeatedly "voted" it one of the most useful courses they have attended as undergraduates.

After benefiting from special attention for a few years the course has unfortunately suffered a descending curve due to staff and budget shortages: in 2005 we have had to cut back this class to 20 hours over 20 weeks, and, due to other commitments the two tutors have had to teach two classes for a semester each. We were faced with the challenge of obtaining the same results in half the time and with the students having to switch tutors half way through the course. The class was structured in the following way:

1. the students read a chapter at home and, following a problem-based logic, attempted a translation practical. The latter was composed of three sections totalling 100 marks: strategic decisions (SDs, marked out of 25), the target text (TT, marked out of 50), and the decisions of detail (DDs, marked out of 25).
2. in class the main points of the chapter were discussed and any problem areas indicated by the students were tackled as a group;
3. examples were given and discussed;
4. the practicals were discussed and compared among students in small groups;
5. a handout (where available) was given out;
6. the students made corrections on their own practical in a different colour pen—in class and at home—and submitted the practical for filing in their portfolio (there are only 6 assessments that are marked by the tutor, the last of these is under exam conditions).

In halving the time available what has been lost are mainly points 3 and 4, i.e. the number of examples given and time available for discussion has drastically been cut. In order to respond to this challenge, based on the knowledge gained during various courses attended over the years, I implemented the following changes in semester 1:

1. One student per week was asked to open the discussion on the week's topic—all students MUST actively participate in the

discussion twice per semester but no marks are given for this activity.

The tutor created the first posting in week 1 in order to give an example of what is required of the students, and would encourage the students to use the online discussion by answering/posting queries. This activity corresponds to Gilly Salmon's "online socialisation" or step 2 of the 5-step Model of Teaching and Learning Online.[4] The lack of tutor assessment/presence of tutor support should enhance the freedom to participate in "interaction [that] through networks break[s] down communication barriers and inhibitions that often stifle the open exchange of ideas in traditional classroom," as Eisenberg & Ely have stated.[5] Or, as Diana Laurillard writes

> an obvious pedagogical advantage over the normal face-to-face tutorial is that students can take time to ponder the various points made, and can make their contribution in their own time. Topic negotiation is possible, as in face-to-face discussion, and a tutor may pursue several lines of discussion with different groups of students in sub-conference, as the topic develops. Student control is therefore relatively high for this medium.[6]

What needs to be created then for this course is what Vygotsky called *a zone of proximal development*[7] out with the classroom (and there is evidence of this in the students' feedback); whether the development is achieved by passive "lurking" as in past years or by active posting and exchange of messages it is too early to know, but the positive aspects of collaborative learning brought about by computer-aided discussion have been studied closely.[8] By reinforcing class work, eliciting alternative

---

[4] For an overview see http://www.atimod.com/e-moderating/5stage.shtml [12/6/2008]. Alternatively see Salmon, G., *E-moderating: The Key to Teaching and Learning Online.* London: Kogan Page, 2004.

[5] M. B. Eisenberg and D.P. Ely, Plugging into the Net. *ERIC* v.21, no.2 (1993): 8-16.

[6] D. Laurillard, *Rethinking University Teaching: A Framework for the Effective Use of Learning Technologies* (London and New York: Routledge-Falmer, 2nd edition, 2002), 148.

[7] L. Vygotsky, *Mind in Society: The Development of Higher Psychological Processes* (Cambridge: Harvard University Press, 1978), 84-91.

[8] See M. Warschauer, L. Turbee, B. Roberts, "Computer Learning Networks and Student Empowerment," *System*, 14 no. 1 (1996): 1-14; M. Warschauer, "Telecollaboration in Foreign Language Instruction." Hawaii: *Second Language Teaching and Curriculum Centre*, 1996; X. Wang and R. Hurst, "An Empirical

translations/language production, acquiring new knowledge from tutors and peers alike, the students should be able to move up to step 3 of Gilly Salmon's 5-step Model of Teaching and Learning Online, i.e. that of "information exchange," and then, as they sway the discussions towards areas of their choice (within the given subject), they should move towards step 4 or the "knowledge construction" step. This new knowledge should then enter the classroom environment for a phase of new development supported by the tutor.

2. students were to place set work on the discussion site and choose the good points from another student's work, giving reasons for choice.

This task leads from the previous one discussed above but starts at step 3 of Gilly Salmon's 5-step Model of Teaching and Learning Online, and again should lead to step 4. The "information exchange" and feedback given by students (and occasionally tutors) should generate an area where "much real learning occurs through observation of other learners engaged in active dialogues."[9]

3. students were to comment on handouts on the discussion site, picking one example that they would adopt and one they would not.

Handouts can go unread or, worse, they can be taken as the "God-given version of a translation"—a notion which undermines the whole foundation of the course where translation is understood to be a subjective exercise. By asking the students to choose a "good" and a "bad" example and discuss it they are first of all forced to read the handout and then to discuss their choices. This should enable the students to analyse and discuss their own decisions better and, again, to learn vicariously from their peers. This should also provide students with greater self-assessment skills.

4. the 5 minute free-writing and the generative writing exercises were implemented where difficulties were experienced last

---

Study of Computer Assisted Discussion: Effects on Social Interaction and Group Dynamics." Paper presented at FLEAT III Conference, 12-16 August, Victoria, British Columbia, Canada, 1997.

[9] T. Mayes, "Dialogue with a Dumb Terminal," *Times Higher Education Supplement*, October 10th 1997 [Athens, 12/6/2008].

year in order to try and minimise problems and provide solutions in class in a limited amount of time.

One of the difficulties encountered in previous years has been to get the students to write their strategic decisions (SDs) in an essay-like form, analysing the linguistic challenges posed by a translation. With the added difficulty of the limited time factor it was decided that Peter Elbow's 5 minute Free-writing exercise allowed the students to generate ideas regarding the source material that need not be linguistically/grammatically correct—translation "jargon" is not important at this stage of the course and would be acquired with time. The students then highlighted what they thought were useful points to expand on in their analysis. At this point Robert Boice's generative writing exercise would be introduced to allow the students to expand on the most important points found in their initial thoughts, justifying their choice and keeping to a set number of words. This quickly provided a much needed writing model for the students to implement in their course work in a limited amount of time.[10]

5. Feedback was extended to long, full sentences where appropriate to provide stronger guidance.

Students of previous years have called for a greater amount of their work to be marked by the tutor (6 assessments) as peer discussion, handouts and self-assessment did not seem to have the same degree of "authority"/guidance. As the number of tutor-marked assessments is already quite onerous for the tutor—marking time stands at 45minutes to 1 hour per student assessment—other means were sought to compensate for this need (one is already discussed at point 3 above). Ivanic, Clark and Rimmershaw's chapter "What am I Supposed to Make of This? The Messages Conveyed to Students by Tutors' Written Comments"[11] certainly provided food for thought, especially where they argued that those tutors who give more feedback "must believe that reading and responding to students' work serves more than just administrative purposes" and has a role in student learning. This chapter also has a section on the way in which responses are given and a few tips have been

---

[10] See P. Nightingale, "Understanding Processes and Problems in Student Writing," *Studies in Higher Education*, 13, no., 3 (1988): 263-83 and C.A. Mullen, "The Need for a Curricular Writing Model for Graduate Students," *Journal of Further and Higher Education*, 25, no.1 (2001): 117-26.

[11] In M.R. Lea and B. Stierer, (eds) *Student Writing in Higher Education* (London: OUP, 2000), 47-65.

implemented: the use of a red pen, which is felt to be very authoritative, is explained in terms of practicality to the students—i.e. it is visible on photocopied work—thus removing its negative "edge;" care is taken to edit the students' work directly on their text; 2 to 4 lines of feedback are given on each of the three sections and final advice is given on the overall piece of work. This will hopefully have the "powerful shaping effect" advocated by the writers and will give the students the feeling that the feedback they receive is enough to inform their future work.

At the end of the first semester I was able to assess the changes implemented and what had not worked and why through:

a. student feedback on the course at the end of semester 1 which was compared to the feedback received the previous year at the end of semester 2. The questionnaire used was the same but there was a discrepancy as to when it was submitted—Semester 1 vs. Semester 2. This disparity could not be overcome as the second semester was taught by another person and there was no guarantee that the changes made would be carried through;
b. a comparison, in terms of structure and content, of the third assessment carried out by students of current and previous years in order to assess what has been learned, how the course has worked, with all its innovations, and to reflect on what can be done for the following year.

Implementation

The students were asked to sign-up to the website before the class started but many still had not created an account by week 3 with a couple of "problem cases" who did not have an account until week 7. Furthermore the book was not available for the first three weeks of the course as it was being reprinted and many students worked on photocopies, etc. This created some disruption but it also allowed me to notice that some students had restricted access to a computer as a lot of work was hand-written, even for the first assessed piece which I requested in printed form. The points which needed to be implemented worked as follows:

1. I hand-picked one student per week to open the online discussion on the week's topic making sure she (there was no male member of class during the year in question) had used an online discussion before and had easy access to a PC—this

obviously ceased to be a problem as we moved into the course as students found university computer rooms and got more accustomed to the site. All students were requested to actively participate in the discussion twice per semester. The results were amazing: for Semester 1 in 2004 the total messages were 13 (at least 8 of which posted by the tutors) while in 2005 the total messages were 91 (at least 18 of which posted by tutors).

2. It proved impossible to ask students to place set work on the discussion site and to choose the good points from another student's work giving reasons for choice as two students had problems with the site throughout the semester. To overcome the problem I asked the students to e-mail me with a short example of their practical work (a couple of lines) but requesting the work, collating it and placing it on the discussion board proved to be too time consuming for the experiment to be repeated. No students provided feedback.
3. Due to the above problems, students were NOT asked to comment on handouts on the discussion site but they used the handouts to self-correct/inform their portfolio practicals as per previous years.
4. The 5 minute free-writing and the generative writing exercise were implemented when teaching how to write Strategic Decisions. The outcome was mixed: the students did learn to identify salient problems in the texts quickly but then had more problems in placing their findings in an essay-like structure (i.e. introduction, analysis, conclusion) preferring to leave their findings in a single paragraph. The percentages in the comparative table that follows show a decrease of 18% in the use of an essay-like structure at assessment 3 stage between 2004 and 2005. However, those students that did implement it in 2005 did so in a more complete manner providing a conclusion at the end of their effort (+ 26%).
5. Feedback was provided through the editing of student assessments and in long, full sentences to provide stronger guidance but there was still one request for more assessed pieces rather than self-assessed practicals in the end of semester questionnaire.

Analysis of assessment results

The assessments were compared on a number of levels.

1. The structure of the strategic decisions (SDs). This showed a decrease in the use of the advocated essay-like structure by 18% (85% of students in 2004 and 67% in 2005) but where it was adopted it was done so more consistently (a conclusion was included in only 31% of the assessments in 2004 while it was included in 53% in 2005).
2. The strategic decisions (SDs) and decisions of detail (DDs) were compared in the assessments to find evidence of the 16 elements covered during the semester. Unfortunately the 2005 group resulted poorer in 12 of the 16 elements taught.
3. The target texts (TTs) were also compared in terms of occurrence of very "visible" errors. These showed that the 2004 group incurred less major errors:
   - the addition/loss of phonic and graphic elements showed a 41% increase in mistakes made;[12]
   - mistranslations showed a 44% increase—denoting a lack of knowledge of source language (Italian);
   - the introduction of a "foreign" element showed a 53% decrease—denoting more lack of confidence with the text;
   - the presence of unidiomatic text increased by 61%.
4. The content of the decisions of details (DDs) were compared and again the 2004 group of students was seen to have a better grasp of the way these should be written in order to give a greater understanding of the students' decision-making process.
5. A comparison of marks—overall and per section—showed that the 2005 group still needed to put in a great deal of effort to close the gap with the previous year.

The overall results suggest that even by halving class hours the implemented changes contained the "deterioration" of results within the 20% mark. Considering that some of the steps deemed necessary to adjust the course to its new time limits were impossible to implement due to intervening factors, this result is quite positive. However, my fear that less students would obtain a 1st class or even 2.1 degree in 2005—the year in question—was unfortunately confirmed.

---

[12] This was calculated by using the following formula: (number of 2005 errors/number of 2005 students)—(number of 2004 errors/number of 2004 students)/(number of 2004 errors/number of 2004 students).

Assessment 3 – Semester 1	Comparison of elements found		2004	2005
Number of assessments			13	15
Strategic Decisions (SDs)	Essay-like structure		85%	67%
	Introduction		85%	67%
	Analysis		92%	67%
	Conclusion		31%	53%
Elements found in Source Text (ST) → Target Text (TT) and mentioned in Strategic Decisions (SDs) and/or Decisions of Detail (DDs)	Genre issues		77%	33%
	Oral vs written		8%	7%
	Semantic issues		77%	53%
	Degrees of translation: literal vs free		62%	60%
	Translation loss		31%	87%
	Cultural transposition (exoticism, calque, cultural transplantation, cultural borrowing)		77%	20%
	Compensation		38%	47%
	Phonic/graphic elements and prosodic issues		92%	73%
	Grammatical level	Words and their formation	62%	47%
		Syntax	77%	93%
	Sentential issues		100%	80%
	Discourse issues		38%	60%
	Intertextual issues		46%	40%
	Literal meaning and translation issues	Synonymy	23%	20%
		Hyperonimy/ hyponimy	23%	7%
		Particularising/ generalising/ partial overlap issues	46%	20%
Target text (TT) occurrence of major errors	Addition/loss of phonic/graphic elements		8	13
	Mistranslations		12	20
	Introduction of "foreign" element (light, sound, etc.)		13	7
	Unidiomaticity		7	13
Decisions of Detail (DDs)	Impersonal style		100%	87%
	Analytical		69%	60%
	Technically correct		100%	93%

Marks	Strategic Decisions avg	18.5/25	13.87/25
	Target Text avg	32.85/50	30.13/50
	Decisions of Detail avg	18.38/25	15.93/25
	Overall avg	69.69/100	59.87/100

Table 10-1. Assessment.

Conclusion

The reduction in class hours has had negative repercussions, as expected; these have been alleviated by some of the measures implemented and unfortunately some were not implemented due to technical problems. However, in hindsight, these extra measures would have added to the home work load that the students already find a burden, as will be detailed below in their feedback. One can safely say that improving pedagogical methods can aid the tutors and students to achieve better results but it cannot be expected to compensate for a halving of contact hours, especially on a problem-based course where the students are asked to do the work and then reflect collectively (this is where the cut in contact time had its greatest repercussions) and privately on it.

The questionnaires received[13] still show that this course is a favourite with students as most respondents used positives to describe it. They also address the lack of class discussion/teaching time by giving lower scores to the overall qualities of the class in question 1, i.e. whether the students found the class informative, interesting, valuable; however, having to keep to a much tighter timetable the class was found to be more well-organised (question 1) and the tutor's teaching methods to be more satisfying (question 5). The course pace was found to be "just right" by the majority of students but 91% found it to be "difficult to manage during busy periods" and 9% found it "impossible" to manage—in 2004 there were no students in this category. Many students addressed this area in their written feedback in both years, asking for a reduced work load or weeks with no work—not realising that they are allowed two revision weeks, one of which is during their extended essay submission week. One student in particular addressed me personally and stated that there was "little point in doing all the work in time if it was not going to be discussed in class" and I have noticed a tendency for people not to do some or all class work prior to class, leaving the onus to a few students and making class discussion

[13] See Appendix B.

difficult. I have addressed this with the students, but it is preferable that they do come to class without the work rather than not show up at all.

Suggestions were made to compact the two one-hour classes into a larger one-to-two hour class (as needed) in order to contain the "damages" and to address problem areas. The larger group would provide more opportunities for discussion and avoid the otherwise undesirable but necessary revision of topics to be covered - making the pace slower for the whole class but leading to less learning. The change in structure was not deemed possible in 2006, due to the large cohort of Honours students, this has naturally lead to the class covering less material but with better results.

University of Strathclyde, Scotland

APPENDIX A

Class Descriptor: Italian Language C [34533: *Thinking Italian Translation*]

Class Hours: 20

Aims of the class: the class focuses on translation as process and as product, on cultural issues in translation, the formal properties of texts, language variety, and aspects of contrastive linguistics. It aims: (a) to develop a greater understanding of what language is and how it functions (including English); (b) to provide a foundation for those students wishing to progress to a translation-based professional qualification after graduation.

The content of the class will be negotiated, but is likely to include most of the following: introduction to the concept of translation as process (as opposed to product, with which students will be more familiar); intralingual translation; speed and gist of translation; cultural issues in translation (transposition/compensation); sentential and inter-sentential issues; grammatical and lexical issues; phonic/graphic dimensions; particularizing/generalizing translations; connotative meaning; dialect/sociolect/code-switching; tonal register; subtitling; legal and administrative translation.

Method of teaching: 20 one-hour seminars. The seminars are "practical" sessions, based largely on student papers, delivered by individuals or by groups according to the project.

Assessment: 4 assessed pieces to be handed in, for Semester 1, in week 6, 10 and 12, for Semester 2, in week 4; towards the end of classes there will be one assessment held under exam conditions (week 8). At the end of the course there will be a three-hour examination (week 11). Students will be given a passage which they must comment on the **strategic challenges** presented by writing of kind, provide a **Target Text** of the section indicated, together with an analysis of the **decisions of detail** which they were called upon to make. Marks will be allocated on a 25%, 50%, 25% basis respectively.

Transferable skills: in addition to the translation skills indicated above, students will develop analytical and presentational skills of value in all professions. Additionally, the TIT course should help those students doing literature options to improve their stylistic analysis.

Required reading: students will be required to use a good monolingual Italian dictionary (*c*.2000-page), a similar-sized Italian-English/English-Italian dictionary, an English dictionary and and English thesaurus both for the seminar presentations and for the examination. Seminars will be based on: S. Hervey, I. Higgins, S. Cragie, P. Gambarotta, *Thinking Italian Translation. A Course in Translation Method: Italian to English*, London, Routledge, 2000. This will be supplemented by practical examples of published translations provided by the tutors.

Recommended reading: Mona Baker, *In Other Words: a Coursebook in Translation*, London, 1992 and Susan Bassnett, *Translation Studies*, Routledge, 1991.

APPENDIX B

Questionnaire results

2004 : Total students 13—Number of questionnaires received 6

2005 : Total students 16—Number of questionnaires received 11

Question 1: The class was

	Year	1	2	3	4	5	6	
a) Very informative	2004	67%	17%			17%		Uninformative
	2005	50%	50%					
b) Very interesting	2004	67%		17%	17%			Uninteresting
	2005	30%		30%	40%			
c) Extremely valuable	2004	50%			33%	17%		A waste of time
	2005	40%	20%	40%				
d) Well organised	2004	50%			33%	17%		Badly organised
	2005	73%	27%					

Question 2: What do you think of your course length (i.e. 20 weeks)?

Year	Perfect	Almost perfect	Too long	Too short
2004	50%	33%		17%
2005	46%	36%	9%	9%

Question 3: Was the course pace

Year	Too fast	Just right	Too slow
2004	33%	67%	
2005	9%	91%	

Question 4: Did you find the work load

Year	Impossible to manage	Difficult to manage during busy periods	Just about manageable	Easy to manage
2004		83%	17%	
2005	9%	91%		

Question 5: How satisfied were you with your tutor's teaching methods

Year	Very satisfied	Quite satisfied	Not very satisfied	Not at all satisfied
2004	50%	33%	17%	
2005	55%	45%		

Question 6: What do you think were the major strengths of the class?

2004 a) The class was very interesting and different to other Italian classes as it felt as if we were truly doing something with the language. It also increased my awareness of the many issues involved in translation. More practice in terms of Strategic Decisions (SDs) and Decisions of Detail (DDs) would improve class members' confidence.

2004 b) We had the chance to discuss our homework in class and see what we were doing wrong; the tutor helped us understand the various concepts and use them accordingly in translation.

2004 c) It gave a whole new insight into translation method. I believe I have taken on a whole new approach to translation.

2004 d) That we got to discuss our homework in class and the amount of feedback we received.

2004 e) The class was very helpful and actually helped me to understand the processes that must be done to translate a text.

2005 a) Breaking down "how we translate" was a very interesting thing for me. The message boards were excellent—once I got the hang of them—and contributed greatly to the class.

2005 b) Chance to correct work and improve by sharing ideas.

2005 c) I thought that the class was good in showing the different linguistic aspects of the translation and how to identify them and deal with them in a text. The website was a good way of providing information and sharing information among each other.

2005 d) Demonstrations and work in practice (live examples) of the theory behind the translating.

2005 e) I liked the fact that it focused on the theory behind the translating—something which we had never done before. This also made it more applicable since I study another language and can transfer these skills. It was also nice that the Strategic Decisions (SDs) and the Decisions of Detail (DDs) counted for as much as the actual translation, so that it was more about acquiring the skill of translation rather than your level of Italian.

2005 f) It is good to know that there is no perfect translation, and it is good to have other people's interpretations.

2005 g) The class made me realise there is no perfect translation and it is good to get other people's translations to help you when you're on your own.

2005 h) Enabled discussion and comparison with fellow students and is a good introduction to the complex issues of the process of translation.

2005 i) Explanations in the book and practice exercises with sample answers.

2005 j) The way it improved my awareness of features of text and enabled me to explain the differences between the two languages involved.

2005 k) I feel that I learned a great deal in this class with regard to tackling a translation. It was good to have the discussion board so that we could discuss any problems we had.

Question 7: How would you improve the class for future students?

2004 a) Having a solution for each of the homework assignment set would be helpful for enhancing understanding. In addition, going over what is typically required in an exam question.

2004 b) Avoid spending time doing something that will not appear in the exam, for example a translation on how to change a battery; use materials that we have covered throughout the year for the assessed work as we did with the Buzzati text so that the student will get an idea of the full work rather than just the short ST.

2004 c) To complete all class work and assessments is quite rigorous. Less emphasis on the class work, so student feels happy to come to class every week.

2004 d) Not so many written assignments.

2004 e) I can't help but think this is something that should be introduced sooner, perhaps in third year. If this was done then, by my final year I would be able to tackle a translation better.

2005 a) I would perhaps make the class shorter in length of weeks, and instead have a 1.5 hr/2 hr class weekly, or in fact two classes per week. I think this would help compound what we are learning, as a week is a long time to forget something. This is difficult for timetabling reasons, I know, but I think it would be beneficial.

2005 b) Have done some study of linguistics before this class.

2005 c) I think the class work load could be changed as I found it very difficult to keep up with the work and prepare for the class every week as I had a lot of other work on at the same time and therefore my time was restricted. However, I did feel going over the practicals in class was useful.

2005 d) I would like to have had a week off every now and then. I felt a bit as though I was always struggling to hand one piece in as well as complete the work for class. Especially since it takes me quite a long time to complete each piece of work.

2005 e) More assessed pieces.

2005 f) Have a piece to hand in every 2 weeks instead of every week.

2005 g) If the pace was a little slower, students would have more time to digest each element before they quickly pile up and I was confused as to what I was looking for.

2005 h) The work load is a bit heavy, a smaller exercise relevant to each chapter would make it easier to handle.

2005 i) I think that the exercises were well-chosen but that sometimes the reading in the chapter can be quite dense – thankfully the chapters are generally short!

2005 j) Possibly have less work to do, I do feel that the practical tasks were useful but with the other Italian classes giving us assessed work every week I found it hard to do everything on top of my other subject.

Question 8a: Did you use the online discussion regularly?

Year	Yes	No
2004	67%	33%
2005	100%	

Year	To contribute	To read	To post/start a new discussion
2004	33%	67%	17%
2005	73%	82%	36%

N.B. More than one possible answer.

Question 8b: Did you find the website useful?

Year	Yes	No
2004*	83%	0%
2005	91%	9%

* One student did not answer this question.

If not why?

2005 a) Not often, since I'd generally already finished the exercise (having grappled with the problems and usually resolved them in some way or another) by the time the postings were made.

Question 8c: What "transferable skills" have you acquired with this class?

2004 a) While I wouldn't say the class necessarily instilled new skills, it certainly helped improve analytical skills.

2004 b) In order to do good translations you can't just translate word by word but you also have to think.

2004 c) I believe that I have acquired an ability to translate in far more contexts. I think the class has developed my ability to read and analyse different texts.

2004 d) I have understood the ethical side of translating and that it is much more important to have a good sound translation than one which has been translated word for word and loses the meaning of the text.

2004 e) There is a tendency for me personally to translate things directly instead of trying to seek out the words that I know. This class seems to open your eyes to the fact that we can all translate differently and there is no right and wrong answer.

2005 a) I have actually "stolen" the board's ideas and am using it with my other degree subject class, in order to facilitate meet-ups and ideas.

2005 b) Greater knowledge of linguistics, am now more analytical and aware when undertaking a translating-type of work.

2005 c) I found the translation skills from this class very useful for my other language translation classes and they have made me approach translation in a different and more effective manner.

2005 d) Logical thought processes. Rational thinking. Ability to consider and hopefully see the "big picture."

2005 e) I am more aware of all the small decisions I make when translating something, for example the style of the language, the vocabulary I use, and trying to make these fit the Source Text (ST) as closely as possible. I also read the original piece more carefully and am more methodical—I look for things such as rhyme, assonance, grammar structures which I might not have noticed before.

2005 f) Planning and attention to detail.

2005 g) I also do French and it has helped me think about the way I do translations in that class.

2005 h) Hopefully it has "opened my eyes" to salient features of different types of texts and improved my analytic abilities as well as widening my own mother tongue language by constant referrals to my English thesaurus!

2005 i) The ability to analyse texts and not just read them and also pay greater attention to detail! Also to devise a plan for your work before actually stating something.

2005 j) A much higher awareness of translation losses and the difficulties involved with translation—this can be applied to cultural situations as well. The greater awareness of texts can be applied to any situation where text analysis is needed, eg. intertextual translation—turning government statistics literature into a report suitable for non specialists.

2005 k) How to analyse and look at something from different angles.

Other comments

2004 a) Although at first I was struggling, in the end this course proved to be the one I most enjoyed. Nevertheless, I think that the exam did not do me justice. The paper was definitely harder than all the other assessments including the mock test.

2004 b) The course structure and teaching methods were good. The textbook is extremely helpful too. The workload I found a little heavy, particularly if asked to revise errors before handing in. The assessed pieces were very fair however, as was the marking.

2004 c) Ability to analyse texts, to think more rationally about translation, seeing texts and translation from another perspective, encouraged me to think more.

2004 d) That both tutors should be commended for the work that they have done this year and the time that they spent in correcting and clarifying points. The course was interesting and enjoyable and has given us an interesting insight into the world of translating.

2004 e) There is a tendency for me personally to translate things directly instead of trying to seek out the words that I know. This class seems to open your eyes to the fact that we can all translate differently and there is no right or wrong answer.

2005 a) I think the class is useful in regards to showing how to approach translation in this way and how to incorporate the linguistic elements which many people have not come into contact with before. However, the class work load is maybe too much to manage and some of the practical exercises could be only for class discussion and not for preparation before. Also perhaps more examples for the linguistic elements could be provided to avoid confusion and help identifying them and using them in translation. Other than that the class has been very useful.

2005 b) I enjoyed this semester's teaching but it is very demanding and if professionally translating outside of university, you would have considerably longer to familiarise yourself with the entire piece in question and then many mistakes in context and subject matter etc. would be more likely to be avoided by the end!

CHAPTER ELEVEN

TRANSLATION IN TEACHING ITALIAN AS L2: EVOLUTION OR INVOLUTION?

SANDRO SCIUTTI

Ever since modern European languages started to be taught to foreigners, the use of translation in teaching and learning foreign languages has known a chequered history, to the extent that its changing fortunes have often been compared to the swinging movement of a pendulum[1]. As a matter of fact, throughout the different stages of the contemporary history of foreign language teaching, translation has passed from being extolled as virtually the one method to learn languages effectively to being rejected altogether, making it bear the brunt, together with other old-fashioned techniques such as dictation, of all the attacks concerning the failures of foreign language learning. Therefore, being translation a discipline with such a long-lasting tradition in the field of foreign language teaching and learning, including it among the "new methodologies" to teach Italian as a foreign language appears somewhat contradictory at the turn of the twenty-first century, whence the question contained in the title of this article.

Taking the foregoing facts into account, the aim of the present paper is to shed light on the current trends of foreign language teaching related to the use of translation, moving first of all from a brief overview of the status that translation enjoyed in the various methods that have marked the modern history of language teaching. Then, having acknowledged the misuse of translation in the past language teaching methods and cleared the way of the common misconceptions that still surround translation today as a language teaching tool, the advantages of this technique will be

---

[1] D. Bowen, "Pendulum swings in language teaching and translation", in *Translator and Interpreter Training and Foreign Language Pedagogy*, ed. P.W. Krawutschke. Ata Scholarly Monograph Series, III. (Binghampton: Binghampton Press, 1989), 26-38.

examined in the light of the opinions shared by several experts in the sector of language teaching as well as by official publications such as the *Common European Framework of Reference for Languages*. Particular emphasis will be placed on teaching Italian as a foreign language, especially to learners with previous knowledge of another romance language, such as French, Spanish, Portuguese or Romanian, either as their mother tongue or as an additional foreign language, dealing with the role of translation in addressing the issue of interferences either from the students' mother tongue or from another foreign language they know.

Translation in foreign language teaching: a historical overview

Although the germ of the hoary debate over the use of translation in foreign language teaching can be traced back to at least the sixteenth century, when Latin gave way to the different European vernaculars as tool of communication between the peoples and the first theoretical discussions on the teaching of foreign languages arose, it is especially since the end of the eighteenth century that the controversy has grown particularly heated. The first method in the history of modern language teaching is generally agreed upon as the so-called "**grammar-translation method**," which resulted from transferring the same techniques used to teach ancient languages such as Latin and Greek to the teaching of modern European languages. The actual name chosen makes it quite clear that within the framework of this method grammar and translation were considered to lie at the core of the language learning process, the latter being exclusively reduced to a mechanical and sterile application, usually from the students' mother tongue to the foreign language, of the grammatical rules outlined at the beginning of each lesson. Such nearly word-for-word translation involved in most cases very short sentences taken out of their original context, usually a literary one, or even made up for the sake of the grammatical exercise, thus making them sound unnatural if not utterly meaningless.

The detractors of such an extreme and naïve approach to foreign language teaching soon made their voices heard quite strongly in the attempt to rescue the discipline from its pitiful state. As a result of the deep sociological changes brought about by the massive flux of immigrants witnessed by countries like the United States or France, as well as of a turning toward a more practical attitude in theoretical discussions on the process of learning a foreign language, a totally opposite method appeared onto the scene towards the end of the twentieth century, referred to as **Direct Method**. Brought to its full success chiefly by Berlitz, this new method claimed the absolute priority of the spoken language over the written one and was based on a more down-to-earth and global approach to the task of learning a foreign language, which was deemed perfectly identical to the process leading to the acquisition of the L1. From such a perspective, the language lesson consisted solely of enhancing the communicative skills of the students through repetition and conversation, leaving no room whatsoever for grammatical explanations or the use of the L1 of the students, with the consequent total ban on translation, which was thought to hinder the ability to think directly in the foreign language. As can be observed, in its attempt to purify the process of language learning from its most negative and undesirable traits, the Direct Method went right to the opposite extreme, stigmatising any rational or analytical approach to language learning, such as resorting to grammar and translation. It was only thanks to the work of three European phoneticians, namely H. Sweet, O. Jespersen and H. Palmer, that the otherwise quite blunt statements made by the convinced promotors of the new method were softened and a more balanced view on the use of grammar and translation in language learning was attained, thus recognising some positive sides to translation in the process of language learning and preventing it from being totally discarded as a useless or even harmful technique. In particular, H. Palmer's stance on the subject is noteworthy, in that it reveals an exceptional reasonableness and farsightedness for his times, as it stands clear from the following remarks, very much ahead of the views commonly held by the linguists who were among his contemporaries:[2]

> Shall we translate? We can learn much from translation; it affords us many types of interesting and valuable exercises. Or shall we ban translation? For we know that under certain conditions translation may foster and encourage more than one vicious tendency. [...] At appropriate moments and for specific purposes, make the fullest use of all sorts of translation work; at other moments, and for other specific purposes, banish translation entirely.

However, such a balanced and tolerant attitude did not yield many results at least judging from the practical applications of the new linguistic theories, for the **"Reading Method"** that consequently emerged from the rather blurred and chaotic scene of language learning in the period

---

[2] H.E. Palmer, *The Principles of Language Study* (London: Oxford University Press, 1974).

between the two wars proved to hold much in common with the Grammar-Translation Method. As a matter of fact, once again it privileged an analytical and deductive mode by focusing mainly on written texts, which were broken down to their major components in terms of grammar and vocabulary for the close examination on the part of the learners. Hence the use of the L1 of the students was re-established, as well as the recourse to translation for the sake of the correct understanding of the texts, although this was more the case during the initial phases of the learning process, relying more and more on the context as the students' knowledge of the L2 increased.

Soon, though, in the wake of the intervention of the United States in World War II, a new method to learn foreign languages was developed, to allow the American troops sent to the far-flung war zones to learn to speak the local languages rapidly and effectively. Thus, the so-called **Audio-Oral Method**, which closely resembled the Direct Method, came into existence, stemming on one hand from Skinner's behaviourist theories in the field of psychology and, on the other, on Bloomfield's structuralism in the field of linguistics. From this perspective, language was considered a habit acquired by means of repeating a series of correct stimulus-response associations over and over again, until the mechanism was interiorised as an automatic and unconscious reflex (known as *overlearning*); the language to be learnt was viewed as a mere taxonomy of a limited number of fundamental structures, expandable through lexical variations and ranked on the basis of their graded difficulty, to be mastered through repetition, imitation and manipulation exercises (the *pattern-drills*). In addition, the process of acquisition of a L2 was viewed as similar yet distinct and parallel to the acquisition of L1, as for each language different mental habits had to be developed, having little or nothing in common with the ones already interiorised for other languages. As a consequence, translation was a strictly forbidden exercise, in that the advocates of the Audio-Oral Method deemed any use of the students' L1 as generating hazardous interferences with the learning process involving the L2. Nevertheless, as pointed out by several authors,[3] the position of many promoters of the Audio-Oral Method, Lado amongst others, actually betrayed an underlying paradox concerning translation, since the interlinguistic comparison between the systems of the L1 and the L2, known as Contrastive Analysis, lay at the very core of the theoretical assumptions of the method, albeit only as a heuristic technique: the choice

[3] M.V. Calvi, *Didattica di lingue affini: italiano e spagnolo* (Milano: Guerini, 1995), 30. E. Lavault, "Traduire en classe: pourquoi ou pour qui?" in *The Role of Translation in Foreign Language Teaching* (Paris: Didier erudition, 1991), 50.

and the ranking of the linguistic structures that made up the syllabus of coursebooks were in fact carried out following the principle of presenting first of all the structures which were similar in both languages and later on those with an increasing degree of divergence.

Starting from the late fifties, and even more so throughout the sixties, a new wave of changes in both psychological and linguistic theories concerning the process of acquisition of a second language began to prevail under the labels of **cognitivism** and **generative-transformational linguistics**, the leading figure in this school of thought being the American linguist Noam Chomsky. Quite contrary to behaviourism, the new linguistic current held that language was an inborn feature of all human beings, who were endowed from birth with a Linguistic Acquisition Device (LAD) enabling them to process the linguistic input through a kind of trial-and-error procedure, consisting of forming hypothesis as to the mechanisms at the root of linguistic expression and checking those hypothesis against further observations of the same linguistic phenomenon as well as against the network of knowledge already constituting the subject's cognitive resources. This new conception of language learning not only stressed the creativity of the speaker, who, having inferred the basic rules governing the functioning of the verbal expression in a given language, could generate an infinite amount of utterances by combining the limited elements at his/her disposal differently, but also made it possible, in view of the retrieval of the rational and conscious components of language learning, to re-evaluate the role of the L1 and consequently of translation in the process of acquisition of a L2. Such renewed interest in translation in the context of learning a L2 was mainly due to the fact that in the eyes of the generative-transformational linguists, the process leading to the acquisition of a L2 differed significantly from the one responsible for the acquisition of the L1, inasmuch as while the latter ran parallel with the person's overall cognitive development, the former could rely on a series of cognitive resources already available, resulting from the acquisition of the L1 or another L2. Therefore, in the network of knowledge constituting the cognitive make-up of a person, the information relating to the L1 and any of the L2s learnt earlier on were regarded as closely interrelated. This meant that stubbornly preventing the learners from resorting to their L1, hence to translation, would be not only pointless, but also potentially harmful to the quality of the learning process, since it would run counter to the cognitive strategies naturally deployed by the students. On account of this, within the framework of the cognitive method that developed from the applications of the generative-transformational linguistic theories, translation played a significant role both as a way of consolidating and rationally synthesising the grammatical rules previously inferred, and as a means to compare the structures of the L2 with the structures of the L1.

Next in the chronology of methods comes the **communicative approach**, to which contemporary language teaching still owes so much. It started to become common practice in foreign language classes from the early seventies onwards, and was a turning point in the way language was conceived. As a matter of fact, quite at odds with the mainstream idea that prevailed up to then, language was no longer considered to be an abstract system of merely linguistic structures, but in a wider sense a way of acting through verbal communication, of conveying intentions and requests affecting the recipient's behaviour and determining a specific response on his/her part. In other words, for the first time ever the stress was placed on the contextual features surrounding linguistic utterances, that is the actual socio-situational variables of the verbal interchange in terms of time, place, characteristics of the speakers and their relationship, contents and vehicle of the message, aims of the communication, etc., without neglecting cultural constraints, so crucial to an effective communication. Thus the very notion of what constituted success in learning a foreign language underwent a radical change, since what was previously identified with linguistic competence, that is the ability to create formally flawless utterances, now came to be replaced by communicative competence, defined as the ability to select in the wide range of structures available to the speakers of a given language, those most suited to the actual features of the communicative interchange. The communicative approach had its most direct and practical application in the notional-functional method, organised around a series of conceptual and grammatical notions and of linguistic functions, corresponding to the particular way the language is used to achieve a specific purpose. Within this framework, translation was mainly used to compare the communicative situations of a given linguistic act in the L2 and the L1.

The most recent trends in the history of language learning, those developed particularly from the decade of the eighties onwards, can be grouped together under the common denomination of "**humanistic-affective methods**," equivalent to that of "alternative methods." They include, among others, the *Community Counselling*, the *Total Physical Response*, the *Silent Way* and the *Suggestopedia*. Although quite different from one another in some cases, all the same they share a series of features which set them apart from the so-called conventional or traditional methods, thus entailing a veritable breakthrough in the field of language learning. For the first time, in fact, these methods focused more on how the learning process was conducted rather than on what was actually taught; special attention was given to the psychological components of learning, above all the presence of a positive, relaxed, friendly and cooperative atmosphere, combined with a lack of competitiveness, as well as of the fear of the teacher's corrections or of being mocked by the other students. The role attributed to translation by these methods is rather negligible, its main use being confined to preventing a potentially anxiety-inducing situation for the students. However, despite the recurrent accusations of naivety and exclusion of the rational reflection on the L2, the most significant merit of the humanistic-affective methods and the legacy they have passed on to contemporary language teaching trends lies in fostering the idea of the absolute priority of the student, whose characteristics, needs, purposes and preferences determine the particular configuration of the learning process. It is in this frame of mind that the present rehabilitation of translation as a language teaching technique finds its full legitimacy and its point of strength, as the following in-depth analysis of the current, widely shared positions on translation will show.

Translation in foreign language teaching: current trends

From a close examination of the contemporary scene of foreign language learning, a conspicuous phenomenon can be detected, namely the disappearance of a univocal, all-embracing method in favour of what can be described as an eclectic and tolerant attitude, which does not stick blindly to one way of viewing things, but rather makes full use at all times of each and every existing procedure by choosing each time the one most suited to the particular characteristics of the learning process. In this line of thought, Bowen[4] states that "the method used to teach a language makes very little difference; the results are what count," and Popovic[5] echoes this by highlighting that "comparative method studies have failed to produce evidence that one particular method results in more successful learning than another". This conviction is also supported by Ciliberti,[6] who expresses herself in these terms:

> Il metodo migliore, quello che produce i risultati più soddisfacenti, è sempre un metodo misto, difficile da definire in quanto il suo successo sta nei dettagli, nella dosatura, nell'elasticità, e la cui scelta è basata sulla

[4] D. Bowen 1989, 35.
[5] R. Popovic (2004), *The Place of Translation in Language Teaching*, www.sueleatherassociates.com/pdfs/Article_translationinlanguageteaching.pdf
[6] A. Ciliberti, *Manuale di glottodidattica* (Firenze: La Nuova Italia, 1994), 83.

> considerazione delle caratteristiche specifiche della situazione di apprendimento/insegnamento—caratteristiche che sono difficilmente generalizzabili.[7]

Amongst these features of the learning process, a crucial role is played by the student, whose needs, objectives and characteristics determine the choice of the particular procedure to be followed, much in line with the student-oriented language learning philosophy of our days, summed up by Hédiard[8] with these words:

> Dans un enseignement centré sur l'apprenant, le rôle de l'enseignant consistera à guider l'étudiant dans le choix des stratégies à privilégier. Ce choix dépendra de differents facteurs: la phase d'apprentissage dans laquelle se trouve l'apprenant, le contrôle qu'il exerce sur la grammaticalité de sa production, la perception de la distance linguistique qu'il possède et enfin la capacité de conceptualiser dont il fait preuve.[9]

The present balanced and bias-free attitude clearly noticeable in today's language learning cannot but involve also the use of translating techniques, which, far from still being the scapegoat of the fierce opponents of an analytical procedure, is currently experiencing an increasingly strong revival, as witnessed by Popovic:[10]

> It seems now that the general attitude towards translation has become to change: those who touch upon it unanimously profess that translation is a legitimate pedagogic tool [...] and that it deserves to be rehabilitated.

Looking into the causes of such a renewed interest, Desideri[11] explains:

---

[7] The best method, the one producing the most satisfying results, is always a mixed method, hard to define in that its success lies in details, balancing different elements, in flexibility. Its choice rests on weighing up the specific characteristics of the learning/teaching situation—which more often than not cannot be generalised.

[8] M. Hédiard, "Langues voisines, langues faciles?" *Studi italiani di linguistica teorica ed applicata*, XVIII, no. 1-2 (Padova, 1989): 228.

[9] Within learner-oriented teaching, the teacher's role consists of guiding the student in the choice of strategies to favour. This choice will depend on several factors: the learning stage the learner finds himself/herself at, his/her control over the grammatical correctness of his/her productions, his/her perception of linguistic distance and finally the ability to conceptualise that he/she shows.

[10] R. Popovic (2004).

[11] E. Borello, *Teorie della traduzione. Glottodidattica e scienze della comunicazione* (Urbino: Quattroventi, 1999), 11-2.

> Le ragioni di questo dilagante sviluppo, di cui un effettivo segnale è il proliferare di convegni e dibattiti sia in Italia che all'estero, sono molteplici. Da una parte le nuove teorie linguistiche e glottodidattiche, la recente ricerca psicolinguistica sui processi di transcodificazione tra lingue e culture lontane, le attuali posizioni dell'antropologia e dell'etnologia; dall'altra l'esigenza, peraltro molto concreta, di automatizzare i processi traduttivi per rendere sempre più rapida ed efficace—grazie ai processi tecnologici—la comunicazione interculturale tra lingua di partenza e lingua di arrivo, comunicazione della quale il mondo contemporaneo ha ormai un bisogno irreversibile, a causa dell'infittirsi dei rapporti internazionali, dei rapidi e radicali cambiamenti geopolitici degli ultimi tempi.[12]

A powerful testimony of the recent surge of interest in translation from the viewpoint of language learning is also provided by the ***Common European Framework of Reference for Languages***, a document drawn up by the Council of Europe in 1996 to provide "

> a common basis for the elaboration of language syllabuses, curriculum guidelines, examinations, textbooks, etc. across Europe [...] thus promoting international co-operation in the field of modern languages."[13]

Its inspiring approach is described as a pluringual and a pluricultural one, in the sense that[14]

> *it* emphasises the fact that as an individual person's experience of language in its cultural contexts expands, from the language of the home to that of society at large and then to the languages of other peoples [...], he or she does not keep these languages and cultures in strictly separated mental compartments, but rather builds up a communicative competence to which

[12] The reasons for this widespread development, one telling indicator of which is the proliferation of conferences and debates both in Italy and abroad, are manifold. On one hand the new linguistic and language learning theories, the recent psycholinguistic research on transcoding processes between distant languages and cultures, the current positions of anthropology and ethnology; on the other the need, very concrete indeed, to automate translation processes in order to allow intercultural communication between source and target languages to become more and more rapid and effective, using new technology. Today's world has an irreversible need for this kind of communication, on account of international relations becoming closer and of the latest rapid and radical geopolitical changes.

[13] Council of Europe, *Common European Framework of Reference for Languages: Learning, Teaching, Assessment* (Strasbourg: Modern Languages Division. Cambridge: Cambridge University Press, 2001), § 1.1.

[14] *Ibidem*, § 1.3.

> all knowledge and experience of language contributes and in which languages interrelate and interact.

From such a perspective, both the use of the L1 and translating techniques have the right to exist in a foreign language class, as proved by the fact that the *Framework* includes mediation activities among the competences possessed by a learner of a L2,[15] for they "occupy an important place in the normal linguistic functioning of our societies."[16] Expanding even further the reasons of such a decision, the authors state:[17]

> The learner of a second or foreign language and culture does not cease to be competent in his or her mother tongue and the associated culture. Nor is the new competence kept entirely separate from the old. The learner does not simply acquire two distinct, unrelated ways of acting and communicating. The language learner becomes plurilingual and develops interculturality. The linguistic and cultural competences in respect of each language are modified by knowledge of the other and contribute to intercultural awareness, skills and know-how. They enable the individual to develop an enriched, more complex personality and an enhanced capacity for further language learning and greater openness to new cultural experiences. Learners are also enabled to mediate, through interpretation and translation, between speakers of the two languages concerned who cannot communicate directly.

The adoption of such a plurilingual and pluricultural approach, with a constant and conscious reference during the learning process to all the languages known by the speaker, may even facilitate, in the eyes of the authors, the task of learning a L2, as pointed out by the following enlightening remarks:[18]

> Pluringual and pluricultural competence also promotes the development of linguistic and communication awareness, and even metacognitive strategies which enable the social agent to become more aware of and control his or her own "spontaneous" ways of handling tasks and in particular their linguistic dimension. In addition, this experience of plurilingualism and pluriculturalism [...] leads to a better perception of what is general and what is specific concerning the linguistic organisation of different languages (form of metalinguistic, interlinguistic or so to speak

---

[15] *Ibidem*, § 6.1.3.
[16] *Ibidem*, § 2.1.3.
[17] *Ibidem*, Ch. 4, 43.
[18] *Ibidem*, § 6.1.3.3.

> "hyperlinguistic" awareness. [...] It may, therefore, to some degree accelerate subsequent learning in the linguistic and cultural areas.

To quote just one example of the recent revaluation of translation and of the application of the sound principles outlined in the *Framework* to the present structure of Italian as a L2 courses, it is worthwhile mentioning that the University for Foreigners of Perugia, the oldest institution in the field of Italian as a L2 in Italy, currently includes translation from the four main European languages (English, French, German and Spanish) and Russian into Italian amongst the optional subjects, along with history, literature and art, to be taken at C1 and C2 levels.

Translation in foreign language teaching: why?

Having established that the latest shared beliefs in terms of language teaching are marked by the rehabilitation of translation as a teaching technique, it is now time to take a closer look at the reasons why translation can be considered beneficial to language learning. To begin with, it may be useful to clear the ground of three main false accusations that have been unfairly levelled at translation through the centuries, by refuting them and explaining why they lack any sensible foundation. In this regard, it can be said that translation:

1) does not contribute significantly to the incidence of **negative interferences** from the L1, for these are an inevitable and normal feature of the learning process. On the contrary, the use of translating techniques actually reduces the likelihood of negative transfers from the learner's L1 in that it enables the student to keep the two codes separate in his/her mind and to reflect consciously on the differences between the two languages and on the wrong strategies leading to interferences.[19]

2) is not **an unnatural procedure** in learning a L2. As seen before, cognitive psychology has proved once and for all that the process leading to the acquisition of a L2 substantially differs from the process of acquiring the L1: unlike learning the L1, whilst learning a L2 an individual relies on an additional set of knowledge deriving from any previous language learning experience, first and foremost from learning the L1. Thus the learner's L1 is an inescapable feature of the learning process of a

[19] P. Vijayaraghava Reddy, "Role of translation in SL teaching," in *Art and science of translation*, ed. J. Venkateswara Sastry (Hyderabad: Centre of advanced study in linguistics, Osmania University, 1994), 58. M. Hédiard, 230.

L2.[20] This being the case, preventing the learners from actively resorting to their L1 and therefore to translating techniques whilst learning a L2 would be tantamount to upholding a repressive, harmful and counterproductive idea of teaching:[21] as a matter of fact, students would be denied the possibility of implementing an approach that to all intents and purposes falls within the range of the normal and spontaneous cognitive strategies they deploy when confronted with the task of learning a L2.[22] In other words, quoting Popovic,[23] "attempts to interfere with the students' approach to learning could have extremely negative effects on such learners". Quite to the contrary, translation provides an excellent opportunity to back up the learners' automatic and natural tendencies by channelling them in the right direction and in compliance with the sound criteria to achieve the best results.[24]

3) does not hinder the development of **linguistic automatisms**. As a matter of fact, these occur during the initial phases of the process of learning a L2, when the recourse to translation should be minimised. At a

---

[20] N. Perini, "Tradurre: una 5ª 'abilità' da sviluppare in glottodidattica?", in *Processi traduttivi: teorie ed applicazioni*. Atti del seminario su "La traduzione", Brescia, 19-20 novembre 1981 (Brescia: La Scuola, 1982), 239.
E. Lavault, 50.
[21] E. Roulet, *Langue maternelle et langues secondes. Vers une pédagogie intégrée* (Paris: Crédif-Hatier, 1980), 23.
[22] V. García Yebra, "La traducción en la enseñanza de lenguas afines", in *La identidad del español y su didáctica*, ed. M.V. Calvi and F. San Vicente (Viareggio: Baroni, 1998), 116-18.
J.M. O' Malley and A.U. Chamot, *Learning Strategies in Second Language Acquisition* (Cambridge: Cambridge University Press, 1990), 127.
A. Danchev, "The Controversy over Translation in Foreign Language Teaching", in *Translation in Foreign Language Teaching*. Round Table FIT-UNESCO (Paris, 1983), 37-8.
A. Ballester Casado and M.D. Chamorro Guerrero, "La traducción como estrategia cognitiva en el aprendizaje de segundas lenguas", in *El español como lengua extranjera: de la teoría al aula. Actas del III Congreso Nacional de ASELE*, ed. S. Montesa Peydró and A. Garrido Moraga (Málaga: Ministerio de Educación y Ciencia, Universidad de Málaga, 1993), 396.
[23] R. Popovic R. (2004).
[24] C. Titford, "Translation – a post-communicative activity for advanced learners", in *Translation in Foreign Language Teaching and Testing*, ed. C. Titford and A.E. Hiecke (Tübingen: GNV, 1985), 78.
A. Ballester Casado and M.D. Chamorro Guerrero, 397.
P. Vijayaraghava Reddy, "Role of translation in SL teaching," in *Art and science of translation*, ed. J. Venkateswara Sastry (Hyderabad: Centre of advanced study in linguistics, Osmania University, 1994), 58.

later stage, once the basic linguistic structures have been interiorised, translation can contribute to consolidating and honing the existing automatisms by introducing an analytical, conscious side to the acquisition of a L2, which is unanimously considered as an indispensable component to achieve a full mastery of a L2. Consequently it can be said that "un'assimilazione cosciente di una lingua, fatta di riflessione e di razionalità, che trascenda la pura automatizzazione di certe abilità verbali di base, non può fare a meno della traduzione."[25]

The commonest misconceptions about translation in language teaching having thus been debunked, we must still consider why it is not only a harmless technique, but also a beneficial one. Its main advantages can be summed up in the following points:

- Translation stimulates the learner's **metalinguistic reflection** and makes it possible to carry it forward in an interesting way, circumventing the often dull grammar explanations. This notion is supported by the recognition that noticing the differences and similarities between two ways of speaking and thinking is an extremely fascinating activity, as it exploits curiosity, a typically human trait.[26] In this way learners may be awakened to even the slightest and seemingly most trivial nuances in the L2 (e.g. prepositions), which were it not for translation, could run the risk of being utterly missed out within a strictly monolingual approach.[27]
- A constant translation activity considerably enriches the learners' **range of vocabulary** both in the L2 and in their L1. By having them select a lexical item among a series of synonyms appearing absolutely interchangeable at face value, the translation exercise allows the students

---

[25] A conscious assimilation of a language, which involves reflection and rationality and goes beyond the mere automation of certain basic verbal abilities, cannot do without translation. [R. Titone, *Il tradurre dalla psicolinguistica alla glottodidattica* (Roma: Armando, 1998), 31].

[26] M. Danesi and R.J. Di Pietro, *L'analisi contrastiva per l'insegnamento della seconda lingua* (Roma: Armando, 2001), 15.
P. Sewell, "Translation in the Curriculum," in *Teaching Translation in Universities. Present and Future Perspectives*, ed. P. Sewell and I. Higgins (London: CILT, 1996), 139.

[27] Z. Zohrevandi, "Translation as a Resource for Teaching English as a Foreign Language", in *Language, Discourse and Translation in the West and Middle East*, ed. R. de Beaugrande, A. Shunnaq and M.H. Heliel (Amsterdam: John Benjamins, 1994), 181-88.
M.V. Calvi, "Il problema della traduzione nella didattica dello spagnolo," in *La traduzione nell'insegnamento delle lingue straniere* (Brescia: La Scuola, 1984), 461-62.

of a L2 to gain more insight into its complex lexical structure and into the even more complex connections between this and that of their L1. As a result, they could be stimulated to test the equivalences they have already established theoretically between the two systems and to discover the existence of false superficial correspondences, such as those involving the so-called "false friends." All of this will improve the lexical precision of their output in the L2.

- Translation exercises are closely intertwined with **intercultural analysis**, since they "not only offer intensive and very active practice in interpreting texts and messages, but they also force students to become aware of the cultural differences between one language and another."[28] Such differences often entail that whole sentences in a text must be changed or radically re-phrased in order to make them fit the particular idiomatic usage of the L2 or the specific local customs; in other instances it may be simply impossible to find exact equivalences of meaning or apparently well-tried correspondences may turn out to be not so viable in all kinds of contexts. In a nutshell, as Parks[29] very fittingly points out,

> the exercise of translation forces one to come to grips with the problems. The fact that there are no obvious answers may itself be the most significant lesson.

- Translation is an effective tool to develop or reinforce the learners' **textual competence** in the L2, as it tangibly shows the students that:[30]

1) any text closely depends on the specific context in which it has been produced and therefore the features of the context must also be thoroughly examined to understand the true meaning of the text;
2) any text possesses a communicative intention which must be kept unchanged as much as possible when translating the text from a language into the other;
3) any translation inevitably involves a loss of information which nevertheless must be minimised;
4) there can be several equally acceptable translations of any given text.

- Translation from a L2 into the learners' L1 provides the teacher with a precious opportunity to double-check the kind of **strategies** they

[28] G. Parks, "The role of translation in the communicative approach," in *Miscellanea n. 2*, ed. G. Parks (Trieste: Scuola Superiore di Lingue Moderne per Interpreti e Traduttori, Università degli Studi di Trieste, 1995), 243.
[29] *Ibidem*, 244.
[30] E. Borello 1999, 64-5.

adopt in decoding a written text in the L2, highlighting the elements that hinder the correct comprehension—such as false correspondences between L2 and L1, for instance—as well as the students' hypothesis on the patterns of the L2.[31] Furthermore, it is an excellent method for an activity of intensive reading in L2, leading to a more careful analysis of the features of the source text than is allowed by a superficial reading of it.[32]

- Finally, translation may play a significant role in developing the learners' ability to reflect consciously on the **learning mechanisms**, so as eventually to reach a stage in which they are handled and mastered autonomously, which is the ultimate aim of contemporary language teaching.[33]

Translation in foreign language teaching: how and when?

If, on one hand, translation can be a useful pedagogical tool, on the other, it is fundamental to make it clear how it should and should not be used in order for it not to relapse into the wrong and detrimental applications made by the supporters of the grammar-translation method. Hence re-evaluating translation by no means implies that the whole foreign language class ought to revolve around a comparison with the learners' L1, but that under certain circumstances it may prove advantageous to leave some room for translating activities, beside those aimed at globally developing the students' communicative skills.

As for the kind of translation to be favoured, it would be advisable to opt for the one defined as "**communicative**" by Newmark[34], whose aim is to convey the communicative intentions from the source text to the target text, so as to maintain the same overall effect on the recipients. However, it is important to note that for the purpose of language learning translation must always be viewed as a **means** and never as a target in itself: in other words, what really matters is the translating process with its implications on the learning of the L2, rather than the final outcome of such a process, which can even remain incomplete. This means that learners should to be warned that it is of little importance to refine the translation to the last detail, and that every time the exact features of the source text are not

---

[31] M.V. Calvi, "La traduzione nell'insegnamento linguistico," in *Interpretar. Traducir textos de la(s) cultura(s) hispánica(s).* Atti del convegno internazionale di Forlì, 21-23 ottobre 1999, ed. A. Melloni, R. Lozano and P. Capanaga (Bologna: CLUEB, 2000), 330-33.

[32] E. Lavault, 54.

[33] A. Ciliberti, *Manuale di glottodidattica* (Firenze: La Nuova Italia, 1994), 95-6.

[34] P. Newmark, *Approaches to Translation* (Oxford: Pergamon Press, 1982).

reproduced in the target text, it is because of substantial differences between the two languages involved, and not simply to achieve a better style, fluency or elegance. However, the priority granted to communicative translation does not totally exclude other types of translation; **literal translation**, for instance, may be used from time to time to increase the students' awareness of the particular configuration of certain structures of the L2, although it would be recommendable to do so after focusing on the meaning first.[35]

Regarding the direction in which to carry out the translating activity, it is generally agreed that it would be preferable to give priority to that **from the L2 into the L1**, as by doing this the risk of interferences is lower, a careful reflection can be conducted both on the structures of the L2 and on those peculiar to the L1 and the students would not be confronted with a task they might feel inadequate on account of their limited active competence in the L2. However, in this case too **translation into the L2** is not altogether ruled out from the foreign language classroom, since its sporadic use may help the students improve their production abilities in the L2, particularly in terms of grammar and vocabulary, to a greater extent than merely spontaneous production activities can. As a matter of fact, when talking spontaneously, students tend to simplify their sentences in the L2 discarding structures seen as complex if they do not feel sure about them, whereas translation into the L2 forces them to come to terms with problems, such as the need to convey the exact meaning of the source text, which would probably have been totally bypassed within a general production activity.[36]

On the subject of the **stage of the learning process** at which it is the most appropriate to introduce the practice of translation, it seems that the advanced level has to be prioritised. At this point, the fundamental linguistic structures of the L2 have already been assimilated, at least partially, and so the use of translation does not run the risk of either interfering with the creation of linguistic automatisms or fostering the idea that speaking in a L2 would be equal to translating all the time from the L1. Moreover, resorting to translation does not cause as much anxiety to advanced students as to elementary or intermediate ones, who may not yet

---

[35] W. Butzkamm, "The use of formal translation equivalents in the teaching of foreign language structures," in *Translation in Foreign Language Teaching and Testing*, ed. C. Titford and A.E. Hiecke (Tübingen: GNV, 1985), 89.

[36] L.S. Barhoudarov, "The role of Translation as a Means of Developing Oral and Written Speech Habits in the Senior Years of Instruction at a Language Teaching College," in *Translation in Foreign Language Teaching* (Paris: Round Table FIT-UNESCO, 1983), 13-4.

feel ready to deal with a far greater task than their actual competences in the L2. In any case, anxiety can be significantly reduced by translating texts the students are already familiar with because they have previously worked on them: it is well known, in fact, that learners' apprehension depends to a great extent on the lack of confidence they experience when confronted with some kind of novelty.[37] Being confined to an advanced learning phase, translation can thus be described as a "post-communicative" activity, as Titford[38] explains:

> In my use of "post-communicative" I conceive of the term both as referring to a third stage of a teaching programme, and as describing an activity appropriate only with a third "level of learner"—the advanced learner. With this level of learner, and at this stage in the teaching programme, translation consolidates what has been learnt in previous stages of (monolingual) activities by facilitating retention of what has already been encountered through reference to L1 communicative norms.

The consolidating effect brought up by Titford is achieved by highlighting the underlying reasons of certain linguistic mechanisms the students have already come across, although without going beyond their merely superficial traits. By virtue of such a deeper analysis, translation offers the matchless advantage of uprooting persistent mistakes in the students' interlanguage, which in time might become fossilised in the absence of a conscious reflection on the L2 structures.[39]

As far as **testing** is concerned, translation does not appear as a suitable tool to assess the students' linguistic level for three main reasons. Firstly because it is not consistent from a methodological point of view: it is wrong to use a technique to check factors having nothing to do with its sphere of action and purposes. In this sense, the nature of translation consists of transferring the contents of a text from a language into the other, and not of applying grammatical rules. Secondly, translation may be conducive to anxiety and is not meant to properly measure the level of the

---

[37] R. Titone, "La traduzione e l'insegnamento delle lingue straniere: problemi psicolinguistici e glottodidattici", in *La traduzione nell'insegnamento delle lingue straniere* (Brescia: La Scuola, 1984), 73.

[38] C. Titford, "Translation—a post-communicative activity for advanced learners", in *Translation in Foreign Language Teaching and Testing*, ed. C. Titford and A.E. Hiecke (Tübingen: GNV, 1985), 75.

[39] L.S. Barhoudarov, "The role of Translation as a Means of Developing Oral and Written Speech Habits in the Senior Years of Instruction at a Language Teaching College," in *Translation in Foreign Language Teaching* (Paris: Round Table FIT-UNESCO, 1983).

abilities actually possessed by the students, who under such stressful circumstances and for fear of committing mistakes are likely to be discouraged from taking unnecessary risks and to stick to what they know for sure, thus giving a reduced idea of their real competence in L2.[40] Lastly, correcting a translation is no easy task, since it is hard to find assessing criteria which are both objective and reliable.

A last observation has to do with whether it is feasible to view translation as a sort of **fifth linguistic ability** to put beside the four basic ones and to introduce among the objectives of a general foreign language course, not aimed specifically at the profession of translator and/or interpreter. Although this is a matter still under discussion, an ever increasing number of language learning experts would welcome such a possibility, on the grounds that translation is intimately connected with all the basic linguistic abilities, which could be enhanced even more thanks to the practice of translation.[41] Besides, some practical reasons must be taken into account: in our era marked by growing globalisation, international relations in the field of politics, economy and culture are becoming more and more numerous and intense, with the result that any learner of a L2 will be inevitably asked, at some point or another, to perform some kind of translating activity. This leads to the conclusion very fittingly reached by Weller:[42]

> If the general public's awareness of the importance of correct translating is to be enhanced, this can hardly be achieved only by organizing more courses for professional translators. Since the number of language learners far exceeds the number of students in special translation courses, inclusion of translation in a regular curriculum provides an excellent opportunity to make language learners more aware of the skills required to be a good translator.

---

[40] G. Anderman, "Finding the right word. Translation and Language Teaching," in *Translation and Language Teaching. Language Teaching and Translation*, ed. K. Malmkjær (Manchester: St. Jerome, 1998), 39-48.
[41] M. Snell-Hornby, "Translation as a means of integrating language teaching and linguistics," in *Translation in Foreign Language Teaching and Testing*, ed. C. Titford and A.E. Hiecke (Tübingen: GNV, 1985), 24.
Popovic R. (2004), *The place of translation in language teaching*, www.sueleatherassociates.com/pdfs/Article_translationinlanguageteaching.pdf
[42] G. Weller, "Some polemic aspects of translation in foreign language pedagogy revisited," in *Translator and Interpreter Training and Foreign Language Pedagogy*, ed. P.W. Krawutschke. Ata Scholarly Monograph Series, III (Binghampton: Binghampton Press, 1989), 45.

Translation in teaching Italian as a L2

All the remarks of the preceding paragraphs concerning a sensible use of translation in language learning naturally find their application also in teaching Italian as a L2, and even more so if the learners' L1 is a Romance language such as French, Spanish, Portuguese or Romanian. The same can be said for students who, despite having a non-Romance language as their L1 (e.g. English or German), possess a knowledge of one or more of such languages as their additional L2, which is often the case. As a matter of fact, it is well-known that interferences may be generated not only by the L1 but also by any L2 known by the speaker, especially if the latter belongs to the same language typology as the L1 or if it is in a dominant position over the L2 being learnt.

Contrary to popular belief, the difficulties of learning a L2 closely resembling one's L1 cannot be overstated. If on one hand it is undeniable that the similarities between the two languages and cultures make it easier to develop satisfactory communication skills from the earliest learning stages, on the other the strong feeling of confidence engendered by the sense of familiarity may in all likelihood lead students to underestimate the efforts needed to achieve total mastery of the L2, which is not limited to effective conversation exchanges, but also includes a reasonable degree of formal correctness of the utterances in L2. This is particularly true of the teaching of Italian as a foreign language, which on account of its distinctive nature belongs more to the sphere of linguistic education than to that of linguistic instruction. Balboni[43] sheds some light on this matter by pointing out that while the latter focuses mainly on practical and short-term targets, i.e. the achievement of effective communicative abilities, the former entails a much more ambitious plan, being closely associated with the learners' maturation and a certain degree of integration in the L2-speaking community. From this perspective, whereas in teaching English as a L2 it may be viable to adopt the instruction standpoint, since it is a language which is very widely studied and in most cases for eminently pragmatic reasons, teaching Italian as a L2 necessarily involves the concept of education, thanks to which it still makes sense to learn a language which, from a strictly utilitarian point of view, would be useless on the international scene. Therefore, in order for the teaching of Italian to be still meaningful, and without overlooking the fact that Italian grammar usually poses more problems to students than, say, English grammar, it

[43] P.E. Balboni, *Didattica dell'italiano a stranieri* (Roma: Bonacci, 1994), 21-5; 51.

seems essential to focus the learners' attention on the formal correctness of their production, much more than one would do with students of English as a L2, for example. This is especially the case when two or more similar languages are involved in the learning process. In actual fact, a lack of metalinguistic reflection could easily lead to continued repetition of the same mistakes,[44] to the extent that they may become fossilised and be responsible for the learning process coming to a standstill, which would condemn the learners to a state of perennial limbo, as Hédiard[45] pointedly acknowledges:

> S'il est vrai que la ressemblance entre les langues peut faciliter l'apprentissage dans la phase initiale, il n'en demeure pas moins que cette même facilité risque de provoquer très vite une stagnation due au fait que l'apprenant, se fixant comme stratégie de communication une compétence réduite qui lui permet de "se débrouiller," a tendance par la suite à se contenter du niveau qu'il a atteint et à fossiliser ses erreurs.[46]

Given this fact, translation may constitute a powerful and valid resource to stimulate the learners' **metalinguistic reflection**, allowing them to rationally compare the languages involved in the learning process and to become more aware of both similarities and differences, thus acquiring a more accurate and objective perception of the real distance between the languages. This is especially true if applied to "false friends," collocations or to tricky grammar structures which may not seem particularly hard to grasp at first. I will only quote some examples taken from my own experience as a teacher of Italian L2 to Spanish-speaking students. As for collocations, it may be interesting to note that the Spanish equivalent of the Italian phrase "all'aria **aperta**" (in the open air) uses a different adjective, being "al aire **libre**." As far as the verb system is concerned, in the following sentence the use of the "imperfetto indicativo"

---

[44] For a classification of the most common mistakes made by Spanish-speaking learners of Italian, you may refer to S. Bailini, "Análisis de errores en las producciones escritas de estudiantes españoles de italiano L2. Reflexiones sobre una experiencia didáctica," in *En obras 2. El error. Experiencias didácticas*, ed. Daniela Carpani (Salerno/Milano: Oèdipus, 2003), 145-47.

[45] M. Hédiard, 225.

[46] If it is true that the similarity between the languages can make learning easier in the initial phase, it is also undeniable that the same ease of learning runs the risk of leading very quickly to a deadlock due to the fact that the learner, adopting as a communicative strategy a reduced competence enabling him to "get by", then tends to be satisfied with the level that he/she has reached and to fossilise his/her mistakes.

of the verb "dovere" followed by a present infinitive is not often immediately understood by Spanish-speaking students, who would use a past infinitive instead in their L1, as the comparison with the Spanish sentence clearly shows:

> Non dovevi **lasciare** la porta aperta! È entrato il gatto e ha fatto un guaio.
>
> ¡No tenías que **haber dejado** la puerta abierta! Ha entrado el gato y ha hecho un desastre.

Something similar can be said concerning the use of the future tense after the conjunction "se" in the first type of the if- sentences (periodo ipotetico di primo tipo). The comparison is valid for English-speakers too:

> Se non **pioverà**, andremo tutti a fare una passeggiata."
> Si no **llueve**, iremos todos a dar un paseo.
> If it **does not rain**, we will all go for a walk.

A third example involves a particular use of the subjunctive in Italian, that is when the subordinate clause introduced by "che" or a question word ("come," "quando," "perché," etc.) is placed at the beginning of the sentence, thus inverting the usual order of the clauses within the sentence, as in the following example, to be compared with the Spanish translation:

> Che tra di loro **sia** tutto **finito**, è ormai chiarissimo.
> A estas alturas está clarísimo que entre ellos todo **ha terminado**.

Finally, the use of translation would also compensate for a common drawback of most textbooks addressed to mixed language classes, that is the failure to take into account the **specific needs** and the progression of the interlanguage of speakers of a given L1. In other words, using the same Italian language course for Japanese-speaking and Spanish-speaking students alike would probably mean that the latter will find the lessons rather slow-paced and boring and will feel the need to progress more rapidly, finding the answers to doubts concerning structures they are already familiar with to a certain degree, but which they have never deeply analysed.

In conclusion, despite being still viewed with distrust by some foreign language teachers, the recent recovery of translation in teaching Italian as a L2 definitely implies more of a progression than a regression. As a matter of fact, having undergone a weighty purification process which has cleared the way of wrong applications, translation now presents itself as a perfectly legitimate technique which can offer countless advantages to learners wishing to progress beyond a superficial knowledge of Italian and achieve real proficiency. Much of this work is left to the teacher's insight and open-mindedness about teaching techniques; at any rate, the inclusion of a correctly judged amount of translation work in the L2 classroom cannot fail to benefit students in the long term.

UNIVERSITY FOR FOREIGNERS, PERUGIA, ITALY

CHAPTER TWELVE

WORDS DON'T COME EASY… ESPECIALLY DURING EXAMS! THE IMPORTANCE OF ADOPTING A DIDACTIC TRANSLATION METHODOLOGY IN THE CONTEXT OF THE 2001 ITALIAN UNIVERSITY REFORM

MARIA CRISTINA CIGNATTA

> In verbis etiam tenuis cautusque serendis dixeris egregie, notum si callida verbum reddiderit iunctura novum.
> You will have written exceptionally well if, by skilful arrangement of your words, you have made an ordinary one seem original.[1]
> —Horace: *Ars Poetica* (vv.46-48)

From Old to New: A Brief Description of the Italian University Reform

Italian University studies were traditionally structured around a one-tier system of qualification, whereby the length of the former 'Laurea' degree ranged between a minimum of 4 years (Languages, Literature, Economics, Law, Science, etc.) to a maximum of 6 years (Medicine, Veterinary Science, Engineering, etc.). Even after the introduction in 1980 of the Ph.D. programme (lasting 3 years) and in 1990 of the University

[1] The translation is my own.

Diploma (2-3 years in length and with a mainly vocational nature), the Laurea still remained the main higher education qualification.

The Ministerial Decree 509/99 established the new framework of the Italian University education system, which came into effect in the academic year 2001-2002. One of the most radical transformations made to the system was the replacement of the former one-tier scheme with the '3+2' unitary two-tier scheme, consisting of a 3-year First Level degree followed by a 2-year Second Level degree. The First Level degree is tailored to provide students with adequate knowledge of general principles and notions, as well as specific professional skills; the Second Level degree aims to provide graduates with advanced education and training for highly qualified professions in specific sectors. After being awarded a Second Level degree students can enrol in Second Level Master courses, Ph.D. courses or Specialisation courses. Another important innovation was the concession of full teaching autonomy to Italian universities: these are now free to decide on the nomenclature of their degree courses and their individual curricula. Thirdly, the Reform pioneered a system of university credits, which represent the total student workload (comprising class time, self-study, practical activities, etc.). Each credit corresponds to 25 hours of total activities, the average full-time workload for one academic year being 60 credits.

The main objectives of the Reform were to bring the Italian University system in line with the European University model and to promote international exchanges. The shorter degree course aimed to increase the number of graduates, lower their average graduation age and reduce drop-out rates.

The First Level Degree in Civiltà e Lingue Straniere Moderne at Parma University

As a mother-tongue English Language teacher, I have been actively engaged in the teaching of translation skills from Italian into English at the University of Parma since 1989. Prior to the Reform, I worked with 3rd and 4th year English Language students on the 4-year Laurea degree course in Lingue e Letterature Straniere; after 2001, with students in their final year of the recently instituted 3-year First Level degree course in Civiltà e Lingue Straniere Moderne.

The traditional 3rd and 4th year translation courses were based on the translation from L1 to L2 of literary texts taken from a plethora of 20th century Italian prose writers. The texts dealt with in class and set in examination papers were unabridged, reflected a wide range of styles and registers within the literary genre and were representative of the various geographical regions of Italy (Pavese and Ginzburg from Piemonte, Cassola from Tuscany, the Roman Moravia and Sicilian Pirandello, to name but a few). On the 4th year course, texts written by more complex authors, such as Svevo, Buzzati, Calvino, Gadda, Pratolini, etc. were worked on. In the 3rd year written examination at the end of the course, students were required to translate into English a literary text consisting of about 250 words, with the aid of a monolingual dictionary (or alternatively a dictionary of synonyms and antonyms) of their own choice within a time limit of 1 hour and 30 minutes. The 4th year written examination entailed a similar type of exercise, except that the source text was more challenging from the point of view of syntax and lexis, slightly longer (about 280-300 words) and with a time constraint of 2 hours.

With the advent of the new 3-year degree course in Civiltà e Lingue Straniere Moderne, a few amendments and innovations have been made to the English Language curriculum. With specific reference to the area of translation, the traditional Italian⇒English translation course has been totally revisited and a parallel translation course from English into Italian introduced on all three years. Considering the professionally-oriented nature and vocation of the new First Level University degrees, and bearing in mind that the majority of the new language graduates who decide to become professional translators will be called upon to translate a wide variety of text types in their everyday working capacity, the scope of the previous syllabus and final examination were extended to cover a variety of text types, ranging from

- Literary texts (fiction, non-fiction, drama, literary criticism);
- Technical and scientific texts (abstracts for specialized science journals, extracts from science text books, science magazine articles for a non-specialist readership, medical texts, instructions from manuals, leaflets, etc.);
- texts dealing with legal, economic and political topics and institutions (agreements, contracts, company profiles, business correspondence, newspaper articles, European Union documents, etc.).

The first consideration to bear in mind is that, with very few exceptions (notably the foreign exchange students studying English at Parma University), the students are translating from their mother tongue (Italian) to a second language (English). Of course, in the case of non-Italian native speakers, the translating process is an even trickier one, in that they find themselves translating from one foreign language into another. Whatever the case, for all students attending the course, English is not their language of habitual use, which means that the transfer process is hardly ever enacted "naturally, accurately and with maximum effectiveness."[2] However, in a real-life situation, most professional translators do in fact translate out of their own language ('service' translation); in this case, extra care must be taken to avoid the risk of producing sub-standard translations packed with inaccuracies, misinterpretations and bad-wording. Translations from L1 to L2 usually need revision and post-editing by a native L2 speaker before submission of the final draft.

The second essential factor to be taken into account is that the students' acquisition of translation strategies and procedures seems to be largely conditioned—sometimes negatively—by the examination looming at the end of the course. My experience of teaching undergraduate students has shown that student performance during the course is for the most part influenced by their fear of failing the examination. When students are given back their assigned work, they invariably ask questions such as: Would this gain a pass mark in the exam? What they usually fail to add is: Why or where did I go wrong? What can I do to improve the quality of my translations? How can I get extra practice in translation? For many students—fortunately not for all—the 18/30 pass mark seems to be the be-all and end-all.

Whatever the nature of the text we are working on, we will inevitably run into a series of problems. Any kind of translation is a multi-faceted entity covering at least two dimensions: first and foremost the semantics and temporal progression of the translation progress, secondly the semiotics and spatial composition of the final product. In short, the translated text involves much more than the re-phrasing of original verbal utterances.

Translation in Teaching Methodology

My experience in the teaching of translation skills has afforded me the opportunity to develop a methodology which has yielded good results in terms of students' exam performance. Of course, no method is infallible and, on the basis of the feedback I periodically obtain from students, this particular method undergoes revision from year to year.

---

[2] Peter Newmark, *A Textbook of Translation* (Harlow: Longman, 2003), 3.

First and foremost, at the beginning of the course, translation material for use in the classroom needs to be accurately selected and classified according to typology (literary texts, techno-scientific texts, legal, economic and institutional texts, etc.) and, within the same typology, according to the degree of difficulty. The different text types are taught in separate modules, each of which is preceded by a brief outline of the theoretical notions linked to that particular typology, as well as an overview of the typical features of the genre.

The first problem facing students is related to **decoding** (i.e. the ability to read, understand and correctly interpret) the source text. This is a particularly delicate phase in which the text needs to be read very carefully, in order to avoid errors of interpretation. During this time they are encouraged to do a preliminary skim reading of the text, and to identify SL text type, style, register and readership. A second scan reading will enable students to organize the text from the point of view of syntax, make a mental translation at least of certain blocks of expression, underline unknown terms and identify any potential stumbling blocks in the passage. In exam conditions, students are given five minutes before the exam officially starts to read carefully through the text, during which time they are not allowed to put pen to paper. We find that, if the 5-minute reading is deducted from the time limit, students tend to panic and will often dispense with this precious preliminary in the fear of not completing the test within the allotted time.

The decoding phase is followed by the **encoding** process. To a large extent, the quality of the translation will be directly proportional to the quality or qualities of the translator; a translation will undoubtedly benefit from the student's ability to read and perfectly interpret a text written in a foreign language, from his/her knowledge of the particular subject that is being dealt with, from his/her sensitivity to both the L1 and L2, and from his/her sound knowledge of the target language and resourceful writing skills in the same language. It is in this last skill in particular that all the translator's linguistic virtuosities come into play. Writing undoubtedly engages all five senses, but more significantly, it includes a sixth sense known as "common sense" which, in the words of Newmark, is a happy combination of "intelligence, sensitivity and intuition, as well as of knowledge."[3]

---

[3] Ibid., 4.

Cloze Method

Literary texts tend to present notorious translational thorns in the flesh, such as syntax, grammar structures, figures of speech, neologisms, idioms, jokes, puns, false cognates, cultural references, etc. In non-literary texts, such as techno-scientific, legal and economic texts, equally taxing issues need to be taken into consideration. Primarily, the inevitable problem of lexis in the shape of **sectorial terminology and jargon**. In the event of a student having absolutely no familiarity with the particular topic at issue, s/he is advised to read around the subject and consult documentary sources (articles in the press or on the Internet, glossaries, experts in the field, etc.) before embarking on the transfer process. Serious incompetence and deficiency of knowledge in the field of medicine, economics, law and technology could result in irreparable consequences in real-life situations.

In lexis consolidation, I have employed strategies such as the **Cloze method**. This method, which has been, and still is, used extensively in listening comprehension, reading comprehension and Use of English exercises, can also be put to profit in translation seminars, where it proves to be a useful tool to assess not only the student's comprehension of the source text (Italian) but also to consolidate lexis and grammar structures in the target language (English). Depending on what the teacher chooses to work on in a particular text, the method can be implemented to focus on certain lexical elements or grammar points or both even, by blocking out from the text the problematic areas under survey. By way of illustration, I propose to look at Texts 1 and 2. I used these particular texts in class as an introduction to sectorial lexis (business English and scientific English).

In the following exercises, all the key words have been blocked out from the text and students are called upon to focus on these specific problem areas, fill in the blanks and justify their choice. They are encouraged to consult all the possible translation resources (monolingual and bilingual dictionaries, glossaries, texts on translation theory and practice, translation software, etc.) and even to compile glossaries of their own, which they will update week by week as they come across new sectorial terms.

Text 1: Profilo di Enel	**Company profile**
Quotata dal 1999 alle Borse di Milano e New York, Enel è la società europea con il più alto numero di **azionisti,** circa 2,3 milioni ed una **capitalizzazione di Borsa**	(1) ….. on the Milan and New York stock exchanges since 1999, Enel is the European company with the largest number of (2) ….., at some 2.3 million. It

di circa 41 **miliardi** di euro al **valore** attuale. E' la più grande azienda **elettrica** del Paese e la terza utility **quotata** d'Europa.

has a (3) ….. of about 41 (4) ….. Euro at current (5) …... Enel is Italy's largest (6) ….. company, and Europe's third-largest (7) ….. utility.

IL BUSINESS

BUSINESS OVERVIEW

Enel produce e **distribuisce** elettricità principalmente in Europa, Nord America e America Latina. Ha circa 53.000 Megawatt di capacità **produttiva** e 32 milioni di clienti nell'elettricità. Enel è anche il secondo **distributore** di gas naturale in Italia, con oltre 2,2 milioni di clienti e una **quota di mercato** del 12% circa.

Enel produces and (8) ….. electricity mostly in Europe, North and Latin America. Enel has 53,000 Megawatts of (9) ….. capacity and has 32 million customers in the power business. Enel is also the second-largest Italian (10) ….. of natural gas, with over 2.2 million customers and a 12% (11) ….. market share.

Lavorano in Enel circa 52.000 persone che **gestiscono** 46 **centrali termoelettriche**, 500 **idroelettriche**, 32 **geotermiche**, 17 **eoliche** e 4 **fotovoltaiche** e oltre un milione di chilometri di **linee di distribuzione**.

The company has about 52,000 employees and (12) ….. 46 (13) ….., 500 (14) ….., 32 (15) ….., 17 (16) ….. and 4 (17) ….., in addition to more than a million kilometres of (18) …..

Nel 2005 Enel ha **prodotto ricavi** per 34 **miliardi** di euro, con un **utile netto** di 3,9 **miliardi** di euro.

In 2005, Enel (19) ….. (20) ….. of 34 (21) ….. Euro, while (22) ….. stood at 3.9 (23) ….. Euro.

Per prima al mondo, Enel ha avviato la sostituzione a tutti i suoi clienti dei tradizionali **contatori elettromeccanici** con moderni contatori elettronici che consentono la **lettura dei consumi** in tempo reale e la **gestione a distanza** dei contratti. Una innovazione che ha permesso la **proposta** di **tariffe multiorarie** che offrono un **risparmio** nelle ore serali e nei fine settimana, e che ha attirato l'interesse di molte utilities in tutto il mondo.

Enel was the first utility in the world to replace its customers' traditional (24) ….. with modern electronic (25) ….. that make it possible to take (26) ….. in real time and (27) ….. contractual relationships (28) …... This innovation has enabled Enel to (29) ….. (30) ….. electricity (31) ….., which offer customer (32) ….. for evening and weekend electricity use, an initiative that has attracted interest from many utilities around the world.

Text 2: Biodiversità

Biodiversity

La biodiversità è la varietà di **organismi** considerati a tutti i livelli, dalle **varianti genetiche** di ciascuna **specie** fino ai ***phyla***, passando per i diversi livelli **tassonomici**. Dall'origine della vita sulla Terra, i processi di **speciazione** ed **estinzione** hanno **avuto come risultato** un aumento progressivo, sebbene **con sussulti**, della biodiversità della Terra.

Biodiversity is the variety of (1) ….. on every level, ranging from the (2) ….. of each (3) ….. to the (4) ….., across the various (5) ….. levels. Ever since life originated on Earth, the processes of (6) ….. and (7) ….. have (8) ….. a gradual, though (9) ….., increase in the Earth's biodiversity.

Attualmente, non siamo a conoscenza del numero di **specie** che **abitano** la Terra. Ne sono state **catalogate** più di 1,4 milioni, ma il numero totale stimato da diversi autori **varia** tra i 5 milioni e più di 30 milioni. Molte di queste non saranno mai conosciute, perché **si estingueranno** prima che qualche naturalista possa **raccoglierle** e **dar loro un nome**, figurarsi poi capire la loro **biologia** ed **ecologia**. Se la distruzione della natura progredisce al **ritmo** attuale, si calcola che, verso l'anno 2020, un 20% della biodiversità **globale sarà andato perduto**.

At present, we have no knowledge of the exact number of (10) ….. that (11) ….. the Earth. Over 1.4 million have been (12) ….. but the total number estimated by different authors (13) ….. 5 million to over 30 million. Many of these will remain unknown, because they (14) ….. before some natural scientist can (15) them and (16) ….. them, let alone gain any understanding of their (17) ….. and (18) ….. traits. If the destruction of nature advances at the present (19) ….., it is calculated that, by the year 2020, about 20% of (20) ….. biodiversity (21) …..

Le ragioni per **proteggere** la biodiversità sono numerose. Molte **specie** hanno un valore di utilità pratica. Occorre distinguere i **batteri**, i **funghi**, vegetali od animali che producono **sostanze con valore farmaceutico**. In questo senso, l'**estinzione** di **specie** equivale a distruggere una **raccolta medica** scritta in una lingua che **non è ancora stata decifrata.**

There are many reasons for (22) ….. biodiversity. Many (23) ….. are useful from a practical point of view. It is important to distinguish (24) ….., (25) ….., plants or animals which yield (26) ….. In this sense, the (27) ….. of (28) ….. is tantamount to destroying a (29) ….. written in a (30) ….. language.

Un'altra ragione fondamentale per **conservare** la biodiversità e il suo valore **ecologico**. L'**estinzione** di alcune **specie** può provocare cambiamenti a livello

Another fundamental reason for (31) ….. biodiversity is its (32) ….. importance. The (33) ….. of certain (34) ….. is likely to cause changes within the (35) ….. to dell'**ecosistema** di cui fanno parte. Ad esempio, l'estinzione delle **micorrize** nei boschi **caducifogli** europei, a causa della **pioggia acida**, colpirà senza dubbio il **bilancio** di **sostanze nutritive** di questi **ecosistemi forestali**. L'**estinzione** di **specie-chiave**, come la **nutria marina** nelle **foreste di laminarie della California**, può cambiare completamente queste comunità.

which they belong. For instance, the extinction of (36) ..... in European (37) ..... forests due to (38) ..... will inevitably affect the (39) ..... of the (40) ..... in these (41) ...... The (42) ..... of (43) ..... like the (44) ..... in the (45) ..... can cause radical changes in these communities.

The Cloze method has also proved to be an invaluable tool for consolidating **grammar** structures in the target language. As all EFL teachers know, structures such as the use of the conditional present in the "Future in the Past," the translation of the Italian subjunctive, the use of modal verbs, etc., represent notorious stumbling blocks for all Italian students translating into English. The following passage from Alberto Moravia's *La Noia* (Text 3) can be used as a starting-point to illustrate these particular problem areas. As can be seen, all renderings of the "future in the past," subjunctives and modals have been conveniently omitted from the English text: the rationale of this exercise is to make students concentrate exclusively on these corresponding verbal patterns in English, without them having to mull over a thousand other issues raised by the text as a whole. Students then proceed to fill in the blanks and justify their choice—it must be made clear to them that they will be penalised for guessing! Once they have mastered the procedure, they should be able to identify and tackle similar structures in other texts.

Text 3:

ALBERTO MORAVIA: ***LA NOIA***

Intanto, però, c'era un problema, piccolo ma angoscioso: **dovevo** telefonare per primo o **dovevo** aspettare **che lei mi telefonasse**? Cecilia aveva l'abitudine di telefonarmi tutti i giorni sempre alla stessa ora, la mattina verso le dieci, per salutarmi e confermarmi l'appuntamento del pomeriggio. Io potevo dunque certamente aspettare anche quel giorno la sua

But in the meantime there was a trivial yet distressing problem: (1) ..... be the first to call or (2) ..... wait (3) .....? Cecilia was in the habit of telephoning me every day, always at the same time, about ten o'clock in the morning, to say hello and confirm our afternoon date. Therefore, I could quite rightly expect a phone call from her that morning, but at

telefonata, ma al tempo stesso temevo **che non si facesse viva** e **uscisse**, e così, quando **mi fossi deciso** a telefonarle io stesso, **non ci fosse** e io **avessi** a rimanere tutto il giorno nell'incertezza ormai sicuramente molto dolorosa della sua venuta. Anche per questa faccenda del telefono, d'altro canto, mi accorsi che i termini del mio problema si ripetevano identici: io volevo **che Cecilia mi telefonasse** per prima per poter continuare a considerarla inesistente appunto perché disponibile; se invece **fossi stato io** a telefonarle, **avrei dovuto** pensare a lei come a qualche cosa di reale, appunto perché problematico e sfuggente. Alle tre del pomeriggio ero ancora immerso in queste riflessioni, quando udii il telefono, laggiù in fondo allo studio, **squillare** ripetutamente, dolcemente, querulamente, ironicamente, come per dirmi che ciò che contava non erano i miei pensieri, **per quanto** lucidi, ma il suo squillo. Mi alzai, andai a staccare il ricevitore e subito udii la voce di Cecilia: "Finalmente, ma dov'eri?"
Risposi con voce molto bassa: "Ero nello studio, ma non ti **avevo udito**."
Ci fu un momento di silenzio; poi lei disse: "Non ti ho telefonato stamattina perché il telefono era guasto. Allora ci **vediamo** oggi alla solita ora."
Non potei **fare a meno di esclamare** con qualche vivacità: "Ma ieri perché non sei venuta?"

the same time I was afraid (4) ..... and (5) ....., with the result that, by the time I (6) ..... to phone her, she (7) ..... and I (8) ..... to remain for the rest of the day in the uncertainty, by now truly painful, of her visit. As for this business of the telephone, moreover, I was aware that the basic problem was repeating itself in identical terms: I wanted (9) ..... first, so that I could go on thinking of her as non-existent, just because she was available. If instead I (10) ..... the initiative, I (11) ..... to think of her as something real, in that she was ambiguous and elusive. At three in the afternoon I was still turning these thoughts over in my mind when, at the far end of the study, I heard the phone (12) ..... repeatedly, softly, querulously, ironically, as if to tell me that what counted were not my thoughts, lucid (13) ....., but its ringing. I got up, went and lifted the receiver and at once heard Cecilia's voice: "About time, too! Where were you?"
I replied in a very low voice: "I was in the study but I (14) ..... you."
There was a moment's silence; then she said: "I didn't call you this morning because the phone was out of order. (15) ..... you today then at the usual time."
I could not (16) ..... in a sharp tone of voice: "But what happened to you yesterday?"

Multiple Choice

Other important issues are, of course, **register, style, setting** (i.e. where the text is typically published) and **readership**. Students need to ask themselves questions like: Where would this text be published in the TL? What would be a TL equivalent to the SL journal, magazine or textbook? What sort of person am I translating for—is s/he an expert, an educated layperson or a person with no knowledge at all of the topic?

Multiple choice is a type of exercise which can be successfully adapted for the purpose of illustrating these key issues. Multiple choice questions usually include a phrase or stem followed by 3-5 options. Learners are required to select the appropriate option/options in order to complete the sentence both grammatically and semantically. The method is best illustrated with a few examples. The passages in question have been taken from Giovanni Guareschi (*Gente Così*) and Italo Svevo (*La Coscienza di Zeno*) respectively. Certain parts of the text have been omitted and students are called upon to select from a list the option(s) that most closely correspond to the source text in terms of style and register. In other words, within the confines of what may be generally considered to be grammatically correct, students are asked to discriminate and discuss each of the options in terms of suitability for that particular context. Given that they will be asked to justify their choice, they are well aware that they will be penalised for guessing.

Text 4:

La Jo' era una donna **impegolata fino agli occhi dentro la politica** e, siccome aveva del temperamento, **riusciva agevolmente a fare** non solo la sua parte ma anche quella del marito.

Suo marito era morto di malattia lasciandola sola con un bambino di tre anni appena: ma il dolore procuratole dalla perdita del coniuge doveva essere stato ampiamente compensato dal fatto che la Jo' aveva potuto **tirare un colpo mancino al prete** portando il morto al cimitero con funerale civile, al suono di "Bandiera rossa."

La Jo' era piuttosto una bella donna e non arrivava ai trent'anni: avrebbe potuto trovarsi un altro marito e campare meglio. Ma non avrebbe mai rinunciato al suo disagio: sentiva che il disagio andava in tanto veleno, e l'odio per gli avversari cresceva di giorno in giorno e la sosteneva perché l'odio era la sua fede.

Si arrangiava come poteva: mietitura, trebbiatura, pigiatura, eccetera. E nella morta stagione fabbricava ceste di vimini che poi andava in giro a vendere.

Lavorava con ferocia e anche gli uomini più rozzi **badavano a non stuzzicarla** perché la Jo', oltre a **essere lesta di mano**, era capace di tirar fuori parolacce **da far rimanere senza fiato** i più celebrati campioni di turpiloquio.

GIOVANNI GUARESCHI: *GENTE COSÌ*

(1) Jo was

A) committed to politics
B) up to her neck/eyeballs in politics
C) highly politicised
D) into politics in a big way

and, being strong-willed,

(2) she

A) had no difficulty in doing
B) had no trouble doing
C) performed with the greatest ease
D) could easily do

not only her part but her husband's, too. Her husband had died of an illness, leaving her with a child of barely three years old. But the grief caused by his death must have been fully made up for by the fact that

(3) Jo had been able to

A) play a nasty/dirty trick on
B) get one up on
C) seek revenge on
D) retaliate against

the priest, by having the corpse taken to the cemetery without a religious ceremony, to the accompaniment of "Bandiera Rossa" ("Red Flag"). Jo was quite an attractive woman and she wasn't thirty yet: she could have found another husband and lived a better life. But she would never have lived without her inner turmoil: she felt that it fired her with venom and her hatred for her opponents grew day by day and kept her going because hatred was her credo.

(4) She

A) managed to subsist by
B) managed to make ends meet by
C) did her best to get by
D) eked out a living

reaping, threshing, grape-crushing, and so on. During the off season she made wicker baskets, which she then went around selling.

(5) She worked tirelessly, and even the most vulgar men

A) were reluctant to provoke her
B) made sure they didn't rouse her
C) kept out of her way
D) were loath to provoke her

(6) because, as well as

A) being somewhat belligerent,
B) having a good left hook,
C) being rather aggressive,
D) being quick with her fists,
Jo was capable of churning out swear-words that would outdo the most renowned champion of coarse language.

Guareschi's zippy, idiomatic "Valpadana" type of language obviously requires a similar type of rendering in English. Therefore our choice is likely to be directed towards a fairly simple syntax in which there will be a predominance of co-ordinate clauses, with the use of idioms, popular expressions, phrasal verbs, contracted forms, etc. For example, students will be given credit for singling options B) and D) in sentence (1) and options A) and B) in sentence (3), etc.

Text 5:

Una sera della fine di marzo arrivai un po' più tardi del solito a casa. Niente di male: **ero caduto nelle mani** di un dotto amico che aveva voluto **confidarmi** certe sue idee sulle origini del Cristianesimo. Era la prima volta che **si voleva da me ch'io pensassi** a quelle origini, eppure **m'adattai alla lunga lezione** per **compiacere l'amico**. Piovigginava e faceva freddo. Tutto era sgradevole e fosco, compresi i Greci e gli Ebrei di cui il mio amico parlava, ma pure **m'adattai a quella sofferenza** per ben due ore. La mia solita debolezza! Scommetto che oggi ancora sono tanto incapace **di resistenza**, che se qualcuno **ci si mettesse sul serio** potrebbe **indurmi a studiare** per qualche tempo l'astronomia.

Entrai nel giardino che circonda la nostra villa. A questa si accedeva per una breve strada carrozzabile. Maria, la nostra cameriera, m'aspettava alla finestra e sentendomi avvicinare gridò nell'oscurità:

"E' lei, signor Zeno?"

Maria era una di quelle fantesche **come non se ne trovano più**. Era da noi da una quindicina d'anni. Metteva mensilmente alla Cassa di

Risparmio una parte della sua paga per i suoi vecchi anni, risparmi che però non le servirono perché essa morì in casa nostra poco dopo il mio matrimonio sempre lavorando.

ITALO SVEVO: ***LA COSCIENZA DI ZENO***

One evening at the end of March I arrived home slightly later than usual. There was nothing wrong:

(1) I had simply
A) fallen into the hands/clutches of
B) been detained by
C) bumped into
D) come across
a learned friend of mine,

(2) who had insisted on
A) giving me the low-down on
B) filling me in on
C) making me partake of
D) confiding to me
some of his ideas on the origins of Christianity.

(3) This was the first time
A) I had been requested to reflect upon
B) someone had got me thinking about
C) I had been called upon to reflect on
D) they'd asked me to think about
those origins,

(4) nevertheless
A) I let myself get carried away
B) I let him go on talking
C) I raised no objection to his long lecture
D) I was quite prepared to listen to the long lecture

(5)
A) in order to please my friend.
B) just to keep in with my friend.
C) so as not to offend my friend.
D) because I didn't want to fall out with my friend.

It was drizzling with rain and cold. Everything was dreary and gloomy, including the Greeks and Jews about whom my friend was talking,

(6) yet
A) I put up with it
B) I stuck it out
C) I suffered the pain
D) I endured the ordeal

for two long hours. My usual lack of willpower!

(7) I bet that even nowadays I am still so incapable of
A) reacting
B) fighting back
C) refusing
D) saying no

(8) that, if someone really
A) put his mind to it,
B) meant business,
C) did his utmost,
D) persisted,

(9) he could
A) seriously persuade/convince me to study
B) talk me into reading up on
C) get me going on
D) seriously induce me to study
astronomy for a certain amount of time.
I entered the garden surrounding our villa. The house could be reached by a short carriage road. Maria, our housekeeper, was waiting for me at the window and, as she heard my footsteps, she shouted in the dark:
"Is that you, Master Zeno?"

(10)Maria was one of those servants that are
A) hard to come across
B) few and far between
C) a rarity
D) are virtually impossible to find

nowadays. She had been with us for over fifteen tears. Every month she used to put away part of her wages in the local bank for her retirement. However her savings were to be of no use to her, because she died in our house, when she was still in service, shortly after my marriage.

Svevo's language, on the other hand, is formal, with a subtle vein of irony and understatement and is best matched by a similar type of language in the English rendering of the text (a richer type of syntax with a predominance of subordinate clauses, neutral expressions as opposed to idioms and popular expressions, single Latinate verb forms as opposed to phrasal verbs, absence of contracted verbal forms, etc.) To give a few examples, students would be given credit for having chosen options C) and D) in sentence (2) and options A) and C) sentence (5).

Error Correction

This is a procedure that has traditionally been in the hands of the teacher, who has the specific task of correcting errors made by students. In actual fact, this method tends to be viewed by some as being unilateral and hierarchical and not 100% effective in language teaching. Evidence of this is the fact that students do not always learn by their mistakes and tend to reiterate the same errors corrected and explained by the teacher. It is undoubtedly more effective for students to identify and correct their own mistakes, in that any information arrived at inductively (by their own reasoning) is more likely to be retained over the long term.

Students are provided with a source text (in Italian) and a translation of the same text in the target language. The latter may be an authentic text translated by one of the students in the class (in which case it will remain anonymous), or alternatively a text in which errors have been deliberately included by the teacher. The students are then set the task of editing the target text, purging it of all possible errors and inaccuracies and maybe improving the parts of the text which are grammatically correct but could be expressed more appropriately. For this purpose, both students and teacher should ideally have a common shorthand for error correction.

Correction Key

T	=	tense
P	=	punctuation
WO	=	word order
Prep	=	preposition

WW	=	wrong word
FF	=	false friend/false cognate
GR	=	grammar
Λ	=	word missing
SP	=	spelling
WR	=	wrong register

The first time students tackle an exercise of this sort, it is not unusual for them to "hypercorrect," i.e. they "correct" words and expressions that are perfectly accurate, while completely ignoring eye-catching errors in the text. As they gain familiarity with the procedure, they tend to become more self-confident and gradually learn to separate the wheat from the chaff, as it were. The following text from *I Pomeriggi del Sabato* by Antonio Tabucchi is provided as an illustration:

TEXT 6: ERROR CORRECTION	TEXT WITH ERRORS	**EDITED TEXT**
Era una domenica mattina. La mamma si era messa una veletta nera, perché era già pronta per la messa, stava immobile su una sedia e guardava fisso davanti a sé, oltre la zia Yvonne che le sedeva di fronte, oltre il buffet del salotto che stava dietro la zia Yvonne, e faceva di sì con la testa lentamente, con calma e rassegnazione, e con un'aria di comprensione e di tenerezza. Le domeniche erano diventate molto più tristi, senza le visite della zia Yvonne. Almeno quando veniva lei c'era un po' di movimento, magari di confusione, perché piombava all'improvviso e il telefono squillava finché lei restava in casa,	**It was on one Sunday morning. My mother wore a black small veil, because she was already ready for the function, she was sit on a chair without moving looking firmly in front of her, beyond the sitting room's buffet that had been placed behind aunt Yvonne, and slowly nodded, quietly and hopelessness, and in an understanding and tender mood.** **Sundays has become much more sadder, without aunt Yvonne coming to meet us. At least when she came to us there was a bit of movement, maybe of noise, because she suddenly came into and the telephone rang until she stayed at home and even after she had gone. Besides she wore a special**	It was a Sunday morning. Mother had just put on her black veil, ready for Mass, and was sitting motionless on a chair staring straight in front of her, past Aunt Yvonne, who was sitting opposite/in front of her, past the sideboard in the lounge behind Aunt Yvonne, and she nodded slowly, calmly, with a resigned look/expression of understanding and tenderness/affection. Sundays had become much sadder without Aunt Yvonne coming to visit us. At least when she came there was a bit of excitement, chaos even, because she would arrive/drop in/land on us out of the blue and the phone never stopped ringing all the time she was with us, and even afterwards; also, she would put on/don a kitchen apron, which

e anche dopo; inoltre si metteva un grembiuletto da cucina che risultava buffissimo su quei vestiti di gran classe che usava—lunghe gonne di seta, camicette di chiffon, il cappellino elegante con la camelia di organza—e conciata in quel modo dichiarava che avrebbe preparato un manicaretto francese, mousse Versailles, per esempio, visto che in casa nostra il cibo era 'di una ovvietà raccapricciante'. Poi succedeva che all'ultimo momento la mamma doveva ricorrere all'ovvietà raccapricciante, fettine al limone e piselli al burro, perché fra una telefonata e l'altra la zia Yvonne avrebbe finito la mousse alle quattro del pomeriggio e io e la Nena, impazienti, ci aggiravamo per la cucina rubacchiando grissini e quadretti di formaggio. Ma anche così tutto quel trambusto metteva almeno un po' di allegria, anche se poi alla mamma toccava lavare sei o sette pirex; ma ad ogni modo la mousse restava per l'indomani, ed era proprio squisita.	**woman's kitchen garment that seemed to us very ridicolous on her high-quality clothes she used to wear—long silk skirts, tiny blouses of chiffon, the small elegant cop with the camellia of a transparent fibrous substance—and dressed in that way she told us she'd have prepaired a very special and good french food, mousse Versailles, for example, as we saw that in our home food was as distasteful as obvious. Then it occured that at the last time my mother was obliged to repair with the distasteful obviousness, thin slices with lemon and little green beans with butter, because among a phone call and another aunt Yvonne would have had the mousse ready by four o'clock in the afternoon and I and Nena, impatient, were wandering round the kitchen stealing thin slices of bread and little pieces of cheese. But, even in this way, all that noise set on the air at least a bit of joy, even if it was my mother's duty washing up six or seven pirex; but in any way we had the mousse left for the day after, and it was very good.**	looked really funny on top of the posh/elegant/sophisticated clothes she used to wear—long silk skirts, chiffon blouses, that elegant hat with its organza camellia – and dressed up/rigged out/dolled up like that/in that fashion, she would declare that she was going to/would prepare/make some French delicacy for us, mousse (à la) Versailles, for example, seeing that the food in our house was horribly/depressingly ordinary/mundane/down-to-earth/banal.' Then at the last minute, Mother always ended up having to/it always ended up with Mother having to resort to something 'disgustingly banal', like steak with lemon juice and buttered peas/peas with butter, because what with one phone call and another Aunt Yvonne would never finish preparing the mousse until four in the afternoon and Nena and I would go/be going impatiently round/would hang/be hanging around impatiently in the kitchen, pinching bread-sticks and lumps of cheese. But even so, all that turmoil/upheaval at least brought a bit of/a little joy into our lives, even if Mother had to wash up six or seven Pyrex dishes; and anyway, we had/would have/would be having the mousse the next day and it was absolutely delicious.

Back Translation

Sometimes it can be useful to take an L1 text translated from an L2 text and set students the task of re-translating the text back into the L2. For example, students can be asked to re-translate into English an Italian translation of a passage from Oscar Wilde's *The Importance of Being Ernest* or a passage from Shelagh Delaney's *A Taste of Honey*. It goes without saying that the exercise must be performed without any prior knowledge of or reference to the original text. When the students have completed the translation, then their work can be compared with the original English text and all deviations and discrepancies vis-à-vis the original text can form a topic of discussion in the following translation seminar.

TEXT 7: Oscar Wilde: *The Importance of Being Ernest*	**Compare students' versions with original English text:**
ALGERNON: E, a proposito della scienza della Vita, hai fatto preparare i tramezzini al cetriolo per Lady Bracknell?	**Algernon**. And, speaking of the science of Life, have you got the cucumber sandwiches cut for Lady Bracknell?
LANE: Sì, signore. (Glieli porge su un vassoio).	**Lane**. Yes, sir. [Hands them on a salver.]
A: (Li controlla attentamente, ne prende due e si siede sul divano). Oh! a proposito, Lane, dal tuo registro contabile risulta che giovedì sera, quando erano a cena da me Lord Shoreman e il Signor Worthing, siano state consumate otto bottiglie di sciampagna.	**Algernon**. [Inspects them, takes two, and sits down on the sofa.] Oh!... by the way, Lane, I see from your book that on Thursday night, when Lord Shoreman and Mr. Worthing were dining with me, eight bottles of champagne are entered as having been consumed.
L: Esatto, signore. Otto bottiglie ed una pinta.	**Lane**. Yes, sir; eight bottles and a pint.
A: Come mai succede che nella residenza di uno scapolo è sempre la servitù che beve lo sciampagna? Lo chiedo soltanto a titolo di informazioni.	**Algernon**. Why is it that at a bachelor's establishment the servants invariably drink the champagne? I ask merely for information.
L: Lo attribuisco alla qualità superiore del vino, signore. Io ho spesso notato che nelle dimore degli ammogliati difficilmente lo sciampagna è di prima	**Lane**. I attribute it to the superior quality of the wine, sir. I have often observed that in married households the champagne is

qualità.

rarely of a first-rate brand.

A: Santo Cielo! E' così avvilente il matrimonio?

Algernon. Good heavens! Is marriage so demoralising as that?

L: A quel che so, è una condizione molto piacevole, signore. Io personalmente ne ho avuto pochissima esperienza finora. Sono stato sposato una volta sola. Ciò fu il risultato di un malinteso tra il sottoscritto e una certa signorina.

Lane. I believe it IS a very pleasant state, sir. I have had very little experience of it myself up to the present. I have only been married once. That was in consequence of a misunderstanding between myself and a young person.

A: (con un'aria di stanchezza) Non so se veramente me ne importi tanto della tua vita familiare, Lane.

Algernon. [Languidly.] I don't know that I am much interested in your family life, Lane.

L: Certo, signore. Non è un argomento molto interessante. Io personalmente non ci penso mai.

Lane. No, sir; it is not a very interesting subject. I never think of it myself.

A: E' evidente, ne sono convinto. E' tutto, Lane, grazie.

Algernon. Very natural, I am sure. That will do, Lane, thank you.

L: Grazie, signore. (Esce Lane).

Lane. Thank you, sir. [Lane goes out.]

A: L'atteggiamento di Lane nei confronti del matrimonio mi sembra un tantino leggero. Insomma, se non ci danno il buon esempio i ceti più umili, a che diavolo servono? Come classe sociale, a quanto pare, non hanno il pur minimo senso di moralità.

Algernon. Lane's views on marriage seem somewhat lax. Really, if the lower orders don't set us a good example, what on earth is the use of them? They seem, as a class, to have absolutely no sense of moral responsibility.

TEXT 8: Shelagh Delaney: *A Taste of Honey*	**Compare students' versions with original English text:**
(Helen entra in cucina e smanetta con il fornello.) Oh, Jo, non mi ricordo più come si faceva ad accendere quest'accidente.	(Helen enters kitchen and fiddles with stove.) Oh Jo, I've forgotten how we used to light this thing.
Jo: Apri tutti i rubinetti. Stai attenta a non intossicarti col gas.	Jo: Turn on all the knobs. Mind you don't gas yourself.
Helen: Ancora non ci riesco.	Helen: I still can't do it.
Jo: Ci pensa Geof ad aggiustarlo. Helen: No, fa lo stesso.	Jo: Geof'll fix it. Helen: No, it's all right.
Jo: Helen. Helen: Dimmi.	Jo: Helen. Helen: Yes.
Jo: Forse il bambino sarà nero.	Jo: My baby may be black.
Helen: Cos'hai detto, tesoro? Jo: Il mio bambino sarà nero.	Helen: You what, love? Jo: My baby will be black.
Helen: Ma non dire cavolate, Jo. Ti farai venire gli incubi. Jo: Ma è la verità. Lui era nero.	Helen: Oh, don't be silly, Jo. You'll be giving yourself nightmares. Jo: But it's true. He was black.
Helen: Lui chi? Jo: Jimmie.	Helen: Who? Jo: Jimmie.
Helen: Vuoi dire che … quel marinaio era un negro? … Cristo! Ci mancava solo questa. Ma mi ci vedi a spingere una carrozzina con dentro un … Dio mio, devo bere qualcosa.	Helen: You mean to say that … that sailor was a black man? … Oh my God! Nothing else can happen to me now. Can you see me wheeling a pram with a … Oh my God, I'll have to have a drink.
Jo: Cosa pensi di fare?	Jo: What are you going to do?
Helen: Non lo so. Annegarlo magari. Chi sa di questa faccenda? Jo: Geoffrey.	Helen: I don't know. Drown it. Who knows about it? Jo: Geoffrey.
Helen: E l'ostetrica? Sarà un po' uno shock per lei, non credi?	Helen: And what about the nurse? She's going to get a bit of a shock, isn't she?

Jo: Beh, veramente, anche lei è nera. Helen: Meno male, forse lo vorrà adottare. Dio mio!	Jo: Well, she's black too. Helen: Good, perhaps she'll adopt it. Dear God in heaven!
Jo: Se non ti piace, puoi andartene via. Non ti ho chiesto io di venire.	Jo: If you don't like it you can get out. I didn't ask you to come here.
Helen: Dove ce l'ho il cappello? Jo: In testa.	Helen: Where's my hat? Jo: On your head.
Helen: Ah, sì … non so cosa farmene di te. Non lo so proprio.	Helen: Oh yes … I don't know what's to be done with you. I don't really.

A Typical Translation Seminar

My translation seminars tend to rely heavily on debate and discussion. After the preliminary skim and scan readings of the text have been dispensed with, students are called upon individually to venture an oral rendering of the text. The other members of the class will then discuss each student's contribution, in terms of grammar, syntax, lexis, style and register and evaluate the most suitable *ad hoc* translation strategies. The student has to "defend" his/her work against criticism. At this stage, it is the class that claims the lion's share in the spoils, as it were, although the seminar is continually monitored by the teacher, who is free to offer comments and suggestions and to ask questions. The class takes notes and evaluates the validity of the different versions that come to the fore during the discussion phase.

The students are then given a week to make all the necessary amendments and produce a final draft of the translation analysed and discussed in class. During this time, students are encouraged to consult all their translation resources. In the following lesson, the teacher will carry out a final revision, bringing to light the good solutions the students have come up with on the one hand and the shortcomings and *faux pas* on the other.

In the final stage, the accent is very much on naturalness. It must be impressed on the students that primarily their renderings must make sense and secondly that they must read naturally, having been written in the appropriate grammar and lexis for that particular type of situation. In order to achieve this, I advise students to read through their final draft as if it were a piece of writing in its own right, completely detached from the SL text.

Evaluation and Assessment

Translations are assessed according to the following criteria:

- ***A. Comprehension, accuracy and register***
  Once the meaning of the ST has been decoded, it must be encoded accurately. Criteria such as rendering of the text, choice of register, lexis, transfer of idioms should reflect the spirit and intention of the ST. Misinterpretations and omissions are penalised (maximum of 10 marks assigned).
- ***B. Grammar, cohesion, coherence and organisation of work***
  Errors of grammar and syntax and over-adherence to ST patterns and sentence structures weigh heavily against the student in this phase (maximum of 15 marks assigned).
- ***C. punctuation, spelling, transfer of names, dates, figures, units, etc.***
  These are typical errors that tend to distort the meaning of the TL text. Also, the use of abbreviations or contracted forms such as "doesn't" or "isn't" should be avoided unless of course they are appropriate to the original (maximum of 5 marks assigned).
  Students are therefore assigned a total mark out of 30.

It is certainly a wise course of action to classify the kinds of errors made or difficulties encountered by students. Whereas textual omissions and misinterpretations should be severely penalised, on the other hand credit should be given for

- creative solutions to translation problems
- correct application of translation procedures in the transfer and rewording process
- appropriate lexical, semantic, grammatical, graphemic and cultural transfer.

Conclusion

In conclusion, from a pedagogical perspective, translation has proved to be a useful means of improving not only students' reading and writing competence but also their cross-cultural and cross-linguistic awareness.

The interest and enthusiasm with which the students attend and actively participate in classroom seminars seem to bear witness to the fact that translation—with all its technical hitches and bugbears—remains a highly stimulating, rewarding and pleasurable language-learning activity.

UNIVERSITY OF PARMA, ITALY

CHAPTER THIRTEEN

TEACHING ITALIAN AS A FOREIGN LANGUAGE FOR ACADEMIC AND PROFESSIONAL PURPOSES. JURIDICAL AND INFORMATIVE LANGUAGE. TEACHING SUGGESTIONS FOR STUDENTS AND LEGAL PROFESSIONALS

MANUELA VISIGALLI

Specialized language defines a variety of language used by a community of subject specialists in a particular field of scientific or academic knowledge. Its function is to communicate a message with the utmost precision and it allows the speaker to recognize other competent speakers as members of a group that shares the same microlanguage and style. Specialized language can be seen from two angles, one which considers the variety of content and distinguishes between various languages for special purposes e.g., financial, legal or IT language and the other which defines socio-pragmatic varieties in each subject area according to the level of specialization contained in the text taking into account the sender-receiver relationship. A specialist text can have an informative purpose (for instance instructions for appliances) and be comprehensible to a broad public; it can show a medium level of specialization (e.g., a letter from a lawyer to a client), and be comprehensible not only to specialists in the field in question but also to those who are competent in similar areas. Finally it can be addressed exclusively to experts and therefore exhibit the maximum level of specialization.

Analyzing and comparing the original text of the smoking ban law published in the Gazzetta Ufficiale and an article published by the Italian daily newspaper "La Repubblica," I will focus on lexical and morphosyntactic features that differenciate them: I will identify and analyze potential difficulties in terms of comprehension and reading skills were these texts to be given to students or specialists attending a course of Italian for lawyers. The specialist text is characterized by a large number of precise technical terms and by the use of specific grammatical structures that require a different type of communicative and linguistic competence from the one usually required by the language of common understanding.

1. Analysis of legal texts. Features of Italian legal language

The text in Appendix A is a copy extract of the smoking ban law that was first published in the "Gazzetta Ufficiale" on 20th January 2003. It is a set of public policies, including legal sumptuary prohibitions, occupational safety and health regulations, that restrict tobacco smoking in workplaces and public spaces. It belongs to the category of administrative juridical texts and exemplifies a perfect model of what characterizes legal language, because of its morphosyntactic and its lexical features.

From a morphosyntactic point of view, the text makes wide use of passive constructions. The preference for passives here is due to the need for depersonalization, since legal language is more impersonal than non-specialised language. In the text we read:

> I locali riservati (…) devono essere contrassegnati (…) essere delimitati (…) essere dotati. L' aria non è riciclabile (…) ma deve essere espulsa. Nei locali sono collocati cartelli (…) i cartelli sono integrati…

The abundant use of nominalization is one of the chief characteristics of Italian legal language. In contrast to what is found in unmarked language, the style of written legal Italian is highly nominal, meaning that noun groups are preferred to verbal forms and that the verbal range of tenses and aspects is reduced. The fact that verbs are semantically emptied is also proved by the frequent use of copulative forms such as *essere, diventare, consistere, significare, rappresentare,* etc. Examples may be found throughout the text (all nouns are in italics):

> I *locali* per *fumatori* devono essere dotati di idonei *mezzi* meccanici di *ventilazione* forzata, in modo da garantire una *portata d'aria* di *ricambio* supplementare esterna o immessa per *trasferimento* da altri *ambienti* limitrofi dove è vietato fumare. (…) La *portata* di *aria* minima da assicurare è pari a *30 litri/secondo* per ogni *persona* che può essere ospitata nei *locali* in conformità della *normativa* vigente, sulla base di un *indice di affollamento* pari allo 0,7 *persone/mq*. All'*ingresso* dei *locali* è indicato il *numero* massimo di *persone* ammissibili, in base alla *portata* dell'*impianto*.

Legal language relies also on the rare use of pronouns. The reason for normally using pronouns is to avoid repetition and thus to make the text less tedious to read. However, it is generally argued that it may be dangerous to use pronouns in a legal document when there is a possibility of reference to two or more people. For this reason legal texts avoid them and exhibit greater use of the present and past participle. An example is provided in the following (substantives and verbal participles are in italics):

> *Visto* (participio passato) il *parere espresso* (participio passato) dalla *Conferenza* permanente per i *rapporti* tra lo *Stato*, le *regioni* e le *province* autonome di Trento e Bolzano nella *seduta* del 24 luglio 2003 sullo *schema di decreto* del *Presidente della Repubblica recante* (participio presente) «*Regolamento di attuazione dell'art.* 51…

From a lexical point of view, the recurring use of abstract nouns and common words with uncommon legal definitions is also noticeable.

> Alle infrazioni al divieto previsto dal presente articolo si applicano le sanzioni…—Al fine di consentire una adeguata attività di informazione, da attivare d'intesa con le organizzazioni di categoria più rappresentative…

Furthermore, the rhythm of juridical prose is slowed down by repetitions of adverbial and prepositional phrases.

When textual coherence and cohesion are taken into account, anaphoric reference is undoubtedly the most recurrent aspect that can be noted. It is typically rendered by an internal reference to a specific point in the text. The following example can serve to illustrate this feature:

> I locali riservati ai fumatori, di cui all'art. 51, comma 1, lettera b) della legge 16 gennaio 2003, n. 3 devono essere contrassegnati…—…le disposizioni di cui ai commi 1, 2, primo periodo, 3 e 5 entrano in vigore decorso un anno dalla data di entrata in vigore del regolamento di cui al comma 2.

The above findings of syntax, lexis and, to some extent, pragmatics will probably be sufficient to warn the reader that legal Italian can be extremely complex. Having considered a number of characteristics, we may end by arguing that teaching legal usage of Italian should be based on the knowledge of the textual features mentioned above. Teachers may take into consideration both the juridical vocabulary and legal language register in the students' L1, as well as the general terminology of L2, which students might already be familiar with.

2. Analysis of the journalistic text. Features of informative language

The informative text that appears here is an in-depth article published on the website of the Italian newspaper "La Repubblica" (www.repubblica.it) on 10th January 2005 (Appendix B). Its purpose is to inform the general reader of the new smoking ban law by summarizing the main points and paraphrasing the content. It may be considered both a descriptive text and an argumentative one as it includes features which are typical of both text types.

On the basis of the example below, it can be argued that the informative language often uses rephrasing and paraphrasing in order to make juridical syntax more comprehensible:

> Nei bar, ristoranti e alberghi che vorranno accogliere i fumatori, così come nei luoghi di lavoro, gli spazi riservati a chi non riesce a separarsi dalle sigarette dovranno essere contrassegnati. Dovranno inoltre essere delimitati e separati con pareti dagli spazi in cui non si può fumare. Se vi è un solo locale, o se non è possibile assicurare una idonea separazione degli ambienti, il divieto di fumo è assoluto.

Verbs appear in finite forms and subjects are always expressed. The use of subjects has a double purpose; on the one hand their primary goal is clear and simple communication, on the other they add connotations to the denotative content of the legal text (for instance, "chi non riesce a separarsi dalle sigarette").

On a lexical level some juridical terms are maintained while metaphors and euphemisms are introduced when required. Thus, it is necessary to specify that the *legalese* cannot be defined as highly "technical" and reach the status as scientific language. Common words are frequently used with uncommon legal definitions; terms do not have one fixed syntactic relationship and texts are open to interpretation. Since the danger of producing an undetermined communicative act is not eliminated, legal language cannot be referred to as mono-referential.

The newspaper article includes expressions such as,

> dovranno garantire una quantità di aria supplementare minima di 22 litri al secondo per ogni persona che può essere ospitata nel locale, sulla base di un indice di affollamento di 0,7 persone per ogni metro quadrato.

and lists the places where the law will have to be enforced:

> C'era già in ospedali, scuole, autobus e metropolitane, sale di attesa delle stazioni, sui compartimenti ferroviari riservati ai non fumatori, nei cinema e nei teatri, in musei e biblioteche. Adesso le sigarette vengono bandite anche dagli esercizi aperti al pubblico e dai luoghi di lavoro, con particolare riguardo per alberghi, ristoranti, bar ed esercizi di pubblico ristoro in genere, uffici e altri luoghi di lavoro.

Anaphoric references have disappeared and information is presented in a functional way. The four paragraphs that compose the article are recognizable, clear and simple to read because each of them focuses on a particular aspect and attempts to explain the topic by mentioning its main points. As a further aid a brief heading—in boldface—has been added at the beginning of each paragraph to further help the reader.

3. Law students' difficulties vs professionals' difficulties

Being aware of the characteristics of legal texts is fundamental for non-expert learners who are not familiar with this type of authentic legal materials. Students' difficulties in reading and understanding specific features of legal Italian slow down the process of interpreting the contents of the documents. This ability is a prerequisite for a lawyer and therefore it has to be developed and acquired by a student in this field. In order to overcome the morphosyntactic obstacles, learners should first work on an informative text like the article mentioned above. A variety of activities can be suggested:

- **Activities on textual organization**:[1] recognizing how information is organized in the text through matching exercises between headings and paragraphs.
- **Grammar exercises on passive forms**: teachers can ask learners to recognize all the examples of passive forms present in the text and prepare transformation activities to turn active forms into passive forms.
- **Activities on vocabulary development**: learners focus on identifying hyponyms and hyperonyms.
- **Development of specific terminology**: learners work on synonyms (both through matching exercises and through their personal creation of synonyms and paraphrases of a number of terms).

---

[1] See Exercise 1 in Appendix C.

- **Comparing informative texts and legal texts**: learners have to recognize content that is expressed in both documents. For instance, a set of similar questions can be presented: How is the same idea expressed in the article and in the legal document? In which paragraph/s is this particular aspect mentioned? Where is the equivalent of the article's first paragraph in the legal document, what are the differences? Are these content or syntactic differences?

If the learner is a professional person who is familiar with technical juridical texts, there are different difficulties to take into consideration. Probably the learners can easily recognize the text format and the recurrent fixed expressions that exist in their mother tongue as well. For example, learners whose L1 is French or Spanish probably have fewer difficulties. Here the following examples of a series of corresponding phrases present in Italian, Spanish and French:

ITALIAN	SPANISH	FRENCH
Conforme a	conforme a	conforme à
In virtù di	en virtud de	en vertu de
In conformità	con de conformidad con	en conformité avec

Since the intended audience should be the primary concern of a speaker in deciding which words to use to express himself/herself intelligibly, it is important that he/she understands that spoken language and written language are different.

Lawyers who aim at an informative and effective direct speech have to be aware of the fact that oral communication is a spontaneous interaction between speakers while written communication is the result of an intellectualizing process. As a legal professional, a lawyer will use the language in a number of different circumstances and will change the use of it depending on the situation. For instance, he/she will talk to his/her clients in a different manner than to colleagues at a conference and he/she will write a letter to a client differently than he/she will write a memorandum to other lawyers in the office. If the audience is not acquainted with the juridical subject, the speaker should be able to choose and use lexical and morphosyntactical features that characterize informative texts. In order to obtain an easily comprehensible message, many paraphrases are needed together with a consistent reduction of all the legal textual features. This set of exercises to practice this skill and reach a satisfactory knowledge of registers can be suggested:

- **Activities on texts registers**:[2] matching exercise in which learners have to combine expressions with the same meaning but using a different register. This way they can compare the informative and the technical text from a lexical and pragmatic point of view.
- **Activities on textual organization**: learners have to divide the legal text into paragraphs according to its contents. Afterwards, they have to find the same information in the journalistic text and compare how the texts are organised and divided up
- **Grammar exercises on active forms**: in contrast to the exercise suggested for law students, learners have to recognize passive forms of the verbs and transform them into the active form.
- **Activities on vocabulary development**: teachers can use the same kind of exercises suggested for non-professional learners. Students work on hyponyms, hyperonyms and synonyms with the new aim of eliminating technical terms or phrases.

Conclusion

By studying methods and approaches applied to teaching a language for academic and professional purposes, I have understood the importance of a deep knowledge of how specialized languages are organized and how they function.

Informative language has the goal of transmitting a clear message; therefore it is characterized by those textual morphosyntactic and lexical strategies that enable straightforward comprehension. Perspectives change in technical and scientific fields since the most important function of legal language is performative rather than informative, meaning that the primary goal is not popular understanding but legal accuracy. Legal language loses its spontaneity and differs significantly from the language of common understanding—as principles of oral interactions do not apply any longer.

Learners have to be capable of recognizing these differences and can

---

[2] See Exercise 2 in Appendix C.

be helped by a series of specific exercises prepared by teachers who stimulate them to make use of their critical skills. By analyzing materials, they can be asked to point out textual structures, internal textual organization, style, linguistic and rhetoric conventions because this knowledge enables them to gain a superior command of the language and to use it effectively. In this way learners do not only work on general comprehension skills, but focus on inductively extracting the specific features of technical and informative texts.

Different types of students need different teaching strategies. What is difficult for a student can turn out to be within a professional expert's capabilities; in his turn the expert may struggle with registers that are more familiar to the student. Previous linguistic and technical knowledge plays an important part in the learning process and can be used to compensate for possible learners' weaknesses. Understanding who the learner is and identifying his learning needs is the first step towards a valid and effective teaching process.

UNIVERSITÀ CATTOLICA DEL SACRO CUORE, MILAN, ITALY

References

AA VV. *Lingua italiana per la formazione professionale*. Quaderni di "percorsi." Dic.2001, 1-35.

Cortellazzo, Michele. A. *Lingue speciali: la dimensione verticale*. Padova: Unipress,1994.

Gotti, M. *I linguaggi specialistici.* Firenze: La nuova Italia, 1991.

Sobrero, Alberto A. *Lingue Speciali,* in *Introduzione all'italiano contemporaneo. La variazione e gli usi.* Roma-Bari: La Terza, 1993.

On Line sources

http://www.governo.it/GovernoInforma/Dossier/fumo_divieto/art_51.html
http://www.repubblica.it/2004/l/sezioni/cronaca/fumo/regole/regole.html

APPENDIX A

DECRETO DEL PRESIDENTE DEL CONSIGLIO DEI MINISTRI 23 Dicembre 2003 Attuazione dell'art. 51, comma 2 della legge 16 gennaio 2003, n. 3, come modificato dall'art. 7 della legge 21 ottobre 2003, n. 306, in materia di «tutela della salute dei non fumatori».

Pubblicato sulla Gazzetta Ufficiale n. 300 del 29-12-2003

IL PRESIDENTE DEL CONSIGLIO DEI MINISTRI
Visto l'art. 5 della legge 23 agosto 1988, n. 400; Visto l'art. 51, comma 2 della legge 16 gennaio 2003, n. 3, e successive modificazioni, in materia di «tutela della salute dei non fumatori»; Visto il parere espresso dalla Conferenza permanente per i rapporti tra lo Stato, le regioni e le province autonome di Trento e Bolzano nella seduta del 24 luglio 2003 sullo schema di decreto del Presidente della Repubblica recante «Regolamento di attuazione dell'art. 51, comma 2, della legge 16 gennaio 2003, n. 3; Visto l'accordo tra Stato, regioni e province autonome di Trento e Bolzano sulla tutela della salute dei non fumatori, di cui all'art. 51, comma 2 della legge 16 gennaio 2003, n. 3, sancito nella seduta della Conferenza permanente per i rapporti tra Stato, regioni e province autonome del 24 luglio 2003; Sulla proposta del Ministro della salute, di concerto con il Ministro dell'economia e delle finanze;
Decreta:

Art.1
1. Il presente decreto recepisce l'Accordo tra Stato, regioni e province autonome di Trento e Bolzano sulla tutela della salute dei non fumatori, sancito nella seduta della Conferenza permanente per i rapporti tra Stato, regioni e province autonome del 24 luglio 2003.

Art. 2
1. Sono definiti nell'allegato 1, che costituisce parte integrante del presente decreto, i requisiti tecnici dei locali per fumatori, dei relativi impianti di ventilazione e di ricambio d'aria e dei modelli dei cartelli connessi al divieto di fumare.

Roma, 23 dicembre 2003

p. Il Presidente del Consiglio dei Ministri
Letta
Il Ministro della salute
Sirchia
Il Ministro dell'economia e delle finanze
Tremonti

Allegato 1
REQUISITI TECNICI DEI LOCALI PER FUMATORI, DEI RELATIVI IMPIANTI DI VENTILAZIONE E DI RICAMBIO D'ARIA E DEI MODELLI DEI CARTELLI CONNESSI AL DIVIETO DI FUMO.

1. I locali riservati ai fumatori, di cui all'art. 51, comma 1, lettera b) della legge 16 gennaio 2003, n. 3 devono essere contrassegnati come tali e realizzati in modo da risultare adeguatamente separati da altri ambienti limitrofi, dove è vietato fumare. A tal fine i locali per fumatori devono rispettare i seguenti requisiti strutturali: a) essere delimitati da pareti a tutta altezza su quattro lati; b) essere dotati di ingresso con porta a chiusura automatica, abitualmente in posizione di chiusura; c) essere forniti di adeguata segnaletica, conforme a quanto previsto dai successivi punti 9 e 10; d) non rappresentare un locale obbligato di passaggio per i non fumatori.
2. I locali per fumatori devono essere dotati di idonei mezzi meccanici di ventilazione forzata, in modo da garantire una portata d'aria di ricambio supplementare esterna o immessa per trasferimento da altri ambienti limitrofi dove è vietato fumare. L'aria di ricambio supplementare deve essere adeguatamente filtrata. La portata di aria supplementare minima da assicurare è pari a 30 litri/secondo per ogni persona che può essere ospitata nei locali in conformita' della normativa vigente, sulla base di un indice di affollamento pari allo 0,7 persone/mq. All'ingresso dei locali è indicato il numero massimo di persone ammissibili, in base alla portata dell'impianto.
3. I locali per fumatori devono essere mantenuti in depressione non inferiore a 5 Pa. (Pascal) rispetto alle zone circostanti.
4. La superficie destinata ai fumatori negli esercizi di ristorazione, ai sensi dell'art. 51 della legge 16 gennaio 2003, n. 3, deve comunque essere inferiore alla meta' della superficie complessiva di somministrazione dell'esercizio.

5. L'aria proveniente dai locali per fumatori non è riciclabile, ma deve essere espulsa all'esterno attraverso idonei impianti e funzionali aperture, secondo quanto previsto dalla vigente normativa in tema di emissioni in atmosfera esterna, nonché dai regolamenti comunali di igiene ed edilizi.
6. La progettazione, l'installazione, la manutenzione ed il collaudo dei sistemi di ventilazione devono essere conformi alle disposizioni legislative e regolamentari vigenti in tema di sicurezza e di risparmio energetico, come pure alle norme tecniche dell'Ente italiano di unificazione (UNI) e del Comitato elettrotecnico italiano (CEI). I soggetti abilitati sono tenuti a rilasciare idonea dichiarazione della messa in opera degli impianti secondo le regole dell'arte ed in conformità dei medesimi alla normativa vigente. Ai fini del necessario controllo, i certificati di installazione comprensivi dell'idoneità del sistema di espulsione, e i certificati annuali di verifica e di manutenzione degli impianti di ventilazione devono essere conservati a disposizione dell'autorita' competente.
7. Nei locali in cui è vietato fumare sono collocati appositi cartelli, adeguatamente visibili, che evidenziano tale divieto. Ai fini della omogeneità sul territorio nazionale, tecnicamente opportuna, tali cartelli devono recare la scritta «VIETATO FUMARE», integrata dalle indicazioni della relativa prescrizione di legge, delle sanzioni applicabili ai contravventori e dei soggetti cui spetta vigilare sull'osservanza del divieto e cui compete accertare le infrazioni.
8. Nelle strutture con più locali, oltre al modello di cartello riportato al punto 7, da situare nei luoghi di accesso o comunque di particolare evidenza, sono adottabili cartelli con la sola scritta «VIETATO FUMARE».
9. I locali per fumatori sono contrassegnati da appositi cartelli, con l'indicazione luminosa contenente, per le ragioni di omogeneità di cui al punto 7, la scritta «AREA PER FUMATORI».
10. I cartelli di cui al punto 9 sono comunque integrati da altri cartelli luminosi recanti, per le ragioni di omogeneità di cui al punto 7, la dizione: «VIETATO FUMARE PER GUASTO ALL'IMPIANTO DI VENTILAZIONE», che si accendono automaticamente in caso di mancato o inadeguato funzionamento degli impianti di ventilazione supplementare, determinando la contestuale esclusione della scritta
indicativa dell'area riservata.
11. Il locale non rispondente, anche temporaneamente, a tutte le caratteristiche tecniche di cui ai punti precedenti non è idoneo all'applicazione della normativa di cui all'art. 51 della legge 16 gennaio 2003, n. 3.

LEGGE 16 gennaio 2003, n. 3
Disposizioni ordinamentali in materia di pubblica amministrazione
Gazzetta Ufficiale N. 15 del 20 Gennaio 2003

Art. 51.
(Tutela della salute dei non fumatori)
1. È vietato fumare nei locali chiusi, ad eccezione di:
a) quelli privati non aperti ad utenti o al pubblico;
b) quelli riservati ai fumatori e come tali contrassegnati.
2. Gli esercizi e i luoghi di lavoro di cui al comma 1, lettera b), devono essere dotati di impianti per la ventilazione ed il ricambio di aria regolarmente funzionanti. Al fine di garantire i livelli essenziali del diritto alla salute, le caratteristiche tecniche degli impianti per la ventilazione ed il ricambio di aria sono definite, entro centottanta giorni dalla data di pubblicazione della presente legge nella Gazzetta Ufficiale, con regolamento, da emanare ai sensi dell'articolo 17, comma 1, della legge 23 agosto 1988, n. 400, e successive modificazioni, su proposta del Ministro della salute. Con lo stesso regolamento sono definiti i locali riservati ai fumatori nonché i modelli dei cartelli connessi all'attuazione delle disposizioni di cui al presente articolo.
3. Negli esercizi di ristorazione , ai sensi del comma 1, lettera b), devono essere adibiti ai non fumatori uno o piu' locali di superficie prevalente rispetto alla superficie complessiva di somministrazione dell'esercizio.
4. Con regolamento da emanare ai sensi dell'articolo 17, comma 1, della legge 23 agosto 1988, n. 400, e successive modificazioni, su proposta del Ministro della salute, possono essere individuati eventuali ulteriori luoghi chiusi nei quali sia consentito fumare, nel rispetto delle disposizioni di cui ai commi 1, 2 e 3. Tale regolamento deve prevedere che in tutte le strutture in cui le persone sono costrette a soggiornare non volontariamente devono essere previsti locali adibiti ai fumatori.
5. Alle infrazioni al divieto previsto dal presente articolo si applicano le sanzioni di cui all'articolo 7 della legge 11 novembre 1975, n. 584, come sostituito dall'articolo 52, comma 20, della legge 28 dicembre 2001, n. 448.
6. Al fine di consentire una adeguata attivita' di informazione , da attivare d'intesa con le organizzazioni di categoria piu' rappresentative, le disposizioni di cui ai commi 1, 2, primo periodo, 3 e 5 entrano in vigore decorso un anno da lla data di entrata in vigore del regolamento di cui al comma 2.
7. Entro centoventi giorni dalla data di pubblicazione della presente legge

nella Gazzetta Ufficiale, con accordo sancito in sede di Conferenza permanente per i rapporti tra lo Stato, le regioni e le province autonome di Trento e di Bolzano, su proposta del Ministro della salute di concerto con i Ministri della giustizia e dell'interno, sono ridefinite le procedure per l'accertamento delle infrazioni, la relativa modulistica per il rilievo delle sanzioni nonché l'individuazione dei soggetti legittimati ad elevare i relativi processi verbali, di quelli competenti a ricevere il rapporto sulle infrazioni accertate ai sensi dell'articolo 17 della legge 24 novembre 1981, n. 689, e di quelli deputati a irrogare le relative sanzioni.
8. Le disposizioni di cui al presente articolo non comportano maggiori oneri a carico del bilancio dello Stato.
9. Rimangono in vigore, in quanto compatibili, le disposizioni di cui agli articoli 3, 5, 6, 8, 9, 10 e 11 della legge 11 novembre 1975, n. 584.
10. Restano ferme le disposizioni che disciplinano il divieto di fumo nei locali delle pubbliche amministrazioni.

APPENDIX B

Fumo, ecco cosa cambia con le nuove norme
ROMA—Le nuove norme che sono entrate in vigore ridisegnano i doveri a cui dovranno attenersi i fumatori nei luoghi pubblici.
Divieto assoluto di fumo. C'era già in ospedali, scuole, autobus e metropolitane, sale di attesa delle stazioni, sui compartimenti ferroviari riservati ai non fumatori, nei cinema e nei teatri, in musei e biblioteche. Adesso le sigarette vengono bandite anche dagli esercizi aperti al pubblico e dai luoghi di lavoro, con particolare riguardo per alberghi, ristoranti, bar ed esercizi di pubblico ristoro in genere, uffici e altri luoghi di lavoro. I divieti valgono anche per gli spazi pubblici destinati ad attività ricreative e per i circoli privati nei quali lo statuto lo preveda.
Zone riservate ai fumatori. Nei bar, ristoranti e alberghi che vorranno accogliere i fumatori, così come nei luoghi di lavoro, gli spazi riservati a chi non riesce a separarsi dalle sigarette dovranno essere contrassegnati. Dovranno inoltre essere delimitati e separati con pareti dagli spazi in cui non si può fumare. Se vi è un solo locale, o se non è possibile assicurare una idonea separazione degli ambienti, il divieto di fumo è assoluto. Lo spazio destinato ai fumatori dovrà essere inferiore alla metà della superficie complessiva aperta al pubblico.
Cartelli luminosi. Le zone riservate ai fumatori dovranno essere indicate da cartelli luminosi e dovranno riportare la scritta "Area per fumatori." In caso di guasto all'impianto di ventilazione, un altro cartello luminoso dovrà accendersi automaticamente indicando l'eventuale divieto di fumo. Nei locali per non fumatori basta esporre il cartello "Vietato fumare,"con il riepilogo delle sanzioni per i trasgressori.
Impianti di ventilazione. In tutti gli esercizi pubblici e i luoghi di lavoro dovranno essere installati impianti per la ventilazione e il ricambio dell'aria: dovranno garantire una quantità di aria supplementare minima di 22 litri al secondo per ogni persona che può essere ospitata nel locale, sulla base di un indice di affollamento di 0,7 persone per ogni metro quadrato. I locali per i fumatori devono essere in depressione non inferiore a 5 Pa (Pascal) rispetto alle zone circostanti e l'aria proveniente da questi dovrà essere espulsa all'esterno. Gli impianti dovranno infine essere verificati annualmente ed i relativi certificati dovranno essere sempre disponibili per i controlli.
(*10 gennaio 2005*)

APPENDIX C

EXERCISE 1: Activity on textual organization. Law students have read the journalistic text and are familiar with its content. They are given the headings of the article and three extracts of the smoking ban law. Their task is to find the information in the legal text and afterwards match the headings with the right extract.

1. Divieto assoluto di fumo.

A. Negli esercizi di ristorazione , ai sensi del comma 1, lettera b), devono essere adibiti ai non fumatori uno o più locali di superficie prevalente rispetto alla superficie complessiva di somministrazione dell'esercizio.	**B.** I locali riservati ai fumatori, di cui all'art. 51, comma 1, lettera b) della legge 16 gennaio 2003, n. 3 devono essere contrassegnati come tali e realizzati in modo da risultare adeguatamente separati da altri ambienti limitrofi, dove e' vietato fumare.	**C.** E' vietato fumare nei locali chiusi, ad eccezione di: a) quelli privati non aperti ad utenti o al pubblico; b) quelli riservati ai fumatori e come tali contrassegnati.

2. Zone riservate ai fumatori.

A. Gli esercizi e i luoghi di lavoro di cui al comma 1, lettera b), devono essere dotati di impianti per la ventilazione ed il ricambio di aria regolarmente funzionanti.	**B.** I locali riservati ai fumatori, di cui all'art. 51, comma 1, lettera b) della legge 16 gennaio 2003, n. 3 devono essere contrassegnati come tali e realizzati in modo da risultare adeguatamente separati da altri ambienti limitrofi, dove e' vietato fumare.	**C.** I locali per fumatori devono essere dotati di idonei mezzi meccanici di ventilazione forzata, in modo da garantire una portata d'aria di ricambio supplementare esterna o immessa per trasferimento da altri ambienti limitrofi dove e' vietato fumare.

3. Cartelli luminosi.

A. A tal fine i locali per fumatori devono rispettare i seguenti requisiti strutturali: a) essere delimitati da pareti a tutta altezza su quattro lati; b) essere dotati di ingresso con porta a chiusura automatica, abitualmente in posizione di chiusura; c) essere forniti di adeguata segnaletica, conforme a quanto previsto dai successivi punti 9 e 10; d) non rappresentare un locale obbligato di passaggio per i non fumatori.	**B.** I soggetti abilitati sono tenuti a rilasciare idonea dichiarazione della messa in opera degli impianti secondo le regole dell'arte ed in conformità dei medesimi alla normativa vigente. Ai fini del necessario controllo, i certificati di installazione comprensivi dell'idoneità del sistema di espulsione, e i certificati annuali di verifica e di manutenzione degli impianti di ventilazione devono essere conservati a disposizione dell'autorità competente.	**C.** I cartelli di cui al punto 9 sono comunque integrati da altri cartelli luminosi recanti, per le ragioni di omogeneità di cui al punto 7, la dizione: «VIETATO FUMARE PER GUASTO ALL'IMPIANTO DI VENTILAZIONE», che si accendono automaticamente in caso di mancato o inadeguato funzionamento degli impianti di ventilazione supplementare, determinando la contestuale esclusione della scritta indicativa dell'area riservata.

4. Impianti di ventilazione.

A. I locali per fumatori devono essere dotati di idonei mezzi meccanici di ventilazione forzata, in modo da garantire una portata d'aria di ricambio supplementare esterna o immessa per trasferimento da altri ambienti limitrofi dove e' vietato fumare. L'aria di ricambio supplementare deve essere adeguatamente filtrata.	**B.** Ai fini del necessario controllo, i certificati di installazione comprensivi dell'idoneità del sistema di espulsione, e i certificati annuali di verifica e di manutenzione degli impianti di ventilazione devono essere conservati a disposizione dell'autorità competente.	**C.** Con regolamento da emanare ai sensi dell'articolo 17, comma 1, della legge 23 agosto 1988, n. 400, e successive modificazioni, su proposta del Ministro della salute, possono essere individuati eventuali ulteriori luoghi chiusi nei quali sia consentito fumare, nel rispetto delle disposizioni di cui ai commi 1, 2 e 3.

(Key: 1-C; 2-B; 3-C; 4-A)

Once students have finished the exercise, another set of activities can be suggested.

Students work on each combination of texts, every time focusing on different features:

1. Exercise on hyponyms and hyperonyms
2. Exercise on passive and active forms
3. Exercise on text features and style.
4. Exercise on synomyms.

Examples.

1. Compare the paragraph *Divieto assoluto di fumo* in the journalistic text and extract C from the previous exercise.
In the legal text we read, *è vietato fumare nei locali chiusi.* What can *i locali chiusi* be? Find examples in the newspaper.

LOCALI CHIUSI
•
•
•
•
•
•
•

Organize the names. Put the names you found in the right group:

LUOGHI DI SVAGO	LUOGHI DI LAVORO	LUOGHI DI STUDIO	MEZZI PUBBLICI

Do you know other names? Add them in the right groups.

2. Compare the paragraph *Zone riservate ai fumatori* in the journalistic text and extract B from the previous exercise.

Both "La Repubblica" and the legal text use passive forms; write sentences in the active form starting with the word given by the exercise.

PASSIVE	ACTIVE
... gli spazi riservati a chi non riesce a separarsi dalle sigarette dovranno essere contrassegnati.	I proprietari dei locali..................... ....
... dovranno inoltre essere delimitati e separati con pareti dagli spazi in cui non si può fumare.	Le pareti..................................... ....
... i locali riservati ai fumatori devono essere contrassegnati come tali e realizzati in modo da risultare adeguatamente separati	Si*.. ....

*Si impersonale

3. Read the texts carefully and answer the following questions. Compare your answers with the ones of other students.

Which text do you understand better? Why in your opinion?

____

Which text would you quote in a letter addressed to other lawyers? Why?

____

How is the same idea expressed in the article and in the legal document? Write at least three differences.

____

4. Compare the paragraph *Impianti di ventilazione* in the journalistic text and extract A from the previous exercise. You have four words taken from the legal text; find four equivalent expressions in the article.

A. quantità	
B. impianti	
C. ambienti limitrofi	
D. immessa per trasferimento	

(Key: A. portata; B. mezzi meccanici; C. zone circostanti; D. proveniente)

EXERCISE 2: Activity on text registers . Professional students work with expressions taken from the smoking ban law text and are asked to focus on synonyms and paraphrases. Through this type of exercise learners can compare legal textual features with informative speech characteristics and be more aware of how they need to use the language if their goal is an easily comprehensible message for a general audience.

1. Complete sentences in column B so that they keep the same meaning of the sentences in column A.

A (LEGAL TEXT)	B
A tal fine i locali per fumatori devono rispettare i seguenti requisiti strutturali	____________ i locali per fumatori devono essere costruiti secondo determinate regole
... secondo quanto previsto dalla vigente normativa ... nonché dai regolamenti comunali di igiene ed edilizi	... secondo quello che dice la legge in vigore ______ quello che dicono i regolamenti dei comuni per quanto riguarda l'igiene e l'edilizia.
I soggetti abilitati sono tenuti a rilasciare idonea dichiarazione ...	I proprietari dei locali in regola ___________ rilasciare la dichiarazione adatta ...
I locali per fumatori devono essere dotati di idonei mezzi meccanici di ventilazione forzata	I locali per fumatori devono ___________ dei mezzi adatti per la ventilazione
All'ingresso dei locali è indicato il numero massimo di persone ammissibili	All'entrata del locale è scritto il numero massimo delle persone ___________

Alle infrazioni del divieto previsto dal presente articolo si applicano le sanzioni di cui all'articolo 7...	Chi ______________ il divieto di fumo contenuto in questo articolo di legge, verrà ___________ secondo quello che dice l'articolo 7 ...
Restano ferme le disposizioni che disciplinano il divieto di fumo ...	Le leggi che ______________il divieto di fumo ______________ ...
... sancito nella seduta della conferenza permanente	... ______________ durante la riunione della conferenza permanente

As an alternative, students can be given a list of terms that they need to select and put in the right sentence.

punito/per questo motivo/stabilito/avere/devono/non rispetta/regolano/e anche/che possono entrare/non cambiano

PART IV:

TEACHING ITALIAN CULTURE

CHAPTER FOURTEEN

VISUAL LITERACY: TEACHING ITALIAN CULTURE THROUGH IMAGES[1]

DANIELA BARTALESI-GRAF

"Verba volant, IMAGINES manent"
—RAI website[2]

"It's not that photographs are not good. They are too good. […] They contain everything. We have worked out techniques to digest verbal data, but what can we do with photographs?"
—John Collier[3]

Introduction: why visual literacy in C2?

The quote from RAI highlights the precedence that the visual world has gained over SCRIPTA, the written words; Collier's words, on the other hand, express a general frustration: though surrounded and often overpowered by IMAGINES, even educated people might feel that, while perfectly able to interpret a written text, they lack the skills to look critically at an image.[4] Visual literacy, first discussed in 1968 by Debes in his paper on audiovisual pedagogy,[5] is not naturally developed but must be

---

[1] I would like to acknowledge the support received by the Critical Thinking Program of Tufts University (Susan Russinoff, Director) during Summer 2007.
[2] Advertisement flyer of RAI's web site: www.linguaitaliana.rai.it (not dated).
[3] John Jr. Collier, *Visual Anthropology: Photography as a Research Method* (New York: Holt, Rinehart and Winston, 1967), 6.
[4] Lavonne Mueller, "Language as Arts and Arts as Language," in *English Journal* v. 66, no. 7 (1977): 49-51; Jacqueline N. Glasgow, "Teaching Visual Literacy for the 21st Century", *Journal of Reading* 37, no. 6 (March 1994): 494-5.
[5] J.L. Debes "Some Foundations for Visual Literacy," *Audiovisual Instructions* 13 (1968): 961-4. For a full discussion and definition of visual literacy, see also Maribe Robert Branch, "A Taxonomy of Visual Literacy," *Advances in*

formally taught, just like language literacy is; in other words, in order to be able to read an image correctly, one must know the meaning assigned by any given culture to the single units that compose that image, just like one must be able to recognize the letters of the alphabet in order to be able to read a written text.[6] Visual literacy also requires strong critical thinking and analytical skills, since images, just like any written text, may present multiple levels of meanings.[7]

Becoming visually literate in C2 presents a unique set of difficulties: being geographically removed from the target country, students may suffer the same disadvantage as those individuals who live in a pictureless environment, and who cannot recognize objects unless they have already seen them.[8] In other words, students may have some degree of visual literacy in their own culture but, when they approach the study of C2, they are visually illiterate, unable to recognize and read correctly many of the basic elements that belong to a visual world unfamiliar to them.[9] Even advanced students, competent at reading complex written texts in L2, unless explicitly instructed in visual literacy, may still lack the skills to decode the visual world of the target country; they will be bound to stumble and possibly get lost as they navigate the foreign culture they study, like someone who, completely ignorant of the Bible or of classical myths, tries to understand Renaissance Italian art. Traditional courses in L2 and C2 are not designed to bridge this gap. The resistance, on the part of many language programs, to adopt curricula that do not explicitly prepare students to the study of literature is perhaps the greatest obstacle

---

Reading/Language Research 7 (2000): 377-383.

[6] Katherine Arbuckle, "The Language of Pictures: Visual literacy and Print Materials for Adult Basic Education and Training (ABET)," *Language Matters* 35, no. 2 (2004): 445-57.

[7] Branch, 380-1; Glasgow, 499; David Considine, "Visual Literacy and the Curriculum. More to it than Meets the Eye," *Language Arts*, no. 6 (October 1987): 634-640. David N. Perkins, *The Intelligent Eye, Learning to Think by Looking at Art* (Santa Monica: The Getty Center for Education in the Arts, 1994), 3-5.

[8] Branch, 385. Research on literacy programs for adults has demonstrated that the only way to overcome visual illiteracy is to increase exposure to images and interpretations of images (Arbuckle, 453). See also the interesting experiment performed on blind people who could suddenly see, but were able to recognize a sphere and a cube only through touch and not sight alone [in Genelle Morain, "Visual Literacy: Reading Signs and Designs in the Foreign Culture," *Foreign Language Annals*, no. 3 (1976): 210-1].

[9] Morain provides a few poignant anecdotes to illustrate the faux pas a student of C2 might make if she/he has not learned this skill in the area of visual literacy. See Morain, 212-4.

that students and teachers alike encounter on the path to visual literacy in C2. The old mentality reflected by the saying *pictura est laicorum literatura* certainly plays a part in considering the visual culture of a country as inferior and subordinate to the written culture.

In this contribution, I will discuss the place of visual literacy in L2 and C2 acquisition. In particular, I will draw on my experience in teaching courses in Italian language and culture, and on theoretical studies in the field, to show that becoming visually literate in Italian (or in any foreign language), is the *sine qua non* to becoming culturally literate, and vice versa: in order to read an image I must know its cultural background.

The importance of teaching culture side by side with language is a postulate long established in second language acquisition research and literature.[10] By ignoring culture, we teach a "hollow language," i.e. a system of communication that disregards the content of the message.[11] However, the definition of culture is often, at best, fuzzy and vague: the term is commonly used to include almost everything, from geography to architecture, to local folk stories and anecdotes.[12] A clear definition of culture is therefore necessary as a theoretical premise. Nelson Brooks makes a distinction that might be obvious but that is often overlooked in discussions of C2 pedagogy: culture is NOT a condensed, abridged version of the history, literature, art or economy of a certain country, but it is all of the above, plus the individual. "In culture—Brooks contends—we never lose sight of the individual."[13] Culture, therefore, comprehends all the ways in which the individual relates to his/her environment—and history, literature, and all the other disciplines in the humanities are certainly expressions and manifestations of this relation between man/woman and his/her world. We might add that culture is also the hierarchical order that society gives to the individual's needs, duties and rights: what is considered essential or inessential, or what constitutes the "good life" might be very different from culture to culture, hence the way

---

[10] Nelson Brooks, "Teaching Culture in the Foreign Language Classroom," *Foreign Language Annals* 1, no. 3 (1968): 204-17; Ciccarelli, Andrea, "Teaching culture through Language," *Italica* 73, no. 4 (winter 1996): 563-76; Paula R. Heusinkveld, ed., *Pathways to Culture: Readings on Teaching Culture in the Foreign Language Class* (Yarmouth, ME: Intercultural Press, 1997), passim.

[11] Gail L Robinson, "The Magic-Carpet-Ride-to-Another-Culture Syndrome: An International Perspective", in Heusinkveld, ed., 78-9.

[12] See Lafayette's goals in C2 acquisitions in elementary classes (in Robert Lafayette, "Integrating Teaching of Culture into the Foreign Language Classroom," in Heusinkveld, ed., 123).

[13] Brooks, 22.

individuals place themselves vis-à-vis their environment, in order to satisfy those needs, will be very different. Using this theoretical framework, we could draw the following examples to illustrate the distinction between Italian culture and other disciplines: in a history class, we may teach how WW II ended in Italy, but if we teach culture we will discuss, among other topics, how women coped at home with severe shortage of food during the same time; in an art history class, we may discuss the architecture of a 19th century farmhouse in Tuscany, but studying how people use the house to organize family life, celebrations and holidays, etc. is learning Italian culture. In an economics course, we might explore the causes of high unemployment in some southern Italian cities, but we teach culture when we discuss how young people in those cities cope with the prospective of not having a job.

Consequently, if the objective of our courses is to teach language as intrinsically connected to culture, then the traditional classroom setting, instead of facilitating learning, becomes one of its main impediments. Both language and culture are complex systems rather then sets of rules or concepts that can be explained in a linear and logical argument, and are ill suited for the artificial environment of the classroom, where learning is not achieved through real life interactions. In L2 teaching, we overcome this obstacle by reproducing and imitating natural verbal exchanges with natives in a variety of situations. In a similar way, if we want to teach culture, we must virtually bring culture into the classroom, i.e. people and the environment that surrounds them. This is the point in which visual literacy interacts with the teaching of C2. Carefully selected images (photographs, posters, reproductions of works of art, etc.) are brought into the classroom as virtual ambassadors of the culture studied.[14] They are a

[14] Images, it might be objected, are already used in textbooks, and classrooms are already equipped with posters from the country studied. However, even a cursory survey of elementary and intermediate textbooks in Italian reveals that most pictures reproduced are post-card-like images of Italy that attract the viewers to the beauty or quaintness of a certain place, but teach very little about Italian culture, because they do no represent individuals in their environment (see the definition of culture discussed above). For example, the two colored inserts in Annamaria Moneti & Graziana Lazzarino, *Da Capo*, 6th edition (Boston: Thomson-Heinle, 2007), an intermediate textbook for college students, contain a total of 31 photographs, of which 16 are post-card-like pictures (landscapes, church façades, city scenes), 8 represent people, and the rest represents objects or places without people (smartcar, motorcycles, shop windows, etc.). It should be noticed that the two inserts are separate from the text and can be easily ignored; they function as "intermezzo" or diversion from grammar. Lafayette also notices that, even when photos are reproduced in textbooks, they are never accompanied by cultural

window through which students observe people as they interact among themselves and with their environment, the physical spaces people occupy when they work or they are at rest, the visual world that they have created to interpret or describe their lives, to express emotions, to make others aware of political and social issues. The process of reading, decoding and analyzing these images can become a powerful learning tool in C2 courses.[15] Cultural literacy and visual literacy are the products of a circular process, in which each learning phase becomes the motivator and the starting point for the next; in order to read correctly an image, an individual must master important facts about that specific cultural background, and conversely, a correct reading of an image will provide invaluable information about the culture.[16] In conclusion, by acquiring visual literacy in C2, students become speakers of a *third* language, a code of communication that, in our postmodern world, has begun to overtake the written or spoken language.

Eight points of visual literacy in C2

I would like to propose the following eight general areas that visually literate students of C2, should ideally master in order to recognize all aspects of the human environment they are studying:

1. Identify correctly the general subject of any photograph representing people in their interaction with a variety of environments—at work, at rest, at worship, at home, on vacation, etc.—and among themselves. In teaching this skill, we are not concerned with the artistic merit of the image, but mainly with its subject. Students should be able, in other words, to answer the question: "what are these people doing?" For example, being visually literate in Italian should mean being able to read the following images: a crowd marching behind a statue in the street of a small village is a religious procession; a stream of cars honking at night with passengers waving colored flags out the window is a celebration of the victory of a soccer team; people strolling up and down main street around 6pm in a

---

activities and vocabulary (Lafayette, 129); this is precisely because the function of the photo in the textbook is mainly ornamental and not educational.

[15] Several studies have shown that those learners who process information mainly with the right hemisphere of the brain benefit greatly from the use of images in the classroom [Richard Sinatra, "Using visuals to help the second language learner," in *The Reading Teacher* (February 1981): 540-1].

[16] My definition of visual literacy in C2 is therefore much broader than Morain's: in his article, he limits it to the ability to recognize body language, environmental elements and object language.

small provincial town are enjoying their daily *passeggiata* before the evening *aperitivo*.

2. Interpret and analyze political posters and advertisements. These artifacts mirror a culture's social fabric,[17] and being able to read them is tantamount to observing a culture from within, through the eyes of the people who live in it. This skill allows students to explore people's values, desires and goals, and analyze how these are exploited to attain persuasion for political or commercial purposes. Thus the deconstruction of political posters and advertisements requires a correct reading of the symbolism carried by each sign used to compose the image, a skill that must be distinguished from skill 1. above, i.e. the ability to read photographs as representations of a human environment or as substitutes for "being there."

3. Interpret and analyze selected objects of art produced in C2, especially those that occupies public spaces, that are charged with widely shared emotions and feelings, or that are particularly relevant for the understanding of a certain social reality or problem. In this skill, just like in 2., we examine the visual world that surrounds people who live in C2.

4. Recognize the different manifestations of "visual figurative language" in any given work of art. According to Mueller, who argues for the teaching of visual literacy in L1, students should be taught to recognize irony, satire, metaphors, etc. in art, just like they are taught to recognize figurative language in literature.[18] This skill is even more critical in C2 learning. Figurative language is very culturally specific: irony, for example plays a uniquely prominent role in American humor; Italian comedians, instead, prefer slapstick based on regional differences and dialects. Being able to recognize figurative language in the visual world, and in the written and spoken language as well, will help students develop a stronger cross-cultural awareness.

5. Date an image correctly. Students should be able to use different visual hints to date a photograph, such as: shops and open markets in a city or a village, the furniture in a house interior, how people are dressed, what means of transportation they use, etc.

6. Place an image in the correct geographical area (north, centre, south, city, small town, village or countryside, etc.), and setting (home, office, public place, place of worship, etc.) where it originated.

7. Identify the type of relationship among people in an image: friends, colleagues, members of the same family, club or political party, etc.

8. Recognize objects, their function and/or their symbolism.

---

[17] Glasgow, 499.

[18] Mueller, 50.

All the above skills are not sequential or mutually exclusive; on the contrary, they are complementary and overlapping: a visual text can be read, just like a written text, using different perspectives, i.e. utilizing one or more of the skills discussed. In the following sections, I will show how, through the process of deconstructing a few selected images, the explicit teaching of visual literacy goes hand in hand with the teaching of cultural literacy.

A historical photograph: people and space, objects and values (figure 1)

"Pre-reading" exercises

A few important "pre-reading" exercises should be done before analyzing a historical photograph, like the one by Franco Pinna (figure 14-1):[19]

- Students should take a few "thinking minutes" to look at the photograph, and should jot down at least three elements that (1) surprised, (2) interested, and (3) puzzled them in the image; [20] they should also write at least three questions about the image. This first "reading" phase should be revisited at the end of the analysis so that students can reflect on the whole learning process.
- Students, individually or as a group, should give the photo a title.[21] Many titles can be given in the class (by individuals or groups or decided by a class vote). If done at the very beginning, the title will reflect students' gut impression. At the end of the analysis students should be asked if they want to revise their title. Final titles, when compared with initial ones, will often reveal the

---

[19] The best reproduction of this photo by Franco Pinna is found, to my knowledge, in Luca Criscenti and Gabriele D'Autilia, *Autobiografia di una nazione. Storia fotografica della società italiana* (Rome: Editori Riuniti, 1999), 316. I am grateful to Dott. Giuseppe Pinna of Archivio Franco Pinna who informed me that this photo was taken in Rome, in January/February 1956 (e-mail personal exchange, December 4th, 2006).

[20] Perkins makes this suggestion, among others, in relation to the analysis of a work of art; this practice is just as relevant in relation to cross-cultural analysis. See Perkins, 64.

[21] Scanlan suggests giving pictures a title *after* the discussion (see Timothy M. Scanlan, "Another Foreign Language Skill: Analyzing Photographs" in Heusinkveld, ed., 351-62).

direction taken by class discussion, and will highlight initial assumptions that students have later revised.

- The relationship of the photographer with his/her subject(s) should also be discussed in this initial phase. Is the photographer part of the scene or is he/she an outsider? Is the photo staged or non-staged? Are subjects aware that they are being photographed? What angle has the photographer chosen for this image?[22]
- Students should also describe in detail the photograph. This first phase should involve as little interpretation as possible. Students should be encouraged to observe the image closely in each detail. During this phase, the teacher will provide new vocabulary items, such as nouns and adjectives, connectors to describe the relative position of people and objects, action verbs to identify gestures and activities. Chart 1, "Pre-Reading of the Image," in the APPENDIX, has been designed for this purpose, and is easily adaptable to the study of different images.

"Reading" the image

Students of visual literacy will need to use skills 1, 2, 5, 6, 7 and 8. In order to "read" this photo beyond the descriptive level discussed above. The activity this group of people is engaged in (skill 1.) leaves little space for ambiguity: they are obviously watching a TV program. Placing this image in its correct setting (skill 6.), instead, requires some analysis. Asking students: "Where does this scene take place?" can generate many types of answers, such as: in a café-bar, in a restaurant, in a community center, in the basement of a church, in the headquarters of a political party, in a club, etc. After an initial phase of brainstorming, teachers can organize a debate in which students are asked to side with one of the hypothesis presented: the class is physically divided into sections (one per each hypothesis) and students are asked to join the section of their choice.

[22] This last question will challenge the common assumption (often shared by students) that a photograph is a faithful copy of reality. Students should understand that the photographer chooses his/her subject(s), a certain angle and light, and that, finally, he/she edits his/her work. What we see, therefore, is not an objective representation of reality, but a version of that reality filtered through the photographer's eyes, and then in turn filtered through our mind's eyes. This doesn't mean that the process of reading a photograph is pointless: we can still learn a great deal about a culture through photographs, provided that we keep in mind the above limits.

Students should then be asked to motivate their choice using their general knowledge of Italian culture, information derived from other sources, and elements taken from the photo. Factors that will be considered in the debate are, for example: the presence and the content of the sign above the door ("Assistendo alle trasmissioni TV è obbligo consumare") and of advertisements on the wall, the type of furnishing and wall paneling, the high position of the television set, placed to allow the view by a large group of people, the sitting in rows, the number, age, gender and type of people occupying this space, the type of TV show being broadcast. At the end of the debate, the teacher can reveal the exact setting of the photo (in this case, a room in the back of a bar-café). In determining the "winner" of the debate (if the class decides in advance that there should be a winner), the class (or the teacher, depending on the debate rules defined in advance) should consider the group that argued in the most forceful and convincing way rather than the group that had the right answer. The hypothesis and arguments brought up by students will reveal many pre-existing ideas of what Italian public and/or private spaces and settings might look like.

After this phase, a more culturally specific inquiry will follow, and students should start to draw inferences from the photo in order to define the "nature" or "essence" of the Italian bar-café; their inquiry, in other words, should go beyond the descriptive level, i.e. the drawing of a list of all the physical or human elements that can be found in a bar-café, as discussed in the "pre-reading" charts above. The starting question will be: What can I learn from this picture about the place of the bar-café in Italian society, in family and community life, its multiple roles as an organizer and deliverer of entertainment, a gathering place for people of all ages, and a dispenser of refreshments? [23] These are only some of the questions that will help unveil the "essence" of the Italian bar-café (largely unchanged since the 50s), and consequently support our claim that this scene takes place in a bar-café. Chart 2, "The Place: Interpretation", might be used for this purpose or adapted to many types of images. If time allows, students might decide to expand their research; using different sources, they could investigate, for example, historical cafés in different cities, or the origin of

---

[23] It's also interesting to compare Scanlan's deconstruction of a photo taken in a contemporary French café with my deconstruction of this historical photograph of an Italian bar-café in the 50s. Scanlan suggests that the teacher provide most information about the "the role of the café as a meeting place for socialization and relaxation as well as basic alimentary function" (Scanlan, 355), whereas I suggest that students (with teacher's help) infer directly from the image these cultural information.

varied terminology such as *osteria, taverna, trattoria, caffè, bar, locale,* etc.

The following phase involves a process of cross-cultural awareness. What public place in your own country is most similar to this place? If students' country of origin is the US, a bar or a restaurant or a community center will be mentioned. Students should bring to class a photo of an American bar or restaurant taken from a magazine and use it to reflect on similarities and differences.[24] The following exercise could be done dividing students in pairs: each student imagines to be one of the customers in each photo (one of the people watching TV in Pinna's photo, and one of the people in the American photo); he/she describes the place and his/her experience in that place to the other student.[25] This exercise will highlight the function and nature of each place from the point of view of the Italian and American customer. Chart 3, "The Place: Cross-Cultural Evaluation," can accompany this final stage.

In conclusion, in order to Place this image in its correct setting (skill 6.) students might go through the following phases: (1) brainstorming: where do you think this scene takes place? (2) Debate: students take side; (4) cultural definition (in the case examined: "what is a bar-café?"); (5) cross-cultural comparison ("does a place like this exist in the US?").[26] The analysis of a single image can give rise to a domino effect: if we start

---

[24] Scanlan suggests the use of American photos because these "will lead to a discussion of how the scene depicted would differ in a foreign context," (Scanlan, 352-3) I suggest the opposite: students should start from a "foreign image," then search for an image of a similar situation in their culture, and finally compare the two.

[25] This exercise is similar to the one proposed by Scanlan. However, Scanlan's objective is to increase students' oral production through dramatization, whereas my objective is, above all, to have students deepen their definition of the Italian bar-café with an exercise in cross-cultural awareness. The imaginative level based on speculation and unverifiable hypothesis suggested by Scanlan, though beneficial for language production, should be avoided in the deconstruction of historical photographs because we want to reach a very accurate historical and cultural reading of the image. See Scanlan 357-9.

[26] Lafayette has devised a template of questions to elicit students' response to images; questions are divided into three groups (*Description. Information Gathering. Comparison*). In the last section, *Comparison*, students are encouraged to draw cross-cultural comparisons. See Lafayette, 130. Scanlan's template also contains three levels of interpretation: the literal level of understanding (observable facts), the interpretative-applied level (highly probable inferences drawn from the facts) and the imaginative level (speculation and unverifiable hypotheses). See Scanlan, 356-7.

asking culturally relevant questions, more will emerge, and the limit will only be a self-imposed one. At the end of this inquiry, students will have explored important tenets in Italian culture, while learning just as much about their own culture.[27]

A different process of inquiry should be used to recognize the central object in this photo (skill 8.). Though clearly a TV set, when this photo was taken people used this object in a very different way than they do in today's Italy (or in the US). In Pinna's photograph, watching TV was a communal event that involved several generations, and the entertainment or learning that came from TV programs was shared in a public space.[28] Unlike the movie theater of today, the room shown in this photo was not solely designed for showing TV programs: it was well light and brightened by posters, people could come and go, other activities were likely to take place nearby, beverages could be consumed; finally, it's easily imaginable that people would have commented aloud what they watched on the screen. TV was not used for private entertainment within a household; its function in a bar-café, as the focus of entertainment and socialization as well, has been completely lost today. In conclusion, students will recognize that two objects may share the same dictionary definition (they both are "electronic system(s) of transmitting [...] images together with sound over a wire or through space [...]),[29] yet, when used in different cultures or different periods of time, they are in fact *different* objects, symbolically and functionally. Chart 4 ("The Object: Cross-Cultural Evaluation") in the Appendix, is an adaptable tool for the analysis of any object in a historical photograph. The following written exercise can accompany this discussion: imagine you are one of the customers in this photo; write a page of his/her diary by the title "What I did last night at the bar-café." Students could also be asked to write a page of their own diary after an evening watching TV (at home by themselves, with friends, at the local bar, perhaps watching a sport event, in their frat house, etc.), and then compare the two diaries.

In order to date this photo correctly (skill 5.) and to place it in its correct geographical area (skill. 6), students must embark on further

[27] See Scanlan, 355-6 on the importance of learning about one's own culture while learning C2.

[28] For a discussion of the role of television programs in the late 50s, see Paul Ginsborg, *Storia d'Italia dal dopoguerra a oggi* (Torino: Editori Riuniti, 1989), 326-8.

[29] This definition is found in Philip Babcock Gove, ed., *Webster's Third New International Dictionary* (Springfield, MA: G. & C. Merriam Company Publisher, 1968).

questioning and research. Most of them will easily recognize that it was probably taken a few decades ago, though very few will be able to place it in its correct time period. An excellent exercise to motivate language production and to sharpen analytical skills is to have students brainstorm the kinds of questions they should answer in order to date this photo, and to determine, at least approximately, in what part of the country it was taken. Relevant questions should be: When did TV programs start in Italy? When did families start buying TV sets, and when did TV sets become common household items? How expensive were TV sets compared to average income? When did films with Stan Laurel (his characteristic figure and top heat are visible on the screen) start being broadcast? Was the television signal immediately available all over the country, in cities, as well as smaller centers and in the countryside?

These factual questions should later give rise to a more analytical discussion. Students in visual literacy should be able to motivate their answers beyond the citation of historical dates and facts easily found on *google* (just like they did in establishing the correct setting of this scene). They need to explore important aspects of the Italian after-war society and culture in order to support their claim that this picture was taken in the late 50's. For example: why does this scene fit in with the culture of the 50s, and not of the 60s or the 70s? Did the bar-café-with-TV-room satisfy a popular need in the 50s? (For example, by creating or reinventing a place for communal entertainment, after long years of cultural deprivation caused by fascism first, and then by the war; or did it rather respond to the need, felt by large masses that had recently migrated from the countryside, to find some kind of communal life in the unknown city?) Other areas of inquiry that can be explored are the following: What was TV's impact on family life? Did it have any influence on cinema as a form of art? What audience did TV programs attract? What is the significance of the presence of women in a public place like this during that time?

An accurate reading of this picture forces students to decipher a complicated web of social relations and environments (see Chart 5 "Dating the photo" in the Appendix). Such analysis has the power to transform this photograph (or any other) into a window opened on a real world where people act and interact in front of us: words are not spoken or written, but we are confronted with a multiplicity of signs, often overlapping and contradictory, at least on the surface. Our task is to give meaning to all of them, so that at the end of the process the visual language of this image will be intelligible, in its single unit and as a whole.[30]

This photo by Franco Pinna can be analyzed even further. The advertisement visible in the background (figure 14-2.) allows us to exercise skill 2, i.e. the analysis of artifacts produced by a culture in a certain period of time. Glasgow has studied a method to analyze advertisements in C1, and has devised a template to "deconstruct" visual signs in advertisements.[31] Chart 6 ("Reading a Coca Cola Ad, 1956") is an adaptation of her chart to the study of the symbolic language of advertisements in C2. The first section "Reading and interpreting" invites students to describe in details people, objects, places and actions portrayed in the poster, to reflect on their symbolical connection with the product advertised, and to draw conclusions on the appeal that this product might have on consumers. In this initial phase, students are also asked to decide on a "title" for this poster, and on its intended target. The second section "Making Inferences: from Poster to Culture and Back" invites students to connect everything they have observed and discussed to larger cultural questions. Finally, students can enter into a more creative phase of their analysis: they can "narrate" the ad from the point of view of one of the customers in Pinna's bar-café, or they can create their own coca cola ad for the 21st century consumer. Further cross-cultural or historical comparison can add to the analysis of this advertisement: for example, students could compare this ad with one from the 50s in the USA. And, by reverse, they could decide if any of today's coca cola ads could have been used in the 50s.[32] Once again, the analysis of an image generates a circular process: from image we learn about culture, and we can use our knowledge of culture and history to further interpret the image.

Teachers can use photography in innumerable other ways in C2 classes. For example, they can ask students to carefully select and bring to class a photograph that they believe is representative of one or more aspects of American culture they would like to share with one Italian peer. If some students have traveled to Italy, they can bring to class one picture they have taken there, that they deem representative of some aspect of

[30] The three phases described above (identify the place, the object and the date) are somewhat artificially separated for clarity, but it goes without saying that, in the healthy messiness of a regular classroom discussion, they will overlap. It is important, however, that teachers keep the distinction clear in their mind so that they can lead a more successful in-class discussion.

[31] Glasgow, 497.

[32] A good selection of historical and contemporary coca cola ads can be found in the official site of The Coca Cola Company Store: http://www.coca-colastore.com/

Italian culture they observed. Students could be given disposable cameras and asked to construct their visual story of life on campus for a hypothetical (or better, real) newly arrived freshman from Italy. Students should always be asked to motivate their choices: Why have you chosen this specific shot? What did you want to capture? What intrigued you? These types of exercises will produce better results if planned *after* a careful analysis of a historical photograph like the one by Pinna detailed above.

Political posters: persuasion, art and allegory (figure 3.)

This poster by the Italian political party *Rifondazione Comunista* (1992) is particularly interesting for our discussion, because its message is just as obscure to students of C2 as it is transparent to the majority of Italian voters. In order to "read" it, students must be able to decipher a case of personification allegory (skill 4.). Students will be puzzled by this Mediterranean looking woman, wearing a crown in the shape of city walls; most Italians would easily recognize in her a version of the *Italia Turrita*, a very common personification allegory of Italy; she is found in countless works of art, and is very familiar to Italians primarily because of a series of popular stamps issued continuously from 1953 till 1988.[33] The thread that connects the birth of this allegory in classical times to the present runs through poetry, literature, and art.[34] Marcus, in her study on the Italian body politics, traces the success of this allegorical female personification in literature and art through the centuries. We can find her in Dante, Petrarch and Leopardi, down to modern Italian cinema.[35] This woman has represented over the centuries the evolution of the idea of Italy as a utopian (or real) political entity: she is always recognizable for her stately

---

[33] "La Storia delle Poste e del Francobollo" available on the official site of Poste Italiane S.p.A., 2002:
http://www.poste.it/azienda/storia/solotesto/solotesto5.4.html. The *Italia Turrita* of the stamp first issued in 1953 is also called Siracusana because she is cast on a Greek coin from the IV century B.C.E., found in the area of Siracuse in Sicily.

[34] The first literary reference to this allegory is found in Virgil's Aeneid 6.781-87. In this passage Aeneas goes to the underworld where the ghost of his father Anchises foresees to him the birth of the city of Rome, described as a woman crowned with a castle representing the Seven Hills of Rome united under one rule.

[35] Millicent Marcus, "The Italian Body Politics is a Woman: Feminized National Identity in Postwar Italian Film" in *Sparks and Seeds: Medieval Literature in its Afterlife*, ed. D.E. Stewarts and A. Cornish (Turnhout, Belgium: Brepols Publishers, 2000), 329-47.

and plump body, her wavy hair, her round and regular face, the archetype of a Southern peasant woman; yet, she can take on different personalities: she has been portrayed as a dispenser of bounty, a sort of earth goddess carrying a cornucopia, or as a wounded or violated woman, or a triumphant heroine. This *Italia* has been exploited in so many contexts through the centuries that the majority of Italian easily recognizes her to this day, though her origin might be unknown to many.

The message of this political poster, then, is particularly effective. *Rifondazione comunista* asks its voters, "Do you want an Italy that will have no voice if it becomes "authoritarian, ruled by the Lega Nord, or ruled by a Presidential (rather than a Parliamentary) political system?" The answer is found in the word *rifondata* (renewed, founded anew), a clear reference to the party Rifondazione Comunista, but also a direct connection to this long allegorical tradition. Present and past literature, art and politics have thus concurred to create a powerful message recognizable, however, only if one understands its cultural background; its deconstruction can enable students to travel through many areas of Italian culture. Once again, students could be inspired to draw some cross-cultural comparisons, by reflecting on the following questions: What personification allegories are used for your country? How would you compare Lady Liberty to this woman? If you had to draw a political poster for voters in your country, and wanted to use a personification allegory of your nation, what image would you choose? Chart 7 "Decoding a political poster," derived from Chart 6 ("Reading a Coca Cola Ad"), can be used to analyze any image intended to sell a political program.[36]

From literature to art, and back: "visual figurative language" in one painting by Carlo Levi (figure 4.)

Learning to recognize "figurative language"—allegory, metaphors, irony, satire, etc.—might be easier in art than in a written text, at least for students of L2 and C2. Through his/her work, an artist communicates to us

---

[36] A final note on the use of charts in the Appendix. The process of pre-reading and analysis plotted in the charts is intended to counteract the tendency to cast only a passing glance at an image; yet this might seem a little cumbersome and artificial. Students should use the charts as tools, and not as complicated machineries that control one's thinking rather than promoting analysis and discussion. Teachers might decide to use some sections of the charts for their own preparation, to train their eyes at looking more closely at an image in order to be more prepared for in-class discussion. Charts can also be split and manipulated in several ways in order to serve different pedagogical needs.

his/her unique view of reality, using a personal esthetic choice. A work of art can also teach a moral lesson or promote awareness of a social problem. However, unlike a written text, a piece of art will always speak a language made of signs that are universally readable. Therefore, students can rely on the universality of the language of art to approach figures of speech that might have been harder to recognize if found in a written text. Using visual metaphors and visual irony, Levi manages to convey in one image the complexity of a local culture, a task he accomplishes in his novel through several passages written in a highly poetic (and difficult) language.

"Testa di vitello" is a little known painting by Carlo Levi, dated September 5th, 1935.[37] Levi's authoritative and unambiguous title contrasts sharply with the actual subject of this painting. Are we really looking at the head of a calf? Our puzzlement doesn't result from a lack of realism in the technique used by Levi, but from the almost palpable ambiguity of this portrait: this disembodied head of an animal is so disturbing because it appears to be alive and because some of its traits are clearly human or, at least, recall a mythological satyr, whose nature crosses the boundaries between animal and human: the rosy color of the skin, the mouth open almost in a grin, the eyes, set apart, yet vivid and alert, as if mocking the viewer, the tufts of auburn hair; all these elements challenge Levi's title; we are observing something that is alive and dead at the same time, that has human, mythological and animal elements. Presented on a cloth and filling the whole space of the painting, lacking any background, this head of an animal-human-satyr could have the function of a precious object of cult. Yet, Levi tells us: this is the head of a dead calf. Through one single image, and the skillful use of visual irony, Levi conveys the essential characters of the complex peasant culture of Aliano, where death is not opposed to life, and animals, humans and divinities all partake of the same nature. Levi writes in his *Christ stopped at Eboli*:

> [...] gli dei dello Stato e della città non possono aver culto fra queste argille, dove regna il lupo e l'antico nero cinghiale, né alcun muro separa il mondo degli uomini da quello degli animali e degli spiriti [...] tutto è legato da influenze reciproche, [...] ogni cosa è un potere che agisce insensibilmente, dove non esistono limiti che non siano rotti da un influsso magico. [I contadini] vivono immersi in un mondo che si continua senza determinazioni, dove l'uomo non si distingue dal suo sole, dalla sua bestia,

[37] Carlo Levi, *Carlo Levi e la Lucania. Dipinti dal confino 1935-1936* (Roma: De Luca Edizioni d'Arte, 1990), Tav. 10.

> dalla sua malaria [...][38] [The deities of the state and the city can find no worshippers here on the land, where the wolf and the ancient black boar reign supreme, where there is no wall between the world of men and the world of animal and spirits [...] here where all thing are held together by acting upon one another and each one is a power unto itself, working imperceptibily, where there is no barrier that can not be broken down by magic. [Peasants] live submerged in a world that rolls on independent of their will, where man is in no way separate from his sun, his beast, his malaria [...][39]

The analysis of this painting is not meant to substitute for an appreciation of Levi's beautiful prose. Being able to recognize visual figures of speech enables students to reach a deeper appreciation of art itself, but also to understand the often contradictory and complex world represented in a painting. Students may comprehend, laboring through Levi's text, many aspects of the culture of Aliano, but through this painting they can feel them immediately, and return to Levi's prose more prepared to tackle figures of speech and multiple meanings in his highly poetic prose.

Levi's case is of course unique: a great writer and an accomplished painter who painted many of the subjects found in his prose. It is easy to see how his paintings might be excellent visual representation of his prose—a unique asset for the L2 and C2 student. However, all literary texts, when presented to our students could be accompanied by some kind of visual representation of their cultural/historical context. This does not mean that teachers should adopt illustrated edition of the texts they assign; rather, the analysis of selected images (photographs and works of art) will provide C2 students with that cultural contextualization that native speakers might naturally have. The following discussions will serve as illustrations of my point.

Three final anecdotes: closet and *catoico*, cotton candy and spindle, a village in sub-Saharan Africa and a village in southern Italy

I would like now to report and analyze three anecdotes from an advanced Italian class, to show how students, through visual literacy,

---

[38] Carlo Levi, *Cristo si è fermato a Eboli* (Torino: Giulio Einaudi Editore, 2001), 68-9.

[39] Carlo Levi, *Christ Stopped at Eboli*, translated by Frances Frenaye (Harmondsworth, England: Penguin Books Ltd., 1982), 79.

might become more aware of their own (often unconscious) false assumptions and stereotypes. Before students read a passage in *Christ stopped at Eboli* by Carlo Levi, where the author describes the typical peasant's house,[40] I showed a photograph of a the interior of a house in Matera from 1958[41] (little had changed in the South during the 20 years following Levi's *confino*): a single room is almost entirely occupied by a large bed; from an opening in the wall behind the bed, a man leads a horse inside the house. Students' amused reaction was the following: "These people keep a horse in the closet!" The reading of Levi's relevant passage revealed that the "closet" is in reality a "catoico," a word in dialect of Greek origin that designates a space "besides the house" occupied by animals. The photograph without Levi's words would have been meaningless, and Levi's description could have remained obscure without the visual backing of the image. Students' comments also revealed the common tendency to explain puzzling aspects of another culture using well-known elements of one's own culture; naturally, what one sees every day is often assumed to be universal, and using what is known to explain the unknown provides a certain level of comfort. Using a photograph in this context taught students not only that closets are generally not found in Italian houses, but that even the most obvious assumption about every-day objects and spaces (what we think of as universal ingredients of human existence) are culturally specific.

The second anecdote is a further illustration of this point. During a discussion of the aftermath of *Risorgimento* in the south, I used a print by Bartolomeo Pinelli to show how *briganti* were seen by most poor peasants in the south: a kind of Robyn Hoods who took from the poor to give to the rich, the opposite of the blood-thirsty bandits found in official documents. This popular print shows two *briganti* as they are carrying a big chest belonging to a young rich lady to an old lady who is spinning wool on a spindle. One of the *briganti* is holding the young rich lady by the hand and points to the old lady, while his companion carries on his shoulder the heavy chest. The young lady, her eyes downcast, appears remorseful, as she is learning a good moral lesson; the *brigante* at the center, tall and handsome, is represented as a good judge who redresses social injustice. Students could not really understand the meaning of the scene, though they could read most of their discrete parts. Their obstacle was the activity the old woman was engaged in. No one in this junior class of students from Tufts University could recognize the spindle and the act of threading wool.

---

[40] Levi (2001), 107-8.

[41] Franco Barbagallo, *Il Sud. Storia fotografica della società italiana* (Roma: Editori Riuniti, 2001), 193 top.

Most students thought that the old woman was sitting holding cotton candy. The use of the spindle, and the woman's clothes were the only indicators of her social class, as opposed to the long white tunic worn by the young woman, a symbol of aristocracy. The failure to recognize the spindle, an object so common in peasants' culture till a few decades ago, prevented a correct reading of the image. Cotton candy, just like the closet, is an object familiar to American students, but totally foreign to peasants traditional life. Only an image could highlight how culturally specific these objects are, and be instructive to students, teaching them that their visual world is far from being universal, and that in order to become visually literate they cannot filter images in C2 through the lenses of the visual world that is familiar to them; on the contrary they must question constantly their own assumptions, even about such common and taken-for-granted objects as closets and cotton candies.

A final anecdote will show the power of images to challenge subconscious stereotypes about other cultures. After reading the first 10 pages or so from the *Christ stopped at Eboli* by Carlo Levi, I showed students some photographs of Aliano. They were genuinely surprised because, they told me, they had formed a very different mental image of Levi's village. They didn't think Aliano would be a village with houses made of stones and tiled roofs. Instead, they thought Aliano's houses would be simple huts made of mud with straw roofs. Students further explained that malaria is characteristic of sub-Saharan Africa where people mostly live in mud houses; hence, they thought that Aliano, also affected by malaria during Levi's time, would have the similar types of dwellings; thus they had formed a solid mental image of a Southern Italian village that resembled a stereotypical African village. Had I not shown these photos, students would have been totally unaware of their stereotypes and faulty logic, since these may have never surfaced during in-class discussion.

Conclusions

Through images instructors bring people, places and objects inside the classroom infusing the teaching of language with the teaching of culture. Images have the unique power to present multiple meanings in a flash whereas a written text might require the reader to follow the long logical path of an argument. But it's not only economy that makes images so important for the teaching of culture. An image has the power to elicit a sudden emotional reaction and personal involvement on the part of the student, identified by Robinson as "the process of cognitive discovery, cognitive dissonance, or intellectual challenge combined with emotional experience";[42] personal involvement, in turn, has a positive effect on motivation and attitude, with beneficial results for L2 acquisition and production.

A discussion of the role of TV and of the influence of American culture in the after-war period, or of the living conditions in a southern Italian village would have been dangerously abstract if not supported by the use of images. On the other hand, the same images, without the support of their historical, literary and cultural background would remain more or less appealing artifacts, signs written in an unknown alphabet that students might appreciate for their elegance and complexity, but that remain mute, unable to communicate any intrinsic meaning.

"Words are stones" ("Le parole sono pietre") said the mother of a mafia victim to explain her son's death;[43] he had dared speak up against large land owners, and his words were powerful and dangerous actions, for which he received the ultimate punishment; images can be just as powerful and dangerous, thus we must be able to judge the weight they carry in C2, in order "to catch" them correctly, as if they were stones and, if need be, "to throw" them in the right direction.

TUFTS UNIVERSITY, USA

---

[42] Robinson, 85.

[43] Carlo Levi, *Le parole sono pietre* (Torino: Giulio Einaudi Editore, 1956), title.

APPENDIX

Choosing images for use in Italian language and culture courses

Though all photographs are valuable means to communicate meaning, not all are equally rich in their cultural content. Two criteria should guide our selection of photographs for our C2 classes:

- We should chose among the ones that Italians themselves have considered representative of their history and culture. The photo by Franco Pinna, for example, has been reproduced in several publications, and is relatively well known;
- photos should include, as discussed above, people in a variety of situation. One can imagine how little meaning Pinna's photograph would convey if it showed the same bar-café without customers. Teachers should avoid postcard type pictures, and prefer those that depict an environment where people have left their mark. For example, a view of Piazza del Campo in Siena at sunset can make a beautiful postcard, but tells us little about culture. A photo of the same piazza the morning after a youth concert tells us much about the way this space can be used in contemporary Italy.

The following publications offer excellent selections of culturally and historically rich photographs:

- De Luna, Giovanni and Diego Mormorio, ed. *Storia fotografica della società italiana.* Roma: Editori Riuniti, 2000
- De Luna, Giovanni, Gabriele D'Autilia and Luca Criscenti. *L'Italia del Novecento. Le fotografie e la storia.* Torino: Giulio Einaudi Editore, 2005

An excellent selection of political posters that can be downloaded for non-commercial purposes is found on the web site of the Istituto Gramsci Emilia Romagna: www.manifestipolitici.it

Chart 1—"Pre-Reading" of the Image

People

Total number:

Each person

Sex:	Age:	Body position (sitting, standing, etc.):	Gestures:	Facial expression:	Clothes:	Hair style:	Visible part(s) of the body:	Activi-ty

Within each subgroup

Distance between individuals:	Verbal interaction (meeting or leaving, talking, listening, lecturing, arguing, etc.):	Bodily interaction: (hugging, holding/shaking hands, kissing, etc.):	Relative body position (facing each other, in a row, side by side, aware of each other, etc.):	Relation between this subgroup and others (ignoring, aware of each other, interacting, etc.)	Activity

Chart 2—The Place: Interpretation

Place

Indoors (general description):

Smaller than…	Bigger than…	Doors	Windows	Furniture	General appearance	Private	Public	Other

Outdoors (general description):

City …	Small town…	Village …	Countryside…	Mountains…	Coast…	Other …

Objects

Objects that I recognize

List of objects and general description:	Possible function:	Relation to the people (individually or as a group)

Place

Objects that I DO NOT recognize

General description:	Hypothesis on possible function:	Relation to the people (individually or as a group)
My narrative description of this photo (people, place, objects, etc.)		

Chart 3—The Place: Cross Cultural Evaluation

From photo to culture: discover the "cultural essence" of this place

General function of this place	Used when? (general times and days)	Activities not allowed here	Activities allowed in this place	Who can be there and who cannot and why	Relation that each individual in the photo has with the place	Relation that other people outside the photo might have with the place	Relation that society at large has with this place	This place in history: what I know and what I would like to find out

Cross-cultural evaluation of a place (above chart, plus following boxes)

From an Italian point of view	Emotions I have towards this place (positive and negative)	What I think of the equivalent place in the US (emotions: positive and negative)	Symbolic value this place might have for me
From an American Point of view	Emotions I have towards this place (positive and negative)	What I think of the equivalent place in the ITALY (emotions: positive and negative)	Symbolic value this place might have for me

Chart 4—The Object: Cross-Cultural Evaluation

From photo to culture: discover the "cultural essence" of this object

General use of this object	When it is not used	When it is often used	Who can use it and who can't	Possible symbolism of the object	Relation that each individual in the photo has with the object	Relation that other people outside the photo might have with the object	Relation that society at large has with this object	This object in history: what I know, what I would like to find out

This object now in the USA (same as above)

Has the object changed name since the time of the photo? In the USA? ______________________ In ITALY? ______________________

Chart 5—Date the Photo

Hypothesis: this photo was taken around _______ (year)

Elements I base my hypothesis on:

People:	Place(s)	Object(s)	General mood of the photo

Questions I need to ask to verify:

1. 2. 3. 4. etc.

Conclusion (was my idea correct? If not, what elements mislead me?)

Needs, values and aspirations of that time and in connection to:	
Place (how did that place satisfy the above needs, values, etc.?)	Object(s) (how did those objects satisfy the above needs, values, etc.?)

Chart 6—Reading a Coca Cola Ad

Reading and Interpreting

Give a title to this ad:	Target of this ad (general population or a specific age, class, gender, etc.):

Image: description of objects, people and places (mainly nouns and adjectives)	*Image*: what happens? (use of verbs, adverbs, connectors)	*Image*: possible meaning of objects, people, place and actions to the Italian consumer of 1956	*Image*: connection with product advertised	*Image*: possible appeal to Italian consumers of 1956
Text	*Text* (its position in relation to images)	*Text*: explicit or implicit message	*Text:* connection with product advertised	*Text*: possible appeal to Italian consumers of the 50s

Making Inferences: From Poster to Culture and Back

What I already know about the culture of the time that might help me decode this ad	Questions I need to answer	From images and text: my inferences on aspirations of the Italian female consumers in the 50s	From images and text: my inferences on larger cultural trends	Elements that strike me about this political poster

My narration of this ad:

One of the people in Pinna's photograph: *his/her* narration of this coca cola ad:

Would this ad work now in the USA? Why? Analyze a 21st century coca cola ad. You can use or adapt for this purpose a real coca cola ad, or … create your own:

My narration of *my* own coca-cola ad:

My target group or my consumer:	Their needs or problems:	The images I would use (description of people, objects and actions)	The text I would use	Connection between images/text and ↓ consumers' needs/problems

Chart 7—Deconding a Political Poster: Rifondazione Comunista, 1992: Reading and Interpreting

Give a title to this political poster:	Target of this political poster (voters at large or a specific group or class)

Image (description)	*Image* (symbolic/ allegorical value)	*Image* (explicit and implicit message)	*Image* (connection with political party)	*Image* (appeal to Italian voters)

Text	*Text* (its position in relation to image)	*Text* (explicit or implicit message)	*Text* (connection with political party)	*Text* (appeal to Italian voters)

Making Inferences: From Poster to Culture and Back

What I already know about the history and culture of the time that might help me decode this political poster	Questions I need to answer:	From images and text: my inferences on strategies, ideology, political platform and objectives of this party	From images and text: my inferences on political issues of concern at the time, and on larger cultural trends	Elements that still puzzle me about this political poster

My narration of this political poster:

Italian voter from 1992, favorable to PRC: *his/her* narration of this political poster:	Italian voter from 1992, NOT favorable to PRC: *his/her* narration of this political poster:

Would this poster work now in the USA, and why?
Create your own political poster:

<table>
<tr>
<td>My political objectives</td>
<td>My voters' needs/ problems</td>
<td>The images I would use (description of people, objects and actions)</td>
<td>The text I would use</td>
<td>Connection between images/text and
↓ ↘
<table><tr><td>My political objectives</td><td>My voter's needs/problems</td></tr></table></td>
</tr>
<tr>
<td colspan="5">My narration of my political poster:</td>
</tr>
</table>

Figure 14-1. Photograph by Franco Pinna.

Figure 14-2. Advertisement visible in the background.

Figure 14-3. Poster by Partito Rifondazione Comunista (1992). From *Archivio Marco Pezzi*, Comune di Bologna.

Figure 14-4. ***Testa di vitello*****, Carlo Levi (September 5th, 1935), © SIAE**

CHAPTER FIFTEEN

A *VISUAL* SOCIO-CULTURAL APPROACH TO ITALIAN WOMEN'S STUDIES

FLAVIA LAVIOSA

Introduction

Visual Sociology and Cultural Studies are academic areas both interested in the visual and cultural dimensions of people's life, and concerned with photography, visual art, and documentary filmmaking as cultural manifestations within sociological contexts. These disciplines include the study of materials illustrating the world and the use of visual tools in their research and teaching methodologies. Therefore the film, video and photo cameras become powerful means well suited as information gathering technologies to record and preserve data of interest for social and cultural inquiries. Further, visual recording technology, a versatile channel of information, facilitates the study of phenomena conveyed through images (i.e. art, photographs, film, video, advertisements, computer icons, landscape, architecture, machines, fashion, makeup, hair style, facial expressions, tattoos), and produced as expressions of the complex visual communication system generated by members of a society.

The use and understanding of images is governed by socially and culturally established symbolic codes and such images may be read as texts in a variety of ways, may be constructed and deconstructed, or analyzed with techniques developed in different fields such as literary criticism, art theory and criticism, or ethnography. Given the pervasiveness of media in the world today, a balanced approach to visual texts would examine their artistic value (i.e. their textual dimension); would analyze their contextual aspect, that means exploring the texts from the point of view of production (i.e. the socio-economic, technolgical and cultural apparatus from which they emerge); and would discuss the visuals from the perspective of the reception (i.e. the various channels and modes of consumption). The methodological principles and epistemological framework described above constitute the theoretical and pedagogical foundations of the visual socio-cultural inquiry implemented in the teaching approach developed for the upper intermediate Italian course *Women in Italy*.[1]

Throughout the 1990s, institutions of higher education in the United States experienced an unprecedented and steady student demographic growth in Italian departments and programs as the result of a renewed academic interest for the Italian language, culture, art, economy and politics. Those were the years when also the Department of Italian at Wellesley College, in Massachusetts, was confronted with a rapid and significant increase in its student population in the first two years of the language requirement. These students needed to be motivated and persuaded to enroll in upper division culture courses, therefore the Department made the decision to enhance the program by diversifying its curricular offerings, and increasing the number of faculty to accommodate larger enrollments and sustain such promising expansion. These major transformations involved also a radical academic paradigm shift leading to the formalization of the new Department of Italian Studies. This name change was meant to acknowledge the existence of various possibilities within the newly and broadly redefined area of Italian studies, to establish a wider ranging program, and envision further developments through the establishment of study abroad opportunities in Italy.

Such transition, from a regionalized characterization of Italian to a more inclusive description of Italian Studies, pushed traditionally conceived disciplinary boundaries by incorporating a larger spectrum of fields, while fostering collaboration among departments across the 'buildings' on the campus. The College recognized the scope of such revival of interest for Italian culture and the new academic centrality of Italian Studies in the world. Consequently the College administration facilitated the institutionalized strengthening and modernization of the Department's major and minor requirements, provided resources to increase curricular offerings, and favored extra- and co-curricular activities and experiential forms of learning.

This intellectually coherent and more viable academic program has allowed the design and experimentation of innovative interdisciplinary courses in the Department of Italian Studies since the mid-1990s. As a result of such climate of academic cross-fertilization, *Women in Italy*

[1] All translations of Italian texts and citations are mine.

represents the product of that propulsive creative force and strong administrative support, and sets an example for the groundbreaking educational initiatives that have inspired the steady development of the Department of Italian Studies for over ten years. Keeping with Wellesley College's stated mission—"to provide an excellent liberal art education for women who will make a difference in the world"—Italian Studies 211 *Women in Italy* is a course reflecting interdisciplinary methodologies, and cultural studies oriented forms of inquiry in approaching issues about Italian society.

Topics, Goals, Materials, Methodology

Women in Italy is a fifth semester culture course recommended to students who have completed two years of the Italian language requirement,[2] master Italian at least at the high intermediate[3] level of language proficiency, intend to minor or major in Italian Studies, and plan to spend one semester or a full academic year with one of the study abroad programs in Italy approved by the College. The course is taught in Italian and students' participation is in Italian. The course meets twice a week for 70 min. per class and over a period of fifteen weeks. Students earn 1 credit unit, and the cap is limited to twenty students. The course is also cross-listed in the Department of Women's Studies at Wellesley College. Offered since the 1999/2000 academic year, the syllabus of *Women in Italy*[4] has been subject to regular updates that would include texts discussing contemporary social and cultural changes occurring in the country, add materials analyzing the recent legislative reforms implemented in Italy, and incorporate current visual documents illustrating these changes.

The complete title is *Women in Italy 1930s-2000s: history, sociology, law, anthropology, cinema, dance and songs*, and the course covers a broad range of topics including:

- Women's Roles, Duties and Rights in the Fascist Era

---

[2] This course is also recommended to students who may have placed out of the forth semester of the language requirement by passing the institutional Italian placement test, or to students who have successfully passed the Advancement Placement Test in Italian with a score of 5.

[3] As defined in the ACTFL OPI Guidelines.

[4] A recent version of the syllabus is available in the Appendix. The original syllabus is in Italian, but it has been translated in English for the purpose of this publication.

- The Post-WWII Era and the Economic Boom
- Beauty Pageant and National Identity
- Women Stars in Italian Cinema
- The Italian Feminist Movement and Women's Rights in the 1970s
- Slogans, Images and Leaflets of the Feminist Struggle in the 1970s
- Changes in the Feminist Movement and Legislative Reforms in the 1980s
- The Feminist Movement and Legislative Reforms in the 1990s
- Violence Against Women: Law n. 66, 1996
- Mobbing Against Women in the Work Place
- Women in the Mafia: Victims or Collaborators?
- Prostitution: Illegal and Flourishing
- Tarantism: Myths and Healing Practices
- The New Italian Families
- The Declining Birth Rate in Italy
- Bioethics and Medically Assisted Reproduction: Law n. 40, 2004
- A New Generation of Women Singers: Pop and Rock in the 2000s.

The educational goal of this course is to elaborate a multi-faceted definition of being a woman in Italian society across generations and historical times, transcending ideological boundaries and bringing together Italian women's shared life experiences over a period of eighty years of national, political and social history, starting in the 1930s and culminating in the 2000s. Organized around social, political, cultural, and artistic themes, the purpose of *Women in Italy* is to examine documented experiences that denounce and protest against violence and abuse, expose hypocrisies, and address the consequences of cultural conflicts and changes for women's lives in Italy from the Fascist era to contemporary times.

In this course a variety of interrelated topics, encompassing a complex spectrum of concurrent socio-cultural phenomena, is presented through different media and discussed in broad historical and socio-political contexts. In addition, this course lends itself to a cross-disciplinary approach by connecting several areas of research such as history and law, sociology and anthropology, cinema and media, music and dance. More specifically, *Women in Italy* covers areas pertaining to women's gender issues, civil rights and equal access to work versus social and cultural injustice, health and reproduction, mental health and traditional healing practices, domestic violence and sexual abuse, women victims and collaborators in organized crime, traditions, taboos, and prejudices versus rebellion and awareness, prostitution and exploitation, fashion and beauty myths, art and music.

With regards to materials, *Women in Italy* includes a range of texts and media illustrating the hybrid expressions of modernity, while paying special attention to Italian women's shifting roles. The variety and combination of texts selected for this course represent historical and cultural manifestations situating philosophical arguments on questions of women's psychology, sociology, anthropology, and sexual politics. These issues are examined through the works of philosophers, political leaders and legislators, social critics, scientists, specialists in media and cultural studies, film directors and artists whose ideas, writings, and art have been relevant to the feminist discourse in Italy.

Women in Italy is also a quintessentially visual course for the employment of diverse instructional media and texts, as the use of visual resources becomes fundamental to teach students how to sharpen their observational skills, to develop reading literacy and viewing fluency of the inter-textual and iconographic meanings of images, and to critique messages expressed in visual forms. Socio-economic, governmental and legislative changes about women's issues are studied in this course through the reading of selected essays,[5] a series of research tasks as well as a number of approaches and media such as:

- the aesthetic and critical viewing of feature films, documentaries, television programs, or video-recorded theater performances and dance shows;
- the commentary of live-interviews with scholars, legislators and film directors;
- the analysis and evaluation of a variety of visual media such as internet-texts and data, newspaper/magazine articles, advertisements, and images, illustrated educational leaflets, political posters, militant slogans, private and journalistic photos, national postal stamps, postcards, comic strips, banknotes, murals and graffiti, LP recording, CD, VHS, and

[5] Articles are both in English and Italian languages.

DVD jackets from the several historical periods covered in the course;
- the cultural analysis of traditional dances and forms of music therapy;
- the ideological examination of militant songs;
- the artistic evaluation of video-recordings of concerts rock/pop lyrics as well as contemporary expressions of world-music.

These audio-visual texts, portraying, describing, and analyzing socio-cultural phenomena, are examined and interpreted as essays documenting Italian women's social conditions and achievements. *Women in Italy* therefore introduces students to a multi-disciplinary investigative approach, while learning visual sociology and cultural studies forms of inquiry, and exploring how media, as representations of cultural practices, can be fundamental to the (trans)formation of social realities.

From a methodological perspective, *Women in Italy* is also highly interactive. Teaching is designed around a pedagogically sound and balanced combination of instructional approaches and learning assignments comprising, in addition to a lecture style presentation delivered to introduce new topics each week, the following several planned activities and projects:

- guided in-class discussions, when students provide prepared answers to pre-assigned questions, and reflect critically on issues introduced during the lecture and discussed in the readings or illustrated in the films of the week;
- students' independent research projects of their choice involving interviewing or search for additional authentic materials and documents;
- students' oral presentations on topics of their research assignments in which they use visual materials (e.g. film clips, pictures/photos, excerpts of video recordings) to illustrate their subjects and support their arguments;
- mid-term and final extensive papers of critical analysis on one of the topics discussed in the course, written in Italian and including illustrations, references to visual media analyzed in the course, and quotations from interviews with experts that they have conducted outside the classroom.

Therefore, the critical and relevant features of this course lie in the fact that learning is fundamentally experiential and strongly connected with learners' projects carried out beyond the classroom as much as it is with students' intellectual abilities. Academic teaching and learning are typically methodical, sedentary and claustrophobic when conducted exclusively within the walls and halls of one's institution. The novelty of this course rests precisely in the fact that it engages students in a modality of learning that allows them to experience the topics beyond the rigid academic disciplinary boundaries and away from the confining classroom settings. Finally, the teaching method employed in *Women in Italy* promotes students' efforts to understand important content, recognizes and develops their intellectual interests, helps them think critically and visually, and assesses their work in ways that inspire further studies. Instruction in this course models intellectual curiosity and rigor, fosters interdisciplinary and collaborative inquiry, and encourages sensitivity to the variegated dimensions of learning, while exploring the specific contents of the course.

Accomplishments of the Italian Feminist Movement

The following overview and commentary of the legislative changes occurred in the 1970s and throughout the 2000s provides examples for the multiplicity of interrelated themes covered in *Women in Italy*. The militant feminist principles, that inspired the struggle for the right to vote for women in 1945, as well as the battles to protect working mothers in the 1970s, to prevent sexual discrimination and guarantee equal opportunity for women in the work place in the 1980s, to incriminate sexual offenders in the 1990s, and to contest the legislation restricting access to medically assisted reproduction techniques to married women in the 2000s, are some of the topics illustrated through broad national socio-economic transformations.

Feminism in the 1970s opened a larger space for female voices, and the women's movement generated practices of individual and collective authorship of art, militant music and cinema, and feminist critical writings and publications. Political activists, from the Movimento Femminista in Rome, the Gruppo Musicale del Comitato per il Salario al Lavoro Domestico in Padua, and the Collettivo Femminista in Bologna, for example composed and recorded a new genre of feminist songs of protest and struggle.[6] While the musical production and distribution of these lyrics

[6] See the syllabus in the Appendix for details on the titles of the songs.

remained circumscribed to a particular era, the songs represent a valuable patrimony of women's political militancy through musical experimentation. Similarly, in the more commercial channels of *musica leggera* (popular music), new singing voices and innovative performing styles emerged, while novel texts were written for a young generation of singers with distinct musical talents like Mina, and captivating personalities with impressive stage presence like Rita Pavone, Patty Pravo, Caterina Caselli, and Mia Martini. Italian political songs and pop music have been object of study by historians and sociologists, and in *Women in Italy* students are exposed to the 'sung word' from a literary and socio-cultural perspective in order to understand the impact of the phenomenon on young generations of women.

In the 1970s Italians witnessed the development of a philosophical model inspired by the concepts of civil freedom, dignity and equality. Such ideals led the feminist movement to achieving important reforms thanks to major legislative changes that improved the living and working conditions of Italian women in the family and in society.[7] March 8 had been recognized as International Women's Day in Italy since 1945, but it was not until 1975, when the United Nations began celebrating International Women's Day[8] that this date was officially celebrated also in Italy. The tradition of the mimosa flower, as the symbol for women's struggle and accomplishments, is typically Italian.[9] The 1970s were also

---

[7] The milestones of the Italian feminist movement in the 1970s are:
- 1970, Law 898 on the legalization of divorce.
- 1971, Law 1204 on Protection of Working Mothers (Protezione delle madri lavoratrici).
- 1971, Law 1044 on the institution of state funded day-care centers (Asili Nido).
- 1975, Law 151 on New Family Rights (Nuovo Diritto di Famiglia).
- 1975, Law 405 on the institution of socio-sanitary structures (Consultori Familiari) meant to offer protection to women's health.
- 1977, Law 903 on Equality in the Work Place (Uguaglianza nel posto di lavoro).
- 1978, Law 194 on the legalization of free and medically assisted abortion (Aborto libero ed assistito).

[8] The United Nations General Assembly proclaimed 1975 as International Year for Women, followed by the decade for Women and the international women's movement was born at the first World's Women's conference in Mexico City, Mexico.

[9] The Socialist International, meeting in Copenhagen in 1910, established a Women's Day to honor the movement for women's rights and universal suffrage. The proposal was approved by women from 17 countries, which included three women elected for the Finnish parliament. International Women's Day was marked for the first time in 1911. More than one million rallied in Austria,

years of inflamed feminist battles and heated debates, animated by the powerful terms and fiery tones of feminist language. The tense political climate of the mass protests, national marches and large organized demonstrations is effectively represented in the vivid footage of events in the documentary *Gli anni '70: sogno e tragedia* (1996),[10] by Giuliana Gamba, and in the commentary of major historical moments in *Bellissime II* (2006), by Giovanna Gagliardo.

Until the mid-1970s, the political discussion within the Italian feminist movement focused on the dichotomy of the theoretical principles of emancipation versus liberation. The concept of equality was understood as inseparable from the concept of the difference between sexes. Equality and difference were therefore viewed not as opposite, but as interdependent. In other words, the movement's position was that equality without difference brings emancipation, but not liberation. Judith Adler Hellman[11] claims that the emancipation movement was seen in Italy as limited and reformist, while the liberation movement was understood as radical and revolutionary. The goal of emancipation was to make women equal to men in the sense that each had equal status under the law. On the contrary, the Italian liberation movement rejected the idea of emancipation or homologation, believing it would lead to a woman's sub-culture conforming to prescribed male models. Therefore, the liberation movement intended to change society with a political platform that respected equality and also recognized the difference between sexes. Political manifestos, published in the format of posters and flyers, verbally and visually expressed these crucial concepts, as it can be observed in photos and video-recordings of political meetings and rallies organized in Rome and Milan in those years. Further, a rich production of newspapers and pamphlets became available at gatherings and demonstrations. Distributed freely in the streets, these publications started a new way to

---

Denmark, Germany and Switzerland. In addition to the right to vote and hold public office, women demanded the right to work, to vocational training and an end to job discrimination. On March 25, 1911 the Triangle Fire in New York City killed 140 working women, mostly Italian and Jewish immigrants. This event and the working conditions leading up to it are still invoked during observances of International Women's Day.

[10] Materials from the Archivio Audiovisivo del Movimento Operaio e Democratico.

[11] Judith Adler Hellman, "The Originality of Italian Feminism," in Ada Testaferri, ed., *Donna: Women in Italian Culture* (Toronto and Ottawa: University of Toronto, Italian Studies and Dovehouse Editions, 1989), 21.

reach out and involve women from different social classes and levels of education in local and national political activities.

After a decade of intense activism, a thorough ideological critique led to new approaches and strategies. During the 1980s, a strong feminist school of thought further analyzed the political theorization of the concept of sexual difference aiming to develop what Raffaella Lamberti called "politics of women citizens."[12] Such philosophical orientation, characterized by a dynamic intellectual and academic debate in Italy, generated a number of programs that elaborated the vast knowledge of the feminist movement. Women's Studies departments were established in universities,[13] female judges discussed *se il diritto sia sessuato o no* (if law is gendered or not), and women in the editorial offices of newspapers, radio and TV stations created spaces to express their opinions. Moreover, women in trade unions at regional and local levels initiated centers for discussions on women's issues, and promoted a platform through a dialogue among working women at all professional levels. Other groups were involved in *Consultori Familiari* (health-care centers) and found answers to health, reproduction, and sexuality needs.

During the early 1980s the Italian women's movement divided itself into a variety of different political orientations.[14] In those years, the feminist movement chose separateness and differentiation while protecting freedom and integrity in the elaboration of a new vision of women's roles.[15] This separation and autonomy in various forms of organization led

---

[12] Luisa Passerini, "The Women's Movement in Italy and the Events of 1968," in Mirna Cicioni & Nicole Prunster, eds., *Visions and Revisions* (Providence, RI: Berg Publishers, 1993), 181.

[13] In the 1980s, women's study groups like *Virginia Woolf* in Rome and *Diotima*, a philosophical community of academic and non-academic women at the University of Verona, were founded. The *Libreria della Donna* in Milan was instituted and in 1987, the association for a *Libera Università delle Donne* (Free University of Women) started research groups in Milan. The year 1988 saw the birth of several new initiatives: the group *Osservatorio sul Lavoro delle Donne* (Observatory on Women's Work), active in the discussion of the absence of female social justice in the work place; and the magazine *Lapis*, interested in exploring the unconscious and the political relationship between psychoanalysis and feminism.

[14] Some joined the Communist Party and the Radical Party, while others organized themselves into new associations within different institutions.

[15] Some groups carried out a systematic theoretical analysis of the facts and events of political life. Other groups started to operate in response to conflicts caused by women's presence in institutions such as universities, court or political parties, and health-care centers. Other women gathered to work on initiatives that would

some feminists to thinking of the 1980s as the dark years that witnessed the disintegration of the feminist movement and the "repression of the desire for revolution,"[16] or as a time of "disorientation, devastation, and suicide."[17] It can be argued instead that these were years of self-reflection and change of strategies and means of expression in spite of ideological disagreement or disengagement.[18]

Compared to the earlier decade, the 1980s were less productive from a legislative point of view, although political activism was still progressing. The reason for this was that national and European orientations stressed the need to support the existing legislation with more concrete and focused interventions, thus strengthening the control for the implementation of equal opportunity in the job market. Under such European recommendations, Italy started to examine and elaborate new ways of modifying pervasive sexual discrimination in the work place and improving the distribution of jobs for women. Concrete actions that implemented the political orientation for *pari opportunità* (equal opportunity) of work among men and women were elaborated. These actions were called *azioni positive* (affirmative action) or *promozionali* (promotional), which, in addition to increasing female employment, guaranteed the actual improvement of opportunities for the professional advancement of working women.[19]

---

guarantee women's rights and translate their needs into progressive legislative proposals.

[16] M. Mottalini, "Il lavoro del gruppo A," *Il foglio del paese delle donne* VIII, 3, 4 (1995): 4.

[17] Passerini, 181.

[18] Moreover, women became active in the political and social arena and, while working in new professional fields, they had the opportunity to develop feminist thought and apply it in practical situations.

[19] - 1981, Law 121 presented new regulations that allowed women, in total equality with men, to participate in the State Police.

- 1983, the "National Committee for the implementation of equal treatment and equal opportunity between working men and women" was instituted with a decree by the Ministero del Lavoro e della Previdenza Sociale.

- 1984, a "National commission for the implementation of equality between men and women" was established with a decree by the Italian Prime Minister. This Commission had the function to promote equality between the sexes and to remove all forms of direct and indirect discrimination against women according to Art. 3 of the Constitution.

- 1987, the first bill on the promotion of affirmative action, as an instrument meant to reach equal opportunity through initiatives supported by private companies, public sectors or trade unions, (developed by the Ministero del Lavoro) was

In the 1990s, political and economic goals aimed at the elaboration of a new operational definition of women's value. The law, which put into effect *Azioni Positive,*[20] to favor female employment and reach real equality in the job market, was meant to eliminate situations that hindered equal opportunity, and to appeal to judiciary authorities to verify and punish actions and behaviors that objectively or indirectly discriminated on the basis of sex. As Ada Grecchi, member of the Committee on Equal Opportunity at the Ministry of Work and Social Security, suggested, "a new cultural reading of equal opportunity is to view sexual difference not as a limit, but as a resource."[21] It is worth mentioning that a commemorative national postal stamp, titled *Pari Opportunità*, was issued in 1997 to commemorate Emanuela Loi (1967-1992), a police officer[22] who died in the line of duty while serving the country in the war against the mafia. She was remembered as a heroic figure and as the first victim of an Equal Opportunity position granted to women. Similarly, a new banknote, in the former Lire 1,000 denomination, had been issued from 1990 to 1999, replacing Marco Polo, to honor the work of philosopher, doctor, scientist, feminist and educator Maria Montessori (1870-1952). This has been the only banknote ever dedicated to a woman in Italy.

The passing of a new law on sexual violence marked another major legislative victory in the 1990s.[23] It took twenty years of political debate and feminist battles to reach juridical consensus on a revised definition of the philosophical and ethical nature of the crime. In the previous legislation, sexual violence was described as an offence against the abstract concept of morality, therefore there was no physical victim and the offender could avoid imprisonment by paying a fine. With the new law, sexual violence is defined as a crime against the dignity and integrity of a person, and therefore more severe forms of punishment are inflicted. The nature of this crime is graphically denounced in the theater performance of the dramatic monologue *The Rape* (1982) by Franca Rame. In this autobiographical piece, Rame tells the experience of the horrific events surrounding her abduction, rape and torture at the hands of

---

presented to the Senate. This bill also protected women not only from the more explicit and direct forms of inequality, but also from the *discriminazioni indirette* (when women are victims of a prejudice or are proportionally under-represented in comparison with men) that took place, even in the regular application of the law.

[20] 1991, Law 125 on Affirmative Action and Equal Opportunity.

[21] Ada Grecchi, *Pari Opportunità* (Milano: Franco Angeli, 1995), 28.

[22] April 1, 1981, Law 121. See note 16 for more details.

[23] 1996, Law 66 on Sexual Violence.

four men in the back of a van.[24] An equally brutal, explicit and detailed representation of gang rape against a young woman at the eve of her wedding, is the more recent film *The Wedding Dress* (2004), based on a true story, and directed by Fiorella Infascelli. This feature film explores also the traumatic psychological effects of rape, the character's slow emotional recovery and the troubled process of her social reintegration.

The 2000s bear witness to a shift of ideological perspective and political alignment with regards to women's rights and reproductive health rights. Italy had made great strides for both rights in the past several decades; therefore the recent philosophical debate and legislation on *Medically Assisted Reproduction*,[25] in relation to women's freedom of choice and limited access to technologies for sterile couples, generated a profound political, ethical and medical controversy.[26] A crucial point in the debate pertains to what is stated in *Article 5*: Paragraph 1 explicitly limits access to reproduction techniques to sterile "couples of age and different sex, married or living together, in potential fertile age and both alive." This article prohibits couples in which one of the partners is irremediably sterile, those in which the woman enters into premature menopause or has passed the child-bearing age, various singles, such as widows, separated or divorced women, and homosexual couples, to engage in fertility treatment. The fundamental reason for excluding single women is that the new born child cannot be fatherless.

Unquestionably, the complex mix of legislative and bioethics issues challenges the meaning of fatherhood and motherhood and forces rethink the biological and philosophical definitions of the relationship between

---

[24] In 1973, she was the victim of a cruel assault and subjected to repeated sexual violence perpetrated by right-wing extremists, an act of intimidation culminating a series of politically motivated life threats against her and her husband Dario Fo.

[25] 2004, Law n. 40 on Medically Assisted Reproduction (Tecniche di Procreazione Assistita). Starting in January 1999, the House of Deputies discussed a unified Bill *Project Bolognesi* (named after Mrs. Bolognesi, who proposed it) which went through different political administrations, was subject to a number of amendments in May 1999, June 2000 and March 2002, until the Senate approved the Bill on *Assisted Reproduction* on December 11, 2003. The text of the Bill then returned to the House of Deputies for minor technical changes on two articles and was passed on 19 February, 2004.

[26] The law forbids heterologous fertilization and prohibits sperm donation and egg harvesting, it assures the right to birth of the fetus, and denies couples the possibility to revert their choice once the egg has been fertilized. Experiments on embryos and human cloning are also forbidden and severely punished. Penalties are up to 20 years' imprisonment and a fine of one million Euros for the transgressors.

parenthood and procreation. At the same time the juridical, ethical, medical and sociological debates around the recognized right to procreation and the right to free use of one's body, as well as the child's rights to acquire the status of child, have a stable family, know one's biological origins and not to be subject to manipulations of his/her genetic patrimony, generated great national and international discussion.

The pragmatic, political debate on sexual difference in the 1970s turned into a theoretical analysis of *il pensiero della differenza sessuale* (the ideology of sexual difference) in the 1980s; and while the legislation of the 1970s aimed at protecting women with a policy of *tutela* (protection), the legislative reforms in the 1990s enforced a policy of *promozione* (promotion) of women. Thus, the 1970s initiated processes that addressed the subject of work, re-examined work inside and outside the home, and produced a new political and economic definition of working hours, all of which led to a discussion on equal opportunity in the 1980s and legislation on affirmative action in the early 1990s. With its historical revolt, the Italian women's movement led to changes, both *de jure* and *de facto*.

The Italian Families

The changes occurred in the structure of the family are another topic fully explored in *Women in Italy*. The Italian media and cinema have turned their attention to the family contradicting centuries of rhetoric on the beautiful Italian family. Populated with new members, the family presents itself with a modern genetic and social map, the product of a metamorphosis that, over the past several decades, since the legalization of divorce in 1970, has changed its socio-economic as well as psychological and biological structure. According to sociologist Anna Laura Zanatta, Italian society is experiencing a "transition from the golden age of marriage to the dawn of cohabitation"[27] together with a shift from the centrality of the parents-children binomial to a plurality of family forms. These topics are at the centre not only of demographic and sociological studies, but also of cinematic representations as expressed in the works of directors such as Francesca Archibugi, Cristina Comencini, and Gabriele Muccino.

---

[27] Anna Laura Zanatta, *Le nuove famiglie. Felicità e rischi delle nuove scelte di vita* (Bologna: Il Mulino, 2003), 7.

Nowadays, sociologists tend to refer more often to "*families* than to *family* to point out the plurality of new ways of living, and family experiences."[28] Rather than being concerned with the dissolution of the family, as the primary social cell and a place of loving and affectionate relationships, demographers use the plural form, *families*,[29] to underline the profound transformations redefining this institution. Starting in the mid-1960s, Italians began experiencing the phenomenon of the post-modern family and felt increasingly estranged from the traditional family, which was founded on marriage and children. Sociologists explain that this change has its roots in a number of interdependent socio-economic and cultural transmutations. The former can be identified in advanced industrialization, urban civilization, and the mass entrance of women into the work force. The latter can be traced back to an erosion of Christian values, a greater acceptance of a pluralism of ideas, the attention paid to the needs of individuals and couples, and an emphasis on the ideal of romantic love.[30] Zanatta argues, "In spite of the weaker stability of conjugal life, the forming of a couple, married or unmarried, stable or temporary, with or without offspring is still the most preferred human condition."[31] Therefore, it is more appropriate to refer to the decline of a certain *archetype* of the family, rather than to a crisis of the family in general.

The *postmodern* family has become anthropologically multifaceted, sociologically variegated, psychologically complex, and biologically composite. In fact, the concept of family has acquired a broader connotation and the word family needs further descriptors in order to be accurately defined.[32] A single person, young or old, and living alone, for example, constitutes what has been termed the *famiglia unipersonale*. A single parent, living in a situation of independent parenthood, *monogenitorialità*, forms the *famiglia monoparentale,* while couples without children represent an example of the micro-nuclear family, *famiglia micronucleare*. Increasingly common is the phenomenon of the extended family, *famiglia lunga*, composed of two or more generations living in the same household, usually parents with their adult children who may be single or divorced. Paul Ginsborg explains that this "model of relationships between parents and children is not based so much on

---

[28] Ibid., 10.
[29] Ibid., 10.
[30] Ibid., 11.
[31] Ibid., 19.
[32] Elisabetta Cioni, Maria Carla Meini, Alessandra Pescarolo, Paola Tronu, *Famiglie in mutamento. Le fonti e i dati 1971-1991* (Milano: FrancoAngeli, 1997).

emancipation *from* the family, as on emancipation *within* the family"[33] as its members establish new intra-family relationships, re-negotiate their private space and manage to protect their own lifestyles. The extended family has also been defined as a form of business, *famiglia impresa*,[34] where parents and children elaborate an inter-generational exchange of emotional care, and strengthen their economic interdependence. As a complex support system of prolonged solidarity and shared resources, this family form takes on the responsibilities of a defaulting society and an absent state.

New realities emerge especially when the family adds step-parents or social parents, *genitori sociali*, to the biological parents. Defined as blended, *famiglia ricomposta*, unlike the traditional step family resulting from the death of one of the spouses,[35] this form of family sees its members, usually parents with children from previous marriages or relationships, living together with children born from their new relationship, experimenting with different family structures in the effort to establish a loving coexistence. The members of a blended family attempt to define new caring roles and to share responsibilities of co-parenthood, *cogenitorialità*,[36] while the emotional presence versus the physical absence of the former spouse, together with the sharing of educational and financial duties between biological and social parents, lead couples to explore forms of plural parenthood, *plurigenitorialità*.[37] This family structure comprises several father and mother figures cohabiting with siblings and new half-siblings, thus acquiring a richer landscape of family relationships. The effort to function as an operational family in a new kind of kinship is the challenge that contemporary Italian society faces.

The wide spectrum of possibilities, ranging from the one-person to the micro-nuclear childless household, to blended nucleuses and the multigenerational family, indicates that the concept of family has developed a broader connotation beyond its traditional structure. Sociologists Anna Laura Zanatta,[38] Valerio Pocar[39] and Paola Ronfani[40] as

---

[33] Paul Ginsborg, *L'Italia del tempo presente. Famiglia, società civile, Stato 1980-1996* (Torino: Einaudi, 1998), 157.
[34] Ibid., 157.
[35] Zanatta, 78.
[36] Valerio Pocar e Paola Ronfani, *La famiglia e il diritto* (Roma-Bari: Laterza, 1998), 171.
[37] Ibid., 193.
[38] Anna Laura Zanatta is sociologist and professor of Demographic Sciences at the University La Sapienza of Rome.

well as directors Francesca Archibugi and Cristina Comencini discuss issues pertaining to the Italian socio-demographic aspects, families *de facto*, homosexual couples, divorce and child custody rights, the wound of separation, relationships in blended and multigenerational families, childhood and adolescence, in the dvd *Società Famiglia Cinema* (2005) produced by Flavia Laviosa.

Tarantism: Myths and Healing Practices

The historical origins, anthropological characteristics, and artistic manifestations of the phenomenon of Tarantism, as a myth and musical practice with healing effects is another interesting topic explored in *Women in Italy*. The tarantula spider is said to take its name from the Apulian sea harbour of Taranto, situated on the Ionian Sea where the Apulia and Calabria regions meet. According to local traditions, people, typically women, bitten by the tarantula were called 'tarantati'. Tarantism, dance disease or dance of the 'tarantati', is a therapeutic and cathartic ritual, as well as a multifaceted anthropological and artistic phenomenon.

According to the myth, in the hot summers, a spider bites women working in corn fields and tobacco plantations, causing a complex syndrome characterized by diarrhea, tremors, convulsions, and delirium, or neuro-pathologic symptoms like depression, paranoia, hysteria, epilepsy, and even schizophrenia. The spider associated with the tradition of tarantism, and the one most commonly referred to in the literature, is the *Lycosa Tarentula*. The spider hides in the lentisk, in the tobacco leaves, in the faggots, in the cracks of the parched ground, in the dry stonewalls of rural houses, but predominantly in the labyrinth of the mind. It bites at midday, like a meridian demon, arousing senses and unleashing unexpressed desires. However, the Italian *Lycosa* tarantula is a small, harmless spider. Therefore, what is interesting is that in most cases, no actual spider bite occurred.

Tarantism has been considered a healing ritual for those affected by the hypothetical or real tarantula bite since the XIV century. For centuries, the cult of tarantism was the sole source of relief for those (supposedly) 'bitten' or 'possessed' by the tarantula, and the only means to free women from alienation caused by poverty, social marginalization, or personal

---

[39] Valerio Pocar, jurist and professor of Sociology of Law in the Department of Law and Economics at the University of Milan-Bicocca.

[40] Paola Ronfani is professor of Sociology of Law in the Department of Political Science at the State University of Milan.

problems. The long and exhausting expiatory ritual, connected with the choreography of dance and music therapy,[41] usually took place in private homes. People claimed that the spider's poison could be expelled and relief assured only through music. Therefore, when a woman felt displaced and manifested hysterical symptoms, the family called the band to avoid madness, feelings of suffocation and in some cases death. The musicians played a kind of music, called 'tarantata' or 'pizzica tarantata'[42] which consisted in a series of beats that would awake the 'taranta' (spider) in the bitten person. The tempo of the music provoked the 'taranta', thus forcing the possessed to dance incessantly. At the end, the dance freed the woman from disease and spell, allegedly caused by the tarantula bite, and from neurosis.

There were fewer real spider bites than women stricken with tarantism, as documented in De Martino's[43] research conducted in the 1960s. It is therefore evident that situations of psychological submission, social status and economic poverty, harsh working conditions in the fields, along with personal dramas connected with love, family and sexuality that characterized the life of these women, were the real causes of their alienation. Consequently, the ritual of tarantism can be described as societal treatment for depression, which validated madness, did not marginalize the sick, and was recognized as a way of embracing mental illness within the community rather than banishing it.

Since the 1960s, the sacred and ancient ritual of tarantism has been the object of the curiosity of the mass-media, visitors, anthropologists and ethnographers, all photographing, audio-recording, filming and documenting both private and public manifestations of the phenomenon. Subsequently, rich photographic records of tarantism include the famous and aesthetically impressive ethnographic reportages by Chiara Samugheo, Annabella Rossi, Sebastiana Papa, Marialba Russo, and Lello Mazzacane,[44] conducted in the 1970s. The dramatic impact of the vivid images from artistically poignant photographs by these professional reporters leave an indelible memory of the powerful, yet unsettling

---

[41] According to German naturalist W. Katner, who took part in De Martino's expedition to the South in the 1960s, tarantella first appeared in Taranto in the XVII century. Chopin, Liszt, Weber, and other composers used the rhythm of the dance in the form of a *perpetuum mobile.*

[42] Giorgio Di Lecce, *La danza della Piccola Taranta: Cronache da Galatina 1903-1993* (Roma: Edizioni Sensibili alle Foglie, 1994), 30.

[43] Ernesto De Martino, *La terra del rimorso* (Milano: Il Saggiatore, 1961).

[44] Complete collections of original copies of their extensive works are available at the Museo Nazionale delle Arti e Tradizioni Popolari in Rome.

moments of folly and helplessness of people cured through the practice of tarantism. These visual documentations of the phenomenon are complemented by a variety of ethnographic documentaries such as *La taranta* (1962) by Gianfranco Mingozzi, and cinematographic representations of tarantism in films such as *Pizzicata* (1996) and *Sangue vivo* (2000) by Edoardo Winspeare, which instead offer fictionalized and romanticized narratives of the ancient rituals.

Conclusion

Women in Italy is a significant and original contribution in the development of Italian women's and cultural studies. Innovative in the content, original in its cross-disciplinary approach, and pioneering in the use of visual media, this course draws from a number of academic fields, such as Cultural Studies, Film and Media Studies, Visual Sociology, and Anthropology. *Women in Italy* is in essence a visual cultural studies course as the teaching is delivered and the learning takes place through the wide, systematic and effective analysis, interpretation and discussion of visual texts, images and graphic representations of historical and cultural value.

Women in Italy has inspired students in the Department of Italian Studies to embark on further studies in the Italian culture, choose to spend their junior year in Italy, and experience the topics discussed in the course first hand during their time in the country, get involved in faculty-student collaborative research projects leading to publication of their work, and opt to write honors theses to acquire more in depth knowledge and critical understanding of crucial issues pertaining to what it entails to be a woman in contemporary Italian society.

The inter-disciplinary approach implemented and diverse media resources employed in *Women in Italy* could serve as a model for courses in other areas of Italian studies, as well as a prototype in comparative courses in the history of women's battles and accomplishments across cultures. Finally, the extensive and effective use of multiple kinds of media could also provide an example of how courses in other disciplines could be taught with an academically sound visual-cultural approach, and how students could be inspired to produce original multi-media based intellectual work.

Dedicated to my nephew Salterio Laviosa

WELLESLEY COLLEGE, USA

APPENDIX

Department of Italian Studies
Wellesley College
Wellesley, MA-USA
Italian Studies 211

Women in Italy
history, sociology, law, anthropology, cinema, music, dance, songs

Flavia Laviosa
Senior Lecturer

Readings: copies of articles and texts of songs will be given by the instructor
Films & documentaries: VHS (Pal, NTSC) and DVD (Regions 1, 2) with Italian and/or English subtitles are available on reserve in the library.

Final grade:

- Attendance and participation 30%. Bi-weekly oral presentations of projects. A total of 3 presentations per student.
- Mid-term 30%. Essay on a topic selected from those discussed in class: 1,500 words
- Final 40%. Essay on a topic chosen from those discussed in class, previously submitted to and approved by the instructor: 2,000 words.

Week I Introduction to the course

Week II Women's Roles, Duties and Rights in the Fascist Era
Readings: "Governing Reproduction," *Social Bodies*, D. Horn, 1994, pp. 66-94
"La legislazione della donna nel periodo fascista," *La donna italiana,* E. Sarogni, 1995, 135-14
"Casalinghe e omosessuali al tempo del consenso," *Una giornata particolare*, T. Kezich e A. Levantesi, 2003, 43-53
Song: *Mamma*, by Beniamino Gigli, 1940
Film: *Una giornata particolare/A Special Day*, by Ettore Scola, 1977

Week III The Post-WWII Era and the Economic Boon
Reading: Italian women gain the right to vote
"1945: cittadine per legge," Miriam Mafai, 57-60
Documentary: *Bellissime I*, by Giovanna Gagliardo, 2004

Social discrimination against working women
Film: *Renzo e Luciana,* episode I, in *Boccaccio '70*, by Mario Monicelli, 1961

Week IV Women Stars in Italian Cinema
Beauty Pageant and National Identity
Readings: "Feminine Beauty, National Identity and Political Conflict in Postwar Italy, 1945-1954," Stephen Gundle, *Contemporary European History*, 8, 3, 1999, 359-378
Photos: Miss Italia 1945-2006
Film: *Miss Italia*, by Duilio Coletti, 1950
TV program RAI 1: *Miss Italia 2006*; *Miss Italia in the World* 2006
Readings: "Fame Fashion and Style: The Italian Star System" 309-326; "Two Ideas of Stardom," *Italian Cultural Studies*, Stephen Gundle, 1996, 347-349; "Sophia Loren, Italian Icon" *Historical Journal of Film, Radio, and Television*, 15, 3, 1995, Stephen Gundle, 367-385
Gina Lollobrigida, M. Ponti, 1982
Sofia Loren, S. Masi e E. Lancia, 2001
Anna Magnani, M. Hochkofler, 2001
Silvana Mangano Il teorema della bellezza, G. Cimmino e S. Masi, 1994

Week V The Italian Feminist Movement and Women's Rights in the 1970s
Songs and videos: *Brava* 1965, by Mina; *Nessuno mi può giudicare* 1966, by Caterina Caselli; *Datemi un martello* 1964, by Rita Pavone; *Ragazzo triste* 1966 and *Bambola* 1968, by Patty Pravo; *Gli uomini non cambiano* 1970 and *Padre davvero* 1971, by Mia Martini
International Women's Day–March 8–1991-2007
Photos and Posters: marches, protests, slogans
Documentaries: *Gli anni '70: sogno e tragedia*, by Giuliana Gamba, 1996
Bellissime II, by Giovanna Gagliardo, 2006
Reading: "1970s: a Decade of Legislative Reforms for Italian Women's Protection and Equality", *Italian Politics and Society*, Flavia Laviosa, 1997, 57-63

Week VI Slogans, Images and Leaflets of the Feminist Struggle in the 1970s
Feminist songs: 1972-1976
Umanità, *Felicità*, *Noi siamo stufe*, *Stato e padroni*, *Avete mai guardato*, *Storia di una cosa*, *8 marzo*, *Bambini pianificati*, *Il parto*, *Abortire*, *Aborto di stato*, *Ma verrà un giorno*, *Il divorzio*, *Il mestiere più antico* (song for prostitute sisters, 1973), *Mi guardo in uno specchio* (song for lesbian women, 1972) by Movimento Femminista Romano, Gruppo Musicale del Comitato per il Salario al Lavoro Domestico di Padova, and Collettivo Femminista Bolognese
Changes in the Feminist Movement and Legislative Reforms in the 1980s
Reading: "The Challenge of Italian Women in the 1980s and 1990s: Resolving the Paradox of Legislation on Affirmative Action in a Reality of Unequal Opportunity," *Italian Politics and Society*, Flavia Laviosa, 1998, 61-70

Week VII The Feminist Movement and Legislative Reforms in the 1990s
Equal Opportunity
Reading: "Sintesi della Legge n. 125, 1991 sulle *Azioni Positive-Le Pari Opportunità*"
Italian Postal Stamp: *Pari Opportunità*, 1997 to commemorate Police Officer Emanuela Loi (1967-1992) who died in the line of duty fighting against the mafia
Banknote: Lire 1.000 (issued 1990-1999) dedicated to Maria Montessori, (1870-1952)
Mobbing Against Women in the Work Place
Reading: *Il lavoro molesto*, Daniele Ranieri, 2003
Film: *Mobbing, mi piace lavorare*, by Francesca Comencini, 2003

Week VIII Violence Against Women: Law n. 66, 1996
Reading: "Violence against Women and the Response of Italian Institutions" Tina Lagostena Bassi, *Visions and Revisions*, 1993, 199-213
Video-recording of theater performance: *Lo stupro/The rape* (1982), by Franca Rame, as part of *Sesso? Grazie, tanto per gradire*, presented at the Teatro Smeraldo in Milano, 8 March, 1995
Film: *Il vestito da sposa/The Wedding Dress*, by Fiorella Infascelli, 2004

Week IX Women in the Mafia: Victims or Collaborators?
Readings: "Introduction," "Camorra Godmothers," *Mafia Women*, Clare Longrigg, 1997, pp. X-21
"Women with the mafia," *Secrets of Life and Death. Women and the Mafia*, Renate Siebert, 1996, 107-130
Video recording: Interview with Renate Siebert, 2004
Films: *Un complicato intrigo di donne, vicoli e delitti*, by Lina Wertmηller, 1985; *Angela*, by Roberta Torre, 2002

Week X Prostitution: Illegal and Flourishing
Readings: "La regolamentazione fascista," 61-63; "Dagli anni '50 al femminismo in Italia," 71-97; "Proposte di legge degli anni '80," 107-112; "Intervista a Roberta Tatafiore," 180-191, *Prostituzione dal Diritto ai diritti*, Roberta Sapio, 2002;
"La prostituta c'è ma non si vede," *Santa Pazienza*, Marta Boneschi, 1999, 270-275; *Io Puttana. Parlano le prostitute*, Isabel Pisano, 2001; "Emigrazione femminile e prostituzione," *Il mercato delle donne*, Paola Monzini, 2002, 89-102
Films: *Adua e le compagne*, by Antonio Petrangeli, 1960
Le Italiane e l'amore, episode *Il prezzo dell'amore*, 1961
Mare nero, by Roberta Torre, 2006

Week XI Tarantism: Myths and Healing Practices
Readings: "Tarantism: Representations of Popular Culture and Rituals in Italian Cinema," Flavia Laviosa, *Film Representations of Popular Culture*. Ed. By Flavia Brizio-Skov, (Under preparation)

Photos: Ethnographic documents by Chiara Samugheo, Annabella Rossi, Sebastiana Papa, Marialba Russo, Lello Mazzacane, André Martin, and Franco Pinna
Documentary: *La taranta*, by Gianfranco Mingozzi, 1962
Films: *Pizzicata*, by Edoardo Winspeare, 1996
Sangue vivo, by Edoardo Winsperare, 2000
***Neo-tarantism* and World Music**
RAI recording: *La Notte della Taranta*, Melpignano, 2006
Video: *Arakne Mediterranea*, Theater performance: dance and singing, Lecce, 2003

Week XII The New Italian Families
Readings: *La fine della famiglia*, Roberto Volpi, 2007
"Traiettorie di vita familiare ieri e oggi," *Le nuove famiglie*, Anna Laura Zanatta, 2003, 7-23;
"La permanenza prolungata: fenomeno antico, ragioni moderne," Giorgio Campanini, *Giovani in famiglia tra autonomia e nuove dipendenze*, a cura di E. Scabini e G. Rossi, 1997, 97-108
PACS (French): Pact of Civil Solidarity
DICO: Rights and duties of people living together. (Diritti e doveri delle persone stabilmente conviventi). Text of the Bill, February 8, 2007.
DVD: *Società Famiglia Cinema*, 2005, by Flavia Laviosa
Interviews with sociologist A. L. Zanatta and P. Ronfani; and directors F. Archibugi and C. Comencini

Week XIII The Declining Birth Rate in Italy
Reading: "Emanciparsi in famiglia," *Le donne fanno paura*, Chiara Valentini, 1997, pp. 67-82
Documentary: *Population Transition in Italy*, BBC, 1996

Week XIV Bioethics and Medically Assisted Reproduction: Law n. 40, 2004
Reading "Commentary to the Italian Law on Medically Assisted Reproduction," Flavia Laviosa, 2005, (Unpublished paper)

Week XV A New Generation of Women Singers: Pop and Rock in the 2000s
Live concerts in dvd: Carmen Consoli, 2001; Fiorella Mannoia, 2003 & 2005; Paola Turci, 1998 & 2004; Giorgia, 2003/04 & 2005; and Elisa, 2003

CHAPTER SIXTEEN

BUILDING AN INTERCULTURAL IDENTITY IN A CROSS-CULTURAL TRANSITION: A SHORT TERM STAY CASE STUDY*

BARBARA SPINELLI AND ROBERTO DOLCI

Introduction

The increasing globalisation stresses more and more the importance to enhance international exchanges among educational institutions. One of the meaningful outcomes of this internationalization is the development of "interculturally-competent students."[1]

International documents and organizations such as the *Common European Framework of Reference,* the ACIIE *American Council on International Intercultural Education*, among others, encourage teachers and institutions to develop their students' *intercultural competence* in order to make them aware of "the complexities of the target culture as well as conscious of their own cultural identity as *intercultural mediators.*"[2] This competence can be enhanced in different ways: 1) by including

---

*Barbara Spinelli and Roberto Dolci jointly wrote the following sections of the article: Introduction, Data analysis and interpretation and Conclusion.
Barbara Spinelli wrote the sections on: What is intercultural competence?; Case Study: a short term experience; Intercultural approach: a pedagogical path; Social Communication activities.
Roberto Dolci wrote the sections on: Becoming intercultural: a dynamic process; Assessing intercultural competence.

[1] Darla K Deardoff, "Assessing Intercultural Competence in Study Abroad Students," in *Living and Studying Abroad*, eds. Michael Byram and Anwei Feng (Clevedon: Multilingual Matters, 2006), 232.

[2] Ewa Bandura, "An Intercultural approach to foreign language teaching—a challenge for textbook writers," in *Bližina Drugosti—The close otherness*, ed. Lucija Čok (Ljubljana: Knjižnica Annales Majora, 2006), 351.

intercultural activities into the curriculum; 2) by developing meaningful intercultural communication through virtual environments; 3) by creating short or long-term study abroad programs; 4) by involving all these components in a broader educational project.

This study will focus on 12 American university students in a short-stay (two months) abroad program in Italy. There are many students involved in these types of programs but the ways in which they perceive this experience is not well known. Additionally, even though one of the main implicit purposes of these projects is to build up students' intercultural competence, this objective is not specifically identified as an expected outcome of such a learning experience.

Our research study aimed to analyze this formative path by attempting to answer the following questions:

- What does Intercultural Competence really mean?
- What psychological and social processes affect students' adjustments while living in a host country?
- What factors can inhibit or facilitate such processes, i.e., block or encourage the development of an intercultural identity?
- What challenges do students encounter in this cross-cultural transition and what strategies can support them in their adaptation journey?
- How can we modify our teaching and our pedagogical choices in order to facilitate this personal development?

In order to investigate these research questions we decided to adopt a quantitative and a qualitative case-study design which we will describe in the following sections. This case study incorporates research from sociology, anthropology, psychology, and language education; together, they encompass a range of theories and models conceptualising cross-cultural adaptation and intercultural competence development.

What is Intercultural Competence?

Intercultural Competence is a very complex concept to define since it consists of a wide range of components. This is the reason why there is a great breadth of definitions among intercultural experts.

The factors implicated in the development of an Intercultural Competence, include:

- *Knowledge:*
  - *Declarative knowledge*: factual information about culture such as customs, traditions, stereotypes, values, etc.
  - *Procedural knowledge*: knowing how to behave in specific communicative contexts and how to interpret different norms of language use which include sociolinguistic and pragmatic awareness.
- *Skills:*
  - *Cognitive skills:* to analyze, interpret, relate, observe, and compare;
  - *Critical skills.*
- *Attitude*:
  - *respect* in valuing the diversity;
  - *openness* to people of other cultures;
  - *curiosity* which entails the tolerance of ambiguity and the predisposition to take a risk.

The desired outcome of the learning process based on the components mentioned above can be *internal* and *external.* The *internal outcome* includes *adaptability* or adjustment to the new environment, *flexibility* selecting the appropriate communication style and *empathy* seeing the world with others' eyes. The internal shift can produce an *external outcome* which is observable and can be described as "behaving and communicating effectively and appropriately"[3] or, using Byram's words, "the ability to interact effectively with people from cultures that we recognise as different from our own."[4]

This intercultural growth from a personal level (attitude) to an interpersonal level (outcome) is a total living experience which involves the individual as a whole, as the *Common European Framework of Reference for Language* points out:

> it is a central objective of language education to promote the favourable development of the learner's whole personality and sense of identity in response to the enriching experience of otherness in language and culture.[5]

---

[3] Deardoff, 244.

[4] Michael Byram, ed. *Routledge Encyclopaedia of Language Teaching and Learning* (London: Routledge, 2001), 297.

[5] Council of Europe, *Common European Framework of Reference for Language* (Cambridge: Cambridge University Press, 2001), 1.

Therefore the intercultural approach integrates a *cognitive*, an *operational*, and an *affective* dimension, and eclectically incorporates elements from different approaches, such as:

- An ethnographic approach, which equips the students with necessary *knowledge, attitudes* and *skills* in order to prepare them to become independent participants in, observers of, and commentators on any culture.
- A comparative approach, in which students are constantly expected to make *cross-cultural* comparisons, and gain critical awareness of one's own cultural norms, as well as those of other cultures.
- An experiential approach, which promotes learning from immediate experience and *engaging* the learners in the process as whole persons, both *intellectually* and *emotionally.*[6]

Becoming *intercultural* requires a cross-cultural adaptation, a phenomenon of a complex nature which involves social and psychological factors we will describe in the following section.

Becoming *Intercultural*: a dynamic process

The process of crossing cultures challenges individuals "as cultural beings"[7] and asks them as newcomers to give responses to an unfamiliar and new milieu, to experience existential otherness, and to cope with a sense of inadequacy and frustration which can occur in changing environment.

The physical and psychological dislocation during the cross-cultural adaptation can be an ambivalent and difficult process but it can also represent a privilege. It is a process of *becoming*, of *transformation*, of *self-discovery,* in which individuals have the opportunity to expand the boundaries of their existence. Studies on cross-cultural adaptation go from an almost exclusive focus on negative perception of otherness such as the sense of loss and frustration (*cultural shock*[8]) to a more enthusiastic

---

[6] Bandura, 352.
[7] Young Y. Kim, *Becoming Intercultural: An Integrative theory of communication and cross-cultural adaptation*, (London: Sage Publications Inc., 2001), 5-9.
[8] Kalervo Oberg, "Cultural shock: Adjustment to new cultural environments," *Practical Anthropology*, no. 7, (1960).

interpretation of the phenomenon as learning and growth (*transition shock*[9]).

Kim[10] reconciles this dualistic view and underlines that this adaptive journey is a multidimensional, contradictory and dynamic phenomenon which incorporates progression and regression, integration and disintegration, construction and deconstruction. The transformation of the individual is a creative and dynamic process which consists of three strictly interrelated steps: *stress-adaptation-growth*. Transformation implies stress and allows renovation. The model which represents this progression is not linear but cyclical and continuous (see Fig. 16-1).

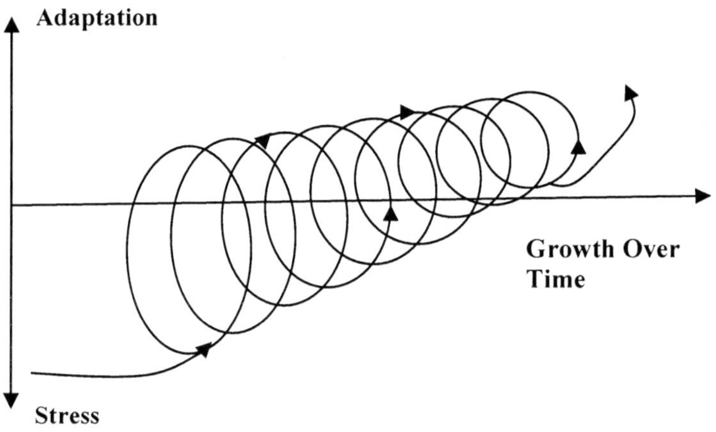

Figure 16-1. ***Stress-adaptation-growth process.***

Therefore cross-cultural adaptation can be defined as:

> the dynamic process by which individuals, upon relocating to new, unfamiliar, or changed cultural environments, establish (or re-establish) and maintain relatively stable, reciprocal, and functional relationship with those environments.[11]

---

[9] Peter S. Adler, "Culture shock and the cross-cultural learning experience," in *Toward internationalism: Readings in cross-cultural. communication*, ed. Louise Fiber Luce and Elise C. Smith (Cambridge, MA: Newbury, 1987).
[10] Kim, 57.
[11] Kim, 31.

This transaction leads the individual from the original cultural identity to a broader *intercultural* identity which does not imply the loss of what he/she was but a progressive enrichment of what he/she will be.

Long-term and short-term adaptations deal with different challenges. Hosts expect more conformity from long-term sojourners. However studies in the field demonstrate that the three-step process described above represents a common path for both long-term and short-term incomers. Therefore, we will refer to this model to analyze our short-term experience.

Case study: a short-term experience

The case used in the present study is a group of Columbia University undergraduate students in a study abroad program at Università Ca' Foscari di Venezia in Italy. The program lasted two months. These 12 American students aged 20-30 arrived in Venice in June 2007 after having studied the Italian language for at least two semesters. Most of them had already studied abroad in some capacity and only a few of them had never been abroad.

In June, students with an elementary knowledge of the language were placed in an intensive intermediate language course while more advanced students attended an Italian literature course. In July, all students were required to take two courses in Italian Art History and Architecture. For this reason, a part of the intensive intermediate course was devoted to the study of the Italian language in the specific field of Art History.

The literature course adopted an interdisciplinary approach involving theatre, cinema and broader cultural activities in Venice such as visits to museums, daily trips to historical places mentioned in the course, etc. All activities and readings (of Italian and foreign writers) were focused on Venice history and life. Students were also asked to keep a reading notebook in which they could reflect on the dialectic contrast between the public dimension of the historical view and their own private emotions, becoming more and more experienced observers of their environment.[12] The art history and architecture courses used the rich authentic context of the city as a setting for their classes.

Within the framework of an Intercultural Approach the main goal of the program was to involve American students as much as possible in the socio-cultural setting provided by a multi-faceted city like Venice, and to

---

[12] The literature course syllabus was designed by Professor Paolo Valesio.

further contacts with the local environment. To this end, the program adopted the following strategies:

1. an online site was created where American students could find detailed information about Venice and establish prior contact with Ca' Foscari staff;
2. "new figures" were introduced, such as the *cultural partners* (seven students of Ca' Foscari University aged 20-30), who fostered the connection with the city and local society;
3. students were hosted in Ca' Foscari dormitories so that the American students could have the same experience as the Italian students, and have more opportunities to get in touch with them;
4. students were led to discover the 'reality' of Venice and the Venetians through specific tasks and small group projects.

In the following section, we will explain in detail the steps of the pedagogical path mentioned above.

Intercultural Approach: a pedagogical path

As we have already pointed out, the adaptation is a dynamic three-step process (*stress-adaptation-growth*) and it depends on a wide range of factors which are summarized in Kim's structural model (Fig. 16-2). Such factors include: predispositional characteristics (attitude, individuals' expectations, and ethnic proximity), the vital role of the host environment and community (host communication), and the relationship with the ethnic group (the American students of Columbia University in this specific case). These factors can facilitate or inhibit the adaptive journey which leads individuals to intercultural transformation. The heart of this process lies in the individual's *communication competence* which is the ability to interact effectively with people from another culture, as we have already described.

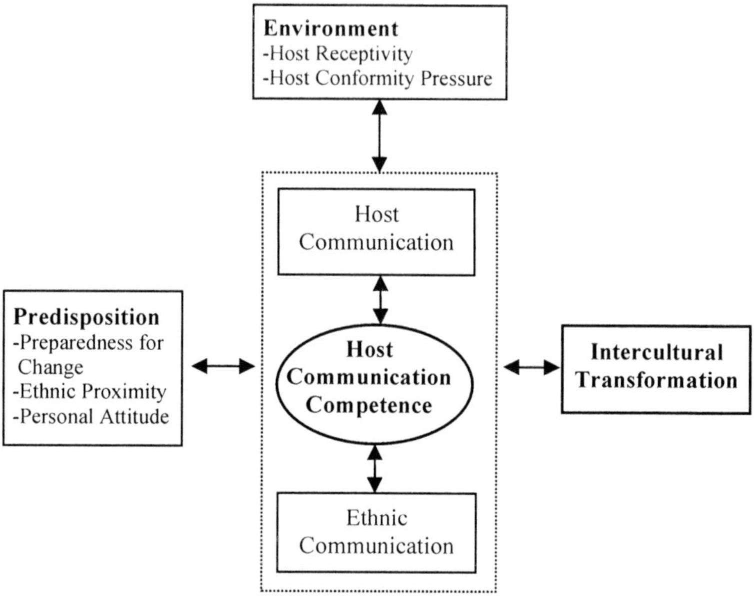

Figure 16-2. Factors Influencing Cross-cultural Adaptation. A structural Model. (Kim 2001, 87. Our adaptation).

Taking into consideration all of these factors, our main objective was to find pedagogical solutions to facilitate this process. According to Kim "successful adaptation hinges on conditions established even prior to our embarking on cross-cultural move."[13] In order to prepare our students for a smoother transition to the new environment, we created an online interactive site which provided detailed information about Venice and the host academic context. On this site, they could also familiarize themselves with their partners, the Italian students, and with the communication system: the Italian language. They were supposed to exchange biographical information, talk about their interests, ask for specific details about the program, etc. This primary exchange is a meaningful phase and can be enhanced, for instance, by promoting a forum discussion on readings of writers who have experienced cross-cultural transition journeys.

---

[13] Kim, 222.

Pre-departure meetings were also organized by the University to introduce the program, to investigate students' expectations and to discuss the challenges they would probably face when estranged from home.[14]

As mentioned above, the host environment has a crucial role for students' "new life." Once there, they are affected by it and depend on it. Communication competence is directly connected to the participation in the interpersonal activities of the host environment, which can provide students with point of references for checking and validating their own and the natives' behaviours. Students have to create a new set of relationships among their ethnic group and with the host community.

To foster these contacts we placed the American students in Ca' Foscari University of Venice dormitories. To further this aim, we involved a group of Ca' Foscari students, namely the *cultural partners*. These partners represented both a support system and an opportunity for the American students: through them, students had assistance in handling difficulties, finding additional contacts, and opportunities to improve language and culture learning. To this end, the *cultural partners* organized many activities to expose their American partners to a set of social rituals by which they could familiarize themselves with different habits and behavioural rules (for instance, participating in Italian academic events and social practices, discovering typical places of socialization such as the "bacari" a sort of Venetian "pubs," etc.).

Cultural partners provided an important support system when American students were confronted with highly uncertain and stressful situations, e.g., a need for language assistance. They also represented an opportunity to enhance communication skills. Students could practice their communicative skills by taking risks and increasing the sense of control at the micro level of social communication with their Italian partners before being exposed to various social groups. *Cultural partners* also participated in the language class activities and they were involved in group or pair work with American students. This created an opportunity for them to be exposed to a more "real" target language and culture in the limited environment of the classroom.

Many of the language class activities had been planned to develop intercultural competence and they were integrated in a communicative syllabus whose purpose was to develop all skills (speaking, listening, reading and writing) and to analyze grammar in language use.[15] The main

---

[14] Meetings were organized by the Global Office of Columbia University directed by Dean Kathleen McDermott.

[15] The Language course syllabus has been designed by Barbara Spinelli and Elena Ballarin.

goal of these activities was to cross the boundaries of the classroom and to build a bridge between the internal more "artificial" reality and the external more authentic world. Students were asked to accomplish tasks by collecting data from the local people through interviews, phone calls, surveys, and interactions in public places. Every week the syllabus introduced a new cultural topic which students explored through intercultural perspectives, with a focus on the development of speaking skills.

Social communication activities

As we underlined, the adaptation process heavily depends on individual factors such as *openness*. This psychological component allows individuals to be more receptive to new learning. Even though cultivating *openness* is not a mere intellectual exercise, *social communication activities* in class can create facilitative conditions in order to break down stereotypes and to emphasise the importance of looking at the world from multiple angles.

Amplifying voices and involving a wide range of perspectives are fundamental pedagogical strategies of an intercultural approach.[16] An example of this approach is the following activity.[17]

The cultural topic of week 3 was "The immigration phenomenon and its consequences on society." We analyzed this theme in the Venetian context. We started by watching a short-movie on Venetian life produced by Ca' Foscari students who wanted to portray Venice as a commuters' city. Its soundtrack was a piano solo of Italian contemporary classical music.

First, students and *cultural partners* listened to the soundtrack without watching the movie and made some assumptions about its content. A lot of stereotypical images of Venice came out of the first discussion such as a romantic affair, San Marco square with pigeons and tourists, etc. Second, they watched the movie with the soundtrack. After this, they compared their different (initial) interpretations with the movie's real subject, and talked about Venice as a city populated by a large number of commuters. Some of the *cultural partners* were commuters as well and they could

[16] Barbara Spinelli, "Il 'Quadro' e lo sviluppo di una prospettiva interculturale," in *Integrazione linguistica in Europa*, ed. Marco Mezzadri (Torino: UTET, 2006), 187.

[17] All the activities mentioned in this study have been planned by Barbara Spinelli and Michele Daloiso.

enrich the debate by providing their own experiences and personal responses to the phenomenon.

Afterwards, students and *cultural partners* in mixed groups were asked to prepare some questions to use in interviews outside the classroom. The questions were designed for Venetians and immigrants living in the city (Africans, Chinese, Arabs, etc.) in order to investigate their experiences about social change. The purpose of this activity was to collect authentic data from "real" people. These data were then analyzed and compared in class. The result was an interesting cross-analysis of a mosaic of perspectives:

- the students' perspectives as newcomers;
- the *cultural partners'* perspectives as commuters or as Venetian students;
- the immigrants perspectives;
- Venetians' points of view about the immigration phenomenon.

The intercultural dialogue is also a negotiation between proximity and distance.[18] Simmel affirms that a newcomer possesses the contradictory quality to be "near" and "far."[19] Kim adds that an increased understanding of similarities between the host culture and the home culture is a clear successful step ahead in the initial phase of the *stress-adaptation-growth* process.[20]

In order to reflect upon this sense of *nearness* we adopted specific pedagogical techniques. During week 1 the language syllabus proposed to analyze and interpret the concept of "love" in the Italian cultural context. First, students watched an excerpt of an Italian movie, "Manuale d'amore" and commented on the Italian rituals that characterize the initial phase of "courting." Then they answered some questions accomplishing the task described in Table 16-1.

---

[18] Spinelli, 169.

[19] Georg Simmel, "The stranger," in *The sociology of Georg Simmel*, ed. Kurt H. Wolff (Glencoe, IL: Free Press, 1950), 402.

[20] Kim, 60-1.

DISCUTIAMO INSIEME! I SENTIMENTI NELLA MIA CULTURA		
Azioni	➢ *Quali passi bisogna fare per conoscere/conquistare una persona?* ➢ *Cosa fanno le giovani coppie durante la fase di innamoramento?* (Per esempio: dove vanno di solito? Cosa possono fare in pubblico?)	
Idee e valori	➢ *Che cosa è "romantico" nella tua cultura?* ➢ *Che valore ha il matrimonio nella tua cultura?* ➢ *Che relazione c'è tra le giovani coppie e le loro famiglie?* ➢ *Quali opere d'arte* (canzoni, film, romanzi, ecc.) *hanno influenzato la concezione dell'amore nella tua cultura?*	
Oggetti	➢ *Quali sono i simboli dell'amore nella tua cultura? Ci sono oggetti che hanno un particolare significato?*	
Lingua	➢ *Fai una lista di 10 parole o espressioni che sono usate nella tua lingua per descrivere i rapporti d'amore* (es. ragazzo/a vs. fidanzato/a) ➢ *Pensa a 3 proverbi nella tua lingua che hanno come tema l'amore*	

Table 16-1. "Discutiamo insieme" questionnaire.

For this exercise, students and *cultural partners* were divided into small groups. After this initial phase they were asked to compare their interpretations and then to find common habits and behavioural rules using the circles representation of Fig. 16-3.

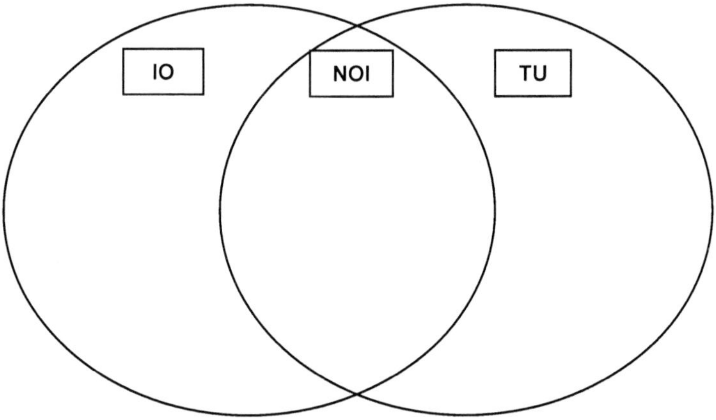

Figure 16-3. Venn diagram comparing cultural habits.

Social communication occurs on many levels. It takes place at the macro level through television, newspapers, and movies (i.e., through *mass media communication* as described above). This level of communication is never neutral and it has to be analyzed *critically*. Social communication also takes place at the micro level throughout the environment: workplaces, classrooms, shops, and informal interactions with the locals. Micro-level social communication also occurs when newcomers simply observe people on the street and in daily life.

We encouraged this level of communication by using the external environment as much as possible. An example of this activity is a task that students were asked to accomplish in week 4. The theme of the week was "Work and unemployment." By considering the subject, we focused the discussion on the young people's values in order to analyze the main issues they have to cope with upon entering the work force. In the initial phase of this task, students performed free associations using the grid represented in Table 16-2.

GUARDA CON GLI OCCHI DELL'ALTRO! -Per gli studenti: *Immagina di essere italiano. Associa ad ogni valore almeno tre parole che secondo te rappresentano la cultura italiana.* -Per i cultural partners: *Immagina di essere statunitense. Associa ad ogni valore almeno tre parole che per te rappresentano la cultura statunitense.*	
AMICIZIA	
BENESSERE MATERIALE	
DIVERTIMENTO	
FAMIGLIA	
INDIPENDENZA	
LAVORO	
POTERE	
SALUTE	
SOLIDARIETA'	
VIAGGIARE	

Table 16-2. "Guarda con gli occhi dell'altro"grid.

The purpose of this pedagogical technique is to activate a decentralization process from individuals' "cultural ego" in order to experience otherness "taking the place of" and developing empathy. During the first comparison, American and Italian students had to explain their choices and the images they wanted to translate through their words. They were asked to reflect upon where these images arose from, for instance: cinema, literature, television, school, direct experience in the host country, etc. Afterwards, students were asked to play the role of observers, with the support of *cultural partners*. In 30-45 minutes they had to collect as much information as possible. This information included flyers, advertisements and brochures (mostly found on student notice boards) focused on young people's principal interests, needs, and issues. Once in class they had to integrate the information from the preliminary discussion with their new findings which ostensibly represented the fruit of their direct observation. They selected the most interesting information they found, and this included cross-cultural comparisons such as political engagement and labor studies.

The few examples we provided above show that the main goal of social communication activities is to improve the *skills* (to analyze, to interpret, to relate, to observe, to compare) needed to become independent participants in, observers of, and commentators on any culture as we described previously. These *skills* represent the essential foundation of an intercultural identity.

In summary, we can conclude that the pedagogical path we adopted aimed to:

- improve student access to the host culture;
- improve student interpersonal communication with the host environment and community;
- increase intercultural awareness.

Assessing Intercultural Competence

The holistic nature of the approach and pedagogical activities we implemented involves the learner as a whole. Therefore the exclusive use of language proficiency tests or pre- and post-survey made by the University would have been too reductive to understand the students' complex language and cultural learning progress throughout the two-month study abroad program.

Jeffrey and Craft[21] underline the importance of a *learner inclusive approach*, Tarp[22] adds that transferring this concept to student exchanges means focusing on:

---

[21] Bob Jeffrey and Anna Craft, "Teaching creatively and teaching for creativity: distinctions and relationships," *Educational Studies* Vol. 30, no. 1 (2004): 84.

- what to investigate about the host culture
- how to investigate it
- how to evaluate the exchange

Alongside the *instrumental* tools we described in the previous section, we developed *awareness* tools in order to include students in the exchange process as autonomous subjects and as responsible authors of their own intercultural *growth.*

To this end, we used both a quantitative and a qualitative approach. We collected the quantitative data (collection of information such as how many languages students knew, how many months/years they spent abroad and where, ranking scale evaluation about housing, academics, onsite support, etc.) using pre and post-surveys, and evaluation forms provided by the university.

The qualitative approach comprised:

- a pre-questionnaire to investigate students and *cultural partners*' expectations; stereotypical images of foreign culture, preparation, descriptions of previous experiences living abroad, purpose of and attitude to exchanges;
- students' diaries about their daily experience in the host environment;
- individual semi-structured video interviews based on the analysis of students' narrative diaries;
- group semi-structured video interviews to compare students' emotional and practical responses to the host environment;
- students' literature reading notebooks and written productions (different *genre*: newspaper articles; poems, papers, etc.) focused on their Venetian experiences;
- *cultural partners'* video interviews focusing on their own responses to the exchange experience, on the occurred intercultural issues, and on their comments as observers of the host culture;
- a video interview of teachers from both the home and host culture who compared similarities and differences in adopting diverse approaches and analyzed their consequences on students' learning process.

---

[22] Gertrude Tarp. "Student perspectives in Short-Term Study Programmes Abroad: A Grounded Theory Study," in *Living and Studying Abroad*, eds. Michael Byram and Anwei Feng (Clevedon: Multilingual Matters, 2006), 167.

As Pearson-Evans[23] points out, diaries are a useful tool to underline the connections between variables and their incidence on students' stories and individual cross-cultural adjustments. Importantly, diaries are also an instrument which provides unpredictable data. Diary methodology heavily depends on students' motivation and continuous encouragement from the teacher. She suggests to use a more structured format in order to collect more reliable data.

Thus we provided students with a guideline to support them in their perception of their *stress-adaptation-growth* process. The guideline has been adapted by Byram's[24] and INCA's[25] portfolio structure. It consists of three main areas of analysis where students can find some suggestions to focus on *feelings*, *knowledge*, *actions* (Table 16-3) which reflect the *affective*, *cognitive* and *operational* dimension of the *Intercultural Identity*.

The following list can help you to describe your experiences and encounters.
La lista seguente ti può aiutare a descrivere le tue esperienze e i tuoi incontri.

List of subjects to reflect on / Lista di argomenti su cui riflettere.

A. ***Feelings***

1. Ways in which my curiosity and interest were aroused: (examples from ordinary daily life, especially when they made me re-consider my own culture)
2. Periods when I felt uncomfortable/homesick (what made me feel like this, with particular examples if possible)
3. Periods when I felt at home and comfortable (what made me feel like this, with particular examples if possible)

B. ***Knowledge***

1. The most important things I learned about social life and/or life at the University
2. The most important things I have learned about Venice
3. What I have learned about customs and conventions of talking with people (topics which interest them, topics to avoid, how to greet people and take leave from them)

C. ***Actions***

1. Incidents or problems which I resolved by explaining different cultures

---

[23] Aileen Pearson-Evans, "Recording the Journey: Diaries of Irish Students," in *Living and Studying Abroad*, eds. Michael Byram and Anwei Feng (Clevedon: Multilingual Matters, 2006), 63.

[24] Michael Byram, "Assessing Intercultural Competence in Language Teaching", *Sprogforum*, Vol. 6, no. 18 (2000): 8-13

[25] CILT, "INCA Project (Intercultural Competence Assessment)," Leonardo da Vinci, European Training in the UK, http://www.incaproject.org

	to people, helping them see the points of view of different cultures and how misunderstandings can happen.
2.	Examples of times when I have had to ask questions and work out my own answers (from "asking the way" to understanding cultural customs and beliefs)

Table 16-3. Diary Guideline (Byram 2000: 12. Our adaptation).

Students were asked to use the guideline to record their actual intercultural experiences during the sojourn using the following module, focusing on how it influenced their development of intercultural awareness (Table 16-4):

Date	Description of experience or encounter
Place	
How this influenced me (what I felt, though or did, as a consequence)	

Table 16-4. Diary record form; (INCA Portfolio. Our adaptation).

We have already pointed out that this adaptive journey includes periods of great stress in which incomers work out new ways of handling problems and strive to meet the challenges by acting and responding to the new milieu. Facing adaptive stress and developing self-awareness of frustrating moments means recognizing that stress is more than just a part of the experience: it is a necessary condition for our adaptation and a key of personal growth. We used diaries and interviews for this purpose.

We collected diaries every week and we interviewed students every fortnight. The entries were supposed to focus on and reflect upon specific issues that arose in their narratives. They had the chance to decode and to share their emotional, mental states, and their challenges with their interviewer or peers. Diaries and interviews heightened awareness of stressful but also rewarding moments authorizing students to partake in the active development of new cultural understanding and habits.

Additionally, we used literature students' reading notebooks to analyze how the bridge between classroom, external world and private emotional responses could interfere with their personal growth. In order to enrich our collection of data and to amplify voices we also interviewed the *cultural partners*.

Kim[26] states that "the openness and strength of personality fosters, and is fostered by, yet another psychological orientation, *positivity*." This positive outlook was guaranteed by *cultural partners* who encouraged their partners' optimism and discouraged destructive anger; they represented the "supportive climate." But this role was not always trouble-free. *Cultural partners* had been prepared to accomplish this task through briefing workshops but differences challenged *their* cultural identity as well. By being positive, American students could help natives to develop their own communicative competence *interculturally* and increase their understanding of American cultural communication practices.

Thus, their relationship was fundamentally interdependent. Having *cultural partners'* feedback was crucial to interpret the whole adaptive process and the universal understanding of human differences. In order to enhance this knowledge in the future it would be helpful to ask *cultural partners* to use narrative diaries as well.

In addition, we used a video interview in which teachers compared the methodology adopted in the host and home culture. In this interview, teachers considered the pedagogical variables which can affect the learning process of the specific L2 context and they sought to better understand how intervening *before-during-after* the study abroad experience would better *prepare-support-maintain* the continuous formative process.

Data analysis and interpretation

To analyse and to interpret our data we decided to adopt Kim's structural model (Fig. 16-2) which shows the influencing factors of the *stress-adaptation-growth* journey. We labelled everything we found interesting and relevant, using colour coding to highlight personal students' responses to the different components along the two-month adaptive process: predisposition (preparedness to change, ethnic

[26] Kim, 232.

proximity, and personal attitude), environment receptivity and conformity pressure, host communication, intercultural transformation, noting when and if changes occurred. Besides taking into consideration this path vertically within the students' individual stories we also compared horizontally the different experiences and events across their diaries, interviews, reading notebooks and written productions. We also considered when and how our pedagogical interventions might have affected that process.

As Kim asserts:

> individuals crossing cultures can be described as experiencing a degree of existential alertness. Many people struggle to cope with feelings of inadequacy and frustration in their change environment.[27]

According to students' initial perceptions, those feelings are associated with living in a hostile receptivity environment represented by the city and its inhabitants as some of them pointed out during the first week of the program:

> *Venetians can tend to stay to themselves and not be as open to talk to strangers or Americans…* (I., diary)

> *I felt a little isolated or singled out and not someone to talk to…* (L., diary)

> *I've been faced everyday with anti-American graffiti and I've always felt like I had to apologize for myself…* (F., diary)

Some individuals resist the change. For instance, dealing with or understanding new social and behavioural norms becomes a stressful experience:

> *I had to pay a fine for not validating the train ticket. Apparently it is imperative to validate the train ticket before boarding. I'm not quite sure why it is important or what purpose it serves exactly. All I know is that T. and I were supposed to pay a 25 Euro fee each… It was a very frustratingly quintessential Italian experience.* (C., diary)

> *In a clothes store the sales lady followed us around the whole time and I felt uncomfortable I learned that this is normal. However, it still makes me really uncomfortable.* (J., diary)

---

[27] Kim, 5.

Others react to the conformity pressure required by the new environment with a "go native" attitude which can generate the same sense of failure, according to the following student's statement:

> *I really wanted to be the same person here as at home and not fall into "tourist made"... I will continue to study so that I can be recognized by the locals as a student instead of a tourist... I must have a cell phone in order to have a social life here as text messages are the way that invitations are sent out, so I will get one promptly.* (F., diary)

This pressure can be also interpreted as a restless need of identification due to ethnic proximity (personal component) with the target culture, since the above-quoted student has Italian roots.

Even though all students were motivated to participate in the program, their individual factors greatly influenced their adaptive potential. Most people, however, learn to identify similarities and differences between their new surroundings and the home culture which is a significant sign of their becoming proficient in handling situations they encounter. This comparison remains mostly neutral and underlines how, initially, the knowledge of the host culture tends to be simplistic:

> *Watching the ritual of the vaporetto stops remind me that I come from a culture that regards line-cutting as a terrible sin and confirms that for Italians is not.* (H., diary)

> *So far it seems like the only news most Italians would hear about the US is celebrity gossip or Bush's (infamous) international policies/affairs. This is sort of frustration but it does help me realize why many Italians may believe most of the stereotypes about Americans. It also works both ways. In the US Italy is mostly, in the (popular) press for stories on the mafia or other spectacular news that might also enforce stereotypes.* (B., diary)

Kim's structural model identifies as a central engine of the cross-cultural adaptation journey the *host communication competence,* as this factor directly affects all the other factors operating in that process. This competence is the newcomer's ability to be engaged in *host communication* events in accordance with the *host communication* system.

The sense of frustration is mainly caused by a weak *host communication competence* such as the misinterpretation of the host community pragmatic and sociolinguistic code. This can cause intercultural misunderstandings and a lack of communication, as the following examples show:

I was buying shoes in Lido and the saleswomen were so rude. I was trying to communicate in Italian and they laughed at me when I called the vetrina a finestra... They kept interrupting me by helping other people to the point where I confronted them about it and asked if there was a problem... They become angry...I just hate it when they say "Dimmi". I don't think it's appropriate and it makes me feel rushed. (F. diary)

In a snobby restaurant I used the "tu" instead of the "lei" and received a bad reaction. It was strange because I have heard that foreigners aren't expected to use the "lei" but since I was speaking Italian I should have used it. (J. diary)

Our pedagogical solutions took into account these factors, identifying approaches and conditions which could facilitate the transition process. As we have already described, we tried to foster contacts with the external world and to enhance the students' knowledge of verbal and nonverbal codes and rules of the target culture through class design, as well as through the invaluable support of the *cultural partners*.

By creating a "friendly" environment we tried to compensate the first perception of hostile environment receptivity:

The whole first day, the orientation, made me feel comfortable and it allowed me to relax. (I. diary)

Professors are so available (...) and I see them in the halls. It is such a pleasure to meet and talk to them every day (D. diary)

Cultural partners intensify the contacts with the surroundings, involving students in other social groups (colleagues, friends, families, etc.):

G. (cultural partner) *told me I could come to the library with her and meet her friends there which I have done! I will continue to study there so that I can be recognized by the locals as a student...*(F. diary)

(...) we not only ate gelato but got to talk with M.'s parents (M. is a cultural partner and his parents hold a "Gelateria"). *His mother told us stories about M. when he was little (at my request) and she also asked us many questions about ourselves and families. She only spoke Italian so we spoke in Italian with her* (I. diary)

Saturday we went to a night club with the cultural partners and the others. We had fun. I didn't feel uncomfortable being with the others (M., diary)

Class activities and trips bridged the gap with the external world and involved the students in significant experiences, breaking down stereotypes:

> *I had a very good time on this trip. It was interesting to see how one of the authors that we read actually lived. This visit gave more depth to work done in class by adding a more personal dimension.* (D. diary)

> *I have an experience here how to learn the language, the culture and then to see culture, speak the language. You get submerged into the real life.* (G., video interview)

> *In the literature course I liked the readings on Venice, Da Ponte... Walking into the town I felt connected with the lectures.* (F. video interview)

> *I liked M.'s classes where we compared Italians and Americans' habits, customs...* (I., video interview)

> *In quelle lezioni abbiamo sfatato molto "miti"...* (cultural partner, video interview)

Class activities also helped to strengthen the ethnic group (the American students) relationships. Kim points out that an environment which has a good influence on newcomers can also include the ethnic group as it "provides strangers with support during the initial transition period." [28]

> *I really love the trips (...). I also think they help the group dynamic to grow. It is a chance to get to know one another better...* (D., diary)

> *It's interesting to hear some of the other group members' opinion about how the people are here in Venice. Some say they are cold and closed, some say if you make an effort to speak Italian, they will be more open and welcoming.* (G., diary)

Cultural partners played a special role to assist students with their language issues and to discover communication rules:

> *I asked S.* (cultural partner) *how people meet people (my age) in Venice. People don't just say "how are you" on the street, it's too personal. This made me realize why people would look at me so crazy when I'd say*

---

[28] Kim, 82.

"come stai?" In Italy it is really asking how the person is "personally," not superficially as in USA... (I., diary)

I was nervous going into the tutoring session, as I was and are still having a hard time making myself speak in Italian. I know I can only get better by practicing (...). I made a lot of progress facing this during the tutoring and especially afterwards in the garden (it is a University garden). *The cultural partners did a good job of making me comfortable.* (A. diary)

By enhancing their language competence, students realized that any communication encounter is affected by different contributing factors such as the interlocutor's communication competence, the nature of their relationship, etc. Their positive attitude could help natives to participate more actively:

I went in and realized that it was difficult to explain in Italian that I was interested in joining a gym. I asked the lady at the desk if she spoke English: she said "not very well" she was really kind and even though my Italian is not fluent, she understood. Now every time I walk in the door, she says "ciao L." (L., diary)

Personally I feel the resident Venetians have been friendly, especially when I make an attempt to speak the language... (G., diary)

Such development is reflected in an advanced and more sophisticated language use which includes not only the understanding of the language *per se* but also the knowledge of pragmatic rules which reflect cultural connotations such as jokes and humour:

B. and I were doing some shopping and the saleslady at the store was so excited to learn that we were studying Italian. She indulged us by allowing us to practice, she spoke slowly and I felt like, for the first time, I had succeeded at communicating, I even told a joke in Italian and made her laugh. (F., diary)

The development of *host communication* allows students to meet their physical, psychological and social needs. It empowers them and confers them a specific status. It contributes to the development of a sense of belonging, of becoming "a part of", and of autonomy:

I got to play soccer with little boys. Playing sports with locals is doing something they do everyday and doing something where people are truly themselves. We spoke Italian and they spoke some English. They were nice and a boy showed us his family... (I, diary)

It was so great to know Italian well enough to know what was happening during a play in Italian. And after the show I talked with the performers. They were very nice. (I, diary)

One of the few times I felt a native. Venetians extend an offer of friendship. It was very nice. And we returned the offer at food. Walking across bridge and hanging out together like everyone else during Redentore was a bounding experience. I felt like I was getting the real Venetian experience. (A., diary)

American students (students from another university study abroad program) *invaded the Residenza and Ca' Bembo* (University of Venice dormitory and building) *and we had to teach them how to say "dove"! The one place where I felt I could interact with Italians and be recognized as a different type of visitor has now become Camp America. My experience of submersion has been seriously compromised ...* (F., diary)

By comparing cultures, students became more critical and judgemental with their own culture:

(…) *it seems to me that Americans show a particularly ugly inclination toward acting incredibly entitled – like making demands n English.* (H., diary)

Really the spritz is a very interesting drive. It took me a while to get used to the taste, but I soon realized it's the social aspect of drinking the spritz that is important, because I don't think the drink is really that great. I really appreciate how often I see teenagers and college students gathering to socialize without being obnoxious (something hard to escape from on most weekends at Columbia) (G., diary)

As we have seen the adaptation process is an individual journey and it is affected by the mutual relationship of personal components and external environment.

Despite the common pedagogical path and the facilitative conditions we attempted to create, a student of the Program failed in facing the challenges of the new milieu and returned home prematurely (after one month). She experienced emotional and social isolation from the new environment even though she had the same support we provided for the other students. Defensive responses to the adjustment are shaped by our own predisposition and they can have different levels of severity which can lead the individual to a mental and physical uneasiness and to a regressive process of change. Studies of immigrants and foreign students demonstrate that they increase their level of adaptation once they have successfully managed the initial phase. We can conclude that this initial phase helped the student to consider her failure not as a permanent condition but as an essential step for her mental and emotional growth. She might have a second chance in her future as she hinted in her poem on Venice

> *La Serenissima mi ha detto "non puoi visitarmi"*
> *Lei si è voltata ed ancora sta sorridendo*
> *Forse quando sono vecchia e coriacea, come lei*
> *diventeremo amici fedeli*
> (E., poem)

On the other hand, some students' transition process was made smoother by their "transversal competences,"[29] skills they developed in other circumstances which facilitated the transfer from a language and culture system to another, such as the capacity to deal with misunderstandings and cultural conflicts. This ability can be enhanced while living in an alien environment as she points out:

> *I've done a lot of travelling before; I did handle situations with a lot of resistance or expectation (...) I learned to be patient, for me it is just an exercise in that (...) my previous experiences definitely helped me a lot... You cannot say "I don like that," "that's stupid" "it is so much better in the USA" I learnt that this is not the right way to adjust...* (F., video interview)

The outcome of this complex cross-cultural adaptation process, when it occurs, is an intercultural transformation which entails the three components we have already mentioned in this study: *affective*, *cognitive* and *procedural*. These aspects are interrelated but do not necessarily develop simultaneously. However, the development of one component can facilitate the growth of others. All these components clearly appear in our students' final comments on their transition experience. The first sign of intercultural growth is the breakdown of simplistic stereotypes toward a more accurate and more detailed knowledge of the host culture:

---

[29] Spinelli, 174

I don't know what to say about Italians in general now because here we are talking about Venetians that are very different from my friends in Puglia, completely different. (F., video interview)

I came to Venice some times, which was enough to solidify my opinion of the place as pretty and interesting, but found it and myself suffocated by tourists and the tourists industry. Beginning with my determination to turn down every path on Giudecca, no matter how forbidding and never discouraged by dead ends, I have found not only that solitude exists in Venice, but that a living breathing city survives here. (H., diary)

I don't know if this is true, but I feel like people in Roma are nicer than the people in Venezia. They are both very touristy town but Roma seems nicer and Roman Italian accent is very clear... (I., diary)

The intercultural transformation is more evident in changing cultural practices and habits, or with new acquisition of factual knowledge, while a change in basic values is extremely difficult and rare:

If you don't call for the waiter they won't bring the bill for an hour and a half. They are just letting you relax. (C., diary)

When walking past, it is normal for people to look right at you. I like this though because it's more straightforward. (J., diary)

È un' esperienza senza parole per una studentessa che studia storia dell'arte. Ora posso dire di averla vista e posso spiegarla. (L., video interview)

The richness of the intercultural transformation includes the sense of appropriation of new codes, new metaphors to interpret the world and to enlarge our own social rules:

I have been to the Commedia dell'Arte performance (...) you can see Arlecchino, Pantalone, everywhere. They are universal. (I., video interview)

Rarely do me and my friends go to a café or bars and just stay there for hours and have a good time with each other. When I go home I will suggest to those we do it like the Italian kids! (G., diary)

Therefore, interculturality brings self-discovery and renovation which entails adaptability, flexibility, empathy and intercultural self-awareness.

This is the outcome of a complex mediation and negation process between the internal and the external world:

> *Any tourist in his non-native country is a fish out of water, and must be patiently forgiven his cultural faux pas.* (H, diary)

> *(...) I have also learned to not take things so personally (...) If I'm making the effort to have a conversation with someone in a shop or at a restaurant and they don't seem very responsive or are impatient with my Italian speaking. I try not to get frustrated. I feel like I can find many others who are interested in speaking with me.* (F., diary)

> *People are so different. It's very difficult to explain what I felt and learnt but when go home it's gonna be interesting how I will act with my family and friends...* (L., video interview)

> *Living in a foreign country makes you grow.* (D., video interview)

In some cases the transformation process seems to entail four basic stages: an initial stage characterized by optimism and elation followed by a stage of uneasiness and hostility, a consequent recovery stage, and a final stage were the adjustment is complete in which new customs are enjoyed. The four stages are commonly known as "U curve hypothesis"[30] and are summarized in the following student's consideration from her literature reading notebook:

> *Senza dubbio ho avuto qualche fase di transizione molto simile all'esperienza del protagonista di Morte a Venezia, Aschenbach. Prima era euforia iniziale della città, poi il disagio di un nuovo posto, e finalmente, ho assorbito tutta la cultura fantastica trovandoci comodità (e vi ho trovato conforto). L'esplorazione, il perdermi, vedere cose nuove, essere a disagio con le mie abilità di lingua, tutte sono state la migliore avventura. Queste esperienze aiutano a svilupparsi e migliorarsi come persone.* (G., reading notebook)

However, as we have described in this article, students' lives in the new environment do not always begin with a euphoria stage. Our findings testify that the progress can be more complex as Kim underlined by her spiral representation (Fig. 16-1) which includes many "U curve" periods

---

[30] Michael Brein and Kenneth H. David. "Intercultural communication and the adjustment of the Sojourner," in *Psychological Bullettin*, 76, no 3 (1971): 215-30.

with moments of dis-integration and reintegration[31] of the experience over time.

In this dynamic and creative process of self-reinvention, students discover new forms and symbols of life with which to forge new intercultural identities.[32]

Conclusion

The main purpose of this study was to illuminate how students actually experience short stays abroad in university exchanges and how educational institutions and teachers can pedagogically intervene to make this experience more rewarding by facilitating the integration process.

We emphasized the importance to pay attention to both internal and external factors which can affect the transition by adopting instrumental and assessment tools. Assessing the meaningful outcomes of sending students abroad and getting access to their "voices" has a twofold purpose: 1) the identification of the improvement needed for the program so that students can benefit significantly from the study abroad; 2) the development of students' intercultural awareness.

Students were constantly encouraged to reflect upon their language, cultural, and intercultural learning. This heightened their awareness of their strengths and weaknesses as intercultural communicators and encouraged them to find new responses to the new milieu which can improve future encounters across cultures.

We included *cultural partners* and teachers in our cross-cultural adaptation process assessment because we believe the effectiveness of the program depends on all participants. The comments of the partners and the teachers enriched our analysis with their perspective as external observers of American students' transition, and their own experiences as cultural interlocutors.

Living and studying abroad is a challenging experience which leads the individual to a transformation process. Although in this journey students had to face stress, frustration and sense of failure, they developed (in most of the cases) a broadened persona with an increased capacity to see situations, others, and themselves with new eyes.

---

[31] Sidney M. Jourard, "Growing awareness and the awareness of growth," in *Ways of Growth approaches to expanding awareness*, eds. Herbert H. Otto and John H. Mann (New York: the Viking Press, 1968).
[32] Kim, 70

The asymmetrical relationship between themselves and the external conditions entailed a continual back and forth, downward and upward movement in the direction of increasing growth.

COLUMBIA UNIVERSITY, NEW YORK, USA
UNIVERSITY FOR FOREIGNERS, PERUGIA, ITALY
CA' FOSCARI UNIVERSITY, VENICE, ITALY

Other References

Byram, Michael. *Teaching and assessing intercultural communicative competence*. Clevedon: Multilingual Matters, 1997.

Dolci, Roberto and Barbara Spinelli, eds. *Educazione linguistica e interculturale in nuovi ambienti di apprendimento*. Supplemento Monografico Rivista Itals, Anno III, No. 9, Perugia: Guerra Ed., 2005.

__________. "La dimension idioculturelle des micro-communautés d'apprentissage en ligne". *Lidil*, No. 36 (2007)

Jourard, Sidney M. "Growing awareness and the awareness of growth". In *Ways of Growth approaches to expanding awareness*, edited by. Herbert . Otto and John H. Mann, 1-14. New York: the Viking Press, 1968.

Oberg, Kalervo. "Cultural shock: Adjustment to new cultural environments", *Practical Anthropology*, No. 7 (1960): 170-179

Spinelli, Barbara and Roberto Dolci. "Developing a Multilevel Language Learning in a Powerful Environment: a Case Study". *Mosaic*, 9, No. 2 (2007): 11-20

Zarate, Geneviève, Aline Gohard-Radenkovic, Denise Lussier and Hermine Penz, eds. *Cultural mediation in language learning and teaching*. Strasbourg: Council of Europe, 2004

CHAPTER SEVENTEEN

EVALUATING CULTURAL PROFICIENCY IN AN UPPER LEVEL ITALIAN CULTURE COURSE

ROMANA CAPEK-HABEKOVIĆ
AND SANDRA PALAICH

Part I: General Observations

Position of Culture within Second Language Instruction

Culture as an integral element in today's second language courses is recognized and accepted both by instructors and students as an irreplaceable arena for a context-based curriculum. Research and practice demonstrate that learners' acquisition of second-language linguistic codes is facilitated if they are taught and assimilated in a wider cultural context. Cultural references had their humble beginnings as brief cultural notes at the end of grammar-heavy chapters in different textbooks some thirty years ago. Nowadays, culture is integrated in today's language textbooks in a meaningful manner, and sophisticated technology is used to deliver cultural information. Culture has undoubtedly earned a central place in the process of students' acquisition of language skills, as well as their becoming citizens of the world. The National Standards for Foreign Language Learning (1996)—Communication, Culture, Connections, Comparisons, and Communities—provided much-needed guidelines for formulating successful second language curricula in which culture would be given its long-overdue legitimacy.[1]

---

[1] National Standards in Foreign Language Education Project. *Standards for Foreign Language Learning: Preparing for the 21st Century* (Yonkers, NY: The American Council on the Teaching of Foreign Languages, 1996).

Definitions of Culture in Second-Language Curricula

In spite of students' enthusiasm for learning about the target language culture, the methodology of the inclusion of culture into the curricula still remains an issue of concern and debate among L2 scholars and instructors. Much has been written about culture, and it is by no means our intent to offer an exhaustive overview of the concept of culture in L2 classrooms. We were, like so many colleagues of ours, faced with the dilemma of what culture means for us, and what it is within the context of our course. Perhaps the reason for this lies in the multifaceted and somewhat elusive nature of culture, which must be addressed first. Lang and Paige (2003) define culture by saying: "Culture is complex and elusive, incorporating as it does elements such as attitudes, beliefs, ideologies, and perceptions, ways of behaving and thinking, and values."[2] Paige (1993) also points out that

> Any discussion of cultural differences could cause language learners to change their own ways of thinking and behaving. In other words, culture takes the learning experience far beyond the realm of comfort, experience, and interest of both teacher and the learner.[3]

Seelye (1993) defines culture as "a broad concept that embraces all aspects of human life, from folktales to carved whales."[4] Paige et al. (2003) offer a particularly comprehensive definition of the process of acquiring cultural competence which was very useful to us:

> Culture learning is the process of acquiring the culture-specific and culture-general knowledge, skills, and attitudes required for effective communication and interaction with individuals from other cultures. It is a dynamic, developmental, and ongoing process which engages the learner cognitively, behaviorally, and affectively.[5]

---

[2] Dale L. Lange, L. Dale, R. Michael Paige, ed., *Culture as the Core. Perspective on Culture in Second Language Learning* (Greenwich: Information Age Publishing, 2003), Introduction, x.
[3] R. Michael Paige, (ed.), *Education for the Intercultural Experience* (Yarmouth. ME: Intercultural Press, 1993), 1-19.
[4] H. Ned Seelye, *Teaching Culture: Strategies for Intercultural Communication* (Lincolnwood, IL: National Textbook Company, 1993), 26.
[5] Robert C. Lafayette, ed., *The National Standards for Foreign Language Learning* (Lincolnwood III, National Textbook Company, 1996), 178.

In other words, in order to become an efficient culture learner, a person must engage in acquiring knowledge and skills which are more general in their nature and transferable across cultures, as well as those relevant to the specific target culture in question. This multidimensional nature of culture learning is also mirrored by Neuner (1997) who states that the dimensions of culture learning are pragmatic, i.e. skills, cognitive, i.e. knowledge, and emotional, i.e. attitudes.[6]

A long standing but frequently repudiated definition of two kinds of culture—the little *c* culture and the big *C* culture—is helpful in clarifying the complexity of the notion of culture. The little *c* culture was often defined as the one that deals with people's everyday life, common social practices and conventions, such as eating habits, interaction among people in different situations, workplace behavior, religious practices, and other pragmatic sociocultural concepts. As such, its treatment in an L2 classroom was at times reduced to generalizations and stereotyping. The big *C* culture, on the other hand, denoted important works of art, literature, music, and other artistic and scientific achievements of national and international importance. For a long time learning a second language was viewed by both teachers and students as a necessary tool for acquiring a competence in the big *C* culture. In other words, linguistic competence was viewed as a tool which will enable the learner to access the big *C* culture. As the small *c* culture became integrated into language instruction in more meaningful ways, it confirmed the realization that learning another language does not only mean the acquisition of grammatical, lexical, syntactic, and phonetic properties of that language. Instead, research and practice demonstrated that the learners' acquisition of second language linguistic codes is facilitated if they are taught and assimilated in a wider cultural context. As the National Standards outline, language learners cannot truly master a foreign language until "they have also mastered the cultural context in which the language occurs" (p. 27). In short, the need for a culturally contextualized second language instruction is widely accepted, which brings us to the essential role of culture in the second language curricula. Culture has therefore proven to be the principal agent of context, in essence a medium that enables learners to put into practice their newly acquired linguistic competence in oral and written communication and become effective readers of cultural codes.

---

6 Michael Byram, Geneviève Zarate and Gerhard Neuner, *Sociocultural Competence in Language Learning and Teaching* (Council of Europe Publishing, 1997).

Goals of Culture Learning

Despite easy accessibility of cultural information in today's world of fast communications and free-flowing information, integrating culture in an L2 classroom is often quite a daunting task. In a foreign language classroom it often means that both the teacher and the students have to engage in a multi-layered process of self-analysis and understanding of their own culture, as well as the target culture. As suggested by Bayram and Zarate (1997) one must be willing "to relativise one's own cultural viewpoint and cultural system of values" (Introduction, p. xx) in order to engage in a meaningful intercultural communication. The teacher must furthermore decide how to include culture in the curriculum and how to objectively evaluate students' cultural proficiency. These are just a few key problems, but there are many more of both a pedagogical and a practical nature that need to be addressed prior to engaging in the process of culture learning.

One of the principal issues in approaching the teaching of culture is the goal of such instruction. What exactly are language/culture learners expected to master? Defining the desired goals of culture learning will enable instructors to more clearly outline the teaching methodology employed, and the techniques of evaluation and assessment of cultural proficiency. The National Standards identify the culture goals as follows:

> **Standard 2.1:** Students demonstrate an understanding of the relationship between the practices and perspectives of the culture studied;
> **Standard 2.2:** Students demonstrate an understanding of the relationship between the products and perspectives of the culture studied.
> **Standard 3.2:** Students acquire information and recognize the distinctive viewpoints that are only available through the foreign language and its cultures.
> **Standard 4.2:** Students demonstrate understanding of the concept of culture through comparisons of the cultures studied and their own.

It can be concluded that understanding ideas, values, mores and behaviors of a foreign culture is one of the important goals of foreign language instruction. It is important at this point to emphasize that the goal of L2 instruction is therefore primarily the *understanding* of a foreign culture and not necessarily the ability to imitate the said culture. In contrast, attaining sociopragmatic and sociolinguistic competence—in other words being able to *behave, act* and *react* appropriately in interactions with the target culture—would primarily be the goals of full immersion programs. This kind of competence is very difficult to accomplish in a simulated foreign language environment and is best left to individual learners to attain during their stays abroad.

Issues and Concerns

Studies show and the teaching community favors the idea that culture should be introduced from the very beginning of second language learning, but methods and techniques of its implementation are still being debated, and are still largely left to individual instructors, their own ingenuity and familiarity with the technology and resources available. A construction of an objective evaluation and assessment system also rests upon the teacher. The compiled sum of difficulties associated with teaching and evaluating culture proficiency quickly erases the initial assumption that culture offers an easily attainable context for L2 instruction.

Once culture becomes an element of context in the second language curricula, attention also must be lent to technology and different media which play a major role in delivering cultural realia. Nowadays, many language departments in the United States have multimedia classrooms and well-equipped media and computer facilities manned with capable staff at hand. Technology and especially the use of computers (internet, blogs, virtual reality) make it easier to present cultural content in class. At the same time, instructors are faced with the challenge of selecting appropriate cultural content in an infinite expanse of information which can be quite overwhelming. It is our responsibility, as instructors, to learn to manage this informational overload if we are to present culture in a measured, meaningful and pedagogically justified manner. The most useful purpose of the internet in L2 classrooms lies in the fact that it allows instantaneous access to authentic materials. Filmic materials, with or without subtitles, are also good tools to present different aspects of culture; listening to music scores in target language provides excellent practice for listening comprehension skills. Computer-based activities dealing with a specific cultural theme are also very effective instructional tools, because they capitalize on students' computer literacy and their desire to individually explore the internet, which brings culture directly to their dorm rooms. In addition, more recently published textbooks are written with popular culture in mind. They frequently focus on themes drawn from everyday life of the country whose language students learn. Furthermore, many students travel and study abroad and thus come in direct contact with social practices of that country. In spite of an overall positive interrelationship between technology and teaching culture, there remain lingering questions that call for further study and analysis, such as:

How much culture should be presented to the learner? In which format? How to deal with controversial issues that involve politics, race and gender? How can instructors help students become more accepting of another culture and not see it solely through the prism of their own upbringing and society? How can teachers step aside and become facilitators in the process of bridging the gap between one's own cultural experience and the target culture? How to most effectively engage in cultural comparisons rather then limiting the role of the instructor to the delivery of factual information? To summarize, learners' exposure to popular culture inside and outside of the L2 classroom is intense and multifaceted. At times it seems that they are bombarded with information. This begs the question of how they process and retain this information, and finally how instructors evaluate the acquired cultural knowledge.

There are several questions that instructors often ask themselves: "Why do we need to evaluate cultural proficiency at all? Isn't it enough that we expose students to another culture through diverse media?" Some of the obvious answers are: we need to evaluate cultural proficiency in order to assess the degree of students' retention of the informational input; to diagnose the level of their understanding of cultural information; to identify their ability to draw comparisons between their culture and the target one, and to verify their progress in thinking without stereotyping.

Part II: A Case Study

Framework: an Upper Level Culture Course

The case discussed here is a third-year Italian culture course at a college level in the United States taught in the target language (see the syllabus in the Appendix). It is a 3-credit-hour course in which most of the students are Italian majors and possess modestly developed linguistic skills. Their reading skills are adequate for the reading and the understanding of most academic topics and concepts. Their speaking skills differ greatly, and depend entirely on their individual foreign language experiences. They may vary from quite fluent—due to attending study abroad programs, or longer expatriations to attend full immersion programs—to experiences limited to the acquisition of the language exclusively at an academic institution in the home country. Similarly, their listening comprehension exhibits the same differences, while their writing skills are generally adequately developed for writing about academic subjects, explaining and defending one's own views and opinions, and performing analyses and comparisons. Their research skills are generally modest.

Defining Culture

In order to ensure that the expectations of the students generally match those of the instructor, we suggest that at the beginning of the semester students be asked the following question: what do you understand under the term "culture"? We did just that, and compiled a list of students' answers. We present it unedited, in the order it was delivered:

> Race, ethnicity, food, religion, traditions, holidays, customs, characteristics that define a people, language, shared values, way of life, establishing relationships, communication, politics, shared history, art, music, dress, technology, literature, industry, economy, education, upbringing, mass behavior, pop culture, current events, news, celebrities, trends, youth.

This list points to the fact that our students' understanding of the concept of culture was very wide and sort of all-encompassing. We were not surprised at this, because we believe that it shows that a large number of young people today subscribe to the view that individuals determine what culture is according to their own view of the world, their needs and experiences. Given the list provided by the students, we could conclude that their notion of culture largely overlapped with ours and that their expectations of the course were realistic. This was later confirmed in their course evaluations.

As a clarification, it is useful to explain that the word *cultura* has an additional meaning in Italian, namely that of a person's education and learning. Similarly, the terms *cultura popolare* and "popular culture" do not carry the same connotations. This notion was emphasized throughout the course.

Goals of the Course

Like many courses taught in the target language, the course we are describing has a dual purpose: the development of students' sociocultural competence, as well as fine-tuning of their linguistic proficiency. This brings up the first question in the mind of the instructor: what exactly do we hope to achieve in such a course? We propose that the goals of a course whose core is culture must be multifold: to help students develop into intercultural speakers by means of a parallel development of linguistic and sociocultural skills. First, the students are expected to learn how to think about a foreign culture in general. They are expected to develop a certain level of intercultural awareness, understanding and tolerance. Clearly, culture is not a sum of facts about a specific country; however, students are expected to acquire a certain amount of factual information that they will need in order to understand the target culture at a deeper level. For example, knowing unemployment rates in different Italian regions could help learners to discuss the economic differences between the North and the South. Learning about the history of those regions would help them contextualize these economic differences and think about their root causes. Similarly, familiarity with the birth rate decline and immigration patterns would enable them to better understand some of the demographic and social changes under way in Italy. Familiarity with statistics related to family, marriage and divorce would help learners understand the changes in the structure of the Italian family. Knowing the makeup of the Italian economy in terms of company size, labor laws and work practices would also foster their understanding of Italy's place within the framework of the European Union and the country's current economic difficulties. We believe that acquiring the appropriate factual content is critical if we hope to foster an informed exchange of opinions about the target culture.

In addition to acquiring factual knowledge, instructors would like to see their students gain insight into Italian social practices and norms, traditions, values and behaviors. This would help students overcome the urge to recycle stereotypes and perpetuate traditional images of Italy which no longer hold true. Furthermore, learning about the enormous variety that the country presents would challenge the old notion of one uniform "Italian" culture and language. It is important that the students develop an ability to understand the target culture utilizing the knowledge acquired, and that they be able to develop an affective relationship with the target culture. Consider for a moment the emotional and cultural charge carried by words such as *extracomunitario, Berlusconi, mammone, Padania, terrone*. Ideally, the students would be able to understand the connotations of words such as these and gain an educated and affective insight into their meaning, much like they would into similar concepts in their native language and culture.

When establishing the goals of the course, a teacher must, however, keep a realistic perspective. Some goals may be outside of the scope of such a course. It may not be realistic to expect that a course taught at an academic institution in the United States will, for instance, be able to attain the goal of teaching sociopragmatic competence. Immersion in the target culture is in many cases the only means for reaching this particular goal.

However, it is realistic to expect that the students will develop a better understanding of social norms and practices of that culture and thus be able to achieve the desired level of sociopragmatic competence once in direct contact with the target culture.

From the linguistic point of view, the goal of this course is to hone the students' linguistic skills through the reading of authored and authentic texts, analysis and discussion of textual materials, acquisition of new vocabulary, exposure to and analysis of authentic audio and video materials, pair and group communicative activities, independent research of authentic sources, delivering cultural presentations in class and the writing of compositions. The aim of developing these linguistic skills is not self-serving. They have the purpose of enabling the learners to react to stimuli in an appropriate manner not only linguistically, but culturally as well.

Course Content and Its Function

Textual Materials

The textbook used in this course, *Parola a te!*,[7] contains a number of authored texts on a large variety of topics. The texts were written keeping in mind the needs of third-year college students in the United States. The underlying structure of the textbook is a survey of a number of Italian regions with the focus on different cities from these regions and various people that were born in the regions. The rationale for such an approach was to cover the widest variety of aspects of life in Italy through the selection of regions, cities and personages, and to offer insights into less commonly known contents related to all aspects of life in Italy: history, geography, society, economy, politics, sports, entertainment, customs and traditions. Furthermore, the texts are tailored to address the vocabulary building needs of students, and they follow a progression in the complexity of syntactic and lexical structures.

Students are also required to access a number of authentic texts in different media: books, newspapers, magazines, government and private institutions' web sites, company web sites and blogs, all readily available online. Ideally, this course would be taught in a multi-media classroom, which enables the instructor and the students to instantaneously access the desired media.

---

[7] Romana Capek-Habeković and Sandra Palaich, *Parola a te!* (Boston: Heinle Cengage Learning, 2009).

Audio and Video Materials

In addition to the previously cited textbook, students are also exposed to a variety of audio and video materials such as native-read texts followed by comprehension activities, textbook video components, and authentic audio and video materials available online. These resources vary from watching Italian television programs (news, debates, interviews, and different entertainment and educational programs), listening to Italian radio and watching excerpts from Italian films online, to viewing Italian films outside of class. Even silent video materials can be useful, such as live webcam feeds from different Italian cities showing the weather, the atmosphere in the streets, the way people dress, vehicles driven and store fronts; in short, the dynamics of everyday living. The purpose of these materials is to hone the students' aural comprehension skills and to motivate them to interpret visual imagery of the target culture. In this way, learners can improve their sociocultural competence by means of observation of interactions in the target culture and acquire knowledge of current events and their protagonists. These materials also provide stimuli for classroom debates and discussions, and thus help develop students' speaking proficiency. Audio and video tools also furnish topics for essays, which in turn foster the development of writing skills.

Issues and Concerns

One of the first concerns in a culture course taught in the target language is the issue of language learning vs. culture learning. These two dimensions of the learning process occur simultaneously and are very much interdependent, but there are also areas in which their development can be independent of each other. An area of culture learning independent of language learning is, for example, the students' willingness to open their minds to the other culture's values and attitudes, or their readiness to engage in a relationship between their own culture and the target culture. Every instructor should therefore make a determination as to the value placed on each of these two dimensions of learning and their role in the assessment process.

Another problem encountered by most instructors who teach upper level culture courses, as well as those who incorporate culture into elementary language curricula, is the fact that they are very difficult to evaluate. The achievement vs. proficiency testing dichotomy, which is easily applicable to language classes, is seemingly less clear here. If the teacher wants students to acquire a grammatical structure such as the *passato prossimo* for example, it is relatively easy to assess their performance through achievement or proficiency tests. They can test how well students have mastered the *passato prossimo* forms through various achievement tests, and how proficiently they use it in conversations and writing through proficiency testing. However, what instructors expect students to acquire in a culture course is not as easily measured.

Adding another dimension to the problem of assessment is the fact that instructors also deal with different media of content delivery and student output. In other words, they evaluate what students have learned, but also in what way they internalize this content and how they make it their own. In addition, when introducing certain cultural content in the classroom, the instructors must decide whether in their assessment they will concentrate on the entire content of the presented information, or only one particular aspect of it. For example, students watch a portion of Italian television news covering the death of internationally-known Italian tenor Luciano Pavarotti. The broadcaster talks at length about Pavarotti's life and when he became famous. He mentions the star's frequent performances in the United States and the operas for which he was best known. After pre-viewing activities in which students practice the essential vocabulary needed to understand the segment, and after watching the news, the instructor must decide whether assessment will focus on recalling the information from the segment in its entirety or partially, whether it will focus on the presenter's accent and manner of speaking, or whether it will focus on background imagery and cultural references present in the piece. The follow-up will also be fashioned depending on the skills practiced (i.e. aural comprehension vs. speaking or writing) and the format chosen (individual vs. pair/group work).

The challenges are, therefore, multifold. To resolve them instructors must decide whether they consider one aspect of evaluation more important than the other, or if they place equal pedagogical value on each component. However, the issue at hand is still how to bridge the gap between the cultural content acquired, which is difficult to measure or quantify, and the current assessment system at our disposal, which is anchored in numerical quantification.

Assessment of Cultural Proficiency

Given the multi-dimensional nature of a culture and language course, assessment must deal with multiple aspects of learning as well. If our goal is to help develop successful intercultural speakers, we must assess not only the abilities developed by the students, both linguistic and sociocultural, but also their attitudes.

There are several formats in place to test cultural proficiency. The following are adoptees from language assessment models: written tests, compositions, oral in-class presentations, individual and pair or group interviews with the instructor. Clearly, none of these are completely objective or comprehensive and they all carry their own innate limitations. Task-oriented projects and activities, as well as a combination of different examination formulas can serve as additional instruments of evaluation. Which of these mechanisms are selected in a particular situation would depend on the level of students' linguistic competency and on the specifics of the cultural information that the instructor wants the learners to process and retain. The decision should be made also with regard to the four linguistic skills acquired (listening, reading, speaking, and writing) and to the use of target language or English in the classroom and during evaluation. These are just a few issues that arise from the complex quandary of how to effectively test and evaluate cultural proficiency.

The decision on the testing format will also be conditioned by the specific medium used in the transmission of the cultural information For example, if students read an authentic newspaper article about the game of soccer in Italy, one of the possible models could be a multiple choice comprehension test. The test could be written either in English or in Italian and the learners could be asked to answer either in English or in Italian. It could focus solely on the cultural content of the piece, or the language of its delivery as well. This brings us to one of the principal dilemmas of testing for cultural proficiency: should the instructor place equal, less, or no value on the students' mastery of linguistic skills in expressing their knowledge and understanding of culture? We think a certain degree of language proficiency assessment needs to take part in the evaluation process, but should be secondary to the acquisition and adoption of cultural knowledge. Therefore, all the testing models in our case study are in the target language and require student output in the target language as well. Additionally, in order to objectively assess students' performance in an upper level culture course we found that a combination of several testing formats is paramount. However, the complexity of this issue requires further research and data.

One of the questions posed frequently in this particular context is: what constitutes a mistake in the evaluation of cultural proficiency? The logical answer seems to be that a mistake is the perpetuation of stereotypes and engaging in generalizations and simplifications. This determination can be made by each individual instructor. However, for the purpose of evaluation within this context, an instructor might characterize the following as deficient student performance: lack of understanding of the material, factual errors, failure to recognize relationships and draw conclusions, inability to draw meaningful comparisons with one's own culture, failure to engage in a relationship with the target culture, failure to observe a culture analytically, severe linguistic deficiencies affecting intercultural communication, and finally failure to comply with any of the class requirements. Some of these deficiencies are culture-general, while others are culture-specific. However, learners should never be penalized for expressing their own critical views of the target culture, as long as their opinions are anchored in facts and supported by valid arguments.

Proposed Models of Testing and Assessment

The following testing models are a result of classroom practice and experimentation, and thus should not be viewed as all-inclusive or exclusive. We found that the combination of these formats offers the most comprehensive evaluation platform, and that it addresses the need to assess sociocultural proficiency, as well as linguistic proficiency.

A. Reading Assignments

While students love audio and video materials, we find them to be slightly resistant when asked to read textual materials. This is due to the fact that such an endeavor is often time-consuming for students, because it requires the use of a dictionary, re-reading certain portions of the text, understanding idiomatic expressions, knowledge of various linguistic registers, interpretation of cultural and other references, as well as attempting to understand unfamiliar syntactic structures. Furthermore, reading of such texts requires background knowledge that many students lack. All of these elements can occasionally lead to students' frustration, and thus a loss of interest.

One way of mitigating this problem is to select interesting readings that deal with topics related to popular culture, are moderate in length and are age-appropriate for college students. Often times the instructors are able to select very interesting and engaging readings accessible online that can capture the students' attention. Another way to ensure that the students complete the reading assignments prior to coming to class is to place adequate emphasis on classroom participation and preparation for class by tying it to a good portion of their overall course grade. In an upper level culture course, it is recommended that the students complete the reading assignments at home so that class time can be utilized for accompanying activities. By experimenting with different formats, we found that frequently administered pop quizzes are the most effective assessment tool for this particular aspect of the course. The pop quiz is a very simple multiple choice test given to the class unannounced. The shortcoming of this testing method is the fact that it only requires the learners to reproduce the facts from the readings, and does not evaluate their deeper understanding of the textual content.

B. Class Blog

In order to ensure that the students have indeed done their reading before the class session, we require them to post their reactions to the reading on the course web site in form of a blog. The comments must be posted prior to the class, as specified in the course requirements. The blog may consist of responses to questions posted by the instructor, as is the case in our course, or be completely free-style. We found that structured and guided posts work much better that free posts in that they allow the instructor to solicit reactions to specific and relevant aspects of the reading. In addition to verifying the students' completion of the reading assignment, the blog is a very useful tool for assessing the progression of their cultural awareness and the development of their analytical thinking. We often find posts that state "I didn't know that...," "I was surprised to learn that...," "I found it interesting that...," "I was shocked to learn that...," and similar reactions. All of these utterances indicate the growth of interest in the material, as well as the development of an affective relationship with it. We do not necessarily assess the linguistic quality of the post, because that would mean introducing a new variable into the evaluation and possibly curtail the freedom of students' expression and reactions. If the structural correctness of their language were graded, it may curb their desire to venture outside of their linguistic comfort zone and express their opinions and emotions in an immediate and natural way, which is one of the goals of the blog.

C. Written Assignments

Compositions are a very valuable format for assessing sociocultural competence in combination with linguistic proficiency. Both aspects are graded in compositions, and the weight of each component varies according to the specific needs of the individual instructor. In written assignments, students are able to show how they have processed and internalized the cultural content to which they were exposed, to express their opinions about it, and to draw comparisons between their own culture and a target culture. Student compositions enable the instructor to assess the level of learners' critical and analytical thinking in light of the newly-acquired cultural content and their intercultural awareness. Compositions also provide a means to assess other aspects of student writing, such as the organization and development of ideas, the richness of lexical elements, the correctness of syntactic structures and the overall fluidity of written expression. All of these aspects can be evaluated if the instructor finds them advantageous to student learning in an upper level culture course. The varying degrees of importance of these elements in their assessment can be determined by the instructor. However, a solid composition is usually well-organized in paragraphs, its ideas are presented and developed in a clear and logical fashion, it exhibits a depth of understanding and analysis of the subject matter, and its lexical and syntactic elements are adequately complex and appropriate for the level. As is desirable with all testing formats, a rubric should be given to students ahead of time so they can have a clear understanding of what is expected of them. Our proposed rubric is as follows: content and ideas 40%; organization and flow 10%; syntax 15%; lexis 20%; grammar 15%.

One of the great advantages of student papers as instruments of assessment is their endless versatility and flexibility. The topics of compositions, as well as their frequency, length and scholarly level, can be tailored to the needs of every individual instructor and course. Their complexity can also vary depending on whether they are written in the course of the semester or as the final essay at the end of the course. For example, one composition assignment might read as follows: "Based on what you have learned in the course, what is your analysis of the changes under way in today's Italian society?" Another assignment may say: "What are the differences between traditional images of Italy in the 20th-century works of literary fiction and cinema, compared to the reality of Italian society today?" Another possibility is: "Politics as a reflection of life in Italy." If these seem too ambitious for the level of student preparation, they may be adjusted to read: "What are some of the economic and social differences between northern regions, such as Lombardy and Piedmont, in relation to some of the southern and insular regions, such as Calabria, Sicily and Sardinia?" Or simply: "Is there such a thing as the *Italian cuisine*?" or "The Italian youth: challenges, opportunities, comparisons." The possibilities are indeed endless, but we would like to offer one simple idea: it might be very interesting to assign a composition at the very beginning of the course to establish the students' preexisting knowledge, views and perceptions of various aspects of Italian life and later repeat a similar assignment at the end of the semester. This would offer a snapshot of students' perception and understanding of the target culture at the beginning of the instruction, and provide a valuable insight into the progression of their learning. This tool might also prove valuable in tailoring the course syllabus to reflect the needs of that particular group of students, their background knowledge and interests.

D. Task-based Assignments: Independent Research and Cultural Presentations

Another model of assessment of students' acquisition of a particular aspect of culture are task-based assignments presented in class as oral reports. Learners can use any Italian resource they find appropriate and applicable to their choice of topic and talk freely about their findings. However, they could be asked to actively use multi-media materials in their presentations, such as the internet, or audio and video content. In reality, the vast majority of learners chose to peruse the internet in search of cultural information. The value of this model lies in the fact that students explore their own interests in researching the topic of their report, that they deal with authentic materials written or spoken in contemporary Italian, and that they are required to deliver it to their classmates in a clear and understandable fashion. Some instructors may prefer that student reports be presented in English, with the focus solely on the cultural information and intercultural references. We favor the former solution, as it enables us to evaluate linguistic competence as well. Smaller-scale independent research can also be used to provide background information for small-group discussions in which students will compare their findings and discuss their meaning. This enables the instructor to evaluate not only the quality and depth of the research, but also the students' speaking skills.

A successful cultural presentation is visually interesting and engaging, and goes beyond mere reproduction of the facts obtained. The student engages in an active relationship with the material, proposes opinions, analyzes and assesses the material, and exhibits a clarity of language necessary for full comprehension by his or her classmates. The suggested grading rubric is the following: mastery of the material 40%; organization and flow of information 10%; visual appeal 10%; lexis 20%; grammar and syntax 20%.

E. Class Participation

Class participation is a wide category that covers a variety of aspects of the learning process. In this context, it refers mainly to the level of student participation in the class, which will largely depend on several factors: their preparation for class in the form of reading of the assigned material, their completion of written and task-based homework assignments, and their willingness to actively participate in classroom discussions and debates. It is our opinion that oral expression in the classroom should remain as free and unencumbered as possible. Most students already experience elevated levels of anxiety when speaking in a foreign language with their classmates and even more so when speaking to the instructor, or in front of the whole class. It is therefore advisable to place only moderate importance on linguistic correctness when evaluating classroom participation. Students should be encouraged to speak liberally and without restraint, to express themselves as they see fit, and they usually do so if they know that they will not be continually corrected while speaking.

Class discussions and debates occur mostly in pairs and small groups. This is the ideal format for accomplishing meaningful and lively conversation, with the instructor in the role of an unobtrusive moderator. The instructor makes note of the content of student conversations, occasionally prompts them to think in this or that direction, encourages drawing of intercultural comparisons, solicits differing opinions and stimulates meaningful debates. We consider this an invaluable aspect of a culture course, in that it enables the instructor to carefully monitor the students' progression and their understanding of the material, as well as provide valuable personal input.

Good class participation therefore implies that students are able to conduct a dialogue with their classmates, that they are able to express their ideas and opinions with sufficient clarity and articulation, that their opinions are logical and grounded in facts, that they show mastery of the material presented in class and they are conversing in a respectful manner. Participation should be graded in a clear and transparent manner, just like any other testing format, even though its evaluation places higher demands on the sensibilities of the instructor. However, it may be useful to consider these guidelines: 90-100% student is always prepared for class, actively participates in small-group discussions, frequently volunteers, uses only Italian in communication with the instructor and his or her peers; 80-89% student is mostly prepared for class, but seldom volunteers, participates in small-group activities in a slightly more passive manner, occasionally resorts to the use of English; 70-79% student frequently unprepared for class, seldom volunteers, is mostly passive in small-group activities, frequently resorts to the use of English; 60-69% student is almost never prepared for class, is passive in small-group activities, frequently uses English and never volunteers.

Numerical Grading

All of the earlier mentioned models offer solutions and ideas for a meaningful and fair assessment of students' performance in a culture course. However, the final outcome of assessment must be a numerical value. How do we put a number on students' cultural competence?

We believe that this can be accomplished through a combination of the suggested models. They represent a blend of objective and subjective modes of assessment, which, when put together, offer an acceptable solution for the dilemma of grading. Pop quizzes, for instance, are a very objective model of evaluation, which provides immediate feedback to students who can then adjust their engagement in the class—as well as possibly their expectations. Other modes of assessment offer opportunities for creative expression and thoughtful demonstration of knowledge. They are evaluated in a more subjective manner and depend on the predisposition and inclination of the individual instructor. We find that students appreciate a variety in grading methods and that this may result in a more positive attitude toward the course.

With all this in mind, we find that the following grade break-down represents a fair assessment of all aspects of the course: classroom participation 30%; pop quizzes 10%; class blog 5%; written papers 30%; cultural presentation 10%; final essay 15%.

Conclusion

Creating an objective and comprehensive model for the assessment of learners' cultural proficiency poses multifold challenges, from purely technical, to pedagogical and methodological. On the other hand, it is possible to compensate for the relative shortcomings of individual assessment models by combining them with various other evaluation formats. The cumulative value of diverse formats of evaluation of cultural proficiency is an essential tool which the instructor can use to verify the learners' understanding of cultural information, their progress in acquiring intercultural awareness, as well as the linguistic output produced in the process. Going back to achievement vs. proficiency testing, we can conclude that even in a culture course, these models can indeed be applied in a somewhat modified form. Achievement assessment can be understood to refer to simple blog posts and pop quizzes, and can be used to closely monitor the acquisition of individual content units on a basic level. Proficiency assessment, on the other hand, can apply to the evaluation of written assignments and in-class cultural presentations, or areas where students are required to show a deeper understanding of the material, its synthesis, internalization and treatment. Through these assignments students can demonstrate their understanding of the historical, geographical, socio-economic, demographic and linguistic diversity present in Italy today and the reflection of that diversity in everyday life. If the goals of the course are achieved, the students will be able to form affective relationships with the target culture, develop an increased awareness of what constitutes a culture and draw comparisons with their own culture. They will be able to replace simplifications, generalizations and stereotyping with informed opinions about Italy based on the knowledge acquired in class and through their own independent research. This is what we understand by cultural proficiency in the context of the course presented.

UNIVERSITY OF MICHIGAN ANN ARBOR, USA

APPENDIX

IT 275:
STUDIES IN CONTEMPORARY ITALIAN CULTURE
Syllabus Fall 2008

Instructor: **Sandra Palaich**
Section: **001**
Office: **MLB 4044 (phone 647-9804)**
Days/Time: **TTh 11:30-1:00**
Office hours: **MF 10:00-11:00, TTh 10:00-10:30**
Room: **4153 USB**
E-mail: **spalaich@umich.edu**

COURSE DESCRIPTION AND OBJECTIVES: This course is content-based and its purpose is to deepen the students' understanding and knowledge of the Italian culture. Readings and class discussions will cover a wide array of topics on numerous aspects of Italian life: from geography, history, arts and music, to sports, entertainment, media, politics and economy. The course will concentrate on contemporary aspects of Italian life. Readings will be followed by numerous communicative activities, and a strong web component is introduced to foster independent research as well as comprehension of various authentic audio, visual and textual materials. The grade will be based on active class participation, several short papers, a presentation and a final essay.

REQUIRED TEXTS: *Parola a te!* by Romana Capek-Habekovic and Sandra Palaich, Heinle Cengage Learning, 2009.

REQUIRED MATERIALS:	A good Italian-English/English-Italian and Italian-Italian dictionary. A recommended on-line resource is www.garzantilinguistica.it.
SUGGESTED RESOURCES:	Book companion web site: www.academic.cengage.com/italian/parola Sandra Palaich's web site: http://sitemaker.umich.edu/palaich

LANGUAGE RESOURCE CENTER

The Language Resource Center (LRC), located on the second floor of MLB, is a facility you can use to do research, homework assignments and create presentations. The hours of LRC are as follows:

Monday-Thursday	8:30 a.m. to 10:00 p.m.
Friday	8:30 a.m. to 5:00 p.m.
Saturday	CLOSED
Sunday	12:30 to 10:00 p.m.

Grading

In order to pass this course, students will be required to obtain a **minimum of C-**. The course grade is calculated as follows:

Class Participation	45%	30% preparation for class, completion of assignments, active participation in all class activities, and regular attendance. 10% pop quizzes, 5% class blogs.
Papers	30%	There will be three 500-word papers.
Presentation	10%	One 10-minute presentation on one of the topics from the Italian culture studied in class.
Final Essay	15%	A final 1000-word essay.

Participation

A thorough preparation for class and active participation in class activities and discussions are **paramount**, as well as completed homework assignments and regular attendance. Contribution to the class blog will also be required on a regular basis. There will be several pop quizzes to check the preparation of the material.

Attendance

Attendance in class is required. If you are not in class you cannot participate, and therefore you will be unable to attain the course's objective. You are allowed **two unexcused** absences in the semester. Every absence beyond that will lower your participation grade by four points. With 10 unexcused absences (37% of class sessions) the student will automatically fail the course. Excused absences are those due to a documented illness (UHM notes only), death in the family and official religious holidays listed on http://www.provost.umich.edu/calendar/religious_holidays_07-08.html. Family vacations or events and job interviews are NOT considered excused absences. If you anticipate missing class for observance of religious holidays, inform your instructor ahead of time and remember that you are still responsible for learning the material acquired in class on that day, and for a timely turn-in of any material due.

Presentation

Each student will prepare and deliver a cultural presentation on a topic chosen together with the instructor. An expansion of any cultural topic studied in class is welcome, but must be run by the instructor first. The presentation must be approximately 10 minutes long. Incorporating visuals is strongly encouraged. Students will be able to use the Internet for their presentation and are encouraged to do so. Absolutely no notes are allowed. At the end of the presentation, the presenter will verify class comprehension by asking at least three questions about the content of the presentation.

What is graded: the content of the presentation, its visual appeal and organization, as well as the correctness of grammar, vocabulary and pronunciation. It is suggested that the presentation be thoroughly rehearsed before hand to ensure proper timing. Students are strongly discouraged from writing their presentation out in English and then translating it in Italian. Research for the presentation must be done in Italian to ensure that correct terminology is used. Any search engine will do; www.yahoo.it or www.google.it are good places to start. Your textbook will have many additional resources.

Papers

There will be three papers in the course of the semester related to the material covered in class. Each paper must be deposited on Ctools (under Assignments) by 5 pm on the day it is due. There will be a 10-point deduction for late turn-ins. The compositions must contain at least 500 words, be double-spaced with one-inch margins and written in Times New Roman 12 font. The instructor will grade it using the grading chart attached to this syllabus.

You may receive help on writing assignments for this class provided you abide by the following conditions:

- All sources (bibliographical, Internet or other) must be cited at the end of each writing assignment.
- It is **unacceptable** to ask someone else to **translate**, **write** or **edit** any parts of your assignment.
- It is **unacceptable to use any computer program that translates sentences from English into Italian.**
- It is **acceptable** to have someone in your same class give you feedback on your paper. When your editor is a peer at the same level, he/she may provide his/her opinions. It is your responsibility to decide whether you want to accept your editor's feedback or not.
- It is **acceptable** to use an online dictionary to look up individual words.

Violations to these guidelines will be considered cheating as outlined by the Code of Academic Conduct and will be reported to the Office for Student Academic Affairs.

Final Essay

The topic for the final essay will be chosen at the end of the semester. It may require independent research. The format will be the same as the other papers, but the length must be 1000 words.

CODE OF ACADEMIC CONDUCT

Students suspected of cheating, plagiarism, or aiding others in dishonest academic behavior will be brought before the Academic Judiciary Committee. You are responsible for reading and understanding the Code of Academic Conduct (see pg. 25 of the 1995-6 University of Michigan Bulletin). If your instructor believes that academic dishonesty may have taken place, he or she will present the evidence to the coordinator, who will inform the Academic Judiciary. Examples of academic dishonesty include, but are not limited to, plagiarism, cheating, and aiding and abetting dishonesty. An example of plagiarism would be to submit a composition which in part or in whole is not entirely the student's own work without attributing the source. Cheating includes allowing another person, such as tutor or friend, to help with or to do one's work and to submit the work under one's own name.

GRADING SCALE

A+ = 98-100
A = 93-97
A- = 90-92
B+ = 88-89
B = 83-87
B- = 80-82
C+ = 78-79
C = 73-77
C- = 70-72
D+ = 68-69
D = 63-67
D- = 60-62
E = 59--

PROGRAM

Date	Class Content	Important Dates
Sept. 2	Introduzione al corso. Lettura del sillabo. Discussione sul concetto di cultura.	
4	**Capitolo 1**: Il Piemonte. Profilo della regione.	
9	Città, cittadine e paesi: Torino. Asti.	
11	Alcuni piemontesi famosi: Primo Levi. Giovanni Agnelli.	
16	**Capitolo 2**: La Lombardia. Profilo della regione.	**Consegna primo saggio.**
18	Città, cittadine e paesi: Milano. Monza.	
23	Alcuni lombardi famosi: Dario Fo. Oliviero Toscani.	
25	Silvio Berlusconi. Sulla strada.	
30	**Capitolo 3**: Il Veneto. Profilo della regione.	
Oct. 2	Città, cittadine e paesi: Venezia. Padova.	
7	Alcuni veneti famosi: Marco Polo. Giacomo Casanova.	
9	Roberto Baggio. Sulla strada.	
14	**Capitolo 4**: L'Emilia-Romagna. Profilo della regione.	**Consegna secondo saggio.**
16	Città, cittadine e paesi: Bologna. Rimini.	
28	Parma. Alcuni emiliani e romagnoli famosi: Giuseppe Verdi. Umberto Eco.	
30	Federico Fellini. Sulla strada.	
Nov. 4	**Capitolo 5**: La Toscana. Profilo della regione.	
6	Città, cittadine e paesi: Firenze. Siena.	
11	Alcuni toscani famosi: Oriana Fallaci. Roberto Benigni.	
13	**Capitolo 6**: La Liguria. Profilo della regione.	
18	Città, cittadine e paesi: Genova. Sanremo.	**Consegna terzo saggio.**
20	Alcuni liguri famosi: Cristoforo Colombo. Renzo Piano.	
25	Niccolò Paganini. Sulla strada.	
Dec. 2	Presentazioni.	**Presentazioni.**
4	Presentazioni.	**Presentazioni.**
9	Presentazioni.	**Presentazioni.**
FINAL ESSAY DUE ON TUESDAY, DECEMBER 11TH, BY 5:00 PM ON CTOOLS		

CLASS PARTICIPATION EVALUATION CRITERIA

90-100% The "A" student:

1. Initiates interaction and participates actively in discussions and group activities.
2. Only uses Italian for asking/answering questions, in class discussions and group activities.
3. Is always prepared, answers readily when called upon.
4. Frequently elaborates on answers using appropriate vocabulary and structures and is always easily comprehensible to other students and instructor.

80-89% The "B" student:

1. Participates actively in group activities but passively in discussions.
2. Occasionally resorts to use of English (i.e. vocabulary) but only uses Italian for asking/answering questions, in group activities and class discussions.
3. Is almost always prepared, usually answers when called upon.
4. Elaborates somewhat on answers, uses mostly appropriate vocabulary and structures, and is mostly comprehensible to other students and instructor.

70-79% The "C" student:

1. Participates more passively then actively in group activities and discussions.
2. Occasionally resorts to use of English (i.e. vocabulary) and/or does not always ask questions in Italian.
3. Is not always fully prepared, sometimes unable to answer.
4. Some elaboration of answers with an attempt to use vocabulary and structures but is sometimes not comprehensible to other students and instructor.

60-69% The "D" student:

1. Rarely participates in group activities and class discussions and generally does not cooperate in class activities.
2. Speaks English in discussions and small group activities.
3. Lacks adequate preparation and has difficulty answering questions.
4. Minimal or no elaboration of answers with little attempt to use vocabulary and structures, and is not comprehensible to other students and instructors.

0-59% The "E" student:

1. Frequently absent from class and/or
2. Fails to comply with the above participation requirements.

WORKSHEET FOR EVALUATION OF COMPOSITIONS

CATEGORY	DESCRIPTION	POINTS
CONTENT	Well thought-out ideas, substantiated and appropriate to assignment.	40-30
	Limited to adequate ideas, but not developed enough, lacking supporting facts, repetitions may be present.	29-15
	Minimal ideas lacking substance, superficial and undeveloped.	14-10
	Incoherent or off target.	9-0
	MAX	**40**
ORGANIZATION	Well-organized paragraphs, convincing, easy to follow.	10-5
	Good to fair evidence of structuring of paragraphs.	4-1
	No evidence of planning in structure of paragraphs.	0
	MAX	**10**
STYLE/SYNTAX	Well-developed sentence structure, sentences varied, well connected and flowing naturally, aptly incorporated into the whole.	15-10
	Very basic sentence structure, unnatural sound to them, abrupt passages between sentences.	9-5
	Sentences translated verbatim from English, the original text showing through, impeded comprehensibility.	4-1
	Garbled syntax.	0
	MAX	**15**

VOCABULARY	Broad vocabulary, precise and effective word use and choice. Mastery of words learned in class.	20-15
	Erroneous word use or choice leads to confused meaning, somewhat limited use of vocabulary studied in class.	14-10
	Very basic, inadequate, repetitive, contains incorrect or invented words.	9-5
	Unintelligible vocabulary, words and expressions left in English.	4-0
	MAX	**20**
GRAMMAR	Few errors overall, mostly minor errors present, broad use of grammar studied, work well-edited for grammatical accuracy.	15-10
	A few gross mistakes (verb forms and tenses, agreement) and a reasonable number of minor mistakes (prepositions, spelling, gender); evidence of partial use of grammar studied, but no incomprehensible parts.	9-5
	Gross mistakes in basic grammatical structures (verb forms and tenses, auxiliaries, subject/verb agreement), incomprehensible sentence parts; poor use of grammar studied.	4-1
	No evidence of grammatical structures, unintelligible.	0
	MAX	**15**
	TOTAL	**100**

Naming your compositions:
last name. composition number   smith.I.doc

Accents (for all vowels):
Grave accent (è) = press ctrl and ` (accent under ~) at the same time, release, type the vowel; acute accent (é) = press ctrl and '(apostrophe) at the same time, release, type the vowel.

CHAPTER EIGHTEEN

CULTURAL ACQUISITION AND LANGUAGE LEARNING: THE IVC, *CHIAVI DI LETTURA* PROJECT

CHRISTINE RISTAINO
AND JUDITH RAGGI-MOORE

In the increasingly globalized community in which we live, the United States is losing ground in comparison to other countries. Thomas L. Friedman, in his article "It's a Flat World, After All" describes globalization in terms of free access to and exchange of information. According to Friedman, nations much smaller than the U.S., with more limited resources, are gaining economic power and prestige through effective use of digital media and technology. Friedman states that the most exciting aspect of globalization involves "the fact that we are now in the process of connecting all the knowledge pools in the world together…."[1] Friedman describes, however, a nagging concern about America's place within the global market. He quotes Bill Gates,

> When I compare our high schools to what I see when I'm traveling abroad, I am terrified for our workforce of tomorrow. In the international competition to have the biggest and best supply of knowledge workers, America is falling behind.[2]

Yet, why is this the case? The recent release of findings by a committee commissioned through the *Modern Languages Association* in 2004, in response to what it defines as a language crisis resulting from 9/11, summarizes how, despite our leading role in the electronic age, our

---

[1] Thomas L. Friedman, "It's a Flat World, After All," *New York Times*, April 3, 2005.

[2] Ibid.

teaching strategies fail to communicate cultural understanding or provide us with skills necessary to correctly interpret information we are exposed to on a regular basis:

> "The need to understand other cultures and languages" was identified by Daniel Yankelovich as one of five imperative needs to which higher education must respond in the next ten years if it is to remain relevant.... Senator Daniel Akaka made a similar point: "Americans need to be open to the world; we need to be able to see the world through the eyes of others if we are going to understand how to resolve the complex problems we face."[3]

The report declares that rather than following the traditional two-tier college tracks, which divide language and literature into lower and upper levels of language acquisition, language departments must change their structure to promote the learning of culture, language, and literature together. The report states,

> Replacing the two-tiered language-literature structure with a broader and more coherent curriculum in which language, culture, and literature are taught as a continuous whole, supported by alliances with other departments and expressed through interdisciplinary courses, will reinvigorate language departments as valuable academic units central to the humanities and to the missions of institutions of higher learning.[4]

Although this report was issued in May 2007 to address growing concerns about language teaching in America, at Emory University many language programs are already accomplishing the committee's recommendations with very positive results. Because of initiatives at the Emory College Language Center combined with a university mission statement that encourages interdisciplinary and intercultural collaboration, the university Italian Studies Program has developed a dynamic and innovative interdisciplinary textbook and pedagogy, catching the attention of educators and students alike with its novel, creative, and highly effective method. Use of the textbook and methodology for the past three years has been so successful on an academic level that the university, through its Office of Technology Transfer, has released it for purchase to colleges and high schools throughout the United States.

---

[3] Report from the MLA Ad Hoc Committee on Foreign Languages, 2007, "Foreign Languages and Higher Education: New Structures for a Changed World," Modern Languages Association, http://www.mla.org/flreport.

[4] Ibid.

Figure 18-1.Textbook cover.

The basic premise of the IVC (Italian Virtual Class), *Chiavi di Lettura* method is to allow Italians to describe Italy and Italian culture and to bring their perspectives, culturally intact via internet and web technology, to Emory students so that they may learn the language and culture of Italy in an authentic and natural setting.

Inspired by the *CULTURA*[5] Project, which facilitates active web-based conversational exchanges between students of two partner schools (one abroad and one in the United States) to explore language through in-depth discussions of cultural topics, from the very first day of class students of the Italian Virtual Class are asked to research and compare regional differences and similarities and given the opportunity to see into the lives and professions of Italians from every region, and every walk of life. In each class they discover the profound influence of Italian culture—its history, its literature, its artistic expression—as well as how those influences play a role in the Italy of today.

Over the course of the academic year, IVC, *Chiavi di Lettura* students discuss literature, religion, immigration, Italian politics, art, architecture,

---

[5] To learn more about this innovative project, please visit its website: http://cultura.mit.edu.

economic conditions and concerns, history, regional traditions, and a number of other interdisciplinary subjects, discovering how these topics relate to the realities projected by Italians from every region as well as numerous professions, social and economic backgrounds, and belief systems. Students have the opportunity to compare regional influences, values, histories and preferences and contrast them with their own belief systems and ideas. From the very first day, each class is taught only in Italian and the students engaged in this advanced cultural exploration are not upper level Italian students. Instead, they are first-year students who have become so taken with the idea of cultural acquisition that language acquisition develops more naturally than it could using more traditional second language acquisition (L2) teaching methods, for it is a result of a practical need for language skills, the same practical need that occurs in a live, full-immersion experience when a study abroad student steps off the plane in a new country. In the IVC, *Chiavi di Lettura* class, students need language in order to negotiate the cultural tasks they have been charged with investigating. They rise to the challenge of creating their own continuous anthology of Italian culture using the highly interactive medium of the internet, which, as a result of its digital format, allows them to overcome language obstacles.

Italian Studies at Emory University has devised a teaching method that utilizes inductive teaching strategies and the combination of a written and on-line interdisciplinary textbook aimed at teaching students how to learn grammatical structures and interpret the cultural information embedded in these structures. The IVC, *Chiavi di lettura* method is presented to students through the window of an existing study abroad program at Emory. Video clips, photographs, paintings, music, literary texts, film, and interviews meaningfully bring the culture and language to students.

Within any academic day, students move through classes that make age-appropriate demands on them, and it would therefore be academically counterproductive to present foreign languages in an oversimplified elementary cultural context, signaling to students that the teaching of foreign languages, and even more dangerously, the teaching of foreign cultures, is not a rigorous intellectual endeavor. Educators and publishers have been equally responsible for allowing this trivialization to persist. Much like the linguistic and cultural negotiations a student must undertake when arriving in a foreign country, the Italian Virtual Class method teaches within a virtually presented authentic world, fully immersing students in Italian language and culture from day one.

The IVC, *Chiavi di lettura* project comes at a time when there is an increased national emphasis on curriculum structure, teaching methodologies, and learning environments and their relation to real-world applications. The American Council on the Teaching of Foreign Languages states that the elements employed to teach language classes should "enable the student of languages to participate in multilingual *communities* at home and around the world in a variety of contexts and in culturally appropriate ways"[6] and the Italian Virtual Class, *Chiavi di lettura* method accomplishes this goal on many levels.

The fives Cs that make up the American Council on the Teaching of Foreign Language's recommendations (Communication, Cultures, Connections, Comparisons, and Communities) play a critical role in the method's ability to teach language and culture as an indivisible unit. The IVC, *Chiavi di lettura* program provides a communicative environment, while at the same time gives students the tools to build the language skills necessary to achieve ACTFL proficiency goals at every level. The Council's assertion that communication should be at the heart of second language study[7] reminds us of the singular most important motivation for L2 acquisition.

In an article titled "Inductive Teaching and Learning Methods," Michael J. Prince and Richard M. Felder discuss first language acquisition and the manner in which children first attain meaning from language:

> In social constructivism, whose principal proponent is Vygotsky, language and interactions with others—family, peers, teachers—play a primary role in the construction of meaning from experience. Meaning is not simply constructed, it is co-constructed.[8]

The IVC, *Chiavi di lettura* method utilizes the concept of co-construction in every activity and lesson. The instructor must act as facilitator, directing students in their quest for meaning and working with students to co-construct meaning in a natural, authentic manner.

The Council asserts that students "…cannot truly master the language until they have also mastered the cultural contexts in which the language

[6] Council on the Teaching of Foreign Languages, "Standards for Foreign Language Learning: Executive Summary, 1996," American Council on the Teaching of Foreign Languages, Inc., http://www.actfl.org/i4a/pages/index.cfm?pageid=3324.
[7] Ibid.
[8] Richard M. Felder and Michael J. Prince, "Inductive Teaching and Learning Methods: Definitions, Comparisons, and Research Bases," *Journal of Engineering Education* 95, no. 2 (2006): 123-38.

occurs."[9] Through co-construction and as a result of the partnership for meaning established between teacher and student, the context of the IVC method becomes a key element, for it establishes a baseline from which meaning is constructed. In the IVC package, the overall context is modeled on a real and virtual study abroad trip, supplemented by a number of student and faculty authored and edited videos. Each video series is regionally based and includes interviews with native speakers in natural settings using authentic language. The textbook consists of authentic cultural texts in which content is not simplified or sacrificed to student linguistic competence.

All of the internet research and the visual component of the content are essential parts of the continuous cultural track. Art, art history, history, music, folklore and traditions featured in the curriculum are period and region specific and support this cultural track. Students and faculty work together to co-construct meaning as well as to meaningfully connect the cultural elements of this context to students' growing cultural knowledge. Because the emphasis is on cultural acquisition rather than on grammar, students do not study grammar outside of its cultural context and thus, the cultural element and the grammar remain connected and are learned as a unit.

Students are also given the opportunity to create *comparisons* and *connections* between their own culture and the Italian culture, between the various representatives from each of the twenty regions of Italy, as well as between Italian as a discipline and the disciplines that Italy's rich past has inspired. According to the Council on the Teaching of Foreign Languages, "Learning languages provides *connections* to additional bodies of knowledge that may be unavailable to the monolingual English speaker."[10] The program's interdisciplinary focus on literature, art, architecture, history, political science, theater, opera and religion, allows students to make comparisons across disciplines, drawing on the observations of their peers and their interactions with Italians on the virtual screen to aid them in forging these new connections.

---

[9] Council on the Teaching of Foreign Languages, "Standards for Foreign Language Learning: Executive Summary, 1996" American Council on the Teaching of Foreign Languages, Inc., http://www.actfl.org/i4a/pages/index.cfm?pageid=3324.

[10] Ibid.

LETTURA: Selinunte: L'asta del pesce.

Da secoli Selinunte è un villaggio di pescatori. La pesca è la principale risorsa della zona. Tutte le notti, ci sono i pescatori nel mare con le loro piccole barche e le loro reti. Loro pescano tutta la notte. La mattina presto ecco che i pazienti pescatori di Selinunte sono nuovamente al porto con il loro pesce. Quasi tutte le mattine c'è del pesce fresco da comprare. Come da tradizione, anche oggi l'asta del pesce è un evento caratteristico del paese di Selinunte. Il pesce è in piccole cassette di legno che tutti possono osservare. L'atmosfera dell'asta è caotica ma ha un rituale antico molto preciso. La compravendita del pesce è basata su gesti e sguardi veloci e quasi invisibili. Il battitore scandisce i prezzi, ed i pescatori hanno varie offerte dalle persone presenti. L'offerta più alta diventa il costo finale della cassetta di pesce. Questo è il guadagno giornaliero di un pescatore. Non è molto, vero? Ecco perché il lavoro dei pescatori è tanto arduo e loro non sono mai ricchi! Durante l'asta ci sono decine di cassette di pesce da vendere, ma in meno di un'ora non c'è più pesce! Il pesce adesso è nella cucina delle case e dei ristoranti di Selinunte.

Uno degli studenti universitari, Colin, vuole fare un'esperienza personale e partecipa alla negoziazione per una cassetta di gamberi abbastanza grossi. Colin è un ragazzo coraggioso e intraprendente. Quando il battitore dell'asta annuncia il prezzo iniziale, Colin alza la sua mano. Poi un'altra persona alza la mano ed allora il battitore alza il prezzo della cassetta. Colin insiste ed alla fine vince lui! Per cena questa sera Colin mangia del buon pesce fresco con i suoi amici! I gamberi freschi pescati nei mari siciliani sono proprio squisiti!

Table 18-1. An authentic cultural reading from the *Italian Virtual Class* first semester textbook discussing the city of Selinunte's fish auction.

Although Communication, Cultures, Connections, Comparisons, and Communities act as the glue that keeps the culture and language from breaking apart during language acquisition in the IVC, *Chiavi di lettura* method, constructivist strategies are the instruments incorporated to help students build upwards and outwards from the body of linguistic knowledge that they already have. As the Italian Studies faculty has adopted more of a facilitator role in the classroom, Italian instruction at Emory has successfully become learner or student-centered. In their article, Prince and Felder define this approach as promoting an environment that imposes more responsibility on students for their own learning than did the traditional, deductive approaches. These inductive strategies are what Prince and Felder call "constructivist" methods, where students learn class materials by constructing tables, charts, or paradigms that work within their own cognitive framework rather than memorizing those created by an author or professor. In this manner, students are able to internalize the material and make it their own, as opposed to simply memorizing it for the test.

According to J. Biggs, and in alignment with constructivist pedagogy, there are four important principles of effective teaching: 1) Students need to learn information in a meaningful way—in other words, in context and somehow relating to their own lives. 2) Material should be organized in a spiral manner, rather than in a linear one, that is, students should be asked to revisit or return to critical concepts often in order to glean a higher level of understanding from the material with each visit. 3) Students should be asked to fill in gaps in the material and extrapolate rules from information provided in the textbook and by the instructor. In this manner, instructors make students independent rather than dependent on them and this strategy promotes self-learning. 4) Finally, collaborative and cooperative learning are essential tools that move students exponentially to new levels of understanding through discussion of the material with their peers.[11]

The IVC method combines listening, reading, writing, and speaking skills to accompany teaching instruction in and out of the classroom and the method fits into the four constructivist categories that Biggs describes. While constructivist methods have been used to teach languages in the past, the primacy of a continuous cultural presentation and of cultural acquisition over grammar acquisition makes the approach by Emory's Italian Studies program unique. Through tasks that involve the four language skills, the instructor of the Italian Virtual Class, *Chiavi di Lettura* method creates the scaffolding necessary for students to discover grammatical structures. The focus remains from start to finish, however, on culture and communication about this culture.

Cultural acquisition is about learning a language hermetically; that is, constantly revisiting and expanding one's own body of knowledge in order to accommodate and internalize new information in a natural manner. Since the methodology itself is free of language, and can be transposed to any other language or discipline, the potential for access and participation in this technology is unprecedented. IVC, *Chiavi di Lettura* authors are committed to educational reform within the United States and inspiring a more effective and powerful way to learn—one that makes the student self-sufficient and provides the learner with the tools to continue active inquiry outside the classroom.

Students of the IVC method are asked to classify and encode new information based on what they already know and all exercises, activities, interviews and readings refer in some manner to the overall context. These strategies allow students to link new information to information already

---

[11] J. Biggs, "Enhancing Teaching Through Constructive Alignment," *Higher Education* 32, no. 3 (1996): 347-64.

present in their cognitive structures. Using the bank of personal experience and academic knowledge that all students bring to class with them, the teacher and students work together to locate linguistic keys to new knowledge. Once these keys are in place, students continue to use the knowledge that they already have to forge new connections, coming to understand language in a very personal manner. Students consistently return to passages, recordings, and websites in order to deepen their knowledge and understanding of the language. Material is thus constantly recycled and expanded upon to permit review and re-entry, and with every re-read, students bring knowledge and tools that are different from those they brought to an earlier reading of the same passage, because they are culturally and linguistically more mature.

A guided inductive teaching strategy is employed at Emory University in order to teach Italian culture and, through culture, the Italian language. Students are first exposed to grammar structures passively. Target grammar structures are embedded in cultural readings and exercises prior to being introduced formally to students. In a more active phase, students are asked to identify and categorize structures in cultural readings. Students then work with the teacher to co-construct rules by creating their own paradigms. Once the students have grappled with the rule, produced it, and made it their own, they may talk about the details of the structure. Students solidify their skills with open-ended web research, readings, and exercises, and they negotiate all names and details about their new world in the target language.

Prepariamo i bagagli! Cosa conosci già sul contenuto della Lettura?
Inserisci subito tutto il tuo lavoro nel tuo I.V.C. Quaderno degli esercizi.

I.V.C.online	Sicilia	La Vita	Asta del pesce

Durante la cena, Orazio parla di una antica tradizione di Selinunte, l'asta del pesce. Tu ed i tuoi compagni di studio sapete che questo paese ha una lunga tradizione di pesca, e che molti selinuntini sono pescatori. Siete curiosi di osservare questo aspetto della loro vita e, la mattina dopo, voi vi svegliate molto presto! Alle 6:00 del mattino siete già al porticciolo di Selinunte. Alle 6:30, voi osservate i pescatori che rientrano dopo una notte di duro lavoro di pesca. Alle 6:45 si organizza l'asta del pesce. Alle 7:15 inizia l'asta e voi potete vedere come i pescatori vendono tutto il pesce che hanno pescato durante la notte.

1) Per conoscere meglio questo lavoro, tu fai domande ad uno dei pescatori. Lui ti descrive questa vecchia tradizione.
   a) Osserva attentamente il video sull'asta in: **I.V.C.online => La Vita**. Osserva attentamente come il battitore vende le cassette di pesce dei pescatori.
   b) Prepara una lista di parole utili per parlare della pesca, dei pescatori, e di questa vecchia tradizione. Prepara una lista di minimo venti parole ... usa la fantasia ed il tuo fedele dizionario!

2) Crea una sezione speciale in: **"il mio dizionario, capitolo III"** intitolata: "I mercati, le aste, i negozi... la compravendita".

Attenzione! Usa la fantasia ed il tuo dizionario, e poi impara questi vocaboli nuovi a memoria!

3) Leggi le seguenti domande, poi ascolta nuovamente il segmento video "Asta del pesce," ed infine rispondi alle domande con frasi intere.
   a) Cosa ha il battitore in mano?
   b) Quali sono i tre prezzi finali di vendita delle tre cassette che noi vediamo?
   c) Quali altri numeri che il battitore dice tu puoi riconoscere! Scrivili con parole.
   d) Come si chiama la moneta della compravendita? È l'euro?
   e) Ti piace comprare il tuo pesce all'asta dei pescatori o al supermercato? Perché?

Table 18-2. Students return to the topic of the auction with a new level of knowledge.

The text's spiral movement requires students to engage in a more profound reading and understanding of the material with each return visit. Furthermore, the constructivist techniques adopted by the IVC, *Chiavi di lettura* method provide students with the tools to engage the language in a natural manner, involving minimal student stress. Students are not required to understand everything they see, hear, or read right away. The method conditions them to search for linguistic keys or clues to aid them in their understanding. The teacher/student partnership in co-constructing patterns of meaning and a spiral movement through the text relieves students of the pressure they often feel to understand everything all at once. By the final visit, students will have a profound understanding of meaning, both linguistic and cultural, and the subtleties that accompany this meaning.

In ascolto #1: cosa ci raccontano i nostri amici siciliani?

I.V.C.online	Sicilia	Le Interviste	Orazio-domanda #3 Cristina-domanda #3

1) Vai alle risposte di Orazio e Cristina alla prima parte della domanda #3, il piatto preferito. Ascolta tante, tante, tante ... volte.
2) Leggi queste domande e poi ascolta le risposte di Orazio ancora una volta.
   a) Qual è il piatto regionale preferito di Orazio?
   b) Quale pesce è l'ingrediente principale?
   c) Orazio spiega il perché di questa preferenza; qual è la ragione?
   d) Qual è il piatto regionale preferito di Cristina?
3) Rispondi con frasi complete alle domande dell'esercizio #2.
4) Domande di curiosità culturali!

I.V.C.online	Sicilia	Curiosità	La cucina siciliana La gastronomia siciliana

Tramite I.V.C.online cerca informazioni sui piatti menzionati da Orazio e Cristina.
   a) Puoi trovare la ricetta del piatto preferito di Orazio?
   b) Puoi trovare delle ricette per i pesci preferiti di Cristina?
   c) Porta queste ricette in classe con fotografie dei piatti preparati

Asta del pesce, Selinunte. I famosi gamberi di Colin.

Table 18-3. Extension exercises after the fish auction reading, which include authentic interviews, individualized and personalized student web research, and real photos taken by students who visited the auction during their summer study in Italy.

There has been extensive research into the efficacy of constructivist methods, with a particular focus on inquiry learning, strategy training, lifelong learning, learning style knowledge, and the idea of a universal grammar base which learners may draw upon to hypothesize about language structures. There is also a compelling body of knowledge outlining the principles behind inductive learning, task-based learning, and communicative approaches. The most comprehensive source is Judith Shrum and Eileen Glisan's *Teacher's Handbook*, which outlines the history of language pedagogy to the present day.[12] Although research often focuses on various methods and how they effectively address listening, reading, writing, and speaking as well as the 5 Cs, the concept of cultural acquisition was coined by IVC textbook authors to express a learning technique that had not been addressed by the profession at that point and thus had no formal terminology.

With the Italian Virtual Class method, students work together to produce vocabulary lists, visual learning aids, paradigms, timelines, outlines, photographs, plays, descriptions, book covers, songs, poetry, short films, interview questions and interviews, and so on. Students are involved in all aspects of authorship of the IVC, *Chiavi di lettura* textbook and, since the text is a dynamic presence in the classroom, teachers are able to focus on student interests and thus make the material individually meaningful, using student homework and research in class to foster learning and growth.

At Emory University, the IVC, *Chiavi di lettura* method has been fully integrated into the Italian program's first year courses and it has been highly successful in the classroom. The method's success is supported by a study that compares the performance of students who studied with the IVC, *Chiavi di lettura* textbook to that of students from an equivalent program who studied using traditional methods. One year of testing showed that IVC students performed significantly better on a scale measuring the retention of grammatical structures and the acquisition of listening comprehension skills in the elementary Italian classroom.

Just as first language (L1) learners do not experience one skill in isolation, IVC, *Chiavi di lettura* students focus on the language as a hermeneutic unit rather than in isolated parts. Its spiral movement through a text, combined with inductive inquiry into linguistic structures (such as recognizing cognates, identifying and demystifying unfamiliar grammar, and utilizing familiar words to understand unfamiliar ones), teach students

[12] J.L. Shrum and E.W. Glisan, *Teacher's Handbook: Contextualized Language Instruction* (Boston: Heinle & Heinle, 2000).

valuable techniques for decoding a language and lead students naturally and independently to proficiency and communication. Furthermore, because the method is taught using the same empirical strategies often employed in science classes, students ultimately learn *how* to learn a language; they become less reliant on the teacher and more trusting of their own knowledge bank and skill sets to solve problems and decode language DNA. They realize just how skilled they are at interpreting the language puzzle. They acquire Italian in the same manner they did their first language—not as a series of individual grammar points or components to be memorized, but as a dynamic, living language born of necessity and curiosity. They learn that the study of another culture is not limited to the observation of a series of random episodes, but is the commitment to understanding its full breadth of development. They quickly acknowledge that the study of Italians and Italy today is infused with the riches of 3,000 years of cultural evolution.

The IVC, *Chiavi di lettura* method introduces students to reading, writing, listening, and speaking skills, but not in a vacuum. By accessing these language skills through their cultural context and in a united chorus of sounds, sights, and flavors, students learn Italian grammar with its cultural DNA[13] intact, providing for real communication abroad.

EMORY UNIVERSITY, USA

[13] A concept that first presented itself in Richard Dawkins discussion "Memes: the new replicators," from his book entitled *The Selfish Gene* (Oxford: Oxford University Press, 1989), 189-201.

CHAPTER NINETEEN

FROM THE PAST TO THE PRESENT: HISTORY OF THE ITALIAN CULTURE

NICLA RIVERSO

The course that I propose is an interdisciplinary survey of the Italian culture from the pre-Roman origins to the contemporary age, and aims at explaining the relevance of the Italian culture in the development of the Western Civilization. The course focuses on the study of the background of Italian culture in order to provide students with an understanding of the current values, traditions, behaviors and ideological points of view. Its basic task is to contextualize literary and artistic events in order to underline their influence and contribution to the evolution and transformation of the Italian culture. The course introduces literary and artistic works as a product of the historical, economic, social and political context.

The course objectives are:

- Develop a considerable insight into the history, literature and art of Italian culture
- Encourage a continuous exchange and interaction of discipline (history/literature/philosophy/art)
- Gain a more complete understanding of the various forms of cultural expression
- Ensure an awareness of Italian culture diversity based on the plurality of ethnic groups that entered Italy during different epochs
- Emphasize the importance of historical, political, religious and economic events and their impact on literary and artistic work.

The class is organized in order to:

- Engage in a cooperative learning
- Encourage debates and discussions
- Provide ability to communicate in written and spoken form effectively
- Enable to use the information for research and communication
- Encourage to use feedback to improve performance
- Provide a preparation for a further study

The discussion about the readings and other class material is conducted seminar-style with exchange of questions and explanations of the key events. The in-class discussions are complemented with individual and group activities. The individual activities encourage students to study and analyze independently the topics covered during the class and reflect on particular issues. The group activities help students to share their views with their peers. The group activities are based on activity sheets with some very open-ended questions regarding the instructor's lecture and the preparatory reading. The main points that arise through the group discussions can help to emphasize particular issues which may not have been featured, but are important to the subject.

Assessment is based on the following: class activities, quizzes, essays and final project. It is recommended for this course ongoing student assessment in order to identify effective teaching strategies and detect any particular problem regarding preparation or uncertainty of the main subject matter. The assessment occurs on two different levels. First, what the students are learning from the class activities (interactive lectures and discussions) is assessed and secondly, an assessment is done in order to determine which skills students are developing by working by themselves. The assessment is administrated in the form of quizzes, essays and final project. The quizzes are based on short in-class questions designed to test basic student comprehension of the materials presented. The essay assignments are designed to test for deeper comprehension and critical thinking. The final project is a collaborative research about a selected topic in which students integrate class material collected from lectures, readings and activities into a development of a research. Moreover, such project is geared towards the exchange of knowledge and expertise among the students. In addition, each group of students presents its final project to the class at the end of the quarter.

Students are also evaluated for the quality of their contribution and their overall commitment to class discussion and activities during a ten week quarter. Every topic needs to be contextualized in its particular timeframe. Use of audio-visual material and maps are encouraged (see the syllabus in the APPENDIX).

I outlined some of the most relevant historical, social, economic, religious and literary events that determined the development of the Italian culture through the ages. The class is based on the presentation of these events in order to explain how many factors influenced the process of the Italian civilization and how literary and artistic works are closely connected with the social and historical milieu in which they were produced.

Weeks 1, 2

Convention holds that the Middle Ages began in A.D. 476, when Romulus Augustulus, the last Emperor of the Western half of the Roman Empire was deposed. Odoacer, the chief of the barbarian soldiery that composed the Roman army in Italy, was responsible for this deposition. Odoacer had not intended to bring about the end of the Roman Empire: he thought that the Emperor of the Eastern half of the Empire would simply control the Western half as well. In fact, he sent the Imperial Standards of Romulus Augustulus to Constantinople, where Zeno was on the throne.

The transformation of Italy from a Roman civilization to a new one had begun several centuries before, through the invasion of German populations from North, the diffusion of Christian thought from the East, the weakening of Roman administration and academic systems, and through the emergence of cultural and linguistic substrates that had survived the pressure of Roman domination. Before the subjugation of Italy by Rome, the territory from the Alps to Sicily had been invaded by Indo-Europeans of two different branches. Prior to that, minor groups of pre-Indo-European comers such as the Ligures, the Asili, the Elimi, the Sicanians and the Camuni had arrived. As such, when the citizens of Rome proceeded to subjugate the rest of Italy piece by piece in order to protect themselves and acquire new lands, they were facing a number of different populations that spoke a range of different languages.

The Ligures, who were pre-Indo-Europeans, prevailed in the Western part of the Northern area; the Celts, who were Indo-Europeans that had arrived in Italy during the first half of the first millennium B.C. prevailed in the centre and Southeast of the same area; and the Venetians, who were Indo-Europeans that had come from the plains of Danube during the second millennium B.C., inhabited the Eastern part. The Etruscans, who were of unknown provenance, lived on the Peninsula, the tribes of the branch of Indo-Europeans generally known as Latino-Siculi lived in the Western and Southern regions; the Sabine and Umbrian tribes lived in the central and Southern regions and Greek colonies lined the shores of Sicily and Southern Italy. Although each of these groups spoke a different language and had their own ways of living, there were strong resemblances between the different languages and cultures.[1]

The Romans created a number of colonies in the more strategic and prosperous regions of Italy after having subjugated all of these groups. Each of these colonies was a city composed of citizens from Rome or the Latium, and had temples to Roman deities, baths, schools that taught Latin and classical literature, theatres, and other buildings for public performances in the style of Rome. From these colonies, Roman language, literature, religion, civil values and laws irradiated throughout the country and minor towns and villages, and large numbers of indigenous populations adopted the usages, language, ideas and the religion of the colonists. When the Empire began to decay, however public services no longer functioned well, local authorities went missing and were replaced by bishops, schools began to lack teachers so that young people could no longer learn to read and write, the classics were abandoned, Roman literature was forgotten and old ways of speaking re-emerged. Pre-Roman phonetics emerged from the uneducated populace and were applied to Latin words, pre-Roman words as well as new words introduced by German (mainly Lombard and Frankish) invaders found their way in the common language, and a simpler syntax ousted the complicated one of classical Latin. In Southern Italy, Greek heritage mingled with Latin in an oral language that was not supported by writing.

While the Church tried to sustain the use of Latin for its own needs throughout the first half of the Middle Ages, the inhabitants of different regions slowly developed an elaborate oral vernacular. This vernacular had some resemblance to Latin, in part because of the persistent prevailing of churchly language. The Church had still a prestigious position and influenced the cultural and social life of the peninsula.[2] Fragments of this

---

[1] An exhaustive enquiry on these languages was made by Vittore Pisani in *Le lingue dell'Italia antica oltre il latino* (Turin: Rosenberg and Sellier, 1966-2nd ed., 1951 first ed.). On the language of Etruscan, see Piero Bernardini Marzolla, *L'etrusco, una lingua ritrovata* (Milano: Mondatori, 1984); Alessandro Moranti, *Le ascendenze indoeuropee nella lingua etrusca* (Roma: Gruppo Archeologico Romano, voll. III, 1984-1985); G.Pugliese Caratelli, M.Pallottino and others, *Rasenta, storia e civiltà degli Etruschi* (Milano: Libri Scheinwiller, 1986).

[2] See Donald Logan, *A History of the Church in the Middle Ages* (London: New York: Routledge, 2002).

vernacular are still extant in notarial papers of the period. Evidence of its use in the 12th century, vernacular can be found in short narratives, poems and communal papers. During this period, the growth of workshops and commercial activities in the towns created a strong need for facts, deeds, and transactions to be recorded in this vernacular. As the need for literate people grew and the written language developed, Italian as an autonomous and written language was born.

Weeks 3, 4

The towns of Northern Italy and Tuscany attained great riches through commerce and industry in late Middle Ages. These riches afforded them the means to pay for good schools and teachers and to build monuments embellished by sculptures and pictures.

The court of Emperor Frederick II in Sicily and Naples was an exemplar of this splendor in Southern Italy and helped shape a new cultural life differentiated by local vernaculars and styles, but connected by the general effort of reviving the Latin language, and the remembrance of the ancient glory of Rome. The content of the poetical compositions of this age was supplied by French literary production that wandering minstrels had brought through the Alpine passes while journeying with merchants or with Norman soldiers looking for adventures in Southern Italy and Sicily. They had carried the songs of the Round Table and King Arthur, the adventures of Roland and other paladins of Charlemagne, the poetical recounting of the war of Troy and so on. These songs produced in French (or *langue d'oïl*) from a more developed literary tradition, stimulated the thinking of early Italian minstrels and cultivated people wishing to effect similar production in the vernacular languages of the Italian countries.

Some of the more important cultivated men of this era were Jacopo de Cessulis, Bonvesin da Riva, Albertano da Brescia, Jacopo da Varazze, Salimbene from Parma, Peter Cantinelli, Rolandino da Padova, Albertino Mussato, Richard from Saint Germain, Jamsilla, Saba Malaspina, Francis of Assisi, Uguccione da Lodi, Gerardo Patecchio, Peter de Bescapè, James of Verona and Jacopone da Todi.[3]

The development of Italian literature during the 12th and 13th centuries reached its highest point in the works by Dante Alighieri (*Vita*

[3] For more information on the early development of Italian literature before Dante Alighieri see Arturo Pompeati, *Storia della letteratura italiana* (Turin: U.T.E.T. 1958), 151-378.

nova, *Rime*, *Convivio*, *Comedia*). His treatise *De vulgari eloquentia*, in Latin, is a learned discussion of the vernacular languages used in Italy and of their characteristics and merits. The *Comedia*, written in the vernacular language of Florence, was a large poetical work that encompassed the whole of the Christian world view and showed, in its richness that the Florentine vernacular was a noble and satisfactory instrument for expressing and describing all sorts of topics and refined feelings, and for proclaiming religious, moral and patriotic ideals. This work was a linguistic triumph, which gave this vernacular a dignified place alongside the Frankish languages *oïl* and *oc* and the Latin used by monks, priests and notaries. Teachers in the schools of the more cultured towns now had a warranted lexicon and grammar worth teaching, and chroniclers in the service of republican governments or of kings and churchly authorities had a reliable instrument for recording facts, rules and admonitions.

During the 14th and 15th centuries the increased standard of living in Italian towns allowed people the wealth and leisure to learn to read and write. Guarino Guarini and Vittorino da Feltre were among the best scholars who became teachers in order to fulfill the educational needs of their contemporary society. Schools proliferated, teachers were easily found, and there was competition between teachers for places in the public administration of towns (notaries, chroniclers, writers of public acts and official letters) that offered better salaries. Rich families also competed for the best existing teachers within their own towns, or even in neighboring ones. Latin was still nonetheless preferred for official and nobler purposes.[4] As such, in the 14th century, the vernacular suffered a setback in Italy. Literary production in Latin was preferred to the Italian one. Petrarch, who was an extremely refined and cultivated Italian poet, imagined himself worthy of poetical laurels primarily because of his Latin works. Boccaccio, whose *Decameron* quickly became a masterpiece of Italian literature, felt it necessary to supplement his works in the vernacular with more ostensibly erudite research written in Latin.

The increasing wealth of the towns was manifested not only in the works of literate people living outside of the cloisters and engaged in civil and commercial life, but also in the great amount of money that was devoted to civil and religious buildings, particularly cathedrals and churches. As of the 11th century, Milan could be proud of its Basilica of

---

[4] I have illustrated in *Alfabetizzazione e Umanesimo nell'Italia dei secoli XIV e XV* (Gaeta: Biblioteca di Gabriele Chiusano Editore, 1997) the process that led Italian towns to the development of schools and diffusion of literacy, with the growing competition among teachers, who improved their Latin through the use of works by ancient writers particularly by Cicero.

Saint Ambrose; in the 12th century, Pavia was enriched with the Basilica of Saint Michael, Como with the Basilica of Saint Abbondio, Modena with the Cathedral of Saint Gemignano, and Parma with a cathedral and a baptistery. In the same century, Venice began to build its Basilica of Saint Mark, Florence its Baptistery of Saint John and Pisa began constructing its cathedral. All of this construction was very complex work that engaged great numbers of people from different professions: architects, stonecutters, sculptors, mosaicists, painters, and carpenters. These projects were so large that for the first time, expert workers and artists arranged themselves into teams. The resultant abundance of sculpted and painted figurations had the role of teaching illiterate people the Christian truths (*Bibliae pauperum*), of stimulating religious emotions and of promoting moral and pious behavior.

Weeks 5, 6, 7

The increase in the number of schools both for teaching Latin and the vernacular was of great consequence for the development of science and art in Italy and for the education of growing numbers of citizens who were increasingly admiring of refined behavior and conversation.

The invention of the printing press and the installation of typographies in a number of towns in Italy contributed greatly to the diffusion of books and of learning among the younger generations. Literacy was no longer confined to the cloisters. Respectable citizens not only felt obliged to wear rich embroidered clothes, mount beautiful horses, lead hunting parties with hundreds of dogs, live in sumptuous houses and to have poets in their retinue who were able to magnify their deeds in fine-sounding verses, but also to be able to speak and write good Italian and Latin (and preferably to read Greek as well) in order to engage in conversations on erudite topics and learned subjects with noble ladies and illustrious gentlemen.

In *The book of the Courtier,*[5] Baldassar Castiglione, who lived in several Italian courts during the Renaissance, describes the ideal character of an Italian gentleman in the age of the Renaissance.[6] The courtier of the Italian Renaissance was the man or woman who had an honorable place in the household of a rich, powerful man (whether endowed with a noble title

---

[5] Baldassar Castiglione, *Il libro del Cortegiano* (Milano: Rizzoli, 1987).

[6] The fundamental work for studying Renaissance in Italy is the one by Jacob Burckardt, *The Civilization of the Renaissance in Italy* (London: The Folio Society, 2005). For the life in the Italian courts see also Alison Cole, *Virtue and Magnificence: Art of the Italian Renaissance Courts* (New York: H.N. Abrams, 1995).

or not) who ruled an autonomous town. The figure of the courtier ousted the paradigm of human excellence that in the Middle Ages had been demonstrated in the figure of the monk and the knight, and announced a new age of refinement and of progress. In his *Letter to Paul from Middelburgh,* Marsilio Ficino describes this achievement and refinement. This human achievement had been described by Marsilio Ficino as the source of the era's importance and power. He wrote:

> Should we qualify our age, we would name it golden; it is undoubtedly so because it produces golden minds and discovered marvelous things. It is golden because it brought to light noble disciplines that had been almost dead: grammar, poetry, rhetoric, picture, sculpture, architecture, music, ancient songs comparable to the ones by Orpheus. This in Florence. In old times all this was respected but afterwards almost cancelled, it united wisdom with eloquence, prudence with smart warfare.[7]

In fact this was a time during which Italian soil sprouted great numbers of brilliant women and men who emerged as giants in many arenas. Veronica Franco, Machiavelli, Pulci, Tullia d'Aragona, Gaspara Stampa, Veronica Gambara, Vittoria Colonna, Castiglione, Ariosto, Pico della Mirandola, Bruni, Michelangelo and Leon Battista Alberti are examples of those who were largely renowned for their great intelligence, learning, refined behavior and conversation and able use of the sword.

Improvements in architecture and design during this period resulted from the needs of architects who could only study the perspective of buildings that they were constructing on two-dimensional plains.[8] These improvements aided in the preparation of cartoons for frescoes and the forging of figures and forms that had to be extracted from marble or cast in bronze. It also helped in the development of technology through improved

---

[7] "Si quod igitur seculum appellandum nobis est aureum, illud est procul dubio tale quod aurea passim ingenia profert. Id autem esse nostrum hoc seculum tanquam aureum liberales disciplinas ferme iam extinctas reduxit in lucem, grammaticam, poesiam, oratoriam, picturam, sculpturam, architecturam, musicam, antiquum ad Orphicam lyram carminum cantum. Idque Florentiae. Quodve apud priscos fuerat venerandum, sed iam prope deletam, sapientiam coniunxit cum eloquentia, cum arte militari prudentiam." Marsilio Ficino, *Letter to Paul from Middelburgh* in Marsili Ficini, *Opera omnia* (Basileae: Ex officina Henricpetrina, 1576, vol. II), 944.

[8] On this topic see Jacob Burckhardt, *The Architecture of the Italian Renaissance*. Revised and edited by Peter Murray; (London: Secker & Warburg, 1985); Christoph Luitpold Frommel, *Architecture of the Italian Renaissance* (London: Thames & Hudson, 2007).

machinery. More fully developed language was useful for a better, more precise description of the anatomy of plants, animals and of the internal structures of the human body. Surgeons, students of medicine and even painters exploited the growing art of design. The best known of these designers was Leonardo da Vinci.[9]

The lives of commoners from among whom great men emerged, was described in detail by Benvenuto Cellini in his *Life*. The picture of events is placed in a context of disorder and violence, in which everybody did their best to survive, earn money, succeed in their enterprises and help their families. Cellini shows us a world in which commoners appear to be endowed with a sort of wisdom that had no theoretical foundation and no religion as its basis. Renaissance Italy during this period had not attained political unity. No stable monarchy had firm control, or could govern through a solid legal code. This fact must certainly have favored the free development of human possibilities in a climate of competition in all productive fields. Sometimes this freedom generated aberrant fruits, as in the case of Aretino who although never producing works of durable credit, applied his exuberance to the forging of poems rich in the most extravagant statements which were sometimes vulgar and offensive that helped keep the spirit of rebelliousness, inventiveness and creativeness alive.

The disorder and lack of national unity among the Italian people lasted for centuries. It had been a source of concern and angst for humanists and literate men since the time of Dante and Petrarch, all of whom indulged in evoking the strength and glory of ancient Rome. By the end of the 16th century, as a result of its lack of unity, Italy could not keep on producing new forms of art and increasing the riches and the power of its towns because other European countries exercised a growing pressure on its markets and political life. Turkey took an ever-increasing share of land and riches from Italy's eastern shores, while other countries whose ships navigated the oceans successfully exploited the gold and silver of Central and South America and the spices of Indian and Indonesian shores. The disordered and contrasting tendencies prevailing in Italy during this epoch were also responsible of the lack of political unity that led to the conquest of Italy by France and Spain. Nonetheless, for our purposes, the monuments that Italy continued to build were the best investments of Italy's decreasing riches.

---

[9] For a more intensive study on da Vinci's visual thinking see Martin Kemp, *Leonardo da Vinci: Experience, Experiment and Design* (Princeton: Princeton University Press, 2006).

Presently we can admire the works that are evidence of the successive stages of Italian painting, sculpture and architecture from the late Middle Ages to the mature Renaissance. Among the painters of whom we should take note: Cimabue, Boninsegna, Cavallini, Giotto, Simone Martini, Peter and Ambrose Lorenzetti, Masaccio, Botticelli, Giorgione, Mantegna, il Perugino, Tiziano and Raphael. One of the foremost architects of the Italian Renaissance was Filippo Brunelleschi. Among the sculptors (although he was a painter and an architect as well) Michelangelo was the most celebrated and he was remembered as a polymath (*homo universalis*) along with Leonardo da Vinci.

In the impoverished Italy of the late 16th and early 17th century, as the Pope and churchly authorities became the greatest sources of riches outside of the royal courts, the church had the means to finance artists and builders. The result was that new monuments in Italy were mostly churches, monasteries and belfries. Pictures and sculptures representing saints, the Virgin Mary, Christ and scenarios inspired by the Bible were created to adorn churches and holy palaces, or princes' buildings. The Godhead was also sometimes figuratively represented. During this epoch, the technique for painting with oils came from the Low Countries to Italy and was soon preferred by painters and used in the portraits of which nobles and churchly authorities were so fond.

In Rome during the 17th century, Sixtus V encouraged the urban and artistic improvement of Rome in order to reassert the power and authority of the Catholic Church after the difficult period of the Reformation and Counter-Reformation.[10] Moreover, the imminent celebration of the jubilee led Rome itself to experiment with a renewal in artistic production. During this period, the Catholic Church had a large influence on the production of books, in order to genuinely reform the moral life of the clergy and Catholic people, thus effecting a deep revision of dogma as elaborated from Holy Scripture and the works of the Church's Fathers and theologians. Many popular literary works (such as the *Comedy,* the *Decameron,* and l'*Orlando Furioso*), as well as philosophical, political and historical works were banned, and only religious books that were considered to be ideologically correct were allowed to be produced, published and put on the market. The Church was responsible for the

[10] See Steven Ostrow, *Art and Spirituality in Counter-Reformation Rome: the Sistine and Pauline Chapels in S. Maria Maggiore* (New York: Cambridge University Press, 1996).

cultural changes of the 17th century because it strictly controlled intellectual production during this period.[11]

Week 8

The Renaissance in Italy was not only an age of artistic achievement but also of scientific research and philosophical attainments. Art, science and philosophy developed together and design connected them as expressions of logical relations and mathematical operations, and as a preparation for the handiwork and craftsmanship that created pictures, sculpted shapes and arrangements of stone. Men of the age relied heavily upon images, and images were saturated with emotions because emotions were imagined and expressed through sketches, paintings and sculptures.[12] Conceiving was imaging, sketching and picturing in the mind. Giambattista Vico, who lived between the 17th and 18th centuries, declared in his *New Science* that "imagination is more robust in proportion as reasoning power is weak,"[13] but he took into account only the emotional import of images, not the technical ones, that could support calculation and confrontation; in fact, reasoning drove the creation of images that were transformed into material works. The designs by Leonardo da Vinci and the ones still extant of architects that designed buildings and cathedrals are evidence of how graphic representation was used for the preparation of thoroughly-reasoned plans for machinery and buildings that had to be described by words.

This sort of reasoning, through design and calculation developed by artists, found application in the interpretation of the material world and its phenomena and inaugurated the naissance of modern science.[14] Artists experimented in their workshops not only through the mixing of colors extracted from different hearths and finely ground, not only in the hardness of stones that had to be cut, not only through new methods for melting bronze and casting it in a mould, but also through experimentation

---

[11] For an inquire about the role of the Inquisition in Italy and in the rest of Europe see *Inquisition and Society in Early Modern Europe* edited and translated by Stephen Haliczer (London: Croom Helm, 1987).

[12] See James Hall, *A History of Ideas and Images in Italian Art* (London: J. Murray, 1983).

[13] Giambattista Vico, *The New Science*, Revised Translation of the Third Edition (Ithaca, NY: Th. G. Bergin and M.H. Fisch, Cornell University Press, 1968), 71.

[14] See Thomas Kaufmann DaCosta, *The Mastery of Nature: Aspects of Art, Science, and Humanism in the Renaissance* (Princeton, N.J: Princeton University Press, 1993).

having to do with relations between lines, angles and curves. Leonardo learned a great deal as a pupil in Andrea Verrocchio's workshop and attempted the inscription of polygons inside of a circle through the figurative and manual method that prepared the argumentative demonstrations of classic geometry. In fact, Leonardo was a friend of Luca Pacioli who studied the *divine proportion*[15] much loved by artists.

Italian philosophers of the Renaissance were deeply concerned with the interpretation of nature. They were divided into two groups: Aristotelians and Platonists. Aristotelians followed the interpretation of Aristotelian texts supplied and interpreted by Averroës that insisted that God was the generative force that created all creatures (*causae secundae*).[16] The followers of Aristotle, whose chief representative was Peter Pomponazzi, favored the study of nature through accurate observations and analysis, though their views were frequently supported by arbitrary imagination and insufficient evidence.

The Platonists, who had a greater appeal for artists and poets, were the more successful of the two groups. Platonists derived their inspiration mainly from the works by Plato, Plotinus and the ones attributed to Hermes Trismegistus. The Platonic dialogue of the most interest for the study of natural sciences was the *Timaeus*. Hermes was supposed to have been an Egyptian prophet during the times of Moses who supplied much evidence favorable to Christianity and who left many treatises on alchemy, magic, chemical transmutations, the structure of the world and many other things. The most renowned of these treatises in the time of the Renaissance went under the name of *Corpus Hermeticum* and was brought to Florence by a friar and presented to Cosimo dei Medici who urged Marsilio Ficino to translate them from Greek into Latin. This translation was very soon read by learned people in Italy and Europe at large, who found in them innumerable cues to develop speculations from the vantage point of magic on the nature of the world, the planets, the central position and dominance of the Sun and many other subjects.

Magic went together with Cabbala and its research into the numbers and geometrical figures that were the concern of artists and astronomers.

---

[15] Luca Pacioli wrote a *Summa* and a book *Divina proportione, Opera a tutti gl'ingegni perspicaci e curiosi necessaria*. We know that he collaborated with Leonardo in some of his enquires.

[16] Among Islamic thinkers, this participation was denied by the followers of al-Ghazali, whose contention was that only God could be the cause of all things that happen. It is easily understood that if creatures have no causative power, it is pointless to try to discover natural causes, and the whole study of nature is thus in vain.

The tendency to apply such research to nature resulted in the introduction of measurability into natural phenomena. Time, length, distance, speed and weight had to be measured through elementary unities, and reciprocal confrontation had to be effected through measured quantities. Everything that happened in nature had to be considered not as an expression of Godly intentions or as intentions formulated by minds animating material things, as Platonists contended, but as a mechanical process transmitting movement.

In Italy, learned men who had profited from the progress of technical design and who tried to exploit mechanical cues suggested by the work of Aristotle and Archimedes, further developed mechanical research. In the late 16th century, Bonamico, a professor of philosophy in Pisa, wrote a ten book treatise on movement in which he treated it as a quality that one object received from another. The great founder of modern mechanics, however, was Galileo Galilei who wrote a book on mechanics and local movements.[17] Known by Marin Mersenne, Descartes and all the learned people of his time, this book inaugurated the methods of modern science in which phenomena are described and calculated through the discovery of rules that can be exploited through the construction and predisposition of congruous conditions. Its practical utility was shown by Galileo in his description and calculation of parabolas that could be applied to artillery.[18]

Evangelista Torricelli was another important learned man living in Italy in the first half of the 17th century and contributed to the development of science by introducing a practical method for measuring the pressure of air at different heights.

Weeks 9, 10

The 17th and 18th centuries were not a bright period for Italian culture. Commerce no longer passed along the shores of Mediterranean; Spain, France, England and the Austrian empire (or Sacred Roman Empire) had mastered the political life of Europe and enjoyed a splendid flourishing of literature and baroque art. England fought successfully to take a large share of lands and riches in different parts of the world. Italy had not succeeded in becoming unified, although all of its regions now used the same vernacular as a written language. The diffusion of schools was poor, illiterate people spoke in many differing dialects, monks and friars were

---

[17] See Galileo Galilei, *Discorsi e dimostrazioni matematiche intorno a due nuove scienze, attinenti alla Meccanica e i movimenti Locali. Appresso gli Elzeviri, in Leida MDCXXXVIII* (Turin: Boringhieri, 1958).

[18] Ibid., 551-78.

concerned mainly with teaching children Christian doctrine together with only rudiments of Italian reading and writing. Seminars founded by bishops in order to propagate obedience to the Council of Trent provided religion-focused education for middle-class families. Industrial activities did not develop in concurrence with the industrial powers of other European countries, and commerce was sluggish. Overall, production was mainly agricultural and in some regions such as Lombardy and Tuscany, people with money preferred to invest it in the improvement of lands and methods of cultivation. Southern Italy was particularly depressed because of Spanish domination and baronial exploitation. With the exception of Naples, which in the course of the 18th century was ruled by the Bourbons who adopted enlightened ideas of government, the inhabitants of Southern Italy were generally illiterate, primitive, and dominated by superstition and ignorance. The Bourbons could effect only limited improvement. Learned men succeeded in attaining intellectual achievements only through strain and exertion. This was the case of Giambattista Vico from Naples who wrote a masterpiece of philosophy under the name of *Principles of a New Science on the nature of nations.*[19]

During the second half of the 18th century, a new literary influence from northern Europe began to be felt among literate people of Italy and stimulated emotions and excitement that prepared the ground for what became Romanticism. Giuseppe Parini, Vittorio Alfieri, Giovanni Pindemonte, Carlo Botta, Vincenzo Monti, Ugo Foscolo were among the most noted poets and writers of this period who absorbed and assimilated this influence during the time in which the French Revolution and Napoleon's adventures spread the ideas of freedom, human equality, greatness of fatherland, glorious performance and loyalty to one's own country throughout Europe.[20]

The need for a unified and free Italy became clear among the literate Italian citizenry. Writers discussed and worked to refine and enrich the Italian language. Alessandro Manzoni occupied the best part of his life in writing a novel (*The Beloved*, or *I Promessi Sposi*) that summarized the moral ideals of simple people living in the country, and supplied a linguistic model that the literate people of the whole peninsula had adopted.

John Berchet, Silvio Pellico, Federico Confalonieri and many other writers discussed both the problems of freedom and of the unification of Italy and of its language. Manzoni wrote an important essay called "On the

---

[19] First edition 1725, revised in 1730, third edition 1744.

[20] See Mario Puppo, *Romanticismo italiano e romanticismo europeo* (Milano: Istituto propaganda libraria, 1985).

unity of Italian language and of the means to enlarge its usage." In fact, even in the second half of the 19th century, less educated people still spoke only in local dialects and even writers only used Italian only to write. In southern Italy the Bourbon Kings did not use Italian in their court or within their family, and the use of dialect was common in the tribunals among judges and barristers. The schools inaugurated after the unification of Italy faced a very big task: the Italian people had to learn the Italian language.

The language systematized by Manzoni in his novel, poems and in other essays became the standard form of Italian for the unified, new nation and only late in the 19th century did literate people begin to react against his style.

Supported by classic reminiscences and by strong patriotic and ethic ideals, Italian literature flourished throughout the 19th century. Giacomo Leopardi, Vincent Gioberti, Antonio Rosmini, Massimo D'Azeglio, Niccolò Tommaseo, Ippolito Nievo, Alfredo Oriani, Giosuè Carducci, Giovanni Verga, Luigi Capuana, Antonio Fogazzaro, Luigi Pirandello and Gabriele d'Annunzio analyzed and discussed the spiritual problems of the young Italian nation that strove for internal social balance, the productivity with which to supply its population the means for survival, and a recognized place amongst the worldly consortium of modern nations. The Neoclassicism in art had its best representation in Antonio Canova for the sculpture and in Andrea Appiani for the painting. The Romanticisms had its most important painter in Francesco Hayez renowned for his great historical paintings and political allegories.

The effort to create a strong and united nation was frustrated by the two wars of the 20th century that damaged Italy's economy and impaired its self-confidence and basic values. The literary production of this time is the best evidence of its extant spiritual problems. The new spirit that was emerging in the literary life was dominated by a strong feeling of dissatisfaction for the existing way of conceiving of the world and facts, of representing and describing them by speech. This existing way of conceiving and speaking had come to be called modernity or modernism and rationality. It was the ripe fruit of a prolonged effort of refining and organizing the means for the interpretation and description of reality. These means produced science and technology and led Europeans to the conquest of the "new world" of Americas in modern times and to the enhanced production of goods by orderly, coherent and continuous procedures in workshops that mathematics and formal logic could control and improve. This was the procedure that operated the dissolution of everything still existing in western culture that could be charged with the fault of irrationality, incoherence or superstition. This was also the procedure that went with a madly rigorous coherence to the worst performances of militarism during the war in the countries occupied by Nazis and Fascists.[21] The rationalism, the extolling of the technology and the loathing of the thoughts and art of the past express themselves through the futurism that was a movement that explored every form of art from painting to sculpture, from architecture to music, from poetry to theatre. The futurism movement started when Filippo Tommaso Marinetti published the *Manifesto of Futurism* in the 1909.[22] The futurism lasted for years and several interesting futurist buildings were built between the 1920 and 1940.

After the war the dominance of order, rationality and functionalism supported by the Futurism have been found responsible for the shaping of modern towns, in which much of what is human and can be felt as human is lacking. The dissatisfaction for all this needed has been called anti-modernism or postmodernism. The postmodernism expressed the rebellious tendencies of post-war generations that opposed the rationality and logical representation of modernism. The dominant aim of the postmodern artists was the one of upsetting, disconcerting, stupefying and disturbing the observers by paintings, constructions, ornamentations, and the readers by linguistic products and by images and emotions stimulated by verses and prose. Writers experimented with new techniques with varying degrees of effectiveness and brought an important and original contribution to the post-war culture. Italo Calvino, Alberto Moravia, Pier Paolo Pasolini, Carlo Emilio Gadda and Leonardo Sciascia are among the writers who best represent the post-war culture.

Because Italy has a great cultural heritage in the Western world, nowadays it is working toward a form of modern culture that grows separately from its glorious past without ignoring it. The conflict of values of nationhood and identification with the state and the progressive process of accommodation within a historical globalized identity has helped to overthrow national barriers against incorporating the multicultural experience that reflected in literary and art production.[23]

The massive influx of international and multi-racial immigration in a short period of time has been the most conspicuous aspect of globalization

---

[21] See Adrian Lyttelton, ed. *Liberal and Fascist Italy, 1900-1945* (Oxford; New York: Oxford University Press, 2002).

[22] The *Manifesto* was composed in 1908 and published the following February on the front page of the most prestigious French daily newspaper, *Le Figaro*.

[23] See Patrick McCarthy, ed. *Italy since 1945* (Oxford; New York: Oxford University Press, 2000).

in Italy, and it has taught Italians to consider human problems, cultures, traditions, religions from the perspective of a multiform humanity. Italians are slowly learning to appreciate the immigrants' presence in their country and accepting their different cultural heritage and perspectives that can enrich and improve Italian understanding of the world. Consequently, Italy is starting its active role in a world wide process of internationalizing the culture and organization of a global social system where every single person will be respected and appreciated for the different cultural heritage that he or she bears.

The topics that I included are the most relevant and suitable to introduce the history of the Italian culture in a contextualizing way. Every instructor who will consider teaching this course is invited to adjust this framework to his/her needs. I suggest that you do not overload the content and prepare a clear lecture outline to show to the students at beginning and during the class. It is also recommended to provide, at the end of the class, a summary of the main points covered during the lecture.

The instructor in order to have a positive student's response needs to consider the following factors:

- Making the teaching session interesting
- Selecting and organizing reading and instructional materials suitable for the course
- Developing students' enthusiasm for knowledge
- Giving clear explanations
- Making appropriate assessment and feedback
- Giving direction to student learning
- Making clear goals
- Allowing for flexibility in learning activities.

Upon completing the course successfully, students will:

- Have a broad and comparative knowledge of the history and the cultural heritage of the different Italian regions
- Be able to set literary and artistic production within their historical, political and social context
- Be able to place historic events in their chronological order and in their correct geographical location
- Be aware of the history, politics, philosophy, science and religion that form the context from which the artistic, architectural and literary heritage belonging to contemporary Italian society can be best understood

- Be able to engage critically with historiographic material
- Be able to produce well-structured arguments supported by appropriately referenced visual, textual and other evidence.

The class aims at instilling in the students an appreciation for the Italian culture and helping them to understand how Western civilization is deeply indebted to it. The class gives the students the opportunity to learn about Italian literature and art in a global and broader context thanks to an across-disciplinary approach. In a time where countries are seemingly moving closer together, particularly in Europe, with the disappearance of borders, it is important to make the students aware of the role of Italy and its contribution to the contemporary culture during an age of globalization.

UNIVERSITY OF WASHINGTON, USA

APPENDIX

Syllabus

WEEK 1: **Pre-Roman habitants, Ancient Rome and the waning of the Roman Empire**.

1. Indo-European population in the Italic peninsula
2. Hellenic civilization in Southern Italy
3. Etruscans and their contribution to the Roman civilization
4. Political and cultural development in the Roman Empire

Visual material: Greek city-states in *Magna Grecia*; Etruscan tombs, Gregorian Etruscan Museum (online); the Roman Forum, Pompeii, Herculaneum.

WEEK 2: **Latin heritage and Christian influences in the troubled years of the early Middle Ages.**

1. Christianity in the Roman Empire
2. The Church in the Middle Ages

Visual material: The catacombs; the churches of the Santi Quattro Coronati, San Bartolomeo and San Lorenzo fuori le Mura (Rome).

WEEK 3: **The development of the language from Latin to the vernacular**

1. The vernacular languages of the Italic peninsula

2. *De Vulgari Eloquentia* and the relationship between Latin and vernacular; Italian as a literary language: prose and poetry through the *Decameron* and *Canzoniere*

WEEK 4: **From the background for the naissance of Italian culture under Lombard and Frankish domination to the humanistic civilization of the peninsula**

1. The classic culture and the birth of lay schools: Guarino Guarini and Vittorino da Feltre

2. Humanism in art and literature and social and economic background

Visual material: The Basilica of Saint Ambrose (Milan), the Basilica of Saint Michael (Pavia), the Basilica of Saint Abbondio (Como), the Cathedral of Saint Gemignano (Modena), the Cathedral of Santa Maria Assunta and the Baptistery (Parma), the Basilica of Saint Mark (Venice), the Baptistery of Saint John (Florence), and the Cathedral of Santa Maria (Pisa).

WEEK 5: **The flourishing of painting, sculpture, architecture and poetry in Italy from the 15th to 16th centuries. The development of new paradigms of life**

1. The man's new conception: *Oration on the Dignity of Man*
2. The portrait of the courtier in *The Book of the Courtier* and *De Amicitia*

Visual material: Paintings by Masaccio, Botticelli, Giorgione, Mantegna and il Perugino; Sculptures by Donatello; Loggia dell'Ospedale degli Innocenti and Cupola di Santa Maria del Fiore by Brunelleschi.

WEEK 6: **Italian culture in the Renaissance**

1. Gigantism in Renaissance culture: Marsilio Ficino, Ludovico Ariosto, Leonardo da Vinci and Michelangelo

2. Courtesans, mothers and poets: Tullia d'Aragona, Gaspara Stampa, Vittoria Colonna, Veronica Franco e Veronica Gambara

Visual material: Paintings by Tiziano and Raphael; drawings by Leonardo da Vinci's; St. Peter's Basilica and the Sistine Chapel; Il Perseo by Cellini.

Audio material: Music by Giovanni da Palestrina and Giovanni Gabrieli.

WEEK 7: **Italian culture and the Baroque Age**

1. Crises of Renaissance values: *Jerusalem Delivered*
2. Against the authority of the Counter-Reformation papacy: *History of the Council of Trent*

Visual material: Caravaggio's and Carracci's paintings; Bernini's sculptures; the Cathedral of Siracusa, the Churches of Saint Ignazio di Loyola and Saint Andrea al Quirinale (Rome), the Church of Gesù Nuovo (Naples), the Church of Santa Croce (Lecce).

Audio material: Music by Claudio Monteverdi e Antonio Vivaldi.

WEEK 8: **The development of Italian culture as seen through the philosophy and science of the 16th and 17th centuries**

1. From magic to science: Galileo and Torricelli

2. The power of the imagination: *New Science*

WEEK 9: **A new era for Italian culture during the 18th and 19th centuries: the political unification of the Peninsula**

1. The birth of the Italian historical novel: *The Betrothed* and *Ettore Fieramosca*

2. Patriotic and ethic ideals in the unified Italy: writings by Berchet, Pellico, Confalonieri and Nievo

Visual material: Sculptures by Antonio Canova; paintings by Andrea Appiani and Francesco Hayez.

Audio material: Music by Giuseppe Verdi (*Va, pensiero*)

WEEK 10: **Italian culture in the 20th century towards an age of globalization**

1. The technological triumph of people over nature: Marinetti

2. Values and identities in crises: writings by Calvino, Gadda and Siascia.
   From a racially homogeneous society to a multi-ethnic one: Italian traditions and globalization

Visual material: Paintings by Umberto Boccioni and Carlo Carrà.

Audio material: Music by Luigi and Antonio Russolo

PART V:

TEACHING ITALIAN CULTURE THROUGH FILM

CHAPTER TWENTY

ITALIAN LANGUAGE AND CULTURE IN CLOSE-UP: USING FILM AT ALL LEVELS OF PROFICIENCY

KERSTIN PILZ

Introduction

This paper is based on the recent curriculum revision of the Italian programme at Macquarie University (Sydney, Australia), which was undertaken with the aim of opening the programme up to the needs and expectations of a changing student body. Typically, the majority of today's students no longer enrol in language courses to pursue a major; instead, they often pursue degrees in a wide range of areas and elect to study a language to increase their compatibility in a global context where intercultural competence is highly valued. A particular aim of the restructuring process therefore was to broaden language study in order to make it relevant to a large group of learners from diverse academic backgrounds. This meant first and foremost restructuring the programme to offer an integrated approach, linking language, content and intercultural competency in meaningful ways at all levels. The existing curriculum, which had followed a traditional grammar-centred and teacher-led approach, was replaced by a multidimensional curriculum that advocates student-centred learning strategies and demonstrates language in multiple and authentic contexts. This paper examines how film was integrated into the curriculum as an important medium to break the traditional language-content dichotomy and to facilitate an understanding of cross-cultural values. It illustrates how film can serve as a resource to develop the four language skills at all levels of proficiency.

New directions for Language Departments

The issues raised in the restructuring process at Macquarie University echo the recent debate and recommendations by a panel of experts assembled by the MLA Executive Council to address the crisis in teaching foreign languages in North American colleges and universities. The panel found the traditional two-tiered literature-language model to no longer be appropriate in today's world, which requires graduates with a broader understanding of a foreign language, including knowledge of a foreign culture's history, society and economic system in favour of specialized literary skills. It concluded that in order to remain relevant and to produce graduates with skills that meet the current employment market, today's foreign language departments need to offer a language major structured in such a way as to produce "educated speakers who have deep translingual and transcultural competence."[1] The study foreshadows a radical curricular reform that will lead to an integrative approach where language study is situated in "cultural, historical, geographic, and cross-cultural frames within the context of humanistic learning."[2] A main emphasis is the incorporation of content and cross-cultural reflection at all levels.[3]

While the radical curriculum reform envisioned by the MLA panel may not be achieved immediately—a major hurdle is the hierarchy of tenure track professors in charge of teaching content at the upper levels, with language teaching largely being left to teaching assistants who have little or no input in the curriculum—many departments around the world have already begun to adopt progressive multidimensional curricula. As is illustrated below, foreign language teachers can benefit from the experiences of ESL teachers who have long since used a holistic approach to teaching language and culture and who have provided some very valuable literature in the field.

Peter Bondanella, who pioneered Italian Film Studies outside of Italy, points out that the introduction of film into Italian Studies programmes was one of the most important changes in a curriculum that until not too long ago focused exclusively on Dante, the Renaissance and highbrow literature. The integration of Film Studies helped to usher in progressive Italian Studies programmes that embrace the study of culture and contemporary society in addition to literature and history. The study of

---

[1] MLA Ad Hoc Committee on Foreign Languages, "Foreign Languages in Higher Education: New Structures for a Changed World," May 2007, www.mla.org/flreport (accessed 30 September, 2007), 3.

[2] Ibid., 4.

[3] Ibid., 5.

Italian film, Bondanella explains, began in earnest in the early 1970s when "a small but determined group of Italianists resolved to add Italian film to the Italian curriculum."[4] Until then, little scholarship of Italian national cinema existed in English (or in Italian), making it difficult to design monographic courses on Italian cinema. Under Bondanella's lead the area has flourished over the past three decades to the extent that North American film scholarship has made a significant impact on the study of Italian national cinema.[5] As a result, and unlike other major European language programmes, Italian film courses are now a staple in most Italian Studies programmes, having over the last decade also permeated the language curriculum. This in turn has led to a proliferation of textbooks and manuals that provide resources for using Italian language films in meaningful and integrated ways in the language classroom. They demonstrate that film is no longer used as a motivational filler, but has an important role to play in the language classroom, if used in a structured way.

The advantages of film in language teaching: The Macquarie experience

At Macquarie University the curriculum was revised to adopt up-to-date teaching methods that allow for student-centred learning and expose students to authentic texts that facilitate incidental learning. Particular attention was paid to film, which, by its very nature of being multilayered, integrates well with contemporary teaching methods that stress a blended approach of language, content and experiential and communicative activities. As Baltova points out, this approach

> is supported by the belief that L2 acquisition is enhanced through the incidental learning of language from contextually rich verbal input while students are focusing on the meaning rather than on the form of the input.[6]

Film is particularly useful in this context as it allows students to absorb language whilst focusing on content and other stimuli such as visual and

---

[4] Peter Bondanella, "New Directions in Teaching Film in Italian Studies Programs," *Italica* 83, no. 1 (2006): 7.
[5] Ibid., 8.
[6] Iva Baltova, "Multisensory Language Teaching in a Multidimensional Curriculum: The Use of Authentic Bimodal Video in Core French," *The Canadian Modern Language Review/La Revue canadienne des langues vivantes*, 56, no. 1 (1999): 33.

audio cues, as well as observing a foreign culture in action. Broadly speaking, film allows for a blended approach to language learning as it can be used effectively to stimulate all four language skills as well as raise intercultural awareness.

The integration of film in the foreign language classroom also has the advantage of being generally perceived as fun and engaging. Students are very familiar with the medium of film, and its integration into the curriculum responds to the needs of a changing student body that is literate in visual and electronic media. Film, however, should not be used in place of but in addition to print media in order to promote multiple literacies. Language instructors need to be careful to integrate film in meaningful ways that are aligned with the objectives of language study. It is essential that audio-visual activities based on authentic films are perceived by the language learner as a challenge requiring effort and that the activities are carefully prepared.[7] At Macquarie University we decided to integrate at least one feature film per semester at all levels, in addition to the base textbook (*Espresso* 2 & 3 at intermediate and advanced levels) and other print-based texts (eg. plot summaries, film reviews and at upper-advanced level a novel and screenplay). This allowed students to study a given film in depth and to fully exploit the learning opportunities offered by the material. At the beginner level we trialled individual scenes from a variety of films based on the speech acts they illustrate (ie. greeting, introducing etc.), as well as the first chapter of *Manuale d'amore*.[8] An end-of-semester survey confirmed what in-class observations had shown: students were more enthusiastic and stimulated to view authentic film clips than the specifically scripted educational video accompanying the textbook *Prego*.[9] Students welcomed the stimulation and challenges provided by the

---

[7] Christine Canning-Wilson, "Practical Aspects of Using Video in the Foreign Language Classroom," *The Internet TESL Journal*, no. 11 (2000): 5 http://iteslj.org/Articles/Canning-Video.html (accessed November 2000).

[8] For useful examples see Francesca Laura, "Io non ho paura: usare i film senza timori," *Studi d'italianistica nell'Africa australe. Italian Studies in Southern Africa* 18, no. 2 (2005): 144-72.

[9] Some would argue against using films as isolated clips as it poses an injustice to the filmmaker (ie. Tania Convertini, "Insegnare lingua con il cinema: una prospettiva alternativa," *Italica* 83, no. 1 (2006): 26). While I agree that it is certainly better to present films as a complete work or text, I would counter argue that the use of film clips is comparable to the standard practice of using excerpts from works of literature to model language. In my opinion, it is better to expose students to a lot of different films, especially if they are available for complete viewing in the library, as this tends to motivate students to make an effort to watch extra Italian language films in their spare time.

authentic material and the embedded knowledge they picked up through incidental learning (ie. culturally specific behaviour and colloquialisms).

It is generally accepted that classroom scenarios that engage students emotionally in authentic and meaningful conversations are more successful in stimulating real learning.[10] Carefully chosen films allow students to relate to characters and situations and to make comparisons between their own situations and cultural contexts and those on screen, facilitating a deeper appreciation of intercultural differences.[11] Films should engage students and present situations, stories and characters that they can relate to. Our trial showed that films with clear, conventional storylines (ie. love stories, journey films, coming of age films etc.) and films that show children (*Io non ho paura*, *Ciao professore*, *Cinema Paradiso*, *La vita è bella, Alla luce del sole*), teenagers and young adults (the first chapter of *Manuale d'amore*, *Caterina va in città*, *My name is Tanino, Ovo sodo*, *Quando sei nato non ti puoi più nascondere*, *L'ultimo bacio*) work very well. Interestingly, while our students generally show less enthusiasm for films that are not representations of contemporary Italy (especially black and white films), films such as *La vita è bella*, *Cinema Paradiso*, *Mediterraneo* and *Il postino* remain all-time favourites due to the combination of strong story lines and characters (especially the child protagonists in *La vita è bella* and *Cinema Paradiso*) and a pervasive sense of sentimentality and nostalgia. These may not be films that I would usually choose for their cinematographic merits or for their representations of recent Italian history, yet they nevertheless provide excellent occasions for addressing the questions of representation of history and national identity.[12]

Film has been recommended for its multisensory appeal, stimulating multiple skills and forms of intelligence: it offers audio as well as visual stimuli that aid recall and comprehension. Researchers have long argued the importance of visual cues in order to involve both hemispheres of the

---

[10] See for example Convertini, 24 and Antonio Vitti, "Il cinema come complemento di insegnamento," *Italica* 83, no. 1 (2006): 82.

[11] Susan Stempleski and Barry Tomalin, *Video in Action. Recipes for using Video in Language Teaching* (Cambridge: Prentice Hall International, 1990), 4.

[12] For example, in one of the written assignments at upper-advanced level, students had to critically discuss and compare *La vita è bella* and *Una giornata particolare* as well as comment on their personal reactions to both films. Predictably most students preferred *La vita è bella*, but interestingly, this included even those students who ranked *Una giornata particolare* as the better film for its cinematographic merits and subtlety and original approach to dealing with the Fascist period and its victims.

brain for more effective learning.[13] At Macquarie University we experimented with sound-only versus sound-and-image situations.[14] At different competency levels classes were divided into pairs of 'listeners' and 'viewers'. One student in each pair was asked to sit with their back to the screen and concentrate only on the sound of a given film clip, while the other student had access to sound and image without subtitles. Students were then asked to collaborate on piecing together the whole sequence, with viewers describing what they had seen and listeners describing what they had heard. When collaborating in this way it soon became clear that viewers who had access to sound and image had the clear advantage. Another activity, where the listeners asked the viewers information about the scene to reconstruct it from the pieces of dialogue they had heard, demonstrated that viewers were also able to fill in the missing dialogue and overall had achieved better comprehension of the scene—despite not having access to subtitles—than students exposed to sound only. Listeners on the other hand performed better in subsequent creative writing exercises (ie. imagine and write the script to the next scene; imagine the outcome of the characters' interactions; imagine a follow-on dialogue between characters etc.), as clearly the sound-only experiment had stimulated their creative intelligence.

Film also has the advantage that it allows for authentic communicative interactions while facilitating intercultural learning, as students are able to hear and see language used in meaningful contexts that illustrate how language and culture are linked. For example, film portrays a range of emotions and culturally specific interactions that would be difficult to portray through print-based media.[15] A brief, carefully chosen film clip can expose students to a vast range of cultural symbols, references, and stereotypes, as well as culturally specific facial expressions, body language and uses of humour. While cinematographic speech is typically scripted, which makes it problematic to refer to as authentic speech, the fact that it is spoken by native speakers for native speakers makes it nevertheless a model of authentic speech that is preferable to the dialogues designed for L2 learners which are unnaturally slow and stilted. Cinematic speech, like authentic speech, provides teachers and learners with a rich

---

[13] See for example Iva Baltova, "The impact of video on the comprehension skills of core French students," *The Canadian Modern Language Review* 50 (1994): 507-32.

[14] The activity was inspired by Stempleski and Tomalin, *Film* (Oxford: Oxford UP, 2001), "Split viewing" 4.

[15] See also Jane Sherman, *Using Authentic Video in the Language Classroom* (Cambridge: Cambridge UP, 2003), 12-4.

repertoire of linguistic registers including slang and vulgar language, colloquialisms, idioms and examples of regionally inflected speech or dialect, delivered at natural speed. In addition, showing subtitles for the hearing impaired, apart from facilitating comprehension at lower proficiency level, can be a useful exercise to draw students' attention to the discrepancy between colloquial speech and grammatically correct speech. In addition to shortening spoken dialogue, these types of subtitles often present 'censored' or grammatically 'corrected' versions of oral speech, whereby colloquialisms and strong language are edited out.

Review of recent textbooks for teaching language through film

As part of our curriculum review process, we carefully evaluated and trialled existing materials before deciding on strategies for the integration of one or more films at each proficiency level. The expanding market of manuals for learning Italian through film can be broadly divided into two categories: film study guides on single films (the individual volumes of the *Quaderni di cinema italiano per stranieri* series edited by Paolo E. Balboni for Guerra edizioni; and the *Film Study Programmes* by Edizioni Farinelli); and a range of more comprehensive textbooks comprising 10-16 chapters on individual films (ie. *Italian Through Film* vols 1&2; *Ciak ... Si parla italiano*; *L'italiano al cinema* etc).[16] Most of these volumes are designed as ancillary textbooks to be integrated, along with other linguistic materials, into multidimensional semester-long language courses. All of these volumes have their obvious strengths and shortcomings, their main point of distinction being their respective approaches to studying film as a series of individual scenes (ie. the individual film guides by Guerra edizioni and Edizioni Farinelli) and on focusing on global viewing and comprehension.

We were able to make a direct comparison between the two approaches at each competency level by trialling one of the individual film guides with the same group of learners in conjunction with the corresponding chapter from *Ciak si parla italiano* and *Italian Through Film*.[17] The trial

[16] Piero Garofalo and Daniela Selisca, *Ciak ... si parla italiano* (Newburyport: Focus Publishing, R. Pullins Co, 2005); Antonello Borra and Cristina Pausini, *Italian Through Film* (New Haven: Yale UP, 2004); *Italian Through Film: The Classics* (New Haven: Yale UP, 2007); Cristina Maddoli, *L'italiano al cinema* (Perugia: Guerra Edizioni, 2004).

[17] The individual film guides trialled were: at intermediate level Elda Buonanno, *L'ultimo bacio. Film Study Program*; *Ciao Professore. Film Study Program* (NY:

showed that students responded best to collective in-class viewing activities based on individual scenes, and were less enthusiastic about the whole film response method. For example, the comprehension questions in Borra and Pausini's two volumes require students to recall minute details of a certain scene or character (ie. what they ate, what they did at a certain point in the film), whilst at the same time expecting them to speak confidently in the same session about the entire film at some distance from the original viewing—which due to time constraints will have to occur outside of class time. The trial demonstrated very clearly the advantages of eliciting student responses immediately after viewing to retain active engagement. Film is such a powerful tool for language teaching exactly because the combination of sound, image and narrative, especially when emotionally engaging, stimulates our cognitive faculties, senses and emotions simultaneously, which is lost when talking about a film at some distance. The trial also demonstrated that while Borra and Pausini's volume provides very useful vocab-building exercises and interesting discussion topics, on the whole, it stopped short of fully exploiting the material to creatively engage students.[18] Most importantly, it lacks effective, relevant exercises that creatively stimulate oral and written production.

The second volume, *Italian Through Film: The classics*, is enhanced through a certain number of creative follow-on exercises in the "Adesso reciti tu!" section accompanying some, but regrettably not all, films. *Ciak ... si parla italiano* is more consistent in this respect, as each film is accompanied by short creative writing and oral activities. In the "Ma ora il regista sei tu ... e vuoi cambiare tutto!" section of each chapter, students are asked to rewrite the film to provide a new ending or slant on events, followed by the invention of a new title, while the "Quattro chiacchiere con ..." section in each chapter asks students to imagine a dialogue or

Edizioni Farinelli, 2006); at advanced level Paola Begotti and Graziano Serragiotto, *Nuovo cinema paradiso. Quaderni di cinema italiano per stranieri* (Perugia: Guerra Edizioni, 2002) and Maria Valentina Marasco and Nicoletta Santeusanio, *Pane e tulipani. Quaderni di cinema italiano per stranieri* (Perugia: Guerra Edizioni, 2003); at upper-advanced level Begotti and Serragiotto, *La vita è bella* (Perugia: Guerra Edizioni, 2003), Beggoti, Serragiotto and Paolo Torresan, *Mediterraneo* (Perugia: Guerra Edizioni, 2004). In addition, at upper advanced level students choose two chapters from Borra and Pausini, *Italian Through Film: The Classics* (ie. *Il sorpasso* and *Una giornata particolare*).

[18] See also Elisabetta D'Amanda, review of *Italian Through Film. A Text for Italian Courses*, by Antonello Borra and Cristina Pausini, *Italica* 83, no. 1 (2006): 122-23. She points out the schematic nature of the exercises which fail to fully engage students creatively and to make valid cultural comparisons.

interview with a given character of each film. Our trial has shown these types of activities to be particularly useful, especially if they provide direct engagement or identification with characters and situations presented in the films and opportunities to expand on the socio-linguistic and cultural contexts in creative and personalized ways.

As a result of the trial, it was decided to adopt one of the individual film guides per semester, despite their shortcomings (eg. all tend to lack follow-on discussion topics and activities relating to the whole film, and the available follow-on activities for cross-cultural observation tend to be badly integrated). Ultimately however, the single film guides provide more flexibility as ancillary materials and they have the advantage of breaking feature films up into a series of scenes that can be presented more usefully within the limited time of class sessions. The focus on transcript-based language awareness activities (eg. cloze listening comprehension tasks, reordering jumbled dialogue etc.) is particularly useful, as these are otherwise time-consuming to prepare. On the other hand, whole film-based tasks and creative oral and written activities can be easily added by the instructor, as is illustrated below. Furthermore, the volumes have the advantage of providing answer keys which make them suitable for independent study.[19] Of the individual film guides we preferred those of the *Quaderni del cinema italiano per stranieri* series over those by Edizioni Farinelli.[20] What makes these volumes more attractive is the systematic division of each sequence into several progressive phases: a first viewing is followed by simple multiple choice comprehension questions; the second viewing is followed by gapfill listening comprehension exercises; next there is room to practice relevant vocab and linguistic structures (which may not always integrate well with the level of

---

[19] At Macquarie University this is another crucial criterion for the selection of teaching materials, as all of our language courses are now offered for external study in online delivery mode. External students are required to purchase the DVD in addition to one of the single film volumes, and to then complete exercises in self-study and through discussion exchanges and online quizzes comprised of comprehension questions in various formats: gapfill, multiple choice, true and false statements and short answer questions. In the few cases where we have access to off-air recordings, which give us copyright free access to the films, we are able to integrate selected film clips in digital form with web-based activities.

[20] The volumes of the Edizioni Farinelli series have useful listening comprehension and written exercises (ie. gapfilling, plot summary of each scene etc.) based on single scenes, but regrettably the volumes make limited use of the material at hand. They lack consistent vocab-building exercises and creative follow-on exercises for oral and written practice and the supplementary material—both the grammar exercises and cultural information—is badly integrated.

instruction but serve as additional revision exercises); and finally each sequence is concluded with a 'verifica della sequenza' activity, which provides opportunities for writing and creative follow-on exercises.

How to integrate feature films: approaches and strategies

The trial demonstrated that the most successful strategy for integrating a whole film in language classes is a combination of the two approaches reviewed above (ie. responses to individual scenes and whole-film-based activities). This can be achieved by showing films in a sequenced fashion in class, broken up into several different viewing exercises spread out over the semester, followed by one or more end-of-semester sessions on whole film response activities.[21] Before the end of the semester, all students are expected to have seen the entire film (preferably as a group outside of class time). In this way precious class time is not wasted and students are given the chance to study a given film in more depth in order to benefit from the whole range of activities and learning strategies it offers. From week to week students are asked to keep a film journal which helps keep track of plot events and provides a record of students' reactions to characters, events, and settings, as well as allowing students to practice their writing skills etc.[22] I have found it useful to ask students collaboratively—or if there is no time, individually in their film journals—to prepare plot summaries after each scene. At the beginning of each new session and before viewing a new clip, the whole class brainstorms the last clip they have seen. This helps students who have missed a class to resume the film viewing and opens opportunities for student-centred activities (eg. the student who missed a class is encouraged to ask specific questions of the others: what did characters wear and say, what music was played, how did the plot evolve etc.). Studying a whole film this way also provides many opportunities for ongoing assessment and other written activities to be completed individually between sessions (eg. write a letter to a

[21] See also what Sherman calls "salami tactics," p. 19; and Stempleski and Tomalin "Film viewing project," *Film*, 136-7.

[22] Film journals are useful to stimulate students to truly engage with the material at hand and to participate in discussions. More introverted students in particular can benefit from the opportunity to collect their thoughts and find appropriate language for articulating their feelings (Stempleski and Tomalin, *Film*, 132-32). Summerfield observes that students are usually more stimulated by the ability to write freely about a topic, rather than by exercises where they must provide specific answers. Ellen Summerfield, *Crossing Cultures Through Film* (Yarmouth: Maine: Intercultural Press, 1993), 38.

character, describe the next scene, take sides with a character and recall a scene from their point of view) and expanded orally as a whole group or small group activity (ie. roleplay) in the next class.

Alongside the available Italian language materials we also tried out a range of activities and strategies adapted from several ESL books on film. Stempleski and Tomalin's volume *Film* (2001) offers easily adaptable generic whole-film-response and scene-based activities graded according to competency level, as well as a series of templates (some of which have been included below).[23] They argue that the level of language should not be the primary concern when selecting materials, instead emphasis should be on matching the level of activity to the level of the class. Given the clues offered by the images, in addition to music and dialogue, film clips are very flexible if used with the right activity.[24] For example, we used with some reservation *Ciao professore* at intermediate level, yet surprisingly it was very popular with students, despite the prevalence of Neapolitan dialect which remains largely inaccessible (even to Italian native speakers).[25] The emphasis here was clearly not on language awareness and listening comprehension, but on training global comprehension and stimulating oral and written production. Students were engaged by the child protagonists, the sentimentality of the story and the intercultural aspects it brought out, and they became active participants in creative follow-on exercises (ie. They related the story from one of the character's points of view; wrote the letter the Professore writes back to the children once he has relocated North etc.).

Ideally we aim to use material that lends itself to being matched to students' linguistic ability. Sherman's volume *Using Authentic Video in the Language Classroom* (2003) is very useful in providing a wide range of activities, focusing on both understanding the parts (listening comprehension, vocab and language structures) and on global comprehension activities of individual clips and whole films. Selecting clips on the basis of the language they model is, by necessity, time-consuming. Sherman advocates reusing material that has been used for other activities and, once it is understood well, utilising it for language

[23] The volume has the advantage of focusing also on the techniques of filmmaking, paying attention to editing, lighting and sound and the ways in which these elements influence and guide our viewing experience; this hones analytical skills and helps prepare students for the monographic film course they can take at third year level.

[24] Stempleski and Tomalin, *Video in Action,* 9.

[25] Released in Italy as *Io speriamo che me la cavo*, Lina Wertmuller, 1992.

focus activities.[26] This can be done even at a considerable distance from the original viewing and we have found that the advantage of studying one film per semester lies in the flexibility it gives us to keep a log of scenes for the language production activities they offer and to reuse these at a later stage (even at the next proficiency level) to model particular speech acts and structures.

Types of activities

1. Activities for working with film clips

1.1. Students predict and anticipate what they will see and hear
Asking students to make predictions about scenes, characters, plot events and dialogue is a powerful way of engaging students creatively and emotionally and of stimulating curiosity. Research supports the importance of 'advance organizers,' in order to facilitate guided and active viewing to achieve deeper learning.[27] Broadly speaking, advance organizers are a range of pre-viewing tasks that provide students with a context and background to the scene or film they are about to see, or with lexical items that focus their viewing and listening skills. Advance organizers can include the following:

- instructors provide a list of key words or ask students to brainstorm vocab for a particular semantic area;[28]
- students brainstorm culturally specific concepts or behaviour patterns (ie. the role of women in Italian society for *Pane e tulipani*);
- students brainstorm historical (*Mediterraneo* and *La vita è bella*) and social contexts (North-South divide, mafia etc. for *Ciao professore*);
- the instructor provides a brief plot summary in single sentences on the board;

---

[26] Sherman, 47.
[27] Carol Herron, "An Investigation of the Effectiveness of Using an Advance Organizer to Introduce Video in the Foreign Language Classroom," *The Modern Language Journal*, 78, no. 2 (1994): 190-98.
[28] The vocab building exercises at the beginning of each chapter in both of Borra and Pausini's volumes are excellent advance organizers that stimulate students to expect to see and hear certain events, culturally specific concepts and characters etc.

- the instructor writes a list of items that students will see or hear on the board. These can include real things (objects, monuments, people etc.) and abstract things (emotions and concepts), of which 2 or 3 are actually not present in the scene and serve as distractors. Students determine which items belong to the scene;[29]
- students read over a list of comprehension questions (ie. multiple choice, true or false statements, short answer questions) and create expectations about characters, events and culturally specific concepts they are about to see and hear. *Italian through Film* and *Ciak ... si parla italiano* are very useful here, but it is also relatively easy for instructors—especially when working with beginner level students—to quickly write up six true or false statements, when wanting to elicit scene-specific responses;
- students hypothesize about the storyline, plot, and actions and decisions of characters (see example below).

1.1.2 Analysing a film trailer and predicting the opening scene

When using films that none of the students are familiar with—or films that students have seen a while ago and can not recall in much detail—I often begin by having students predict the opening scene. This also works well as a one-off exercise with films that will not be studied in detail as an entire film. Students can be prompted in a variety of ways to imagine the opening scene of a film, including visual and verbal clues. DVD covers, film posters, advertisements and trailers can serve as visual triggers, while plot summaries of the entire film—either in written form for students to read, or summarized freely by the instructor in oral form—can serve as verbal triggers.[30] Film trailers, now available on most DVDs, are particularly useful, as they allow students to make hypotheses about the entire film, view some of the key characters and understand how music, images and editing are used to tell a story and to manipulate our expectations and emotions.[31]

---

[29] Stempleski and Tomalin, *Video in Action,* 123.
[30] Stempleski and Tomalin, *Film*, 47-9.
[31] Ibid., 31-4.

Example: *Caterina va in città* (intermediate and above)

Students are shown two trailers of the film. First, they are shown a thirty second trailer and are asked to complete the worksheet.

WORKSHEET 1 **ANALISI DI UNO SPEZZONE PUBBLICITARIO DI FILM (trailer)**[32]	
Qual è il titolo del film?	
Quando viene rivelato il titolo del film? Perché?	
Quali informazioni vengono date sui personaggi del film?	
Che genere di musica viene usato? Che cosa rivela la musica a proposito della trama del film?	
Che tipo di informazione viene data alla fine dello spezzone pubblicitario? Perché viene data alla fine?	

Table 20-1. Worksheet 1.

The trailer is shown several times and after the second viewing students consult in pairs to complete the worksheet. A brief plenary discussion clarifies what their expectations are about the film. At this stage students are led to believe that the film involves a lot of kissing and is centred around family dynamics. Students are then shown the longer version of the trailer (1.5min) and must add the new information to their worksheets. In pairs they are asked to compare their expectations about the film and then they are given the second worksheet and must decide, in pairs, and based on the information in the trailer, what the first scene will be: where will it be set, which characters will be in it, what the key events will be, what the characters will say and what will happen in the next scene.

[32] Freely adapted, ibid., 33.

WORKSHEET 2 INDOVINATE LA PRIMA SCENA[33]	
AMBIENTAZIONE Dove e quando sarà ambientata la prima scena?	
PERSONAGGI Quale personaggio apparirà nella prima scena e come si comporterà?	
AVVENIMENTI CHIAVE Cosa accadrà nella prima scena?	
DIALOGO Cosa si diranno le persone nella prima scena?	
ALTRO Elencate altri dettagli che pensate faranno parte della prima scena.	
LA SCENA SUCCESSIVA Cosa accadrà nella seconda scena? Dove sarà ambientata e quali saranno i personaggi coinvolti?	

Table 20-2. Worksheet 2.

In a plenary discussion students compare their hypotheses. Most students at this stage assume that the first scene will be in Caterina's hometown, showing her and the family engaged in preparations for the impeding move to Rome. One pair of students observed that while the shorter trailer led them to believe the emphasis of the film would be on the family dynamics, the longer trailer led them to believe that the emphasis would be on the school, both for Caterina and her father. One pair actually worked out that the father would have to be present in the first scene. Students are then shown the first scene and most will be very surprised to find that it is set in the father's classroom, on his last day at his old school before relocating to Rome, and he is telling his students in no uncertain terms that they had been the worst class of his life. Students will be emotionally engaged as the scene shows Italian students in a classroom situation and interesting student-teacher interactions, and it draws on their ability to think creatively and anticipate content. Completing this activity as a challenge between groups can also work well to awaken a competitive spirit and encourage students to come up with creative scenarios. Students

[33] Freely adapted ibid., 49.

in this class had just learned the use of indirect speech and were asked as a follow-up written activity to write the dialogue between one of the pupils and a parent in which the pupil recounts the outraged farewell speech by the teacher to one of his or her parents later that day.

1.2. Describing scenes and characters

Example: *Manuale d'amore* (Beginner to advanced level)

Manuale d'amore works well at all levels of competency, as it represents young characters in situations that students can easily identify with and that they are curious about. Introducing the chapter as a series of clips is effective as student interest is maintained from week to week, with students keen to find out more about the characters and what will happen to Tommaso's seemingly ill-fated courtship of Giulia. In week one, beginner level students, who have just learned the future tense, are given a worksheet that asks them to identify the characters they are going to see in the opening scene.

WORKSHEET 3

CHI SONO I PERSONAGGI?[34]

Guarda lo spezzone di *Manuale d'amore* e scrivi l'informazione richiesta per ogni personaggio.

	PERSONAGGIO 1	PERSONAGGIO 2	PERSONAGGIO 3
NOME			
RUOLO NEL FILM			
SESSO			
ETÀ			
LAVORO (cercate di capire o indovinare che lavoro fa questo personaggio; parlatene con il vostro compagno di banco)			

[34] Freely adapted ibid., 125.

DESCRIZIONE FISICA Com'è questo personaggio? (p.e. alto, bello, biondo, occhi blu ...) Com' è vestito?			
PERSONALITÀ Com'è questo personaggio? (simpatico, antipatico, tranquillo ...)			

Table 20-3. Worksheet 3.

The clip is shown at least two times. The first time students simply observe. During the second viewing students take notes and in pairs try to complete the worksheet providing simple information regarding the name, sex, occupation, age, and physical appearance of characters. I encourage students to give detailed descriptions of the characters and to comment in detail on their behaviour (eg. Tommaso è preoccupato, stressato, teso; Giulia è sicura di sé etc). It is useful to provide students with a vocab list of possible adjectives and descriptors (or ask students to refer to the relevant pages in the textbook).[35] As a group, students then compare their answers and reactions to the characters, observe culturally specific behaviour (the black cat crossing Tommaso's path; his efforts of courting Giulia etc.) and speculate about the characters' next moves. This can also be done as a written follow-on exercise: students write three sentences in the future tense about what will happen next (eg. they will/will not meet again; what they will say when they meet again; how they will react etc.)

---

[35] A variation of this activity at a beginner level is to have students conduct a trivia quiz about the scene, whereby the teacher gives a brief outline of the scene (a guy on a motorbike encounters two girls outside one of their homes, there is a cat etc). In teams students write up a list of trivia questions ("Di che colore era lo scooter del ragazzo? Cosa indossava la ragazza con lo scooter? Di che colore era il casco? Che cosa ha detto il ragazzo quando ha visto le due ragazze?" etc.). See Susan Stempleski and Barry Tomalin *Video in* Action, 111. A variation of this is "I spy," where students call out objects starting with a particular letter, as suggested by Sherman, 177-78.

Love stories such as *Manuale d'amore*, *L'ultimo bacio*, *Pane e tulipani* are particularly suitable for activities of anticipation and predicting future actions. As the stories unfold, there are many entertaining moments that offer opportunities for instructors to pause and ask students in pairs to predict what will happen next.

1.2.2 Activities on film characters

Activities based on film characters are successful with students at all levels, as they encourage identification and provoke strong emotional responses that ensure active student engagement. What follows is a list of activities that were variously adapted with all of the films we used in our trial process:

- interview with character;
- give advice to character;
- summarise a scene from the point of view of one of the characters. This works well for practicing reported speech, for example when students need to relate to a friend (real or immaginary) a scene played by their chosen character with a lot of dialogue. As an alternative, scenes without much dialogue can be used to get students to sum up the actions of a scene from a character's point of view, and this can help with practicing the past tense.
- imagine you are one of the characters: what would you have done and said in their place? (this lends itself for practising the 'periodo ipotetico').
- roleplay (focus on gestures that are used to communicate meaning and how they differ from their own culture);[36]
- write a letter (ie. the professore in *Ciao professore* writes a letter back home talking about his experience in Corazano; 'adopt' one of the soldiers stranded on Kastellorizon in *Mediterraneo* and write the letter he writes back home to his mother, wife or girlfriend; in pairs act out the scene; write the letter that Rosalba in *Pane e tulipani* writes to her son explaining her choice to stay in Venice etc.);
- imagine the character to be of a different nationality (ie. Come avrebbero reagito Giulia e Tommaso di *Manuale d'amore* se fossero australiani?);

[36] For useful guidelines on how to conduct effective roleplays ee also Stempleski and Tomalin, *Video in Action*, 90.

- imagine the character's interior monologue (for example in the first episode of *Manuale d'amore* Tommaso gives us a running commentary of his emotions through his interior monologue, while we can only deduce Giulia's thoughts from her lines of dialogue and body language; students complement Tommaso's interior monologue by providing one for Giulia);
- students identify and describe emotions displayed.[37]

The above activities are very flexible and can be adapted relatively easily to most films without too much modification.

1.3 Listening and grammar-based tasks

Films offer many opportunities for language awareness activities. Sherman observes that using film clips to model language structures and to prompt production has a deeper learning effect, as it shows language in action in authentic contexts.[38] Close comprehension exercises require students to listen out for words and language structures. They are useful in order to identify what Sherman refers to as language "black spots" or "patches of incomprehension."[39] Sherman suggests a range of activities that can be done alongside global comprehension exercises without much preparation.[40] Below is a list of exercises I have found particularly useful:

- Wordhunt:[41] a short sequence with suitable language is selected and after several viewings students are asked to listen out for one type of word or language structure (eg. verbs, adjectives, colloquialisms, idiomatic expressions, subjunctive etc.).
- Listening for vocab: ask students to listen out for particular words or how a particular concept is expressed; provide students with definitions of words but not the word itself; ask students to identify the word;[42] using subtitles for the hearing impaired, ask students to identify the differences between the words they hear and the words they see on screen.
- Progressive dictation and gapfill:[43] students watch a scene with a very short dialogue (3 sentences) and call out words as they

---

[37] See "Show your emotions," Stempleski and Tomalin, *Film*, 52-3.
[38] Sherman, 47.
[39] Ibid., 122.
[40] See "Understanding the words," ibid., 120-22.
[41] Ibid., 268.
[42] Ibid., 121.
[43] Ibid., 122.

hear them; the instructor writes them on the board and during successive viewings the students gradually piece together the complete dialogue which the instructor or another student writes up on the board, gradually filling all gaps.

2. Activities for working with whole films

2.1. Favourite scenes

An engaging follow-on activity I like to do with my students once they have seen the whole film—including the scenes that were not studied in class—is to list and discuss their favourite scenes.[44] The class is divided into groups of three students and each student is encouraged to suggest at least one or more scenes, which are then discussed by the whole group in order to arrive at a ranking of the three best scenes preferred by the whole group. I then hand out the worksheet, which the group completes together. Ideally each person in the group will be given the chance to report back to the class, describing one of the scenes selected by the group. Inevitably there will be some overlap, as many students will prefer the same key scenes. This is an excellent activity that enables the instructor to learn about students' reactions to films and the kinds of situations and characters that engage them emotionally. This activity usually leads to lively discussions as students disagree and challenge each other on their preferences. As a variation of this, with films that present a lot of characters (eg. *L'ultimo bacio*; *Ciao professore*; *Mediterraneo*, *Manuale d'amore*), students can be asked to talk about their preferred character.

---

[44] See Stempleski and Tomalin, *Film*, 79.

WORKSHEET 4 Scene preferite[45]			
	Scene 1	**Scene 2**	**Scene 3**
L'AMBIENTAZIONE Dove si svolge la scena? (descrivete l'ambiente: p.e. le cose che si vedono, i palazzi, i monumenti; le località geografiche; l'ambiente sociale etc)			
I PERSONAGGI Nominate e descrivete i personaggi più importanti e commentate il loro ruolo			
AZIONE Descrivete come si svolge la scena (cosa accade, quando, come, perché etc)			
COLONNA SONORA Musica Provate a ricordare i brani musicali Dialogo Cercate di ricordare alcune battute e commentate le cose che si dicono i personaggi (ci sono voci fuori campo, monologhi interiori etc. ?)			

[45] Freely adapted ibid., 80.

PERCHÉ Motivate la vostra scelta (che cosa vi piace di questa scena? Qual è la sua importanza all'interno del film?)			

Table 20-4. Worksheet 4.

As Stempleski and Tomalin point out, at lower proficiency level, it may be preferable for the instructor to prepare a list of memorable scenes to jog students' memories and to provide verbal cues.[46] I find that it works well to run the students through the 'scene select' menu on the DVD, as the images and scene titles help students to recall their reactions to a particular scene and to remember the not-so-prominent scenes.

2.2 Discussion topics

While the available textbooks for studying Italian through film (e.g. *Italian through Film*; *Ciak ... si parla italiano*) are very useful in providing film-specific discussion topics that help consolidate subject specific vocab-building, the generic catalogue of discussion topics provided by Stempleski and Tomalin is a handy base list that can be used as is; alternatively it can be easily expanded and adapted by the instructor to suit a particular film.[47] Below is the version I have used with my students and circulated amongst colleagues to adapt to their particular materials. In small groups students select and discuss 2-3 questions. One or two students act as spokespersons, reporting back to the whole class after about 10-15 minutes. The discussion topics are also useful for written practice. I have found it constructive to ask students to prepare a short paragraph for each of the 2-3 selected questions at home before the next class. In this way students are given the opportunity to reflect at length on a given film and to prepare their answers with the help of a dictionary. This method allows students especially at advanced level to practice particular verb forms such as the periodo ipotetico (e.g."Se potessi incontrare uno dei personaggi, chi vorresti incontrare e cosa gli diresti?") both in written and oral form. In the next class, students are then asked to discuss their answers freely without reading from their prepared answers, while the

[46] Ibid., 79.
[47] Ibid., 78.

instructor circulates to provide feedback on the written versions. At Macquarie University where we use on-line discussion boards and email exchanges with our external students, we make the catalogue of questions available online and students, who are paired up over the course of the semester in an ongoing discussion exchange via email and voice board.

WORKSHEET 5 Argomenti per la discussione[48]
• Cosa ti è piaciuto di più in questo film? Perché? • Che cosa non ti è piaciuto? Perché? • Quale personaggio hai trovato più simpatico/antipatico? Perché? • Se avessi la possibilità di incontrare uno dei personaggi, chi vorresti incontrare e che cosa gli diresti? • Che cosa non hai capito di questo film? • Ti è piaciuto il finale del film? Perché sì/ Perché no? • Se fossi tu al posto del regista cosa cambieresti? • Cosa ti ha insegnato questo film (cosa hai imparato?) • Quali aspetti interculturali (differenze culturali) ha messo in luce questo film? • Ti è piaciuta la musica in questo film? Perché sì/ Perché no? • Qual è la tua scena preferita? Perché? • Se avessi la possibilità di incontrare il regista di questo film, cosa gli chiederesti?

Table 20-5. Worksheet 5.

3. Assessment and other written tasks

To ensure that students understand that film is not used merely as entertainment, it is important to make it part of the assessment structure

[48] Freely adapted, ibid., 78.

and to intersperse what are generally perceived as enjoyable oral activities with writing tasks. These can include:

- Plot summaries (done individually or collaboratively at the end of a scene or after viewing the complete film);
- Film reviews (see example below);
- Short answer quizzes (these can be prepared collaboratively and conducted as competitions between teams;[49] analysis and description of characters and events;[50]
- Online quizzes comprised of a mixture of true and false statements, multiple choice comprehension questions and short answer comprehension questions;
- Letter to character (or from character's point of view);
- Research project on historical, cultural or social background;
- Oral presentations subsequently written up (see example below).

3.1 Film reviews

Film reviews can be integrated in different ways, but it is important to familiarize students with the genre before asking them to write one of their own. I find it useful to provide students with several straightforward reviews on a variety of films (including Italian language reviews of the latest box office hit that students are likely to have seen in their own language). In small groups students are asked to analyse the reviews and to deduct information about the general structure, tone and style of a film review, followed by a whole-class summing up session. Once students are familiar with the conventions of film reviews, they are asked to compare different reviews about the film they are studying, followed by writing their own review. At upper intermediate level I provide a pair of students with two different reviews—ideally one favourable and one critical—and ask them to summarise their respective reviews to the other student and to elucidate the point of view of their review, once again paying attention to tone, style etc. Students are asked to comment on the two different points of view and to discuss their own perception of the film. As a follow-on activity they jointly write their own review of the film. The teacher circulates and assists with language.

---

[49] See also "Memory Game," ibid., 44-6.

[50] Here Borra and Pausini's suggestions can be quite useful.

At advanced level I prefer to complete this task as a research activity, whereby students locate film-specific websites and download good quality film reviews. This also trains their skills in understanding Italian print media and hones their independent research skills. I have found it useful to use Tomalin and Stempleski's worksheet (see worksheet 20-6), as it provides a guide for a structured comparison.

Reviews can be written collaboratively in class or independently as part of the written assignment. Student versions are then read to the class and can later be up-loaded onto web-based bulletin boards to be shared with other students. This activity can also be followed by a pro/con panel discussion whereby different teams challenge each other's point of view.

WORKSHEET 6 **Paragonare le recensioni**[51]		
	Recensione A	Recensione B
Qual è il titolo della recensione? Ti sembra appropriato?		
Dov'è stata pubblicata la recensione? Di che tipo di rivista, giornale, o sito internet si tratta?		
Come si chiama l'autore della recensione?		
C'è una locandina? Che cosa fa vedere?		
Di quali aspetti del film parla la recensione?		
Quali aspetti del film vengono discussi in modo positivo? Quali aspetti del film sono piaciuti all' autore della recensione?		

[51] Adapted from Stempleski and Tomalin, *Film*, 94.

Quali aspetti del film vengono discussi in modo negativo? Quali aspetti del film non sono piaciuti all' autore della recensione?		
Questa recensione consiglia la visione del film?		
Che giudizio dà del film (in termini di punteggio?)		
Scrivi due o tre frasi in cui riassumi il punto di vista dell' autore di questa recensione.		
Ora paragona, insieme al tuo compagno, il tuo punto di vista. È diverso dalla recensione? Come?		

Table 20-6. Worksheet 6.

3.2 Synopsis

Writing a film or scene synopsis is a useful activity that can be performed easily in class, as non-assessed homework, as part of the film journals and as part of the written assessment. Again it is helpful to familiarize students with the conventions. With films that the majority of students has seen beforehand (eg. *La vita è bella*), I find it useful to ask students to write a short plot summary in pairs in class, while I circulate to assist and offer corrections. Students are then asked to read their versions out aloud to one another and to compare the types of information given. A sheet with three different published plot summaries (ie. provided by DVD covers, internet sites etc.) is circulated and students are asked to compare them with their own and to identify how professionally written versions differ from their own (eg. use of tenses, types of information, when information is supplied).

3.3 Oral presentation

At upper-advanced level our trial focused on writing about intercultural differences. For this purpose, one of the ongoing assessment tasks required students to imagine they were teaching English abroad and had to present one or more Australian films to their class to illustrate Australian cultural values. As a follow-on activity students had to imagine they were teachers of Italian at an Australian school or college and had to choose an appropriate Italian film that lends itself to the teaching of intercultural values. This was done as a group activity and consisted of an oral presentation (using powerpoint and film clips) to the whole class, accompanied by a written version submitted at a later time and incorporating comments on the discussion that the oral presentation had triggered.

WORKSHEET 7

PRESENTAZIONE ORALE[52]

In coppie scegliete un film italiano che si presta all'insegnamento dei valori della cultura italiana.

In coppie preparate la vostra presentazione:

- scegliete almeno due scene che ritenete importanti da presentare al resto della classe. Scrivete un riassunto di circa 200 parole del film, da fotocopiare e da dare al resto della classe il giorno della presentazione.
- Su internet cercate qualche recensione e spiegate brevemente come il film è stato accolto dal pubblico italiano.

IL GIORNO DELLA VOSTRA PRESENTAZIONE

- dite il nome del film e date altre informazioni utili
- date una copia del vostro riassunto al resto della classe
- lasciate che gli altri studenti leggano il riassunto che avete preparato
- rispondete alle domande che gli altri hanno da fare riguardo al riassunto appena letto
- mostrate almeno due scene chiavi del film al resto della classe e spiegate brevemente
    - cosa succede
    - perché la scena è importante
    - perché avete scelto quella scena

[52] Freely adapted, ibid., 134-35.

- le cose a cui fare attenzione durante la visione
- sviluppo della trama
- sviluppo dei personaggi
- scenografia
- recitazione
- lingua
- valori interculturali

PER CONCLUDERE: Finite la vostra presentazione con una domanda generale che risulti dal film e che potrebbe stimolare una discussione generale. Sta a voi iniziare e guidare la discussione. Nella versione scritta includete anche alcuni commenti e punti di vista suscitati dalla discussione in classe.

Esempio: Presentazione del film *Radio Freccia*. Domanda per la discussione: Immagina di essere un ascoltatore di Radio Raptus. La stazione radio lancia un appello ai suoi ascoltatori a partecipare alla scelta degli argomenti da trattare e discutere in diretta (on air). Quali argomenti proporresti?

Table 20-7. Worksheet 7.

Conclusion

In order to evaluate the use of film in the language classroom, at the end of the semester I conducted group interviews with students at all competency levels. The questions asked included: How did the film-based activities change you as learners? To what extent did the use of film increase your language skills? What other skills do you think you have acquired over the course of the semester? What did you like about the material? Do you have any suggestions for improvement?

Language learning through film was unanimously rated as a very positive and motivating experience. Working with a whole film spread out over the course of the semester was perceived as positive and engaging, as it allowed students to feel comfortable with a particular register of language, regional inflection and diction and to become familiar with storylines and characters, which increased their motivation to participate in creative follow-on exercises. Students reported that they had become more confident speakers and agreed that their listening skills had improved, particularly because they had learned to be less worried about understanding each word in favour of using global comprehension strategies. Students felt that they had been taught to become active learners. Analysing and interpreting individual clips had enhanced their awareness of how the parts make up the whole. This by implication showed how the experience had enhanced students' media literacy and sharpened a whole range of analytical skills, including their critical thinking skills.

Advanced and upper advanced level students in particular, who had previously been used to a grammar-based and teacher-led approach, benefited in quantifiable ways. For example, end-of-semester oral examinations and listening comprehension tests showed improved listening comprehension and oral fluency. Importantly, after their initial resistance towards task-based, student-centred and collaborative activities, students reported that these activities had contributed to making them more independent learners and active viewers.

Asked for further suggestions, students expressed strong views in favour of watching a film together as a group, outside of class time and to use class time for (re)viewing short clips and doing related activities. Students enjoyed the variety of tasks and the mixture of close comprehension and global comprehension exercises and felt that collaborative learning activities had been helpful and enjoyable. Students suggested doing writing and reading activities outside of class time in favour of further clip-based activities in class.

Overall the trial demonstrated the effectiveness of film-based activities in assisting students to systematically build their language, learning and thinking skills. It illustrated the flexibility of film as a medium for language teaching and confirmed the need to integrate film carefully through effective, task-based activities.

MACQUARIE UNIVERSITY, AUSTRALIA

Other References

Textbooks

Balì, Maria and Giovanna Rizzo. *Espresso 2*, Firenze: Alma Edizioni, 2004.

Balì, Maria and Luciana Ziglio. *Espresso 3*, Firenze: Alma Edizioni, 2003.

Lazzarino, Graziana et. al. *Prego! An Invitation to Italian.* 6th ed. New York: McGraw Hill, 2004.

Films

Caterina va in città. Paolo Virzì, 2003.

Ciao professore (*Io speriamo che me la cavo*). Lina Wertmuller, 1992.

Il postino. Michael Radford, 1994.
Il sorpasso. Dino Risi, 1963.
Io non ho paura. Gabriele Salvatores, 2003.
La luce negli occhi, Andrea Porporati, 2001.
La vita è bella. Roberto Benigni, 1997.
L'ultimo Bacio. Gabriele Muccino, 2001.
Manuale d'amore. Giovanni Veronesi, 2005.
Mediterraneo. Gabriele Salvatores, 1991.
My name is Tanino. Paolo Virzì, 2002.
Nuovo cinema paradiso, Giuseppe Tornatore, 1988.
Ovo sodo. Paolo Virzì, 1997.
Pane e tulipani. Silvio Soldini, 2000.
Quando sei nato non ti puoi più nascondere. Marco Tullio Giordana, 2005.
Una giornata particolare. Ettore Scola, 1977.

CHAPTER TWENTY-ONE

TEACHING VISUAL THINKING, IN AND OUT OF THE ITALIAN CANON

THOMAS ERLING PETERSON

In this essay I investigate the teaching of cinema in terms of the notion of visual thinking. My point of departure is a pursuit of the specific cognition that comes about by viewing films with classes in context. I suggest that it is incumbent on students to negotiate paradoxes and ambiguities in their descriptions and analyses of the cinematic artefact, and to engage in aesthetic responses that incorporate the dramatic, historical, visual and narrative components of film. Citing examples from the Italian cinema of the 20th century, I explore the connection between Italian film history and the legacy of Italian humanism and suggest, through this example, how visual thinking can reclaim the authenticity and particularity of artistic culture in the university classroom.

Filmic Logic and Visual Thinking

I have witnessed two extremes in the teaching of film: the formalist and the sociological. The first focuses on theory; whether semiotic, psychoanalytic, aesthetic or ideological, this focus drives the film into a "reading" that students are asked to make. Such interpretations are steered by criteria that often have no compelling or coherent relationship with the film itself. The 1960s and 1970s witnessed an explosion in film theory which resulted in a frequent bias in the classroom as professors passed on their theoretical perspectives in such a way as to distance students from the immediate consideration of the films' complexity. Conversely, the sociological approach to teaching film I witnessed tended to regard the film naively as a container of information, usually a narrative, analyzable in terms of the events it referenced. The question of how a film is made was sacrificed for the sake of the representational mirror it holds up to society and its problems. What these approaches share is a certain tendentiousness, a pursuit of an *interpretation* even before an adequate *description* or *analysis* can be made.

As Edgar Morin writes in *The Cinema, or the Imaginary Man*, there has been a widespread tendency among intellectuals to judge films on the basis of their political or historical usefulness. Under such skewed criteria, the most "valid" films communicated a message of immediate legibility and thus lacked ambiguity. A corollary to this (I am still reflecting on my experience as a student and teacher) is that teachers assemble survey courses that represent moments in political-sociological history, assuming in the process that the action represented in the films is close enough to reality to accept as real. As with the formalist approach, the sociological approach distances the films from the immediate consideration of the student. In my opinion, both of these approaches undervalue the image and thus suppress the native curiosity and creativity of students. As an alternative to this didactic polarity I propose the engagement of *visual thinking* in the study and teaching of film. I do not mean to commit the inverse error and simply reject the use of formalistic or sociological criteria; but I do mean to prioritize the pedagogic and scholastic activity of describing and analyzing films before interpreting them. This in turn means recognizing that films are primarily visual documents.

Visual thinking originates in perception, in the sensory-motor phenomenon of sight and the vividness of space-time. Such perception is more complex, mysterious and ambiguous than is commonly acknowledged, not being the mere reception of information but its encoding and interpretation. Visual thinking is also a matter of cognition, of the processing and integration of cultural signs; as such it implicates the symbiosis (or convergence) of ocular-retinal and imaginary functions. In this composite way, visual thinking mediates between "common sense" approaches to the role of sight in the construction of knowledge and the more scientific discussions of specialists. By focusing on the perceptive and cognitive processing of the filmic image, the educator can gain access to the multiple and parallel learning capacities—the visual thinking—of the student.

Yvette Biró has written in this regard of a "filmic logic" which instructors can employ as the basis for the teaching of film. The classification of filmic logic includes semantics and aesthetics: filmic logic is analogical and is concerned with drawing comparisons and homologies from among a variety of patterns. This is in contrast to formal logic, which is digital and syntactic in nature, and classifies by means of reduction and elimination. As Biró argues, most of the information humans take in is analogic and iconic in nature: "We receive more than eighty percent of all our information throughout our eyes. This is why seeing is naturally the foremost medium of thought."[1] The paradox which arises in the film classroom is that while students are typically saturated with visual media from an early age, rarely have they been asked to articulate how visual messages work to communicate ideas and emotions, or how film sequences are constructed into works of art.

In order to orient students to filmic logic, I ask them to prepare sequential expositions of films. In this way, they appropriate works in terms of their concrete structures without presuming to enter into the subjectivity of the characters or filmmaker. Sequential expositions help to sort out problems of articulation of space and time in film, enabling access to the film's deeper signifying structures. Other empirical questions include: When was the film made, in what genre, in what social-aesthetic-historical context? What are its raw physical characteristics? If it is a narrative, what are its dramatic components? Who are the characters, how do they behave and interact? What is the timeline? What other salient aspects concern the film's production and distribution?

Such questions lead naturally to a discussion of technique and style. While most students are unfamiliar with technical vocabulary, they *are* sensitive to the mechanics of shots, framing, movement, and duration or visual rhythm; many will be led to acquire a critical sensitivity to editing style and the manipulation of photographic values (such as depth of field, focal length and image tonality). These factors are sufficient to ensure that students' descriptions take on density and shape, that filmic transitions become memorable, that representational details become emblematic of something larger. As students arrive at the verbal means to describe and analyze visual phenomena, they acquire a critical sense and thus a sense of accomplishment. As one's satisfaction with a film is expressed, one passes from issues of vocabulary and context to questions of interpretation. Here one can also respond to the emotional impact of the work of art, entering into the subjectivities of the characters. If analysis means avoiding the moment of judgment, interpretation requires it, as it concerns the film's actualization in the world.

Filmic logic and visual thinking involve deontic, performative language, the language of gestures and the nonverbal, as do poetry and the other arts. Part of the problem of defining visual thinking has to do with the term "thinking" itself, with its centuries of acceptance as

---

[1] Yvette Biró, *Profane Mythology: The Savage Mind of the Cinema*, trans. Imre Goldstein (Bloomington, IN: Indiana UP, 1982), 45.

"ratiocination," which does not get to the heart of cognition. Thinking as cognition entails the sensory-motor mechanism of the eye, the unconscious decisions of the perceiver, the recollection of repeated scenarios and the assumptions of "common sense."

Maurice Merleau-Ponty's reflection on the visual as the basis for cognition stands at the advent of a phenomenology of perception that paralleled emerging developments in psychology, philosophy and the arts in the mid-20th century. In his more topical studies of film he defends the viewer's capacity to spontaneously comprehend the forms, behaviors, emotions, facts and ideas of a film and to interrelate them coherently, respecting the film's rhythms and ambiguities.

> Movies [...] always have a story and often an idea [...], but the function of the film is not to make these facts or ideas known to us. Kant's remark that, in knowledge imagination serves the understanding, whereas in art the understanding serves the imagination, is a profound one. In other words, ideas or prosaic facts are only there to give the creator an opportunity to seek out their palpable symbols and to trace their visible and sonorous monogram. The meaning of a film is incorporated into its rhythm just as the meaning of a gesture may immediately be read in that gesture: the film does not mean anything but itself.[2]

Merleau-Ponty opposes both empiricism and intellectualism. If empiricism boils down the act of vision to a passive reception of external stimuli, or little more than an act of observation (as in the sociological approach to cinema), intellectualism interiorizes the visual within the subject who produces or "constitutes the world" on the basis of speculation (as in the formalistic approach). The alternative to empiricism and intellectualism locates in the visual and other senses a potential "union of mind and body" that benefits from the perception of groups, gestalts and configurations.[3] This alternative does not support the outdated views of classical psychology (including behaviorism) or speculative philosophy, but seeks to consider the film as a perceptual object that guides the sensitive viewer to its meaning.[4]

---

[2] Maurice Merleau-Ponty, *Sense and Non-Sense*, trans. with pref. H. L. Dreyfus and P. A. Dreyfus (Evanston, IL: Northwestern University Press, 1964), 57.

[3] See Martin Jay, *Downcast Eyes. The Denigration of Vision in Twentieth-Century French Thought* (Berkeley: U of California P, 1993), 297-327, for a discussion of Merleau-Ponty's positive view of vision, including his film theory.

[4] See Edgar Morin, *The Cinema or the Imaginary Man*, trans. L. Mortimer (Minneapolis: U of Minnesota P, 2005), for an anthropological study of the development from the 19th century "cinematograph" to the 20th century "cinema,"

Film History: the Case of Italian Cinema

In his essay, "Film History," Raymond Williams argues against the "assumption that there is a significant unitary subject, film, with reasonably evident common properties," and he critiques the tendency of those who, in considering film history, are "likely to pass over 'history' and put a defining emphasis on 'film.'"[5] Williams divides his pursuit of "an actual, rather than an ideal or categorical history" of film, into four areas: "(a) the actual technology and its uses; (b) film and popular culture; (c) film and established culture; (d) film and modernist culture" (135). As concerns technology Williams notes, "Already in the earliest years the basic elements of the technology were being used for the radically different purposes which were inherent in what was never a series but always a scatter of inventions" (136). In the popular culture, which is altered vastly by periods of industrialization, Williams notes the importance of melodrama, with its continuation of theatrical techniques of mime and "visual acting" along with "acrobats, conjurors, tumblers and dancers, who carried on both old and new tricks in film; the performers of farces and sketches in the music-halls; the skilled horse-riders, prominent in the circus..." (139). In general, the economic reality of the cinema industry has worked against the popular culture, absorbing it and utilizing it for its own ends. Williams notes how the "established culture" of the "metropolitan centres" clung to higher forms of theater while the cinematic art developed elsewhere, in a way that was "quite remarkably liberating;" because of the reproducibility of cinema, "there could be a simultaneous high investment of both talent and resources in any single production" (141). Thus a new medium was born in spite of an intransigent establishment. On the margins of the new industry one finds the culture of modernism, in which a great cultural transformation was taking place that involved "profound perceptual shifts," in cinema, painting, and the other arts. Modernist cinema explored dispersed narratives and shifting points of view and, through editing and montage, provided non-representational imagery that had much in common with modernism's "rejection of the forms of bourgeois theatre and representational painting" (143).

---

the latter typified by metamorphoses of time, space, and of the notion of their representation, in contrast to the relatively simple documentation of reality that is presumed to have been accomplished by the former. Morin's study builds on the work of Merleau-Ponty.

[5] Raymond Williams, *What I Came to Say* (London: Hutchinson Radius, 1989), 132.

Generally speaking, film history in Italy has confirmed this pattern of developments. Yet one doesn't find the intransigence that Williams writes of in the early years (perhaps due to the lateness and incompleteness of the industrial revolution in Italy). From the earliest years of documentaries and magic shows, melodrama and epics, Italian cinema crossed barriers between the established and popular cultures. Pastrone's 1914 *Cabiria*, a three-hour epic that introduced the tracking shot and radical innovations in lighting, was based on Livy's account of the Second Punic War, but it was named after a slave girl. One sees in Pastrone's use of Livy a general truth, that when films are based on classic texts the references to the source text take on an iconic quality: deviations from the text can be more interesting than fidelity to it.[6] *Cabiria* represents the "expressionist" school of Italian film, while there developed in parallel a "realistic" school, which eventually leads to Neorealism. Though the fascist regime certainly subjugated the popular culture, much creative activity continued to occur. With the foundation in 1935 of Cinecittà and the Centro Sperimentale di Cinematografia in Rome, the young generation of filmmakers was provided a valuable center of activity.

Neorealism was a liberating break from the established culture, accomplished by a group of filmmakers whose ethical judgments were never absent from their aesthetic choices. As André Bazin was quick to see, the shift to realism was nothing if not paradoxical, since the films themselves were inimical to naive assumptions about what constituted the real. When teaching Neorealist cinema, therefore, one must introduce the various and conflicting definitions and interpretations of that term; one must remind students that realism depends on fantasy and the oneiric as much as on historical reenactments based on the popular culture. As with literary Neorealism, the new cinema presented a "chorus of voices" from the broad "variety of Italys" that existed beyond and beneath the veneer of official Italy.[7] There is Luchino Visconti, whose 1941 *Ossessione* recovers

---

[6] Pasolini's *Il vangelo secondo Matteo* (1964) stands as the classic example of this problem. The text of Matthew's Gospel is subjectively reordered with scenes skipped and others expanded. This manipulation also concerns the problems of contemporary Christianity in its relationship to the past.

[7] See Italo Calvino, "Prefazione" to *Il sentiero dei nidi di ragno* (Milano: Garzanti, 1987), 9: "Il 'neorealismo' non fu una scuola. (Cerchiamo di dire le cose con esattezza). Fu un insieme di voci, in gran parte periferiche, una molteplice scoperta delle diverse Italie, anche—o—specialmente—delle Italie fino allora più inedite per la letteratura. Senza la varietà di Italie sconosciute l'una all'altra—o che si supponevano sconosciute, senza la varietà dei dialetti e dei gerghi da far lievitare e impastare nella lingua letteraria, non ci sarebbe stato 'neorealismo.'"

the popular genre of melodrama, and whose love of opera is combined with the political theme of the Risorgimento in *Senso* (1954). There is Roberto Rossellini, who learns his craft making documentaries for the regime, then emerges with *Roma, Città aperta* (1945) and *Paisà* (1946), whose stark mise-en-scéne style culminates in the stark *Viaggio in Italia* (1953). And there is the tender, wrenching pathos of Vittorio De Sica whose *Ladri di biciclette* (1948), *Umberto D* (1951) and *Miracolo a Milano* (1950) are masterfully choreographed portraits of the urban poor set in "real time." Subsequently there is Fellini, who contributes an amusing anti-clerical chapter to *Paisà*, and comes of age showing his debts to burlesque, popular theater and religious ritual with *Luci del varietà* (1950), *La strada* (1954) and *Le notti di Cabiria* (1956).

Amid so much variety and change, even within the *oeuvre* of individual directors, it is very hard to generalize about Neorealism or Italian cinema. This seems to confirm another observation by Raymond Williams, that a "sense of diversity and contradiction must be firmly sustained against the forms of any unitary 'aesthetics of film' or unitary developmental history" (144). Given the individualism and auteurism Italian filmmakers, the critic in search of unifying trends or styles is best advised to look at the iconic or figurative means by which, in Merleau-Ponty's terms, the movie means itself; for it is only through that process of self-signification and self-framing that it represents or stands for something else, which is invariably to some extent, Italy and the Italian artistic-humanistic patrimony. As Andre Chastel writes:

> Il posto occupato da registi quali Antonioni, Visconti fa in gran parte riferimento ad una ricca eredità, ad un senso della composizione e dei colori, che induce a considerarli come gli eredi dell'attività di Piero della Francesca, Correggio o i Carracci. L'utilizzazione per i film delle risorse della pittura sembra naturale ai cineasti italiani. È assieme un'attitudine a cogliere i momenti pregnanti dell'esperienza umana.[8]

With the advent of Neorealism one moves from an emphasis on product to an absorption in process (also because of the lack of production facilities after the war). As Deleuze has written, the "direct time-image" of modern cinema starts with Neorealism, when the purely optical takes over, abandoning any slavish relation to a *text* and involving a "slackening of

[8] André Chastel, *Storia dell'arte italiana* (Bari: Laterza, 1996), 628.

sensory-motor connections."[9] Renato Barilli has written of the new cinema's

> scrupulous attention to the search for its own material, whether this is understood as a valorization of plastic and spatial effects worthy of the visual arts or for mundane, banal materials, in which it would reveal, as in an epiphany, the purest state of existence.[10]

Thus the problem for educator is two-fold: to train the attention and to educate to the history. As seen above, "film history" needn't be qualified in terms of a national canon. Just as one adjusts one's thinking about a period of cinematic history, so one's teaching can be altered to focus on the importance of visual cognition in the making of films.

The Italian literary canon existed for centuries before unification, offering a sense of identity and unity to a people beset by foreign domination, factionalism and unstable political structures. Yet the language of this canon was never truly spoken by large numbers of people. More than in any other European country, the *questione della lingua* in Italy was conditioned by the phenomena of bilingualism (the stratification of national language and dialects proceeding diachronically through time) and bistylism (the synchronic presence of high and low registers in the literature). There was a pervasive formalism and classicism in the literature and a perceived need for canonical self-reference, but there was also a strong popular, regionalist and anti-classical reaction against it. After the Counter-Reformation, the Italians emerged as guardians of the world's art, the sometimes listless curators of a dusty realm of the dead. Achieving nationhood, Italy's *matria*, the motherland of the popular and provincial cultures, grew estranged from its *patria*, the overarching institutional and state apparatuses of the dominant culture.[11] After the

---

[9] Gilles Deleuze, *Cinema 2: The Time-Image*, trans. Hugh Tomlinson and Barbara Habberjam (Minneapolis: U of Minnesota P, 1989), 1-13.

[10] Renato Barilli, *A Course on Aesthetics*, trans. Karen E. Pinkus (Minneapolis: U of Minnesota P, 1993), 115.

[11] Andrea Zanzotto, *Fantasie di avvicinamento* (Milan: Mondadori, 1991), 310, uses the matria/patria dichotomy with reference to the contrast between one's maternal language and the language of the nation-state. Renato Poggili, "The Italian Success Story," in *The Spirit of the Letter* (Cambridge, MA: Harvard UP, 1965), 199-221, discusses the "patriotic myth" in the Italian national literature in terms of "fatherlands" which are destined to be artificial constructs designating the futility of a struggle with the past, while the "motherlands" that emerged in the *dopoguerra* and with Neorealism, in cinema and in literature, expressed hope and invoked the future.

debacle of fascism, this fact of a fundamental disunity was openly acknowledged in art, literature and film; but the crisis was not resolved and the Resistance aspirations for national renewal were frustrated. Despite the economic miracle of the 1950s, vast social inequities among Italians persisted, especially between North and South. In addition to economic differences, one found something akin to what Octavio Paz has called "a multiple other" that allows the alterity of various groups in society to be likened to that of the individual who confronts an existential or spiritual crisis.[12]

In Neorealism it is the civic intention of directors to represent cultural change and learning with an eye to the multiple other of Italy. Filmmakers disseminate a new ethical message that hovers at the margins of the collective consciousness, as did the great figurative artists of the past, trusting in the values of the image, the strength of analogy and the power of ambiguity. One finds encapsulated in the great Italian films a certain allegory of learning, a representation of how one learns to learn. In these pedagogical situations the figural element takes over, accomplishing what words cannot. As the subliminal and intentional facts of cognition are transmitted through filmic images, so does the viewer interiorize the filmic other by processing the spatio-temporal continuum on the screen. Figurality does not pit the word against the image, just as filmic logic does not exclude the rational coherence of the verbal component. Rather, as Lyotard puts it, figurality involves "a (discursive) principle of readability and a (figural) principle of unreadability shared one in the other"; but this sharing cannot be equated with a simple harmony: "[The figural] is not attached to the visible, nor to the I-You of language, nor to the One of perception, but to the Id of desire. And not to the immediate figures of desire but to its operations."[13] In his defense of the Id in the name of unreadability, Lyotard posits "the figural as an internal principle of disruption, which pits the materiality of signifiers against what they try to

---

[12] Octavio Paz, *Configurations*, trans. G. Aroul et. al. (New York: New Directions, 1971), 111: "peasants, women, oppressed nationalities, submerged cultures, Dostoevski's underground man—the Other that each one of us constitutes, sexuality and its contradictory complement: the aspiration toward the divine, the beliefs that we call irrational, poetry—in a word, all the areas where exception and difference are the rule, the world of Others and the Other. The multiple other that Marx was unable to recognize."

[13] Jean-François Lyotard, "Interview," *Diacritics* 14, no. 3 (1984): 17, cited by Jay, 564; and Lyotard, *The Lyotard Reader*, ed. Andrew Benjamin (New York: B. Blackwell, 1989), 23, cited by Jay, 566.

signify."[14] If one applies these insights to the pedagogical situation, one might infer that any approach to teaching cinema that does not offer wide berth to the figural, will fail to accurately reflect the emotional and psychological force of the medium.

Biró has written, "[mere] verbal maturity does not constitute a measure of thinking ability."[15] Using as her example the development of language in children, she notes that the so-called semantic and verbal levels of language evolve in inverse proportions: neither in their chronology nor in their inner structures do mental images agree with logical structures. The verbal builds from word to sentence, while the semantic moves from the sentence to the word. Sensory cognition is not a storage mechanism or conveyor belt for information. Thought has characteristics that are not served best by words. When film narratives venture into the pedagogical situation, one may see a picture, or "strong metaphor," of the learning system itself, akin to what Biró calls (with Ferenc Mérei) "experience-thought:"

> In both experience-thought and cinematic expression the stuff of presentation is made of sequences of action, islands of happenings, and remnants, discontinuous and fragmentary bits of events. We may not find in them the usual economy of the flow of images, the strict separation of essential and nonessential elements, yet the chain of events shows a peculiar continuity. Only now the selection is determined not by an external, rational consideration, but by a more internal, invisible, and emotional decision. [...] Both in experience-thought and in the film *a certain lack, the poverty of verbal expression*, is what leads to experiencelike presentation.[16]

Let us consider in this regard Visconti's *Rocco e i suoi fratelli* (1960). There are five brothers in the Parondi family; the oldest, Vincenzo, is living in Milan when the others arrive there from Lucania with their mother, internal emigrants like so many others in these years. The father has died and the sons need to earn a living in the Milan winter. Rocco and Simone, the two next-oldest brothers, will struggle for a livelihood in contrasting ways, the one virtuous the other outside the law. The story takes the form of a melodrama, rich in histrionic gesture and bodily hyperbole. There is something epic about the moral drama of Rocco, who is engaged not just in a battle for survival and love, but for Simone's salvation. In terms of experience-thought, Rocco's character possesses a

---

[14] Jay, 568.
[15] Biró, 22.
[16] Biró, 14-15. My emphasis.

fully efficient form of consciousness that is not a prelude to logical thought or anything else. To be immersed in his story serves as a gateway into the collective consciousness and unconscious of the time. As one sees Simone and Rocco train in the boxing gym one is cast into a learning matrix in which the brothers are educated to the art of boxing, the socio-economic laws of urban Milan, the laws of the underworld, and their own internal demons. Amidst the blight of Simone's corruption, Rocco learns of the limits of family loyalty. While Visconti's script is based on texts by Pratolini, Dostoevsky and Thomas Mann, as well as Antonio Gramsci's essay on the "Southern Question," the force of the film is due to the concreteness of its images and the coherence of its filmic logic. As students chart the narrative lines of such a film, they encounter factors that are hard to describe, which verge on the ineffable or the horrible, as in the rape and murder scenes of Nadia. By confronting "unreadable" aspects of the filmic language, they learn to confront the limits of their own rational expression. They recognize the value of *obscuritas* in visual learning, as in the lengthy nighttime shots without dialogue, in which darkness and silence take shape (as in the Nō theater).

The great pioneer in the field of negative visual space is Michelangelo Antonioni, whose 1950 *Storia di un amore* defies preconceptions about Neorealism. Despite a conventional plot, Antonioni

> refuses to unfold the information we seek in any logical order; chance plays a greater role than cause and effect; and the true drama resides not in the plot's unfolding but in the complex emotional reactions to what are often unexplained events.[17]

Antonioni casts us into the silences of characters whose painful and conflicted relations strike a resonant chord with the modernist sensibility, for which the divide between the conscious and unconscious mind is a familiar reality. Antonioni's films provide students a new incentive to look and feel the weight and measure of the nonverbal, and thus to gain access to feelings perhaps known but never formulated as such. Like Visconti he introduces a new sort of cinematic text, the reading of which must be undertaken dynamically and with deference to the figural tradition and its symbolic density.

The sort of median approach we are recommending is descibed in Angelo Principe's essay on his teaching of Italian cinema (with a focus on Neorealism) over three or more terms of concentrated study. The essay's

---

[17] Peter Bondanella, *Italian Cinema from Neorealism to the Present* (New York: Continuum, 1995), 109.

title, "From Image to Concept," reflects the author's respect for constitutive elements of cinema—or what we have labeled filmic logic—as the curriculum moves slowly toward concepts so as to not overwhelm the student and to preserve the "training" to visual thinking required, an element too often ignored in cinema classes, or too rapidly "theorized" or simply considered as intuitive. Writes Principe,

> most students taking Italian cinema need to be trained (alerted) to respond to moving images critically and creatively, enabling them to make the necessary leap from image to concept.[18]

The Book as Filmic Symbol

The experience-thought and filmic logic I am discussing depends on icons or symbols. If "symbolization" can be defined as "a level of figurativization which may involve elements such as mirrors, eyes, and/or windows as metaphors for the forces behind the text," another example of such a metaphor is the book itself.[19] Viewed as an image in a film, the book is an icon of the unstated, the purely potential or the opaque. As a physical object it is a vehicle of ambiguity and a powerful means of representing the nature of relationships among people. What sorts of books do we see figured in films: primers, manuals, masterpieces, gospels, oracles, diaries? As phenomenal images what symbolic quality do they import into the narrative and viewing experience?

Umberto Eco, in a synopsis of the evolution of semiotics from the late 19th century forward, asks,

> But what, after all, is a sign? A word? A sentence? Peirce will say that even a whole book is one. And if signs are not that which is indicated but rather serve to indicate (or to recall) that which is not there, are ideas signs as well?[20]

The answer is obviously yes, and it leads Eco to anticipate the evolution of general semiotics after Peirce and Saussure: "we [now] know

---

[18] Angelo Principe, "From Image to Concept: Teaching Italian Cinema to Undergraduates," *Romance Languages Annual* 4 (1993): 340-44; 340.

[19] Francesco Casetti, *Inside the Gaze. The Fiction Film and Its Spectator*, introd. Christian Metz, pref. Dudley Andrew, trans. Nell Andrew with Charles O'Brien (Bloomington, IN: Indiana UP, 1998), 141.

[20] Umberto Eco, "Looking for a Logic of Culture," in *The Tell-Tale Sign: A Survey of Semiotics*, ed. Thomas A. Sebeok (Lisse: Peter de Ridder Press, 1975), 9-17; 11-12.

that it is impossible to establish a typology of signs as if they were entities, whereas in fact they are *relations*."[21] Thus books in films are signs of their own signifying capacity, of the formal logic that is not adhered to by visual logic, which endows them with a sense of incommensurability. One might say that the filmic book signifies its own absence; or perhaps, that the book-as-object signifies in its indeterminacy the concrete human relations of those that use it. In this respect the filmic book possesses iconicity and symbolic pregnance (even more when closed than open!).

The book may serve as an icon of authority or notoriety, obscenity or erudition. Consider the pawnshop registry one sees in *Ladri di biciclette*: in this weighty book are contained the future fortunes of the protagonists, who exchange part of their trousseau to acquire a bicycle needed for a new job. Or the account book of the Camorra boss that comes into the hands of the hapless signor Picone in Nanni Loy's 1983 *Mi manda Picone*. This book contains all the secrets—the debits and credits of a vicious crime boss; as such the book serves as a guide into the Neapolitan underworld, and sets the stage for an unlikely love story. The book may serve as an icon of an illicit love, a *galeotto* (or go-between) as in the Paolo and Francesca episode filmed by Peter Greenaway in *Dante's Inferno* (1993). As Francesca speaks the camera zooms in diagonally, focusing finally just on her mouth as she pronounces the fatal words—"that day we read no further." The readings of the teenage protagonist of *Ernesto* (1979) to his coarse-skinned laborer-lover in Samperi's adaptation of Saba's autobiographical portrait of 1898 Trieste serve as an amorous go-between and narrative catalyst. The great black comedy of manners *Sedotta e abbandonata* (1961) begins with the lustful swain Peppino reading a poem by Giovanni Pascoli to the vulnerable Agnese, another *galeotto* that opens and precipitates the entire plot.

Such opaque signs are examples of the cinematic convention that Pier Paolo Pasolini called the "im-segno" or image sign. Pasolini theorizes that cinema employs nothing other than the "language of reality:"

> Film is fundamentally oneiric because of the elementary nature of its archetypes (which I will list once again: habitual and thus unconscious observation of the environment, gestures, memory, dreams), and because

[21] Eco, 13. Peirce defines "icon" in a way compatible with our use of "symbol" and "figure." The icon is an eidetic image; it is two-faced in a positive sense like Janus, it is self-similar and looks fore and aft.

of the fundamental prevalence of the pregrammatical qualities of objects as symbols of the visual language.[22]

In his *Decameron* (1971) Pasolini cast himself as the storyteller leafing through Boccaccio's great book; in these scenes—which divide the episodes—one senses the director's depiction of the book as a symbol of the storytelling tradition itself and as an alphabetizing, pedagogical tool. In numerous other examples I could draw from, the book stands as an icon of Italian struggles: for a fully realized modern nationhood, universal literacy and justice for all citizens; in numerous other examples the book is used as a prop, a red-herring or a McGuffin (a false lead that advances character development).[23]

---

[22] Pier Paolo Pasolini, *Heretical Empiricism*, ed. Louise K. Barnett, trans. Louise K. Barnett and Ben Lawton (Bloomington, IN: Indiana UP, 1988), 171.

[23] Fascism itself may be seen as a denial of honest pedagogy, a tragedy of national life, as figured in *Il giardino dei Finzi-Contini* (1970) when the Jews are marched away from the Torah in their homes to a local school where they wait for the trains northward. And Francesco Rosi's *La tregua* (1997), based on the book by Primo Levi, opens with the burning of books at Auschwitz. In Gianni Amelio's *Porte aperte* (1990), based on the eponymous novel by Leondardo Sciascia, Gian Marie Volontè plays a judge in a capital murder case in Sicily during the early years of the fascist regime after the passing of the Rocco Law, which reinstated the death penalty. The judge's solitary reflections on the great books of the past, from Beccaria's *Dei delitti e delle pene* to the *Avvertimenti cristiani* of Argisto Giuffredi (a 16th century opponent of the death penalty), possess a solemn and provocative counter-balance to the violence of the perpetrator, a state bureaucrat and loyal fascist who had been unjustly dismissed by his victim. *Porte aperte* can be used as a part of cluster of films set in Sicily; Rosi's *Salvatore Giuliano* (1962), Visconti's *La terra trema* (1948) and *Il gattopardo* (1963). These could also include films about the mafia. I have used Alexander Stille's book *Excellent Cadavers: the Mafia and the Death of the First Italian Republic* (New York: Pantheon, 1995) in teaching about the war against the Mafia in the 1980s, and the Mafia's killing of Judges Falcone and Borsellino; I also include the accounts of public reactions against the killings in Paul Ginsborg, *Italy and its Discontents: Family, Civil Society, State, 1980-2001* (New York: Palgrave Macmillan, 2003). Two films address the subject: Ricky Tognazzi's *La scorta* (1993)—in which one can trace meaningful continuities with *Porte aperte*—and *Excellent Cadavers*, a 1999 HBO movie on which Tognazzi collaborated. These works dramatize the importance of the law, as contained in books and interpreted by human beings, often under the threat of violence. Another valuable resource in this cluster is provided by the prize-winning photographs of Letizia Battaglia, a city council member in Palermo. One might combine these painful and even gruesome images with a parody of the Mafia in the form of a musical, the 1997 *Tano da morire* directed by the Milanese Roberta Torre, as well as with Torre's 2002 drama on the mafia subculture in

Ettore Scola's *C'eravamo tanto amati* (1974), is a culturally panoramic yet highly personal film which reflects on the ironies of commitment and the confusions, enthusiasms and tested loyalties of the *dopoguerra*. When Nicola, a Neapolitan professor of Italian cinema (hopelessly seeking a publisher for his book on that subject), appears on Mike Bongiorno's game show "Lascia o Raddoppia," he responds incorrectly to the final question. Asked why the character Bruno in *Ladri di biciclette* (1948) had broken out in tears, instead of saying it was because the father's bicycle was stolen, Nicola responds literally, saying it was because the director put cigarette butts in the boy's pocket. While the TV host and his audience enter into the filmic logic, the professor has answered "by the book" ignoring the fictional context. The error signifies a non-communication between the world of the intellectual and that of the mass culture. Scola seems to suggest with this character that leftist intellectuals were ultimately powerless in addressing the social issues exposed in *Ladri di biciclette*. Scola's film is effective both as an engaging tale of friendship and love, gained and lost, and as a metacinematic allegory of recent Italian history. It works "in and out" of the Italian canon, problematizing assumptions about regional and class identities and about recent film history (Neorealist films were never blockbusters). It also offers the student penetrating lessons concerning issues of viewer reception and temporal stratification (the title, *C'eravamo tanto amati* is in the past perfect). Whether in the freeze-frame theatrical framing device, the allusions to classical cinema or the swift resumés of actions that define the "Italianness" of the major characters, one is challenged to go beyond a stereotyped description of the events so as to enter into the experience-thought of the characters.

Books may refer in the Italian context to canonical literary texts taught in the schools. In the opening scene of Bellocchio's *Diavolo in corpo* (1986) a young African woman, crazed and babbling, is about to jump from a rooftop next to the high school classroom of Andrea Raimondi, whose professor is glossing Pascoli's "La tovaglia" (a poem in which, the professor says, the dead are not frightening but are welcomed warmly into the home). On the terrace below the anguished scene another young woman, Giulia, succeeds in calming the woman on the roof who, when she realizes she is in danger, collects herself and comes down to safety. This opening precipitates the meeting and eventual love affair between Andrea and Giulia. Their situation is complicated by the fact that Giulia is the

---

Palermo, *Angela*. The effect of mixing these various sources, genres, historical periods and approaches, renders the eventual portrait of Sicily more palpable and accessible, both to the student's cognitive side and to the imaginative sensibility.

patient of Andrea's father, a psychoanalyst, and she is engaged; her fiancé, Giacomo Pulcini, is currently a defendant in a maxi-trial of presumed terrorists, but will soon be released for turning state's evidence. In short, the love affair is threatened simultaneously by the institutions of school, family and state. The film ends with Andrea's oral exam for his high school diploma, where he needs to gloss the two tercets which open Cacciaguida's prophecy to Dante in *Paradiso* xvii:

[Andrea:]	La contingenza sarebbe il corso degli eventi contingenti che sono propri del mondo materiale-terrestre. Questa contingenza tutta presente, dipinta, appunto, nella mente di Dio.
[Professore:]	Esattamente. Ab eternum.
[Andrea:]	E tuttavia da questa prescienza divina il corso degli eventi contingenti non prende carattere di necessità, come una nave, appunto, che, discendendo la corrente di un fiume, non deriva la necessità del suo movimento dallo sguardo dell'osservatore che la contempla.
[Professore:]	Bene, a quale teoria, qui, si riferisce Dante in questi versi?
[Andrea:]	Alla teoria del libero arbitrio.
[Professore:]	Lei dà risposte logiche, ineccipibili, per il tono, anzi il monotono, ch'è poi un po' monotono, con cui risponde, mi lascia un po' perplesso, come se a Lei Dante interessasse poco o nulla.
[Andrea:]	Quanto basta per passare l'esame.

This final scene takes the viewer back to the place of the opening scene the classroom where a reading of Pascoli was interrupted by the threatened suicide of the woman on the roof. If one reflects on the cited lines of Cacciaguida, it seems that the protagonists have been transformed, spiritually awakened by their love. Andrea's answers are "correct" but do not satisfy the professor; his experience-thought and use of the book transcend the institutional context. The professor suggests that Andrea has chosen for ideological reasons not to appreciate Dante's message. He asks him if he is a Marxist or a member of the catholic youth group Comunione e liberazione; Andrea responds that he is neither and has answered properly for the context of the exam, which does not require an examination of conscience. He has also demonstrated in the course of the film, in his relationship with Giulia, that he is a highly mature young man, well qualified in exercising his free will.

While shooting *Enrico IV* (1984), says Bellocchio, he gradually distanced himself from Pirandello's text as they found their cinematic form; he states that for him the central problem was not that of Madness but of Fiction, of the mask one must wear in the world. He has not abandoned Pirandello's text; rather he has engaged in the true spirit of adaptation and provided a paradigm of visual learning. As the film opens we see the foil and rival to Henry, the Baron Belcredi, urinating by the side of the highway, reciting Carducci's classic poem "Il bove" and listening to stock market quotes on the radio, as an aerial shot rises above the car to an adjacent field where Henry had his fall from a horse twenty years earlier. In this dramatic fusion of separate time-frames we are introduced to the intellectual problem at the basis of Pirandello's text in a way that encapsulates it cinematically.[24] The classic play by the Sicilian is broken down by Bellocchio, who can only be faithful to the literary message by altering it, attenuating its tragic resolution and sanctioning Henry's rejection of contemporary society once he has regained his lucidity. Bellocchio lives the filmmaking process as a collaboration and has consistently challenged critics to step outside the conventional limits of their métier. He is an ideal contemporary to employ in teaching visual thinking in the Italian context, also as concerns his use of literary texts and books as Janus-faced icons of the vastness of experience-thought with respect to formal logic.

"Some possible pedagogy of the imagination"

The above examples of the book-as-object resonate as invitations to visual thinking, highlighting the role of experience-thought and filmic logic in several Italian films.[25] By considering the context and use of the book symbolically, filmmakers are free to expand their reflections on their subject matter (character, story, action, theme) into areas more intrinsic to

[24] Sandro Bernardi, *Marco Bellocchio* (Milan: Il Castoro, 1998), 123, writes in this context of "un cronotopo, in cui due tempi diversi della vita stanno per sovrapporsi."

[25] See Robert Richardson, *Literature and Film* (Bloomington: Indiana UP, 1969), 68: "Between the film's use of imagery and its literary uses there are both significant similarities and differences. Imagery is used both for vividness and for significance; and one might say that literature often has the problem of making the significant somehow visible, while film often finds itself trying to make the visible significant."

their medium and its capacity to instruct visually.[26] What is exacted of film is a spontaneity of percept that directly confronts the aesthetic sensibility or imagination. Jean-François Lyotard addresses this idea in commenting on Cezanne's series of paintings of the Montagne Sainte Victoire:

> Its singularity lies in how irrelevant for painting pictures are such values as meaning, consistency, likelihood, recognition, identification—one's only concern is to glance at the birth of colors, like the dawn of a cloud on the horizon. The equivocity of the English term "touch" brings together perfectly the idea of an agonistic, loving contact between the flesh of the painter and what Merleau-Ponty called the flesh of the world and the connotation of a singular style.[27]

In his essay on "Visibility," Italo Calvino begins with Dante's invocation of the "*imaginativa*" in *Purgatorio* xvii, where the imagination is something lofty, divinely inspired. There is a film-like quality, says Calvino, to Dante's poem, in which Dante the poet sees the actions of Dante the actor played out before him as in the cinema.[28] Calvino also discusses St. Ignatius' *Spiritual Exercises* and his practice of contemplation, in which the active practice of visualization attains for the first time in the devotional practices of the Catholic Church

> the shift from the word to the visual image as a way of attaining knowledge of the most profound meaning. [. . .] The believer is called upon personally to paint frescoes crowded with figures on the walls of his mind, starting out

---

[26] See Principe, 344: "Through cinema we are able to perceive (see) images, communicate concepts, and experience feelings. A trichotomy, which far surpasses the dichotomy of written or spoken language. Because of this, the cinematic world is always both periphery and centre at the same times: the individual icon, taken by itself, is the centre of its universe; but, engulfed in a general concept, it becomes periphery in the orbit of a larger universal meaning. Hence the cinematic world is always multicentric and monoperipheral."

[27] Jean-François Lyotard, *Peregrinations. Law, Form, Event* (New York: Columbia UP, 1988), 19.

[28] Italo Calvino, *Six Memos for the Next Millennium* (Cambridge, MA: Harvard UP, 1988), 83: "A film is the outcome of a succession of phases, both material and otherwise, in the course of which the images acquire form. During this process, the "mental cinema" of the imagination has a function no less important than that of the actual creation of the sequences as they will be recorded by the camera and then put together on the moviola. This mental cinema is always at work in each one of us, and it always has been, even before the invention of the cinema. Nor does it ever stop projecting images before our mind's eye."

> from the stimuli that his visual imagination succeeds in extracting from a theological proposition or a laconic verse from the gospels (86).

As regards the relation between the visual image and verbal expression, Calvino posits two opposing views of the imagination: as a communication with the world soul and as an instrument of knowledge. The latter view requires one to

> divide what can be known into two parts, leaving the external world to science and isolating imaginative knowledge in the inner self of the individual (88).

While he acknowledges both tendencies at work in his writing—both the rational plotting out of a verbal plan and the imaginary search for a spontaneous logic of images—here he lands on a *third* possibility:

> the imagination as a repertory of what is potential, what is hypothetical, of what does not exist and has never existed, and perhaps will never exist but might have existed.I believe that to draw on this gulf of potential multiplicity is indispensable to any form of knowledge (91).

Here, he says, lies a skill shared by poet and scientist alike, though one increasingly at risk today, when fewer people are capable of

> *thinking* in terms of images. I have in mind *some possible pedagogy of the imagination* that would accustom us to control our own inner vision without suffocating it or letting it fall, on the other hand, into confused, ephemeral daydreams, but would enable the images to crystallize into a well-defined, memorable, and self-sufficient form, the *icastic* form. This is of course a kind of pedagogy that we can only exercise upon ourselves, according to methods invented for the occasion and with unpredictable results (92).

It has been precisely in the pursuit of a pedagogy of the imagination that I have questioned certain assumptions about the teaching of film. As seen, such assumptions relate to broader educational questions of epistemology, selfhood and ethics. The position taken in this chapter has been that visual thinking is involved in consciousness, awareness and perception; in how one recognizes reality in films and is compelled to respond; in the cognitive decoding of the images and codes of cinematic language; and, in the discernment of historical and cultural context, which involves the delineation of a syntax, a semantics and an ideology.

This seems an accurate précis of the epistemological problem of cinema and the opportunity it offers in the classroom. If one is able to undo certain assumptions and habits and unlearn the restrictive and ego-centered, category-centered method of analysis, one may come to achieve a keener, more compassionate and ethical student-teacher-text relationship. By abandoning exogenous or imposed views—such as those discussed in the opening of this paper—this method would reveal the visual sense as that which cannot be abstracted. It was that sort of semantic liberation that occurred, amidst all its mimetic and diegetic paradoxes, in the grand era of neo-realism, when the movie camera discovered in Italy what Eugene Minkowski called "lived synchronism," that is, the penetration of screen time into the real time of the entire country.[29]

Conclusion

In analyzing the stratified nature of the cinematic message, students should dwell comfortably with metaphors, for analogical thinking is frequently the quickest and most effective means for them to articulate responses to those phenomena observed in the film that manifest *differences* from their own reality. By remaining faithful to the economy of the image one is led directly into the sensibility and repository of knowledge of the student. And at this point the instructor can contribute his or her expertise to an inquiring classroom.

When presenting a film to a class, much can be accomplished by exploring student reactions to the viewing experience in open discussion; trust in the initial response is the instructor's friend, as it provides the palette and starting point against which the class will map out its experience of what is unfamiliar or "foreign." The detection of difference concerns more than just language; it concerns patterns of audio-visual kinetic sequences that are bearers of historical, aesthetic and cultural information. Thus one asks for rudimentary descriptions in the form of a sequential exposition of films. What this uncovers for all concerned is that the classroom viewing is tacit but not passive; it is a critical experience that must be heeded as such by the instructor. One needn't dwell on sociological, aesthetic or linguistic issues for the film to have an impact in these areas, since these issues do not present themselves as separate contents within the image. Rather they interpenetrate—even in the documentary film—in the language of metaphor and symbol.

[29] Eugène Minkowski, *Il tempo vissuto* (Turin: Einaudi, 1983), 20.

It has been shown that the instruction of cinema manifests some truths concerning education generally: that only the integration of a confluence (or clashing) of disciplinary perspectives can hope to describe the real; that paradoxes and ambiguities are always part of the raw material of learning; that dialogue is indispensable in the critical evaluation of the art work, that artists and critics are themselves bound by the historical and social conditions of their particular societies. Cinema allows us the opportunity to enhance our teaching of language, literature and culture by integrating into it elements of history, anthropology, aesthetics and ethics.

UNIVERSITY OF GEORGIA, USA

CHAPTER TWENTY-TWO

MEMORY ON THE MARGINS: REFLECTIONS ON ITALY (1938-1943) IN SCOLA'S *UNA GIORNATA PARTICOLARE* & OZPETEK'S *LA FINESTRA DI FRONTE*[1]

MARY ANN MCDONALD CAROLAN

Preparing to teach Ferzan Ozpetek's film *La finestra di fronte* (*Facing Windows,* 2003) in a course on contemporary Italian cinema, I realized the striking thematic and stylistic similarities between this recent release and Ettore Scola's film *Una giornata particolare (A Special Day*, 1977*)*. Ozpetek's tale, which weaves together the lives of a young married couple, a confused elderly gay man, and an intriguing male neighbor, recalls the German round-up of Roman Jews in the ghetto on October 16, 1943. Ettore Scola's film describes the encounter between a fascist housewife and her homosexual neighbor in a deserted apartment complex when Hitler paraded through Rome on May 6, 1938. When taught together the two films provide students with the historical background needed to understand Italy under fascism as well as to analyze the persistent preoccupation with memory in the works of Italian filmmakers. *La finestra di fronte* and *Una giornata particolare* both bear witness to particular historical events through the lens of marginalized individuals such as women, homosexuals, and Jews. The witnesses' marginality enriches our students' understanding of the time period while calling into question the culture of consent officially associated with fascism.

---

[1] All citations from the films are taken from *Una giornata particolare: Un film di Ettore Scola. Incontrarsi e dirsi addio nella Roma del '38*, ed. Tullio Kezich and Alessandra Levantesi (Turin: Lindau, 2003) and Gianni Romoli and Ferzan Ozpetek, *La finestra di fronte* (Milan: Idea Books, 2003).

This cinematic coupling also provides fertile ground for the analysis of film techniques such as flashbacks and voiceover narration; it also offers a model for the analysis of the gaze, which is essential for understanding notions of spectatorship in film. In addition to film courses, the pairing of *Una giornata particolare* and *La finestra di fronte* would enhance courses on contemporary Italian culture and modern Italian history, as well as seminars on gender and sexuality.

Una giornata particolare: Reading Fascism in Italy

Scola's film provides students of Italian culture with insight into the reception of fascist programs by Italians. The protagonists of *Una giornata particolare* provide the most salient examples of the fascist social agenda: Antonietta (played by Sophia Loren) represents the highly prescribed life of an ideal fascist wife and mother and Gabriele (Marcello Mastroianni), a former state radio announcer at EIAR (*Ente Italiano per le Audizioni Radiofoniche*), embodies the precarious situation of homosexuals under fascism. Antonietta's fugitive myna Rosmunda serves as the couple's *galeotto* by uniting the heterosexual woman and homosexual man who live across the courtyard from one another. Brought together first by the bird, the pair also shares the alienation that comes from not participating in the celebrations occasioned by Hitler's visit to Rome. The unlikely couple makes love on this special day that ends as Antonietta, alone in the kitchen as in the beginning of the film, watches as Gabriele, accompanied by two fascist officials, leaves for exile.

Scola's protagonists, with the exception of Gabriele, illustrate the culture of consent among Italian citizens under fascism. *Una giornata particolare* begins with evidence of popular support of Mussolini's political and military agenda through the LUCE (*L'unione cinematografica educativa*) footage that shows thousands of Italians gathered to welcome Hitler. The film also demonstrates Italian acquiescence to fascist social policy in the initial scene in which Antonietta wakes each of her six children to prepare for the day's celebrations. Her many progeny and their names—Littorio, Romana, and Adolfo for her hoped-for seventh child—demonstrate the regime's deep penetration into the national psyche. Scola further underscores the fascist connection by casting Benito's granddaughter, Alessandra Mussolini, in a cameo role as Maria Luisa, one of Antonietta's daughters. Antonietta's portrait of Mussolini fashioned out of buttons and her album filled with news articles about the Duce attest to the cult of the totalitarian dictator. In this fictional tale Scola demonstrates the regime's insistence on physical fitness and hygiene through the morning gymnastic routine of Antonietta's husband Emanuele (played by John Vernon) and the fascist salutes exchanged by parade goers.

Una giornata particolare reveals that the regime's dictates extended to language as well. Emanuele's insistence on the "italianization" of foreign sounding words such as pompom ("*pompóno*") highlights the linguistic xenophobia of the regime that sought to eliminate foreign words such as *cachet, drink,* and *weekend.*[2] Antonietta avoids using *Lei* to conform to Mussolini's attempt to rid Italian of Spanish influence. She reminds Gabriele of this prohibition when he, ever the subversive, addresses her with *Lei* before switching to the more informal *tu.*

Scola's film showcases fascist iconography as a pervasive presence in clothing, flags, and the calendar. Emanuele's black uniform, emblazoned with the insignia MVSN (*Milizia Volontaria Sicurezza Nazionale*) and those of his children with the symbols of their respective youth groups in GIL (*La Gioventú Italiana del Littorio*), identify this as a fascist family. In fact, the couple's youngest son, Littorio, wears the uniform of the *Figlio della Lupa*, the same one that the six-year old Scola wore to the festivities on May 6, 1938.[3] Antonietta's family, like the rest of the palazzo's inhabitants, are dressed to celebrate Hitler's visit, an occasion marked by the red banners with black swastikas that symbolize the union of Germany and Italy. The fascist custom of dating events from the inception of the fascist reign in 1922 is also noted as Gabriele reads aloud an entry from Antonietta's scrapbook dated "agosto '37, XVI E.F. (*Era Fascista*)."

Una giornata particolare also catalogues fascist social advances and military conquests. The film's set, an enormous palazzo complex on Viale XXI Aprile, exemplifies the regime's response to the need for urban housing in the 1920s and 1930s. Emanuele's position in the *Ministero dell'Africa Orientale*[4] demonstrates Mussolini's expansion of the government bureaucracy. The radio announcer reports that all EIAR stations, including the newest one in Addis Ababa, are covering the historic meeting between Hitler and Mussolini. This reminds listeners of the quick and decisive victory of the African campaign that made Italy a

---

[2] See Alfredo Panzini, ed., *Dizionario moderno delle parole che non si trovano negli altri dizionari*, VII (Milan: Hoepli, 1935) for the identification of foreign words in Italian at that time.

[3] For a discussion of the autobiographical resonances in this film see Ettore Scola, "Parla l'autore," in Kezich and Levantesi, ed., 145-52.

[4] Antonietta has the wrong title for her husband's office, which is really *Ministero dell'Africa italiana* according to Tullio Kezich and Alessandra Levantesi, "Vademecum per la visione," in Kezich and Levantesi, ed., 129. This office was only abolished in 1953, thirteen years after Italy lost its territories in Africa.

colonizing force and signaled its intention to become a world power. Of course, the regime was also effective at creating the perception of success by its manipulation of the media through the use of LUCE clips and EIAR broadcasts like the ones that document the historical background of *Una giornata particolare.*

Women's Role in Fascist Demographic Policies

The fictional family in *Una giornata particolare* illustrates the influence of fascist demographic policy on the lives of Italians, both male and female. Scola's film reflects the national imperative to increase the birthrate in order for Italy to realize autarky, or self-sufficiency, and to establish an empire. As the fascist regime moved closer to the Third Reich, with its emphasis on war making and colonization, population growth became critical. Women were essential to the success of this plan. Yet politically women were powerless. Granted the vote in local elections in 1925, Italian women lost that right when the plebiscite was denied all Italians shortly thereafter. Any progress Italian women had made towards emancipation evaporated with Mussolini's identification of women as breeders, an opinion expressed in one of the clippings found in Antonietta's album: *La Guerra sta all'uomo come la maternità sta alla donna.* At the film's outset there is little doubt that Antonietta has embraced the maternal function: the camera follows her as she wakes her six children one by one.

In May 1927, Mussolini first articulated the regime's demographic concerns in his famous Ascension Day speech, which was subsequently published as "*Numero come forza*" in the newspaper *Il Popolo d'Italia*. In order to increase the Italian population by 20 million for a projected population of 60 million Italians by 1950,[5] fascism directed its pronatalist program at women through policies that combined punitive measures and incentives. The regime repressed information about sexuality and contraception, regulated prostitution, outlawed abortion, and founded organizations to support maternal health such as ONMI (*Organizzazione nazionale di maternità e infanzia*). The primary legal instrument regarding women at this time, the *Codice Rocco* (1930), consolidated legal and financial power in male heads of household, and articulated the punishment of female adulterers, not male adulterers such as Antonietta's husband Emanuele. In March 1937, the Minister of the Interior established the Union of Big Families to encourage heads of families to have more

[5] John Pollard, *The Fascist Experience in Italy* (London: Routledge, 1998), 78-9.

children by offering benefits and low-level government posts like Emanuele's as "*capoufficio del Servizio Uscieri*." If a woman had fourteen children, she was invited to meet the Duce in person. On Mother's Day (December 24), the most prolific mothers of the ninety Italian provinces were honored as part of the celebration in Rome. Those mothers were introduced by Mussolini himself with the number of live births, rather than the women's names, announced to the crowd.[6] In the end, these policies failed to increase the birthrate in Italy. Despite the concerted efforts of the fascist state, the birthrate dropped from 24% in 1935 to 19.9% in 1945.[7]

Migration, rather than population growth, increased the population of Italy's cities during fascism. Rome's population doubled from 700,000 in 1921 to 1,415,000 in 1938, the year in which Scola's film takes place.[8] Housing became an essential part of the demographic campaign as urban population soared. Scola's set, the apartment complex located on 21-29 Viale XXI Aprile, represents the fascist response to the growth of Italian cities in the 1920s and 1930s. Constructed between 1931 and 1937 and designed by the architect Mario DeRenzi, this building complex included 442 apartments, 70 stores, a parking garage and cinema.[9] Although the regime initially tried to stem the migration from countryside to city, because rural families tended to have more children than urban ones, it soon realized the necessity of affordable urban housing. In addition to constructing *borgate* in outlying areas where existing structures were demolished to make way for new neighborhoods with water, sewers, and other utilities, the regime embarked on an ambitious program to provide housing for the burgeoning middle class. The fascist government provided financial incentives to institutions such as banks, insurance companies, and construction firms to build apartments with the understanding that the rents remain affordable for working and middle class Italians. Antonietta and her family rent a typical three-bedroom apartment in one of these *case convenzionate* or conventional homes;[10] she views the addition of a seventh child as a way to receive larger accommodations from the Union of Large Families.

Although fascism focused on the educational system as a means for inculcating its values, many women, like Antonietta, had minimal

---

[6] Victoria DeGrazia, *How Fascism Ruled Women: Italy, 1922-1945* (Berkeley: University of California Press, 1992), 71.
[7] Ibid., 54.
[8] Borden W. Painter, Jr., *Mussolini's Rome: Rebuilding the Eternal City* (New York: Palgrave, 2005), 92.
[9] Ibid., 100.
[10] Ibid., 98.

schooling. In fact, one quarter of all Italian women were illiterate at the time the film takes place.[11] Antonietta acknowledges the marginality of women in the world of ideas by agreeing with the fascist declaration, found in her scrapbook, that "*Inconciliabile con la fisiologia e la psicologia femminile, il Genio è soltanto maschio.*" Antonietta notes that the names of men, not women, fill the history books.[12] Emanuele's affair with a teacher confirms her intellectual inferiority. She describes his infidelity as an insult to her intelligence: "mettersi con una istruita… è come se mio marito… è come dire a una moglie che è una mezzacalzetta, una ignorante." Antonietta readily confesses that she could never write a love letter like the one penned by her husband's mistress. Alienated from the canonical masterpieces that line Gabriele's bookshelves, Antonietta engages in literature at a level that is at once juvenile and popular. After her family leaves for the parade, she dozes off while reading a discarded comic book, *Dick Fulmine tra i pigmei della jungla,* the hero of which is an Italian American giant who fought Capone-style gangsters and other villains in Chicago.[13] This work resonates with the fascist tendency to fill all vehicles of cultural expression with nationalistic, imperialistic ideology. Dick's threatened annihilation of the pygmies amidst racist taunts—he calls them "*musi neri,*" "*cimici*" and "*liquirizia*"—recalls the Italian campaign in East Africa and the May 5, 1936 occupation of Addis Ababa, which then became capital of AOI, or *Africa Orientale Italiana.* Later, Antonietta mistakes Alexandre Dumas's 1844 historical novel, *The Three Musketeers*, for another comic book, *I quattro moschettieri.* This comic, transcribed and illustrated from the eponymous radio show broadcast between October 1934 and March 1937 by Angelo Nizza and Riccardo Morbelli, recounts the adventures of four German aviators who

---

[11] Laura Laurenzi, "Casalinghe e omosessuali al tempo del consenso," in Kezich and Levantesi, ed., 50.

[12] Lesley Caldwell, "Reproducers of the Nation: Women and the Family in Fascist Policy," in *Rethinking Italian Fascism: Capitalism, Populism & Culture*, ed. David Forgacs (London: Lawrence & Wishart, 1986), 125 notes that as part of the larger program to regulate women and work, legislation from 1923 onwards prevented women from serving as heads of middle schools, or teachers of history, philosophy or economics in *licei.*

[13] Carlo Cossio invented the character of Dick Fulmine, the first real Italian superhero. This good giant, who resembled the famous weightlifter Primo Carnera, waged a brutal war against evil. Even though the fascists disapproved of American names, an exception was made for Dick. Mussolini himself asked the creator to make the character more "virile" and that he did, according to the Motta Editore website.

created technologically advanced aircraft to fight crime and evil.[14] Along with Mickey Mouse, *I quattro moschettieri* was one of the most popular radio programs of the era. Gabriele's gift of canonical literature, on the other hand, invites Antonietta to abandon the popular sphere that was essential to the fascist culture of consent in order to experience the romantic adventure found in Dumas's epic tale. As a work of historical fiction, *The Three Musketeers* resembles *Una giornata particolare*, which is essentially a record of an historical event from the distinctly personal perspective of a highly unlikely couple.[15]

Pronatalist Policies: The Role of Men

Although women gave birth to the new generation of Italian fascists it was incumbent upon men to impregnate them. Fascism assigned new meaning to fatherhood; Mussolini served as role model for fascist manhood. In addition to his role as *pater patriae*, like Caesar and Augustus before him, Mussolini was also *pater familias* to his wife Rachele and their five children. Biographers such as Quinto Navarro, Mussolini's butler, have described the Duce's sex appeal that resulted in numerous affairs.[16] Mussolini received between thirty and forty thousand letters each month, most of which were written by women. Now catalogued in an anthology,[17] these letters demonstrate that women of every social strata considered Mussolini a father, sovereign, and godlike figure to be revered. Antonietta's description of her encounter with Mussolini at the Villa Borghese personalizes this experience of the Duce as supreme, almost divine lover:

> Lui passava, a cavallo… Io mi fermai e lui, al galoppo, mi gettò uno sguardo… Diventai tutta una fiamma… stavo con la borsa della spesa, figuratevi… mi sentii le gambe spezzate, mi cominciò a girare tutto interno e … caddi a terra svenuta.

---

[14] Tullio Kezich and Alessandra Levantesi, "Vademecum per la visione," in Kezich and Levantesi, ed., 126.

[15] Millicent Marcus, "Un'ora e mezzo particolare: Teaching Fascism with Ettore Scola," *Italica*, vol. 83, no.1 (2006) 54 explains the irony inherent in the director's presentation of this historical event: "By making this subject position explicit, Scola of course is asserting his antithetical intent in *Una giornata particolare*—the public of his film will be constructed in diametrical opposition to the imagined spectatorship of the Fuhrer."

[16] Quinto Navarra, *Memorie del cameriere di Mussolini* (Milan: Longanesi, 1972).

[17] Giorgio Boatti, ed., *Caro Duce: Lettere di donne italiane a Mussolini, 1922-1943* (Milan: Rizzoli, 1989).

Later that same day Antonietta finds that she is pregnant and here the sly allusion to the Annunciation cannot be ignored.

Gabriele's homosexuality stands in stark contrast to Mussolini's virility. In fact, the gay man uses Mussolini's own words, found in Antonietta's album, in order to explain his difference from the fascist expectations: "C'è una frase nel tuo album. 'L'uomo è marito, è padre, è soldato.' … Io non sono … marito… né padre, né soldato." In fact, the regime directed one of its first attempts to increase population at bachelors like Gabriele by instituting a tax on them in December 1926. This tax, in turn, helped finance programs, such as ONMI, that were developed to encourage more births.[18] The oft-revised law required all single men between the ages of 26-65 to pay a sliding scale tax (tipped heavily towards the youngest and most able to pay) in addition to a 25% deduction from gross income. The regime devised these punitive and homophobic measures to eradicate male celibacy that it found to be "deviant, parasitical, antipatriotic behavior."[19] Gabriele expresses this prejudice when he screams, to no one in particular, in the apartment hallway that he is *"un finocchio, un ricchione, un invertito."* As a bachelor, Gabriele finds the female-gendered space of the kitchen comfortable despite Antonietta's declaration that "La cucina non è posto per uomini." She immediately associates his bachelorhood with the tax, declaring: "Ah. Scapolo! … Allora pagate la tassa sul celibato." Gabriele, ever the subversive, sarcastically notes the connection between solitude and wealth. In fact, it is not only the kitchen that brings the housewife and gay man together, but demographic policy as well.

Gabriele, the antithesis of ideal fascist manhood, represents the precarious situation for homosexuals in fascist Italy. His loss of employment and subsequent exile reveal the harsh measures leveled against those whose sexuality did not conform to the regime's plan. These measures took on an even more nefarious character in the absence of formal laws against homosexuality. An initial attempt at legislation, Article 528, failed in 1931 when the person in charge of the committee investigating this issue, Magistrate Appiani, declared such a statute unnecessary:

[18] Painter, Jr., 91.

[19] DeGrazia, 70.

La previsione di questo reato non è affatto necessaria perché per fortuna ed orgoglio dell'Italia il vizio abominevole che ne darebbe vita non è così diffuso tra noi da giustifcare l'intervento del legislatore...[20]

At the time there were three possible sanctions for homosexuality, in increasing level of severity: once identified by a neighbor, friend, or coworker, a homosexual might receive a verbal warning, then be placed under house arrest for up to two years, during which time he would report daily to the police station and avoid public places and observe a curfew, or, finally, he might be deported to an island such as Favignana, Ponza, Ventotene, Ustica, le Tremiti, or Carbonia in Sardinia, where the fascist officials take Gabriele at the end of the film.[21] Scola's film illustrates the desperation of homosexuals like Gabriele who engage in futile exercises such as dating female colleagues and carrying medical certificates that attest that they are not homosexual. Adherence to fascist dictates, even in the matter of sexuality, determined one's allegiance to the party, and by extension, to the country. Gabriele recognizes the phenomenon when he blames his alienation squarely on the regime, telling Antonietta:

io non credo che l'inquilino del sesto piano sia antifascista, è il fascismo che ce l'ha con lui. Ce l'ha con lui perché non è sposato, tanto per cominciare, e già questo gli getta addosso una luce sospetta e sovversiva.

Fascism's insistence on the personal as political reveals its deep reach into the most intimate aspect of human existence, sexuality.

Fascism and the Media

La cinematografia è l'arma piú forte.
—Mussolini at the dedication of Cinecittà, April 1937

Fascism enjoyed tremendous success with the manipulation and exploitation of the media to manufacture consensus. The *Ministero della Cultura Popolare,* or MinCulPop for short, controlled the news media, the theater, and all literary production. The administration of propaganda through film and radio was quite effective in Italy, a country whose population was largely illiterate. Censorship was an important feature of

---

[20] Quoted in Gianfranco Goretti, "Il periodo fascista e gli omosessuali: il confino di polizia," in *Le ragioni di un silenzio: la persecuzione degli omosessuali durante il nazismo e il fascismo*, ed. Circolo Pink (Turin: Lindau, 2003), 65.

[21] Laurenzi 2003, 43-53.

cultural production during the *ventennio*. The aim of both censorship, which attempts to excise objectionable material, and propaganda, which tries to create preferred expressions of national culture, is to elevate one's own culture while denigrating others.[22] The following dialogue between Antonietta's two sons illustrates the essential role film plays in propaganda as well as Italian cinema's ambivalent relationship to American cinema:

> Arnaldo: 'A papà è vero che ci avremo piú cannoni noi dell'americani?
> Umberto: Certo. Loro so' bravi a fa' er cinematografo ma in fatto di armi… ci hanno ancora i pellirosse co' le frecce.

This exchange also underscores the fact that the year of Scola's narrative, 1938, signaled the end of American film imports because the fascist regime could no longer afford the extremely popular, yet costly, American products.

Scola's film comments in a self-reflexive way on the fascist state's recognition of the power of the media to manipulate public opinion through film and radio. The initial six-minute documentary montage of *Una giornata particolare* that details Hitler's arrival by train in Rome and welcome by the King and Mussolini both historically situates the action of the film and mirrors the reality for cinemagoers in 1937. Part of the regime's propaganda machine included the mandatory screening of LUCE documentaries before feature films. Typically these documentaries featured fascist agricultural policies (and the draining of marshland in particular) directed at improving rural life, traditional folklore and the celebration of work done in the countryside. Mussolini's life, deeds, and travels were also frequently mentioned in this media.[23]

Building upon a cultural tradition established in the 1910s and1920s, Mussolini focused his propagandistic and nationalistic attention on the media, primarily the cinema. Already the regime had established LUCE, giving it power over newsreel and documentary film production in the 1920s. The next decade witnessed the inauguration of the Venice Film Festival in 1932, the foundation of the Centro Sperimentale di Cinematografia in 1935, the takeover of the previously private enterprise of Cinecittà in 1938, and the establishment of funds and awards for the encouragement and support of indigenous film production through taxes

---

[22] Jill Forbes and Sarah Street, *European Cinema: An Introduction* (Hampshire and New York: Palgrave, 2000), 17.

[23] Pierre Sorlin, *Italian National Cinema, 1896-1996* (London and New York: Routledge, 1996), 51-2.

on imported films.[24] The regime promoted anti-bourgeois comedies of manner, didactic films, and other works that educated and lauded the Italian populace in the fascist manner. It also provided an incentive for its citizens to go to the movies by keeping ticket prices unnaturally low, such that the price of admission remained at 2.00 Lire from 1932 until 1937 whereas the price of pasta increased from 2.52 Lire per kilogram to 3.20 Lire in the same five-year period.[25]

Scola's treatment of Hitler's visit to the Eternal City in *Una giornata particolare* recalls the grandiose historical epics, or colossal films, that Italy produced during its first golden age of cinema in the 1910s. This historic visit was truly a spectacular event in terms of cost, organization, and international attention. In the United States, *Time* dedicated three pages in its May 16, 1938 issue to Hitler's six-day visit to Rome, Florence and Naples, preparations for which reportedly cost $20,000,000. Mussolini recognized the iconic significance of the state visit, knowing that the salute by the Italian troops and the Fuhrer's visit to the Tomb of the Unknown Soldier would glorify the military might of Italy by aligning it with the power and organization of Germany.[26] Mussolini paid special attention to the monuments of Rome, the first stop on the Fuhrer's Italian itinerary, in an attempt to associate his reign with the glories of classical Rome. *Una giornata particolare* relays the fruits of this endeavor through the words of the radio announcer Guido Notari:

> Il volto del Fuhrer appare commosso di fronte a questo spettacolo nel quale palpita tutta la storia di Roma: come se nello stesso palco fossero presenti i Cesari e i Consoli che portarono nel mondo la forza e la giustizia di Roma...

Mussolini assumed the role of director for this spectacle with Rome as its stage set. He choreographed Hitler's visit brilliantly, ensuring a nighttime arrival that allowed the Fuhrer to see the illuminated splendor of Roman monuments. The Duce ordered a revamping of the Ostiense train station, which was connected to the Eternal City by the new Viale Adolfo Hitler. He made certain that the route was lined with troops and civilians

---

[24] Ibid., 70.

[25] Ibid., 74.

[26] This visit was an attempt by Mussolini to reciprocate, or perhaps outdo, the hospitality offered him in Germany in 1937. According to the *New York Times* article on May 8, 1938, Mussolini: "has gone Hitler one better and worked out a program which makes his trip to Germany, strenuous though it was, look like a holiday."

and lighted the Colosseum with thousands of red torches held by soldiers standing at attention. The Duce also arranged the dressing of ships, organized 50,000 fascist youths, and presented elaborate musical and opera productions.

Scola employs various cinematic techniques to underscore the historical veracity of the events portrayed. The director's use of voiceover narration in the form of Notari's EIAR coverage that narrates the LUCE montage (essentially a film within a film) compounds the historical sense of this fictional story. The radio broadcast, played in Antonietta's apartment courtyard as it would have been in 1937, appears in some scenes as diegetic but at other points extra-diegetic. Voiceover, typically considered omniscient and therefore authoritative, performs two other critical functions in this film: it reminds Antonietta and Gabriele of the finite nature of their encounter while also underscoring Gabriele's loss of employment as radio announcer. The disembodied voice of the radio realizes its cinematic existence in the body of the former announcer Gabriele. Once a voice without a body, now a body without a voice, Gabriele has been silenced by the fascist dictates about homosexuality.[27]

La finestra di fronte: Holocaust Revisited

Whereas Scola's film showcases Italian society after fifteen years of fascist indoctrination, Ozpetek chooses the end of the fascist regime as subtext for his film. *La finestra di fronte* begins with what the viewer later comes to understand is a flashback of young Davide Veroli running through the streets of the Roman ghetto. Events from the past fade into the present as the film proper opens in contemporary Rome where a young couple, Giovanna (played by Giovanna Mezzogiorno) and Filippo (played by Filippo Nigro), walk the very streets that the youthful Davide raced through that fateful night sixty years earlier. On a bridge over the Tiber, the couple encounters Davide (played by Massimo Girotti) who is now a lost, elderly man. Giovanna, with help from her handsome neighbor Lorenzo (the actor Raoul Bova), unravels the man's identity by tracing his roots in the Jewish ghetto. She assists him in retrieving his memories, and thus his life, by piecing together his identity from the numbers tattooed on his arm and a love note found in his pocket. As a result of her friendship with Davide, Giovanna contemplates an affair with Lorenzo, and

[27] Laurenzi 2003, 48 notes that Gabriele possesses both a radio and a telephone, which was quite unusual at the time since only 13% of the Italian population in the late 1930s had a radio and even fewer had a telephone.

ultimately quits her job at the chicken processing plant to embark on a new career as a pastry chef.

Ozpetek's film addresses a tragic consequence of the fascist union with the Nazis that *Una giornata particolare* depicts. The implementation of the racial laws in the late 1930s, followed by Italy's surrender to the Allies in the summer of 1943, ultimately led to the event to which Ozpetek's film bears witness: the German deportation of Roman Jews to concentration camps in the fall of 1943. Only at the end of the film does the spectator realize that the initial flashback sequence of *La finestra di fronte* reveals Davide Veroli's secret: he murdered his Christian employer, an accomplice to the German plan, in order to alert his fellow Jews to the imminent round-up in the early morning hours of October 16, 1943.

Facing Windows and Voyeurism

At first glance, it may appear that Ozpetek's heroine Giovanna, who has professional and artistic aspirations, has little in common with Antonietta, the classic oppressed housewife of the fascist era. Despite her work outside the house, Giovanna is associated with the kitchen, the space in which she is most often seen and the locus of her passion, baking. This female-gendered space provides the perspective from which both Antonietta and Giovanna spy their male neighbors and would-be lovers. *La finestra di fronte* and *Una giornata particolare* manifest the voyeuristic fantasy that is realized through the facing windows of Ozpetek's title. Ozpetek's screenwriter and collaborator Gianni Romoli described the attraction of this essentially cinematographic gaze:

> Vagliando le varie possibilità si affacciò l'intuizione del palazzo di fronte, di una finestra che si guarda tutto il giorno in cui avviene una vita che non conosci ma su cui puoi fantasticare.[28]

In both films, the act of looking substitutes for, and leads ultimately to, intimate physical contact. Whereas in Ozpetek's film Lorenzo returns Giovanna's gaze, underscoring the heterosexual nature of the relationship, in Scola's film Gabriele initially ignores Antonietta's frantic attempt at attention. She looks at him, but he does not have eyes for her. Men, not women, are his objects of desire, and by extension, the objects of his gaze. Scola's camera compounds Gabriele's disinterest in looking at women by

[28] Romoli and Ozpetek, 2003, 32.

refusing to fetishize the female body even in the most intimate moment of Antonietta and Gabriele's encounter.

Antonietta sees the power of the gaze as erotic substitute. She tells Gabriele of her anticipated pleasure at looking at him when the rest of the fascist faithful leave to attend an upcoming official gathering:

> Guarderò tutti i giorni la tua finestra! Come stamattina, quando sono tornata a casa ti guardavo sempre e non arrivavo a combinare niente... E sabato prossimo, quando vanno tutti all'adunata... Mi basta vederti... starti a sentire.

Here Antonietta's voyeuristic pleasure is expressed as political subversion; she has internalized Gabriele's response to the regime in terms of personal resistance. Giovanna's lust for Lorenzo, on the other hand, is decidedly apolitical. Lorenzo's assignations with other women, which Giovanna watches from her window, establish his heterosexuality. When the two are finally alone in his apartment, intimacy eludes Giovanna as she spies her own life—her husband, her children with her close friend, and eventually her reflection—in the facing window. It is as if Giovanna's own image, looking back at her at the end of the sequence, prevents her from destroying the life she has built for momentary pleasure. In an interesting twist, the heterosexual woman and homosexual man (Antonietta and Gabriele) make love in Scola's film, but two heterosexuals (Giovanna and Lorenzo) do not consummate their affair in Ozpetek's film.

This clever thematization and inversion of voyeurism also provides students with a rich opportunity to explore one of the most self-reflexive aspects of film. Watching films is in essence all about looking. Ozpetek's film challenges received notions of voyeurism as an instrument of male power used to subjugate females by showcasing the homosexual union, albeit in flashback, that Scola's film merely suggests. *La finestra di fronte*, like Ozpetek's previous films *Il bagno turco* (1997), *Harem Suaré* (1999), and *Le fate ignoranti* (2001), accommodates a new homoerotic perspective by emphasizing the male body, with shots of male nudity far outnumbering those of female nudity. This film diverges from the traditional cinematic perspective that champions the male gaze, and, according to feminist film critics such as Laura Mulvey and others, assumes a male spectatorship.[29]

---

[29] Laura Mulvey, "Visual Pleasure and Narrative Cinema," *Screen* 16, no. 3 (Autumn 1975): 6-18.

Film and History: Italiani brava gente?

The Italian response to fascist dictates is perhaps one of the most complex and compelling chapters of recent Italian history. It continues to fascinate, and therefore continues to appear in Italian films. Ozpetek's film in particular comments upon the notion of Italians as "*brava gente*," or essentially good people who were innocent of war crimes.[30] The film unveils an unsympathetic portrait of Italian complicity in German atrocities when, much later in the film, Davide recounts the story behind the initial flashback: Davide's Christian employers at the bakery try to prevent him from escaping and alerting his fellow Jews of the Germans' plans when he overhears the discussion of the imminent round-up. Scola also debunks the notion of Italians as *brava gente* through his portrayal of the nosey, ideological building superintendent. The *portiera* tells Antonietta of her impression of Gabriele:

> l'inquilino del terzo piano è un disfattista! Una mezza cartuccia! Un antifascista! Che in parole povere sarebbe come d': un fijo de na mignotta!

Scola also alludes to the success of civil operations such as OVRA (*Organizzazione vigilanza reati antifascisti*) to instill fear in the Italian populace during the *ventennio*. When Antonietta hears the bell, rung by the *portiera*, she wonders aloud who it might be, explaining her fear to Gabriele:

> No, è che ... quando bussano alla porta mi piglia sempre un po' di paura. Se chiedi "Chi è" quello risponde "Amici"... pure se non l'hai mai visto.

Ozpetek's position as an outsider, a Turk who came to Rome in the 1970s, affords him a more neutral perspective on this chapter in history. Although removed from the highly philological strain of Italian filmmakers by reason of his foreign birth, Ozpetek continues the discourse on the war. He stated in an interview with the RAI that *La finestra di fronte*'s genesis was due, in part, to his actual encounter with a lost man thirty years earlier near the Ponte Sisto in Rome. Ozpetek acknowledged the autobiographical aspects of the film, describing his meeting with the lost man:

---

30 Susan Zuccotti, *The Italians and the Holocaust: Persecution, Rescue, and Survival* (New York: Basic Books, 1987) examines in depth the perception and reality of the Italian response to the racial laws and their consequences.

> Mi disse che erano vent'anni che non usciva di casa. Trovai la sua abitazione e lo riportai indietro. Io racconto sempre le cose che vedo e che sento, partendo magari dai fatti che mi sono accaduti. In questo film mi sono esposto molto, ci ho messo molto di mio...

Ozpetek also revealed that his reading of Giacomo DeBenedetti's personal account of the deportation of Roman Jews in *16 ottobre 1943,*[31] another narrative of an historical event, informed his writing of *La finestra di fronte.*

Scola's connection to Italian film legacy is different. Born in 1931 in solidly fascist Italy, Scola not only attended the very ceremony he showcases in *Una giornata particolare*, but also acknowledged his gratitude to the neorealist master Vittorio De Sica by dedicating his most successful film *C'eravamo tanto amati* (1974) to him. In an interesting parallel, Ozpetek also claims indebtedness to De Sica after whose protagonist in *Umberto D.* (1952) he modeled Davide Veroli's character.[32] Even if Ozpetek does not acknowledge the influence of Scola's *Una giornata particolare*, the striking similarities between the two films are impossible to ignore. Perhaps Ozpetek has internalized the message and stylistics of that earlier film, for according to Romoli, Ozpetek

> non vuole influenze dirette da altri registi. Preferisce conservarsi la memoria di quello che ha visto, di cui rimane—come per ogni ricordo—la sensazione emotiva più che la "lettura" tecnica della realizzazione. [33]

Memory on the Margins in Scola and Ozpetek (*Il segreto della memoria*)

Ozpetek's contemporary film, like Scola's earlier work, depicts two marginalized figures: a homosexual man and a heterosexual woman. Both Ozpetek's and Scola's male protagonists find themselves in danger. They have lost the possibility of love through the intervention of the fascists (*Una giornata particolare*) or the Nazis (*La finestra di fronte*). Ozpetek's Davide is doubly marginalized as a homosexual Jew.[34] Davide explains

---

[31] Giacomo DeBenedetti, *16 ottobre 1943* (Turin: Einaudi, 2001).
[32] Tilde Corsi and Gianni Romoli, *La finestra di fronte* (Milan: Idea Books, 2003), 30.
[33] Ibid., 36.
[34] The viewer notes the similarity between Davide's surname and that of the ancient Roman Jewish family by the name of DiVeroli. See chapter entitled "A Family of the Ghetto: The DiVerolis of Rome," in Alexander Stille, *Benevolence and*

that the motivation to save his religious brethren from the Nazis was not entirely altruistic. Rather, his decision to alert the community, instead of going directly to his lover Simone, stemmed from the need to vindicate himself from their disdain for his homosexuality. According to Davide,

> Quelle stesse persone che ridevano di me, che non credevano ai miei sentimenti, che non accettavano che io potessi amare Simone… Volevo che mi capissero, dovevo dimostrargli che ero degno di loro… Salvarli era il mio riscatto… e per salvare loro ho perso lui!

Giovanna interprets Davide's painful remorse for this sacrifice as a rationale or encouragement for her to have an affair with the man she lusts after, Lorenzo.

For both Antonietta and Giovanna, the interaction with a gay man effects an invidious comparison to coarse and boorish husbands whose attachment is primarily sexual rather than emotional. Antonietta describes the sad state of her marriage:

> Mio marito con me non parla, ordina. È da quando eravamo fidanzati che non ci siamo piú fatta una risata insieme. Lui ride fuori casa. Con le altre.

The spectator sees the subversive power of humor that eludes both Antonietta and Gabriele, who is forbidden from laughing on the air. The afternoon with Gabriele renders Antonietta more critical of Emanuele's chauvinistic behavior, including his nasty comments about her disheveled appearance and lack of industriousness. Giovanna, like Antonietta, lives a traditional, albeit unsatisfied, married life, with children, when she is drawn involuntarily to experience the margins of society through her interactions with Davide. On the surface, Ozpetek's triangulation of the male/female relationship (Giovanna-Davide-Lorenzo) appears to complicate this comparison. Yet despite Giovanna's longing for Lorenzo, the true nexus of shared experience, the one that leads to the consideration of others and eventual self-knowledge, is between Giovanna and Davide. Romoli explains their intention in making this film:

> Inoltre era abbastanza chiaro per noi che la vera storia d'amore del film era quella tra Giovanna e Davide. Per lo meno era l'unica a lieto fine, i due si scambiavano realmente qualcosa, ognuno di loro cambiava grazie all'altro in questo passaggio di "testimone" anche generazionale.[35]

Betrayal: Five Italian Jewish Families under Fascism (New York: Summit Books, 1991), 167-222.

[35] Corsi and Romoli, 35.

The personal connection between the marginalized pair brings the female protagonists to an epiphany. With Davide's help and encouragement, Giovanna realizes her dream of becoming a professional baker. She comes to understand, in Romoli's words, that "Cambiare non è fuggire (a Ischia, dietro la 'storia' di un altro)."[36] Instead, she has learned, at the critical moment at Lorenzo's window, looking into her own life, who she is and what she needs to do. Lorenzo will not solve her problems. She must do that alone in the context of the world she has created with her husband and children. Instead of losing herself in a narcissistic lens, Giovanna assumes the perspective of the viewer of the movie that is her life, perhaps suggesting the redemptive, anti-solipsistic function of cinema. Similarly Antonietta's encounter with Gabriele, and the subsequent examination of her own life and marriage, affords new insight into her role as obedient fascist wife and mother. She now understands that the term "*antifascista*," in Gabriele's case, carries no political significance. His sexuality, not his political views, is suspect in the fascist regime that equates the personal with the political. Scola's film does not reveal the results of this transformative (and potentially transgressive) experience: whether the encounter between a fascist housewife and a "*sovversivo*" will produce Antonietta's much desired seventh child, her little Adolfo.

The absence of memory, rather than the remembrance of the Holocaust per se, is the subject of Ozpetek's film according to Romoli:

> La mancanza di memoria storica delle nuove generazioni era un bel tema, troppo "sociologico" però. Dovevamo rileggerlo all'interno di noi stessi, in termini piú emotivi. Era un'altra la "smemoratezza" che riuscivamo a identificare anche a livello autobiografico: una smemoratezza dei sentimenti, la perdita del progetto originario che lega ogni coppia, ogni sogno, ogni progetto di vita che spesso si perde per colpa dei problemi quotidiani, economici, di sopravvivenza. [37]

Sara, Davide's maid, points out that Giovanna and others of her generation do not know the significance of the date October 16, 1943. Ignorance of such momentous events signals the paralyzing loss of memory, like that suffered by Davide at the beginning of the film. The only way to resuscitate those memories is through bonds such as those forged between Giovanna and Davide. At the end of the film, seated in the garden where decades before the two male lovers exchanged notes,

[36]Ibid., 32.
[37]Ibid., 30-1.

Giovanna reads a letter she has written to Davide. This letter reveals the possibility for memory for those who love on the margins of society:

> Ho ancora bisogno di una tua parola, Davide, di un tuo sguardo, di un tuo gesto. Ma poi all'improvviso sento i tuoi gesti nei miei, ti riconosco nelle mie parole. Tutti coloro che se ne vanno, ti lasciano sempre addosso un po' di sé? È questo il segreto della memoria? Se è così, allora, mi sento più sicura perché so che non sarò mai sola.

Una giornata particolare and *La finestra di fronte* reveal what Giovanna calls "*il segreto della memoria*" by focusing on highly subjective individual experiences of specific historical dates. These films combine fact and fiction like all good narratives. *Una giornata particolare* highlights the growing relationship between Germany and Italy in the spring of 1938. This union resulted in cultural similarities between the two countries, including the introduction of the Roman marching step in imitation of the German goose step and the replacement of the handshake by the Roman salute, and, in the summer of 1938, the institution of Italian racial laws. These laws barred foreign Jews from Italian schools, demanded that Jews who had taken up residence in Italy since 1919 leave the country within six months, discharged Jewish teachers and students from schools and universities and prohibited Jewish intermarriage with Christians.[38] Hitler's visit to Italy also laid the symbolic and political groundwork for the signing a year later in May 1939 of the Pact of Steel that solidified the union of the two totalitarian regimes.

The enforcement of the racial laws led ultimately to the mass deportation of the Roman Jews in the fall of 1943, the subtext of Ozpetek's *La finestra di fronte.* The Germans had come to occupy Rome in the summer of 1943 following the Italian surrender. In an ironic twist, when the Nazi troops entered the city, they marched up the Via dei Trionfi and past the Arch of Constantine, then down the Via dell'Impero to Piazza Venezia, following the same route as Hitler's parade on that special day in May five years earlier.[39] The Germans, now in charge, insisted that the Italians implement the racial laws. At the end of September 1943, the Jews were forced to deliver fifty kilos of gold to the Germans in order to ensure the safety of the Roman ghetto. Despite assurances to the contrary, the Jews faced mortal danger. Early in the morning of October 16, 1943,

---

[38] For a complete description of the racial laws and their impact, see *La persecuzione degli ebrei durante il fascismo: Le leggi del 1938* (Roma: Camera dei deputati, 1998).

[39] Painter, Jr., 147.

German Special Forces surrounded the Roman ghetto, closed all exits and then searched house by house for ten hours. In the end, over one thousand Roman Jews were arrested and deported to Auschwitz; fewer than twenty survived until the camps were liberated.

Una giornata particolare and *La finestra di fronte* memorialize historical events by deliberately focusing on dates. In addition to describing the meeting between Hitler and Mussolini, Scola's film recalls the birthday of Rome, XXI Aprile, the address of the palazzo in which the narrative unfolds. Much attention is paid to the date with which *Una giornata particolare* begins. Yet the film also ends with a date that Antonietta reads aloud from *The Three Musketeers*, Gabriele's gift to her: "Il primo lunedí del mese di aprile 1625, il paese di Meung appariva in completo subbuglio." The beginning of this historical novel coincides with the end of Gabriele's personal narrative in fascist Italy. By concluding the film just as it began, with *una giornata particolare*, Scola underscores the importance of individual human narratives that enrich our collective imagination.

FAIRFIELD UNIVERSITY, USA

Part VI:

Teaching Italian Culture Through Songs

CHAPTER TWENTY-THREE

TEACHING ITALIAN CULTURE THROUGH SONGS: "NON SOLO CANZONETTE"

PAOLA VETTOREL

Songs are like tattoos
—Joni Mitchell, *Blue*

Songs, language and culture

Teaching and learning a language does not mean dealing only with morpho-syntactical structures and vocabulary. Communicative competence goes beyond merely knowing grammar and words: it includes learning about the pragmatic contexts in which they are used. Culture and civilization are part of the complex background knowledge we need to interact with the people who speak that language to be able to share frames of reference and schemata which belong to the hidden part of the iceberg that constitutes culture. In language learning culture has traditionally been seen either as the presentation of a big "C" culture, namely literature and literary products, or as a collection of facts and notions belonging to small "c" culture, being considered in many cases a feature separated from language learning and teaching (Kramsch 1993). However, both "highbrow" and "lowbrow" cultures are complementary sides of the coin and students are more often in contact with pop culture as a real, authentic part of a language. Music, and especially pop songs, already play a part in our students' world in general and in the vision of the language they are learning, too. As concerning Italian in particular, many students, wherever they are from, are already familiar with at least a couple of Italian songs, tunes and words whether more or less recent. It is often their main source of exposure to the language outside the classroom. Many Italian singers do tours abroad[1], taking with their songs a vision of our country that becomes a reference point in people's imaginations. For learners of Italian *Nel blu dipinto di blu*, *Adesso tu* or *Quando si ama*[2] are symbols of Italy as much as tasty food or sunshine. Songs in themselves are a mirror of a culture and society and this is particularly true for Italian songs. Pop music in Italy is a multi-faceted world which includes, on one side, very popular productions and on the other the panorama of the *canzone d'autore*, where the *cantautori*[3] bring poetry and more complex and deeper matters into their music[4]. As Pivato underlines, "a song conveys not so much and not only content, but emotions that in any case refer to well-defined historical periods, situations and characters,"[5] a sort of living document that belongs to the memories of older and younger generations, and that are part of culture.

Including songs in a course of Italian, whether as a foreign or, even more, as a second language can therefore create a variety of unique links both with the use of the language itself and with the cultural and social world they represent. Songs are pervasive, they are "all around us," we cannot avoid hearing them and they "stick in our mind"—a phenomenon that advertisers know very well. They are full of cross-references that mix up "big C" and "small C" culture in a light and at the same time deep way. Being able to recognize these references can be source of pleasure not last for language learners. Songs can bring language learning and its surrounding culture nearer to the experience and life of learners, becoming a long-lasting memory and a living evidence of the different aspects of what learning a language means[6]—not least an affective immersion in its context of life.

---

[1] To mention just a few Paolo Conte, Lucio Dalla, Eros Ramazzotti, Laura Pausini, who are appreciated abroad at least as much as in Italy.

[2] Domenico Modugno's *Nel Blu dipinto di blu*, *Eros* Ramazzotti's *Adesso tu*, or Laura Pausini's *Quando si ama* are witnesses of Italy as much as Tornatore's *Nuovo Cinema Paradiso*, or *Io non ho paura*, the novel by Niccolò Ammaniti made into a film by Salvatores, or Dario Fo theatre, or films by Roberto Benigni.

[3] They are artists who write and sing their own songs, such as Gino Paoli, Fabrizio de André, Giorgio Gaber, Francesco de Gregori. They have given way to what has been defined as *canzone d'autore*, characterized by refined and poetic lyrics which have often been compared to those of poets (Cfr. Pivato 2002).

[4] See amongst others Borgna 1992, Pivato 2002.

[5] Pivato 2002: 215, our translation.

[6] Important in this perspective is also the fact that new technologies and especially internet have made it very easy to trace lyrics and tunes all over the world.

Music and language learning

Music is directly connected to the emotions. Even if the processing of language is situated mainly in the left hemisphere, when that decoding implies emotional or connotative aspects the right hemisphere is also involved in processing meaning. Besides, music activates other areas of the brain including the limbic system, which is connected to the emotions and to long-term memory. In addition, it can contribute to the processes of visualization (right hemisphere) and to induce a state of alpha waves in the brain—the best state to concentrate and intake new pieces of information[7]. Music and songs can be employed to create a relaxed and comfortable learning environment, where students can learn without negative pressure and keep their affective filter low.[8] Music can then be used as a background to individual, pair or group work, or as a break signal between lessons or tasks, or even as an energizing moment before a particularly demanding activity to enhance and support attention and concentration.[9]

Several methodologies, including Dr Lozanov's Suggestopedia, have underlined the value of using music in the classroom.[10] Alfred Tomatis[11] has shown that each language is set on different frequencies. The whole range of these can be perceived by the human ear at birth but this ability becomes restricted as we are exposed to only one language. According to Tomatis, we cannot produce sounds unless we can perceive them. Listening and being exposed to different frequencies through music and songs can therefore stimulate a perception of those languages other than our mother tongue, thereby improving comprehension and pronunciation.

---

[7] See among others Eiffert 1999: 131, Fletcher 2000: 115-16, Lake 2002.

[8] Krashen states that one of the conditions for learning to take place is to create conditions where the affective filter is low so that it does not interfere with the learning process. Cfr. Krashen, S. 1981, 1985a, Lake 2002.

[9] See Norman & Revell 1999.

[10] Dr Lozanov's Suggestopedia recommends the use of particular kinds of music during some phases of the learning process, in particular Mozart, Haydn and Brahms' pieces: researches show that listening to this kind of music creates the so-called *Mozart Effect*, where learning is enhanced. See also Fletcher 2000:117 for further suggestions about pieces to be used, and Smith 1996, 1999 for the development of Lozanov's theory into Accelerated learning.

[11] See Tomatis 1991b. Particularly relevant in our case is the fact that Italian and English are situated in two different ranges of frequency: English from 2,000 to 12,000 Hz, while Italian from 1,500 to 3,000 Hz, missing therefore all the high frequencies which are present in English.

Gardner's theory of Multiple Intelligences[12] includes, in its nine different types, the musical intelligence, which can be stimulated through the use of music in classroom activities. This would also cater for those learners who prefer an auditory learning style. As far as specific language aspects are concerned, songs offer great opportunities to develop automatic and unconscious learning of a foreign language as music supports and enhances the memorization of words, of chunks of language and intonation patterns (see also Schoepp 2001, Fonseca Mora 2000).

Songs can be used: to introduce or expand a topic of grammar, a theme, an area of vocabulary; to support rhythm and intonation; to encourage extensive and intensive listening, reading and writing skills; to set off a class discussion; or, to introduce creative or structured writing.[13] They can also be an alternative to repetitive exercises or pattern drills aimed at consolidating new structures and vocabulary. This is particularly true for young learners, but they can be used also with older students—rap, for instance, is popular with different age groups, in the first place teenagers, and jazz chants[14] can be appreciated by all ages. Last but not least, the kind of language used in songs is generally simple, colloquial, often repetitive, all of which makes it suitable to learners at different levels. It supports the learning of the communicative, lexical, pragmatic and cultural aspects of a language.

Songs and Italian culture: a module course

Songs can be used more or less regularly in the language classroom to integrate coursebook materials or to implement our syllabus. However, a specifically tailored course can be designed to deal specifically with aspects of civilization and culture. Such a course was realized with Erasmus B1-C1 students at the *Centro Linguistico di Ateneo*[15] at Verona University in Academic Year 2005/06. The course consisted of 20 lessons organized around some main themes (Table 23-1):

---

[12] See Gardner 1983.

[13] For a whole range of activities using music and songs see Murphey 1992, Domoney & Harris 1993, Saricoban & Metin 2000, Brewer 1995, Brown 2006, Davanelos 1999, Pasqui 2004.

[14] See Graham 1978, 2006.

[15] The *Centri Linguistici di Ateneo/Interateneo* (University Language Centres) have been set up within Italian Universities to overlook language training for students of most faculties. Most of them are members of AICLU, *Associazione Italiana Centri Linguistici Universitari,* an Association founded in 1997 to coordinate the policy of the centres: http://www.aiclu.it/

Theme	Authors - Songs
Motivation phase	Music is... What do you know about Italian music?
Gli anni '60: L'Italia fra campagna e città The 60s: Italy between countryside and cities	Modugno *Nel Blu dipinto di blu-Volare* Celentano-Conte *Azzurro* Celentano—*Il tuo bacio è come un rock, Il ragazzo della Via Gluck*
Le donne e la canzone Women and songs	Patty Pravo *La Bambola* Mina *Le mille bolle blu* Laura Pausini *Come se non fosse mai stato amore* Giorgia *Un amore da favola* Fiorella Mannoia *Quello che le donne non dicono*
La Città Squares and Cities	Lucio Dalla *Piazza Grande* Antonello Venditti *Roma Capoccia* Francesco Baccini *Le donne di Modena* Francesco Baccini/Fabrizio De André *Genova Blues* Fabrizio De André *Via del Campo* Batistococo *Venezia*
Tuttovasco	*Vita Spericolata* *Sally* *Ti prendo e ti porto via*
Gaber, Jannacci e Fo—La scuola milanese Laughing and crying: Gaber,Iannacci and Fo	*Lo Shampoo* *Vengo anch'io no tu no* *Ho visto un re* *La libertà/Barbera champagne*
L'amore Love	Nek *Lascia che io sia* Zucchero *Donne/Con le mani* Max Pezzali *Eccoti/Canzone d'amore*
Paolo Conte	*Bamboolah* *Bartali* *Via con me*
E se mi lasci? What if you leave me?	Laura Pausini *Come se non fosse mai stato amore* Francesco De Gregori *Rimmel* Alex Britti *Prendere o lasciare*

L'amore 2 Love 2	Lucio Battisti *Dieci ragazze per me* Eros Ramazzotti *Adesso tu/Cose della vita* Negramaro *Solo tre minuti*
Fabrizio de André	*Bocca di Rosa* *Via del campo* *Genova Blues*
Estate Italiana Italian summers	Alex Britti *La vasca* Luna Pop *50 special* Ligabue *Certe notti* Francesco Baccini *Sotto questo sole* Gino Paoli *Sapore di sale*
Il dialetto Dialects	Pitura Freska *Pin Floi* Batistococo *El telefonin* Pino Daniele *Napule è* De André *Creuza de Ma*

Table 23-1. Themes.

The above themes and songs were chosen as they offer the opportunity of introducing aspects which are relevant for Italian culture and society. The songs were presented using music and lyrics integrated with material such as articles, essays, interviews and pictures, which opened up continuous and sometimes hyper-textual connections with different and variegated aspects of culture. The teaching techniques were based on a humanistic approach and were therefore student-centred. They included individual work, *Cooperative Learning* techniques, group and pair work. Songs were used also for listening comprehension practice applying a range of different techniques drawn from the examples in the following paragraph.

Classroom activities with songs

Depending on the song and the topic, one or more of the following were employed in pre-, while and post listening activities. The songs were considered as a fundamental tool to create connections to present and reflect on those socio-cultural dimensions involved in the theme. A varied list of possible techniques that can be used depending on the class, level, materials chosen and kind of song is given below. Different techniques might be suitable and can be adapted to the learning context.

Key-words listening activity

Choose some relevant key words from the song. The words or the ideas are written on the blackboard, or alternatively on a sheet/flashcards, which are then shown to the students to test their knowledge of the vocabulary. The students are then asked to predict the story of the song. While listening, the students rearrange the words/images in the correct order/sequence.

Using rhymes and phonetic symbols

Take the last word of each rhyming line and ask the students to insert them in the table according to the corresponding sound (phonetic symbol), e.g.

/za/	/sa/	/ʃ/
rosa	rossa	lascia
cosa	fossa	coscia
casa	cassa	angoscia

Table 23-2. Phonetic symbols.

Let the students listen to the song. Divide the class into groups of four and give each student in the group a few lines of the song, different for each student. They then dictate it to the others so that, between them, they can make up the whole text. They listen to the song again, and then time is allowed for correction of peer versions. Finally distribute to all students a correct and complete version of the lyrics.

Running dictation

Write part of the lyrics of the song on a sheet of paper. This can be done using the IPA phonetic symbols, if students are familiar with it. Hang copies of the text on the classroom walls. Divide your students into pairs. One student will have to read the text and memorize it in order to dictate it to his/her partner; roles are swapped halfway through the text.

Different versions

Divide the students in pairs. Each partner in the pair will have a different version of the song: a) different missing words; b) some different words.

Reading the lines, the students make up a correct version of the text, which will then be checked listening to the song.

Jumbled lines/stanzas

Re-write the lines (or the stanzas) of a song jumbling them up. Ask your students, who will be working in pairs, to reconstruct the correct sequence of lines, using as clues textual elements such as cohesion markers, linkers, punctuation marks. When the students have finished, they compare their version with that of another pair. Finally, they listen to the song to check their versions, more than once if necessary. The listening activity can also be done at the beginning as a guide to reconstruct the correct order of the lines.

Linking words

Give the students a list of verbs and nouns, or nouns and adjectives, from the song lyrics. Ask them to match them in what they think the correct collocations are. Then let them listen to the song to check their predictions, and finally give them the complete lyrics text.

Grammar and songs

Choose a song dealing with an aspect of grammar which you want either to introduce to the class or reinforce through practice. Then you can erase the words connected to this aspect (e.g. the verb forms, or adjectives, or prepositions) and ask the students to complete the cloze text, or prepare a set of multiple choice options for each cloze for the students to choose from. First let the students listen to the song and ask them to make predictions about the title. Write their ideas on the blackboard, and finally give them the real title. Then ask them to complete the cloze exercise while listening to the song again. When they have finished, check the answers and play the song again. Finally, the students can be asked to write another line or stanza using the grammar function you have been dealing with.

Find the mistake

Rewrite the lyrics of a song substituting a number of words with others of your choice (the focus can be phonology, grammar, vocabulary, etc.). Ask the students to work in pairs to find the mistakes in the text; then play the song to complete the task and check their predictions. There could be a competition amongst the pairs where the winning pair is the one who finds the greatest number of mistakes.

Remakes

Play the song, more than once if needed, asking the students to note down some key-words and then to use them to write a text containing the main ideas of the song. Then give the class the lyrics and tell the students they have two minutes to read and memorize them. At this point distribute a text where the words in some lines are jumbled up and ask the students to work in pairs to put them in the correct order. Finally play the song again.

Follow-up activities

Change the mood

Ask the student to work in small groups to rewrite the text changing its mood (e.g. from sad to happy or vice versa).

Talking songs

The students in small groups make up a role play about the theme of the song, or prepare an interview with the protagonist of the song or with the singer/group. Then they act it out.

Video Music

Ask the students to design the storyboard of a video clip: pictures, setting, characters, dialogues. Should you have the original video for the song, play it and compare the ideas of the students with the official one. The video-clip could be realized in practice as a project if appropriate equipment is available.

Time for ads

The students work in groups of four and choose or are assigned a song. They think about a product the song could be associated with in a radio or TV ad. They then design the ad and present it to the classroom. Some real ads could be presented to the students beforehand, and they could be encouraged to discover unusual associations.

Make it personal

Choose a song you particularly like and listen to it together with the students. Explain the reasons why you particularly like it. Then ask the students to do the same in turn. Ten minutes of a lesson, once a week/fortnight, could be devoted to the activity.

Examples of lessons

We will give here some examples of the way in which the units in the Module were structured. Apart from the first motivational phase, most units maintain the same format, i.e. starting from a song, links and connections are made to the relevant aspects of culture and society through the use of other material, both written and visual.

1. Motivation phase: Music is...

Part of the first lesson was centred around the role music plays in the lives of the students and to brainstorm about their previous and present knowledge of Italian music and songs. After this brief brainstorming session, the following texts[16] were presented to the students:

Aldo Nove, novelist

Vengo anch'io no tu no	Enzo Jannacci
Quando sarai grande	Edoardo Bennato
The Robots	Kraftwerk
With or without you	U2
Hyperballad	Bjork

Ho ancora una foto in cui porto un paio di occhiali grossissimi che erano di mio zio. Facevo finta di essere Enzo Jannacci, io da grande volevo essere Jannacci. Poi è nata un'amicizia, ho scoperto che a lui piacciono le cose che scrivo. Insomma non sono riuscito a diventare lui, ma in qualche modo sono riuscito a emularlo.

Ferzan Ozpetec, film director

Strangers in the Night	Frank Sinatra

[16] These texts were chosen amongst others as the characters are outstanding men of culture in the Italian panorama, and the songs they mention are not only Italian but provide a link to a cross-cultural view in this first motivational phase.

Bugiardo e incosciente	Mina
La seconda primavera	Sezen Aksu
La donna cannone	Francesco de Gregori
Come nosso pais	Elis Regina

La prima canzone che mi viene in mente è Strangers in the Night. Ero alle elementari, avevo un'amichetta con cui uscivo sempre. In quegli anni a Istanbul andavano molto di moda i locali con i tavolini all'aperto e l'orchestra, chiusi da tende di cinta, dove suonavano musica americana. Io e lei ci arrampicavamo sugli alberi per spiare, ricordo una cantante che andava per la maggiore, cantava i pezzi di Sinatra. Anni dopo ho rivisto quell'amica e lei mi ha fatto capire che io ero stato il suo primo amore. Non me n'ero reso conto. Strangers in the Night è rimasta per me il simbolo di quelle situazioni che capisci solo a distanza

Gianni Vattimo, philosopher

Il cielo in una stanza	Mina
Ma mì ma mì	Ornella Vanoni
Oltre il ponte	Italo Calvino
La Zolfara	(di Amodei-Straniero) Ornella Vanoni
La mauvaise herbe	Georges Brassens

Dice, la canzone di Brassens, io sono l'erba cattiva che non si raccoglie. E' così evidente perché mi è sempre piaciuta: è l'idea di non essere parte del sistema, di non stare dove si deve stare. E' un'idea romantica che si ha in gioventù, e che continua ad appartenermi[17].

After an individual reading phase, the students were invited to discuss the ideas with a partner and, subsequently, to write a similar paragraph about five important songs in their life. The ideas were then shared first in small groups and then in plenary. Where Italian songs and singers had been included in the list by students, their choices were discussed in more detail and supplemented with some extra information when necessary. Amongst the most common references, and already part of the students' background, were Domenico Modugno's *Nel Blu Dipinto di Blu*, the San Remo Festival, Caruso, Pavarotti, Bocelli and the opera, Laura Pausini, Eros Ramazzotti and Vasco Rossi.

[17] Polese: 2005: 256-58.

2. Gli anni '60: L'Italia fra campagna e città— The 60s: Italy between countryside and cities

Starting from the fact that most students know or had heard *Nel blu dipinto di Blu*, better known as *Volare*, after a first listening the teacher introduced some ideas related to why it is considered as the starting point of the modern age in Italian songs. With the help of pictures and OHP slides the main traits of the pre-Modugno typical songs, plus the birth of the San Remo Festival, were looked at. This underlined how the Italy represented in songs like *Papaveri e Papere* (1952) and Nilla Pizzi's *Vola colomba vola* (1953) was mainly an agricultural, patriarchal and parochial country where love and rural landscapes were the norm[18]. But with the 60s and the economic boom things take a different direction: television sets become a more widespread commodity and TV music programmes like *Canzonissima* are a great success, the music industry explodes, and a series of Festivals are set up, like the *Cantagiro* (1962), the *Festivalbar* and the *Disco per l'Estate* (1964), some of which still survive today. Modugno's *Volare* was the first breach with tradition both for the vaguely surrealistic words and for his inflection and body language; the song has therefore become a symbol[19] which was to become famous all over the world. After this introduction, the students listen to the song again, first just noting down any words they understand, and then reading the full text. The song to follow is *Azzurro* by Celentano-Conte: it represents another piece of reality of those years, with the *oratorio*[20] and the hot summers which will later on become a synonym of holidays at the seaside. This time the song is given in jumbled stanzas to be reconstructed in pairs while listening, and then comprehension is followed with the explanation of the above elements. The figure of Adriano Celentano is also introduced with the support of a picture accompanied by the following extract of one of his monologues *Rock... e Lento:*[21]

---

[18] And where, from a linguistic point of view, the regular rhymes were "cuore-fiore-amore" (heart-flower-love).

[19] Cfr. Borgna 1992: 225-28.

[20] The *oratorio* is a meeting place run by the parish, usually next to the church, where young people meet and play, particularly important as such in the 60s and 70s.

[21] The monologue is divided into sections, which were each broadcasted by RAI UNO during the programme *RockPolitick* completely run by Celentano in 1995.

IL CANNONE **E' LENTO**, I FIORI **SONO ROCK..**
L'ODIO **E' LENTO E** IL BACIO **E' COME UN ROCK**
LA FANFARA **E' LENTA,** IL ROCK **E' ROCK**
ZEMAN **E' ROCK,** CASSANO **E' ROCK,** ADRIANO **E' ROCK,**
MOGGI **E' LENTO.**
LE POLPETTE **SONO ROCK,** L'HAMBURGER **E' LENTO**
LA VESTAGLIA **E' LENTA,** LA MINIGONNA E' ROCK
IL DIRETTORE **DELLA SCUOLA E' LENTO,** LA MAESTRA E' ROCK
LA FORMICA E' LENTA, LA CICALA E' ROCK
LA TORTURA E' LENTA, LENTISSIMA... LA PIETA' E' ROCK
VALENTINO ROSSI E' ROCK, PORTO CERVO E' LENTO
LO ZOO E' LENTO, LA FORESTA E' ROCK
CHI SI SOSPENDE E' LENTO CHI SI DIMETTE E' ROCK
IL 26 E' LENTO, IL 27 E' ROCK
LA CARBONARA E' ROCK, LA MINESTRINA E' LENTA
PAPERINO E' ROCK, TOPOLINO E' LENTO
IL SILICONE E' LENTO, E QUELLE VERE SONO ROCK.[22]

The monologue was read and commented on and the many cultural references explained—some of which by the students themselves, who were already familiar with expressions like "Zeman, Cassano, Moggi, minigonna, carbonara". The students were then asked to produce in pairs a mini-sample of a rock-lento monologue, which was then exchanged with class-mates.

A final song, *Il ragazzo della Via Gluck,* was introduced. The vocabulary in this case is quite simple and the topic generally familiar, so comprehension was easier. Finally the class listened to *Il tuo bacio è come un rock* to have an example of the innovation in rhythm this song represented in the 60s.

3. La città–Squares and cities; Il dialetto–Dialects

First, there was a brief brainstorming session to recall and integrate students' existing knowledge about cities in Italy, with the support of pictures of famous squares and their location on a map. Then the class was presented with a passage about the significance and meaning of the "square" in Italian culture.[23] A picture of Piazza Maggiore in Bologna accompanied Lucio Dalla's song *Piazza Grande* (cloze technique activity) with the reading of an extract by Loriano Macchiavelli,[24] and a picture of a

[22] Source: http://www.rockpolitik.it/home.html
[23] See MATDID website http://www.scudit.net/mdindice1_40.htm
[24] Macchiavelli 2005a: 78-9; 2005b: 8-9.

skyline in Rome accompanied Antonello Venditti's *Roma Capoccia.* Pictures and brief notes about the two *cantautori* were also given, highlighting their role in the Italian musical scene.[25] In the case of *Roma Capoccia*, the text contains quite a few words in dialect, which created the occasion to reflect upon this aspect of the language still well widespread in Italy. At the end of the lessons other examples were given with the following: Pitura Freska *Pin Floi,* Batistococo *El telefonin* (both in Venetian dialect, with which the students were already in some way familiar, living in Verona), Pino Daniele *Napule è* (Naples) and Fabrizio De André *Creuza de Ma* (Genua dialect). The third piece in this unit was Francesco Baccini's *Le donne di Modena*, which presents an ironic portrait of women living in four Italian big cities. The presentation phase was here too accompanied by a picture of the singer, and the comprehension was followed by a group reading of an interview with Baccini where he explains how the song was born and the reactions he had after the song became popular[26]. The song also opened up an interesting discussion about stereotypes and images of women in Italy.

An expansion of this unit could also include material about Genoa, e.g. Francesco Baccini/Fabrizio De André's *Genova Blues*, Fabrizio De André's *Via del Campo* and Paolo Conte's *Genova per noi.*

4. Estate Italiana—Italian summers

Italian summers have a special flavour. These are often linked to melodies that resonate everywhere, on the radio and on the beaches, from bars to shopping malls. The tunes and words stick in your mind and are sung by everybody for a season.

> It [summer] has always been the most sung season: but in Italian music summer has also been able to imprint a very special mark, a different, original one, different from anywhere else in the world, made of sonorities and lexical choices able to define a genre, to picture an age, to set a fashion (Gentile 2005:1).[27]

Summer songs exploded in the 60s, linked to the economic boom that allowed families to go on holiday to the seaside, and, since then, have

---

[25] See Borgna 1992: 353-58, 379-82.

[26]Source: http://www.galleriadellacanzone.it/canzoni/anni90/schede/donnedimodena/donnedimodena.htm

[27] Our translation.

become a symbol of the prosperity of those years, together with the *Fiat 500* and the *Vespa*. Festivals and radio broadcasting supported the spread of easy-to-remember and easy-to-sing melodies: *Festivalbar*, *Un Disco per l'Estate*, *Cantagiro* as examples of the former and *Per Voi Giovani* and *Bandiera Gialla* by Gianni Boncompagni/Renzo Arbore and as radio programmes, to mention just the most significant ones.[28]

The Unit was introduced with pictures of Italian seaside resorts in the 60s, of a *Vespa* and a *Fiat 500* packed with a family going on holiday. At the same time some key ideas were pointed out about what it was like to have a seaside holiday in those years and what remains today of that spirit. The first two songs to be contextually introduced were Gino Paoli's *Sapore di sale and* Nico Fidenco's *Legata a un granello di sabbia* as both portray very well the atmosphere of those years. After a first listening eliciting the students' impressions and comments, the lyrics were distributed (with a "Find the mistakes" activity). Then Francesco Baccini's *Sotto questo sole* was presented, followed by Luna Pop's *50 special.* The latter in particular was an opportunity to see if habits and atmosphere relating to young people have changed, and if so how; and also to make some points of comparison between the fabulous 60s and the 80s and 90s. At this point a passage by P. Vittorio Tondelli, *Adriatico Kitsch*[29], was introduced and read collectively, followed by a discussion involving the experiences of Italian beaches in the summer by the students themselves. Finally, Alex Britti's *La vasca* was played and the students were asked to recognize in the lyrics those elements referring to typical activities of Italian young people during a holiday at the seaside. Things like singing around a bonfire, a midnight swim, waiting for sunrise before having a *cornetto and cappuccino* opened up an interesting conversation in the whole group about habits and free-time entertainment. An interesting possible expansion of this topic could be that of summer nights, with Ligabue's *Certe notti*, accompanied by the reading of Tondelli's "Modena" (1990:76-80), Ligabue's "Le strade blu dell'Ameribassa" (2004: 120-25) and of a passage about the role the Via Emilia has had in socio-cultural and musical terms.[30]

---

[28] See Gentile 2005, Borgna 1992: 298-302.
[29] Tondelli 1990: 98-101.
[30] E.g. M. Smargiassi, 1995 in AAVV: 14-21.

Conclusions

The experience of the course was definitively positive,[31] as it gave the students an unusual point of view on matters of Italian culture that could then be found in their everyday lives any time they heard a song on the radio, TV, in the street or while having a drink in a bar. The course, besides being fun, achieved a high level of involvement both at a cognitive and an affective level. It also gave the students some tools to help them to pay conscious attention and interpret elements of the surrounding socio-cultural reality they experienced during their stay in Italy. Even from a linguistic point of view the course was positive:

> When coupled with a visual image, music can become a very powerful learning tool. Perhaps that is why television programs [and ads] that dramatize contemporary songs have been so successful as a medium in reaching youth culture. Whether it is a positive or negative message, the input sticks (Lake 2002:6).

In this course there was a variety of significant inputs that, stemming out from a pop culture as a starting point, all added cultural elements: frames, schemata and knowledge of the world "encyclopaedia". These are as important as linguistic knowledge to become a competent user of a language. Italian culture, in the eyes of our students, is a kaleidoscope of components: some belonging to "big C" culture such as art, literature, classical music, opera; and others belonging to what is traditionally considered "small c" popular culture, which plays an important part in the minds and everyday lives of students.

"La chanson est un art de synthèse. Elle doit son identité à 'la magie conjuguée du texte et de la musique'" (Delière & Lafayette 1985:413). Exploiting these two highly evocative elements together with the numerous deep links pop songs and *canzone d'autore* have with society and culture can offer valid and powerful tools in language teaching. In turn this can create connections across all the linguistic and cultural aspects of learning a language, enabling learners to use language effectively as well as to understand the realities it conveys.

---

[31] A questionnaire about the course was distributed at the end of the experience. The results confirmed that the level of interest and motivation had been high throughout the lessons and the materials highly appreciated. Some suggestions about other possible topics and songs were given by the students, a further sign of the impact of the course on cultural awareness.

UNIVERSITY OF VERONA, ITALY

References for songs cited

Baccini, F. *Le donne di Modena.* 1990. ed. Insieme/Sugarmusic.
—. *Sotto questo sole* (Baccini-Belli, Prandi). 1990. EMI.
Baccini, F. and De André F. *Genova Blues.* 1990. CGD.
Batistococo. *El telefonin* (A. De Fanti, G. Bertan). 1999. New Boys Production.
—. *Venezia.* (M. Musoni). 1999. New Boys Production.
Battisti, L. *Dieci ragazze per me* (Battisti-Mogol). 1970. Ricordi.
Britti, A. *La vasca,* 2000, Universal Music Italia.
—. *Prendere o lasciare.* 2006. Universal Music.
Celentano, A. *Il ragazzo della Via Gluck,* (Celentano-Beretta-Mariano), 1966, Ed. Clan.
—. *Il tuo bacio è come un rock,*(Vivarelli-Fulci-Celentano), 1959, Ed. Mascotte.
—. *Azzurro,* (Conte-Pallavicini), 1968, Ed. Clan.
Conte, P. *Bartali*, 1979, BMG Ariola.
—. *Bambolah.* 2004. Warner Music Italia.
—. *Via con me.* 1981. RCA.
Dalla, L. *Piazza Grande.* (Baldazzi-Bardotti-Dalla-Cellamare). 1972. BMG Ariola.
Daniele, P. N*apule è.* 2002. CGD East West.
De André, F. *Bocca di Rosa.* 1970. BMG Ricordi.
—. *Creuza de Ma,* (De André-Pagani), 1984, Ed. Jubal/Fado.
—. *Via del Campo.* (Musica di Enzo Jannacci). 1980. Ricordi.
De Gregori, F. *Rimmel.* 1975. Sony BGM Music Entertainment Italy.
Fidenco, N. *Legata a un granello di sabbia.* (Fidenco-Marchetti), 1961, Sony BGM Music Entertainment Italy.
Gaber, G. *Barbera champagne.* (Gaber-Luporini). 1970. Ed. Curci.
—. *La libertà* (Gaber-Luporini). 1974. BMG Ricordi.
—. *Lo Shampoo* (Gaber-Luporini). 1972. Carosello Records.
Giorgia. *Un amore da favola.* 1997. Dischi di cioccolata/BMG Ricordi.
Jannacci, E. *Ho visto un re* (Fo-Esposito). 1966. Ed. Redi/Bella Ciao.
—. *Vengo anch'io no tu no.* (Fo-Fiorentini-Jannacci). 1967. BMG Ariola.
Ligabue, L. Ce*rte notti.* 1995. WEA Records.
Luna Pop. *50 special.* (Cremonini). 2003. Pibedeoro.
Mannoia, F. *Quello che le donne non dicono* (Ruggeri-Schiavone). 1987. Sony BGM Music Entertainment Italy.

Mina. *Le mille bolle blu* (Pallavicini-C.A. Rossi). 1961. Ed. C.A. Rossi.
Modugno, D. *Nel Blu dipinto di blu* (Migliacci-Modugno). 1958. Ed.Curci.
Negramaro. *Solo tre minuti*. 2005. Sugar.
Nek. *Lascia che io sia*. 2005. Warner Bros.
Paoli, G. *Sapore di sale*. 1963. BMG Ariola.
Pravo, P. *La bambola*. 1968. RCA.
Pausini, L. *Come se non fosse mai stato amore*. 2004. Warner Music.
Pezzali, M. *Eccoti*. 2004. Atlantic.
—. *Canzone d'amore*. 2001. CGD EastWest.
Pitura Freska *Pin Floi*. (Skardy-Verardo). 1991. Psycho Records.
Ramazzotti, E. *Adesso tu* (Cassano-Cogliatti-Ramazzotti). 1986. Sony BGM Music Entertainment Italy.
—. *Cose della vita* (Ramazzotti-Cogliati-Cassano). 1993. BMG Ricordi.
Rossi, V. *Sally*. 1996. EMI.
—. *Ti prendo e ti porto via*. 2001. EMI.
—. *Vita Spericolata* (Rossi-Ferro). 1983. Ed.Star/Targa Italiana/Curci.
Venditti, A. *Roma Capoccia*. 1972. Ed. IT Dischi/BMG Ariola.
Zucchero. *Donne*. 1985. Polydor.
—. *Con le mani*. 1987. Polydor.

References

General

Eiffert, D. S. *Cross-Train your Brain*. New York: Amacom, 1999.
Gardner, H. *Frames of Mind, the Theory of Multiple Intelligences*. New York: Basic Books, 1983.
Kramsch, C. *Context and Culture in Language Teaching*. Oxford: Oxford University Press, 1998.
Krashen, D. S. *Second Language Acquisition and Second Language Learning*. Oxford: Pergamon, 1981.
—. *Principles and Practice in Second Language Acquisition*. Oxford: Pergamon, 1982.
—. *The Input Hypothesis: Issues and Implications*. Harlow: Longman, 1985a.
—. *Language Acquisition and Language Education*. San Francisco: Alemany Press, 1985b.
Revell, J. and Norman S. *In Your Hands – NLP in ELT*. London: Saffire Press, 1997.

Revell, J. and Norman S. *Handing Over—NLP-based activities for Language Learning*. London: Saffire Press, 1999.
Smith, A. *Accelerated learning in the Classroom.* Stattford: Network Educational Press, 1996.
—. *Accelerated learning in Practice.* Stattford: Network Educational Press, 1999.
Tomatis, A. A. *L'oreille et le langage*. Paris: Editions du Seuil, 1991a.
—. *Nous sommes tous nés polyglottes*. Paris: Editions Fixot, 1991b.

Music and songs in the (language) classroom

Ahola, S. K. 2001. "Digging deeper into Songs: a writing activity." *The Internet TESL Journal* Vol. XI no. 2 (2001). http://iteslj.org/lessons/Ahola-Songs.html (accessed September 20, 2007).
Brewer, B. C. *Music and Learning: Integrating Music in the Classroom*, 1995. http://www.newhorizons.org/strategies/arts/brewer.htm (accessed September 20, 2007).
Brown, J. L.M. "Rhymes, stories and songs in the ESL classroom." *The Internet TESL Journal* Vol. V No. 11 (2006). http://iteslj.org/Articles/Brown-Rhymes.html (accessed September 20, 2007).
Caon, F. *Canzone pop e canzone d'autore per la didattica della lingua, della cultura italiana e per l'approccio allo studio della letteratura*, Modulo FILIM – Formazione degli insegnanti di lingua italiana nel mondo. Venezia: Laboratorio Itals, Università Cà Foscari, 2007. http://venus.unive.it/filim/index.php?name=EZCMS&page_id=1&menu=1 (accessed September 20, 2007).
Cardona, M. "Accrescere la competenza lessicale attraverso l'uso della canzone." *Bollettino Itals* Anno I No. 3 (Settembre 2003) http://venus.unive.it/italslab/modules.php?op=modload&name=ezcms&file=index&menu=100&page_id=109 (accessed September 20, 2007).
Carter R. *6 Pop Songs for you*. Crawley: Helbling Languages, 2005.
Cassano R. "La Lingua della musica pop." *Europa Vicina* Anno XI No. 15 (2007):26-27.
Cranmer, D. and Laroy, C. *Musical Openings*. Harlow-Canterbury: Longman-Pilgrims, 1992.
Cullen, B. "Song Dictation." *The Internet TESL Journal* Vol. V No. 11 (1999).

http://iteslj.org/Techniques/Cullen-SongDictation.html (accessed September 20, 2007).
—. "Music and song in discussion." *The Internet TESL Journal* Vol. XII No 4 (1998). http://iteslj.org/Techniques/Cullen-Music.html (accessed September 20, 2007).
—. "Song Dictation." *The Internet TESL Journal* Vol. V No 11 (1999). http://iteslj.org/Techniques/Cullen-SongDictation.html (accessed September 20, 2007).
Cunningham P. A. "Student created song exercises". *The Internet TESL Journal* Vol. VII No 4, 2001. http://iteslj.org/Lessons/Cunningham-SongsExercises.html (last accessed September 20, 2007)
Davanelos, A. "Songs." *English Teaching Professional* Issue no.13 (October 1999).
Delière J. and Lafayette R. C. "La Clef des chants: thèmes culturels et techniques pédagogiques pour l'einsegement de la civilisation par la chanson." *The French Review* Vol. LVIII No. 3 (1993): 411-25.
Domoney L. and Harris S. "Justified and Ancient: pop music in the EFL classroom." *ELT Journal* Vol. 47/3 (1993):234-41.
Ferencich R. "Alcuni spunti sull'uso della musica." *Bollettino Itals* Anno I No.3 (Settembre 2003). http://venus.unive.it/italslab/modules.php?op=modload&name=ezcms&file=index&menu=79&page_id=114 (accessed September 20, 2007).
Fletcher, M. *Teaching for Success*. Folkestone: English Experience, 2000.
Ferradas Moi C. "Materials for Language Through Literature. Rocking the Classroom: Rock Poetry Materials in the EFL Class." In *Developing Materials for Language Teaching*, ed. Tomlisnon Brian, 221-33. London: Continuum, 2003.
Fonseca Mora, C. "Foreign Language Acquisition and melody singing." *ELT Journal* Vol. 54/2 (2000):146-52.
Gigante, L. and Turri G. *Prestami Orecchio. L'uso della canzone nel dialogo tra le generazioni*, Molfetta: La Meridiana, 2005.
Graham, C. *Jazz Chants*. Oxford: Oxford University Press, 1978.
—. *Jazz Chants for children*. Oxford: Oxford University Press, 1979.
—. *Jazz Chants Fairy Tales*. Oxford: Oxford University Press, 1988.
—. *Let's Chant Let's Sing*. Oxford: Oxford University Press, 1994.
—. *Creating Chants and Songs*, Oxford: Oxford University Press, 2006.
Iotti, P. "Sono solo canzonette? Come e perché il canto mi fa dire 'sono portato per le lingue': teoria, esperienze, considerazioni." *Annali della Facoltà di Scienze della Formazione* 1 No. 2 (2004): 573-92, Macerata: Università di Macerata.

Lake, B. "Enhancing acquisition through Music." *The Journal of the Imagination in Language Teaching and learning Vol.* VII (2002). http://www.njcu.edu/CILL/vol7/lake.html (accessed September 20, 2007).

Ludlow, K. and Reilly, P. *10 Original Pop Songs*. London: Heinemann ELT, 2005.

Medina S. L. "The Effect of Music on second Language Vocabulary Acquisition." *ESL Through Music Website*, 2002. http://www.forefrontpublishers.com/eslmusic/articles/06.htm (accessed September 20, 2007).

Murphey, T. *Music and Songs*. Oxford: Oxford University Press, 1992.

Nicosia, M. P. undated. *Canzoni ed insegnamento di una lingua straniera*.http://it.eduhi.at/didattica/canzdid.html (accessed September 20, 2007).

Pasqui, R. "L'utilizzo della canzone in glottodidattica." *Bollettino ITALS* Anno I no.3 (Settembre 2003). http://venus.unive.it/italslab/modules.php?op=modload&name=ezcms &file=index&menu=100&page_id=116 (accessed September 20, 2007).

—. "Risorse tecnologiche per l'insegnamento/apprendimento di una L2/LS attraverso le canzoni: suggerimenti per l'italiano." *Bollettino ITALS* Anno II no.6, Settembre 2004. http://venus.unive.it/italslab/modules.php?op=modload&name=ezcms &file=index&print=1&page_id=120# (accessed September 20, 2007).

Puchta, H. and Rinvolucri, M. *Multiple Intelligences in EFL*,. Crawley: Helbling Languages, 2005.

Saricoban A. and Metin E. "Songs, verse and games for teaching grammar." *The Internet TESL Journal* Vol. VI no. 10 (2000). http://iteslj.org/Techniques/Saricoban-Songs.html (accessed September 20, 2007).

Schoepp, K. "Reasons for Using Songs in the ESL/EFL Classroom." *The Internet TESL Journal* Vol. VII no. 2 (2001). http://iteslj.org/Articles/Schoepp-Songs.html (accessed September 20, 2007).

Suk Mei Lo, Regina and Chi Fai Li, Henry. "Songs enhance Learner Involvement." *Forum* Vol. 36 No. 3 (1988): 8-14.

Tomlinson, Brian (ed.). *Developing Materials for Language Teaching*. London: Continuum, 2003.

Vettorel, P. "Canzoni in classe: la vita non è (tutta) fuori." *LEND Lingua e Nuova Didattica* Anno XXXV/1, Febbraio 2006.

Walker, Robin. "Going for a Song." *English Teaching Professional* Issue n. 43 (March 2006).
Wingate, Jim. "The Power of Music." *English Teaching Professional* Issue n. 36 (January 2005).

Italian music and songs

AA.VV. *L'Italia del Rock.* Roma: Ed. La Repubblica, 1994.
—. *Bologna e dintorni. Il rock della Via Emilia.* Roma: Ed. la Repubblica, 1995.
Antonellini, M. *Non solo canzonette, Temi e protagonisti della canzone d'autore italiana.* Foggia: Bastogi, 2002.
Assante E. and Cataldo G. (eds.). *La grande storia della canzone italiana.* Roma: Il Corriere delle Alpi/Gruppo Editoriale l'Espresso, 2005.
Berselli, E. *Canzoni. Storia dell'Italia leggera.* Bologna: Il Mulino, 2007.
Borgna, G. *Storia della canzone italiana.* Milano: Oscar Saggi Mondatori, 1992.
Borgna G. and L. Serianni. (Eds.). *La Lingua Cantata. L'italiano nella canzone dagli anni Trenta ad oggi*, Roma: Garamond, 1994.
Bozzone Costa R. *Viaggio nell'italiano.* Torino: Loescher, 2004.
Buono Hodgart L. *Capire l'Italia e l'italiano.* Perugina: Guerra Edizioni, 2002.
Capasso E. *Andare lontano... Luoghi e non luoghi della canzone italiana.* Foggia: Bastogi, 2005.
AA.VV. *Storia e Canzone in Italia: il 900.* Venezia: Comune di Venezia, Assessorato all'Istruzione, Itinerari Didattici, 2000.
Gentile, E. *Legata a un granello di sabbia, Storie e amori, costume e società nelle canzoni italiane dell'estate*, Milano: Melampo, 2005.
Jachia, P. *La canzone d'autore italiana 1958-1997.* Milano: Feltrinelli, 2006.
Maraone, P. and Maddeddu, P. *Una lacrima sul viso...*Milano: Kowaski, 2006.
Morozzi, G. *L'Emilia o la dura legge della musica.* Parma: Guanda, 2002.
Pivano, F. *I miei amici cantautori.* Milano: Mondadori, Milano, 2005.
Pivato, S. *La Storia Leggera.* Bologna: Il Mulino, 2002.
Polese, R. (Ed). *La Musica che abbiamo attraversato.* Almanacco Guanda. Parma: Guanda, 2005.
Smargiassi M. "La via Emilia è sull'atlante dell'anima". In AAVV. *Bologna e dintorni. Il rock della Via Emilia:* 14-21. Roma, Ed. La Repubblica, 1995.

Biographies and narratives

Baccini, F. *Nudo*. Milano: Bompiani, 1993.
Brizzi, E. and Marzaduri, L. *L'altro nome del rock*. Milano: Oscar Mondatori, 2001.
Jovanotti, L. *Il grande Boh*. Milano: Feltrinelli, 1998.
Ligabue, L. *Fuori e dentro il borgo*. Milano: Baldini Castaldi Dalai, 2004.
Macchiavelli, L. *Sarti Antonio e la ballata per chitarra e coltello*. Monferrato: Sonda Ed, 2005a.
—. *Sarti Antonio e il diamante insanguinato,* Monferrato: Sonda Ed, 2005b.
Tondelli, P. V. *Un weekend post-moderno*. Milano: Bompiani, 1998.

Collected songs to teach Italian as a Foreign/Second language

Costamagna, L. *Cantare l'italiano*. Perugia: Guerra Edizioni, 1990.
Mezzadri, M. *Cantagramma* (elementary level, intermediate level). Perugia: Guerra Edizioni, 2006.
Naddeo, C. M. e Trama G. *Canta che ti passa*. Firenze: Alma Edizioni, 2000.

Italian songs-Useful websites

http://www.italica.rai.it/monografie/canzone_italiana/index.htm
The page is part of the RAI International online course *Italica*–Learning Italian as L2/LS. It offers a rich selection of materials connected to the Italian "canzone d'autore."

http://rockol.it/musicaitaliana.com/
The website is entirely devoted to Italian music. It offers links to other significant websites, both official and unofficial, of many artists.

http://www.galleriadellacanzone.it/
The website has been created by *SugarMusic* publishing house and is devoted to the history of Italian pop music. It includes songs lyrics (the ones published by *Sugar*), photos and stories connected to songs from the 1940s to today.

http://www.italianissima.net/directory/storia_della_canzone/
Italianissima.net is devoted to Italian music, and Italian songs in particular. It contains information, news, links to sites of various singers, *cantautori*,

groups, and musicians. Particularly interesting the link to the history of Italian songs at:

http://www.sanremo.rai.it/R2_HPprogramma/0,,1067026,00.html
San Remo Festival's official website
http://www.radioitalia.it
Radio Italia–only Italian music–official website.

http://www.artemotore.com/index-9.html
The website offers links to various singers and *cantautori*'s official websites. It contains also a section with reviews and 'specials' on some artists.

http://www.girodivite.it/antenati/xx3sec/cons_son.htm
Notes on Italian music and songs between 1945 and 1990.

http://www.italia.ms/musica2000/
Numerous links to official home pages of Italian artists and to other sites connected to music.

http://www.lacanzoneitaliana.it/
The website contains many interesting sections on Italian artists, and includes characters, stories and reviews. It also offers links to some important festivals such as Sanremo, Festivalbar, Premio Tenco.

http://www.romaexplorer.it/divertimento/musica/musica_italiana.htm
The page contains various interesting links connected to Italian music and songs.

http://www.lisolachenoncera.it/
This magazine is entirely devoted to Italian music. It contains many relevant links to the home pages of a great number of artists.

http://venus.unive.it/italslab/modules.php?op=modload&name=ezcms&file=index&print=1&page_id=120#
Article by Rita Pasqui which presents a good number of links to other sites and to materials to use songs in the classroom

http://it.eduhi.at/
Website (in German) with a series of activities and lessons using Italian songs.

http://www.scudit.net/mdindice.htm
Matdid site containing a really wide selection of activities to learn Italian, including songs.

Songs lyrics

http://testimania.leonardo.it/
http://www.freeuniverse.it/testi-canzoni.htm (link to various sites)
http://www.tuttotesti.com/italiani/a.asp
http://www.tuttogratis.it/musica_gratis/testi_canzoni_gratis.html
http://www.lyricsondemand.com/

Webliography last updated and accessed 23 May 2008.

CHAPTER TWENTY-FOUR

ITALIAN FREAKS AND PUNKS: HISTORY OF ITALIAN CULTURE FROM 1950S TO 2005 RETOLD BY PROTEST SONGS

SILVIA BOERO

The fact that songs can be a highly effective means of support and can tell much more about a country than any language text is obviously not news; songs have been employed in language teaching for a long time and by many programs all over the world.[1] What I want to emphasize is, to quote Marcella Filippa, that there are particular songs which do not only reproduce reality but they also represent it:

> [Song] reworks it, reformulates certain aspects of it, those which most closely reflect widespread states of mind and perception, or which avoids others. In the Second World War, for instance, which more than any previous war involved the civilian population [...] love songs and escapist songs were widely popular. [...] Many critics have viewed these songs as [...] childish and have referred to them disparagingly as *canzonette*. Similar views were expressed in Italy in the 1960s and 1970s, during the wave of students' and workers' protest, when so-called escapist songs began to be severely criticized. Specialist and musicologists [...] regarded

[1] See the book by C. Naddeo and G. Trama, *Canta che ti passa* (Florence: ALMA Edizioni, 2003). It is an innovative text which uses contemporary Italian music as a way of teaching Italian to beginners and intermediate-level students. The CD contains 15 songs by different Italian artists which are then used as the basis for a number of language-based activities. These include communicative classroom exercises, games, comprehension and free production exercises and grammar practice. What's more there are also biographical notes on each artist. (http://www.italianbookshop.co.uk/italianbooks/series/m1/c1/6/CCTP)

> these songs as the equivalent of a digestive pill, as lacking spontaneity, mirroring the alienated and neurotic modern condition.[2]

In order to represent the complex and composite reality of Italian life in the last half century, I propose to explore songs that marked—historically and culturally if not commercially—some of the most significant moments of the country. Grammar, buttressed by cultural and historical context, can be reviewed and better internalized. My intention is to introduce the students to the dramatic changes the Italian language has undergone, especially during the last fifty years due to the connection with the Anglo-American culture caused by post WWII occupation. Such transformations, together with the immigration upsurge of the last 30 years, deeply affected the Italian social tissue and collective memory. A chronological approach provides for a historical insight that often is overlooked, allowing students to form a well–constructed view of the factual development of the Italian cultural landscape.

In this essay I will analyze some of the songs I use in class, those that in my opinion are the most essential to expand cultural consciousness and to strengthen grammar. Some of them are not exactly protest songs—at one time they were considered even *canzonette*—nevertheless they are symbolic of a specific historic–social–cultural context and mirror striking developments within the country.

Several practical examples help to visualize how the course functions. As one can see in the attached tentative syllabus, I start with a song that denotes a very important moment in the Italian history: establishment of American Navy and Army bases in the South of the country. This was a strategic move closely linked to the Cold War. The song by Renato Carosone, *Tu Vo' Fa' l'Americano* (You want to act like an American) is in Neapolitan dialect[3] and mocks not only Italians for abandoning their culture in trying to adopt American habits, but, tongue in cheek, derides Americans—young and naïve soldiers stationed at the local Navy base together with the rich and patronizing tourists. Carosone's song will be

---

[2] M. Filippa, "Popular Song and Musical Cultures," in *Italian Cultural Studies, an Introduction*, ed. D. Forgacs and R. Lumley (Oxford, New York: Oxford University Press,1996), 328–329.

[3] American troops landed in Anzio, near Naples, in 1944. Naples became the location for the first NATO base in Italy, built in 1949 but officially active since 1951.

analyzed with the film *Un Americano a Roma*[4] (An American in Rome) that narrates the adventures of Nando, a Roman youngster who is blindly enamored of the USA and everything that is American according to his imagined and imaginary world. His dreams about becoming an American citizen—a Joe Di Maggio or a John Wayne—are shattered by the encounter with real Americans living in still occupied Italy. Carosone himself was in love with American popular music—a love he openly declared in this song that is an authentic Dixie Jazz. However, he reminded the Italian public, youngsters *in primis*, that being Italian can still be "cool" and invited the audience to mingle with the occupying forces, but only to a certain extent. *Tu vo' fa' L'Americano*, today a classic, was and is intended to be thought provoking under a playful guise. The ending lines "*Ma si' nat' in Italy* [...] *Sent' a me, nun c'è sta' nient' a fa OK Napulitan*" (But you were born in Italy [...] Listen to me, it does not take anything to say OK, Neapolitan),[5] is a friendly exhortation to both parties, Italians and Americans, to understand each other, and to learn how to live together in a destroyed city and country. Another seminal song is *A Tammurriata nera* (lyrics by E. Nicolardi and music by E. Mario; in the syllabus I use Renato Carosone's version, 1950). Here, again, the Neapolitan dialect is in charge of the lyrics. It is the story of a young woman who had a black baby due to her relationship with an Afro-American GI. She decides—to scorn the gossips—to call her baby boy Ciro (candlestick in Neapolitan) displaying colorblindness as a means to fight racism. This song was written in 1945 when in Naples bi-racial relationships and marriages were quite frequent among the low classes. The music, a typical *tarantella*, mocks the bigotry of the locals, calls for an interclass and interracial society, and sends a message intended for a wider audience: "*Addó pastine 'o grano, 'o grano cresce/Riesce o nun riesce semp'è grano chello ch'esce*" (It does not matter who sows wheat or where it has been sown, wheat it will always be). In other words, black or white, this is a child, and nothing else matters. By comparing the dialect to the standard Italian, students are invited to review and rethink Italian history from a linguistic point of view, remembering that only in the last sixty years Italy has been more or less linguistically unified. Both songs are also a message of peace that does not imply, however, the obliteration of the devastations the World War II. Students will have then to confront

[4] Directed by Steno, on a screenplay by Ettore Scola and Lucio Fulci; released in 1954, produced by Carlo Ponti. The song *Tu vo' fa' l'Americano* was released in 1956, loosely inspired by the film.
[5] All translations are mine.

and discuss issues that, unfortunately, are universal and recurrent in an eerily endless circle.

The songs *La Locomotiva* by Francesco Guccini, and *La Lallera* by Paolo Pietrangeli prove useful when dealing with the subjunctive and the agreement of tenses and moods in main and secondary clauses. *La locomotiva* also offers a good review of past perfect and simple past used together in a narrative context:

> *Non so quanti anni avesse, neppure come si chiamava*
> *Con che voce parlasse, con quale voce poi cantava*
> [...]*E la locomotiva sembrava fosse un mostro strano*
> *che l'uomo dominava con il pensiero e con la mano:*
> […]*Ma un' altra grande forza spiegava allora le sue ali,*
> *parole che dicevano "gli uomini son tutti uguali"*
> *e contro ai re e ai tiranni scoppiava nella via*
> *la bomba proletaria e illuminava l' aria*
> *la fiaccola dell' anarchia,*
> […]*Un treno tutti i giorni passava per la sua stazione,*
> *un treno di lusso, lontana destinazione*
> […] *un treno pieno di signori*
> *Non so che cosa accadde, perchè prese la decisione,*
> […] *dimenticò pietà, scordò la sua bontà,*
> *la bomba sua la macchina a vapore*
> […] *Correva l' altro treno ignaro e quasi senza fretta,*
> *nessuno immaginava di andare verso la vendetta,*
> *ma alla stazione di Bologna arrivò la notizia in un baleno:*
> *"notizia di emergenza, agite con urgenza,*
> *un pazzo si è lanciato contro al treno"*

> (I do not know how old he was, not even his name/How he used to talk, how then he used to sing/And the locomotive looked like a strange monster/that men could dominate with hand and thought [...] But another great force was spreading its wings at the same time/words that said "Humans are all equal"/and against kings and tyrants was blowing in the streets/the proletarian bomb was lighting up the air/the torch of anarchy [...] A train, everyday, used to come by his station/a high class, long distance train/a train full of rich people [...] I do not know what happened, why he made such a decision [...] he forgot his own piety and kindness/the locomotive his own bomb [...] The other train, unaware, was traveling in no hurry/nobody was thinking to be going toward revenge/but in Bologna the news arrived suddenly/"emergency, a madman is running the engine against the train")

An intentional mistake stands out in the incipit of *La Locomotiva*: the lack of tense and mood agreement, the use of imperfect indicative instead of another imperfect subjunctive (a very common pattern in spoken Italian). In this ballad Guccini talks about the true story of a young anarchist railroad worker who in the late 19th century decided to run a steam engine toward a train transporting high society types.[6] The use of the indicative imperfect is intentional; besides using a poetic license, the author wants to speak commonly, like everyday people, echoing in his narration the story as it was probably handed on from worker to worker, peasant to peasant. Hence, this text effectively links directly the two instructional topics: the standard rule and the cultural-historical context. The subjunctive is widely used, especially with questions–from my side–to provoke debate.[7] Students will be asked to use the subjunctive, past perfect and simple past not only during directed conversation but also in the writing assignments that will follow this lesson. Other songs, more openly linked to the protest tradition, are beneficial to explain and reinforce the above-mentioned structures and some of their different uses. *La Lallera* is a perfect example to introduce the students to "if clauses:"

Se le strade cambiassero di nome,
ci sarebbe, tutt'a un tratto
Di sicuro la ragione
di chiamarsi soddisfatto
Se per esempio Corso Umberto si chiamasse
Karl Marx Strasse
Ed una strada che più grande non ce n'è,
Lenin Alè.
[...]*Se ci fosse un po' di Lallera*

---

[6] A message from the daily newspaper "Il Resto del Carlino" July 23, 1893: "Poco prima delle 5 pomeridiane di ieri, l'Ufficio Telegrafico della stazione (di Bologna, ndr) riceveva dalla stazione di Poggio Renatico un dispaccio urgentissimo (ore 4,45) annunziante che la locomotiva del treno merci 1343 era in fuga da Poggio verso Bologna. Lo stesso dispaccio era stato comunicato a tutte le stazioni della linea, perché venissero prese le disposizioni opportune per mettere la locomotiva fuggente in binari sgombri dandole libero il passo in modo da evitare urti, scontri o disgrazie. [...]"Alle 5,10 [la locomotiva] entrava dal bivio e passava davanti allo scalo, fischiando disperatamente, con una velocità superiore ai 50 km. Sulla macchina c'era un uomo che, invece di dare il freno, cercare di fermare, metteva carbone...." The machinist was Pietro Rigosi, twenty-eight years old, from Bologna. He survived the accident, even if terribly disfigured and maimed. When authorities asked him of his crazy action, he only answered: "It is better to die than to be oppressed and imprisoned."
(http://www.avvelenata.it/locomotiva/storialocomotiva.html)

[7] See Appendix. Discussions on assigned readings and grammar review precede the in-class writing activity.

Quest'erba delicata
Tutti vedrebbero chiaro
Mangiandola in insalata

(If roads changed name, there would be, all at once / the good reason to be satisfied / If, for instance, Corso Umberto were named Karl Marx Strasse / and a street that bigger could not be / named Lenin Avenue [...] If there were a little bit of Lallera / this delicate grass / Everyone would see clearly / eating it as salad)

Pietrangeli not only wishes for an immediate future world where streets will be named after the "father" of Communism and his famous follower, but also a society that will freely adopt the habit of using marijuana even as a salad.[8] These poems/songs may lead to in-class debates; appropriate handled, there is no need for this to be awkward or for the instructor or the class. In my own experience it is not possible to present a perfect world to our students, especially when we talk about a country such as Italy that, in less than 60 years, has experienced sudden and dramatic changes and that is still struggling to survive as a democracy.

If *La Lallera* employs a teasing mode, poking mercilessly at the *benpensanti*, *Luna Rossa* (Red Moon) by Banda Bassotti (a group linked to *centri sociali*) does not leave anything to ironic *divertissement*. A punk/ska band whose models are The Clash of the most socially active Joe Strummer, Banda Bassotti try to bring back historic collective memories that often the establishment has tried to hide, if not to erase:

Dice la gente che in piazza Fontana
forse è scoppiata una caldaia
la nella piazza 16 morti li benediva un cardinale
[...] *No, no, no, non si può più dormire*
la luna è rossa e rossa di violenza
bisogna piangere i sogni per capire
che l'unica giustizia borghese si è spenta
[...] *Ieri ho sognato il mio padrone*
a una riunione confidenziale
si son levati tutti il cappello
prima di fare questo macello
Come un vecchio discende il fascismo
succhia la vita ad ogni gioventù
ma non sentite l'urlo sulla barricata

---

[8] *Liberalizzazione* and *Liberalizzatela* (make it free) are the slogans of the most prominent radical and leftist groups who have been campaigning during the last thirty years to make marijuana lawful also for medical purposes.

la classe operaia continua la sua lotta

(People say that perhaps a boiler exploded in Piazza Fontana / there in the square sixteen corpses / a cardinal was blessing them [...] No, no, no, we cannot sleep anymore, the moon is red with violence / we must mourn the dreams to understand that the last bourgeois justice has died out [...] Yesterday I have dreamt about my boss at a confidential meeting / they all took off they hats before this massacre / Just like a mean old man Fascism sucks life from any youth / but can't you hear the scream on the barricades, the working class keeps fighting).

Banda Bassotti narrate the tragedy of Piazza Fontana, Milan, December 12, 1969, when 16 people died due to a neo-fascist bomb blast attributed for a long time to the innocent anarchist Pietro Valpreda, who was jailed for three years while waiting for appeal. Banda Bassotti openly call on to the masses for resistance—not violence—and awareness. While this song might not focus on a specific grammar structure, it offers an option to review several fundamental constructions at the same time; it is also helpful to explore the use of similes and metaphors. The songs/poems mentioned are extremely functional to review that period of Italian history—the so called *anni di piombo*, or years of lead—that is marked by years of terrorism, when the population was torn between the jaws of the extra parliamentary left and right.

Some other songs—harking back to the Italian beat generation—speak the truth still today. Caterina Caselli's *Nessuno mi può giudicare* (No one can judge me) was a controversial success due to a number of factors: she was seventeen when it was released, she had been the leader/bass guitarist of her own teen band, and, most importantly, the the lyrics of her hit were controversial. The text stood up for women who wanted to have options, when choosing their lovers:

Se ho sbagliato un giorno ora capisco che l'ho pagata cara la verità
[...] *Ognuno ha il diritto di vivere come può (la verità ti fa male, lo so)*
Per questo una cosa mi piace e quell'altra no
(la verità ti fa male, lo so)
Se sono tornata a te,
ti basta sapere che
ho visto la differenza tra lui e te
ed ho scelto te

(If one day I have made a mistake now I understand that / I have dearly paid for truth [...] Everyone has the right to live as s/he can / truth hurts you, I know / That's why I like one thing and not another / truth hurts you,

> I know / If I came back to you / it is enough to you to know / that I have seen the difference between him and you / and I have chosen you)

The proto–feminist implication might appear trite today, but at the time—1966—this song represented an authentic statement of rebellion. It is not by chance that the line *ognuno ha il diritto di vivere come può* was the slogan of the Gay Pride parade that took place in Rome in 2000. From a grammatical point of view, this song is excellent to review past perfect; the proper use of auxiliaries *essere* and *avere*; the agreements in the past participle; the direct, indirect and stressed pronouns. I decided to use this song to introduce a discussion on the second wave of Italian feminism. After the Post-Unity polemics in the 1860s and '70s that had seen as protagonists the philosopher Anna Maria Mozzoni and novelists/journalists Marchesa Colombi and Emilia Ferretti Viola, feminism in Italy lay fallow, despite the obvious repression and/or exploitation during the *Ventennio*. The feminist uprising of the 1960s and '70s was no new thing in Italy—as actually so many (especially American students) believe. Rather, it springs from the post-Unitarian women's movements.

Students can be introduced to the big shift that affected Italy in political-social matters, through the late '70s and early '80s, and then Italian punks come on the stage. These are the years that see the birth of *liberismo selvaggio*, the advent of Bettino Craxi and Silvio Berlusconi, and the first seeds of globalization together with immigration from so-called third or fourth world countries to a totally ignorant and unprepared Italy:[9]

> It appears that Italian perceptions of the immigrants, who come from over a hundred countries, and two–thirds of whom are from the South of the World, particularly the Maghreb, West Africa, the Philippines, and Latin America, are filtered through a small number of symbolic categories: *marocchino, zingaro, meridionale* (Southern Italian), *ebreo, africano/negro.* All these "common sense" categories suggest exclusion from the moral community rather than serving to identify any particular group [...]. A Kurdish interviewee recounted a conversation with a bartender who asked him and his friends where they came from. "Iraq, Lebanon and Greece" was the reply. "Oh, you're all African, then" exclaimed the bartender (IRES–Piemonte 1991: 172).

---

[9] Vanessa Maher, "Immmigration and Social Identity," in *Italian Cultural Studies, an Introduction*, ed. D. Forgacs, and R. Lumley (Oxford, New York: Oxford University Press, 1996), 167-70.

A song that despite its intrinsic complexity of language and therefore interpretation is very effective in educating American students (together with Italian) is *Islam Punk* by CCCP of Giovanni Lindo Ferretti. The text demands an in depth analysis and an accurate contextualization. The music, a masterful mix of obsessive punk and eastern sonorities, together with the lyrics targets the closed mindedness of westerners toward immigrants and /or foreign citizens in general. Giovanni Lindo Ferretti, major author of *Islam Punk* (to which guitarist Massimo Zamboni contributed) carefully chose the words to weave a trancelike narration of the protagonist's reversed immigration—a westerner who decides to go East to find himself:

Non mi fermo a pensare
continuo a salmodiare
mi sono perso ad Istanbul
e non mi trovano più
[…]*A Istanbul sono a casa*
ho un passato e un futuro
ho un presente che è Dio
e fa la cameriera

(I do not stop to think / I keep singing psalms / I lost myself in Istanbul / they will never find me […] I feel at home in Istanbul / I have a past and a future / I have a present who is God, and she works as a waitress).

To introduce the '90s and the wide scale of immigration in Italy, it is surely functional to present the class with MAU MAU and their *Paseo Colon*, a song in Piedmontese and Genoese dialects, is the story of the sailing toward the Americas, retold by the *ciurma*—the multiethnic and multilingual crew of Nina, Pinta and Santa Maria—who surely knew how to speak Genoese, *lingua franca* in those times. *Paseo Colon* is a *j'accuse* against Columbus and the *conquistadores* of all times; a song that speaks of *Caribe massacrà* (massacred Caribbeans) and *oû insanguinaû* (blood covered gold). The music, another cross-over between Eastern and Western tradition—a mantra-like tune that brings to mind the monochord chants of rowing sailors—is pedagogical by itself. The band's name, MAU MAU, is a clear reference to the revolutionary Kenyan movement active in the '60s, and to the numerous African residents (since the late '80s) in Turin.

The contrast between dialect and standard Italian as a metaphor of the struggle between state hegemony and local resistance is visibly expressed also by 99 Posse in *Curre Curre Guaglio'* (Run Run Kid):

Un giorno come tanti ma non certo per qualcuno
qualcuno che da giorni mesi anni sta lottando
contro chi di questo stato na gabbia sta facendo
reprimendo ascolta dico reprimendo
chi da solo denuncia e combatte sti fetiente
e sa bene che significa emarginazione
esattamente quanto costa amare un centro sociale
Officina 99
Curre curre guagliò
Siente sti parole d'odio e pure dammore
si nu scatto di manette strette ai polsi dentro a un cellulare
Guaglio'
allora chisto o mumento
[…] *o mumento d'occupà*
Curre curre guagliò
Si pu vivere una vita intera come sbirri di frontiera
in un paese neutrale, anni persi ad aspettare

(A day like another but surely not for someone/someone who has been fighting for days, months, against who is making a cage of this country / oppressing—listen, I say oppressing/who by him/herself is denouncing and fighting these bastards / and knows well what alienation means / exactly how much costs to love a social center / Workshop 99 / Run run kid / Listen to these words of hate and love / the click of the handcuffs you locked inside a prison van / Kid / Then this is the moment […] the moment for occupation / Run run kid / It is possible to live an entire life as frontier cops / in a neutral country, lost in waiting)

Curre Cure Guagliò is an indispensable step in order to introduce students to the almost unknown (at least here in the USA) *Pantera* movement,[10] the reality of *centri* sociali, and their appropriation of American rap (or better, its adaptation to local paradigms) as the main tool to exert active and effective protest:

The most interesting musical phenomenon of the last decade is the emergence of an Italian form of rap. Italian rap has spread through the

---

[10] Italian rap, better identified with "posse" "first emerged as a musical style ant the end of the 1980s, as a result of the occupation of universities and the student movement known as la Pantera, the Panther, and linked to the occupation of social centers by young people. It is an Italian version of politicized rap which originally came from the U.S.A., and it combines the slogans of political demonstrations with the campaigning songs of earlier decades to create a kind of equivalence between Afro-American radicalism and the Italian university occupations. M. Filippa, "Popular Song and Musical Cultures," 338–39.

> alternative network of centri sociali (self-managed social center) and independent record companies [...] Italian rap is committed to protest movements, anti-racist and multi-culturalist. Italian rappers often find dialect more expressive and to the point than standard Italian, and they make large use of it. Historical continuity with the tradition of the campaigning songs has not being broken, and political consciousness still walks hand in hand with populism.[11]

A great part of *canzone di protesta* is linked to the left—as for Paolo Pietrangeli, Banda Bassotti, and 99 Posse—or to anarchy (as in the case of Francesco Guccini and Fabrizio De Andrè). Surely not a leftist, Lucio Battisti always displayed non-involvement into political matters, an attitude that caused him to be quite groundlessly accused of being close to Fascist orientations. Battisti was an extraordinarily gifted musician whose career spanned from 1964 to 1998; he was dedicated to music of highest quality and set himself away from the mainstream or the control and censorship of RAI and of any leading political group. After the skyrocketing success of the '60s, Battisti shunned from the glittering world of the new born Italian VIP system. Always quite aloof, he preferred absence as the tool to reiterate his fundamental presence in the sphere of Italian and European music. In my course I propose Battisti's song *Sì Viaggiare* (Let's Travel):

> *Quel gran genio del mio amico*
> *lui saprebbe cosa fare,*
> *lui saprebbe come aggiustare*
> *con un cacciavite in mano fa miracoli.*
> *Ti regolerebbe il minimo*
> *alzandolo un po'*
> *e non picchieresti in testa*
> *così forte no*
> *e potresti ripartire*
> *certamente non volare*
> *ma viaggiare.*
> *Sì viaggiare*
> *evitando le buche più dure,*
> *senza per questo cadere nelle tue paure*
> *gentilmente senza fumo con amore*
> *dolcemente viaggiare*
> *rallentare per poi accelerare*

[11] Alessandro Carrera, "Folk Music and Popular Songs," in *The Cambridge Companion to Modern Italian Culture*, ed. Z. Baranski and R.J. West (Cambridge: Cambridge University Press, 2001), 333–34.

con un ritmo fluente di vita nel cuore
gentilmente senza strappi al motore.

(That great genius of my friend / he would know what to do / he would know how to fix / with a screwdriver in his hands he makes miracles / he would fix the minimum for you / jazzing it up a little / and you would not beat on the cylinder / not so hard / and you could leave again / perhaps not flying / but surely you could travel / Let's travel / avoiding the worst potholes / without fears / gently without smoke / softly let's travel / slowing down to accelerate again / with a flowing rhythm of life in your heart / gently, without jolting the motor).

Ideal in presenting the conditional mood, this song—a masterpiece of crystalline sonorities and perfectly mastered assonances—reiterates with its light and carefree lyrics the author's "non belonging" and intolerance for any intellectualism, a feature that perhaps attracted so many youths of several generations; to quote Alessandro Carrera "Battisti, as the semiotician Paolo Fabbri put it, did not sing about Italian teenagers; he created them."[12] In the syllabus I introduce this song with a rhetoric question: "Protesta a destra?" not only to underline Battisti's apartness but also to provoke questions and possibly healthy debates about the very concept of protest. This is why, despite fighting against my own personal resistance, I decided to include Delenda Carthago in this course. Openly Neo Nazi-Fascist—as one can easily infer from their website[13] where they sign their messages with "Sieg Heil," Delenda Carthago often play at the meetings of *Forza Nuova*, the party led by Alessandra Mussolini. A few lines from their *L'Invasione* (The Invasion) are quite explicatory:

Si parla continuamente di razzismo e prepotenze,
ma non mi frega un cazzo di Maometto e la sua gente.
non posso tollerare, chi accoglie indifferente,
tutta quella melma, del medio-oriente.
La sola soluzione, fermare l'invasione
Questa è l'altra faccia della globalizzazione.
La sola soluzione, fermare l'invasione
Questo e' un attentato alla nostra Nazione

---

[12] A. Carrera, "Folk Music and Popular Songs," 333.

[13] http://www.delendacarthago.it. The references to Cato's exhortation to destroy Carthago is explicit. When visiting the website mentioned above and scrolling the mouse on the list of contents, flames arouse from the words, an obvious allusion to burn anything "non Italian" or more specifically of African origin. The appropriation of the Nazi symbology, the glorification of Mussolini and his myth are openly displayed throughout their website.

Mi alzo la mattina, apro il giornale
Ecco i risultati del meticciato culturale
Droga nelle strade, rapine a mano armata

(They always talk about racism and bullying / but I don't give a rat's ass of Muhammad and his people / I cannot tolerate whoever welcomes indifferently / All that slime from Middle East / The only solution, to stop the invasion / This is the other face of globalization / The only solution, to stop the invasion / This is an attack to our Nation / I get up in the morning, I open the newspaper / here you have the results of cultural crossbreeding / Drugs in the streets, armed robberies)

The text does not need interpretation; it speaks straightforwardly of racism as the only way for Italy to save herself. Yet the whole song is based on rhythm'n'blues and rock'n'roll sonorities, non-white traditional musical paradigms. Delenda Carthago often indulge, despite their declared white supremacy, in guitar riffs inspired to Jimi Hendrix. It is to be wondered why, in order to be Italian and Fascist "to the bone," they do not research about and employ local traditional sonorities. To their disappointment they would discover that music soars far above any gross nationalism. Nevertheless, Delenda Carthago are a necessary step in this course in order to have students to learn about the multiple—and sometimes shameful—facets of the Italian socio-cultural landscape.

Conclusions

In the early sixties, the influence from the USA and from Great Britain was quite strong on the Italian musical scene. Ironically, those who were the most vocal in their opposition against the *ancient regime* of bourgeoisie and the American *longa manus* clasping Europe, were inspired by the very same Americans who historically made protest music: Pete Seeger, Woody Guthrie and his son Arlo; later Bob Dylan, Joan Baez, and Patti Smith. At the same time the British tradition was also exerting an enormous influence on Italian *cantautori* and bands: primarily the Who, especially those of *My Generation*, in the late '70s and early '80s; the Clash, who are still looked up by Banda Bassotti and Assalti Frontali, another urban rock-band active in cooperation with *centri sociali*. But, despite the obvious influences, our protest songs are exquisitely, genuinely Italian: they keep the traditional imprinting, as it can be clearly seen in songs by Fabrizio De Andrè and Giorgio Gaber[14]—the greatest poets of Italian popular music—or I Nomadi, the band that often accompanied Francesco Guccini on stage. The same can be said for CCCP, later CSI, and their *Unità di Produzione* from the award winning CD *Tabula Rasa Elettrificata.* Most of these songs and authors were (and still are not) commonly heard or seen on RAI, but one could listen to them on private radio stations and TVs, that, at the beginning, were representatives of freedom from the state monopoly, or better, from the intrusion of *Democrazia Cristiana,* that used to control great part of RAI 1. The influence of the leftist parties on *canzone di protesta* was surely strong; however authors were ready to detach themselves from any sort of misuse. It is the case of Edoardo Bennato, a true bluesman, with his LPs *Burattino Senza Fili* (Puppet without strings) and *Sono solo canzonette* (They're just songs). Both are concept albums: the first is the revisited story of Pinocchio; the second of Peter Pan. They are gigantic metaphors and biting satires against the cultural establishment; Bennato derides and accuses all parties—even the leftist like himself, when they try to exploit his success for their own political designs.

I close my course with Francesco Guccini's *Piazza Alimonda*[15] and a new and almost unknown band, Getrò. The word "differing" especially applies to them. Getrò continue the tradition/vocation of the Genoese School made famous by De Andrè, Tenco, Lauzi, and Conte, while they re-invent and re-shape Italian poetry/music. In this course use the text of their *Favola di un uomo* (Fable of a Man) a good example of "neo-hermetism:"

Se penso che son partito col buio per non vedere i ricordi
Ora piango il mio non sapere e la fiducia negli ingordi
Seduto su questo manto con gli occhi lucidi di stupore
Mi ritrovo uomo che alla fine del suo sentiero
Ha cominciato a camminare per davvero
Scoprendo la favola che nessuno mi ha voluto raccontare
Perché la tavola imbandita dal mio lavoro
Contava più del mio libero volo

---

[14] Included in the syllabus but not mentioned in this essay since they deserve a detailed monograph.

[15] The title is the name of a square in Genoa where on July 21st 2001 twenty-three year old Carlo Giuliani was killed by a *carabiniere* while demonstrating against the G8 summit. Violence erupted in the streets, due to still non-identified groups self called "Black Bolks," and to civilian police attacking indiscriminately the demonstrators. Investigations are still ongoing.

(If I think I left in the darkness not to see my memories / Now I mourn my own un-knowledge and my faith in the gluttons / Sitting by this mantle with my eyes shining with stupor / I find myself as a man who at the end of his own path / Started walking for real / To discover the fable no one ever wished to tell me / Because the table lavishly laid with my labor / Was more important than my flight for freedom).

This story/fable is everyone's tale; thanks to the perfect synthesis of innovative yet ancient sonorities, Getrò are able to fuse the visual and aural feelings the rough and tender Ligurian landscape evokes. This is the not-so-common quality of these ground-breaking Italian musical poets: the universality of their language, due not only to the universality of music, but also to their way to incorporate both codes, verbal and non-verbal.

Pier Paolo Pasolini, in the late sixties, mourned a sad departure, the one of *intellettuale organico* from the Italian cultural scene. Perhaps he was too pessimistic in his views. Many Italian musicians/poets of the last fifty years have proven the contrary; "music undoubtedly continues as a chief theater of action and the main vehicle of protest [...] [16] keeping Pietro Calamandrei's words alive: "Ora e sempre Resistenza."[17]

PORTLAND STATE UNIVERSITY, USA

Other References

Bertoncelli, R., Zanetti F. *Avant pop '68. Canzoni indimenticabili di un anno che non è mai finito*. Milano: BUR Biblioteca Univ. Rizzoli, 2008

Borgna, G. *Storia della canzone italiana*. Milano: Mondadori, 1992.

Calamandrei, P. *Lapide ad Ignominia*. http://www.anpi.it/kesselring.htm.

Duggan, C. *A Concise History of Italy*. New York: Cambridge University Press, 1994.

Forgacs, D. Ed. *The Antonio Gramsci Reader*. New York: New York University Press, 1988.

Germano, J.E., Conrad J. Schmitt. *Outline of Italian Grammar*, 2nd edition, New York: McGraw-Hill, 1995.

Giovannetti, P. *Dalla poesia in prosa al rap*. Novara: Interlinea, 2008.

Gramsci, A. *Letteratura e vita nazionale*. Roma: Editori Riuniti, 1971.

[16] M. Filippa, "Popular Song and Musical Cultures", 340.

[17] From "Lapide ad Ignominia" the epigraph by Pietro Calamandrei against the Nazi commander Albert Kesserling, written on a plaque today placed in Montepulciano.

Guglielmi, F. *Voci d'autore: la canzone italiana si racconta.* Roma: Arcana, 2006.
Pasolini, P.P. *Le ceneri di Gramsci.* Milano: Garzanti, 1963.
Pivano, F. *Complice la musica.* Milano: BUR Biblioteca Univ. Rizzoli, 2008.
Saffioli, T. *Enciclopedia della canzone popolare e della nuova canzone politica.* Milano: Teti, 2004.
Straniero, M. *Manuale di musica popolare.* Milano: Rizzoli, 1991.
Testani. G. *Oggi ho salvato il mondo. Canzoni di protesta 1990-2005.* Roma: Arcana, 2006.

http://www.cantilotta.org
http://www.delendacarthago.it.
http://www.ildeposito.org
http://www.italianbookshop.co.uk/italianbooks/series/m1/c1/6/CCTP
http://www.avvelenata.it/locomotiva/storialocomotiva.html
http://www.ondarock.it
http://www.italica.rai.it/cinema
http://www.tuttotesti.com
http://it.youtube.com/

APPENDIX A

Syllabus

Italian Freaks and Punks: History of Italian Culture and Civilization from1950s to 2005 retold by Protest Songs.

A Tentative Syllabus (With Language Feedback)

Class meets three times a week, 75 minutes

REQUIRED TEXTS:

Course pack: Song lyrics and related activities; authors biographies, with historic-social-cultural context, selected material from different sources chosen by the instructor.
Germano, J.E., Schmitt. ***C.J. Schaum's Outline of Italian Grammar***, 2nd edition, New York: McGraw-Hill, 1995.
Italian cultural studies: an introduction/edited by David Forgacs and Robert Lumley. Oxford University Press, 1996: Oxford; New York.
The Cambridge Companion to Modern Italian Culture. **Edited by Zygmunt Baranski and Rebecca J.West**. Cambridge: Cambridge University Press, 2001

RECOMMENDED TEXTS: Duggan, C. ***A Concise History of Italy*** Cambridge [England]; New York: Cambridge University Press, 1994

USEFUL WEBSITES:
www.ondarock.it
http://www.cantilotta.org
http://www.ildeposito.org

COURSE DESCRIPTION AND OBJECTIVES

Content: This course, designed for undergraduate students and/or graduates who have completed four semesters in Italian (or equivalent), is to guide them in the investigation of culture through the protest songs that marked the most critical events of recent history, comparing them, when possible, with films. The Internet will also be a reference for research and consultation. Classes will be taught mostly in Italian. Discussion will revert to English when the students are required to discuss readings that regard cultural matters. Focusing on the lyrics, students are expected to review grammar and strengthen their listening and comprehension abilities without engaging in exercises that often become too mechanical, if not boring. The course will cover not only the four skills—listening, speaking, writing and comprehension—but will also enhance the interest in a culture that, unfortunately, it is still associated with mafia, spaghetti and *mandolino* (with the addition of some Sophia Loren and a bit of Pavarotti here and there). There is another Italy, the one that struggled (and still is) to come out of the darkest periods of her history: the post war reconstruction, the years of terrorism, corruption and neo-liberalism.

This course, though, is not grammar specific; we will address grammatical issues as they arise. For grammar review, we will rely on *Schaum's Outline of Italian Grammar* by J. E. Germano and C. J. Schmitt.

Assignments: In addition to reading assignments, various grammar practice and writing activities will be assigned for homework. Students will also be asked to view films, conduct web-searches and research projects to discover more about the intellectual history and background of the authors and themes explored throughout the semester. This will help to better prepare for classroom activities, oral presentations, and written assignments **(*saggi*).** More specific readings and assignments will be announced in class and posted on the course Blackboard page (BB). Some readings may vary according to specific class needs. Students are responsible for keeping up with the material covered and announcements made on BB. Reading the assigned materials before class will ensure that students are prepared for the communicative activities that we will carry out in the classroom.

Film screenings: In addition to the readings, we will explore aspects of Italian culture and society through film screenings. Films will be put on reserve at the language Lab.

GRADING GUIDELINES:

Calculation of grades: Your performance in the following categories will determine your final grade:

Saggi (4)..40%
Participation, Attendance and Homework.......20%
Presentation 10%
Midterm...15%
Final examination.....................................15%

1. Saggi: There will be **4 IN CLASS** writing assignments, (1.5 pages in Italian) during the semester. The topics and formats will be explained at a later date. They will be graded on content and organization, as well as vocabulary use and grammatical accuracy. **Dictionaries allowed.**
2. Participation and attendance: Active participation in class is essential for language acquisition. It will be graded throughout the semester based on student's effort to use Italian in the classroom, preparation for class, contribution to a cooperative classroom atmosphere, and the quality and quantity of your participation to class discussions and group activities. Daily attendance is crucial for success in learning Italian. **Absences will have a negative impact on grades. A maximum of two absences is allowed in this course to accommodate for illness or personal emergencies**. The absence will count as part of the two permitted, but students will be allowed to make up any missed work. Late arrivals and early departures will also affect class participation grade. **Fifteen minutes after class has begun, will be considered absence**.
3. Missed graded work: **No make up tests will be given**. Exceptions will be made **ONLY** for the following situations: 1) **Written notification** from the **academic dean** of a medical or family emergency; 2) The test is scheduled during a recognized religious holiday and **the instructor must be informed ahead of time** of absence.
4. Presentation: One presentation is required of approximately fifteen minutes each during the semester. We will negotiate topics, times and format during the semester.
5. Homework: It is an essential part of language learning process and it is obligatory. It will be posted on BB. **No late work will be accepted.**
6. Written Exams: There will be one cumulative one-period midterm during the semester and a cumulative final. See scheduled dates and chapters covered. **NO make-ups.** Please note that the final exam is a block exam and is scheduled at a different time than the corresponding class meeting time. **Make your travel plans accordingly. No alternative exam dates will be offered.**

Grade Scale:

100–97 A	**77–74 C**
96–91 A-	**73–70 C-**
90–88 B+	**69–67 D+**
87–84 B	**66–63 D-**
83–81 B-	**62–60 D-**
80–78 C+	**59–below F**

CLASS SCHEDULE

Week 1: ***Introduction to the Course. General Historic Overview of Italy after WW II. The American Influence on Italian Culture.W Gli Americani?***
Renato Carosone: *A Tammuriata Nera* (1950)
Renato Carosone: *Tu vo' fa' l'americano* (1956)
FILM SCREENING: *UN AMERICANO A ROMA* by Steno
Americanized Italian singers: Just like Little Richard:
Little Tony: *Cuore matto* (1965)
Language Feedback: Standard Italian vs. Dialects I. Revisione del tempo presente indicativo.

Week 2: ***The Early Sixties: Italians Can Do Rock'n'roll too, Especially Girls***
Caterina Caselli: *Nessuno mi può giudicare* (1966)
Beyond gender: Patty Pravo: *Ragazzo Triste* (1967)
Language Feedback: Passato Prossimo con pronomi oggetto diretto.

Week 3: ***Still the Sixties: Italian Freaks***
SAGGIO 1
Protest and Demonstrations in Italy: Make Love not War
Fabrizio De Andrè: *La ballata dell'eroe* (1961-64)
Fabrizio De Andrè: *La Guerra di Piero* (1964)
Language Feedback: Imperfetto; pronomi diretti ed indiretti. Imperativo con i pronomi

Week 4: ***The seventies: Home-made Terrorism: The Red, The Black and The Red and Black***
Francesco Guccini: *La locomotiva* (1972)
FILM SCREENING: *1900* by B. Bertolucci
Stefano Rosso: *Colpo di Stato* (1976)
Language Feedback: Congiuntivo e concordanze in tutti i tempi. Passato Prossimo vs Imperfetto. Futuro semplice.

Week 5: ***Still the Seventies: Environmental awareness***
Francesco Guccini: *Il Vecchio e il Bambino* (1972)
Protesta a Destra?
Niente politica, per favore: Lucio Battisti: *Sì Viaggiare* (1977)
Language Feedback: Imperfetto vs.Passato Remoto. Infinito con le preposizioni semplici.

Week 6: ***The Transition: From the Seventies to the Early Eighties***
SAGGIO 2
Joints & Co: Liberalizzatela
Paolo Pietrangeli: *La lallera* (1976)
Comunisti ma non Troppo
Peter Pan has grown up
Edoardo Bennato: *Sono Solo Canzonette* (1980)
Language feedback: Periodo Ipotetico, Ripasso modo indicativo (presente,passato prossimo, imperfetto, futuro)

Week 7: ***The Eighties: Italian Punks***
MIDTERM
CCCP: *ISLAM PUNK/PUNK ISLAM* (1981)
Italian Yuppies: Craxi and The Birth of Neoliberismo Selvaggio
CCCP: Rozzemilia (1984)
Language Feed back: Imperativo con Pronomi diretti. Preposizioni articolate.

Week 8: ***The Late Eighties/Early Nineties: Italiani Brava Gente?***
From a Land of Immigrants to a Land of Immigration
MAU MAU: *Paseo Colon* (1992)
Mafia, Camorra and Tangentopoli; the Second Republic
Fabrizio De Andrè: *Don Raffaè* (1990)
Elio e le Storie Tese: *La terra dei Cachi* (1991)
FILM SCREENING: *TANO DA MORIRE* by R. Torre
Language Feedback: Standard Italian vs Dialects II .Verbi riflessivi al presente e al passato prossimo.

Week 9: ***The Nineties: I Centri Sociali Occupati: Italian Rap and Hip Hop***
99 Posse: *Curre Curre Guagliò* (1992)
Grazie Joe (Strummer)
Banda Bassotti: *Luna Rossa* (1997)
History and Revisionism: The New (?) Left and the New (?) Right
C.S.I.: *Unità di Produzione* (1997)
Language Feedback: Espandere il vocabolario. Figure retoriche: similitudine e metafora. Uso creativo degli aggetivi. "Neapolitialian"

Week 10: ***Berlusconi's Reign: Capitalism is Dead, Long Live Neo-liberism.***
SAGGIO 3
Articolo 31: *L'Italiano Medio* (2003)

Right Wing/Left Wing, Where Are Ya'll?
Giorgio Gaber: *Destra e Sinistra* (2001)
Frankie Hi NGR: *Rap Lamento* (2003)
FILM SCREENING : *CATERINA VA IN CITTÀ* by Virzì
Language Feedback:Espandere il vocabolario Rime ed assonanze. Figure retoriche: metafora e metonimia. Italian Slang I

Week 11: ***Racist Italy? The Extreme Right Wing at the Government***
Delenda Carthago: *L'Invasione* (2003)
Something New Under the Left
Caparezza: *Io Vengo dalla Luna* (2003)
Language Feedback: Italian Slang II.

Week 12: ***Italy in Europe: Globalization and the No Global Movement***
SAGGIO 4
Three Days of Genoa, July 2001
Francesco Guccini: *Piazza Alimonda* (2002)
Revolution from Within: Know Thyself
Getrò: *Favola di un uomo* (2005)
Language Feedback: Revisione di tutti I tempi nell'Indicativo. Imperativo. Uso del Participio passato come Aggettivo.

Week 13: REVIEW AND PRESENTATIONS

Week 14: FINALS

APPENDIX B

Unità didattica 4a settimana

Strutture: concordanza del congiuntivo imperfetto e del condizionale presente. Passato prossimo e passato remoto in un contesto narrativo.
Ascolta la canzone di Francesco Guccini *La Locomotiva:*

Non so che viso avesse, neppure come si chiamava, con che voce parlasse, con quale voce poi cantava,
quanti anni avesse visto allora, di che colore i suoi capelli, ma nella fantasia ho l'immagine sua: gli eroi son tutti giovani e belli,
Conosco invece l'epoca dei fatti, qual' era il suo mestiere: i primi anni del secolo, macchinista, ferroviere,
i tempi in cui si cominciava la guerra santa dei pezzenti
sembrava il treno anch' esso un mito di progresso lanciato sopra i continenti
E la locomotiva sembrava fosse un mostro strano
che l'uomo dominava con il pensiero e con la mano: ruggendo si lasciava indietro distanze che sembravano infinite, sembrava avesse dentro un potere tremendo, la stessa forza della dinamite
Ma un' altra grande forza spiegava allora le sue ali, parole che dicevano "gli uomini son tutti uguali"
e contro ai re e ai tiranni scoppiava nella via
la bomba proletaria e illuminava l' aria la fiaccola dell' anarchia
Un treno tutti i giorni passava per la sua stazione, un treno di lusso, lontana destinazione: vedeva gente riverita, pensava a quei velluti, agli ori, viva, sembrava un giovane puledro che appena liberato il freno mordesse la rotaia con muscoli d' acciaio, con forza cieca di baleno
E un giorno come gli altri, ma forse con più rabbia in corpo pensò che aveva il modo di riparare a qualche torto.
Salì sul mostro che dormiva,
cercò di mandar via la sua paura
e prima di pensare a quel che stava a fare,
il mostro divorava la pianura
Correva l' altro treno ignaro e quasi senza fretta, nessuno immaginava di andare verso la vendetta,
ma alla stazione di Bologna arrivò la notizia in un baleno: "notizia di emergenza, agite con urgenza, un pazzo si è lanciato contro al treno
Ma intanto corre, corre, corre la locomotiva
e sibila il vapore e sembra quasi cosa viva
e sembra dire ai contadini curvi il fischio che si spande in aria: "Fratello, non temere, che corro al mio dovere! Trionfi la giustizia proletaria!"
E intanto corre corre corre sempre più forte
e corre corre corre corre verso la morte
e niente ormai può trattenere
l' immensa forza distruttrice,
aspetta sol lo schianto e poi che giunga

pensava al magro giorno della sua gente attorno, pensava un treno pieno di signori Non so che cosa accadde, perchè prese la decisione, forse una rabbia antica, generazioni senza nome che urlarono vendetta, gli accecarono il cuore: dimenticò pietà, scordò la sua bontà, la bomba sua la macchina a vapore E sul binario stava la locomotiva, la macchina pulsante sembrava fosse cosa	il manto della grande consolatrice La storia ci racconta come finì la corsa la macchina deviata lungo una linea morta... con l' ultimo suo grido d' animale la macchina eruttò lapilli e lava, esplose contro il cielo, poi il fumo sparse il velo: lo raccolsero che ancora respirava, Ma a noi piace pensarlo ancora dietro al motore, mentre fa correr via la macchina a vapore e che ci giunga un giorno ancora la notizia di una locomotiva, come una cosa viva, lanciata a bomba contro l' ingiustizia

Table 24-1. Francesco Guccini's song.

Scrittura guidata:

Chi è Francesco Guccini? Consulta la sua biografia sul suo sito ufficiale: http://www.francescoguccini.it/francesco_guccini.htm
Conosci qualche cantautore americano che ha fatto o fa ancora oggi musica di protesta?

____

____

____

____

____

Secondo te Guccini si è ispirato a qualche cantautore americano?

____

____

____

____

____

Riconoscimento: Sottolinea tutti i verbi al congiuntivo imperfetto, al condizionale presente, al passato prossimo e al passato remoto nel testo della canzone.

Vocabolario: Trascrivi qui sotto tutte le parole che non conosci

____

____

____

____

____

Rispondi alle domande facendo attenzione ai modi ed ai tempi verbali che dovrai usare:

1) In quale periodo della storia italiana si svolge questa storia?

____

____

____

____

____

2) Qual è il mestiere del protagonista?

____

____

____

____

____

3) Rileggi attentamente il testo, come pensi che fosse la sua condizione sociale e perchè?

____

____

____

____

____

4) Quali pensi che siano i motivi che lo hanno spinto ad agire in questo modo?

____

____

____

____

____

5) Dopo aver studiato la parte della storia italiana relativa alla fine dell'800, cosa pensi del movimento anarchico? Credi che gli anarchici fossero tutti violenti? Pensi che ci fossero situazioni in cui la monarchia italiana provocasse reazioni violente da parte del movimento anarchico?

____

____

____

____

____

6) Nella storia americana c'è un fatto simile a questo? Se lo conosci raccontalo brevemente.

____

____

____

____

____

CONTRIBUTORS

JANICE M. ASKI is Associate Professor and Director of the Italian Language Program at The Ohio State University. She specializes in foreign language pedagogy (FLP) and historical Italian/Romance linguistics. She has published a variety of articles in FLP that reflect the most current research in second language acquisition, and she is co-author of the first-year Italian text, *Avanti!*. Her publications in historical Italian/Romance linguistics focus on the social, pragmatic and cognitive aspects of phonological and morphological change.

DANIELA BARTALESI-GRAF holds a Master degree in classical languages and literatures from Tufts University; she is Lecturer in Italian at Tufts University where she has been teaching intermediate and advanced courses in the Italian language and culture since 1992. She has published articles on Italian writers Carlo Levi and Margaret Mazzantini; she is the author of the intermediate/advanced textbook *L'Italia dal fascismo ad oggi: percorsi paralleli nella storia, nella letteratura e nel cinema* (Perugia: Guerra Edizioni, 2005).

CAMILLA BETTONI is Professor of Applied Linguistics at the University of Verona, Italy. She studied in Padua and in Edinburgh, then taught at the Universities of North Queensland and Sydney for 17 years. Her interests are language contact, bilingualism, and second language learning and teaching. Her recent publications include *Imparare un'altra lingua* (2001) and *Usare un'altra lingua* (2006), Bari-Roma, Laterza.

SILVIA BOERO is Assistant Professor of Italian at Portland State University, Portland, Oregon. She received her PhD from the University of North Carolina at Chapel Hill, and in Italy she graduated from the University of Genoa. She has taught Italian Language and Literature, History and Social Studies in Italian public schools for 15 years. Her area of interest is Modernism and Postmodernism; Expressions of Dissent in Literature and Figurative arts during Fascism. In the last years she has been working on music and its employment as a teaching methodology while researching on History of Italian Folk music.

CLELIA BOSCOLO has been teaching Italian as a foreign language at all levels for over 20 years. She has worked as Language Instructor and Co-ordinator of Language Courses in the Department of Italian Studies at the University of Birmingham since 1989. She is author (with A. Bianchi) of *Practising Italian Grammar—a Workbook* (Arnold, 2004), and *Upgrade Your Italian* (Arnold, 2005).

ROMANA CAPEK-HABEKOVIĆ received her PhD from the University of Michigan. She teaches language, literature and culture courses. She is the author of *Tommaso Landolfi's Grotesque Images* and the co-author of *Insieme,* a program for intermediate college Italian. She is also the co-author of *Taped Exercises for Basic and Intermediate Italian.* Her articles on twentieth-century Italian authors have appeared in many scholarly publications. Presently, she is teaching and directing the Italian Elementary Language Program at the University of Michigan.

SILVIA CARLOROSI is an Assistant Professor at the University of Maryland. She received a PhD. in Italian Studies in 2006 from the University of Pennsylvania with a dissertation on *Cinepoiesis*, which focuses on the interactions between cinematic and poetic languages. She has published articles on Italian cinema, amongst which "Neo-Romanticismo in risposta al Postmodernismo? L'influenza leopardiana nella poetica cinematografica felliniana di *La voce della luna*" *Film e Letterature: Rivista di Cinema e Letteratura* (Number 4, 2006).

MARIA CRISTINA CIGNATTA was awarded an Honours Degree in Italian Studies at the University of Reading (Berks). She then graduated in Lingue e Letterature Straniere at the University of Parma where she now teaches English in the Foreign Languages Department. Her academic interests are centred on the theory and practice of translation, comparative grammar, stylistics, discourse analysis and comparative literatures. She is also actively engaged in freelance translation, particularly in the area of literary and scientific texts. Among her main publications are *Targets in Translation—A practical guide for Italian University students of English-(Advanced Level)*, *Towards Autonomy in Translation— A practical guide for Italian University students of English (Proficiency Level), Enemy at Sea* (translation, with H. West, of the short story written by Mario Colombi Guidotti entitled *Nemica al Largo*).

LUCIANA D'ARCANGELI received her PhD in 2007 from the University of Strathclyde, where she has been the Italian Teaching Fellow since 1998. Before returning to full time study she worked in Italian cinema. She specializes in translation and interpreting and in the study of contemporary Italian theatre and cinema. She is author of various articles; amongst them: "L'evoluzione dei personaggi femminili nel teatro di Dario Fo e Franca Rame" (2006); "Madness in the Theatre of Dario Fo and Franca Rame" (2005); "Dario Fo, Franca Rame and the Italian Censors" (2005); "Illustration of the IPA: Italian"—co-authored with Derek Rogers (2004); "Franca Rame: Pedestal, Megaphone or Female Jester?" (2002); 'Franca Rame *Giullaressa*' (2000).

ALISON DAVIES is Research Projects' Officer for the Learning Development Unit at the University of Birmingham. She is responsible for working with and advising LDU project leaders on the design and implementation of evaluation procedures. Her publications include: A. Davies, K. J. Smith 2005, "Drivers and Barriers to the Uptake of Learning Technologies: Staff Experiences in a Research-Led University." O'Donoghue, John (ed) *Technology Supported Learning & Teaching: A Staff Perspective.* USA: Idea Group Inc A. Davies, A, J. Ramsay, H. Lindfield, J. Couperthwaite 2005. "Building Learning Communities: Foundations for Good Practice." *British Journal of Educational Technology* 36, no. 4: 615-27

BRUNO DI BIASE is Associate Head of the School (Languages), School of Humanities and Languages, University of Western Sydney. He studied at Macquarie and the Australian National University. Processabiltity Theory and its application to SLA, bilingualism, language maintenance maintenance, and L2 pedagogy are his interests. With Pienemann and Kawaguchi he contributed to the current extension of PT.

ROBERTO DOLCI is Associate Professor in the Department of Language Sciences at the University for Foreigners in Perugia. His main research areas are language education, theories of language teaching and learning, language teacher training and technology for language teaching with particular attention to e-learning. His work has been published in Italian and International journals and books.

FRANCESCA HELM is a research Assistant Professor at the University of Padova. She has an MA in TESOL from the Institute of Education, London University. She has published articles on technology and language learning, for instance "Technology and Language Learning. What the Learners Say" in *LEAA Lenguas en Aprendizahe Autodirigido* (vol.1) http://cad.cele.unam.mx/leaa/cont/ano01/num01/0101ind.html She has presented at national and international conferences such as Eurocall, IALIC, Online Educa in Berlin and at the Universidad Nacional Autónoma de México.

FLAVIA LAVIOSA is Senior Lecturer in the Department of Italian Studies at Wellesley College. She holds a PhD in *Foreign Language Education* and a Master in *Humanities* (SUNY Buffalo), and a Master in *European Film Studies and Criticism* (University of Edinburgh, Scotland). Her articles on Second Language Education have been published in *Italica, College Board Special Focus, RILA, Tuttitalia, African Association for Language Teaching*, and *Il Forneri*. Her works on Italian cinema and women's studies have appeared in *Studies of European Cinema*; *Italica*; *Rivista di Studi Italiani*; *Kinema*; *Italian Politics and Society*; and *American Journal of Italian Studies*. She has contributed chapters to the edited anthologies *Italian Cinema-New Directions; Watching Pages, Reading Pictures: Cinema and Modern Literature in Italy*; *Incontri con il Cinema Italiano*; *La Scuola Italiana di Middlebury (1996-2005) Passione Didattica Pratica*; *Film Representations of Popular Culture*; and *Italy and the Mediterranean: Transcultural Spaces*. She is also the editor of *Visions of Struggle: Women's Filmmaking in the Mediterranean* (in progress).

NICOLETTA MARINI-MAIO is Assistant Professor of Italian at Dickinson College, USA. She holds a PhD. in Italian Studies (University of Pennsylvania), a MA in Teaching Italian as L2 (Università per Stranieri di Perugia), and a MA in Linguistics (Università di Roma). She authored "Il cinema 'liquido' dei fratelli Frazzi. *Certi bambini*," in V. Zagarrio (ed.), *La meglio gioventù* (Venezia: Marsilio, 2006), 255-63, and "I Sei personaggi siamo noi: Pirandello, o la metamorfosi degli studenti nel laboratorio teatrale in italiano," *Italica* 81, no. 4 (2004): 459-82. She co-edited the scholarly volume *Set the Stage! Italian Language, Literature, and Culture Through Theater* (in press, Yale UP).

MARY ANN MCDONALD CAROLAN is Associate Professor of Modern Languages & Literatures and Director of the Italian Studies program at Fairfield University in Fairfield, CT (USA). A graduate of Dartmouth College, she received her PhD. in Italian Language & Literature from Yale University. Prof. Carolan has published articles on Italian authors Elsa Morante, Grazia Deledda, and Alessandro Manzoni as well as on film directors Michelangelo Antonioni and Sergio Leone. She has also written on the role of women in Italian American comedies.

KATHRYN K. MCMAHON, who holds a PhD. in French from Cornell University, is the Director of Language Programs at the University of Pennsylvania where she oversees language studies in French, Italian, Portuguese and Spanish, and is responsible for the training of graduate student Teaching Assistants. She is co-author of a Spanish textbook, *Lecturas periodísticas,* and has given presentations at ACTFL, AAIS, AATI, AAUSC, and NECTFL on curriculum design, technology and language teaching, intercultural communication, and language program direction.

TOM MEANS is Professor of Applied Linguistics and Italian at Marlboro College, Vermont, and the founder of Means Language Center in New York City. His main interests are instructed second language acquisition and method comparison research. He holds a PhD in Italian and Second Language Acquisition from Rutgers University and is the author of the *Instant Vocabulary Builder* series published by Hippocrene Books.

AMELIA MOSER received her PhD in Italian from Harvard University in 2004 and has taught Italian language and literature at Yale University, Bard College, Iona College, and Columbia University, where she is currently Visiting Scholar in the Department of Italian. She is Co-Managing Editor of the journal *Italian Poetry Review* (Columbia University & The Italian Academy for Advanced Studies in America). Her research interests concern Modern and Contemporary Italian Literature. She has published on Anna Maria Ortese and is currently writing a book on the Fantastic in Ortese's writings.

EMANUELE OCCHIPINTI is Assistant Professor and Director of the Italian Program at Drew University. He holds a *Laurea* in Modern Foreign Languages and Literatures from the University of Florence and received his PhD in Italian Literature from Rutgers University. He has published on Italo Svevo and Igino Ugo Tarchetti and contributed to the *History of Feminist Thought*, forthcoming from Greenwood Press. His area of specialization covers eighteenth to twentieth century Italian Literature, with a focus on travel literature, the Italian American experience, psychoanalysis, film, cultural and comparative studies, and language pedagogy.

SANDRA PALAICH is the coordinator of elementary Italian at the University of Michigan. She earned her undergraduate degree at the University of Zagreb, Croatia, and her MA in Italian Literature at Wayne State University in Detroit, Michigan. She has been at the University of Michigan since 1998, where she teaches first-, second- and third-year Italian courses. She is the co-author of *Parola a te!* (Thomson-Heinle, 2009) with Romana Capek-Habekovic. Her professional interests are translation and application of technology in foreign language teaching.

THOMAS PETERSON is Professor of Italian at the University of Georgia. His books include critical monographs on the works of Alberto Moravia, Franco Fortini and Pier Paolo Pasolini, as well as the topical study, *The Rose in Contemporary Italian Poetry*. His essays include several studies of the poetry of Dante, Petrarch and Tasso. In the area of pedagogy, he has published three essays on the philosophy of education in the journal *Educational Philosophy and Theory*.

KERSTIN PILZ is Head of Italian Studies at Macquarie University (Sydney, Australia), where she lectures in all areas of Italian language, culture and society. She also contributes to interdisciplinary courses on global identity and issues of intercultural communication and most recently designed a course on representations of European identity through film. Her monograph *Mapping Complexity* (Troubador, 2005) examined the relationship of literature and science in the works of Italo Calvino. Most recently her research has focused on Italian cinema and representations of Italo-Australian identity in diaspora cinema. She has just completed a semester aboard *The Scholar Ship*, an oceangoing university, where she taught Intercultural Communication.

JUDITH RAGGI-MOORE is a Senior Lecturer & the Program Director of the Italian Studies Program at Emory University. She is also a Dottore in Lingua e Letteratura Moderne from the Università degli Studi di Roma (1980) in Italian language and cultural studies. Raggi-Moore is the creator of the Italian Virtual Class teaching method & co-author of Italian Virtual Class, *Chiavi di Lettura* Volumes 1, 2, 3 (published through the Emory University Office of Technology Transfer, 2007, 2008, 2008). Raggi-Moore has also authored a number of journal articles and won a number of prestigious teaching awards.

CHRISTINE RISTAINO is a Lecturer and First-Year Language Coordinator & Teacher Trainer for the Italian Studies Program at Emory

University. She has a Ph.D. in Italian Literature from the University of North Carolina at Chapel Hill (2004). Her fields of expertise are Italian cultural studies, cultural acquisition, language pedagogy, the marvelous Baroque, the "Querelle des Femmes," and Italian women writers. Ristaino is co-author of the textbook Italian Virtual Class, *Chiavi di Lettura* Volumes 1, 2, 3 (published through the Emory University Office of Technology Transfer, 2007, 2008, 2008). She is also co-author of the book entitled "Lucrezia Marinella and the 'Querelle des Femmes' in Seventeenth Century Italy," published through Farleigh Dickinson Press (2008). She has authored two articles in the Encyclopedia of Italian Literary Studies as well as a number of journal articles.

NICLA RIVERSO is a teaching associate at the University of Washington. Her study and research are in Comparative literature (English and Italian from Middle Ages to Early Modern), history, philosophy, religion, cultural studies and education. Her current research explores the historical, political, scientific and literary value ascribable to the works of Paolo Sarpi, as well as some of its connections with British Protestantism. Her most important publication is *Alfabetizzazione e Umanesimo: nell'Italia dei Secoli XIV e XV* (Gaeta: Bibliotheca, 1997).

JACQUELINE SAMPERI MANGAN received her PhD from McGill University, specializing in Swiss-Italian literature. She was coordinator of the Italian language and culture courses at the Université de Montréal and has taught for over twenty years in various Canadian universities and colleges. She worked in ministerial projects concerning multilingualism and has collaborated with the Montreal school commissions and with the Quebec ministry of foreign affairs. She has also published numerous literary and linguistic articles and she is active in new teaching technology research at the Université de Montréal.

SANDRO SCIUTTI graduated at the University of Genoa, Italy, with a thesis on the role of translation in teaching Italian to Spanish-speaking students. After teaching Italian at the Italian Cultural Institute in Barcelona (Spain), he went on to teach Spanish and English in state secondary schools in Genoa. At present, he is teaching Italian at the University for Foreigners in Perugia. Besides teaching, he also devotes himself to translation and interpreting from and to English, Spanish and French.

KELLY SMITH is based in the Learning Development Unit of the University of Birmingham. She encourages and supports academics in their use and development of innovative learning and teaching practices including the use of learning technologies. One of Kelly's key roles is concerned with the evaluation of innovative initiatives from staff and student perspectives. Her publications include *Supporting E-learning in Enterprise Education: The TE3 Project* (in press), and A. Davies, K. J. Smith 2005, *Drivers and Barriers to the Uptake of Learning Technologies: Staff Experiences in a Research-Led University.* O'Donoghue, John (ed) *Technology Supported Learning & Teaching: A Staff Perspective.*

BARBARA SPINELLI is the Director of the Italian Language Program at Columbia University, New York. She works as teacher educator, curriculum designer and materials writer. She has taught in universities in the United States and in Italy. Her current fields of research are: Network-based Language Learning, Socio-cultural and Ecological Approach in Second Language Acquisition. In this field she has presented papers at International Conferences and she has published articles in ISL journals. She currently works for the CVCL (Centre for Language Assessment and Certification) of the University for Foreigners in Perugia.

PAOLA VETTOREL taught English to students of different ages and Italian as a second language in the Centro Linguistico di Ateneo of Verona University. She is now a researcher in the English Studies Department of the same University. She is also a teacher trainer. Her works include "Uno, nessuno, centomila: come riconoscere e valorizzare le differenze individuali in classe" in CAON F. (ed). 2006. *Insegnare italiano nella classe ad abilità differenziate*. Perugia: Guerra; "Canzoni in classe: la vita non è (tutta) fuori," *Lend* Anno XXXV/1 Febbraio 2006; "A musical experience," *English Teaching Professional* no.52, (September 2007).

MANUELA VISIGALLI lives and works in Milan as a teacher of Italian as a foreign language in both public universities and private schools. She holds a *Laurea* in Modern Foreign Languages and Literatures from the IULM in Milan with a thesis on translations techniques, and a Master's in *didattica di Italiano come lingua non materna*. Her book *Manuale di Grammatica base* (written with P. Della Putta) has just been published and a second volume *Manuale di Grammatica intermedia e avanzata* will follow.

HEATHER WEBB is an Assistant Professor of Italian at The Ohio State University. She specializes in the literature and cultural history of medieval and Renaissance Italy. Areas of research include Dante, devotional poetry and prose and the history of the body. She is currently working on a book manuscript, entitled *The Medieval Heart: Circulation before William Harvey*. She is a member of the advisory board for the World of Dante web project.

SIMONA WRIGHT holds a *Laurea* in German from Ca' Foscari University, Italy, and a PhD in Italian from Rutgers University. She is Professor of Italian at The College of New Jersey, where she is Co-Chair of the Department of Modern Languages and Director of the Italian program. She has published a volume on Italo Calvino and several articles on Italian women writers, the literature of migration, postcolonial studies, and twentieth century Italian poetry. She is presently NEMLA Director of Italian and serves on the NEMLA Board of Directors.

ASSUNTA GIUSEPPINA ZEDDA is a linguistic expert collaborator in the Language Center at Sassari University where she teaches courses in Italian as second language. Her research interests include task-based and project-based learning and teaching, cooperative learning, group dynamics in language classroom, Interlingua and error analysis, language reflection techniques, SLA and Processability Theory and their didactic implications. She has published articles on these topics in national and international journals (ITALS, LEND, RILA, SLI, Revista de Italianística).